CONTENTS

iii

PROPERTY

 UNIFORM COMMERCIAL CODE

 CREDITORS AND DEBTOR/CONSUMERS

 AGENCY AND EMPLOYMENT

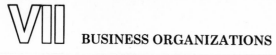

VII BUSINESS ORGANIZATIONS

APPENDIXES

PREFACE

Most students in business law are not headed for legal careers but rather careers that require a knowledge of fundamental principles of law. It is to these students at every level of higher education that *Fundamentals of Business Law* is directed.

To accommodate the needs of today's students, we have attempted several techniques to facilitate the learning of the subject matter. We have used numerous section headings to readily identify subject-matter content. In order to save the students valuable time while utilizing the combination text-and-case approach, a somewhat different method of presenting cases has been adopted. Carefully prepared briefs have been inserted to illustrate the text material. There are approximately six such case briefs for each chapter. There are 229 such cases in this second edition, of which 124 are new. We believe that all the advantages of studying actual cases will result from this format but that they will be more easily understood and more readily followed by students by being presented in this manner.

The text is divided into seven parts so that individual instructors may select those particular subjects with which they wish to deal, in the order of their choosing. It is our intention that the textbook be sufficiently flexible for either the quarter-system school or the semester-system school and that there be adequate material for at least two courses.

Part I, in addition to introducing students to the various sources of law and the judicial system, contains separate chapters on the criminal law and the law of torts. There is a separate chapter on criminal law due to its increasing importance to society as a whole and because so much of the attention and effort of our legal system is in that area. The chapter on torts places special emphasis on the problems of the fault system and the trend toward no-fault in the automobile accident area. In addition, the problems related to malpractice by professional persons are highlighted.

Part II, on contracts, covers the traditional contract subjects; in addition it focuses on many of the new developments of the law under the Uniform Commercial Code. The Code is attached to the text as an Appendix, and the appropriate sections are noted in the text. Students will be able to refer directly to the appropriate Code sections as they study, thus enhancing their understanding and retention of the subject matter. The Code as it relates to contracts is summarized in the last section of each chapter, and the differences between the Code and the common law are noted. We believe this approach to be unique and, from our experience in the classroom, quite helpful to students.

Part III discusses property, including personal property, bailments, real estate transactions, and wills, estates, and trusts. The chapter on wills, estates, and trusts is new to this edition. This portion of the text pays special attention to transactions involving property. Studying property law from a transactional approach is of immediate practical value.

Part IV is devoted to the Uniform Commercial Code. Without repeating those points emphasized under the law of contracts, it covers the traditional subjects of sales, commercial paper, and secured transactions. There is a separate chapter on warranties and product liability, recognizing the major importance of these topics to all businesses in our economy. The discussion of commercial paper places increased emphasis on the liability of the parties in transactions involving commercial paper, especially the liability of banks. It also recognizes the decreased importance of the "holder in due course" concept as the result of the 1976 FTC rule. Because secured transactions are so important to creditors and to sellers of goods, two chapters are devoted to this subject.

Part V contains three quite important chapters that deal with the law as it relates to creditors and debtor/consumers. The special chapter on the laws assisting debtors and consumers gathers in one place much of the recent legislation aimed at protecting consumers. It highlights the new FTC rule on holders in due course and the Moss-Magnuson warranty law. Other material emphasizes the trend from "let the buyer beware" to "let the seller beware." The chapter on bankruptcy is designed to give students a thorough understanding of bankruptcy in practice as well as in theory. An attempt has been made to make students aware that bankruptcy is an uncomplicated and common proceeding in which the debtor is able to keep a substantial amount of his property while ridding himself of his debts.

Part VI, on agency and employment, places special emphasis on several aspects of the employer-employee relationship that have developed in recent years. There is a separate chapter on labor-management relations, covering labor law in detail. This chapter is a significant part of the text because of the extremely important role played by labor unions in the decision-making process of American industry. This part of the text also highlights the legal aspects of discrimination in employment. The chapters dealing with agency place emphasis on the law of torts and workmen's compensation. A special chapter on agency and the law of torts, in recognition of the important role that *respondeat superior* plays in our legal system, is also included.

Part VII discusses business organizations in three stages. In addition to the factors used in selecting the form of organization, these stages are (1) the method of creation of the various forms of organization, (2) the legal aspects of operating the various forms of organization, and (3) the law as it relates to dissolution of business organization. In addition, there is a discussion of special types of business organizations, such as the Sub-Chapter S corporation and the professional service association. There is also a separate chapter on government regulation of business organizations. This chapter, in addition to discussing the power of government to regulate business, illustrates government regulation with a discussion of the antitrust laws. Because antitrust is the legal link with our economy and most business students have several courses in economic theory, we feel this chapter has particular importance. It is also designed as background material for courses in marketing.

Throughout the text, a substantial amount of attention has been given to the public aspects of the law as it relates to business. The heavy emphasis on consumerism and the chapters on labor law and government regulation of business are but a few examples of the emphasis on our legal environment. We believe that a modern course in business law must contain these matters in addition to the generally accepted, traditional content.

We are pleased that Barbara George has written a student workbook to accompany the text. We know that many students will benefit from its use, and we want to express our appreciation to her for its preparation. We also want to express our appreciation to Professor O. Lee Reed of the University of Georgia for assisting in the preparation of the teacher's manual. He brought valuable insight based on a successful teaching career to its preparation. Professor Sanford Searleman of Adirondack Community College (New York) did an in-depth review of the manuscript and we are grateful for his helpful comments. Finally, we want to thank Betty Hampel of Champaign, Illinois, and Donna Weber of Athens, Georgia, for their valuable assistance in the preparation of the manuscript.

Robert N. Corley

William J. Robert

I INTRODUCTION TO THE LAW

1 LAW

Introduction   Before starting the study of business law, one should have an understanding of our legal system—where our laws came from, how they are applied, and how they may be changed. The beginning chapters of this text will discuss the legal system of our society, and the remaining chapters will consider the law as it relates to business.

Now more than ever before in our nation's history, the direct relationship between law and the social problems facing our society has a direct and substantial impact upon business and its decision-making processes. Solutions to many of society's problems are found in laws regulating business activity. For example, the basic approach to solving the problems of air and water pollution is found in the law. In the area of employment, legislation now affects the hiring of employees as well as their promotion, especially with regard to minority groups and women. In the field of consumer protection, new laws have been enacted regulating the debtor-creditor relationship and other matters of consumer interest. These laws have been passed in order to give better protection to many groups of people. The law thus serves as a scheme of social control of the business community.

WHAT IS LAW?

Our view of the law will be a broad one, and our first consideration will be the question: What is law?

In everyday conversation people use the word *law* in many different ways. Actually the word *law* is very difficult to define. There is a field of law that is known as "jurisprudence," which analyzes the concept of

3

law and is concerned with the philosophy of law. Throughout the centuries people have attempted to define *law* and to set forth its role in society.

In attempting to define *law*, it is helpful to look at its purposes or functions. It is fundamental that a basic purpose of law in a civilized society is to maintain order. This is the prime function of that body of law known as the *criminal law*. Another role of law is to resolve disputes that arise between individuals and to impose responsibility if one person has a valid legal claim against another. Between these two extremes of what might be called law and order on the one hand and settlement of disputes on the other, there are many situations that cannot be so clearly defined. For example, the income tax laws require that a person pay an income tax. If he fails to do so, or if he fails to declare all his income or takes improper deductions, he may be subjected to penalties, but he has also failed to live up to his obligations to society. In any event it is important that one bear in mind that the law is not simply a statement of rules of conduct but is also the means whereby remedies are afforded when one person has wronged another.

In one sense all issues and disputes in our society—political, social, religious, economic, or otherwise—ultimately become legal issues to be resolved by the courts. Thus it can be said that law is simply what the courts determine it to be as an expression of the public will in resolving these issues and disputes.

Another view of law is that it is a method of social control—an instrument of social, political, and economic change. Law is both an instrument of change and a result of changes that take place in our society. The law brings about changes in our society. Society also brings about changes in the law. The law—responding to the goals, desires, needs, and aspirations of society—is in a constant state of change. Sometimes the law changes more rapidly than does the attitude of the majority of society. In this event the law and our legal system provide leadership in bringing about changes. At other times our society is ahead of the law in moving in new directions, and changes in the law are brought about by the people. For example, in the field of ecology various groups have put pressure on legislators to clean up the air and water. As a result, laws have been enacted that require that devices be installed to control pollution. Here the public pressure resulted in the enactment of laws and the law was a follower rather than a leader. It is important to note that the law is not static—that it is constantly changing and that the impetus for the changes may come from many different sources.

In still another sense *law* has been defined as the rules and principles that are applied by the courts to decide controversies. These rules and principles fall into three categories: (1) laws that have been passed by legislative bodies, including the federal Constitution and the state constitutions; (2) common law, or case law—the law that is derived from cases decided by the courts; and (3) procedural rules, which determine how lawsuits are handled in the courts and include such matters as the rules of evidence and related issues. The first two elements provide the rules of substantive law that are applied by the courts to decide controversies. The third provides the machinery whereby these rules of substantive law are given effect and applied to resolve controversies.

Classifications of Law

In order to understand the many different aspects of law, it is helpful to look at the various areas or classifications of law. As noted above, laws are sometimes classified as *substantive* or *procedural*. The law that is used to actually decide disputes may be classified as *substantive* law. On the other hand, the legal procedures that provide how a lawsuit is begun, how the trial is conducted, how appeals are taken, and how a judgment is enforced are called *procedural* law. Substantive law is the part of the law that defines rights, and procedural law establishes the procedures whereby rights are enforced and protected. For example, A and B have entered into an agreement, and A claims that B has breached the agreement. The rules that provide for bringing B into court and for the conduct of the trial are rather mechanical and they constitute procedural law. Whether the agreement was enforceable and whether A is entitled to damages are matters of substance and would be determined on the basis of the substantive law of contracts.

Law is also frequently classified into areas of *public* and *private* law. Public law includes those bodies of law that affect the public generally; private law includes the areas of the law that are concerned with the relationship between individuals.

Public law may be divided into three general categories: (1) *constitutional law*, which concerns itself with the rights, powers, and duties of federal and state governments under the U.S. Constitution and the constitutions of the various states; (2) *administrative law*, which is concerned with the multitude of administrative agencies, such as the Interstate Commerce Commission, the Federal Trade Commission, and the National Labor Relations Board; and (3) *criminal law*, which consists of statutes that forbid certain conduct as being detrimental to the welfare of the state or the people generally and provides punishment for their violation. These public-law subjects will be discussed later in this and subsequent chapters.

Private law is that body of law that pertains to the relationships between individuals in an organized society. Private law encompasses the subjects of contracts, torts, and property. Each of these subjects includes several bodies of law. For example, the law of contracts may be subdivided into the subjects of sales, commercial paper, agency, and business organizations. The major portion of this text covers these subjects, which constitute the body of law usually referred to as business law.

The law of torts is the primary source of litigation in this country and is also a part of the total body of law in such areas as agency and sales. A *tort* is a wrong committed by one person against another or his property. The law of torts is predicated upon the premise that in a civilized society people who injure other persons or their property should compensate them for their loss.

The law of property may be thought of as a branch of the law of contracts, but in many ways our concept of private property contains much more than the contract characteristics. Property is the basic ingredient in our economic system, and the subject matter may be subdivided into several areas, such as wills, trusts, estates in land, personal property, bailments, and many more.

SOURCES OF LAW

Introduction The unique characteristic of American law is that a very substantial part of it is not to be found in statutes enacted by legislatures but rather in cases decided by our courts. This concept of decided cases as a source of law comes to us from England. It is generally referred to as the *common law*. Our common law system of heavy reliance on case precedent as a source of law must be contrasted with civil law systems, which developed on the European continent. The civil law countries have codified their laws—reduced them to statutes—so that the main source of law in those countries is to be found in the statutes rather than in the cases. Under the common law system, of course, we have a large number of statutes, but these are only a part of our law.

In our system, statutes must be in keeping with the constitutions—federal and state—and the courts can overrule a statute that is found to violate constitutional provisions. Statutes and constitutions are classified as "written law." Also included under this heading are treaties that by the federal constitution are also a part of the supreme law of the land. Case law, as opposed to written law, is not set forth formally but is derived from an analysis of each case that uncovers what legal propositions the case stands for. It is not proper to call this "unwritten" law because it is in fact in writing. However, it must be distinguished from statutory law in that it is not the product of the legislature but is rather the product of the courts. When a court decides a case, particularly upon an appeal from a lower-court decision, the court writes an opinion setting forth among other things the reasons for its decision. From these written opinions rules of law can be deduced, and these make up the body of what is called case law or common law. The basic characteristic of the common law is that a case once decided establishes a precedent that will be followed by the courts when similar controversies are later presented.

A third source of law is administrative law. Federal, state, and local administrative agencies make law by promulgating rules and regulations as well as by making decisions concerning matters under their jurisdiction.

In summary, our law comes from written laws such as constitutions, statutes, ordinances and treaties; from case law, which is based on judicial decisions; and from the rules and decisions of administrative agencies.

Constitutions   The Constitution of the United States and the constitutions of the various states are the fundamental written law in this country. A federal law must not violate the U.S. Constitution. All state laws must conform to or be in harmony with the federal Constitution as well as with the constitution of the state.

Two very important principles of constitutional law are basic to our judicial system. They are closely related to each other and are known as the *doctrine of separation of powers* and the *doctrine of judicial review.*

The doctrine of separation of powers results from the fact that both state and federal constitutions provide for a scheme of government consisting of three branches—the legislative, the executive, and the judicial. Separation of powers ascribes to each branch a separate function and a check and balance of the functions of the other branches. The doctrine of separation of powers infers that each separate branch will not perform the function of the other and that each branch has limited powers. The system of checks and balances may be briefly summarized as follows: The Senate retains the power to approve key executive and judicial appointments. The legislative branch exercises control through its power to appropriate funds. In addition, Congress can limit or expand the authority of the executive branch or the jurisdiction of the judicial branch in most cases. The executive has the power to veto legislation and to appoint judges (in some states the judiciary is elected). The judiciary has the power to review actions of the executive and to review laws passed by the legislative branch to determine if such laws are constitutional.

The doctrine of judicial review is the heart of the concept of separation of powers. This doctrine and the doctrine of supremacy of the Constitution were established at an early date in our country's history in the celebrated case of *Marbury* v. *Madison.* In this case, Chief Justice Marshall literally created for the court a power that the founding fathers had refused to include in the Constitution. This was the power of the judiciary to review the actions of the other branches of government and to set them aside as null and void if in violation of the Constitution. In creating this power to declare laws unconstitutional, Chief Justice Marshall stated: "Certainly, all those who have framed written constitutions contemplated them as forming the fundamental and paramount law of the nation, and consequently, the theory of every such government must be that an act of the legislature, repugnant to the constitution, is void. This theory is essentially attached to a written constitution and is, consequently, to be considered by this court as one of the fundamental principles of our society." Justice Marshall then decided that courts have the power to review the action of the legislative and executive branches of government to determine if they are constitutional. This doctrine of judicial review has, to some extent, made the courts the overseer of government and of all aspects of our daily lives.

Statutes The power of courts over legislation is not limited to the doctrine of judicial review. Courts also interpret legislation by resolving ambiguities and filling the gaps in the statutes. There would be no need to interpret a statute that was direct, clear, and precise. However, most legislation is by its very nature general, and courts are faced with the problem of finding the meaning of general statutes as applied to specific facts. Interpretation is designed to find the intent of the legislature.

One technique of statutory interpretation is to examine the legislative history of an act to determine the purpose of the legislation, or the evil it was designed to correct. Legislative history includes the committee hearings, the debates, and any statement made by the executive in requesting the legislation. Legislative history does not always give a clear meaning to a statute because many of the questions of interpretation that confront courts were never even considered by the legislature. The real problem often is to determine what the legislature *would have* intended, had it considered the question.

Several generally accepted rules of statutory interpretation are used by judges in construing the legislative intent. For example, there is the rule that criminal statutes and taxing laws should be strictly or narrowly construed. As a result, doubts as to the applicability of criminal and taxing laws will be resolved in favor of the accused or the taxpayer, as the case may be. Another rule of statutory construction is that remedial statutes (those creating a judicial remedy on behalf of one person at the expense of another) are to be liberally construed in order that the statute will be effective in correcting the condition sought to be remedied. The power of courts to interpret legislation means that in the final analysis, it is what the court says that a statute means that determines its effect.

Uniform State Laws   Each state has its own constitution, statutes, and body of case law developed by its court system. There are substantial differences in the law among the various states. It is important to recognize that ours is a federal system wherein each state has a substantial degree of autonomy; thus it can be said that there are really fifty-one legal systems—a system for each of the states plus the federal legal structure. In many legal situations it does not matter that the legal principles are not uniform throughout the country. This is true when the parties to a dispute are citizens of the same state; then the controversy is strictly *intrastate* as opposed to one having *interstate* implications. But when citizens of different states are involved in a transaction (for example where a buyer in one state contracts with a seller in another), many difficult questions can arise from the lack of uniformity in the law. For example, assume that a contract is valid in one state but not in the other. Which state's law controls? Although a body of law called "conflict of laws" (see page 12) has been developed to cover such cases, uniformity is still more desirable.

Two methods of achieving uniformity are possible: (1) federal legislation governing business law and (2) adoption by the legislatures of all the states of the same laws concerning at least certain phases of business transactions. The latter method has been attempted by a legislative drafting group known as the National Conference of Commissioners on Uniform State Laws.

The first uniform state law, the Uniform Negotiable Instruments Law (NIL), was drafted in 1896. Since then over one hundred uniform laws concerning such subjects as partnerships, sale of goods, conditional sales, warehouse receipts, bills of lading, stock transfers, and many others have been presented to the various state legislatures. The response from the state legislatures has varied. Very few of the uniform laws have been adopted by all states. Some states have adopted a uniform law in principle but have changed some of the provisions to meet local needs or to satisfy strong lobbying groups, so that the result has often been "nonuniform uniform state laws."

The most significant development for business in the field of uniform state legislation has been the Uniform Commercial Code. This Code was prepared for the stated purpose of collecting in one body the law that "deals with all the phases which may ordinarily arise in the handling of a commercial transaction from start to finish . . ." The detailed aspects of "the Code," as it is often referred to, constitute a significant portion of this book.

The field of commercial law is not the only area of new uniform statutes. Many states are adopting criminal codes, and other uniform laws dealing with social problems, that contain modern procedures and concepts. In addition, the past few years have seen dynamic changes in both state and federal statutes setting forth civil procedures and revising court systems. The future will undoubtedly bring many further developments to improve the administration of justice. The trend,

9

despite some objection, is to cover more areas of the law with statutes and to rely less on precedent in judicial decisions, or common law, as a source of law. Many of these new statutes tend to be uniform throughout the country.

CASE LAW

Stare Decisis Notwithstanding the trend toward reducing law to statutory form, a substantial portion of our law finds its source in decided cases. This case law, or common law, is based on the concept of precedent and the doctrine of *stare decisis*, which means "to stand by decisions and not to disturb what is settled." This means that the case has established a precedent. The doctrine of *stare decisis* must be contrasted with the concept of *res adjudicata*, which means that the "thing has been decided." *Res adjudicata* applies when, between the parties themselves, the matter is closed at the conclusion of the lawsuit. The losing party cannot again ask a court to decide the dispute. *Stare decisis* means that a court of competent jurisdiction has decided a controversy and has, in a written opinion, set forth the rule or principle that formed the basis for its decision, so that rule or principle will be followed by the court in deciding subsequent cases. Likewise, subordinate courts in the same jurisdiction will be bound by the rule of law set forth in the decision. *Stare decisis*, then, affects persons who are not parties to the lawsuit, but *res adjudicata* applies only to the parties involved.

Stare decisis provides both certainty and predictability to the law. It is also expedient. Through reliance upon precedent established in prior cases, the common law has resolved many legal issues and brought stability into many areas of the law, such as the law of contracts. The doctrine of *stare decisis* provides a system wherein a businessman may act in a certain way with confidence that his action will have a certain legal effect. People can rely on prior decisions and, knowing the legal significance of their action, can act accordingly. There is reasonable certainty as to the results of conduct. Courts usually hesitate to renounce precedent and generally assume that if a principle or rule of law announced in a former judicial decision is unfair or contrary to public policy, it will be changed by legislation. It is important to note that an unpopular court ruling can usually be changed or overruled by statute. Precedent has more force on trial courts than on courts of review; the latter have the power to make precedent in the first instance.

Inherent Problems The common-law system as used in the United States has several inherent difficulties. First of all, the unbelievably large volume of judicial decisions, each possibly creating precedent, places "the law" beyond the actual knowledge of lawyers, let alone laymen.

Large law firms employ lawyers whose sole task is to search the case reports for "the law" to be used in lawsuits and in advising their clients. Legal research involves the examination of cases in hundreds of volumes. Because the total body of ruling case law is beyond the grasp of lawyers, it is obvious that laymen who are supposed to know the law and govern their conduct accordingly do not know the law and cannot always follow it, even with the advice of legal counsel.

Another major problem involving case law arises because conflicting precedents are frequently presented by the parties to an action. One of the major tasks of the courts in such cases is to determine which precedent is applicable to the case at bar and which precedent is correct. In addition, even today, many questions of law arise on which there has been no prior decision or in areas where the only authority is by implication. In such situations the judicial process is "legislative" in character and involves the creation of law, not merely its discovery.

It should also be noted that there is a distinction between precedent and mere dictum. As authority for future cases, a judicial decision is coextensive only with the facts upon which it is founded and the rules of law upon which the decision is actually predicated. Frequently, courts make comments on matters not necessary to the decision reached. Such expressions, called "dicta," lack the force of an adjudication and, strictly speaking, are not precedent that the court will be required to follow within the rule of *stare decisis*. However, dictum or implication in prior cases may be followed if sound and just, and dicta that have been repeated frequently are often given the force of precedent.

Finally, our system of each state having its own body of case law creates serious legal problems in matters that have legal implications in more than one state. The problem is discussed in more detail under the heading "Conflict of Laws."

Rejection of Stare Decisis The doctrine of *stare decisis* has not been applied in such a fashion as to render the law rigid and inflexible. If a court, and especially a reviewing court, should find that the prior decision was "palpably wrong," it may overrule it and decline to follow the rule enunciated by that case. By the same token, if the court should find that a rule of law established by a prior decision is no longer sound because of changing conditions, it may not consider the rule to be a binding precedent. The strength and genius of the common law is that no decision is *stare decisis* when it has lost its usefulness, or the reasons for it no longer exist. The doctrine does not require courts to multiply their errors by using former mistakes as authority and support for new errors. Thus, just as legislatures change the law by new legislation, so also do courts change the law, from time to time, by reversing former precedents. Judges are subject to social forces and changing circumstances just as are legislatures. The personnel of courts change, and each new generation of judges deems it a responsibility to reexamine precedents and to adapt them to the world of the present.

It should be noted, also, that in many cases a precedent created by a decision will not be a popular one and may be "out of step" with the times. The effect of the decision as a precedent can be nullified by the passage of a statute providing for a different result than that reached by the court as to future cases involving the same general issue.

Stare decisis may not be ignored by mere whim or caprice. It must be followed rather rigidly in the daily affairs of men. In the whole area of private law, uniformity and continuity are necessary. It is obvious that the same rules of tort and contract law must be applied in the afternoon as in the morning. *Stare decisis* must serve to take the capricious element out of law and to give stability to a society and to business.

However, in the area of public law, and especially constitutional law, the doctrine is frequently ignored. The Supreme Court recognizes that "it is a constitution which we are expounding, not the gloss which previous courts may have put on it."[1]

Conflict of Laws   Certain basic facts about our legal system must be recognized.

First of all, statutes and precedents, in all legal areas, vary from state to state. For example, in many states the plaintiff in an automobile accident case must be completely free of fault in order to recover judgment; but in other states the doctrine of comparative negligence is used, so that a plaintiff found to be 20 percent at fault could recover 80 percent of his injuries. Second, the doctrine of *stare decisis* does not require that one state recognize the precedent or rules of law of other states. Each state is free to decide for itself questions concerning its common law and interpretation of its own constitution and statutes. (However, courts will often follow decisions of other states if they are found to be sound. They are considered persuasive authority. This is particularly true in cases involving the construction of statutes such as the uniform acts, where each state has adopted the same statute.) Third, many legal issues arise out of acts or transactions that have contact with more than one state. For example, a contract may be executed in one state, performed in another, and the parties may live in still others; or an automobile accident may occur in one state involving citizens of different states.

These hypothetical situations illustrate the following fundamental question: Which state's *substantive* laws are applicable in a multiple-jurisdiction case where the law in one of the states or jurisdictions differs from the law in the other?

The body of law known as conflict of laws or choice of laws answers this question. It provides the court or forum with the

---

[1] Chief Justice John Marshall in *McCullough* v. *Maryland*, 4 Wheat 316, 407.

applicable substantive law in the multistate transaction or occurrence. For example, the law applicable to a tort is generally said to be the law of the state of place of injury. Thus a court sitting in state X would follow its own rules of procedure, but it would use the tort law of state Y if the injury occurred in Y. Several rules are used by courts on issues involving the law of contracts. These include the law of the state where the contract was made; the law of the place of performance; and the "grouping of contacts" or "center of gravity" theory, which uses the law of the state with the most substantial contact with the contract.

It is not the purpose of this text to teach conflict of laws, but the student should be aware that such a body of law exists and should recognize those situations in which conflict of law principles will be used. The trend toward uniform statutes and codes has tended to decrease these conflicts, but many of them still exist. So long as we have a federal system and fifty separate state bodies of substantive law, the area of conflicts of law will continue to be of substantial importance in the application of the doctrine of *stare decisis* and statutory law.

The Law in the Federal Courts

Our dual system of federal and state courts creates a unique problem in "conflicts." The federal courts use their own body of procedural law and their own body of substantive law in cases involving federal law. Decisions of the U.S. Supreme Court on questions involving the U.S. Constitution, treaties, and federal statutes are binding on state courts. Federal courts also have jurisdiction of cases involving citizens of different states even though no federal law is involved. The jurisdiction of federal courts is discussed more fully in Chapter 2. It is noted here that there is no body of federal common law and that in suits based on diversity of citizenship (suits between citizens of different states), federal courts use the substantive law, including conflict-of-law principles, of the state in which they are sitting. As in all cases, the federal courts do use their own rules of procedure, however. Thus, just as the state courts are bound by federal precedent in cases involving federal law and federally protected rights, so also are federal courts bound by state precedent in others.

Full Faith and Credit

One further aspect of the scope of precedent must be noted. Article IV, Section 1, of the U.S. Constitution provides: "Full Faith and Credit shall be given in each State to the Public Acts, Records, and judicial Proceedings of every other State. . . ." This does not mean that the precedent in one state is binding in other states, but only that the final decisions or judgments rendered in any given state by a court with jurisdiction shall be enforced as between the original parties in other states. "Full Faith and Credit" is applicable to the result of a specific decision as it affects the rights of the parties and not to the reasons or principles upon which it was based. Full faith and credit requires that a suit be brought on the judgment in the other state.

The Nature of the Judicial Process In this chapter we have briefly examined the great powers of the judiciary in our society that result from the doctrine of judicial review, from the role of courts in interpreting and applying statutes, and from the very nature of the concept of *stare decisis*. We now turn to an examination of the processes by which these powers are exercised. Recognizing that a court may declare a law unconstitutional, when and why will it do so? Why does a court announce one rule of law or follow one precedent rather than another? What type of reasoning is used by courts? What factors influence the courts in their decisions? Of course, no absolute answers can be given to these questions, but a consideration of them is essential to an understanding of the legal process and is accordingly the subject of this section.

The judicial system has a rather obvious priority of sources. Constitutions prevail over statutes, and statutes prevail over case law. Precedent would prevail over dicta, and dicta would usually be persuasive over mere argument. However, it should be acknowledged that, in spite of our more than two hundred years as a nation, many legal issues are not directly covered by a statute or case precedent. Litigation is frequently brought to challenge the validity of a statute or to seek to change a precedent that does exist. Frequently the decided cases are in conflict, or the case involves issues of conflicting social policies.

Thus the law is not a system of known rules. When many legal issues are presented to a court, the law applicable to those issues is made by the court and not merely found in some statute or case. In the sense that the law is made and not found, the role of the courts is legislative in character. When the applicable law is not known or clearly established the court must examine the rationale, or *ratio decidendi*, of existing statutes and cases and then extend or contract this *ratio* in deciding the case before it.

In describing the nature of the judicial process, Justice Cardozo[2] indicated that there are four forces that influence judges in the application of the *ratio decidendi*. These are logic, history, custom, and utility. The use of logic or analogy has been evident in our common law system and is ordinarily considered to be the chief method employed by courts. Using logic satisfies our desire for certainty and predictability in the law. History and custom have played a major role in the development of business law. Throughout this text, there will be references to the historical development of various concepts and statutes; it should be noted that statutory changes in the law frequently

[2] Benjamin Cardozo, *The Nature of the Judicial Process* (New Haven, Conn.: Yale University Press, 1921).

come about because the law recognizes the customary practices of businessmen. It is interesting to speculate, for example, whether checks not bearing a signature might someday be legal.

The fourth force, utility, refers to the elements of justice, morals, and social welfare. This factor, which Cardozo called the method of sociology, has become the major influence in many areas of the law in recent years. As public policy considerations have played an ever-increasing role in the development of our law, utility can be recognized as the dominant influence in such areas as civil rights, reapportionment, and antitrust actions.

The forces discussed by Cardozo can also be seen in the various kinds of reasoning used by courts in determining a rule of law or its applicability. For example, a court may base its determination upon the literal meaning of words appearing in the rule, upon the purpose of the rule, upon similarities between the facts of the case to be decided and the facts of decided cases, or upon considerations of social policy. Thus, reasoning may be literal, purposive, precedent oriented, or policy oriented.

Few principles are more firmly established in Anglo-American law than the principle of *stare decisis*. Accordingly, many judicial decisions are precedent oriented, and in nearly every case lawyers and judges expend considerable time and energy analyzing and discussing similarities and differences between the facts of decided cases and the facts of the case to be decided.

REVIEW QUESTIONS AND PROBLEMS

1. What are two basic purposes of law?
2. What is the difference between substantive law and procedural law?
3. List three categories of public law.
4. State X enacts an open occupancy law that requires owners of real estate to sell their property to any ready, willing, and able buyer regardless of race, creed, or color. Is this law a part of the public law or the private law? Explain.
5. How does the American common law system differ from the civil law system?
6. What role does the doctrine of judicial review play in the separation of powers concept?
7. Is the judiciary the overseer of the government? Explain.
8. Contrast the application of the doctrine of *stare decisis* in the public area of the law to its application in the private area.
9. What is the function of the body of law known as conflict of laws?
10. What basic trend in the American legal system is contributing toward uniformity among state laws?
11. Why is there a trend toward uniform state laws?
12. When will courts reject *stare decisis*? Give three examples.
13. What are the four forces that Cardozo said shaped the law?

2 THE RESOLUTION OF DISPUTES

Introduction   In our society, a variety of methods can be used to resolve conflicts and disputes. The most common is a compromise or settlement agreement between the parties to the dispute. Conflicts and disputes that are not settled by agreement between the parties may be resolved by litigation. A second important method for resolving conflicts and disputes is known as *arbitration*. Arbitration is the submission of a controversy to a nonjudicial body for a binding decision. Litigation has been the traditional method of resolving disputes, but more and more disputes are being submitted to arbitration. Finally, many issues in our society are submitted to a governmental agency for decision. Some of the disputes submitted to these agencies are between whole segments of society, and thus the decision is of general application in a manner similar to a statute. For example, a ruling by the Federal Aviation Administration that all passengers on airplanes must be searched would be an example of a problem resolved by an administrative agency in a manner that affected all of society. These administrative agencies also hear and decide disputes between individuals and individuals and government. For example, the Equal Employment Opportunity Commission might decide that an employer was guilty of discrimination or the Internal Revenue Service might decide that a taxpayer owed additional taxes. The basic legal principles applicable to these methods of resolving disputes will be discussed in this chapter.

Compromises and Settlements   Most disputes are resolved by the parties involved without resort to litigation or arbitration. Only a small fraction of the disputes in our society end up in court or even in a lawyer's office. There are a multitude of reasons why compromise is so prevalent

16

a technique for settling disputes. Some of the reasons may be described as personal, and others as economic.

The desire to compromise is part of human nature and may be considered to be almost a matter of instinct. Many persons have a fundamental dislike for trouble and a fear of "going to court." The moral and ethical values of a majority of society encourage compromise and settlement. The opinion of persons other than the parties to the dispute is often influential and is a motivating force in many compromises. Thus both internal and external forces exist that encourage people to settle their differences amicably.

Compromise and settlement of disputes is also encouraged by the economics of many situations. Lawsuits are expensive to both parties. As a general rule, each party must pay his own attorney's fees, and the losing party must pay the court costs. As a matter of practical economics, the winning party in a lawsuit is a loser to the extent of the fees he must pay his attorney, and the fees are often quite substantial.

At least two additional facts of economic life encourage business to settle disputes out of court. First, business must be concerned with its public image and the goodwill of its customers. Although the motto "The customer is always right" is not universally applicable today, the influence of the philosophy it represents cannot be underestimated. It often is simply not good business to sue a customer. Second, juries are frequently sympathetic to individuals who have suits against large corporations or defendants who are covered by insurance. Close questions of liability, as well as the size of verdicts, are more often than not resolved against business concerns because of their presumed ability to pay. As a result, business seeks to settle many disputes rather than submit them to a jury for decision.

The duty of lawyers to seek and achieve compromise whenever possible is not usually understood by laymen. In providing their services, lawyers will devote a substantial amount of their time, energy, and talent to seeking a compromise solution of the disputes of their clients. Attempts to compromise will be made before resort to the courts in most cases. Of all the disputes that are the subject of legal advice, the great majority are settled without resort to litigation. Of those that do result in litigation, the great majority are settled before the case goes to trial or even during the trial. Literally, the attempt of the lawyers to resolve the dispute never ends. It occurs before suit, before and during the trial, after verdict, during appeal, and even after appeal. As long as there is a controversy, it is the function of lawyers to attempt to resolve it.

Lawyers on both sides of a controversy seek compromise for a variety of reasons. A lawyer may view his client's case as weak, either on the law or on the facts. The amount of money involved, the necessity for a speedy decision, the nature of the contest, the uncertainty of legal remedy, the unfavorable publicity, and the expense entailed are some other reasons for avoiding a court trial. Each attorney must evaluate the cause of his client and seek a satisfactory—though not necessarily the most desirable—settlement of the controversy. The settlement of disputes is perhaps the most significant contribution of lawyers to our society.

Arbitration   Until recently the law and lawyers tended to prefer litigation to arbitration as a means of resolving disputes. Today more and more controversies are submitted for a final and binding decision to a person or persons other than the judicial tribunals provided by ordinary process of law. For example, a significant portion of all consumer quarrels with businesses are being submitted to arbitration for resolution. The arbitrator in such cases is often a Better Business Bureau.

There are several advantages to using arbitration as a substitute for litigation. For one thing it is much quicker and far less expensive. An issue can be submitted to arbitration and decided in less time than it takes to complete just the pleading phase of a lawsuit. Arbitration also creates less hostility than does litigation, and it allows the parties to continue their business relationship while the dispute is being decided. Finally, under the arbitration process complex issues can be submitted to an expert for decision. For example, if an issue arises concerning construction of a building, by using arbitration it can be submitted to an architect for decision. Besides lawyers, other specialists frequently serve as arbitrators: physicians decide issues relating to physical disabilities, certified public accountants decide those regarding the book value of stock, and engineers decide issues relating to industrial production. Of course a substantial amount of arbitration is also conducted by the academic community, especially in the area of labor relations.

The process of arbitration must be distinguished from *mediation.* Arbitration provides a binding decision, called an award. In mediation the third party assists the parties in seeking a compromise, but the mediator lacks authority to impose a binding solution. The purpose of mediation is to supply unbiased input to the negotiations and to encourage conciliation. The purpose of arbitration is the final solution of the dispute. Awards are enforceable by the courts just the same as a judicial decision. It should be noted that an agreement to submit a dispute to arbitration is usually memorable.

LITIGATION

**The Function
of Courts**   Many controversies cannot be settled by the parties or by arbitration. When other methods for resolving conflicts and controversies cannot or have not succeeded, there must be an ultimate method for accomplishing this goal. Our system of government has selected courts for this purpose. Courts settle controversies between persons and between persons and the state.

The rule of law applied by the court to the facts as found by the jury or court produces a decision that settles the controversy. Although there are obviously other agencies of government that resolve controversies, it is peculiar to our system that for final decision all controversies may ultimately end up in court. Whether the issue is the busing of schoolchildren, the legality of abortions, the enforceability of a contract, or the liability of a wrongdoer, the dispute, if not otherwise resolved, goes to the courts for a final decision.

State Court Systems

The judicial system of the United States is a dual system consisting of state courts and federal courts. The courts of the states, although not subject to uniform classification, may be grouped as follows: supreme courts, intermediate courts of review (in the more populous states), and trial courts. Some trial courts have general jurisdiction; others have limited jurisdiction. For example, a justice of the peace or a magistrate has power to hear civil cases only if the amount in controversy does not exceed a certain sum, and only those cases covering certain specified minor criminal matters.

Lawsuits are instituted in one of the trial courts. Even a court of general jurisdiction has geographical limitations. In many states the trial court of general jurisdiction is called a circuit court because in early

A Typical State Judicial System

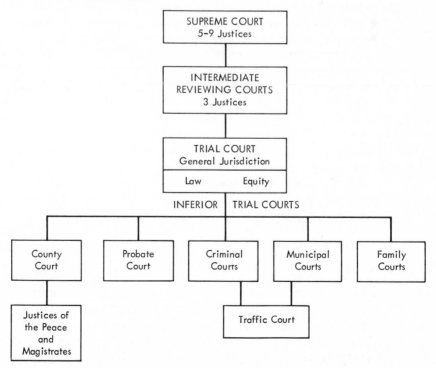

times a single judge sitting as a court traveled the circuit from one county to another. In other states it is called the superior court or the district court. Each area has a trial court of general jurisdiction.

Most states also have trial courts of limited jurisdiction. They may be limited as to subject matter, amount in controversy, or area in which the parties live. For example, courts with jurisdiction limited to a city are often called municipal courts.

Courts may also be named according to the subject matter with which they deal. Probate courts deal with wills and the estates of deceased persons; family courts, with divorces, family relations, juveniles, and dependent children; criminal and police courts, with violators of state laws and municipal ordinances; and traffic courts, with traffic violations. For an accurate classification of the courts of any state, the statutes of that state should be examined. The chart on page 19 illustrates the jurisdiction and organization of reviewing and trial courts in a typical state.

The Federal Court System

The courts of the United States are created by Congress, but their jurisdiction is limited by the Constitution. The Constitution creates the Supreme Court and authorizes such inferior courts as the Congress may from time to time establish. Congress has created eleven United States courts of appeal, the United States district courts (at least one in each state), and others such as the Court of Customs and Patent Appeals, the Court of Claims, and the Tax Court, which handle special subject matter as indicated by the name of the court. The chart on page 21 illustrates the federal court system.

The district courts are the trial courts of the federal judicial system. They have original jurisdiction, exclusive of the courts of the states, over all federal crimes, that is, all offenses against the laws of the United States. The accused is entitled to a trial by jury in the state and district where the crime was committed.

In civil actions the district courts have jurisdiction only when the matter in controversy exceeds the sum or value of $10,000, exclusive of costs and interest, and is based on either diversity of citizenship or a federal question. Diversity of citizenship exists in suits between (1) citizens of different states; (2) a citizen of a state and a citizen of a foreign country; and (3) a state and citizens of another state. The plaintiff or all plaintiffs, if more than one, must be citizens of a different state than any one of the defendants for diversity of citizenship to exist. Diversity of citizenship does not prevent the plaintiff from bringing his suit in a state court, but if the defendant is a citizen of another state, the defendant has the right to have the case removed to a federal court. A defendant, by having the case removed to the federal court, has an opportunity of having a jury selected from a larger area than the county where the cause arose, thus hopefully avoiding the possibility of jurors prejudicial to the plaintiff.

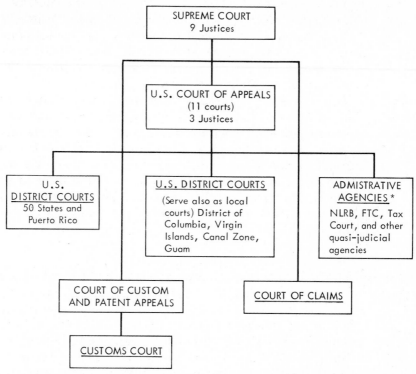

```
                    ┌─────────────────────┐
                    │   SUPREME COURT     │
                    │     9 Justices      │
                    └─────────────────────┘

                    ┌─────────────────────┐
                    │ U.S. COURT OF APPEALS│
                    │     (11 courts)     │
                    │     3 Justices      │
                    └─────────────────────┘
```

| U.S. DISTRICT COURTS 50 States and Puerto Rico | U.S. DISTRICT COURTS (Serve also as local courts) District of Columbia, Virgin Islands, Canal Zone, Guam | ADMISTRATIVE AGENCIES * NLRB, FTC, Tax Court, and other quasi-judicial agencies |

COURT OF CUSTOM AND PATENT APPEALS

COURT OF CLAIMS

CUSTOMS COURT

*The federal administrative agencies are not officially part of the Federal Court System but are included in this chart because their rulings can be appealed to a federal court.

For the purpose of suit in a federal court, a corporation is considered a "citizen" of the state where it is incorporated and of the state in which it has its principal place of business. As a result, there is no federal jurisdiction in many cases in which one of the parties is a corporation. If any one of the parties on the other side of the case is a citizen either of the state in which the corporation is chartered or is doing its principal business, there is no diversity of citizenship and thus no federal jurisdiction.

Federal jurisdiction based on a federal question exists if the lawsuit arises out of rights granted by the Constitution, laws, or treaties of the United States. The federal courts have jurisdiction of federal question cases if $10,000 or more is involved or if the case involves personal rights without reference to money value of the controversy. For example, the amount of the controversy is not a jurisdictional question when the suit is brought by the United States or a federal officer and arises under the Constitution or federal laws and treaties. These civil actions may involve matters such as bankruptcy or setting aside orders of administrative agencies such as the Interstate Commerce Commission. Other federal question cases that do not require that $10,000 be involved are suits based on patents, copyrights, trademarks, taxes, elections, and the rights guaranteed by the Bill of Rights and those rights secured to individual citizens by the Fourteenth Amendment. In addition, by statute the district courts now have original jurisdiction to try tort cases involving damages to citizens caused by officers or agents of the federal government and the power to issue writs of *habeas corpus* and to grant injunctions in a variety of cases. In cases where injunctions are sought, three judges must hear the case.

Direct appeals from the decisions of the district courts to the United States Supreme Court may be made in several situations, such as (1) in criminal cases when the decision of the lower court is based upon the invalidity or construction of a statute upon which the indictment or information was founded; (2) when the lower court has held an act of Congress unconstitutional, in a case in which an agency of the government is a party; and (3) when the lower court consisting of three judges has either granted or denied after notice an interlocutory or permanent injunction. However, in most cases an appeal is taken from a U.S. district court to the court of appeals.

The intermediate courts of appeal from the U.S. district courts are called the United States Courts of Appeals. The federal judicial districts are divided into eleven circuits, and a court of appeals has been established for each circuit. These courts are not trial courts and are limited to appellate jurisdiction.

In most cases the decisions of the courts of appeals are final. Cases in the courts of appeals may be reviewed by the Supreme Court by a *writ of certiorari* granted upon a petition of any party before or after a decision in the courts of appeals. The writ of certiorari to review a judgment of the courts of appeals is within the discretion of the Supreme Court. The writ will be issued when necessary to secure uniformity of decision or to bring cases of grave public concern to the court of last resort for decision.

Courts of appeals decisions may also be reviewed by the Supreme Court in cases in which a state statute has been held unconstitutional and a federal question is presented. In addition, the courts of appeals may by certification seek instructions from the Supreme Court on any question of law in any civil or criminal case.

The U.S. district courts and the courts of appeals cannot review, retry, or correct the judicial errors charged against a state court. Final judgments or decrees rendered by the highest court of a state are reviewed only by the Supreme Court of the United States. State cases appealed to the U.S. Supreme Court must concern the validity of a treaty or statute of the United States or must present a question involving the validity of a state statute on the grounds that the statute is repugnant to the Constitution, treaties, or laws of the United States and that the state decision is in favor of the statute's validity. When a case involves the constitutionality of a state statute or treaty or when a citizen's rights, privileges, or immunities under the constitution or laws are impaired, the case may be brought to the Supreme Court by writ of certiorari. In all other cases the decision of the highest state court is not subject to review.

Law and Equity   Historically, the trial courts in the United States have been divided into two parts—a court of law and a court of equity or chancery. The term *equity* arose in England because the failure of the law courts to provide adequate remedies often made it impossible to obtain justice in the king's courts of law.

In order that justice might be done, the person seeking a remedy sought redress from the king in person. Because the appeal was to the king's conscience, he referred such matters to his spiritual adviser, the chancellor. Such an individual was usually a church official, and in giving a remedy he usually favored the ecclesiastical law.

By such method, there developed a separate system of procedure and different rules for deciding matters presented to the chancellor. Suits involving these rules were said to be brought "in chancery" or "in equity," in contradistinction to suits "at law" in the king's courts. Courts of equity were courts of conscience and recognized many rights that were not recognized by common law courts. For example, trusts in lands were recognized; rescission was allowed on contracts created through fraud; injunction and specific performance were developed.

In a few states courts of equity are still separate and distinct from courts of law. In most states the equity and law courts are organized under a single court with two dockets—one at law, the other in equity. Whether the case is in equity or at law is determined by the remedy desired. Modern civil procedure laws usually have abolished distinction between actions at law and in equity. However, pleadings usually must denote whether the action is legal or equitable because, as a general rule, there is no right to a jury trial of an equitable action. The constitutional guarantee to a trial by jury applies only to actions at law.

Courts of equity use maxims instead of strict rules of law. There are no *legal* rights in equity, for the decision is based on moral rights and natural justice. Some of the typical maxims of equity are:

1. Equity will not suffer a right to exist without a remedy.
2. Equity regards as done that which ought to be done.
3. Where there is equal equity, the law must prevail.
4. He who comes into equity must do so with clean hands.
5. He who seeks equity must do equity.
6. Equity aids the vigilant.
7. Equality is equity.

These maxims serve as guides to the chancellor to use in exercising his discretion. For example, the clean-hands doctrine (4) prohibits a party who is guilty of misconduct in the matter in litigation from receiving the aid of the court.

The decision of the court in equity is called a decree. A judgment in a court of law is measured in damages, whereas a decree of a court of equity is said to be *in personam*, that is, it is directed to the defendant, who is to do or not to do some specific thing.

Decrees are either final or interlocutory. A decree is final when it disposes of the issues in the case, reserving no question to be decided in the future. A decree quieting title to real estate, granting a divorce, or ordering specific performance is usually final. A decree is interlocutory when it reserves some question to be determined in the future. A decree granting a temporary injunction, appointing a receiver, and ordering property to be delivered to such a receiver would be interlocutory.

Failure upon the part of the defendant to obey a decree of a court of equity is contempt of court because the decree is directed not against his property but against his person. Any person in contempt of court may be placed in jail or fined by order of the court.

Equity jurisprudence plays an ever-increasing role in our legal system. The movement toward social justice requires more reliance on the equitable maxims and less reliance on rigid rules of law.

Courts and Change

Many people have the mistaken notion that the law is a set of known rules applied by a judge. To them the problem is simple.

If the judge does not know the law on a particular subject, he need only look it up in one of hundreds of books in his library. This is definitely not so, especially in the area of constitutional law. Law is frequently made and not found. It is also changed from time to time to meet changing conditions. Thus courts are an instrument of social, political, and economic change. The law changes as it is applied to new cases. It may expand or contract its application or take off in a new direction, but it is seldom static. Whole new legal principles that change society may also be created by courts.

Courts at different times play different roles in bringing about changes in our society. Some judges and courts adopt what is usually described as the philosophy of "judicial restraint." This philosophy admonishes courts to change only those rules of law that they must change and to decide only those matters that they must decide. According to this view, change for the most part should be left to the political processes and to the legislative and executive branches, which are responsive to the political process.

The other philosophy of many courts and judges has been often referred to as the "activist" philosophy. According to activist judges, the political processes and the other branches of government either may fail to bring about necessary changes in society or may do so too slowly. They view the law and the courts as being leaders of social, political, and economic change. To them the Constitution must be interpreted in the light of the times and our experience as a people, and not merely by what was said. Some scholars have called this belief that the Constitution is a relative document the sociological approach to constitutional decisions. According to the activist view, the law is not as concerned with what the founding fathers intended when they wrote the Constitution as with what they would have intended had they known of contemporary problems. This view of the court's role as an instrument of social change and of the Constitution as a relative document was graphically illustrated in the school desegregation case of *Brown* v. *Board of Education*, 347 U.S. 497 (1954), in which Chief Justice Warren said in part while discussing the meaning of the Fourteenth Amendment to the United States Constitution:

> In approaching this problem, we cannot turn the clock back to 1868 when the Amendment was adopted. . . . We must consider public education in the light of its full development and its present place in American life throughout the Nation. Only in this way can it be determined if segregation in public schools deprives these plaintiffs of the equal protection of the laws.

Throughout our history, the Supreme Court has at least to some degree followed the activist theory. Some Supreme Courts have been more activist than others. The era of the Warren court from 1954 to 1969 was generally known for its activist majority, but the Supreme Courts of the early thirties were generally labeled as conservative or judicial restraint oriented. The majority of the Burger court of the 1970s has given clear signs of a judicial restraint orientation. The extent to which the Court is an instrument of change will vary from time to time depending upon the makeup of the Court. However, the Court will always be an instrument of change to some degree. For example, the Supreme Court in 1973 held that state laws prohibiting abortions were unconstitutional. In 1972 the same court held the death penalty to be unconstitutional, but in 1976—with a change of only one in the makeup of the Court—it was held that capital punishment may be constitutional. Thus a Court with considerable bent toward judicial restraint has activist tendencies.

**The
Court System's
Major Problem
—Delay**

"Justice delayed is justice denied" sums up the most obvious problem in our court system—court congestion and the delay that results therefrom. In many areas, the backlog of civil cases is so great that a period of several years elapses between the event in question and a jury trial. Such delays cause serious problems for the parties and adversely affect the search for truth. The volume of criminal cases that are awaiting trial or are pending on appeal raise many serious consequences for society, not the least of which is that anyone out of jail on bond is free to commit more crimes while the case is pending.

Chief Justice Burger is seeking to speed up the litigation process in both civil and criminal cases. Among the changes being instituted are (1) reducing the number of written opinions at the appellate level, (2) requiring attorneys to be prepared when the case is first called for trial, and (3) making use of such modern technology as data-processing equipment and computer transcribers to speed up the paperwork of courts.

Many other changes designed to eliminate and reduce court congestion and the backlog of court cases have been proposed. The changes that have had partial acceptance to date include (1) requiring only six-person juries instead of twelve, (2) requiring only majority verdicts instead of unanimous ones, (3) eliminating oral argument on appeal whenever possible, and (4) eliminating jury trials in certain types of cases. In addition, the number of judges has been expanded in many states.

There have been several suggestions made to reduce the caseload of the federal courts. Perhaps the most radical idea is to abolish diversity of citizenship jurisdiction. It is argued that there is no rational basis for putting an automobile accident case in a federal court simply because the parties are citizens of different states. The chief justice has also advocated the elimination of three-judge federal district courts with the right of direct appeal to the Supreme Court.

It has also been proposed that a special court be created to hear petitions for writs of certiorari. This would free the Supreme Court to spend its time deciding the cases before it rather than requiring it to spend a significant portion of its time deciding which cases it wants to hear. Each year the Supreme Court must review over two thousand petitions for writs of certiorari. This new court could consist of courts of appeals justices on a rotating basis.

Other possible changes in the future are (1) the creation of some special courts to handle specialized areas of the law, such as antitrust and consumer protection, (2) the creation of administrative processes to handle complaints of persons in prison, and (3) the use of electronic data-processing techniques to speed up the preparation of transcripts for review purposes, as well as the retrieval of precedent. In regard to the last suggestion, it seems clear that legal research needs to be brought out of the dark past into the last quarter of the twentieth century.

ADMINISTRATIVE LAW

**Administrative
Agencies**   In a complex industrial society, social and economic problems are so numerous that courts and legislative bodies cannot possibly deal with all of them. Legislation must be general in character and cannot possibly cover all the problems and situations that

may arise in connection with the problem or evil the law seeks to control or correct. There must be a method of filling in the gaps in legislation and of adding meat to the bones of legislative policy. Administrative agencies are necessary in order to lighten the burdens that otherwise must be borne by the executive branch, legislative bodies, and courts. The multitude of administrative agencies performing governmental functions today encompasses almost every aspect of business operation and, indeed, almost every aspect of our daily lives. These agencies provide flexibility in the law and adaptability to changing conditions.

The direct day-to-day legal impact on business of the many local, state, and federal administrative agencies is far greater than the impact of the courts and legislative bodies. Administrative agencies create and enforce the greater bulk of the laws that make up the legal environment of business.

Functions The functions of administrative bodies generally are described as (1) rule making, (2) adjudicating, (3) prosecuting, (4) advising, (5) supervising, and (6) investigating. These functions are not the concern of all administrative agencies to the same degree. Some agencies are primarily adjudicating bodies, such as the industrial commissions that rule on workmen's compensation claims. Others, such as the Federal Power Commission, are concerned primarily with a special industry, and still others, such as the Federal Trade Commission, with a particular phase of business. Others are primarily supervisory, such as the Securities and Exchange Commission, which supervises the issue and sale of investment securities. Most agencies perform all the foregoing functions to some degree in carrying out their responsibilities.

In addition to traditional executive functions, the administrative process involves performance of both quasi-legislative and quasi-judicial functions. The *quasi-legislative function* in the administrative process is to make rules and regulations to carry out the purposes of the agency. Such rules and regulations provide the detail necessary to implement the policy as announced in the legislation creating the agency. Courts frequently review the rules and regulations adopted by administrative agencies to determine whether or not they have exceeded their delegated authority. These rules and regulations are in effect laws just as if they had been passed by the legislative body.

The *quasi-judicial function*, as the term implies, involves conducting trial-like hearings and deciding controversies between actual parties. These parties may be an employer and an employee, as in the case of an unfair labor practice charge or a charge of discrimination. On the other hand, one party may be the agency itself, as in the case of an unfair method of competition charge brought by the Federal Trade Commission.

Administrative Hearings As previously noted, administrative agencies conduct two distinct types of hearings. The first type is an integral part of the rule-making function and consists of receiving testimony concerning the need for or the desirability of proposed rules and regulations. Notice of such hearings is usually given to the public, and all interested parties are allowed to present evidence for consideration by the agency. Assuming that the adopted rule is within the delegated authority, the rule cannot be set aside by a court simply because the court does not agree with the rule or because the court believes that a different rule should have been adopted. Courts cannot substitute their judgment for that of the agency because the legislative body has determined that the agency is the expert in the area and is better equipped to make the decision. However, an agency rule that is arbitrary, capricious, and unreasonable will be set aside as being unconstitutional.

The second type of hearing is a quasi-judicial hearing concerning a specific party or parties and the agency. Its purpose may be to find if a rule of the agency or an applicable statute has been violated. For example, a hearing may be for the purpose of fixing liability as in the case of workmen's compensation, which provides employer liability for employee deaths, sicknesses, and injury arising out of and in the course of employment. The quasi-judicial hearings receive detailed evidence and determine the rights and duties of the parties subject to the jurisdiction of the agency.

The rules of procedure used in these quasi-judicial hearings are usually formulated by the administrative bodies themselves and are made available to those who may be interested in them. The hearings are more informal in character than court trials, but on the whole they follow the general pattern set by the courts. The rules of evidence are not as strictly followed because the hearing officer may not have formal legal training. A hearing normally originates with the filing of a petition or complaint. The interested parties are then notified that a hearing will be held at a stated time They are given an opportunity to file pertinent documents and an opportunity to present evidence at the hearing.

The agency often appoints a person to conduct the hearing. He is sometimes called a hearing examiner or trial examiner and sometimes an arbitrator. He receives the evidence, submits his findings of the facts, and makes his recommendations to the board or commission regarding the disposition to be made in the case. The board studies the report and issues such orders as the law in the case appears to demand.

The quasi-judicial function of administrative agencies is the subject of substantial controversy. A frequent complaint is that administrative agencies make a law; investigate to see if it has been violated; serve as prosecutor, judge, and jury; and then act in the manner of an appellate court in reviewing the decision. Lawyers also object that these quasi-judicial hearings are subject to improper influence and that the person conducting the hearing does not always follow the accepted rules of evidence, so that improper and irrelevant evidence may be the basis of a decision. The lack of direct accountability to the people is another often-stated criticism of administrative agencies.

Judicial Review of Agency Decisions

Perhaps the most important question for businessmen in the field of administrative law is: Under what circumstances will the quasi-judicial decision of an administrative agency be changed or reversed by a court? First of all, one must have "standing to sue" before he or she may challenge the decision of an agency. Standing to sue requires a direct financial or property interest in the decision. A local citizen who likes a particular TV program could not challenge an FCC decision on a TV station license renewal.

Second, it must be recognized that courts will review the findings and rulings of the agency only after the remedies and review provided within the agency have been exhausted. For example, a property owner who wishes to challenge the zoning classification made by his local zoning board must appeal to the appropriate city council or Zoning Board of Appeals as the law may provide before a court challenge is possible.

Finally, a court will not reverse the decision of the agency if there is substantial evidence on the record as a whole to support the decision of the agency. If a reasonable result was obtained, the decision will not be changed even though the court on the same evidence would have reached a different conclusion.

REVIEW QUESTIONS AND PROBLEMS

1. What is the difference between *arbitration* and *mediation?*

2. Name four situations in which business may want to include an arbitration provision in a contract.

3. What are the advantages of arbitration over a judicial decision?

4. List three reasons why lawyers encourage business to settle controversies out of court.

5. Give reasons for the large number of governmental administrative agencies.

6. What are some of the objections of lawyers to administrative agencies exercising judicial powers?

7. Under what circumstances may a court reverse the decision of an administrative agency?

8. Compare the philosophies of "judicial restraint" and "judicial activism."

9. Prepare a chart of the judicial system of your state.

10. What is the jurisdictional limit on the amount of money involved in federal court cases?

11. D company is incorporated in Delaware, but its principal place of business

is in Illinois. P, a citizen of Illinois, sues D company for $20,000 in the federal district court for injuries received in using a product manufactured by D. D moves to dismiss on the grounds of lack of federal jurisdiction. What result? Why?

12. Is there a jurisdictional limit on the amount of money involved in all federal question cases? In any federal question cases? Explain.

13. Why did courts of equity develop?

14. Does the Constitution guarantee a trial by jury for all types of cases?

15. If X, a citizen of Illinois, sues Y, a citizen of Indiana, and Z, a citizen of Illinois, does a federal court have jurisdiction if the subject matter of the suit is not a federal question? Why?

16. X, a citizen of Alabama sues Y, a citizen of Mississippi, in the Alabama state court for $7,500. Jurisdiction is obtained by service of process in Mississippi. Can Y have the case removed to the federal courts? Why?

17. X and Y are discussing matters and disagree on the legality of proposed action. X suggests that a suit be filed to determine the legality of the proposed conduct. Will a court settle their dispute? Explain.

18. What is the most obvious problem of today's court system, and what are some of the suggested solutions?

3 LAWSUITS

Introduction   As previously noted, law may be classified as *substantive law* or *procedural law.* Substantive law defines the rights and duties of citizens and is the result of legislative action or judicial action. Procedural law specifies the method and means by which the substantive law is made, enforced, and administered. Procedural rules prescribe the methods by which courts apply substantive law to resolve conflicts. Substantive rights have no value unless there are procedures that provide a means for establishing and enforcing them.

Judicial procedure is concerned with the rules by which a lawsuit is conducted. One common method of classifying judicial procedure is to divide it into two parts—*criminal* and *civil.* Criminal procedure prescribes the rules of law for the apprehension, prosecution, and fixing of punishment of persons who have committed crimes. Civil procedure prescribes the rules by which parties to civil lawsuits use the courts to settle their disputes.

In most cases there are three basic questions to be answered: (1) What are the facts? (2) What evidence is relevant and proper to prove the facts? (3) What rules of law apply to the facts? It is the function of the jury to answer the first question; the court furnishes the answer to the second; and the court provides the answer to the third by instructing the jury as to the law to be applied to the facts as found by the jury.

Jurisdiction   The first requirement in any lawsuit is that it must be brought before a court that has the power to hear the case. This power to hear the case is known as *jurisdiction.*

Jurisdiction has two aspects—jurisdiction over the subject matter and jurisdiction over the parties. Jurisdiction over the subject matter

31

means that the lawsuit is of the type that the court was created to decide. For example, a probate court would not have jurisdiction to determine questions of law involving a civil suit for damages. A criminal court would have no jurisdiction in a divorce matter. Courts may also be limited by the amounts of money involved in the case. For example, federal courts only hear suits for damages that involve at least $10,000.

A court must also have jurisdiction over the parties—the plaintiff and the defendant. Jurisdiction over the plaintiff is obtained when the lawsuit is filed. A plaintiff voluntarily submits to the jurisdiction of the court when the suit is filed.

Jurisdiction over the defendant is accomplished by the service of a summons issued by the court. It is delivered to a sheriff or other person to be served upon the defendant. Jurisdiction over a defendant in some cases may be obtained by publishing a notice in a newspaper. The latter is possible in a limited number of cases, such as a suit for divorce or cases involving real estate in which the "thing" involved is of sufficient importance that notice by publication is deemed sufficient to actually notify the defendant. Publication may also be accompanied by proper attachment proceedings. In such cases, service by publication brings under the court's jurisdiction all attached property of a nonresident defendant that lies within the territorial limits of the court. When this technique is employed, the attached property may be used to satisfy any judgment. Most cases, however, require the actual service of a summons on the defendant in order to give him notice of the suit.

Many states allow a summons to be served at the defendant's home upon any member of the family above a specified age, such as ten years. In such cases, a copy is also mailed to the defendant.

Long-Arm Statutes

Historically, the jurisdiction of courts to enter judgment against a person required actual personal service of the summons on the defendant in the state in which the suit was brought. This was necessary in order to give the defendant notice of the suit and an opportunity to defend. Because the jurisdiction of courts was limited to geographical areas such as a state or a county, power to issue and serve a summons beyond the borders of the state or county did not exist. Extending judicial jurisdiction across a state boundary for the purpose of acquiring jurisdiction over the person of a nonresident was considered a denial of due process of law. Requiring a person to go from his own state or county to another state or county for trial imposed undue burdens on the defendant and was a denial of the right to a fair trial.

Such reasoning limiting the jurisidiction of courts is no longer accepted. Personal jurisdiction over nonresidents has been expanded because modern transportation and communication facilities have minimized the inconveniences to a nonresident defendant who must defend himself in courts beyond his home state. There is no longer any logical reason to deny a local citizen a remedy in local courts for an injury caused by a nonresident temporarily present in the state. The first extension of jurisdiction over nonresidents occurred in auto accident cases. This was done by creating a legal "fiction" that resulted in the summons being served within the state whose court issued the summons. This legal fiction was created by the enactment of statutes that provided that a nonresident, by using the state highways, automatically appointed a designated state official, usually the secretary of state, as his agent to accept service of process. The summons would be served on the secretary of state, who would notify the defendant of the suit, and the defendant was then subject to the power of the court.

These nonresident motorist statutes opened the door for adoption of other statutes, called "long-arm" statutes, which further extend the jurisdiction of courts over nonresidents, whether they be individuals or corporations. Long-arm statutes typically extend the jurisdiction of courts to cases in which a tort injury has been caused by a nonresident "doing business" in the state.

They also usually extend jurisdiction to cases arising out of the ownership of property located within the state. Of course, the conduct of business such as entering into contracts confers jurisdiction. Thus a nonresident individual or a corporation may be subject to a suit for injuries if either has certain "minimal contacts" within the state, so long as the maintenance of the suit does not offend traditional notions of fair play and substantial justice.

What "minimal contacts" and activities are necessary to bring the defendant into a state is a fact question depending upon each particular case. Whatever the basis for the action may be, either in contract or in tort, the court can acquire jurisdiction over the defendant if these minimal contacts are present.

Venue As previously discussed, the term *jurisdiction* defines the power of the court to hear and adjudicate the case. Jurisdiction includes the court's power to inquire into the facts, apply the law to the facts, make a decision, and declare and enforce a judgment. *Venue* relates to and defines the particular territorial area within the state, county, or district in which the civil case or civil prosecution should be brought and tried. Matters of venue are usually determined by statute. In a few states, the subject of venue is covered in the state constitution. Venue statutes usually provide that actions concerning interests in land must be commenced and tried in the county or district in which the land is located. Actions for the recovery of penalties imposed by statute against public officers must be commenced and tried in the county or district in which the cause of action arose. Suits for divorce must be commenced and tried in the county in which one of the parties resides. All other suits or actions must be commenced and tried in the county in which one or all of the defendants reside, or in the county in which the transaction took place or where the wrong was committed. For example, a tort action may be commenced and tried either in the county or district where the tort was committed, or where the defendant resides or may be found. If the defendants are nonresidents, and assuming that proper service can be made upon them under a "long-arm" statute, the suit may be commenced and tried in any county the plaintiff designates in his complaint.

The judge may change the place of trial at the request of either party when it appears from an affidavit of either party that the action was not commenced in the proper venue. A change of venue may also be requested on the ground that the judge has an interest in the suit or is related to any parties to the action or has manifested a prejudice so that he cannot be expected to conduct a fair and impartial trial. A change of venue is often requested in criminal trials when the inhabitants of the county allegedly are so prejudiced against the defendant that a fair trial is not possible. The convenience of witnesses and the parties may also justify a change of venue.

Pleadings   A *pleading* is a legal document filed with the court that sets forth the position and contentions of a party. The purpose of pleadings in civil actions is to define the issues of the lawsuit. This is accomplished by each party making allegations of fact and the other party either admitting the allegations or denying them. The procedure is as follows: The plaintiff files with the clerk of the court a pleading usually called a *complaint*. In some types of cases this initial pleading is called a *declaration* or a *petition*. The clerk then issues a summons that, together with a copy of the complaint, is served on the defendant. The summons notifies the defendant of the date by which he is required to either file a pleading in answer to the allegations of the complaint or file some other pleading attacking the complaint.

If the defendant has no legal basis to attack the sufficiency of the complaint, an answer will be filed in which the defendant either admits or denies each material allegation of the complaint. This answer will put in issue all allegations of the complaint that are denied.

In addition to the admissions and denials, an answer may contain affirmative defenses, which if proved will defeat the plaintiff's claim. The answer may also contain causes of action the defendant has against the plaintiff, called *counterclaims*. Upon receipt of the defendant's answer, the plaintiff will, unless the applicable rules of procedure do not so require, file a reply that specifically admits or denies each new allegation in the defendant's answer. These new allegations are those found in the affirmative defenses and counterclaims. Thus the allegations of each party are admitted or denied in the pleadings.

Allegations of fact by either party that are denied by the other become the issues to be decided at the trial.

Motions Attacking Pleadings The first pleading (complaint), in order to be legally sufficient, must allege facts sufficient to set forth a right of action or right to legal relief in the plaintiff. The defendant's attorney, after studying the complaint, may (instead of answering) choose one of several different ways to challenge its legal sufficiency. For example, by motion to the court the defendant may object to the complaint, pointing out specifically its defects. The defendant, through such motion, admits for purposes of argument all the facts alleged in the complaint. His position is that those facts are not legally sufficient to give the plaintiff the right to what is sought in the complaint. Such motion, called a *demurrer* at common law, raises questions of law, not questions of fact. If the court finds that the complaint does set forth facts sufficient to give the plaintiff what is sought, it will deny the motion. The defendant will then be granted leave to answer the complaint; should he fail to do so within the time limit set by the court, a judgment by default may be entered for the plaintiff. If the court finds, however, that the complaint fails to state facts sufficient to give the plaintiff the relief sought, the court will allow the motion and dismiss the suit but will give to the plaintiff permission to file an amended complaint. The plaintiff will thus be given an opportunity to restate the allegations so that he may be able to set forth a right to recover from the defendant.

In addition to a motion to dismiss for failure to allege a valid cause of action, a defendant may also move to dismiss the suit for reasons that as a matter of law would prevent the plaintiff from winning his suit. Such matters as a discharge in bankruptcy, a lack of jurisdiction of the court to hear the suit, or an expiration of the time limit during which the defendant is subject to suit may be raised by such a motion. These are technical matters that raise questions of law for the court's decision.

Decisions Based on Pleadings Most states and the federal courts have procedures known as "motions for summary judgment" or "motions for judgment on the pleadings" by which either party may seek a final decision without a trial. In hearings on these motions the court examines all papers on file in the case, including affidavits that may have been filed with the motion or in opposition to it, to see if a genuine material issue of fact remains. If there is no such question of fact, the court will then decide the legal question raised by the facts and find for one party or the other. This is possible only when there are no facts in dispute. In such cases there is no reason for a trial, and the issues between the parties are pure questions of law.

35

If a defendant subject to the jurisdiction of the court fails to file an answer either originally or after his motions have been overruled, he is in default, and a court of law may enter a default judgment against him. A court of equity would enter a similar order known as a decree *pro confesso*. A plaintiff who fails to reply to new matter such as a counterclaim is also in default and subject to judgments and decrees.

**Pretrial
Procedures**   During the pleading stage and in the interval before the trial, the law provides for procedures called *discovery* procedures. Discovery is designed to take the "sporting aspect" out of litigation and to ensure that the results of lawsuits are based on the merits of the controversy and less on the ability, skill, or cunning of counsel. Without these procedures an attorney with no case on the facts or law might win a lawsuit through surprise—by keeping silent about a fact or by concealing his true case until the trial. The theory is that the results of lawsuits should not be based on the skill or lack thereof of counsel but on the relative merits of the controversy. Discovery practice is designed to ensure that each side is fully aware of all aspects of the case and of the contentions of the parties prior to trial. With each side fully aware of the strengths and weaknesses of his case, the second of the avowed purposes of discovery—to encourage settlement of suits and to avoid actual trial—is facilitated. Modern discovery procedures result in the compromise and settlement of a large majority of all civil suits.

Discovery practices include the taking of the deposition (questioning under oath) of other parties and witnesses; the serving of written questions to be answered under oath by the opposite party; compulsory physical examinations in personal injury cases by doctors chosen by the other party; orders requiring the production of statements, exhibits, documents, maps, photographs, and so on; and the serving by one party on the other of demands to admit facts under oath. These procedures allow a party to learn not only about matters that may be used as evidence but also about matters that may lead to the discovery of evidence.

Just prior to the trial, a pretrial conference between the lawyers and the judge will be held in states with modern rules of procedure. At this conference the pleadings, results of the discovery process, and probable evidence are reviewed in an attempt to settle the suit. The issues may be further narrowed, and the judge may even give his prediction of the outcome in order to encourage settlement.

THE TRIAL

Jury Selection   Not every case can be settled even under modern procedures. Some must go to trial on the issues of fact raised by the pleadings that remain after the pretrial conference. If the only issues are questions of law, the court will decide the case without a trial by a ruling on one of the motions previously mentioned. If the case is at law and either party has demanded a jury trial, the case will be set for trial and a jury empaneled. If the case is in equity or if no jury demand has been made, it will be set down for trial before the court. For purposes of the following discussion we shall assume a trial before a jury.

The first step of the trial is to select the jury. Prior to the calling of the case, the clerk of the court will have summoned potential jurors known as the *venire*. They will be selected at random from lists of eligible citizens, and twelve of them will be called into the jury box for the conduct of *voir dire* examination. Recent legislation in some states provides for juries of six persons in some types of cases. Such legislation has been held constitutional by the Supreme Court. It should also be noted here that some recent statutes allow for less than unanimous verdicts as well. *Voir dire* examination is a method by which the court and the attorneys for each party examine the jurors as to their qualifications to be fair and impartial. Each side in the lawsuit may challenge or excuse a juror for cause—for example, for bias, prejudice, or relation to one of the parties. In addition, each side will be given a certain number of challenges known as "peremptory challenges," for which no cause need be given. Each side is given an opportunity to question the prospective jurors and either to accept them or to reject them until his challenges are exhausted. The prospective jurors are sworn to give truthful answers to the questions on *voir dire*. The process continues until the full jury is selected.

Introduction of Evidence After selecting the jurors, the attorneys make opening statements. An opening statement is not evidence. It is only used to familiarize the jury with the essential facts in the case that each side expects to prove in order that the jury may understand the overall picture of the case and the relevancy of each piece of evidence as presented. After the opening statements, the plaintiff presents his evidence.

Evidence is presented in open court by means of examination of witnesses and the production of documents and other exhibits. The party calling a witness questions him to establish the facts about the case. As a general rule, a party calling a witness is not permitted to ask "leading questions," questions in which the desired answer is indicated by the form of the question. After the party calling the witness has completed his direct examination, the other party is given the opportunity to cross-examine the witness. Matters inquired into on cross-examination are limited to those matters that were raised on direct examination. After cross-examination the party calling the witness again has the opportunity of examining the witness, and this examination is called redirect examination. It is limited to the scope of those matters covered on cross-examination and is used to clarify matters raised on cross-examination. After redirect examination the opposing party is allowed recross-examination, with the corresponding limitation as to scope of the questions. Witnesses may be asked to identify exhibits. Expert witnesses may be asked to give their opinion, within certain limitations, about the case, and sometimes experts are allowed to answer hypothetical questions.

In the conduct of a trial, the rules of evidence govern the admissibility of testimony and exhibits and establish which facts may be presented to the jury and which facts may not. Each rule of evidence is based on some policy consideration and the desire to give each party an opportunity to present his evidence and contentions without unduly taking advantage of the other party. Rules of evidence were not created to serve as a stumbling block to meritorious litigants or to create unwarranted roadblocks to justice. On the contrary, the rules of evidence were created and should be applied to ensure fair play and to aid in the goal of having controversies determined on their merits. Modern rules of evidence are liberal in the sense that they allow the introduction of most evidence that may contribute to the search for truth.

Motions During the Trial

A basic rule of evidence is that a party cannot introduce evidence unless it is competent and relevant to the issues raised by the pleadings. A connection between the pleadings and the trial stage of the lawsuit is also present in certain motions made during the trial. For example, after the plaintiff has presented his evidence, the defendant will usually make a motion for a directed verdict. This motion asks the court to rule as a matter of law that the plaintiff has failed to establish the case against the defendant and that a verdict should be entered for the defendant as a matter of law. The court can only direct a verdict for the defendant if the evidence taken in the light most favorable to the plaintiff establishes as a matter of law that the defendant is entitled to a verdict. The defendant argues that the plaintiff has failed to prove each allegation of his complaint. Just as a plaintiff must allege certain facts or have his complaint dismissed by motion to dismiss, he must also have some proof of each essential allegation or lose his case on a motion for a directed verdict. If he has some proof of each allegation, the motion will be denied.

In cases tried without a jury, either party may move for a finding in his favor. Such a motion will be allowed during the course of the trial if the result is not in doubt. The judge in ruling on such motions weighs the evidence, but he may end the trial before all the evidence is presented only if there is no room for a fair difference of opinion as to the result.

If the defendant's motion for directed verdict is overruled, the defendant then presents his evidence. After the defendant has presented all his evidence, the plaintiff may bring in rebuttal evidence. When neither party has any additional evidence, the attorneys and the judge retire for a conference to consider the instructions of law to be given the jury.

Jury Instructions The purpose of the jury instructions is to acquaint the jury with the law applicable to the case. Because the function of the jury is to find the facts, and the function of the court is to determine the applicable law, there must be a method to bring them together in an orderly manner that will result in a decision. At the conference, each attorney submits to the court the instructions he feels should be given to the jury. The court examines these instructions and confers with the attorneys about any objections to proposed instructions. The court then decides which instructions will be given to the jury. A typical jury instruction in a case in which a minor is seeking to recover money paid to him in purchase of an item is as follows: The court instructs the jury that contracts of minors may be avoided by the minor upon return of so much of the consideration received by the minor as he has left, providing the consideration is not a "necessary." If you find from evidence that the plaintiff was a minor, that the consideration received by him was not a necessary, and that he has returned so much of what he received as he has left, then your verdict will be for the minor, plaintiff.

In this instruction the court is in effect saying that the plaintiff must prove that he was a minor, that the contract does not involve necessaries, and that he has returned all of what he received that he has left. Thus the law of minors is applied to the facts, and the jury is instructed as to the result to be returned if they find certain facts.

Verdicts and Judgments After the conference on jury instructions, the attorneys argue the case to the jury. The party with the burden of proof, usually the plaintiff, is given an opportunity to open the argument and to close it. The defendant's attorney is allowed to argue only after the plaintiff's argument and is allowed to argue only once. After the arguments are completed, the court reads the instructions to the jury. The jury then retires to deliberate upon its verdict.

Upon reaching a verdict, the jury returns from the jury room, announces its verdict, and judgment is entered. Judgments are either *in rem* or *in personam*. A judgment *in rem* is an adjudication entered against a thing—property, real or personal. The judgment is a determination of the status of the subject matter. Thus a judgment of forfeiture of goods for the violation of a revenue law is a judgment *in rem*. Although a judgment *in rem* is limited to the subject matter, it nevertheless affects the rights and duties of persons. For example, although a decree dissolving a marriage seriously affects persons, it is nevertheless a judgment *in rem* because it affects a "status," the marriage relation. A judgment *in rem* is binding not only on the persons previously concerned with the status or thing but on all other persons.

A judgment against a particular person is a judgment *in personam*. It is limited in its application to such person only, whereas a judgment *in rem* is conclusive on all persons.

Post-trial Motions   After judgment is entered, the losing party starts the procedure of post-trial motions, which raise questions of law concerning the conduct of the lawsuit. These motions seek such relief as a new trial or a judgment, notwithstanding the verdict of the jury. A motion seeking a new trial may be granted if the judge feels that the verdict of the jury is contrary to the manifest weight of the evidence. The court may enter a judgment opposite to that of the verdict of the jury if the judge finds that the verdict is, as a matter of law, erroneous. To reach such a conclusion, the court must find that reasonable men viewing the evidence could not reach the verdict returned. For example, a verdict for the plaintiff based on sympathy instead of evidence could be set aside.

From the ruling on the post-trial motion, the losing party may appeal. It should be noted that lawsuits usually end by a ruling on a motion, either before trial, during the trial, or after the trial. Motions raise questions of law that are decided by the court. The right to appeal is absolute if perfected within the prescribed time. All litigants are entitled to a trial and a review, providing the proper procedures are followed.

Appeals   A dissatisfied party, plaintiff or defendant, has a right to appeal the decision of the trial court to a higher court, provided that he proceeds promptly and in the proper manner. Whether he is plaintiff or defendant, the person who appeals is called the *appellant* and the opposite party is called the *appellee*, or *respondent*. The appellant is often named first in the title of the case on appeal, although in the trial court he may have been the defendant.

Appellate procedures are not uniform among the states, and the appellant must comply with the appropriate statute and rules of the particular court. Appeals are usually perfected by the appellant's giving "notice of appeal" to the trial court and opposing parties.

Most states require that within at least ten days after giving notice of appeal, the appellant must file an appeal bond that in effect guarantees that the appellant will pay costs that may be charged against him on the appeal. This is to protect the respondent so that he may collect his costs if the appellant loses an appeal.

The statutes usually require that within a specified time after the appeal is perfected, the appellant shall file with the clerk of the appellate court what is known as a *transcript*. The transcript consists of a copy of the judgment, decree, or order appealed from, and such other papers as are required by the rules of the court.

The transcript alone is not enough to present the case to the appellate court. The appellant must prepare and file a "brief" that contains a statement of the case, a list of the assignment of errors upon which the appellant has based his appeal, his legal authorities, and argument. The brief contains the arguments on both fact and law by which the attorney attempts to show how the court below committed the errors alleged.

The appellee (respondent) files a brief of like character, setting out his side of the case with points, authorities, and arguments. By such procedure the case on the issues raised gets to the appellate court for decision.

The appellate court upon receipt of the appeal will place it on the calendar for hearing. The attorneys will be notified of the time and will be given an opportunity for oral argument. After the oral argument the court prepares a written opinion stating the applicable law involved and giving the reasons for its decision. The court by its decision may affirm or reverse the court below, or the court may send the case back for a new trial. At the end of each published opinion found in the reports, there will appear in a word or in a few words the result of the court's decision. Such words may be "affirmed," "reversed," "reversed and remanded," and so forth, as the case requires.

Enforcement of Judgments and Decrees

A decision of a court becomes final when the time provided for a review of the decision has expired. In cases in the trial court, it is the expiration of the time for appeal. In cases in a reviewing court, it is the expiration of the time to request a rehearing or to request a further review of the case. After the decision has become final, judicial action may be required to enforce the decision. In most cases the losing party will voluntarily comply with the decision and satisfy the judgment or otherwise do what the decree requires, but the assistance of the court is sometimes required to enforce the final decision of the court.

If a judgment for dollar damages is not paid, the judgment creditor may apply for a *writ of execution*. This writ directs the sheriff to seize personal property of the judgment debtor and to sell enough thereof to satisfy the judgment and to cover the costs and expenses of the sale. The writ authorizes the sheriff to seize both tangible and intangible personal property, such as bank accounts. If the judgment debtor's personal property seized and sold by the sheriff does not produce sufficient funds to pay the judgment, the writ of execution is returned to the court with a statement of the extent to which the judgment is unsatisfied. If an execution is returned unsatisfied in whole or in part, the judgment becomes a lien on any real estate owned by the debtor within the jurisdiction of the court that issued the writ of execution. An unpaid judgment creditor is entitled to have the real estate sold at a judicial sale and to have the net proceeds of the sale applied on the judgment. A judgment creditor with an unsatisfied writ of execution not only has a lien on real property owned by the judgment debtor at the time the judgment becomes final but he also has a judicial lien on any real property acquired by the judgment debtor during the life of judgment.

In recent years many states have adopted a procedure known as a *citation proceeding*, which greatly assists the creditor in collecting a judgment. The citation procedure is commenced by the service of a "citation" on the judgment debtor to appear in court at a stated time for the purpose of examination under oath about his financial affairs. It also prohibits the judgment debtor from making any transfer of property until after the examination in court. At the hearing, the judgment creditor or his attorney questions the judgment debtor about his income, property, and affairs. Any nonexempt property that is discovered during the questioning may be ordered sold by the judge, with the proceeds applied to the judgment. The court may also order that weekly or monthly payments be made by the judgment debtor. Such payments must not violate the laws relating to garnishment. In those states that have adopted the citation proceeding, the difficulties in collecting a judgment have been substantially reduced.

One important method of collecting a judgment is also relevant to the procedures that may be used to commence a lawsuit. This procedure with these dual purposes is known as *attachment*. Attachment is a method of acquiring *in rem* jurisdiction of a nonresident defendant who is not subject to the service of process. The court may "attach" property of the nonresident defendant, and in so doing the court acquires jurisdiction over the defendant to the extent of the value of the property attached. Attachment as a means of obtaining *in rem* jurisdiction is used in cases involving the status of a person, such as divorce, or the status of property, such as in eminent domain proceedings.

Attachment as a method of ensuring collection of a judgment is used by a plaintiff who fears that the defendant will dispose of his property before the court is able to enter a final decision. The plaintiff has property of the defendant seized pending the outcome of the lawsuit.

Attachment and the procedures controlling its use are governed by statutes that vary among the states. The attaching plaintiff-creditor must put up a bond with the court for the protection of the defendant, and the statutes provide methods whereby the attachment may be vacated by the defendant. If the plaintiff receives a judgment against the defendant, the attached property will be sold to satisfy the judgment.

REVIEW QUESTIONS AND PROBLEMS

1. What is meant by the term *jurisdiction*?
2. Upon whom may a summons be served? Where may it be served?
3. What is meant by a judgment by default or a decree *pro confesso*?
4. When is a motion for summary judgment proper?
5. What are the purposes of discovery procedure?
6. What function do the pleadings serve?
7. Who is an appellant? An appellee?
8. What are the purposes of a pretrial conference?
9. Name four discovery procedures.
10. Distinguish between a *verdict* and a *judgment.*
11. What is *voir dire* examination, and what is its purpose?
12. What are instructions for the jury? Why are they necessary? Who finds the facts, and who pronounces the law?
13. What is a writ of execution?
14. What is a motion for directed verdict? What is its function?
15. What are the uses of a writ of attachment?
16. Distinguish *venue* from *jurisdiction.*
17. What is a long-arm statute?

4 THE CRIMINAL LAW

Introduction   The law to a substantial degree is concerned with wrongful acts and omissions. An act or omission (conduct) may be wrongful against society, in which case the conduct is known as a *crime*. On the other hand, the wrongful conduct may not affect society as a whole but only one or more individuals. In such cases, the wrongful conduct is known as a *tort*. Of course, many wrongs are both crimes and torts. For example, an assault and battery is a tort against the victim and is also a wrong against society because of the society's interest in maintaining law and order. In this chapter we will briefly discuss some of the general principles of the law as it relates to crimes. The next chapter will deal with torts.

Classes of Crimes   Because a crime is a public wrong against society, criminal actions are prosecuted by a government on behalf of the people. Historically, upon conviction of a crime, one of the following punishments has been imposed by society: (1) death, (2) imprisonment, (3) fine, (4) removal from office, (5) disqualification to hold and enjoy any office or vote. Among the purposes of punishments and of the criminal law are the protection of the public and the deterrence of crime. Punishment is also imposed simply for the sake of punishment as well as the isolation and suppression of the criminal element of society.

Crimes are traditionally classified as treason, felonies, and misdemeanors. *Treason* against the United States consists of levying war against it or adhering to its enemies, giving them aid and comfort. *Felonies* are offenses usually defined by statute to include all crimes punishable by incarceration in a penitentiary. Examples are murder, grand larceny, arson, and rape. Crimes of lesser importance than felonies, such as petty larceny, trespass, and disorderly conduct, are called misdemeanors. *Misdemeanors* are usually defined as any crimes not punishable by imprisonment, but punishable by fine or confinement in the local jail.

Violation of traffic ordinances, building codes, and similar municipal ordinances for which prosecution takes place before a city magistrate are sometimes termed *petty offenses* or public torts instead of being classified as crimes. The distinction is insignificant because, whether they are called crimes or public torts, the result is the same—the party charged may be fined or put in jail or both.

Terminology   The criminal law has developed some terminology distinct from that used in civil law cases. The word *prosecution* is used to describe criminal proceedings, and *prosecutor* is the name usually given to the attorney who represents the people. Although the proceedings are brought on behalf of the people of a given state or of the United States, the people are generally not called the plaintiff as they would be in a civil case. Rather the case is titled *U.S.* v. *John Doe* or *State of Ohio* v. *John Doe*.

In felony cases the court conducts a preliminary hearing to determine if there is sufficient evidence to establish that the accused committed the crime of which he is charged to justify submission of the case to the grand jury. If the court finds this probable cause, the accused is "bound over" to the grand jury. The function of the grand jury is to examine the evidence against the accused and to determine if the evidence is sufficient to cause a reasonable person to believe that the accused probably committed the offense. If this *probable cause* exists, the grand jury *indicts* the accused by returning to the court what is called a *true bill*. If it is the opinion of the grand jury that the evidence is insufficient to indict, then a *no true bill* is returned to the court. Indictment by the grand jury will be discussed further as a part of the Fifth Amendment discussion later in this chapter.

If the crime involved is a misdemeanor or if the accused waives the presentment of the case to the grand jury, the prosecution may proceed by filing the charges in a document known as an *information*. Both an indictment and an information serve to notify and to inform the accused of the nature of the charges against him so that he may prepare his defense.

The technical aspects of the various crimes are beyond the scope of this text. However, it should be recognized that every crime has elements that distinguish it from other crimes. To illustrate: larceny, robbery, and burglary are crimes with many common characteristics. Yet they are legally distinct. Robbery is theft with force; larceny implies no force. Burglary is breaking and entering with intent to commit a felony (usually larceny). One act may be more than one crime, and it is possible to be convicted of more than one crime for any particular act. Many crimes are actually a part of another crime. Such crimes are known as *lesser included offenses*. For example, an assault would be a lesser included offense of forcible rape.

Criminal cases differ from civil cases in the amount of proof required to convict. In a civil case the plaintiff is entitled to a verdict if the evidence preponderates in his favor. In other words, if when weighing the evidence the scales tip ever slightly in favor of a plaintiff, the plaintiff wins. However, in a criminal case, the people or the prosecution must prove the defendant's guilt beyond a reasonable doubt. Note that the law does not require proof "beyond the shadow of a doubt" or proof that is only susceptible of one conclusion. It does require such a quantity of proof that a reasonable man viewing the evidence would have no reasonable doubt about the guilt of the defendant.

Act and Intent   As a general rule, a crime involves a combination of act and criminal intent. Criminal intent without an overt act to carry it out is not criminal. If X says to himself, "I am going to rob the First National Bank," no crime has been committed. Some act toward carrying out this intent is necessary for the intent to be criminal. It should be noted that if X communicates his desire to Y who agrees to assist X, then a crime has been committed. This crime is known as conspiracy. The criminal act was the communication between X and Y.

Just as a crime requires an act, most crimes also require criminal intent. A legislature may declare an act to be a crime without intent, but crimes that do not require intent are rare. A wrongful act committed without the requisite criminal intent is not a crime. Criminal intent may be supplied by negligence to the degree that it equals intent. For example, if a person drives a car so recklessly that he kills another, his criminal intent may be supplied by his negligence.

Criminal intent is not synonymous with motive. Motive is not an element of a crime. Proof of motive may help to establish guilt, but it is not an essential element of a crime.

Some crimes are known as specific intent crimes. When a crime has a specific intent as a part of its definition, that specific intent must be proven beyond a reasonable doubt. For example, in a burglary prosecution there must be proof of intent to commit some felony, such as larceny, rape, or murder. Also, if a crime is defined in part "with intent to defraud," this specific intent must be proven just like any other element of the crime.

There is a presumption of intention in crimes without a specific intent. The intent may be implied from the facts. In other words, the criminal act implies the criminal intent. (The accused may rebut this presumption, however.) The accused is presumed to intend the natural and probable consequences of his acts. Thus, if one's action causes a result that the criminal law is designed to prevent, he is legally responsible although the actual result was not intended. For example, assume that X dynamites a safe. A passerby, Y, is killed in the explosion. X is guilty of homicide even though he did not actually intend to kill Y because X intends the natural and probable consequences of his act.

Defenses to Criminal Prosecutions A defendant in a criminal case may avail himself of a variety of defenses. Of course he may contend that he did not commit the act of which he is accused. He may present an *alibi*—proof that he was at another place when the crime was committed. He may also contend that if he did the act, it was not done with the requisite intent. There also are many technical defenses used on behalf of persons accused of crimes.

Entrapment is a defense commonly raised in certain crimes, such as the illegal sale of drugs. Entrapment means that the criminal intent originated with the police. When a criminal act is committed at the instigation of the police, fundamental fairness would seem to dictate that the people should not be able to contend that the accused is guilty of a crime. To illustrate, if a police officer asked X to obtain some marijuana, X could not be found guilty because the criminal intent originated with the police officer. Entrapment is sometimes described as a positive defense because the accused must admit that the act was committed as a basis for the defense.

Immunity from prosecution is another technical defense. The prosecution may grant immunity in order to obtain a "state's witness." When immunity is granted, the person receiving it can no longer be prosecuted, and the privilege against compulsory self-incrimination no longer exists. When several persons have committed a crime together, it is common practice for one to be given immunity so that evidence is available against the others. The one granted immunity has a complete defense.

Insanity is a defense involved in many criminal cases. A person cannot be guilty of a crime if he or she lacks the mental capacity to have the required criminal intent. Likewise a person who is insane cannot adequately present a defense, so insanity at the time of trial is also a defense.

The defense of insanity poses many difficult problems for courts and for juries. Many criminal acts are committed in fits of anger or passion. Others by their very nature are committed by persons whose mental state is other than normal. Therefore, a major difficulty exists in defining insanity. In the early criminal law the usually accepted test of insanity was the "right from wrong" test. If the accused understood the nature and consequences of his act and had the ability to distinguish right from wrong at the time of the act involved, he was sane. If he did not know right from wrong or did not understand the consequences of his act, insanity was a defense.

Subsequently the courts of some states, feeling that the right and wrong test did not go far enough, adopted a test known as "irresistible impulse." Under this test it was not enough that the accused knew right from wrong. If he was possessed of an irresistible impulse to do what was wrong and this impulse was so strong that he was compelled by his mental condition to do what was wrong, insanity was a defense.

As psychiatry and psychology began to play a greater role in the criminal law and in the rehabilitation of criminals, many courts became dissatisfied with both the "right and wrong" and "irresistible impulse" tests of insanity. A new rule known as the Durham rule was developed. Under the Durham rule an accused is not criminally responsible if his act was the product of a mental disease or defect. This new test has not received universal acceptance. This in part is due to the fact that perpetrators of some crimes always have some mental abnormality, and the Durham rule thus makes the conduct unpunishable. For example, the crime of sexual assault on a child is only committed by one with some mental deviation. The Durham rule would make prosecution of such cases impossible. Today there is a wide disparity among the states as to which test of insanity will be followed. All three tests have significant acceptance. In the years ahead additional developments in the law of defining insanity are likely.

Intoxication as a defense is quite similar to insanity, but its application is much more restricted. Voluntary intoxication is generally no defense to a crime. Becoming voluntarily intoxicated is simply no excuse for wrongful conduct. However, if the crime charged is one of specific intent, and the accused was so intoxicated that he could not form the specific intent required, then intoxication is a defense of sorts. It can be used to establish lack of the required specific intent. For example, in a prosecution for an assault with intent to rape, intoxication sufficient to negate the intent would be a defense.

It should be noted that it is no defense that the accused was acting for or on behalf of others. It is also no defense that the accused was acting at the direction of another. To illustrate, assume that X breaks into a political campaign headquarters to steal some information. It is no defense that he was working for and under the direction of another. It should also be noted that both parties would be guilty of a conspiracy to commit burglary.

Return of property stolen, paying for damage caused, and forgiveness by the victim of a crime are not defenses. If a person shoplifts some goods and is caught, it is no defense that the goods were returned or that the store owner has forgiven him. Because the wrong is against society as a whole, the attitude of the actual victim is technically immaterial. However, as a practical matter many prosecutors do not prosecute cases that the victims are willing to abandon.

Ignorance of the law is not a defense to a criminal prosecution. Everyone is presumed to know the law and to follow it. No other system would be workable.

The sections that follow discuss matters that in the broad sense are also defenses. These are the various constitutional protections and guarantees available to a defendant. These constitutional guarantees may prohibit or impede prosecution of a case. As a practical matter, they may often make it impossible for the prosecution to obtain a conviction. For example, if evidence of the crime is illegally obtained, that evidence is inadmissible. By preventing the admission of the evidence, the accused may obtain an acquittal.

CRIMINAL LAW AND THE CONSTITUTION

In General The Constitution of the United States is a major source of the law as it relates to crimes. Constitutional protections and guarantees govern the procedural aspects of criminal cases. The Bill of Rights and especially the Fourth, Fifth, Sixth, and Eighth Amendments contain these constitutional guarantees. The Fourteenth Amendment "picks up" the constitutional protections of the Bill of Rights and makes them applicable to the states.

As these constitutional guarantees are studied, two aspects of constitutional guarantees should be kept in mind. First, constitutional guarantees are not absolutes. Every one of them is limited in its application. Just as freedom of speech does not allow one to cry "fire" in a crowded theater, protections such as those against illegal search and seizure and self-incrimination are not absolutes. The protections are in effect limited. Second, in determining the extent of the limitations on constitutional guarantees, the courts are balancing the constitutional protections against some other legitimate legal or social policy of society.

Case: California's so-called hit-and-run statute requires the driver of a motor vehicle involved in an accident to stop at the scene and give his name and address.

Issue: Does this law violate the Fifth Amendment's protection against compulsory self-incrimination?

Decision: No.

Reasons: 1. Conflict between the state's demand for disclosures and the protection of the right against self-incrimination inevitably must be resolved in terms of balancing the public need on the one hand and the individual claim to constitutional protections on the other.

2. Society commands many reports by individuals that include some possibility of prosecution. However, the mere possibility of incrimination is insufficient to defeat the strong policies in favor of a disclosure called for by statutes like the one challenged here.

3. Disclosures with respect to automobile accidents simply do not entail substantial risk of self-incrimination. Furthermore, the statutory purpose is noncriminal, and self-reporting is indispensable to its fulfillment.

4. The act of stopping is no more testimonial—indeed less so in some respects—than requiring a person in custody to stand or walk in a police lineup, to speak prescribed words, or to give samples of handwriting, fingerprints, or blood, none of which are protected by the Fifth Amendment.

California v. Byers, 91 S.Ct. 1535 (1971).

In the foregoing case, the court balanced the protection against compulsory self-incrimination with the need of accident victims to know the identity of the other party. Requiring a person to give his name is a form of self-incrimination to a degree. The court weighed the competing policies in making the decision. In the sections that follow, care should be taken to recognize the policy conflicts involved.

The Fourth Amendment   The Fourth Amendment prohibits illegal search and seizure. Several procedural issues may arise as a result of the protection against illegal search and seizure. Among the more common Fourth Amendment issues in criminal cases are (1) the validity of searches incident to an arrest without a warrant; (2) the validity of search warrants—the presence of probable cause; (3) the validity of consents to searches by persons other than the suspect; and (4) the extent of the protection afforded.

To illustrate the first issue, assume that a student is arrested for speeding. Is it a violation of the Fourth Amendment if the police officer searches the trunk of the car without a search warrant and finds heroin? The answer is yes, and the student could not be convicted of illegal possession of drugs because the evidence was unconstitutionally obtained.

A search may be illegal even if it is conducted pursuant to a search warrant. The Constitution provides that a search warrant may be issued only if probable cause for its issue is presented to the court.

The validity of a consent to search premises without a search warrant is frequently an issue in a criminal case. For example, assume that a parent consents to a police search of a child's room in the family home. Is this a valid waiver of the constitutional protection of the Fourth Amendment? The decision depends on many factors, including the age of the child, the extent of emancipation, and the amount of control the parents have over the total premises. Similar issues are raised when a landlord consents to the search of premises leased to a tenant. As a general rule, such consents are not sufficient to eliminate the need for a search warrant.

The protection afforded by the Fourth Amendment is not limited to premises. It prohibits the use of electronic surveillance equipment to obtain information. For example, in one case evidence of gambling was obtained by listening in on telephone conversations. Such evidence was inadmissible because it was illegally obtained.

Fourth Amendment issues frequently have an effect on the civil law as well as the criminal law. The protection has been extended to prohibit such activities as inspection of premises by a fire inspector without a search warrant. Criminal charges for violating building codes cannot be based on a warrantless inspection of the premises if the owner objects. However, the Supreme Court has held that a search of premises by a caseworker of a welfare recipient is not a violation of the Fourth Amendment. The need of government to know how its welfare funds for a child were being spent by its mother exceeded the need to give additional protection to the Fourth Amendment guarantees.

The Fifth Amendment

The Fifth Amendment is well known for its provision prohibiting compulsory self-incrimination. When a person pleads "the Fifth," almost everyone understands that he is exercising the right against compulsory self-incrimination. The Fifth Amendment also requires indictment by a grand jury for a capital offense or infamous crime and prohibits double jeopardy. In addition, the Fifth Amendment contains the due process clause, which requires that all court procedures in criminal cases be fundamentally fair.

A grand jury has the function of deciding if there is sufficient evidence of guilt to justify the accused's standing trial. It is contrasted with a petit jury, which actually decides guilt or innocence. Grand juries are usually made up of twenty-three persons, and it takes a majority vote to indict a defendant. It takes less proof to indict a person and to require him to stand trial than it does to convict. The grand jury provision contains an exception for court-martial proceedings.

The grand jury provision is limited to capital offenses and infamous crimes. Infamous crimes are ones that involve moral turpitude. The term indicates that one convicted of such a crime will suffer infamy. Most felonies are infamous crimes. The prohibition against double jeopardy means that a person cannot be tried twice for the same offense. A defendant who is acquitted in a criminal case cannot be retried on the same offense. However, a defendant who on appeal obtains a reversal of a conviction may be tried again. The reversal in effect means that the defendant was not in jeopardy.

Notwithstanding the foregoing provisions of the Fifth Amendment, the protection against compulsory self-incrimination is still its most important constitutional protection. The prohibition against being compelled to be a witness against oneself extends both to oral testimony of an accused before and during his trial and to documents and to statements before grand juries, legislative investigation committees, and judicial bodies in civil and criminal proceedings.

A statement or document does not have to be a confession of crime in order to qualify under the privilege. Both are protected if they might serve as a "link in the chain of evidence" that could lead to prosecution. The protection of the Fifth Amendment is the right to remain silent and to suffer no penalty for silence.

To illustrate the extent of the protection provided by the Fifth Amendment, the Supreme Court has held that (1) a prosecutor may not comment on the failure of a defendant to explain evidence within his knowledge; (2) a court may not tell the jury that silence may be evidence of guilt; (3) an attorney may not be disbarred for claiming his privilege at a judicial inquiry into his activities, just as a policeman may not be fired for claiming the privilege before the grand jury; and (4) the privilege protects a state's witness against incrimination under federal as well as state law and a federal witness against incrimination under state law as well as federal law. To illustrate this latter concept, assume that a person is granted immunity from state prosecution in order to compel him to testify. He cannot be compelled to testify if it is possible that his testimony would lead to a conviction under federal law. The granting of immunity must be complete.

The breadth and extent of the Fifth Amendment protection is perhaps best illustrated by a case involving the federal law on the wagering tax.

Case: A defendant was convicted for failing to register and pay an occupational tax under the federal wagering-tax law. Those gamblers paying the tax were listed, and the information was made available to law-enforcement officers charged with enforcing the gambling laws.

Issue: Is the federal wagering-tax law constitutional?

Decision: No.

Reasons: 1. The law is in violation of the Fifth Amendment. It creates real and appreciable and not merely imaginary and unsubstantial hazard of self-incrimination.

2. The defendant's assertion of the privilege against self-incrimination constitutes a complete defense to the prosecution.

Marchetti v. United States, 88 S.Ct. 697 (1968).

Limitations on the protections afforded by the Fifth Amendment are also readily apparent. The hit-and-run driver law previously discussed is one example. In another case it was held that the prosecution can use as evidence in a drunken driving case the analysis of a blood sample taken without consent of the accused. Such evidence is admissible even though the accused, on the advice of counsel, objected to the extraction of blood. The Fifth Amendment reaches an accused's communications, whatever form they might take, but compulsion that makes a suspect the source of "real or physical evidence" does not violate it. In addition, the protection is personal and does not prevent the production of incriminating evidence by others.

Case: A taxpayer delivered her tax records to her accountant for use in preparing her tax returns. The IRS conducted a tax audit and attempted to summon her records. The taxpayer sought to prevent their delivery to the IRS.

Issue: Does the Fifth Amendment privilege against compulsory self-incrimination prevent the production of business and tax records in the possession of an accountant?

Decision: No.

Reasons: 1. Historically, the privilege sprang from an abhorrence of governmental assault against the single individual accused of crime and the temptation on the part of the State to resort to the expedient of compelling incriminating evidence from one's own mouth.

2. The Fifth Amendment privilege is a personal privilege: it adheres basically to the person, not to information which may incriminate him. As Mr. Justice Holmes put it: "A party is privileged from producing the evidence, but not from its production." The Constitution explicitly prohibits compelling an accused to bear witness "against himself": it necessarily did not proscribe incriminating statements elicited from another.

3. In this case, there exists no legitimate expectation of privacy and no semblance of governmental compulsion against the person of the accused. It is important, in applying constitutional principles, to interpret them in

light of the fundamental interests of personal liberty they were meant to serve. Respect for these principles is eroded when they leap their proper bounds to interfere with the legitimate interest of society in enforcement of its laws and collection of the revenues.

Fisher v. United States, 96 S.Ct. 1569 (1976).

The Sixth Amendment

The Sixth Amendment contains several provisions relating to criminal cases. It guarantees to a defendant the right (1) to a speedy and public trial; (2) to a trial by jury; (3) to be informed of the charge against him; (4) to confront his accuser; (5) to subpoena witnesses in his favor; and (6) to have the assistance of an attorney.

The right to a speedy trial is of great concern today. Most states require that a defendant in jail be tried within a minimum period of time—such as four months. This prevents punishment of those not convicted of a crime.

The right to a jury trial does not extend to state juvenile court delinquency proceedings, as they are not criminal prosecutions. However, juveniles do have the right to counsel, to confront the witnesses against them, and to cross-examine them. Thus it can be seen that there are many technical aspects to the Sixth Amendment.

Perhaps no provision of the Sixth Amendment has been given a broader interpretation in recent years than the right to counsel. During this period the Supreme Court in a series of decisions has been confronted with two fundamental questions: (1) At what stage of the proceedings does the right to counsel attach? (2) To what types of cases is it applicable?

For many years, it was thought that the right to counsel existed only during the trial and that it did not exist during the investigation of the crime. During the 1960s the Supreme Court extended the right to counsel to events before the trial.

In *Massiah* v. *United States*, 377 U.S. 201, the Court observed that "a Constitution which guarantees a defendant the aid of counsel at . . . trial could surely vouchsafe no less to an indicted defendant under interrogation by the police in a completely extrajudicial proceeding. Anything less . . . might deny a defendant 'effective representation by counsel at the only stage when legal aid and advice would help him.' " In *Escobedo* v. *Illinois*, 378 U.S. 478, the Court extended the right to an accused under arrest but not under indictment when the accused asked for a lawyer. The Court in that case said that the "guiding hand of counsel was essential when the police were seeking to obtain a confession from the accused." This was the stage when legal aid and advice were most critical. What happened at the interrogation could certainly affect the whole trial because rights "may be as irretrievably lost, if not then and there asserted, as they are when an accused represented by counsel waives a right for strategic purposes."

Subsequent to *Escobedo*, other decisions expanded and clarified the Sixth Amendment protection. Perhaps the best known of these cases is *Miranda* v. *State of Arizona*, 86 S.Ct. 1602, which resulted in the development of what has become known as the "*Miranda* warning." This warning notifies the accused that he has the right to remain silent, that anything he says may be used against him in court, that he has the right to the presence of an attorney and to have an attorney appointed before questioning if he cannot afford one. The *Miranda* case recognized that a defendant may waive the right to counsel, provided the waiver is made voluntarily, knowingly, and intelligently.

Other decisions have required that the *Miranda* warning be given to an accused who was not in custody at a police station but on whom the investigation was centering if the accused was being deprived of his freedom of action in any significant way. Today the right to counsel has been extended to postindictment lineups.

Case: The defendant had been convicted of bank robbery. After his indictment and before the trial a lineup was conducted. The defendant's attorney was not notified of the lineup and was not present when it was conducted. Bank employees identified the defendant at the lineup and at the trial.

Issue: Was the lineup conducted in violation of the Sixth Amendment?

Decision: Yes.

Reasons: 1. The constitutional guarantee that in all criminal prosecutions the accused shall enjoy the right to have the assistance of counsel for his defense encompasses counsel's assistance whenever necessary to assure a meaningful defense.

2. In addition to counsel's presence at trial, the accused is guaranteed that he need not stand alone against the state at any stage of the prosecution, formal or informal, in court or out, where counsel's absence might derogate the accused's right to a fair trial.

3. The presence of counsel at critical confrontations, as at trial itself, operates to assure that the accused's interests will be protected consistently with the adversary theory of criminal prosecution.

4. For a defendant accused of bank robbery, a postindictment lineup was a critical stage of the prosecution at which he was as much entitled to aid of counsel as at the trial itself. Thus both the defendant and his counsel should have been notified of the impending lineup, and the counsel's presence should have been requisite to the conduct of the lineup, in absence of an intelligent waiver.

United States v. Wade, 87 S.Ct. 1926 (1967).

In the mid-1970s the Supreme Court in a series of decisions tended to limit the effect of the *Miranda* decision. For example, the Court held that a confession obtained without the requisite warning being given could nevertheless be used to impeach a defendant who denied under oath committing the crime. The law relative to the *Miranda* warning is still developing, and it is anticipated that more limitations will be imposed in the near future.

The courts have also extended the types of cases to which the right to counsel attaches. Historically, the right existed only in felony cases. Today it extends to any case—felony or misdemeanor—in which the accused may be incarcerated. In addition, the right to counsel extends to juveniles in juvenile proceedings. It also extends to investigations by the Internal Revenue Service. Thus any person charged with any crime for which he may be put in jail or prison has the right to counsel at all stages of the proceedings from the time the investigations center upon him as the accused through his last appeal.

**The Eighth
Amendment**   The Eighth Amendment provides that "excessive bail shall not be required, nor excessive fines imposed, nor cruel and unusual punishments inflicted." Bail is excessive if greater than necessary to guarantee the presence of the accused in court at the appointed time. The function of bail is to not restrict the freedom of the accused prior to trial because of the presumption of innocence. Most states today only require that a small percentage of the actual bail be posted. For example, the law may require that 10 percent of the total bail be deposited with the court. If the defendant fails to appear, the persons signing the bail bond then owe the other 90 percent.

At one time the Eighth Amendment was used as the basis for declaring the death penalty to be unconstitutional. However, many legislative bodies reinstated the death penalty, and some of these laws were later held to be constitutional.

**The Fourteenth
Amendment**   The Fourteenth Amendment is quite general in its language. To the extent relevant here, it provides that "no State shall make or enforce any law which shall abridge the privilege or immunities of citizens of the United States; nor shall any State deprive any person of life, liberty or property, without due process of law, nor deny to any person within its jurisdiction the equal protection of the laws." The three major provisions are known as the "privileges and immunities" clause, the "due process" clause and the "equal protection" clause. Although all three clauses play a significant role in constitutional law, the due process clause and the equal protection clause have been involved in more significant criminal law litigation than has the privileges and immunities clause.

The term *due process of law* cannot be narrowly defined. The term is used to describe fundamental principles of liberty and justice. Simply stated, *due process* means "fundamental fairness and decency." It means that government may not act in a manner that is arbitrary, capricious, or unreasonable.

The issues in due process cases are usually divided into questions of *procedural* due process and *substantive* due process. Substantive due process issues arise when property or other rights are directly affected by governmental action. Procedural due process cases are often concerned with whether proper notice has been given and a proper hearing has been conducted. Such cases frequently involve procedures established by state statute. Due process has been used to strike down such varied state action in criminal cases as forced pleas and trials held with excess publicity. Many of the cases decided by the Supreme Court relating to the Fourteenth Amendment have simply ruled that the federal standard on a given issue was to be the minimum state standard. These cases use the due process clause to "pick up" or to "incorporate" the federal standards of criminal jurisprudence and to make them applicable to the states.

Case: A state was conducting an investigation into gambling. X, who had been previously convicted of gambling, was subpoenaed to testify and was asked certain questions. He refused, asserting his rights against compulsory self-incrimination. He was sentenced to jail for contempt of court.

Issue: Does the Fourteenth Amendment safeguard the privilege against self-incrimination during state action?

Decision: Yes.

Reasons: 1. The Fifth Amendment's exception from compulsory self-incrimination is also protected by the Fourteenth Amendment against abridgement by the states.

2. The federal standard is applicable to state cases.

3. The Fourteenth Amendment secures against state invasion the same privilege that the Fifth Amendment guarantees against federal infringement—the right of a person to remain silent unless he chooses to speak in the unfettered exercise of his own will, and to suffer no penalty for such silence. . . .

Malloy v. Hogan, 378 U.S. 1 (1964).

The equal protection clause is used more often in civil litigation, such as school desegregation cases. It is used to prevent all types of invidious discrimination, such as discrimination based on race, creed, color, sex, or national origin. It has been used in the criminal law where discriminating laws or practices were involved.

Contemporary Problems
The criminal law system has failed to accomplish most of its assumed goals. It has generally failed to act as a deterrent to criminal conduct. Society is faced with an ever-increasing crime rate, especially in larger communities. Crimes of violence as well as the so-called white-collar crimes are constantly in the news. Our penal system has not found the means to rehabilitate convicted offenders, and a significant portion of all crimes are committed by repeat offenders.

Many people believe that the failure of the criminal law results from its failure to provide swift and sure punishment for those committing wrongs against society. Delay in all steps of criminal procedure is quite common. Most delays are probably the result of defense tactics, as time favors the accused. Court congestion also contributes to delay, and vice-versa. Recent decisions such as those expanding the right to counsel have contributed to court congestion also.

One of the more controversial procedures used in the criminal law is commonly referred to as *plea bargaining*. This term describes the technique by which an accused pleads guilty to a lesser offense than that which is charged, or there is an agreement as to punishment less than normal in return for a plea of guilty. Plea bargaining is essential because the caseload is too great to try all cases. However, plea bargaining has many adverse side effects. For example, persons who have committed serious crimes are often almost immediately back on the streets to commit more crimes after only paying a fine or serving a much shorter sentence than would have been imposed if they had been convicted of the crime originally charged.

The increased criminal law caseload has had a great impact on the work of reviewing courts. Today approximately 75 percent of those convicted of crimes appeal their convictions. This increase is largely due to the fact that the indigent defendant is now entitled to a free appeal. We do not have enough judges to handle this caseload properly, and delay is inevitable.

Another inherent problem in our criminal law system arises from the fact that many recent law school graduates join the staff of either the prosecutor or the public defender. Criminal cases are thus frequently tried by lawyers with little experience and a minimum of training. After gaining experience, they leave for private practice. The criminal law has to a significant degree become an internship for training lawyers for private practice.

The free legal services provided to indigents also create some problems. Many people close to the situation believe that the free public defender, who is frequently underpaid by the state and is overworked because of the volume of cases, often does not do an adequate job in defending his or her clients. In addition, these attorneys are to all intents and purposes on the court payroll, which may affect the vigor of their representation of defendants. As a result, an adequate legal defense is a goal that is yet to be achieved for many defendants.

Many other problems have arisen as a result of the failures of our criminal law system. Overcrowded jails, unworkable probation systems, unequal sentences, plea bargaining that tends to favor the wealthy, and the failure of sentencing laws to deter crime are but a few of the obvious ills. Most legal scholars agree that the criminal law system needs a drastic overhaul. In fact, the Supreme Court in its process of reviewing convictions is bringing about many changes. It is requiring prompt trials or the dismissal of charges. Other decisions have reduced the number of appeals that are available to a convicted defendant. Finally, the court is reconsidering many of the highly technical aspects of the Bill of Rights as they affect criminal prosecutions. In many of these cases, the court is balancing the competing and conflicting policies more heavily in favor of the police and the victim of crimes rather than in favor of the accused.

REVIEW QUESTIONS AND PROBLEMS

1. Define the following terms introduced in this chapter: *treason, felony, misdemeanor, indictment, grand jury, information, lesser included offense, true bill, entrapment, illegal search and seizure, double jeopardy, infamous crime, and Miranda warning.*

2. What is the basic distinction between a *felony* and a *misdemeanor*?

3. Compare the burden of proof in a criminal case with the burden of proof in a civil case.

4. Give an example of a lesser included offense to assault with a deadly weapon. To armed robbery.

5. X, in the course of attempting to escape from jail, sets fire to a mattress. His cellmate, Y, dies of smoke inhalation. Is X guilty of murder? Explain.

6. A and B get together and plan to steal a car. They "chicken out" and do not carry out the plan. Are A and B guilty of any crime? Explain.

7. Do all crimes require both act and intent? Explain.

8. Contrast *criminal intent* and *motive.*

9. What is the difference between a *general intent crime* and a *specific intent crime*?

10. List and illustrate four defenses available to an accused in a criminal case.

11. Compare the three tests of insanity currently used by the courts in criminal cases.

12. X, while intoxicated, drove his automobile the wrong way down a one-way street and struck Y's auto, killing Y. Is X's intoxication a defense to the charge of manslaughter brought against X? Explain.

13. Are the constitutional guarantees of the Bill of Rights absolute? Explain.

14. List four issues that may arise under the Fourth Amendment and give an example of each.

15. What is the relationship of the Fourteenth Amendment to the Bill of Rights?

16. List three protections afforded by the Fifth Amendment other than the protection against compulsory self-incrimination. Give an example of each.

17. List the constitutional guarantees to a defendant in a criminal case that are based on the Sixth Amendment.

18. When is a person entitled to an attorney in a criminal matter?

19. What statements must be contained in the warning given to an accused in a criminal case?

20. Does the Fifth Amendment protection against self-incrimination apply to evidence held by a person other than the accused?

21. What does "due process of law" mean?

22. Explain the difference between *substantive* due process issues and *procedural* due process issues.

23. What is plea bargaining?

24. What are some of the problems inherent in the criminal law system?

5 THE LAW OF TORTS

Introduction　The term *tort* is somewhat difficult to define. Traditionally it has been defined as a wrongful act against a person or against his property, other than a breach of contract. The victim of a tort may bring civil action to recover damages for the injuries received because the other party was at fault. The adjective "wrongful" in the definition means that a person has violated a legal duty owed to another and the violation has caused an injury. Torts may be classified as *personal torts* or *property torts*. Personal torts are those that involve an injury to one's body, feelings, or reputation. Property torts involve injuries to both real and personal property.

The distinction between *crime* and *tort* must be kept in mind. A tort is a private wrong for which a civil action is instituted, as contrasted with a crime (public wrong) for which the people bring action.

The same act may be both a crime and a tort. For example, an assault and battery is both a wrong against society and a wrong against the victim of the assault and battery. Society may punish the guilty party, and the victim may sue in tort for his injuries. It must be recognized that the criminal action does not benefit the victim of the crime or compensate him for his injury. Such compensation is left to the civil law of torts.

Theories of Tort Liability　Tort liability is predicated on two premises: (1) that in a civilized society one person should not intentionally injure another or his property; and (2) that all persons should exercise reasonable care and caution in their activities. The first premise has resulted in a group of torts labeled *intentional torts*. Intentional torts

61

may also be explained by another basic assumption of a civilized society— that each member of society is entitled to have certain interests protected. If a member of society invades the protected interests of another, the injured party should have a right to seek damages by bringing a lawsuit for dollar damages for the intentional wrong committed, using the appropriate intentional-tort theory. Some of these protected interests are: (1) Freedom from bodily harm or apprehension of bodily harm, or from impairment of movement. Invasions of these interests are called assault, battery, and false imprisonment. (2) Freedom from injury to property. Invasions of this interest are called trespass to goods, conversion of chattels, trespass to land, and nuisances. (3) Freedom from disparagement of reputation. Invasions of this interest are called defamation, libel, and slander. (4) Freedom from wrongful interference with the right of privacy. (5) Freedom from interference with business relationships. Invasions of this interest include fraud in the inducement of breach of contract, and slander of title and trade name.

In addition to these protected interests, the law sometimes creates new theories of liability when one party's conduct causes injury to another. One such theory is called *outrageous conduct.*

Case: P sued D, a retail store, for mental anguish and emotional distress resulting in two heart attacks. P alleged that her heart attacks were caused by D's attempt to collect from her a debt of her adult son. D had telephoned P late at night and had sent her "threatening" letters.

Issue: Do these facts create a cause of action for P?

Decision: Yes.

Reasons: 1. One who, without a privilege to do so, by extreme and outrageous conduct intentionally causes severe emotional distress to another, with bodily harm resulting from such distress, is subject to liability for such emotional distress and bodily harm even though he has committed no heretofore recognized common law tort.

2. Liability does not exist for every case of hurt feelings or bad manners. Liability exists only where the conduct is so outrageous in character and so extreme in degree, as to go beyond all possible bounds of decency, and to be regarded as atrocious, and utterly intolerable in a civilized community.

George v. Jordan Marsh Company, 268 N.E.2nd 915 (Mass.) 1971.

Some of the other intentional torts will be discussed more fully in later sections of this chapter. It should be noted that all of them have certain elements or legal requirements that a plaintiff must allege and prove before there is a right of recovery from the defendant.

Intentional torts as a group are given special treatment by other branches of the law. For most intentional torts, a complaining party is entitled to exemplary or punitive damages in addition to the actual damages sustained. Thus, intentional torts have a punitive aspect in order to discourage people from committing them. Although there are exceptions, one must keep in mind that recoveries on a theory of intentional wrongdoing are in part designed as a deterrent. Second, judgments obtained on a theory of intentional wrongdoing cannot usually be discharged in bankruptcy. This is another punitive aspect of the law as it relates to intentional wrongs against a person or his property.

The second premise mentioned is the basis for the general field of tort liability known as *negligence*. Liability based on negligence is liability based on fault, just as in the case of an intentional tort. However, because the wrong is of a lesser degree, the theory of damages does not include any punishment aspect as a general rule. For simple negligence, a person is entitled to collect from the wrongdoer such sum of money as will make him whole. He is not entitled to collect money to discourage the wrongdoer from repeating his wrong. In addition, simple negligence claims are dischargeable in bankruptcy. Negligence is discussed further later in this chapter.

A third theory of tort liability is called *strict liability*. Strict liability is not based on wrongful conduct in the usual sense. It is based on the peculiar factual situation and the relationship of the parties. To the extent that an activity by one party causes injury, there is liability in cases that come within this theory. Although one party is not at fault in the sense of wrongdoing, he is at fault in that his actions caused the injuries. For example, the theory of strict liability is imposed in situations where harm is caused by dangerous or trespassing animals, blasting operations, or fire. The theory of strict liability is also being applied in certain product liability cases, as will be discussed later in Chapter 20.

Elements of Tort Liability

While the actual elements of the various torts vary considerably, most torts have the following elements in common: (1) a duty owed to the injured party by the person whose conduct causes the injury, (2) conversely, a legal right in the injured party which has been affected by the conduct of the other, (3) a breach of the duty, (4) an act or omission which is the proximate cause, (5) the injury.

The first two elements of all torts are described as the right-duty relationship. The duty one party owes the other is imposed by law. Moral obligation does not impose a duty or create a right. The duty must be owed to the person claiming injury. For example, an airline owes a duty to its passengers, and the passengers have the right to safe transportation. Assume that this duty is breached and the plane crashes, killing all on board. Assume also that X was the employer of Y, a passenger on the plane, and that Y was a key employee of X. X has no claim or tort action against the airline because the right-duty relationship did not exist.

A tort may consist of either an act or an omission—failure to act. The act or the omission must be wrongful in the sense that another's legal right has been violated, but acts or omissions need not involve moral turpitude, or bad motive, or maliciousness. Moreover, an act or an omission that does not invade another's rights is not tortious, even though the actor's motive is bad or malicious.

Perhaps the most difficult of the elements of a tort to understand is the one known as *proximate cause.* Proximate cause means that the act or the omission complained of is the proximate cause of injury. Problems in applying the rule of proximate cause arise because events sometimes break the direct sequence between an act and the injury. In other words, the chain of events sometimes establishes that the injury is remote from the wrongful act. For example, assume that a customer slips on the floor of a store and breaks a leg. While en route to the hospital in an ambulance, there is a collision in which the customer is killed. The store would not be liable for the wrongful death because its negligence was not the proximate cause of the death, although it was one event in the chain of causation of the death.

The issue of proximate cause must be decided on a case-by-case basis. Proximate cause requires that the injury be the natural and probable consequence of the wrong. Proximate cause means that the injury was foreseeable from the wrong, and without the wrong, the injury would not have occurred. Issues of foreseeability are often difficult. In one recent case, a plaintiff's daughter and granddaughter were killed in an auto accident. The plaintiff suffered a heart attack when informed of the deaths. The court held that he could not collect from the party at fault in the auto accident. His injury was not foreseeable and predictable. He was too remote for there to be proximate cause.

Proximate cause need not be the sole cause or the one nearest in time. Where several causes contribute together to an injury, they each may constitute proximate cause. For example, if two autos, each with a negligent driver, collide and injure some third party, both drivers are liable. The negligence of each is a proximate cause of the injury.

Persons Liable Every person legally responsible is liable for his or her own torts. It is no defense that the wrongdoer is working under the direction of another. Such a fact may create liability on the part of the other person, but it is no defense to the wrongdoer. (The liability of employers for the torts of employees is discussed in Chapter 32.)

Where two or more persons jointly commit a tort, all may be held liable for the total injury. The liability is said to be joint and several. All are liable, and each is liable for the entire damage.

In general, an infant is liable for his own torts. Several factors are taken into account in determining an infant's tort liability—the age of the infant, the nature of the tort involved, and whether the tort is intentional. At common law and in many states, a child under the age of seven is conclusively presumed to be incapable of negligence; and from ages seven to ten, a child is presumed to be incapable, but the presumption may be rebutted. A child older than ten is usually treated as any other person insofar as torts are concerned. Some states use the age fourteen instead of ten for these rules. A minor above the minimum age is held to the same standard as an adult. For example, a minor driving an automobile owes the same duty of due care as does an adult.

Another area of substantial misunderstanding of the law is concerned with the parents' liability for the torts of their children. As a general rule, a parent is not responsible for such torts. Parents are liable if the child is acting as an agent of the parent, or if the parents are themselves at fault. In addition, some states have adopted the "family-purpose" doctrine, which provides that when an automobile is maintained by a parent for the pleasure and convenience of the family, a member of the family—including an infant who uses it for his or her own pleasure or convenience—is presumed the owner's agent, and the owner is responsible for the negligence of the family member. The presumption may be rebutted, however. Other states have gone further and have provided that anyone driving a car with the permission of the owner is the owner's agent, and the owner has vicarious liability to persons injured by the driver. These laws greatly expand the liability of automobile owners, who should take precautionary measures to make sure that this potential risk is adequately covered by insurance.

PARTICULAR TORTS

Trespass The tort of *trespass* is a common one and affects both real and personal property. A trespass to personal property—goods and the like—is unlawful interference by one person with the control and possession of the goods of another. One is entitled to have exclusive possession and control of his personal property and may recover for any physical harm to his goods by reason of the wrongful conduct of another. Closely allied to trespass is the tort of *conversion*. Conversion is the wrongful disposition and detention of goods of one person by another. It may occur by theft, but most conversions occur when a party who legally has possession of goods fails to return them as agreed.

The person in exclusive possession of land is entitled to enjoy the use of that land free from interference of others. Entry upon the land of another is a trespass even if the one who enters is under the mistaken belief that he is the owner or has a right, license, or privilege to enter.

Trespass to land may be *innocent* or *willful.* An innocent trespass would occur when one goes on another's land by mistake or under the impression that he has a right to be there. It is still an intentional wrong because persons intend the natural and probable consequences of their acts. A trespass is willful if the trespasser knowingly goes on another's land, aware that he or she has no right to do so.

In a trespass case, if the trespass is willful, the plaintiff is entitled to exemplary damages. If the trespass endangers lives, these punitive damages may include an amount to deter similar trespasses in the future by making them uneconomical. If no lives are endangered, the exemplary damages include attorney's fees and other related expenses but do not include amounts to deter similar conduct in the future. It should be remembered that except in cases of exemplary damages, every litigant pays his or her own attorney's fees in tort cases.

Case: D had bulldozed P's land, built a road, and destroyed a fence. The jury found the trespass to be willful. It assessed $5,000 as punitive damages.

Issues: 1. Is P entitled to exemplary damages?

2. Do the exemplary damages include an amount as punishment?

Decision: 1. Yes.

2. No.

Reasons: 1. If a willful trespass endangers no lives and D does not have a history of such conduct, damages for deterrence purposes are not allowable.

2. The items included in exemplary damages in such a case are reasonable attorney's fees and other related expenses not ordinarily recoverable plus an amount to reimburse P for the inconvenience of the time and effort in bringing the case.

3. P also obviously is paid for all his actual damages to the real estate.

Cox v. Stolworthy, 406 P.2d 682 (Idaho) 1972.

Nuisances Tort liability may also be predicated upon the unreasonable use by a person of his own property. Any improper or indecent activity that causes harm to another person, to his property, or to the public generally is tortious. Such conduct is usually described as a *nuisance.* Nuisances may be either private or public. A private nuisance is one that disturbs only the interest of some private individual, whereas the public nuisance disturbs or interferes with the public in general. The legal theory supporting tort liability in these areas is that an owner of property, although conducting a lawful business thereon, is subject to reasonable limitations and must use his property so as not to unreasonably interfere with the health and comfort of his neighbors or with their right to the enjoyment of their property. Liability may be imposed for nuisances even in the absence of negligence.

Case: P, the owner and occupant of a private residence, sued D, a manufacturer, for damages suffered as a result of noxious odors emitted from D's plant. The odors on occasion required P to leave home and stay out overnight and also interfered with P's entertainment of friends.

Issue: Is P entitled to damages for loss of use and of enjoyment of a home?

Decision: Yes.

Reason: When premises are occupied by the owner who suffers injury by reason of a nuisance, the measure of damages is the injury caused by the discomfort and the deprivation of the healthful use and comforts of home and annoyance of the plaintiff while occupying the premises. The amount recoverable cannot be gauged by any definite rule. The exact amount is up to the jury.

Schatz v. Abbott Laboratories, Inc., 281 N.E.2d 323 (Ill.) 1972.

In addition to tort liability, the remedy of an injunction is used to abate a nuisance.

Case: D purchased land for the purpose of building a "drag strip" racing track. Persons who lived in the vicinity sought an injunction to prevent the operation of the drag strip.

Issue: Is the operation of a drag strip enjoinable as a nuisance?

Decision: Yes.

Reasons: 1. Drag strip racing is not a nuisance per se, but its operation in the vicinity of residential and agricultural properties may, because of the extraordinary noise during races, constitute a nuisance in fact.

2. The construction of proposed drag strip racetrack can be enjoined where the operation of the track would create such an unreasonable amount of noise that serious interference would be caused owners and occupants of surrounding property in their use and enjoyment of their property.

Gustafson v. Cotco Enterprises, Inc., 328 N.E.2d 409 (Ohio) 1974.

The Right In recent years the law has developed a tort known as *invasion*
of Privacy *of the right of privacy.* The right of one to privacy may be
invaded in numerous ways. Many cases involve the publication
of stories in newspapers or magazines about one's private life. For
example, the publication of a picture of a family at a funeral of a loved
one by a detective magazine would be an invasion of privacy. The tort
must be distinguished from libel and slander. Invasion of privacy does
not involve defamation. It involves the wrongful intrusion into one's
private life in such a manner as to outrage or to cause mental suffering,
shame, or humiliation to a person of ordinary sensibilities. The
protection is for a mental condition and not a financial one. Invasion of
privacy is the equivalent of a battery to one's integrity. Actual damage
need not be proven. Unjustified invasion of privacy entitles the victim
to damages. Punitive damages may be collected if malice is shown.

Case: A husband and wife were separated. The wife obtained a private telephone
line from the telephone company. She informed them of her separation at
this time and that she was employed and would pay the bill. The
telephone company later attached an extension to the wife's telephone
and placed it in her husband's residence at his request. The husband then
listened in on his wife's conversations.

Issue: Is the telephone company liable in tort for invasion of privacy?

Decision: Yes.

Reasons: 1. Eavesdropping on telephone conversations of another by unauthorized
mechanical means or a so-called tap constitutes intrusion or prying into
another's private affairs.
2. One who materially aids or abets a wrongful act by another may be as
responsible as the one who commits the act, and liability may be imposed
on aider or abettor to same extent as if he had performed the act himself.

LeCrone v. Ohio Bell Telephone Co., 201 N.E.2nd 533 (Ohio) 1963.

Business Torts In recent years several torts that may be classified under the
heading "business torts" have arisen or grown in importance.
Such wrongful conduct as fraud, interfering with a business relationship, or violating a statute such as the Sherman Antitrust Act comes
under this general category.

Numerous federal and state laws give a cause of action for dollar
damages to persons who are injured by others in violation of these
statutes. For example, tort liability may be imposed and damages
awarded a person denied equal privileges in using public accommoda-
tions under the Civil Rights Act of 1964.

Fraud as a tort will be discussed with the materials on contracts in Chapter 9. Cases concerned with interference with a contract or other business relationships present complex questions of policy that require a balancing of conflicting objectives. For example, assume that X is employed by a bank as a cashier. Y, a depositor of the bank, tells the bank president that he believes X to be dishonest and suggests that X be discharged. Has Y committed a tort? The policy of protecting employees from wrongful interference with the employment contracts must be weighed against the desirability of ensuring that bank employees are honest. The trend of cases is to allow recovery for all wrongful interferences with the rights of others. Any intentional invasion or interference with the property or contractual rights of others without just cause is a tort. Such torts include not only interference with existing contracts but interference with the formation of contracts as well.

Another business tort is the wrongful appropriation of another's goodwill or business value. For example, it is a tort to infringe on another's patent, trademark, or copyright. In addition, a trade name such as Holiday Inn or Coca-Cola is entitled to protection from theft or appropriation by another. Many cases involving the appropriation of another's business values involve words or actions that are deceptively similar to those of another. It is a tort to use a name or take an action that is deceptively similar to the protected interests of another. Just how similar the mark or name, must appear before a wrong has been committed presents an interesting problem. In general, it can be said that whenever the casual observer, as distinct from the careful buyer, tends to be misled into purchasing the wrong article, an injunction as well as a tort action is available to the injured party.

The remedy of injunction is perhaps more important than the tort action when there is infringement of a patent, copyright, or trademark. The injunction that prohibits the continued appropriation protects not only the owner of the right but the consuming public as well.

Trade secrets are also protected by the law of torts and courts of equity. Information about one's trade, customers, processes, or manufacture is confidential. If a competitor can discover this information fairly through research, study, or observation, he may use it freely in the absence of a patent or a copyright. However, if he obtains such information by bribery of an employee of the first concern or by engaging an employee of the first concern with the understanding that he will use this information, the second party may be enjoined from making use of it.

In this connection it should be emphasized that an idea once exposed to the public may thereafter be used by anyone. The forward march of civilization is dependent upon the freedom with which new ideas are adopted. A book or a magazine article containing new ideas may be copyrighted, but the ideas set forth therein may be used by anyone as long as the language used is not published by another. One who unfolds to an interested party a plan for financing his product or for merging several industries may discover later that the interested party has made use of these ideas without compensating the originator of them. To forestall such a possibility, the originator of the idea should, before explaining his idea, obtain a promise of payment in case his plan is adopted.

**Negligence
Actions**
The field of negligence is frequently broken into degrees, depending on the extent of carelessness involved and the extent of the duty owed. The usual categories are *willful and wanton misconduct* and *simple negligence*. Willful and wanton misconduct is wrongful conduct less than intentional but much more than simple negligence. It is sometimes defined as a conscious disregard of the rights of others. It has been described as such "reckless and wanton disregard of the safety of others" that the actor should know or have reason to know that harm will likely result. For example, A recklessly and knowingly drives through a stoplight at a high rate of speed. B is injured. A is guilty of willful and wanton misconduct.

Simple negligence is best described as the failure to exercise due care and caution. Due care and caution is that which a reasonable man, guided by those circumstances that ordinarily regulate the conduct of human beings, would exercise or would not exercise under the circumstances.

Negligence is the theory of fault upon which most claims for personal injury, especially in automobile accidents, are predicated. A person seeking damages under the theory of negligence is usually required to establish (1) that he was injured without fault of his own (freedom from contributory negligence); (2) that he was injured by conduct of the defendant that was the proximate cause of his injuries; and (3) that the defendant's conduct was contrary to a duty owed to the injured party. This duty is usually expressed in terms of the degree of care and caution that the wrongdoer was bound to exercise for the other party by reason of the factual situation and their relationship. For example, an owner of property would owe a higher standard of care and caution to a business visitor than to a trespasser. Therefore, conduct that might be considered negligence to a business visitor might not be so to a trespasser. Negligence, then, is based on a violation of a duty owed that is the proximate cause of an injury to another.

There are a variety of standards used to describe the duty that one person owes to another. Generally the greater the duty, the higher the standard of conduct.

The various duties owed under the various theories of fault may be summarized as follows:

Theory of Fault	Duty	Degree of Fault for Liability
1. Slight negligence	To use extreme or high degree of care	Failure to use extreme or high degree of care
2. Ordinary negligence	To use ordinary care	Failure to use ordinary care
3. Willful and wanton misconduct	To use slight care	Actions with a conscious disregard for the safety of others (gross recklessness)
4. Intentional tort	Not to intentionally injure another	Actions with intent to harm
5. Strict liability	Not to injure	None

The nature of the duty owed by one person to another is a question of law for the courts. The issue as to whether or not there has been a breach of the duty owed is almost always a question of fact for the jury. Only when reasonable minds could not differ is the latter issue one of law for a court.

Case: A policeman was fatally shot by a burglar while making a security check at a grocery store. The outside of the store was poorly lighted and a mercury light had been disconnected. The policeman's widow sued the owner of the grocery store on a theory of negligence.

Issue: Did the grocer violate any duty owed to the policeman?

Decision: No.

Reasons: 1. Whether or not there exists a legal duty is a question of law for the courts. Liability for negligence is based on fault.

2. The possessor of land has the same duty to a policeman or fireman who is on the premises in the performance of his official duties, at a place where he might reasonably be expected to be, as the duty that a possessor of land owes to an invitee.

3. A possessor of land has liability to his invitees only if he

a. Knows or by the exercise of reasonable care would discover the condition, and should realize that it involves an *unreasonable* risk of harm to such invitees, and

b. Should expect that they will not discover or realize the danger, or will fail to protect themselves against it, and

c. Fails to exercise reasonable care to protect them against the danger.

4. The risk to which the decedent was subjected because of the conditions that existed upon the defendant's premises was the same risk that every police officer encounters while conducting security checks in both residential and commercial areas. The danger of being ambushed by criminals lurking in poorly illuminated areas, in shadows, or behind objects is a risk inherent in the occupation. Hence, the danger to which the decedent was subjected was not an *unreasonable* risk for a police officer.

Fancil v. Q.S.E. Foods, Inc., 328 N.E.2d 538 (Ill.) 1975.

Malpractice Suits —Generally Among the more significant trends in the law of negligence is the substantial increase in malpractice suits against professional persons such as doctors or accountants by their patients and clients. A malpractice suit may be predicated on a theory of breach of contract, but the usual theory is negligence—failure to exercise the degree of care and caution that the professional calling requires. Although professional persons do not guarantee that they will make no mistakes, they are required to meet the standards of their profession. While such suits involve standards of professional conduct, the issue of negligence is nevertheless submitted to a jury for a decision. In many cases, juries find that liability exists even though members of the profession contend and testify that the services performed were all that could reasonably be expected under the circumstances.

medical malpractice Malpractice suits against doctors and hospitals have multiplied so rapidly that they have significantly affected the practice of medicine. In addition, these cases have been a major cause of the spiraling increase in medical costs—which has, in turn been a major contributing factor to inflation. Not only has the number of malpractice suits more than doubled in recent years, but the size of the verdicts has frequently reached astronomical proportions. As a result, the cost of malpractice insurance has risen dramatically. For example, malpractice insurance that cost $1,000 in 1970 might cost as much as $40,000 today.

Many doctors and some hospitals have been unable to obtain adequate malpractice coverage. More significantly, many doctors have been reluctant to attempt difficult medical procedures that could result in a malpractice suit. Because of the trends in malpractice litigation, most doctors are practicing defensive medicine: prescribing tests that are probably not indicated, requiring longer hospital stays, and consulting with other doctors as a matter of routine. Defensive medicine, obviously more costly, adds to the spiraling cost of medical care.

The medical malpractice problem reached crisis proportions in the mid-1970s. A few doctors gave up their private practice. Doctors in some areas withheld their services to protest the high cost of

72

malpractice insurance. Many doctors refused to take high-risk cases. As a result of this crisis, some states have enacted legislation calling for a set maximum limit (such as $500,000) that may be recovered in a malpractice suit. Other states are considering transferring medical malpractice claims to an administrative agency to be handled in a matter similar to workmen's compensation claims. The federal government has also set up guidelines for medical practice which may eliminate much of the negligence that has heretofore existed. None of these solutions have proved to be adequate. As the trend toward more malpractice litigation and bigger and bigger verdicts continues, the problems for society as the consequence of this type of tort litigation are of crisis proportions.

liability of
accountants
While most negligence actions against professional persons are brought by their patients or clients, some suits are brought by third persons who are injured. This is especially true in suits against accountants, since frequently their services are for the benefit of the public as well as the party who retains them. This is especially true of the audit function.

In suits against an accountant by third parties on a theory of negligence, it is necessary to distinguish between third parties that the accountant knew would rely on his work and third parties that may be described as unforeseen. While there is some conflict between various jurisdictions, the majority and better-reasoned rule is that an accountant is liable for negligence in the performance of his services to those persons whose reliance on the financial representations was actually foreseen by the accountant. The Restatement of Torts (second) extends the liability of the accountant to those persons known to the accountant to whom his client intends to supply the product of the accountant's services. For example, if an accountant knows that his financial statements are to be furnished to banks as a part of the process of obtaining a loan, the negligent accountant has liability to a lending bank for negligence in the preparation of the financial statements relied upon by the bank.

The liability of the accountant for negligence is limited to the class of third persons who come within the description "actually foreseen." It is the law in most jurisdictions that an accountant is not liable on a theory of general negligence to "unforeseen" third persons because there is no contractual connection with the third party. Third persons can sue for fraudulent acts of accountants without a contractual connection, but not for mere negligence. There is no liability to unforeseen third parties for mere negligence even though the accountant recognizes that some third party may rely on his work product.

It should be noted that an accountant may also be liable to third persons under the federal securities laws. This statutory liability, which will be discussed later with the materials on corporations, may involve issues of negligence. Under the Securities Act of 1933, an accountant is liable to any purchaser of a security upon proof that the portion of a registration statement attributable to the accountant contains an untrue statement of a material fact or omits to state a material fact necessary to prevent the statements made from being misleading.

However, it is a defense for the accountant that he had, after reasonable investigation, reasonable grounds to believe and did believe that the statements contained in the registration statement were true and that there was no omission to state a material fact required or necessary to make the statements not misleading. In other words, "due diligence" or "lack of negligence" is a defense to an allegation of a 1933 Securities Law violation. In determining whether or not an accountant has made a reasonable investigation, the law provides that the standard of reasonableness is that required of a prudent man in the management of his own property.

**Problems
of the
Fault System**

In recent years the fault system has been widely critized, and major changes in it have been suggested. The criticism and proposed changes have been primarily directed at automobile accident litigation, whether on a theory of negligence or willful and wanton misconduct. The fault system as it relates to auto accident cases suffers from so many inherent weaknesses and resultant injustices that even many lawyers and insurance companies agree that change is essential.

Among the problems inherent in the fault system are (1) court congestion and the inevitable delays caused thereby; (2) the overcompensation of minor claims and the undercompensation of major claims; (3) the high cost of liability insurance; (4) inaccurate testimony and unreliable evidence; (5) inconsistency of juries; and (6) the high cost of operating the system.

Of the criticism directed at automobile accident litigation, perhaps none is more significant than the high cost involved in operating under the fault theory. This high cost is readily apparent in automobile insurance premiums. Verdicts and settlements in auto accident cases frequently are in the hundreds of thousands of dollars. Payments in excess of a million dollars are often demanded and sometimes paid. As a result, the cost of automobile liability insurance has skyrocketed. Many insurance companies have become insolvent due to the number and extent of recoveries against their insureds and because of the lag time in rate increases. The cost of liability insurance has risen to the extent that many auto owners cannot realistically afford to pay the premiums. There are substantial additional high costs to the victim of the automobile accident, to the alleged wrongdoer, and to society as a whole.

Most victims must utilize the services of an attorney in order to collect their damages. The usual fee for such services is contingent on the total amount collected. The contingent fee system means that the attorney is paid a percentage of the recovery. Usual contingent fees are 33-1/3 percent if a trial is held, and 40 to 50 percent if the case is appealed. Contingent fees eliminate the risk of high attorney's fees if the case is lost. However, if the injuries are very substantial and liability is easily established, the fees of the attorney may be unfair and unreasonable. Assume a $300,000 verdict is given for the loss of two legs by a plaintiff. It is difficult to see how the $100,000 fee could have been earned. In addition, the chance of earning large fees has encouraged "ambulance chasing" of potentially big cases, especially in large cities.

The alleged wrongdoer in most tort litigation is usually defended by an insurance company. A substantial portion of the insurance premium dollar is spent on investigations and in trying to prevent payment to the person seeking the damages. Thus both parties to the occurrence are spending considerable sums attempting to determine what, if anything, one must pay the other. Moreover, society must operate an extensive court system and pay judges, court personnel, and jurors to try these cases and to settle these controversies. Thus it is readily apparent that the fault system is a very expensive system to operate.

Studies have been conducted attempting to show that the great majority of automobile accident victims are not appropriately compensated. The theory of damages tells us that the victim of a tort should receive a sum of money that will compensate him for the damage he has sustained. The damages paid should make him "whole." In other words, dollar damages are supposed to place the victim of the tort in as good a position as he would have been in had the tort not been committed. This, of course, is impossible because no amount of money can replace an arm, a leg, or an eye, let alone a life. Therefore, in the very serious cases, especially those that involve substantial pain and suffering, any amount of money damages is probably inadequate.

However, in the very minor cases many plaintiffs are overcompensated. A person with little or no personal injury who brings suit will frequently be overcompensated for his injuries because of the nuisance value of the case. Because it will cost money to investigate and defend the case and because the amount of jury verdicts are highly unpredictable, insurance companies frequently pay some amount to obtain a settlement of a claim even though the claimaint is probably not entitled to the amount paid.

Another problem with the fault system is court congestion. In many large cities the length of time between filing the lawsuit and the actual trial is over five years. Justice delayed is justice denied. These delays tend to cause claimants to settle cases for less than they would be entitled to in some instances. Delay also allows the wrongdoer or his insurance company, as the case may be, to recover a substantial portion of the loss through earnings on the money during the period of delay.

The theory of fault was developed long before there were automobiles. In many auto accident cases the litigation is quite unrealistic. Witnesses usually do not remember exactly what happened, and so they testify as to what they thought and sometimes hoped had happened. Witnesses with faulty memories have their memories refreshed and tend not to testify about what actually happened but about what somebody said happened.

Moreover, witnesses frequently do not know what happened in the split second of the automobile accident. As a result, many factors influence verdicts in these negligence cases. One very important factor is sympathy for the plaintiff or animosity toward the defendant. A very seriously injured person or the next of kin of a deceased is frequently the obvious beneficiary of sympathy. When the testimony is conflicting and the memory of witnesses questionable, sympathy may play a major role. Animosity is frequently just as important. For example, assume that a teenager runs a stop sign and kills an innocent bystander. The jury in such case is likely to award higher damages, especially if they believe an insurance company for the teenager may be required to pay them.

Finally, the fault system in auto accident litigation has traditionally proceeded on the premise that the accident was the defendant's fault and that negligence on the part of the plaintiff did not contribute to the plaintiff's injuries. In other words, the plaintiff has been required to be free from *contributory negligence.* The law has required that the defendant be 100 percent at fault and the plaintiff 0 percent at fault. This all-or-nothing requirement, of course, built an element into any case that encouraged settlement. Today the legislature in some states and the courts in others are abandoning the doctrine of contributory negligence and substituting for it a doctrine known as *comparative negligence.* Under the doctrine of comparative negligence, liability is assessed in proportion to the fault of each party. In some states using comparative negligence, a plaintiff can collect even if equally at fault or more at fault than the other party, but in other states, when the degree of fault reaches 50 percent, a plaintiff is barred from recovery. Thus the fault system varies greatly from state to state in its theories and their application.

**The Trend
Toward
No-Fault** In recent years there have been numerous proposals to eliminate the fault system in auto accident cases. These proposals have taken various forms. Some have recommended that auto accident cases be turned over to an administrative agency for decision. Others have recommended that the fault system be replaced by a no-fault system, or a system of first-party insurance.

Although the approaches to no-fault vary from state to state, most have elements in common. First of all, a party injured in an auto accident collects from his own insurance company just as he would if he were collecting on his own health insurance. Payment is made irrespective of fault. Just as health insurance would pay the hospital bill of a person attempting suicide, so also would no-fault insurance pay the hospital bill of a person injured in an automobile accident even if he were at fault. Second, claimants are entitled to collect their medical bills, lost earnings, and out-of-pocket expenses up to a stated amount. Third, most no-fault laws contain a formula for computing the amount to be paid for pain and suffering. For example, a person may be paid an amount equal to his medical bills for pain and suffering. If the total doctor bill is $500, then he would be paid an additional $500 for pain and suffering. Fourth, tort claims may still be filed in very serious cases. The approach of no-fault to date has been to keep the fault system for serious cases, such as permanent disability, disfigurement, and death. Only the minor cases are usually covered by no-fault legislation. This is accomplished by the law's setting a threshold above which the fault system is retained. Finally, claimants cannot collect their medical bills under no-fault if the medical bills are paid by any other form of health insurance or by workmen's compensation. This eliminates duplicate payment of medical expenses.

The experience to date under state no-fault laws has been quite varied. In some states, such as Massachusetts and Florida, the experience has been that there is a major reduction in the cost of automobile insurance and a substantial reduction in the number of lawsuits being filed. Cost savings are present because of the elimination or reduction of investigative costs and attorneys' fees. Savings have also come from the reduced payments for pain and suffering and from the elimination of duplicate payments of medical expenses. In other states, there has been no reduction in auto insurance rates. No-fault laws in some states have been declared unconstitutional on the ground that they denied injured parties the right to a trial by jury. Low thresholds have encouraged some persons to incur additional medical expenses so that the case is back within the fault system.

Critics of no-fault have been able to delay its enactment in many states and have kept the threshold quite low in others. Among the most often cited objections are (1) that the victims of automobile accidents are receiving substantially less for their injuries under no fault than they would receive under the fault system, and (2) that the elimination of the jury system from auto accident litigation deprives a plaintiff of his very important fundamental right—the right to a trial by jury. Thus it is apparent that no-fault has not been universally accepted and is still in the process of development. It appears that some form of no-fault for auto accident litigation will be enacted in most states in this decade, if not at the federal level. The very serious weaknesses of the fault system previously noted will undoubtedly be fatal to that system as it has heretofore existed.

REVIEW QUESTIONS AND PROBLEMS

1. Can the same act be both a crime and a tort? Explain.

2. List five intentional torts and give an example of each.

3. X intentionally committed assault and battery on Y. Y's doctor bills were $500, but he sustained no permanent injury. Is Y entitled to collect more than $500 from X? Explain.

4. Name two tort actions that are based on the freedom from disparagement of reputation.

5. Explain the theory of damages in a negligence suit.

6. Give two examples of situations in which tort liability is imposed without fault.

7. What five elements are usually present in a case of tort liability?

8. X, a customer, slipped and fell in a restaurant owned by Y. Z, another customer, was injured when he tried to prevent X's fall. Is Y liable for Z's injuries? Why?

9. What factors are useful in determining whether an infant is liable for his own tort?

10. Compare the punitive damages available in a willful trespass that endangers lives with those payable in a trespass that does not.

11. What remedies are available to one who believes that he is a victim of a private nuisance?

12. Contrast a *public nuisance* and a *private nuisance.*

13. Compare the tort of *invasion of the right of privacy* with *defamation.*

14. Give three examples of conduct that could be held to be "willful and wanton" by a jury.

15. Compare the duty an owner of premises owes to a *business visitor* with that owed to a *trespasser.*

16. List five problem areas of auto accident litigation that are being used to support the demand for a change in the system.

17. Explain in general terms the approach of most no-fault systems for automobile accident cases.

18. What are some of the problems associated with the recent increase in medical malpractice claims?

19. X, an accountant, negligently prepared a financial statement for Y, who presented it to Z bank to obtain a loan. Z granted the loan on the basis of the statement, which proved to overstate Y's financial condition. Y defaulted. Is X liable for Z's losses? Explain.

CONTRACTS

6 INTRODUCTION TO CONTRACTS

Nature and Importance of the Contractual Relationship
The law of contracts is concerned with the creation, transfer, and disposition of property rights through promises. The Restatement of Contracts defines a *promise* as an undertaking "however expressed, either that something shall happen, or that something shall not happen, in the future." A *contract* is a promise or a set of promises for the breach of which the law gives a remedy or the performance of which the law recognizes as a duty. In other words, a contract obligation is a legally enforceable promise.

When they enter into a contract, the parties, by mutual assent, "fix their own terms and set bounds upon their liabilities." In a very real sense, the parties create for themselves their own rights and duties, leaving it only to the state to set up the machinery for the interpretation of the contract and the enforcement of the promises.

Although the parties to a contract fix their own terms and set their liabilities, they are subject to limitations. To create a valid contract, the expression of the terms of the contract must be in compliance with rules of law. Many factors enter into the determination of whether or not a promise is in compliance with the law. What is the status of the person who made the promise? How was the promise expressed? Was the promise made orally or was it in writing? Are the necessary contractual requirements and elements present: offer and acceptance, consideration, legal capacity of the parties, and a legal purpose in light of the rules of law and of sound public policy?

This last requirement recognizes that in our society parties do not possess *absolute* freedom of contract. For example, the public interest demands that parties not be allowed to enter into contracts unduly limiting competition or resulting in unreasonable restraint of trade. In addition, inequality of bargaining power between the parties often requires the law to control the terms and provisions of contracts.

Since the law of contracts furnishes the foundation for other branches of commercial law, a study of the general rules applicable to contract law logically comes first in the study of business law. The special rules of law pertaining to agency, sales, commercial paper, corporations, partnerships, and secured transactions are all based upon general principles of contract law. These special areas are discussed in the books that follow this one.

Classification of Contracts

For certain purposes it is desirable to classify contracts according to the characteristics that they possess. They may be classified as follows:

1. Valid, voidable, or unenforceable
2. Executed or executory
3. Bilateral or unilateral
4. Express or implied (in fact or in law)

A *valid* contract is one that is in all respects in accordance with legal requirements and will be enforced by the courts. A *voidable* contract is one that will be enforced unless and until one of the parties who has the right to do so elects to disaffirm the contract. For example, a contract entered into by one who is under legal age is voidable and can be disaffirmed or set aside by the underage party. An *unenforceable* contract is one that will not be recognized by the courts if an action is brought to enforce it. For example, the law requires that some contracts such as contracts for the sale of land be in writing, and they are not enforceable in court if made orally.

An *executed* contract is one that has been fully carried out by the contracting parties. An *executory* contract is one that is yet to be performed. An agreement may be executed on the part of one party and executory on the part of the other. For example, a contract for the purchase of a suit of clothes to be paid on credit following the delivery of the suit is executed on the part of the merchant and executory on the part of the purchaser.

Contracts ordinarily result from an offer made by one party to another and accepted by the latter. A *bilateral* contract involves *two* promises, one made by each of the parties to the agreement. To illustrate: A offers to sell to B certain merchandise at an established price. B, after receiving the offer, communicates his acceptance to A by promising to buy merchandise and to pay the price set forth in the offer. After the promises are exchanged, it becomes the legal duty of each party to carry out the terms of the agreement. Although the parties have only exchanged promises and neither has rendered any performance, the promises constitute a bilateral contract. Most contracts are bilateral in character.

A *unilateral* contract consists of a promise for an act. The acceptance by the offeree (the person to whom the promise or offer is made) is given by the performance of the act requested rather than the promise to perform it. For example, A says to B, "I will pay you $2,500 if you will recondition and repair the air-conditioning system in my building." Only A has made a promise. B's acceptance of the offer is the performance of the requested service.

A contract that results from an oral or written agreement entered into by the parties is said to be an *express* contract. On the other hand, a contract may be entirely *implied* from the conduct and the acts of the parties, the acts being such that a contract may be inferred from them even though the parties have not entered into any express agreement. This is called a contract *implied in fact.* In other instances the contract may be, and often is, partially expressed and partially implied. Thus, if a person delivers his television set to a repairman to be repaired, he impliedly agrees to pay the repairman a reasonable fee for his services and materials. The intention of the parties to contract is clear from the facts and the specific circumstances.

**Implied-in-Fact
Contract**

A contract may be implied in fact whenever one person knowingly accepts a benefit from another person, and the circumstances make it clear that the benefit was not intended as a gift. The person who accepts the benefit impliedly promises to pay the fair value of the benefit that he receives. However, no implied promise to pay arises when the person who receives a benefit is unaware that such a benefit is being conferred. It is the acceptance of benefits at a time when it is possible to reject them that raises the implied promise to pay for them. To illustrate: A, during the absence of B and without B's knowledge, made certain repairs to B's house. B was under no duty to pay for the repairs, although he of necessity made use of them in connection with his occupancy of the property. The use of the house created no implied promise to pay for the repairs because B had never had the opportunity to reject them. However, if B had been present and had watched the repairs being made, his silence might well obligate him to pay the reasonable value of the improvement.

Historically, a typical implied-in-fact contract arose when a seller mailed goods to a buyer who had not requested them, with instructions that the buyer should either pay for the merchandise or return it to the seller. This was a common method of selling religious bookmarks, neckties, and even records. At common law a buyer was not obligated to go to any expense to return the goods and was not obligated to pay for the goods unless he used them as his own. However, use of the goods created an implied-in-fact contract and liability.

To stop this method of selling, the Federal Trade Commission, pursuant to its power to eliminate deceptive practices and unfair methods of competition, has enacted a rule that changes the common law of implied-in-fact contracts. This regulation provides that if a business mails goods to a consumer who has not ordered them, the consumer need not pay for them and need not return them. This regulation has almost eliminated the practice of mail-order businesses sending out unsolicited goods. This regulation is not applicable to cases where goods are mailed by mistake.

Quasi Contract   A contract implied in fact must be distinguished from a contract implied in law, generally known as *quasi contract*. Whereas an implied-in-fact contract is a true contract, quasi contract is not a contract at all. It is simply the name given to a remedy that is used by the courts to do justice and to avoid unjust enrichment as if a contract exists. Quasi contract imposes a duty upon a party and considers the duty as arising from a contract. It is a legal fiction predicated upon reason, justice, and equity to prevent fraud, wrong-doing, or the unjust enrichment of one person at the expense of another. The law in effect infers a promise by a party to do what in equity and good conscience he ought to do, even though he does not in actuality want or intend to do it. There are many situations in which the remedy of quasi contract is made available to a party.

Case: P, who operated an equipment sales company, entered into a contract to sell a tractor to D, a farmer. The tractor was delivered to D, who used it for two weeks during which time he was attempting to borrow money to cover the purchase price. He was unable to raise the money and returned the tractor to P. P claimed that D should pay him for the use of the tractor for two weeks.

Issue: Was D obligated to pay P for the use of the tractor in the absence of any promise to do so?

Decision: Yes. Judgment for the plaintiff. D must pay P $50 for the use of the tractor for two weeks.

Reason: The court said that this case was similar to an earlier case in which a contractor was employed to make improvements and repairs on the owner's building. During the owner's absence in Europe, the roof of the building was partially destroyed by fire through no fault of the contractor, who made necessary repairs for fire damage without knowledge of the owner. In that case the court held that a quasi contract arose obligating the owner to reimburse the contractor for the reasonable cost of material and labor furnished. In this case the court said that D had the use of P's tractor without paying for it, and under these circumstances the law would imply a contract because D would otherwise be unjustly enriched.

Anderson v. Copeland, 378 P.2d 1006 (Okla.) 1963.

To be entitled to the remedy of quasi contract, the plaintiff must prove that a benefit has been conferred on the defendant, that the defendant has accepted and retained the benefit, and that the circumstances are such that to allow the defendant to keep the benefit without paying for it would be unfair and inequitable. A typical case involves the receipt of money that was paid to the recipient by mistake. The person improperly receiving the money would have a duty to return it, and because no actual contract existed, the law would imply one. There are many other situations in which no contract exists, but the quasi-contract remedy is given because one person would be unjustly enriched if he were not required to pay for the benefits received.

Elements of a Contract As noted, a contract is defined in terms of promises. A *promise* is an undertaking that something shall happen or that something shall not happen in the future. The basic elements of a contract are:

1. The *agreement*, which consists of an *offer* by one party and *acceptance* by the other
2. *Consideration*, which is the price paid by each party to the other or what each party receives and gives up in the agreement
3. *Competent parties*, which means that the parties must possess legal capacity to contract (be of legal age and sane)
4. A *legal purpose* consistent with law and sound policy

These elements of a contract will be considered in detail in the chapters that follow. Problems arise when one or the other of the parties to a contract either refuses to perform or does not perform in the proper fashion. A number of legal procedures are used in contract litigation when performance problems arise.

JUDICIAL REMEDIES FOR BREACH OF CONTRACT

Introduction The breach of a contract or the threat thereof defeats the expectations of the parties and may even have consequences that affect persons other than the contracting parties. There is a natural desire to quickly and expeditiously resolve the problems arising from the breach. Three primary methods are used to obtain a resolution: negotiation and compromise, arbitration, and legal action. The third method is one of last resort and is used less frequently than the first. Most differences that arise over breaches of contracts are settled by the parties without litigation. The threat of court action often has a salutary effect on a person who has either breached or threatened to breach a contract and often produces cooperation in effecting an out-of-court settlement.

However, many contract cases do reach the courts, and remedies are provided for the purpose of granting appropriate relief to the injured party. Three basic remedies are afforded for breach of contract: dollar damages, specific performance, and rescission. In general these remedies are exclusive—a party is required to elect one to the exclusion of the others.

Money damages are recoverable in a court of law; specific performance and rescission are equitable remedies. Although damages are always recoverable for loss sustained as the result of a breach of a contract, the equitable remedies are not so readily available and will be allowed less often and usually only if the remedy at law (damages) is not adequate under the circumstances of the case. In other words, if a person can be adequately compensated by receipt of money damages, he will not be allowed the equitable remedies.

The equity court can order *specific performance* of a contract—that the party who has breached actually do what he had agreed to do under the contract. For example, in a contract to sell land, the court will order that the seller execute and deliver a deed to the buyer. This will be discussed further later in this chapter.

Rescission   The other equitable remedy is rescission of a contract, which is disaffirmance of a contract and the return of the parties to the status quo (the position each occupied prior to entering into the contract). For example, rescission is afforded when a contract has been induced by fraud or misrepresentation.

A party who discovers facts that warrant rescission of a contract has a duty to act promptly, and if he elects to rescind, to notify the other party within a reasonable time so that rescission may be accomplished at a time when parties may still be restored, as nearly as possible, to their original positions. A party entitled to rescission may either avoid the contract or affirm it. Once he makes his choice, he may not change it. Failure to rescind within a reasonable time is tantamount to affirming the contract.

Case: D applied for automobile insurance with P company through its agent. In his application, D stated that he had not been convicted of a traffic violation or had his driver's license revoked during the past five years. The

agent knew that D had in fact been convicted for drunken driving. More than a year later, D was involved in an accident in which one person was killed. P company sought to rescind the insurance contract on the basis of fraud.

Issue: Is P entitled to rescind the contract and avoid liability on the policy?

Decision: No.

Reasons: 1. A party who has notice of grounds for the rescission of contract and who elects to rescind it must do so promptly or lose his right to rescind.

2. When a contract has been induced by the misrepresentation by one party, so that the other party has an election whether to affirm the contract or to rescind it, one who retains the payments received and acts in a manner inconsistent with an intent to rescind the contract cannot later seek to rescind the contract.

3. By waiting more than one year after the company had knowledge through its agent, P had lost the right to rescind.

State Farm Fire and Casualty Co. v. Sevier, 537 P.2d 88 (Or.) 1975.

The party who seeks rescission must return what he has received in substantially the same condition in which he received it. Because this remedy is an equitable one, it is subject to the usual maxims of courts of equity.

Damages— Generally   The purpose and the theory of damages is to make the injured party whole. As a result of the payment of money, the injured party is in the same position he would have occupied had the breach of contract not occurred. Damages give just compensation for the losses that flowed from the breach. In other words, a person is entitled to the benefits of his bargain. If a purchaser receives less than he bargained for, the difference between the actual value and the contract price constitutes the damages. Unusual and unexpected damages resulting from peculiar facts unknown to either party at the time the agreement was entered into are generally not recoverable.

The question as to the amount of damages is usually one of fact for the jury. A jury may not speculate or guess as to the amount damage. Damages that are uncertain, contingent, remote, or speculative cannot be used. Loss of profits may be included as an element recoverable damages if they can be computed with reasonable certain from tangible and competent evidence.

A party suing for breach of contract is not entitled to recover amount expended for attorney's fees, unless the contract so provides special legislation permits it. Litigation is expensive, and the party w

87

wins the lawsuit is still "out of pocket," since the legal ε.
usually reduce the net recovery substantially. Court costs,
which include witness fees and filing costs, are usually assesse
the losing party.

Damages— Several terms are used to describe certain types of damages.
Terminology *Nominal damages* are awarded if no measurable actual loss is
established. In such cases one dollar is awarded to the plaintiff
to show that a technical breach has occurred.

The term *liquidated damages* or *liquidated damage clause* is used to
describe the situation in which the parties provide in their contract for
the amount of damages to be awarded in the event of a breach. These
provisions will be enforced unless the court considers the stipulation to
be a penalty for failure to perform, rather than compensation for
damages. Should the court find the term to have been inserted primarily to force actual performance and not to compensate for probable
injury, it will be considered to be a penalty and will not be enforced. In
order to be valid and not as a penalty, the amount of recovery agreed
upon must bear a reasonable relation to the probable damage to be
sustained by the breach. Recovery is allowed for the amount agreed
upon by the parties, although the damages actually suffered may vary
somewhat from those agreed upon in the contract.

Case: P installed a coin-operated phonograph in D's restaurant. The contract
provided that the parties would divide the receipts, that the contract
would extend for a specified period, and that the damages for breach by D
would be the amount of revenue that P would have received for the
balance of the contract period. D breached, and when sued by P, D
contended that the provision for liquidated damages was unenforceable.

Issue: Will a damage provision calling for payment of the amount that would
have been received in the absence of a breach be enforced?

Decision: Yes.

Reasons: 1. Liquidated damages may be collected; a penalty will not be enforced.
2. *Liquidated damages* are a sum that a party to a contract agrees to pay
if he breaks some promise, and which, having been arrived at by a
good-faith effort to estimate in advance the actual damage that would
probably ensue from the breach, are legally recoverable or retainable—if
the breach occurs. A *penalty* is a sum that a party similarly agrees to pay
or forfeit—but which is fixed, not as a preestimate of probable actual
damages, but as a punishment, the threat of which is designed to prevent
the breach, or as security—to insure that the person injured shall collect his
actual damages.

3. Whether a stipulated sum will be treated as a penalty or as liquidated damages may ordinarily be determined by applying one or more aspects of the following rule: "[A] stipulated sum is for liquidated damages only (1) where the damages which the parties might reasonably anticipate are difficult to ascertain because of their indefiniteness or uncertainty and (2) where the amount stipulated is either a reasonable estimate of the damages which would probably be caused by a breach *or* is reasonably proportionate to the damages which have actually been caused by the breach."

4. Here, there was a formula that provides a reasonable estimate of the probable damage in the event of a breach.

Knutton v. Cofield, 160 S.E.2d 29 (N.C.) 1968.

The term *punitive* or *exemplary* damages refers to damages awarded to one party in order to punish the other for his conduct. While it is not the purpose of a civil proceeding to punish a party, punitive damages are sometimes allowed. Punitive damages are frequently awarded in tort cases such as those involving libel or slander but are also allowed in contract cases.

Case: P entered into a contract to purchase a car from D auto company for $2,999. A trade-in allowance of $900 on P's used car was provided. P signed a retail installment form in blank. D auto company filled in the space for the trade-in as $599 instead of $900. The contract was assigned to a bank, and the bank sent a copy of the contract to P. P notified D of the error, but D refused to correct it and subsequently repossessed the car. P sued D, and the jury awarded him $900 actual damages plus $4,999 punitive damages. D appealed.

Issue: Did the facts warrant an award of punitive damages?

Decision: Yes.

Reasons: 1. The legal justification for punitive damages is to serve as a deterrent, and such damages will be allowed when there is a sufficient violation of societal interests.

2. The "trick" of agreeing to a trade-in allowance and having the customer sign a contract in blank in the hope that he will not notice that a different figure had been inserted is "reprehensible." This award of damages may discourage this auto dealer and others from engaging in this conduct.

McGill v. Huling Buick Co., 487 P.2d 656 (Or.) 1971.

Rules Concerning Damages The injured party is duty-bound to mitigate the damages. It is his duty to take reasonable steps to reduce the actual loss resulting from the breach to a minimum. He cannot add to his loss or permit the damages to be enhanced when it is reasonably within his power to prevent such occurrence.

When a contract is willfully and substantially breached after part performance has occurred, there may be some benefit conferred on the nonbreaching party. Furthermore, the benefit may be of such character that the nonbreaching party cannot surrender it to the other. For example, in construction contracts the benefit received from partial performance cannot be returned. Under these circumstances, the law does not require the innocent person to pay for the benefit conferred. As a result, the party who has refused to complete the job is penalized because of the failure to perform.

A different result obtains when the breach is unintentional—resulting from a mistake or a misunderstanding. In this situation, the party may be required to pay for the net benefit received on a theory of quasi contract. The court may award damages in the amount necessary to complete the performance, in which event the defaulting party is automatically credited for the partial performance.

In those contracts where partial performance confers benefits of such a nature that they can be returned, the recipient must either return the benefits or pay for their reasonable value. This rule is applied to willful breaches as well as unintentional breaches.

Specific Performance The legal remedy of dollar damages or the equitable remedy of rescission may not be adequate to provide a proper remedy to a party injured by a breach of contract. The only adequate remedy may be to require the party in breach to perform the contract.

Specific performance is granted in cases when the court in the exercise of its discretion determines that dollar damages would not be an adequate remedy. Specific performance is not a matter of right but rests in the sound discretion of the court. To warrant specific performance, the contract must be clear, definite, complete, and free from any suspicion of fraud or unfairness. Dollar damages are considered inadequate and specific performance the proper remedy when the subject matter of the contract is unique. Since each parcel of real estate differs from every other parcel of real estate, all land is unique, and courts of equity will therefore specifically enforce contracts to sell real estate. Examples of unique personal property are antiques, racehorses, heirlooms, and the stock of a closely held corporation. Such stock is unique because each share has significance in the power to control the corporation.

90

Case: P and D entered into an agreement whereby P was to receive one-third of the stock in a closely held corporation upon payment of $45,000 to D. D refused to transfer the stock, and P sought specific performance.

Issue: Is P entitled to specific performance?

Decision: Yes.

Reason: Closely held stock is not available in the market, so that it is really a unique commodity. As a result, P had no adequate remedy at law and specific performance was the only remedy.

Peters v. Wallach, 321 N.E.2d 806 (Mass.) 1975.

If the subject matter of a contract is goods, specific performance will be ordered whenever commercial needs and considerations make it equitable to do so. The remedy is liberally granted as a matter of policy. However, contracts that involve personal services or relationships will not be specifically enforced—the only remedy in such cases is money damages. Thus courts will not usually order specific performance of employment contracts.

Construction and Interpretation of Contracts

Courts are often called upon to construe or interpret contracts. The basic purpose of construing or interpreting a contract is to determine the intention of the parties. If the language is clear and unambiguous, construction or interpretation is not required, and the intent expressed in the agreement will be followed. When the language of a contract is ambiguous or obscure, courts apply certain established rules of construction in order to ascertain the supposed intent of the parties. However, these rules will not be used to make a new contract for the parties or to rewrite the old one, even if the contract is inequitable or harsh. They are applied by the court merely to resolve doubts and ambiguities within the framework of the agreement.

The general standard of interpretation is to use the meaning that the contract language would have to a reasonably intelligent person who is familiar with the circumstances in which the language was used. Thus, language is judged objectively, rather than subjectively, and is given a reasonable meaning. What one party says he meant or thought he was saying or writing is immaterial, since words are given effect in accordance with their meaning to a reasonable man in the circumstances of the parties. In determining the intention of the parties, it is

91

the expressed intention that controls, and this will be given effect unless it conflicts with some rule of law, good morals, or public policy.

The language is judged with reference to the subject matter of the contract, its nature, objects, and purposes. Language is usually given its ordinary meaning, but technical words are given their technical meaning. Words with an established legal meaning are given that legal meaning. The law of the place where the contract was made is considered a part of the contract. Isolated words or clauses are not considered, but instead the contract is considered as a whole to ascertain the intent of the parties. If one party has prepared the agreement, an ambiguity in the contract language will be construed against him, since he had the chance to eliminate the ambiguity. As an aid to the court in determining the intention of the parties, business custom, usage, and prior dealings between the parties are considered.

In the interpretation of contracts, the construction that the parties have themselves placed on the agreement is often the most significant source of the intention of the parties. "The parties themselves know best what they have meant by their words of agreement and their action under that agreement is the best indication of what that meaning was."

Case: P, a construction company, had a contract with D, the state of New Mexico, to construct a highway for an agreed price. The contract, consisting of four hundred pages, was drafted by P and was heavily loaded in favor of the state. The contract was ambiguous with regard to payment for extra work. D's key employees believed that P was entitled to payment for extras under the contract.

Issue: In case of ambiguity, will a contract be construed against the party preparing it?

Decision: Yes.

Reasons: 1. The law requires the construction of ambiguities and uncertainties in a contract most strongly against the party who drafted the contract.

2. It is logical to assume that the parties to a contract know best what is meant by its terms. Consequently, the construction of a contract adopted by the parties, as evidenced by their conduct and practices, is entitled to great weight, if not the controlling weight, in ascertaining their intention and their understanding of the contract.

Schultz & Lindsay Construction Co. v. State, 494 P.2d. 612 (1972).

THE UNIFORM COMMERCIAL CODE

Introduction The rules and principles of commercial law are of ancient origin. Throughout the centuries, merchants engaged in trade and commerce have recognized many customs and usages that regulate and control their conduct and their relationships with one another. Gradually over the years a body of law developed, based upon the practices of merchants, that was called the law merchant. For centuries the law relating to commercial transactions was based on case law rather than statutes. However, starting in 1896 a number of statutes were drafted relating to certain aspects of business transactions. Today most of these statutes have been replaced by one law known as the Uniform Commercial Code. This *Code*, as it is usually referred to in this text, relates to all aspects of a business transaction.

When there are references to the Code in the text, they will be placed in parentheses. These references pertain to the sections of the law, which is set forth in its entirety as an Appendix at the end of the text. For example, the purposes of the Code are to simplify, clarify, and modernize the law governing commercial transactions; to permit the continued expansion of commercial practices; and to make uniform law among the various states. (1-102) Section (1-102) may be referred to for the exact language of the law.

Although the Code provides definite rules that govern commercial transactions, the parties may, by mutual agreement, provide for a different result. To a large degree the Code provides for those situations that have not been covered by the parties in their contract. Accordingly, the parties to a transaction can, within limits, tailor their agreement to suit their needs. The Code supplies the rules and principles that will apply if the parties have not otherwise agreed.

To accomplish these purposes, the concept of the Code is that a "commercial transaction" is a single subject of the law, notwithstanding its many legal relations. Thus any given transaction could involve a contract for sale, a sale, the giving of a check for a part of the purchase price, and the acceptance of security of some type for the balance. The check may be negotiated by the seller to some other person and at the same time it will pass through a bank for collection. If the goods are shipped or stored, a bill of lading or warehouse receipt or both will likely be involved. In addition, especially in international sales, a letter of credit may be used in connection with the sale and its financing. Thus at the base of a commercial transaction is a sale accompanied by a method of payment for the goods purchased. The Code therefore deals with all the phases that may ordinarily arise in the handling of a commercial transaction, from start to finish.

It is important to note that the Code does not cover every legal problem that may arise in a commercial transaction. Many fields of law are not within the coverage of the Code. Accordingly, the Code provides that it shall be supplemented by the principles of law relative to capacity to contract, fraud, duress, and several others. (1-103) This means that a court will look, for example, at the law of duress, if a problem concerning this subject comes up in the course of a commercial transaction.

It is important to note that the Code is restricted to transactions involving various aspects of the sale, financing, and security in respect to *personal property*. It has very little application to *real property*—land and interests in land. It does not purport to cover all contracts and transactions but only those specified.

The Code contains ten articles, of which eight deal with specific aspects of commercial transactions in detail, one contains general provisions applicable to the whole body of Code law, and one designates those statutes that were repealed by it.

The Code is the law. The drafters of the Code prepared "official comments" for each provision in the Code. The official comments are not law, but they have been looked upon favorably by courts in order to determine what a particular section means or how it is to be interpreted and applied. The official comments are explanatory and often explain what the drafters were seeking to accomplish. The official comments therefore are significant and have had considerable impact on the law of the Code.

This text places special emphasis on Article 2—Sales, Article 3—Commercial Paper, Article 4—Bank Deposits and Collections, and Article 9—Secured Transactions. The other articles are also mentioned in appropriate sections. From the beginning of the study, it must be recognized and firmly kept in mind that Article 2, Sales, is restricted to transactions involving the sale of goods, which are generally defined as "movable" physical property. This definition excludes intangible items of property such as contract claims and also excludes contracts for the sale of investment securities—stocks and bonds.

To facilitate the learning of those special rules of law found in the Code that affect contracts for the sale of goods, there are special sections at the end of the chapters detailing the changes of the common law found in the Code. Each chapter of Book 2, "Contracts," discusses the general principles of contract law. The Code discussion at the end of the chapters covers the special rules applicable to contracts involving the sale of goods based on the Code. The reason for these special rules is that ordinary and general contract principles do not always produce a satisfactory result in a commercial transaction. Accordingly, the Code contract rules have been "tailored" to fit the sale-of-goods transaction.

Special Rules Under the Code The Code specifically provides that a contract clause that calls for unreasonably large liquidated damages is void. To be valid under the Code, a liquidated damage clause must be reasonable in light of the anticipated or actual harm caused by the breach, the difficulties of proof of loss, and the inconvenience or nonfeasibility of otherwise obtaining an adequate remedy. (2-718(1))

Another form of liquidation of damages is the forfeiture of goods when a buyer defaults after paying part of the price or making a deposit as security. The Code provides that, absent a liquidated damage clause, a buyer who defaults and does not receive the goods is entitled to recover from the seller any amount (1) by which his payments exceed 20 percent of the price, or (2) $500, whichever is smaller. (2-718(2)) Thus, if the buyer had made a deposit of $500 on the purchase of appliances for a price of $1,500, he would after his breach and return of the goods be entitled to recover $200 from the seller. If the sale contract contained a liquidated damage clause, the buyer would be entitled to recover the excess of the amount by which his deposit exceeds the amount provided for in such clause. Thus, a buyer who has made a part payment will not be unduly penalized by his breach, and the seller will not receive a windfall.

There is a Code provision relating to the obligations of buyers when there has been a breach by the seller after part of the goods has been delivered. The buyer may, on notifying the seller of his intention to do so, deduct the damages suffered because of the seller's breach from the price still due under the contract. (2-717)

There is a Code provision on the effect of performance on the interpretation of contracts. Any course of performance accepted or agreed to by both parties is relevant to determine the meaning of the contract. However, when it is not possible to harmonize the course of performance with the actual words of the contract, the express terms control over the course of performance. However, the course of performance controls both course of dealing and usage of trade in construing a contract. (2-208)

REVIEW QUESTIONS AND PROBLEMS

1. What limitations are there upon absolute freedom of contract?
2. What are the four classifications of contracts?
3. How is a unilateral offer accepted?
4. What is the difference between a *contract implied in law* and a *contract implied in fact*?
5. What are the basic elements of a contract?
6. What are the three remedies afforded by courts in contract matters?

95

7. D agreed to sell 1,000 shares of the XYZ company, a closely held corporation, to P. D then refused to carry out the agreement, and P sued for specific performance. What result? Explain.

8. D said to P: "I will pay you $500 if you will paint my house." The next day D called P on the telephone and said: "I revoke my offer. I have hired X to paint my house." P contends that he was counting on getting this job and that D had breached the contract. P sued D. What result? Why?

9. A purchased an auto which was represented as new from the XYZ dealership. After driving the auto a few weeks, A discovered that the auto was actually used and that the odometer had been set back. Is A entitled to recover punitive damages from XYZ? Why?

10. A and B entered into a lease in which A agreed to rent an apartment from B for $500 per month for one year. The lease did not mention attorney's fees in the event of a suit for rent. After six months, A moved out and refused to pay any further rent. In a suit for breach of contract, will B be entitled to recover attorney's fees? Why?

11. A and B had a contract in which A promised to repair B's roof before an expected rainstorm. A forgot to make the repairs, and the roof began to leak when the storm arrived. The rains continued for two weeks and caused extensive damage to B's home and furniture. Is A liable for all of B's losses? Explain.

12. The XYZ insurance company provided A with a copy of its automobile insurance policy at the time A purchased the insurance. The policy stated that theft coverage included equipment that was "a part of the vehicle." A's CB radio was stolen from his car. XYZ refused to pay A's claim on the basis that the radio was not part of the vehicle. Is the radio covered by the policy? Discuss.

7 THE AGREEMENT: OFFER AND ACCEPTANCE

FORMATION OF OFFERS

Introduction The first requirement of a valid, enforceable contract is an *agreement* between the parties. Generally, an agreement is reached when one party, the offeror, makes an offer and the other party, the offeree, accepts it. Offer and acceptance are the acts by which the parties have a "meeting of the minds"—they reach an accord as to the terms of their agreement. This is also referred to as *manifestation of mutual assent.* Frequently, parties may have had a discussion with regard to a contract but have not yet indicated their willingness to be bound by any contract.

An *offer* is a conditional promise made by the offeror to the offeree. It is conditional because the offeror will not be bound by his promise unless the offeree responds to it in the proper fashion. The response sought by the offeror is expressed in his offer and will be either (1) that the offeree do something—perform an act; (2) that the offeree refrain from doing something (forbearance); or (3) that the offeree *promise* to do something or refrain from doing something. If the offeree complies with the terms of the offer within the proper time, there is an agreement.

In a unilateral contract, the offeror's promise is conditional upon an act or a forbearance by the offeree. The offeror is promising to do something in return for some performance by the offeree or by the offeree's refraining from doing something (forbearance). To illustrate: A says to B, "I will pay you $500 if you will paint my building." Here, A is not asking for any promise from B, he is simply saying that he will pay B this amount of money if B performs the act of painting the building. To illustrate a forbearance: A promises to pay B $1,000 if B refrains from entering into a business that would compete with a business that B had sold to A. Here A is asking that B refrain from doing something that he might otherwise do. Note that in the unilateral contract situation, there is only one promise and that the response to the promise is either an act or a forbearance from acting. On the other hand, in an offer for a *bilateral* contract, the offeror is asking for a return *promise* from the offeree. Basically, the *offer* in either case is a communication of what the offeror is willing to do for a stated price or consideration to be furnished by the offeree.

Offers Contrasted with Invitations

Not all communications that invite further business transactions are worded so as to constitute offers. Many are of a preliminary character and are designed to encourage the person to whom they are addressed to respond with an offer. Within this class of communications fall most catalogs, circulars, advertisements, estimates, and proposals in which major terms are not included. Also included are oral statements of general terms when it is understood by the parties that the detailed terms will be reduced to writing and signed before the agreement is to be binding.

It is possible for an advertisement to be so worded that it constitutes an offer. To be an offer, the intent to make an offer in an ad must be clear and explicit. Most advertisements do not meet this test, and they are treated as mere invitations to make an offer.

Case: D, an automobile dealer, placed an ad with a newspaper to sell a used car. The price to be listed was $1,795. As the result of a printing error by the newspaper, the advertisement quoted the price as $1,095. P attempted to purchase the automobile for the advertised price and D refused to deliver the car. P sued D for breach of contract.

Issue: Was the newspaper advertisement an offer that P could accept?

Decision: No.

Reasons: 1. A newspaper advertisement that contains only an erroneous purchase price and no other terms is not definite enough to be an offer.

2. While it is quite possible to make an offer for a contract in an advertisement, it is not customary to do so. An advertisement amounts only to an invitation to make an offer.

3. There was no meeting of the minds nor the required mutual assent by the two parties to a precise proposition. There was no reference to several material matters relating to the purchase of an automobile, such as equipment to be furnished or warranties to be offered by the defendant.

Indeed the terms were so incomplete and so indefinite that they could not be regarded as a valid offer.

O'Keefe v. Lee Calan Imports, Inc., 262 N.E.2d 758 (Ill.) 1970.

One reason that advertisements and the like do not qualify as offers is that the parties making them do not intend to enter into a binding agreement on the basis of the terms expressed. The advertiser did not intend that any legal consequences should necessarily flow from his action.

An Offer Must Be Definite Many transactions involve lengthy negotiations between the parties and often an exchange of numerous letters and proposals, as well as conversations. It is frequently difficult to establish the point at which the parties have concluded the negotiation stage and have actually entered into a binding contract. The key question in such situations is whether a definite offer was made and accepted or whether the letters, communications, and proposals were simply part of continuing negotiations. The courts must examine the facts of each case and apply the basic contract rules concerning the requirements of an offer to the facts. An offer must be definite and must be made under such circumstances that the person receiving it has reason to believe that the other party (offeror) is willing to deal on the terms indicated.

One of the reasons for the requirement of definiteness is that courts may have to determine at a later date whether or not the performance is in compliance with the terms. Consequently, if the terms are vague or impossible to measure with some precision or if major terms are absent, no contract results. Time for performance and the price to be paid are important elements of a contract and would normally be specified and not left open. However, their absence will not preclude enforcement of the contract if the court is satisfied from the evidence that the parties intended to be bound by contract. Without a time clause, the court will imply a "reasonable time" for performance; if no price is specified, the court may rule that a "reasonable price" was intended. However, if neither party has yet performed, that is, the contract is executory as to both parties, an agreement in which the price is not specified will normally not be enforced.

An Offer Must Be Communicated An offer is not effective until it has been communicated to the offeree by the offeror. It can be effectively communicated only by the offeror or his duly authorized agent. If the offeree learns of the offeror's intention to make an offer from some outside source, no offer results. Also, to be effective, the offer must be communicated through the medium or channel selected by the offeror.

99

Thus, if A was in B's office and noticed on B's desk a letter directed to him containing an offer, the offer would not have been communicated to A. A would not be in a position to accept the offer.

When does an offer become effective? Assume that A mailed an offer to B on March 1 and stated that the offer would remain open ten days. B received the offer on March 3. When would the offer expire? It would expire March 13—ten days from the date of receipt of the offer.

An offer to the public may be made through newspapers or the posting of notices. As far as a particular individual is concerned, it is not effective until he learns that the offer has been made. As a result, a person without actual knowledge cannot accept the offer. For example, assume that a reward is offered for the arrest of a fugitive. If a person makes the arrest without actual knowledge of the offer of the reward, there is no contract.

An offer is effective even though it is delayed in reaching the offeree. Because the delay normally results from the negligence of the offeror or his chosen means of communication—for example, a telegraph company—he should bear the loss resulting from the delay. However, if the delay is apparent to the offeree, the acceptance will be effective only if it is communicated to the offeror within a reasonable time after the offer would normally have been received. If he knows that there has been a delay in communicating the offer, he cannot take advantage of the delay.

The unexpressed desire to enter into an agreement can never constitute an offer. Thus, writing a letter embodying a definite proposition does not create an offer unless the letter is mailed.

It should be noted that printed material often found on the back of contract forms and occasionally on letterheads, unless embodied in the contract by reference thereto, is not generally considered part of any contract set forth on such a form or letterhead. It is not a part of the contract because it has not been communicated to the offeree by the offeror.

Meeting of the Minds Unless there is a "meeting of the minds" of the parties on the subject matter and terms of the agreement, no contract is created.

To determine whether the minds have met, both the offer and the acceptance must be analyzed. The person making the offer may have had in mind something quite different from that of the person who accepted it. The rule that the minds of the parties must be in accord is limited in one important respect: namely, that the intention of the parties is to be determined by their individual conduct—what each leads the other to reasonably believe—rather than by their innermost thoughts, which can be known only to themselves. It is the objective manifestation of intent rather than the subjective that controls.

Case: P sued D, an insurance company, for specific performance of an alleged oral contract to settle a claim for personal injuries arising out of an automobile accident. D's adjuster had offered P $7,500 to settle the claim. The insurance company had paid P $2,400 in advance payments. The insurance adjuster intended to deduct the advance payments to P from the $7,500 and to pay P $5,100 net. P believed that the $7,500 would be in addition to the payments already received.

Issue: Is there a contract to settle the claim?

Decision: No.

Reasons: 1. It is elementary in contract law that mutual assent must be expressed by the parties to the agreement. When the minds of the parties have not met on any part or provision of a proposed contract, all of its portions are a nullity.

2. The meeting of the minds must be found in the objective manifestation of the parties. The apparent mutual assent, essential to the formation of a contract, must be gathered from the language employed by them, or manifested by their words or acts, and it may be manifested wholly or partly by written or spoken words or by other acts or conduct.

3. The parties to the alleged oral contract in the instant case used the same language, but the overt manifestations reveal that they attached different meanings to their words (a latent ambiguity), and there was in fact never a mutual assent.

4. Where one party meant one thing and the other party meant another, the difference going to the essence of the supposed contract, the court will find no contract in law or equity unless the court should find that one party knew or had reason to know what the other party meant or understood.

Trujillo v. Glen Falls Insurance Company, 540 P.2d 209 (N.M.) 1975.

The minds of the parties are also said to have met when they sign a written agreement. Each person possessing legal capacity to contract who signs a written document with the idea of entering into a contract is presumed to know the contents thereof. Where one who can read signs a contract without reading it, he is bound by the terms thereof unless he can show (1) that an emergency existed at the time of signing that would excuse his failure to read it, (2) that the opposite party misled him by artifice or device, which prevented him from reading it; or (3) that a fiduciary or confidential relationship existed between parties upon which he relied in not reading the contract. Because the act of signing indicates a person's intention to be bound by the terms contained in the writing, he is in no position at a later date to contend effectively that he did not mean to enter into the particular agreement. All contracts should, therefore, be read carefully before they are signed.

101

Offers clearly made in jest or under the strain or stress of great excitement are usually not enforced because one is not reasonably justified in relying on them. Whether an offer is made in jest can be determined by applying the objective standard.

OFFERS IN SPECIAL SITUATIONS

Auctions and Advertisements for Bids
When articles are sold at public auction the offer is made by the bidder, and it is accepted by the seller at the drop of the auctioneer's hammer. Because of this rule, the seller can withdraw his article from sale at any time during the auction. The purchaser may withdraw his bid at any time before the auctioneer has concluded the sale. The seller may, by statements in circulars relating to the sale or by statements made on the part of the auctioneer, prescribe the conditions under which the contract is to be concluded. Thus an auction advertised "without reserve" means that the property will be sold to the highest bidder. The seller has surrendered his right to withdraw an article once it is put up for sale. In any case the bidder has the right to retract his bid any time before the fall of the auctioneer's hammer, and the withdrawal of a bid does not have the effect of reviving any prior bid.

Unless it is otherwise announced before the sale, the seller has no right to bid at his own sale. For him to bid or have an agent do so would amount to fraud, the potential buyers having the right to presume that the sale is held in good faith. If an auctioneer knowingly accepts a bid on the seller's behalf, or if the seller makes or procures such a bid without giving notice of such bidding, the buyer has the alternatives of avoiding the sale or taking the goods for the amount of the last good-faith bid before his.

A related matter is that of bids that are solicited for a particular service or other purpose. When one advertises that bids will be received for construction work, it is held that the person calling for the bids makes no offer but that the party who submits the bid is the offeror.

The one calling for the bids may reject any or all of them, and in the absence of some statute, the bidder is free at any time to withdraw his bid until it has been accepted. Statutes in most states provide that public work must be let to the lowest responsible bidder, but the courts have held that all bids may be rejected.

Options
An *option* is a contract based upon some consideration whereby the offeror binds himself to hold an offer open for an agreed period of time. It gives the holder of the option the right to accept the continuing offer within the specified time. Quite often the offeree pays or promises to pay money in order to have the option—the continuing offer—remain open. The consideration need not be money—it may be

any other thing of value. The significant fact is that the offer has been transformed into a contract of option because of consideration supplied by the offeree. The offer becomes irrevocable for the period of the option. Of course the offeree in an option contract is under no obligation to accept the offer; he simply has the right to do so.

Frequently, an option is part of another contract. A lease may contain a clause that gives to the tenant the right to purchase the property within a given period at a stated price, or a sale of merchandise may include a provision that obligates the seller to supply an additional amount at the same price if ordered by the purchaser within a specified time. Such options are enforceable because the initial promise to pay rent serves as consideration for both the lease and the right to buy, and the original purchase price of goods serves as consideration for the goods purchased and the option to buy additional goods.

THE DURATION OF OFFERS

Lapse An offer that has been properly communicated continues in existence until it lapses or expires, is revoked by the offeror, is rejected by the offeree, or becomes illegal or impossible by operation of law. Also an offer ceases to be an offer and is merged into the contract when it is accepted by the offeree.

An offer does not remain open indefinitely, even though the offeror fails to withdraw it. If the offer stipulates the period during which it is to continue, it automatically lapses or expires at the end of that period. An attempted acceptance after that date can amount to no more than a new offer being made to the original offeror by the original offeree.

An offer that provides for no time limit remains open for a reasonable time—a reasonable time being such period as a reasonable person might conclude was intended. Whether an offer has lapsed because of the passage of time is usually a question of fact for the jury after it has given proper weight to all related circumstances, one of which is the nature of the property. For example, an offer involving property whose price is constantly fluctuating remains open a relatively short time in comparison with property whose price is more stable. Other facts that should be considered are the circumstances under which the offer is made, the relation of the parties, and the means used in transmitting the offer. For example, an offer made orally usually lapses when the conversation ends unless the offeror clearly indicates that the proposal may be considered further by the offeree.

Revocation by Offerors Except in the case of options, an offeror may revoke an offer at any time before it has been accepted by the offeree. This is true even though the offeror has promised to hold his offer open for a definite period. As long as it is a mere offer and not an option the offer can be legally withdrawn, even though morally or ethically such action may seem unjustified.

The courts, however, have sometimes held that it is too late to withdraw an offer after the offeree, in reliance on it, has substantially changed his position, particularly if the offeror promised to hold it open for a certain period.

Case: P, a general contractor, was preparing to submit a bid to build a school building. He requested D to submit a bid for the paving work that would be involved in the project. D offered to do the paving work for $7,000, and P used this subcontractor's offer in making his bid. The contract was awarded to P, but D stated that he would not do the paving for the $7,000. P got another contractor to do the work at a cost of $11,000 and brought legal action to recover $4,000 from D.

Issue: Could D legally withdraw his offer to do the paving work at the specified price?

Decision: No.

Reasons: 1. P's reliance on D's offer made the offer irrevocable.

2. When P used D's offer in computing his own bid, he bound himself to perform in reliance on D's terms. Though D did not bargain for this use of its bid neither did D make it idly, indifferent to whether it would be used or not. On the contrary it is reasonable to suppose D submitted its bid to obtain the subcontract.

3. D was bound to realize the substantial possibility that its bid would be the lowest, and that it would be included by P in his bid.

Drennan v. Star Paving Company, 333 P.2d 757 (Cal.) 1958.

The above case was decided using a doctrine commonly referred to as the *doctrine of promissory estoppel*. It is discussed in detail in the next chapter.

The revocation of an offer by the offeror becomes effective only when it has been communicated to the offeree. The mere sending of a notice of revocation is insufficient. It must be received by the offeree or reach a destination where it would be available to him. But communication of a revocation is effective when actually received regardless of how or by whom it is conveyed. If the offeree obtains knowledge from any source of the offeror's conduct clearly showing an intent by the latter to revoke, the offer is terminated.

An offer made to the public presents a special problem to an offeror who desires to revoke such an offer. It would be impossible to give personal notice of revocation to all persons who may have learned of the offer. Accordingly, the offeror is allowed to withdraw his offer by giving the same general publicity to the revocation that he had to the offer. A public offer made through the newspapers in a certain locality may be withdrawn through the same medium. Although it is thus possible that persons who are made aware of the offer may not actually be made aware of its withdrawal, the result is justified on the premise that the offeror is still the master of his offer and that he has taken reasonable means to give notice of revocation.

Rejection by Offerees

Rejection by the offeree also causes an offer to terminate. An offeree who rejects cannot later bind the offeror by tendering an acceptance. A rejection terminates an offer even though the offeror had promised to keep the offer open for a specified time. For example, if B has paid A for a ten-day option to purchase property at a given price, but on the seventh day tells A that he does not want it, A is immediately free to sell to another buyer.

An attempted acceptance that departs from the terms of the offer is a rejection of the offer. It is a counteroffer because it implies that the terms set forth in the offer are not acceptable. For example, A offered to sell a house to B for $25,000. B responded: "I accept your offer, provided that a new roof is put on the house." Here the acceptance varies from the offer and is therefore not effective as an acceptance but rather it is a counteroffer and a rejection.

It is often difficult to determine whether a communication by an offeree is a rejection or merely an expression of a desire to negotiate further on the terms of the agreement. Thus it is possible to suggest a counterproposal in such a way as to make it clear that the offer is still being considered and is not being rejected. In such a case the offeree wishes a reaction from the offeror to the suggested changes. Also, the offeree may, in his acceptance, set forth terms not included in the offer, but the terms may be those that would be implied as ones normally included in such an agreement. The inclusion of such terms will not prevent formation of a contract.

Case: P leased property from D. The lease contained an option to purchase the premises for $25,000 at any time during the term of the lease. P decided to exercise the option and to purchase the property, and he so notified D in writing. In the writing, P stated that he would pay the purchase price as soon as D furnished him proof of title to the property and furnished him with a deed warranting that the title was good. D refused to sell to P. D contended that P had added conditions to the option with regard to proof of good title, and therefore the purported acceptance was actually a rejection.

Issue: Did P properly accept the offer contained in the option?

Decision: Yes.

Reasons: 1. An option is defined as a right acquired by contract to accept or reject a present offer within the time limited. If the person who holds the option does signify acceptance of the offer within the time limited and upon the terms stated, the obligations become mutual and are capable of enforcement at the instance of either party.

2. Nothing was said expressly in the option regarding the kind of deed or proof of title, but in a real estate transaction a buyer is entitled to both of these. The addition of these in the acceptance did not go beyond what the seller would have had to have furnished in any event.

3. While the lessor did not promise in so many words that he would give a deed or furnish proof of title, the obligation to do so could be fairly implied. The lessee's so-called counter conditions are in reality only suggested ways and means by which his purchase of the premises can be appropriately effected by the lessor.

Department of Public Works v. Halls, 210 N.E.2d 226 (III.) 1965.

A request for further information by an offeree who indicates that he still has the offer under consideration will not constitute a rejection of the offer.

Rejection of an offer is not effective in terminating it until the rejection has been received by the offeror or his agent or is available to him at his usual place of business. Consequently, a rejection that has been sent may be withdrawn at any time prior to delivery to the offeror. Such action does not bar a later acceptance.

Termination of an Offer by Operation of Law There are several events that will terminate an offer as a matter of law. Notice of the occurrence of these events need not be given or communicated to the offeree or to the offeror, as the offer ends instantaneously upon the occurrence of the event. Such events include the death or insanity of either party or the destruction of the subject matter of the offer. The occurrence of any one of these events eliminates one of the requisites for a contract, thereby destroying the effectiveness of the acceptance of the offer to create a contract. Thus, if the offeror dies before the offeree has communicated acceptance to him, the offer is terminated, and the acceptance would have no effect. Another event is the promulgation by a law-making body of a statute or ordinance making illegal the performance of any contract that would result from acceptance of the offer.

There is a distinct difference between the termination of an offer and the termination of a contract. It should be emphasized that death, for example, terminates an offer but not a contract. As a general rule, death of either party does not excuse performance of contracts, although it would in contracts for personal service. To illustrate the effect of the death of one of the parties to an offer: Assume that A offers to sell to B a certain electronic computer for $15,000 and that after A's death, B without knowledge of his decease, mails his acceptance to A and immediately enters into a contract to resell the computer to C for $17,000. The estate of A has no duty to deliver the machine, even though C may have a claim against B for breach of contract if the latter failed to deliver the computer to C. Had B's acceptance become effective before A's death, the executor of A's estate would have been obligated to deliver the computer.

THE LAW AND ACCEPTANCES

Definition A *contract* consists of an offer by one party (offeror) and its acceptance by the person (offeree) to whom it is made. Figuratively speaking, an offer hangs like a suspended question, and the acceptance must be a positive answer to that question. The offeror says: "I will sell you this article for $200. Will you buy it?" The offeree now has the legal power to accept this offer, and if he does so in proper fashion, a contract will result. A contract therefore results when the offeree—acceptor—answers the question in the affirmative. An acceptance is an indication by the offeree of his willingness to be bound by the terms of the offer. Acceptance may, if the offer permits, take the form of an act (unilateral offer), an oral return promise communicated to the offeror (bilateral offer), or the signing and delivery of a written instrument. The latter method is the most common in transactions of considerable importance and in those that are more formal. If a written contract is the agreed method of consummating the transaction, the contract is formed only when it has been signed by both parties and has been delivered.

**Acceptance
of a
Unilateral Offer** As indicated previously an offer may be either unilateral or bilateral. Most offers are bilateral, and when there is doubt as to whether they are unilateral or bilateral, the courts tend to construe them as bilateral.

When an offer is unilateral, the offeror does not desire a promise of performance. He insists on substantial completion of the act or forbearance requested.

As a general rule, substantial performance of the act requested constitutes an acceptance of a unilateral offer. If the offeror ceases performance short of substantial performance, there is no acceptance and no contract.

A difficult question arises when an offeror seeks to withdraw a unilateral offer during the course of the offeree's attempted performance of the act requested. In the early common law, many courts allowed the offeror to withdraw the offer prior to substantial performance by the offeree, but the offeror was liable in quasi contract for any benefits received. Today the generally accepted view is that an offeror of a unilateral offer cannot withdraw during the performance by the offeree. The offeror becomes bound when performance is commenced or tendered, and the offeree has a duty to complete performance. The continuing liability of the offeror is in effect conditioned on the offeree's finishing performance. The underlying theory of this result is that the offer of a unilateral contract includes, by implication, a subsidiary promise that if part of the requested performance is given, the offeror will not revoke his offer. The consideration for this subsidiary promise is the part performance by the offeree. It is the *part performance* by the offeree that gives rise to the obligation of the offeror to keep his offer open. The offeree may incur expense in *preparation* for performance, but this is not the part performance that prevents revocation.

Acceptance of a Bilateral Offer

An offer for a bilateral contract is accepted by a *promise* from the offeree given in response to the promise of the offeror. The offeree's promise is to perform in the manner required by the offer. The promise of the offeree (acceptance) must be communicated to the offeror or his agent and may consist of any conduct on the part of the offeree that clearly shows an intention to be bound by the conditions prescribed in the offer. In construing the language of a purported acceptance, the usual rules of construction, including the principle that ambiguous language is to be construed against the person using it, are applied.

The acceptance may take the form of a signature to a written agreement, even to a nod of the head or any other indication of a willingness to perform as required by the offer. No formal procedure is generally required. If the offer is made to two or more persons, the acceptance is not complete until each of the parties has indicated his acceptance. Until all have responded and accepted, the offeror is at liberty to withdraw his offer.

When it is understood that the agreement will be set forth in a written instrument, the acceptance is effective only when the document has been signed and delivered, unless it was clearly the intention of the parties that the earlier verbal agreement be binding and that the writing act merely as a memorandum or evidence of the oral contract that was already effective and binding upon the parties.

Silence as Assent

As a general rule, the offeror cannot force the offeree to speak. In most cases, therefore, mere silence by the offeree does not amount to acceptance, even though the offeror in his offer may have stated that a failure to reply would constitute an acceptance. However, a previous course of dealing between the parties, the receipt of goods by the offeree under certain circumstances, or the solicitation of an offer could impose a duty on the offeree to speak in order to avoid a contractual relationship.

Case: P construction company entered into a contract to build an apartment building for D and to have it completed by a certain date. Due to extremely bad weather and other circumstances, P asked for extensions of time. These were submitted to D's architect on a printed form. D's architect agreed to some extensions and ignored the request for others. D sought damages because the building was not completed on schedule.

Issue: Was the silence or lack of disapproval a grant of the requests for extensions?

Decision: Yes.

Reason: When the relations between the parties justify the offeror's expectation of a reply or where a duty exists to communicate either an acceptance or rejection, silence will be regarded as an acceptance.

Brooke Towers Corp. v. Hunkin-Corkey Construction Co., 454 F.2d 1203 (1972).

Silence *of itself* does not constitute an acceptance, but silence with intent to accept may do so. For example, the receipt of a renewal fire insurance policy retained by the insured with intent to keep and pay for it constitutes acceptance of the offer to insure for the new period. Mailing out the renewal policy constituted the offer to insure, and the retention of the policy was the acceptance if the offeree intended to avail himself of the insurance protection. Obviously the requisite intent will often be difficult to determine.

Acceptance by Offeree Only the person to whom the offer is made can accept the offer. Offers to the public may be accepted by any member of the public who is aware of the offer. An offeree cannot assign the offer to a third party. Option contracts, however, although a form of offer, are usually assignable and may be accepted by the assignee— the person to whom the option is transferred.

If goods are ordered from a firm that has discontinued business and the goods are shipped by its successor, the offeror (the purchaser) is under no duty to accept the goods. If he does accept them knowing that they were shipped by the successor, then by implication he agrees to pay the new concern for the goods at the contract price. If he does not know of the change of ownership when he accepts the goods, he is not liable for the contract price—his only liability is in quasi contract for the reasonable value of the goods, and of course he could return them to the seller if he so elected.

Variance Between Offer and Acceptance As a general proposition of contract law, to be effective an acceptance must conform exactly to the terms of the offer. If the acceptance contains new terms or conditions, or if it otherwise deviates from the terms of the offer, it is a counteroffer and constitutes a rejection of the offer, unless the offeree explicitly states that it is not to be considered a rejection. Provisions in an offer relating to time, place, or manner of acceptance must be strictly complied with by the offeree. If the offeree does not follow the requirements of the offer, the attempted acceptance will be a counteroffer and, therefore, a rejection of the offer. This requirement has been referred to as the "mirror image rule," which requires exact compliance between offer and acceptance.

Time of Taking Effect A bilateral offer is not accepted until the offeree communicates his acceptance to the offeror. A conflict has long existed in the law as to whether or not the acceptance is effective to create a contract at the moment it is deposited in the mail, or whether its effectiveness is delayed until the offeror actually receives it. The so-called deposited acceptance rule—that an acceptance is effective when deposited in the offeror's channel of communication, for example, the mail—is generally applied.

Case: P leased certain restaurant property to D. The lease provided for an initial term of five years and contained option provisions providing for extensions of two successive five-year periods each. In order to exercise the option to renew, D was required to give P written notice six months before the expiration of the initial term. More than six months before the initial term expired, D prepared, signed, properly stamped and addressed, and deposited a letter notifying P of his intent to exercise the option. P never received the letter.

Issue: Did the exercise of the option require actual receipt of the letter?

Decision: No. The option was an offer, and it was accepted as soon as the letter was deposited in the mail.

Reasons: 1. The option contract is an irrevocable offer, the acceptance of which creates a binding bilateral contract.

2. It is well established that the acceptance of an offer to enter into a bilateral contract is effective and deemed communicated as soon as deposited in the regular course of mail.

Palo Alto Town & County Village, Inc. v. BBTC Co., 110 Cal. Rptr. 93 (1973).

If the offeree uses a diferent means of communication than that used by the offeror, the acceptance is not effective until it is *received* by the offeror.

The deposited acceptance rule has the effect of placing on the offeror any possible loss resulting from failure on the part of the communicating agency to deliver the acceptance. Thus, even though a letter of acceptance is lost in the mail, a contract may exist. The offeror, in such cases, is duty-bound to perform, even though he may have entered into other contracts as a result of his failure to receive a reply from the offeree. He can avoid this result by stating in his offer that the acceptance shall not be effective until it is actually received by him.

It is to be noted that the deposited acceptance rule applies only to *acceptances.* It will be recalled that other communications associated with contracts—revocations of offers and rejections of offers—are not effective until they are received.

Changes Under the Code The Code has made a number of significant changes in the law of offer and acceptance. It must be stressed again that the Code does not apply to all contracts and that those contracts not covered by the Code continue to be governed by the general rules and principles of contract law previously covered in this chapter. The Code is primarily concerned with transactions involving the sale of *goods.*

definiteness The Code recognizes that parties often do not include all the terms of the contract in their negotiations or even in their contract. The Code provides that even though one or more terms are

111

left open, a contract for the sale of goods does not fail for indefiniteness if the parties have intended to make a contract and if there is a reasonably certain basis for giving an appropriate remedy. (2-204) It further provides that an agreement that is otherwise sufficiently definite to be a contract is not made invalid by the fact that it leaves some of the particulars of performance to be determined by one of the parties. Specification of such particulars must be made in good faith and within limits set by commercial reasonableness. (2-311) Unless otherwise agreed, specifications as to the assortment of the goods are at the buyer's option, and those relating to method and mode of shipment are at the seller's option. (2-311(2))

auctions The Code has a separate section that covers sales of goods by auction. In an auction sale, the sale is completed when the auctioneer strikes his hammer—at this point when the hammer falls, the person making the highest bid is entitled to the article and must pay for it. It sometimes happens that while the auctioneer's hammer is falling, but before it has struck the table, another bid is made. In this case, the Code provides that the auctioneer can either reopen the bidding or declare the goods sold under the bid on which the hammer was falling. (2-328(2)) One who is selling goods at auction cannot bid at his own sale unless notice has been given that he retains this privilege. The Code provides that if the auctioneer knowingly receives a bid that has been made by the seller or on his behalf, and no notice has been given that the seller has the privilege of bidding at his own sale, the buyer has a choice of remedies. If the seller's wrongful bidding has bid up the price, the bidder can refuse to be bound by the sale. If he wishes to do so, he could demand that the goods be sold to him at the price of the last good-faith bid prior to the completion of the sale. (2-328(4)) The Code provisions are designed to protect people who bid at auction sales and to prevent them from being defrauded or otherwise taken advantage of.

firm offers The Code contains a provision with regard to a promise by an offeror that his offer will remain open for a specified period. If a merchant states in an offer that the offer will remain open for a stated period, such an offer is called a "firm offer." In such cases the merchant may not withdraw the offer during the stated period, provided it does not exceed three months, or for a reasonable length of time not exceeding three months, if no period is stated. The firm offer must be a signed, written offer, and in the event that the provision stating that the offer will remain open is set forth on a form supplied by the offeree, it must be separately signed by the offeror in addition to his signature as a party to the contract. (2-205) The offeree in a firm offer can rely upon the continuing legal obligation of the offeror and make other commitments on the strength of it. In effect, the firm offer by a merchant is the equivalent of an option.

variance   The Code rejects the mirror image rule of the law of contracts.

Under the Code, a definite expression of acceptance of a written confirmation operates as an acceptance. This is true even though the acceptance states terms additional to or different from those offered or agreed upon, unless acceptance is made conditional upon agreement to the additional or different terms. This means that the additional terms do not prevent the formation of a contract, unless they are expressed in the form of a counterproposal. The terms in question will otherwise be treated simply as new proposals.

However, when the contract is *between merchants*, such terms become part of the contract unless "(a) the offer expressly limits acceptance to the terms of the offer; (b) they materially alter it; or (c) notification of objection to them has already been given or is given within a reasonable time after notice of them is received." (2-207(2))

Case: P ordered adhesive materials from D. These materials were for use in manufacturing celophane bags for holding wet-pack spinach. The printed order forms specified this intended use. D accepted P's, order with a printed order form which stipulated that it did not guarantee the results to be obtained from the use of its products and that there were no warranties. P, upon receipt of this form, did not respond. The adhesive did not work properly, and P sued for breach of warranty.

Issue: Did the new terms become a part of the contract?

Decision: No.

Reasons: 1. Section 2-207 of the Code provides:

(1) A definite and seasonable expression of acceptance or a written confirmation which is sent within a reasonable time operates as an acceptance even though it states terms additional to or different from those offered or agreed upon, unless acceptance is expressly made conditional on assent to the additional or different terms.

(2) The additional terms are to be construed as proposals for addition to the contract. Between merchants such terms become part of the contract unless:

(a) The offer expressly limits acceptance to the terms of the offer;

(b) They materially alter it; or

(c) Notification of objection to them has already been given or is given within a reasonable time after notice of them is received.

2. Here P could have objected to the new terms. The failure to do so and acceptance of the goods with knowledge of the new terms means that P was bound by D's disclaimer of warranty.

Roto-Lith Ltd. v. F. P. Bartlett & Co., 297 F.2d 497 (1962).

The problem of variance arises in three similar situations: (1) where an acceptance states terms additional to or different from those offered, (2) where a written confirmation of an informal or oral agreement sets forth terms additional to or different from those previously agreed upon, and (3) where the printed forms used by the parties are in conflict, especially in the "fine print." The Code takes the position that in all of the above situations ". . . a proposed deal which in commercial understanding has in fact been closed is recognized as a contract." (2-207)

To illustrate the problem of variance in offer and acceptance, and the Code solution, assume the following: Merchant A sends to Merchant B an offer to sell him 1,000 boxes of select Anjou pears at $10 per box, F.O.B. Medford, Oregon (A's place of business). B replies by wire: "Accept your offer to sell 1,000 boxes of select Anjou pears at $10 per box, F.O.B. Champaign, Illinois. Boxes to be made of wood and pears individually wrapped." There are two matters to consider here. First, the terms of delivery were changed. A contract has been formed, and A's provision on delivery (Medford, Oregon) prevails. A had effectively objected to B's proposal, since A had stated the terms of delivery in the offer. The law considers the statement of a term as an objection to a change in that term. Second, there were new or additional terms concerning the boxes and wrapping added in the acceptance. As to these additional terms, they would be included *unless* either (1) A objects to these additional terms within a reasonable time, or (2) the additional terms are found to "materially alter" the contract. If A does seasonably object to the additional terms or if a court finds that they constituted a material alteration, they are not included.

It is to be noted that either party could easily have protected himself against the contingencies posed by this example. A, the offeror, could have expressly stipulated in his offer that acceptance was limited to the terms of the offer, or he could have seasonably communicated to B his refusal to include the additional terms. B, the offeree, could have stated in his acceptance that it was to be effective only if A agreed to ship F.O.B. Champaign, Illinois, and to pack in wooden boxes, with each pear separately wrapped. In this event his acceptance would constitute a *counteroffer.*

In the example, the offeror and the offeree are merchants; if merchants were not involved on both sides, the additional terms would not become a part of the contract unless mutually agreeable. They would simply be proposals for additions to the contract, which A could accept or reject.

unilateral offers   The Code makes some changes in the law of acceptance of unilateral offers. Basically the Code provides that an order for goods may be accepted either by a shipment of the goods or by a prompt promise to ship the goods. (2-206(1)(b)) To illustrate: A merchant who needs several items of merchandise right away mails a letter to a manufacturer asking for immediate shipment of the articles listed. This would be a unilateral offer and it could be accepted by the act of shipment, even though the offeror (the buyer) had no actual knowledge of the acceptance. The buyer, however, could withdraw his offer at any time before the seller's delivery to the carrier, even though the seller might have incurred expense in anticipation of delivery by way of procuring, assembling, or packing the goods for shipment. Under the Code, such an offer may be treated either as a unilateral offer and accepted by shipment, or it may be treated as a bilateral offer and accepted by a promise to ship. The seller under the Code is thus afforded an opportunity to bind the bargain prior to the time of shipment if he wants to do so.

time acceptance is effective The Code retains the deposited acceptance rule and has expanded it to provide that an offer to make a contract shall be construed as inviting acceptance *in any manner* and *by any medium* reasonable in the circumstances. (2-206(1)(a))

REVIEW QUESTIONS AND PROBLEMS

1. The XYZ company mailed one of its catalogs to A. A mailed an order for a new clock described in the catalog. At this point, was there a contract between A and XYZ? Why?

2. A offered to sell to B a boat for $100. B replied, "I think I want the boat, but let me have a week to think it over." A then told B, "OK, I will not sell to anyone else until after one week." Two days later, A sold the boat to C for $150 and notified B that the offer was no longer open. B attempted to accept the offer. Is A liable to B for breach of contract? Why?

3. A was employed as the manager of an office building owned by B. B sold the building to C. A had a conversation with X, C's agent, and offered to continue as manager of the building now owned by C on the same terms that he had with B. Six weeks later C appointed a new manager, Y. This was A's first knowledge that he would not be continued as manager, as C had not responded in any way to A's offer. Does A have any claim against C? Why?

4. A offered, by a letter dated August 13, to sell stock to B. The offer stated: "It is a condition of this offer that it be accepted in writing within five days from this date." B mailed an acceptance on August 18, which was received by A on August 20. A refused to recognize any contract, and B brought legal action. The trial judge ruled that there was no contract. Was this ruling proper? Why?

5. A, who operated a hardware store, placed an order for fifty power saws with B, a manufacturer. The order form supplied by B's salesman stated that the order would not become a contract until accepted by the home office. Thereafter A received a letter from B acknowledging receipt of the order and promising prompt attention. Some time later B wrote to A stating that it could

not fill his order. A then sued B for damages in the amount of the profit he would have made on the sale of the fifty power saws. Should A succeed? Why?

6. A placed an advertisement in the B newspaper for a special sale of fur scarves at the price of $15. When the advertisement appeared, it stated a price of $5. During the period of this sale, A sold forty-eight furs at a price of $5. He now seeks to recover $480 from the newspaper. Should he succeed? Why?

7. A and B had been drinking in a bar. During their conversation, the subject of A's farm came up and B said: "I bet you would not take $50,000 cash for that farm." A replied that he would, and B asked if he would put it in writing. A then wrote a statement to that effect. B seeks to enforce the agreement; A contends that it was all a joke. Would a court grant specific performance to B? Why?

8. A advertised that he would sell his estate at public auction "without reserve." Bids were made, B finally bidding $41,000. At this point A ordered the auctioneer to stop the sale, saying that he would not accept anything less than $100,000. B seeks to obtain a decree that A sell him the property for $41,000. Should he succeed? Explain.

9. A as seller and B as purchaser had been negotiating for the sale and purchase of land. B made an offer and mailed it to A. A accepted the offer and placed the letter of acceptance in the mail, but before B received it, A telephoned B that he would not sell, that B should disregard the acceptance. B contends that A is bound by contract. Is B correct? Why

10. A mailed an offer to B and stated in the offer that unless B responded to the contrary within ten days, his silence would be an acceptance of the offer. B remained silent for more than ten days. Is there a contract between A and B? Why?

11. The XYZ dairy by mail offered to sell A, a retailer, 100 gallons of milk at a stated price. A promptly replied, "Please send immediately 100 gallons of milk in one-gallon plastic containers." XYZ ignored A's reply. Is XYZ liable for breach of contract if the milk is not sent? Why?

8 CONSIDERATION

Introduction   In addition to offer and acceptance, consideration must be present before there is a valid enforceable contract. *Consideration* is defined as the price bargained for and paid for a promise. It usually takes the form of some benefit to the promisor, but it may also consist of a loss or a detriment to the promisee. *Benefit* as used in this context is not limited to tangible benefits but means that the promisor has, in return for his promise, acquired some legal right to which he would otherwise not have been entitled. In addition, the benefit may accrue to a third person. A promise based upon consideration of benefit to a third person constitutes sufficient consideration for promise or agreement.

A person suffers a loss or a *detriment* in the legal sense when he gives up a legal right that he has or takes on an obligation to do something that he was not otherwise required to do. In other words, when a promisee does something he is not legally bound to do or refrains from doing that which he has a right to do, there is a detriment and consideration. In most situations there will be both a benefit to the promisor and a detriment to the promisee.

Case: P was employed by D company and was injured on her job. D promised P that she would be paid the same benefits as those provided under the state's Workmen's Compensation Act, although the company did not participate in the compensation program. Companies that chose not to participate were subject to tort suits by injured employees. D paid compensation for some time but then discontinued payments. P brought suit to enforce the promise, but D contended that the promise was not enforceable and that P's only remedy was in tort.

117

Issue:	Is there consideration to support D's promise to pay an amount equal to workmen's compensation?
Decision:	Yes.
Reasons:	1. By agreeing to accept benefits measured by provisions of the Workmen's Compensation law, P gave up her acknowledged right to sue in tort for her full damage. This is a detriment to the promisee.
	2. D also received a benefit. In consideration of limiting its liability to the equivalent of benefits that might accrue under the Workmen's Compensation Act, D escaped liability in tort for P's full disability.

Tigrett v. Heritage Building Co., 533 S.W.2d 65 (Tex.) 1976.

The Price Paid for a Promise

Consideration has also been defined as the surrender or promise to surrender a legal right at the request of another. It is what each party to a bargain gives to the other. It is the price paid for a promise. Either the performance or the promise to perform an act or the surrender or promise to surrender a right at the request of a promisor is consideration. Without this price paid for the promise, the promisor might be *morally* obligated to carry out his promise, but the law would consider it to be legally unenforceable. For example, a person made a pledge to a hospital development fund. The pledge form recited that it was in consideration of and to induce other pledges. The pledge is not legally enforceable. It is a mere gratuitous promise unsupported by consideration.

The Restatement of the Law of Contracts provides that consideration for a promise may be

a. An act other than a promise, or
b. A forbearance, or
c. The creation, modification, or destruction of a legal relation, or
d. A return promise, bargained for and given in exchange for the promise.

Since consideration is required to make a promise legally binding, a promise to make a gift is unenforceable. The fact that the recipient of a proposed gift must take certain steps to place himself in a position to receive it cannot be substituted for the required consideration. If, however, the promisee of the gift is requested to act in a certain manner, and the action is considered to be the price paid for the promise, the taking of such action as is requested will serve as consideration.

118

Promises Enforced Without Consideration Although consideration is required for a valid contract, there are some exceptions to this requirement and some substitutes for consideration. For example, as we discussed in the preceding chapter, a firm offer is valid and binding under the Code without any consideration. The next section discusses one of the more common substitutes for consideration. In addition, some obligations described as mere moral obligations are enforced because of special facts. These special facts usually establish that the promisor actually received some benefit that justifies the enforcement of the promise.

Case: P, a former ward of D, sued D, his uncle and former guardian, for interest on guardianship funds that D had loaned to himself. When P reached majority, D repaid the principal and promised to pay interest but failed to do so. When P sued for the interest, D claimed that there was no consideration for the promise to pay interest.

Issue: Is the promise enforceable?

Decision: Yes.

Reasons: 1. A moral obligation is a sufficient consideration to support a subsequent promise to pay where the promisor has received a material benefit, although there was no original duty or liability resting on the promisor.

2. P wrongfully took the use and benefit of P's funds. He received a material benefit from them. Therefore there was a moral obligation to pay interest and the promise is enforceable.

Slayton v. Slayton, 315 So.2d 588 (Ala.) 1975.

Promissory Estoppel This chapter is primarily concerned with what is and what is not "good consideration." Before turning to these issues, the significant substitute for consideration commonly known as *promissory estoppel* must be considered.

The doctrine of promissory estoppel is an equitable doctrine used where there is in fact no consideration. It allows enforcement of a promise when the promise is such that the promisor should reasonably expect the promisee to take some substantial action or forbearance in reliance on the promise to such an extent that injustice can be avoided only by enforcement of the promise. The promise without consideration becomes enforceable because of the reliance upon it. That there would be reliance must have been foreseeable by the promisor, and there must be a change of position. For example, X promises his church

119

$1,000 to be used to construct a new building. The church, in reliance on X's promise and on promises and pledges by others, undertakes the construction project. X's promise may be binding because he induced the church to materially change its position on reliance on his promise. However, if his $1,000 pledge were to be used in discharge of an existing mortgage, the promise would likely be unenforceable for lack of consideration. The church did not change its position in reliance on the promise. The doctrine of promissory estoppel is limited in its application and provides only a limited means of enforcing promises that fail to pass the test of consideration.

Adequacy of Consideration

Historically, it has not been a function of law to make value or economic judgments concerning contracts voluntarily entered into by the parties. As a general rule, courts have not attempted to weigh the consideration received by each party to determine if it is fair in the light of that which the other party gave. It has been sufficient in law if a party received something of legal value for which he bargained. The law is only concerned with the existence of consideration, not with its value. It does not inquire into the question of whether the bargain was a good one or a bad one for either party. In the absence of fraud, oppression, undue influence, illegality, or statutory limitation, parties have been free to make any contract they please. The fact that it is onerous or burdensome for one or the other has been immaterial.

Today this philosophy is changed to a substantial degree. The Code provides that contracts that are so one-sided as to be unconscionable are unenforceable (2-302). Courts as well as legislative bodies have attempted to protect consumers by changing this historical view of consideration. These matters will be discussed further in subsequent chapters dealing with consumer protection.

There has always been one exception to the general rule on adequacy of consideration. In contracts that call for the exchange of money between the parties, the adequacy of consideration will be scrutinized. A promise to pay $1,000 in one year in return for an immediate $100 loan would not only be usurious, and therefore illegal, but would also be unenforceable because of the inadequacy of consideration. Money has a fixed value, and there is therefore no basis for holding that the payment of $100 is sufficient consideration to support the promise to pay $1,000. Although it could be argued that the borrower may have needed the $100 so badly that it was worth it for him to promise to pay the larger sum, such has not been an acceptable argument to the courts. It is one thing to indulge in the presumption that the parties have provided for a reasonable relationship between the detriment to the promisee and the benefit to the promisor in ordinary contracts, but the basis for the presumption fails when money alone is involved on both sides. Note, however, that if something in addition to money is provided by the promisee, adequacy of consideration is no longer an issue. Thus, for example, if A pays $100 to B and in addition promises to attend a political meeting in return for B's promise to pay him $1,000, the promise would be supported by consideration.

Recitals of Consideration Most written contracts contain a provision reciting that there is consideration. For example, a contract may state: "For and in consideration of $1 in hand paid, etc." Such a recital of nominal consideration does not conclusively establish the existence of consideration. A recital that consideration exists is not consideration unless it can be proved that the nominal consideration was "bargained for" and the price paid for the promise.

The general rule, therefore, is that a mere recital of consideration may be questioned in an action to enforce the alleged contract. A recital of consideration will stand up in the absence of evidence to contradict the recital, and of course one dollar actually bargained for and paid may be good consideration. Just as a court may examine a contract to determine the presence of consideration, even though consideration is recited, it may also receive evidence of the presence or absence of consideration when the agreement is silent on this score.

Forbearance Consideration, which usually takes the form of a promise or an action, may take the opposite form—forbearance from acting or a promise to forbear from taking some action.

Case: P entered into a contract to purchase stock from D corporation. Thereafter P brought an action against D to rescind the contract and to recover money from the corporation. At the same time of the suit, P attached the corporate bank account. He agreed to release the bank account and not to make any further attachments if the corporation would maintain a special trust bank account of $28,000 to take care of any judgment P might obtain. D sought to avoid its obligation to maintain a trust account.

Issue: Was there consideration to support D corporation's promise?

Decision: Yes.

Reason: The relinquishment of a legal right constitutes sufficient consideration for a contract. Here P relinquished his right to make any further attachments—a forbearance.

Lefton v. Superior Court for Los Angeles, 100 Cal. Rptr. 598 (1972).

The law also considers the waiver of a right or the forbearance to exercise a right to be sufficient consideration for a contract. The right that is waived or not exercised may be one that exists either at law or in equity. It may even be a waiver of a right that one has against someone other than the promisor who bargains for such a waiver.

A common form of forbearance is a promise not to bring a lawsuit, generally referred to as a release or a covenant not to sue. Forbearance to assert a legal claim is good consideration, regardless of the validity of the claim that is surrendered, provided there is reasonable and sincere belief in its validity. Giving up the right to litigate is something of value and a legal detriment even if it is ultimately discovered that the surrendered claim is worthless. However, if the claim is frivolous or vexatious, or if the claimant knows it is not well founded, forbearance to sue would not be good consideration.

There are numerous other examples of forbearances that may constitute consideration. For instance, the relinquishment of alleged rights in an estate will furnish consideration to support a return promise to pay money. An agreement by the seller of a business not to complete with the person who has bought a business from him is another example of forbearance. Mutual promises to forbear are sufficient to support each other. They are commonly used as a part of a settlement of a dispute.

SPECIAL ASPECTS OF CONSIDERATION

Preexisting Obligations The performance of a preexisting contractual or statutory duty does not furnish consideration for a promise. If a promisee receives nothing more than he was entitled to without making the promise, he has not received any consideration for the promise. In other words, doing what one is required to do anyway is not valid consideration. Applying the detriment-benefit test, the promisor who gets only what he was already entitled to has not received any benefit, and the promisee who does what he is already obligated to do has suffered no legal detriment.

The problem of preexisting obligations has arisen in various circumstances. A common situation is one in which one party to a contract refuses to continue performance unless and until the terms of the contract are modified. The other party may, in order to ensure continued performance, assent to the demands and agree to terms that are more burdensome than those provided in the agreement. He may promise to pay more than the contract price or to accept less in the way of performance. Generally a promise to pay more than the agreed price or to accept less is not enforceable. An exception to this rule is discussed in the next section.

Usually an owner who promises a contractor an additional sum to complete a job under contract is not legally bound to pay the additional sum. If, however, the promisee contractor agrees to do anything other than or different from that which the original contract required, consideration is provided. The contractor who agrees to complete his work at an earlier date or in a different manner may recover on a promise by the owner to pay an additional amount. It would also be possible for the parties to cancel the original contract and enter into an entirely new agreement that included the new amount.

Some conflict exists in those cases in which a *third party* promises added compensation to one of the two contracting parties, if such party will perform his obligations under the contract. Most courts hold that a promise made by a third party to pay money to one of the parties to perform an existing contractual obligation offers no consideration. Some recent judicial decisions appear to favor the promisee when the third-party promisor stands to gain by the performance. Of course, if the third party requests the original party to do anything new or different, the promise becomes binding because of the new consideration.

A promise to perform a statutory duty does not support a return promise. Thus, a promise to pay a public official a sum of money in return for his promise to perform the duties of his office would not only be of questionable legality, but would also be without consideration.

Unforeseen Difficulties   The parties to a contract often make provisions for contingencies that may arise during the course of the performance of the contract. They recognize that certain problems may arise and that performance may be rendered more difficult because of the occurrence of these events. They are well advised to exercise this foresight. However, they frequently do not make any provisions at all or make some that do not encompass all the difficulties that may render performance by either party more burdensome than anticipated. In the absence of an appropriate contract clause, two questions are raised when unanticipated difficulties arise during the course of performance: (1) Will the party whose performance is rendered more difficult be required to complete performance without any adjustment in compensation? (2) Will a promise to pay an additional sum because of the difficulty be enforceable?

Excuses for breach of contract are discussed in Chapter 13. For purposes of this discussion, it must be recognized that additional hardship is not an excuse for breach of contract as a general rule. Thus, the answer to the first question is usually yes.

The second question therefore assumes that a promisor, although not required to do so, has promised to pay an additional sum because of the difficulty. Courts have held that where a truly unforeseen difficulty arises and because of it a promise is made to pay an additional sum, such promise will be enforced.

Case: D entered into a contract with a city to collect all the trash in the city for a five-year period for an agreed-upon compensation. The number of required collections increased substantially, and the city agreed to pay an additional $10,000 per year because of the increased amount of trash. P, a group of citizens of the city, objected to the increased payments and sought to recover $20,000 paid over a two-year period.

Issue: Was the promise to pay an additional sum enforceable?

Decision: Yes.

Reasons: 1. The general rule is that a promise to pay more for work already required to be performed is not enforceable. There is an exception to this general rule for unforeseen difficulties.

2. The modern trend of cases recognizes that courts should enforce agreements modifying contracts when unexpected or unanticipated difficulties arise during the course of the performance of a contract, as long as the parties agree voluntarily to the modification.

3. The city was not required to promise to pay an additional sum, but when it did so, the promise was enforceable.

Angel v. Murray, 322 A.2d 630 (R.I.) 1974.

The above result is most often justified on the theory that in effect the parties rescinded the old agreement because of new circumstances and formed a new one. However, it is prudent for the promisee to whom the promise for additional compensation is made to either furnish some new consideration or to have the old agreement formally rescinded and a new one executed. Note in the above example that D did ultimately win but that he was put to the expense of litigation. Had D insisted upon the execution of a new contract and a rescission of the old one, he probably would not have had to go to court at all. It should be emphasized that when unforeseen difficulties do arise, the party who is having the difficulty is obligated to perform at the original contract price unless the other party promises to pay an additional sum.

Unforeseen difficulties are those that seldom occur and are extraordinary in nature. Price changes, strikes, inclement weather, and shortage of material occur frequently and are not considered to fall into this category. Thus it may be that a person who has contracted to build a building finds that the cost of materials has risen since he entered the contract, or he may be faced with a strike by carpenters. He must nevertheless perform at the original price unless he has made provisions in the contract that some relief shall be given him in the event that these things do happen.

Discharge of Liquidated Debts and Claims As previously noted, if the consideration on each side of an agreement involves money, the consideration must be equal. Because of this rule, an agreement between a debtor and his creditor to have a liquidated (fixed in amount) debt discharged upon the payment of a sum less than the amount agreed to be owing is unenforceable. In other words, there is no consideration for the agreement to accept less than the full amount owed. In most states the unpaid portion is collectible even though the lesser sum has been paid. If there is no dispute as to the amount owed, a debtor who sends in a check for less than the amount of the indebtedness and marks on the check "paid in full" will still be liable for the balance due.

Case: P entered into a contract to sell real estate to D for $4,000 payable in monthly installments. After three years P agreed to reduce the price to $2,500, but when D had paid that amount P refused to give a deed to the property and brought a foreclosure suit because D refused to pay any more.

Issue: Was the promise to accept $2,500 in full payment enforceable?

Decision: No.

Reason: The agreement to accept a lesser amount was without consideration. Part payment of a liquidated and undisputed claim even though accepted in full satisfaction thereof does not operate to discharge the debt but constitutes only a part payment. P had agreed to accept less than the full amount of the purchase price, and there simply was no consideration to support a forgiveness of $1,500 of the amount due.

Monroe v. Bixby, 47 N.W.2d 643 (Mich.) 1951.

The payment of the lesser sum is the performance of an existing obligation and cannot serve as consideration for a release of the balance. However, if there is evidence that the creditor made a gift of the balance to the debtor, no recovery of the balance may be had by the creditor. A paid-in-full receipt given to the debtor by the creditor is usually regarded as evidence that a gift was intended. Likewise where the debt is evidenced by a note, the cancellation and return of the note upon receipt of part payment is judged as a gift of the balance due.

125

Just as a promise to pay an additional sum for the completion of an existing contract is enforceable if the promisee does something other than or in addition to the required performance, a debtor may obtain a discharge of the debt by paying a lesser sum than the amount owing if he gives the creditor something in addition to the money. The settlement at the lower figure will then be binding on the creditor. Since the value of consideration is ordinarily unimportant, the added consideration may take any form. For example, payment in advance of the due date, payment at a place other than that agreed upon, surrender of the privilege of bankruptcy, the giving of a *secured* note for less than the face of the debt, have all been found sufficient to discharge a larger amount than that paid. The mere giving of a note for a lesser sum than the entire debt will not release the debtor of his duty to pay the balance. The note is merely a promise to pay, and consequently the mere promise to pay less than is due will not discharge the debt.

Discharge of Unliquidated Debts and Claims A promise to forbear from suing to collect a debt or a claim is sufficient consideration to support a promise to pay for a release, and the compromise results in a binding settlement. The parties are surrendering their rights to litigate the dispute, and this detriment serves as consideration. As a result, when one party has a claim against another party and the amount due is disputed or unliquidated (uncertain in amount), a compromise settlement at a figure between the amount claimed or demanded and the amount admitted to be owing is binding on the parties. Payment of money that one claims is not owing is consideration for the loss of the right to litigate the dispute.

It does not matter whether the claim is one arising from a dispute that is contractual in nature, such as one involving damaged merchandise, or is tortious in character, such as one rising from an automobile accident. The compromise figure agreed to by both parties operates as a contract to discharge the claim. Such a settlement contract is known legally as an *accord and satisfaction*. The dispute as to the amount owed by the debtor must be in good faith, or the rules for liquidated debts are applicable. If the dispute is not in good faith, the creditor could pursue the debtor for the difference, even though the creditor had agreed to settle for a lesser amount.

Accord and Satisfaction An accord and satisfaction is a fully executed contract between a debtor and a creditor to settle a disputed claim. The accord consists of an agreement whereby one of the parties is to do something different by way of performance than that called for by the contract. This accord is satisfied when the substituted performance is completed. Both must be established. The cashing of a check marked "paid in full" when it is tendered to settle a disputed claim is a typical example of an accord and satisfaction.

Case: P had entered into a contract to furnish material and labor for plumbing modifications in D's house. A dispute developed as to the amount that D owed P, and D wrote a check on which he wrote "payment of account in full." When P received the check he crossed out the words "payment in full," wrote on the check the words "paid on account," and deposited it.

Issue: Was there an accord and satisfaction when P deposited the check?

Decision: Yes.

Reasons: 1. It is well settled that when an account is made the subject of bona fide dispute between the parties as to its correctness, and the debtor tenders his check to the creditor upon condition that it be accepted in full payment, the creditor must either refuse to receive the check or accept the same burdened by its attached condition.

2. If the creditor accepts the check and cashes it, he impliedly agrees to the condition.

Burgamy v. Davis, 313 S.W.2d 365 (Tex.) 1958.

An accord may be either oral or written. For an accord and satisfaction to discharge a claim, the claim must be disputed between the parties. If the creditor is not aware of the dispute, the cashing of a check tendered in the usual course of business with a "full payment" notation will not operate as an accord and satisfaction. An accord, like any other agreement, requires a meeting of the minds. An accord will not be implied from ambiguous language. The intent to settle the dispute must be clear.

Composition of Creditors An additional method of satisfying a debt by payment of a lesser sum than the amount claimed or admitted is a "composition of creditors." This is a procedure whereby a person's creditors agree to accept a certain sum of money and/or property in full and complete settlement of the debtor's obligations to them. The creditors prorate the debtor's assets, which are made available to them, and agree with each other and the debtor to accept a percentage of their claims in full satisfaction. The composition is a type of insolvency proceedings enabling a person in debt to satisfy his debts by making most, if not all, of his assets available for distribution to his creditors. Of course, this raises a legal question as to the consideration to support the acceptance of a lesser sum in full satisfaction than the amount admittedly due. The consideration for which each of the assenting creditors bargains may be any one of the following: (1) the promise of each of the other creditors to forgo a portion of his claim; (2) the action of the debtor in securing the acquiescence of the other creditors; (3) forbearance or a promise to forbear by the debtor to pay the assenting creditors more than the stipulated proportion. Thus the law encourages mutual agreements between a debtor and his creditors to the extent of precluding the participating creditors from thereafter collecting the difference between their pro rata share and the amount of the debt.

Past Consideration   Past consideration is insufficient to support a present promise. The consideration must consist of some present surrender of a legal right. Some act that has taken place in the past will not suffice. Hence, an express warranty concerning real property sold, when made after the sale has taken place, is not enforceable, nor is a promise to pay for a gift previously received.

The past consideration rule does not apply, for example, to those cases in which one person requests another to perform some work for him without definitely specifying the compensation to be paid, and after the work is completed, the parties agree upon a certain sum to be paid for the work. Although it would appear that the work done in the past furnishes the consideration to support the promise made later to pay a definite sum, such is not really the case. As soon as the work is completed, the party performing it is entitled to reasonable compensation. His later surrender of this right is consideration for a promise to pay a definite sum. The surrender of the right to receive a reasonable wage is a consideration for the promise to pay a certain sum.

There are other exceptions to the rules of law concerning past consideration. For example, a new written promise to pay a debt that has been discharged in bankruptcy is enforceable without any new consideration. This result is based on special state statutes. Thus A files a petition in bankruptcy and is discharged of all his debts, including his debt to creditor B. B can no longer enforce A's obligation. If A, however, thereafter promises in writing to pay the debt even though it has been discharged in bankruptcy, the promise will be enforced. Many states have a similar statutory provision for a promise to pay a debt outlawed by the statute of limitations.

A creditor who has given a voluntary and binding release of part of a debt may not enforce a later promise by his debtor to pay the balance. If the release of the unpaid portion is considered in the nature of a gift, the rule relating to a promise to pay for a gift previously received renders such a promise unenforceable.

Mutuality of Consideration The mutual promises in a bilateral contract furnish the consideration for each other. That is, the promise made in A's offer to B is the consideration for the promise made by B in his acceptance of the offer. However, each of these mutual promises must be valuable, certain, and not impossible of performance, or they will not suffice as consideration. As a general proposition, if one party is not bound by his promise, neither is bound. A promise is valuable only if it meets the benefit-detriment test previously discussed. The requirement that a promise be definite and certain involves the same issues mentioned in Chapter 7 concerning offer and acceptance. A promise that cannot possibly be accomplished is not a binding promise and does not constitute consideration. However, a promise that has even a remote possibility of being performed may be binding and will be consideration for the other promise.

Sometimes what appears to be a binding promise is only an illusion. The law requires mutuality of consideration, not mutuality of obligation, although many cases indicate that these are two separate requirements. As was previously noted, the law is not concerned with the adequacy of the consideration, only with its actual existence. As a general proposition of contract law, if a party who has given an illusory promise actually performs the promise, the other party is bound to perform also. Lack of mutuality is not a defense to an executed contract; it becomes binding upon the promisor after performance by the promisee. An agreement that is based upon an illusory promise is not a contract. To determine if mutuality of consideration is present or if the purported promise is illusory, a careful examination of the language of the contract and of all the facts surrounding it is required.

Case: P, an eighty-three-year-old married woman, sued D, a seventy-nine-year-old widower, seeking to enforce a contract under which she claimed the right to reside in a house. The house was originally owned by D. D asked P to live with him and conveyed the title to the house to P, subject to a retained life estate.

P and D later quarreled. A reconciliation agreement was entered into by the terms of which each party agreed not to dispossess the other from the premises. D then sought to force P to leave, and she filed this suit.

Issue: Is there consideration for the promise of D not to dispossess P from the premises?

Decision: No.

Reasons: 1. The contract lacked mutuality of obligation, since it was illusory.

2. Since D had a life estate, P could not dispossess him. Therefore she gave no consideration for D's promise not to dispossess her.

129

3. While there appeared to be a promise for a promise, in fact such was not the case. P gave nothing.

Maszewski v. Piskadlo, 318 So.2d 226 (Fla.App.) 1975.

An agreement that gives to one of the parties the right to cancel the contract at any time prior to the time for performance is not binding and is illusory. However, if the right to cancel is not absolute but is conditioned upon whether some event happens or does not happen, the contract is such that neither party may avoid it unless the condition occurs and it is not illusory. Mutuality does not require that a contract be definite in all details or that there be reciprocity or a special promise for each obligation. Nor does it require mutuality of remedies between the parties.

Many promises that appear to assure something of value, but when fully understood do not embody such an assurance, are illusory promises because real mutuality is lacking. Consider the following agreement: B, a trucker, promises to purchase from S all he *wants* of S's gasoline at fifty cents a gallon plus taxes, and S promises to sell all that B *wants* at that price. Careful analysis of this agreement makes it clear that B has not *agreed to buy* any gasoline. He has promised to purchase only in case he wants it, which is equivalent to no promise at all. Since B has thus given S no consideration for his promise, B's promise being illusory, S is at liberty to withdraw, and his withdrawal becomes effective as soon as notice thereof reaches B. Until withdrawn by S, the agreement stands as a continuing offer on his part, and any order received prior to revocation must be filled at the quoted price.

In the above case, if B had agreed to buy his gasoline *needs* or *requirements* from S for a period of one year, the agreement would have been binding. Whenever the buyer is reasonably certain to have needs or requirements, an agreement to purchase all of one's needs or requirements will support the promise to supply them even though the amount to be needed is uncertain. Past experience will, in a general way, aid the seller in estimating the amount required.

Changes under the Code

modification of contracts

The requirement of consideration is often a barrier to enforcement of promises, and the Code has made substantial inroads on the consideration element of a contract, especially with regard to authorizing alteration or modification of contracts without requiring consideration to support the changes.

Under the Code, parties to a binding contract for the sale of goods may change the terms, and if such change is mutually agreeable, no consideration is required to make it binding. (2-209(1)) This means, for example, that if a buyer agrees with the seller to pay more than the contract price for goods purchased, he will be held to the higher price.

To illustrate: A, an automobile manufacturer, entered into a contract with B, a supplier, to purchase a certain number of wheels at a stated price. Thereafter B told A that because of higher production and labor costs, he would need to be paid $5 more per wheel in order to carry on with the contract. If A agrees to pay the additional sum, his promise to do so will be binding even though there is no consideration present.

Nevertheless, consideration is very much a part of the framework of modern contract law, and even under the Code it is a viable element. The Code section that sustains modifications of a contract without any additional consideration could, if not limited in some way, permit a party to a contract with a superior bargaining position to take advantage of the other party. Accordingly the Code provides that the parties must act in good faith, and the exercise of bad faith in order to escape the duty to perform under the original terms is not permitted. The "extortion" of a modification without a legitimate reason therefore is ineffective because it violates the good-faith requirement.

To safeguard against false allegations that oral modifications have been made, it is permissible to include in the contract a provision that modifications are not effective unless they are set forth in a signed writing. (2-209(2)) However, if a consumer enters into such a contract, in addition to signing the contract, he must also sign the restrictive provision to assure that he is aware of the limitation—otherwise it is not effective. If not signed in this fashion, a consumer is entitled to rely upon oral modifications. The provision is apparently designed to protect the unwary consumer against reliance upon statements made to him that certain provisions of the contract do not apply to him or that others are subject to oral change. He is entitled to be forewarned not to rely upon anything but the printed word, and it is expected that the double signing will bring this message to his attention.

The Code allows necessary and desirable modifications of sales contracts without regard to the technicalities that hamper such adjustments under traditional contract law. The safeguards against improper and unfair use of this freedom are found in the requirements of good faith and the "observance of reasonable commercial standards of fair dealing in the trade." There is recognition of the fact that changes and adjustments in sales contracts are daily occurrences and that the parties do not cancel their old contract and execute an entirely new one each time a change or modification is required.

mutuality—
unilateral offers The requirement of mutuality of consideration presents particular problems in unilateral contracts. The promisor-offeror is at liberty to withdraw his offer at any time prior to the requested conduct by the offeree, but he loses his power to revoke after the offeree has performed or tendered performance of a part of what was requested. Thus, the offeror is in a sense bound, whereas the offeree can theoretically either continue performance to completion or

abandon the act of acceptance. The beginning of performance does not constitute an acceptance, but it does bar the offeror's power of revocation. The Code provides that the beginning of performance can be effective as a bar to revocation only if the offeree gives *notice* within a reasonable time that he accepts the offer. Should the offeror not receive such notice of acceptance within a reasonable time, he may treat the offer as having lapsed before acceptance. (2-206(2)) Of course, he also has the option to treat the offer as having been accepted if the offeree does complete performance in response to it.

output and requirements contracts With respect to a term in a contract that measures the quantity by the output of the seller or by the requirements of the buyer, the Code provides that this means such actual output or requirements as may occur in good faith. (2-306(1)) In addition, no quantity unreasonably disproportionate to any stated estimate, or in the absence of a stated estimate, to any normal or otherwise comparable prior output or requirement may be tendered or demanded. In other words, under the Code, quantity must bear a reasonable relationship to estimates given or to past outputs or requirements.

REVIEW QUESTIONS AND PROBLEMS

1. What is *consideration*? How can it be determined whether or not consideration is present?

2. What is an *accord and satisfaction*?

3. A constructed a building for B and presented a final bill in the amount of $500. B questioned the amount and sent a check for $200 marked "paid in full." A crossed out the words "paid in full" and cashed the check. Thereafter he sent a bill for $300. Is B required to pay? Why?

4. A pledged $1,000 to a charitable organization whose purpose was to help needy people. The charity borrowed money on the strength of this and other pledges. A died, and the charity presented the claim against his estate. Should the claim be allowed? Why?

5. A owned a mine in Alaska. He told B that if B would give him $50 so that he could go to Alaska, he would pay B $10,000 if the mine produced gold. The mine produced a half million dollars in gold. Is B entitled to $10,000? Why?

6. A paid 25 cents in return for an option to purchase real estate from B for $100,000. B sought to revoke the option. Can B revoke the option? Why?

7. A had a written contract to manage B's hotel for two years at $18,000 a year. At the end of three months A received a better offer, whereupon B in writing agreed to pay A an additional $5,000 if A remained the full two-year period. At the end of two years, is B liable for the $5,000 if A remained and did an excellent job during the period? Why?

8. X purchased a used automobile from Y on credit, the original debt being $1,000. X discovered that the car had a cracked valve and demanded that Y

correct it. When Y refused to do so, X sent Y a check for $750 marked "paid in full of account." Should Y cash the check? Why?

9. When A returned from vacation, he noticed that one of his employees, B, had done some work not required by the employment contract. A told B, "Since you did this extra job, I will pay you an additional $100 on your next payday." A later refused to pay the extra $100. May B recover the $100 from A? Explain.

10. A owed B $500, which was due on June 15. B called A and stated, "If you will pay me $400 by June 10, I will forget about the rest of the bill." A paid $400 before June 10. Does A's action release him from liability for the original debt? Why or why not?

11. A, a manufacturer of bolts, agreed to furnish B all the bolts that B needed in his business for one year. For several years prior to the agreement, B's needs had been between 2,500 and 3,000 bolts per month, and B continued to order within that range each month. However, after five months, B ordered 10,000 bolts, and A could not honor the request. Is A liable for breach of contract? Why?

9 VOIDABLE CONTRACTS

Introduction   The presence of offer, acceptance, and consideration indicates the existence of a contractual relationship. It does not mean that the contract is enforceable or that a party may not legally cause it to be canceled or disaffirmed. This chapter and those that follow will discuss the rights of a party to rescind or disaffirm a contract, and the circumstances under which a contract is unenforceable. This chapter is generally concerned with the various grounds available for the equitable remedy of rescission or cancellation of a contract previously entered into. Such contracts are known as *voidable contracts*. A party that avoids a contract will be returned to the position that he occupied before he entered into the contract. If he has paid money and received goods, he will be entitled to return the goods and obtain a return of the money paid. Some allied problems, such as suits for damages as an alternative remedy, are also discussed.

The usual grounds for exercising the right to rescind a contract are (1) lack of capacity to contract, (2) fraud, (3) misrepresentation, (4) mutual mistake, and (5) lack of free will. In addition, a major breach of the contract by one party justifies rescission by the other (see Chapter 13).

LACK OF CAPACITY

In General   *Lack of capacity* refers to the mental state of the party to a contract. Minors are presumed to lack the requisite capacity to contract and are thus allowed to disaffirm contracts. Contracts by insane persons are also voidable. The test of insanity for the purpose of avoiding a contract is different from the test of insanity for other

134

purposes, such as those involving the criminal law, making a will, or commitment to a mental institution. In the law of contracts, the test is whether the person has sufficient mental capacity to understand the nature of the transaction. Insanity may be of a temporary nature, such as that caused by intoxication or drug addiction.

If a contract is disaffirmed by an insane person, he must return the consideration received if no advantage has been taken of the insane person by the other. If the contract is unreasonable or unfair advantage has been taken, the party without mental capacity is entitled to rescind by returning so much of what he received as he has left.

Minors' Contracts —Generally

The age of majority and capacity to contract has been lowered to eighteen in most states. However, the statutory law of each state must be examined to determine the age of majority for contracts.

A person below the age of capacity is called an infant or a minor. Minors have the right to disaffirm or to avoid contracts. The law grants minors this right in order to promote justice and to protect them from their presumed immaturity, lack of judgment and experience, limited will power, and imprudence. An adult deals with a minor at his own peril. A contract between an infant and an adult is voidable only by the infant. The right to disaffirm exists irrespective of the fairness of favorability of the contract and whether or not the adult knew he was dealing with a minor. It even extends to contracts involving two minors.

Legislation in many states has in a limited way altered the right of minors to avoid their contracts. For example, many states provide that a purchase of life insurance or a contract with a college or university is binding. Some statutes take away the minor's right to avoid contracts after marriage, and a few give the courts the right to approve freedom of contract for emancipated minors.

Avoiding Contracts by Minors

A minor has the right to avoid or to disaffirm contracts. Until steps are taken to avoid the contract, the minor remains liable. A minor can disaffirm a purely executory contract by directly informing the adult of the disaffirmance or by any conduct that clearly indicates an intent to disaffirm. If the contract has been fully or partially performed, the infant also has the right to avoid it and obtain a return of his consideration. If the infant is in possession of consideration that is passed to him, he must return it to the other party. He cannot disaffirm the contract and at the same time retain the benefits.

The courts of the various states are somewhat in conflict when an infant cannot return the property he purchased in its original condition. The majority of the states hold that the infant may disaffirm the contract and demand the return of the consideration with which he has parted, even though he is unable to return that which he received. A few courts, however, hold that if the contract is advantageous to the infant and if the adult has been fair in every respect, the contract cannot be disaffirmed unless the infant returns the consideration received. These courts take into account the depreciation of the property while in the possession of the infant.

The minor may avoid both executed and executory contracts at any time during minority and for a reasonable period of time after majority. What constitutes a reasonable time depends on the nature of the property involved and the specific circumstances. Many states establish a maximum period, such as two years, by statute.

Ratification *Ratification* means to approve and sanction, to make valid, or to confirm. It applies to the approval of a voidable transaction by one who previously had the right to disaffirm. As applied to contracts entered into by infants, it refers to conduct by a former minor after majority that indicates approval of or satisfaction with a contract. It eliminates the right to disaffirm.

Generally an executed contract is ratified by retention of the consideration received for an unreasonable time after majority. Ratification also results from acceptance of the benefits incidental to ownership, such as rents, dividends, or interest. A sale of the property received or any other act that clearly indicates satisfaction with the bargain made during minority will constitute a ratification. In general a contract that is fully executory is disaffirmed by continued silence or inaction after reaching legal age. Ratification is not possible until the infant reaches legal age because action prior to that date could always be avoided.

Liability for Necessaries The law has recognized that certain transactions are clearly for the benefit of minors and hence are binding upon them. The term *necessaries* is used to describe the subject matter of such contracts. A minor is not liable in contract for necessaries; the liability is in quasi contract. The fact that the liability is quasi-contractual has two significant features: (1) the liability is not for the contract price of necessaries furnished, but rather for the reasonable value of the necessaries; and (2) there is no liability on executory contracts, but only for necessaries actually furnished.

What are *necessaries*? In general, the term includes whatever is needed for a minor's subsistence as measured by his age, station in life, and so forth. Food and lodging, medical services, education, and clothing are the general classifications of necessaries. It is often a close question as to whether a particular item or service is to be regarded as a necessary.

Case: D, an infant, went to P employment agency to seek aid in finding work. D agreed to pay a fee if a job were found for him. P obtained a job for D and presented a bill for $295. D refused to pay.

Issue: Is a contract with an employment agency a necessary?

Decision: No.

Reasons: 1. The services of a professional employment agency may not be considered "necessary," so that a minor may not disaffirm a contract for such services.

2. It makes no difference that D has profited by the efforts of P. P's services were advantageous to D, who clearly was in need of a job when they were rendered; however, it does not appear that they were necessary for him to earn a livelihood.

Gastonia Personnel Corp. v. Rogers, 168 S.E.2d 31 (N.C.) 1969.

Third-Party Rights If an infant sells goods to an adult, the latter obtains only a voidable title to the goods. The infant can disaffirm and recover possession from the adult buyer. At common law, even a good-faith purchaser of property formerly belonging to a minor could not retain the property if the minor elected to rescind. This rule has been changed under the Code. It provides that a person with voidable title has "power to transfer a good title to a good-faith purchaser for value." (2-403) The common-law rule, however, is still applicable to sales of real property by minors. For example, if a minor sells his farm to Y, who in turn sells it to Z, the minor may disaffirm against Z and obtain the farm back. This is not unfair, since the minor's name appeared in the chain of title.

FRAUD AND MISREPRESENTATION

Introduction A contract is voidable if it has been induced by a misrepresentation of a material fact by one party which is relied on by the party to his injury. The misrepresentation may be intentional, in which case the law considers the misrepresentation to be "fraudulent." It may be unintentional, in which case there has been no fraud but only innocent misrepresentation. In both cases, the victim of the misrepresentation may rescind the contract. In the case of fraudulent misrepresentation, the victim is given the choice of the additional remedy of a suit for dollar damages.

While the elements of actionable fraud are stated differently from state to state, the following are those generally required:

137

1. Scienter, or intention to mislead. This is knowledge of the falsity or statements made with such utter disregard and recklessness for the truth that knowledge is inferred.
2. A false representation or the concealment of a matter of fact, material to the transaction.
3. Justifiable reliance on the false statement or concealment.
4. Injury as a consequence of the reliance.

Innocent misrepresentation does not require proof of scienter but does require proof of all the other elements of fraud. The absence of scienter is the reason that a suit for dollar damages cannot be based on such a theory.

Rescission is permitted only in case the defrauded party acts with reasonable promptness after he learns of the falsity of the representation. Undue delay on his part effects a waiver of his rights to rescind, thus limiting the defrauded party to an action for recovery of damages. A victim of fraud loses his right to rescind if, after having acquired knowledge of the fraud, he indicates an intention to affirm the contract. These principles result from the fact that rescission is an equitable remedy.

Scienter   The requirement of <u>intent to mislead</u> is often referred to as *scienter.* This Latin word means "knowingly." Scienter is present in circumstances other than a false statement made with actual intent to deceive. For example, scienter may be found when there has been a concealment of a material fact. Moreover, a statement that is partially or even literally true may be fraudulent in law if it was made in order to create a substantially false impression. Intention to mislead may also be established by showing that a statement was made with such reckless disregard as to whether it is true or false that intention to mislead may be inferred. For example, an accountant who certifies that financial statements accurately reflect the financial condition of a company may be guilty of fraud if he has no basis for the statement. While perhaps he does not actually intend to mislead, his statement is so reckless that the intention is inferred from the lack of actual knowledge.

False Representation   To establish fraud, there must be an actual or implied misrepresentation of a fact. False statements of opinion as opposed to fact do not generally constitute fraud. The misstatement of fact must be material or significant to the extent that it has a moving influence upon a contracting party, but it need not be the sole inducing cause for entering into the contract.

False statements as to matters of opinion, such as a representation as to the value of property, are not factual and are usually not considered actionable. However, an intentional misstatement even with regard to value may be fraudulent if the person making the statement is under some special obligation to be truthful, candid, and honest with the other party. This concept is sometimes used when the person who is allegedly fraudulent is an expert such as a physician or when the parties stand in a fiduciary relationship to each other. For example, assume that a doctor, after examining a patient for an insurance company physical, states that he is of the opinion that the person has no physical disability. If his actual opinion is that the patient has cancer, the doctor is guilty of fraud. He has misstated a fact—his professional opinion. The same is true if a partner sells property to the firm of which he is a member. A false statement of opinion by the selling partner as to the value of the property will supply the misstatement-of-fact element. Each partner is a fiduciary toward his fellow partners and the firm and must give honest opinions.

The misstatement may be oral and may in fact be true in part. A half-truth, or partial truth, that has the net effect of misleading may form the basis of fraud just as if it were entirely false. A partial truth in response to a request for information becomes an untruth whenever it creates a false impression and is designed to do so.

An intentional misrepresentation of existing local or state law affords no basis for rescission. A statement about local law is not a statement of fact in the technical sense. In addition, local law is deemed a matter of common knowledge. A misstatement as to the law of another state or nation, however, is one of fact and may be used as a basis for redress.

A misrepresentation may be made by conduct as well as by language. Any physical act that has for its ultimate object the concealment of the vital facts relating to the property involved in the contract is, in effect, a misstatement. One who turns back the odometer on a car, fills a motor with heavy grease to keep it from knocking, or paints over an apparent defect—in each case concealing an important fact—asserts an untruth as effectively as if he were speaking. Such conduct, if it misleads the other party, amounts to fraud and makes rescission or an action for damages possible.

Case: P sued D to recover actual and punitive damages for fraud in the sale of a used car. The mileage on the odometer at the time of sale was 34,676 miles. The previous owner testified that the car had 74,624 miles when it was traded in.

Issue: Is D's conduct fraudulent and is P entitled to punitive damages?

Decision: Yes, Yes.

Reasons: 1. A representation is not confined to words or positive assertions; it may consist as well of deeds, acts, or artifices of a nature calculated to mislead another and thereby to allow the fraud-feasor to obtain an undue advantage over him.

2. The term "fraud" embraces all multifarious means resorted to by one individual to get advantage over another by false suggestions or suppression of truth, including all surprise, trick, cunning, disassembling, mechanical alterations, and any unfair way by which another is cheated.

3. P is entitled to $200 actual damages and $7,000 punitive damages.

Cates v. Darland, 537 P.2d 336 (Okl.) 1975.

Silence as Fraud Historically, the law of contracts has followed caveat emptor, especially in real estate transactions. The parties to a contract are required to exercise ordinary business sense in their dealings. As a result, the general rule is that silence in the absence of a duty to speak does not constitute fraud.

The law has developed at least three situations in which there is a duty to speak the truth, and failure to do so will constitute actionable fraud. First of all, there is a duty to speak when the parties stand in a fiduciary relationship. A fiduciary relationship is one of trust and confidence, such as exists between partners in a partnership or between a director and a corporation or between an agent and a principal. Because such parties do not deal "at arm's length," there is the duty to speak and to make a full disclosure of all facts.

The second exception is based on justice, equity, and fair dealing. This exception occurs when a vital fact is known by one party and not the other and it is such that if known, there would have been no contract. While this concept is difficult to define or describe, it is not difficult to apply on a case-by-case basis, especially when the suit is in equity for rescission. For example, when there is a latent defect in property—one that is not apparent upon inspection—the vendor has a duty to inform the purchaser of the defect. Failure to do so is fraudulent.

Case: P purchased a residential lot from D. Subsequently it was learned that the lot had been "filled" and was not suitable for construction of a residence. This was not mentioned during the negotiations, nor was any inquiry made by P.

Issue: Does D's failure to inform P of the "fill" constitute a fraud?

Decision: Yes.

Reasons: 1. A party entering into a bargain is not bound to tell everything he knows to the other party, even if he is aware that the other is ignorant of the facts. But if a fact known by one party and not the other is so vital that if the mistake were mutual the contract would be voidable and the party knowing the fact also knows that the other does not know it, nondisclosure is not privileged and is fraudulent.

2. Under the circumstances, justice, equity, and fair dealing demand that D inform P of the condition, regardless of the latter's failure to ask any questions.

3. While fraud is not lightly to be inferred, it does not follow that the inference of fraud cannot be gathered from surrounding circumstances, provided they are of sufficient strength and cogency to overcome the presumption of honesty and fair dealing . . . .We conceive the essential "elements" in proof of constructive fraud by nondisclosure of the existence of a land fill to be: (1) a vendor, knowing that the land has been filled, fails to disclose that fact to a purchaser of the property, and (2) the purchaser is unaware of the existence of the fill because either he has had no opportunity to inspect the property, or the existence of the fill was not apparent or readily ascertainable, and (3) the value of the property is materially affected by the existence of the fill.

Sorrell v. Young, 91 P.2d 1312 (Wash.App.) 1971.

The third exception is that a person who has misstated an important fact on some previous occasion is obligated to correct the statement when negotiations are renewed or as soon as he learns about his misstatement. This exception is really not a true exception to the silence rule because there is in fact a positive misstatement.

The gist of these exceptions is that one of the parties has the erroneous impression that certain things are true, whereas the other party is aware that they are not true and also knows of the misunderstanding. It therefore becomes his duty to disclose the truth. And unless he does so, most courts would hold that fraud exists. This does not mean that a potential seller or buyer has to disclose all the factors about the value of property he is selling or buying. It is only when he knows that the other party to the agreement is harboring a misunderstanding on some vital matter that the duty to speak arises.

Justifiable Reliance   Before a false statement of fact can be considered fraudulent, the party to whom it has been made must reasonably believe it to be true and must act thereon to his damage. If he investigates and the falsity is revealed, no action can be brought for fraud. The cases are in conflict as to the need to investigate. Some courts have indicated

141

that if all the information is readily available for ascertaining the truth of the statements, blind reliance upon the misrepresentation is not justified. In such a case the party is said to be negligent in not taking advantage of the facilities available for confirming the statement.

Case: P bought a newspaper and printing business from D. Thereafter P sought to rescind the contract on the grounds that D had misrepresented the financial condition of the business. P was in possession of certain financial documents that were inconsistent on their face as to the financial affairs of the business.

Issue: Was P entitled to rely upon D's statements as to the financial condition of the business?

Decision: No.

Reason: P could tell from the inconsistencies in the documents that something was wrong. He should therefore have investigated, and in the absence of such investigation he was not entitled to rely on the accuracy of the statements.

Jahraus v. Bergquist, 494 P.2d 110 (Colo.) 1972.

If a party inspects property or has an opportunity to do so, he is not misled if a reasonable investigation would have revealed that the property was not as it had been represented to be. On the other hand, some courts deny that there is any need to investigate and say that one who has misrepresented facts cannot avoid the legal consequences by saying in effect "You should not have believed me—you should have checked as to whether or not what I told you was true." Courts generally agree that reliance is justified when substantial effort or expense is required to determine the actual facts. The standard of justified reliance is not whether a reasonably prudent man would be justified in relying but whether the particular individual involved had a right to so rely, In any case, the issue as to whether or not the reliance is justified is for the jury.

Injury or Damage   In order to prevail, the party relying upon the misstatement must offer proof of resulting damage. Normally, such damage is proved by evidence indicating that the property that is the subject of the contract would have been more valuable provided the statements had been true. Injury results when the party is not in as good a position as he would have been had the statements been true.

In an action for damages for fraud, the plaintiff may seek to recover damages on either of two theories. He may use the "benefit of the bargain" theory and seek the difference between the actual market value of what he received and the value if he had received what was represented. A plaintiff may also use the "out-of-pocket" theory and collect the difference between the actual value of what was received and its purchase price.

Perhaps the most significant aspect of a suit for dollar damages is that the victim of fraud is entitled to punitive damages in addition to compensatory damages. If the fraudulent representations are made maliciously, willfully, or wantonly, or so recklessly as to imply a disregard of social obligations, punitive damages as determined by a jury may be awarded. For example, refer to the previous case of *Cates v. Darland*, pp. 139-40.

MISTAKE

In General   A *mistake* is a state of mind that is not in accord with the facts.

There are a variety of possible mistakes in the law of contracts. They may occur at various stages of a transaction. For example, they may involve errors in arithmetic, or in setting forth the terms of the contract. The mistake may be *bilateral*—both parties are mistaken; or it may be *unilateral*—only one party is laboring under a mistake.

In order that a mistake by one or both of the parties may warrant relief to either of them, the mistake must be a material one. The relief afforded by virtue of the mistake will depend upon a number of factors, including the point of time at which the mistake is discovered; the extent to which performance has already progressed; the extent to which one or the other of the parties has changed his position in reliance on the contract before the mistake was discovered; and the extent to which the parties can be restored to the status quo.

The basic remedy for mistake is rescission. The general rule is that one who has made a mistake and wishes to rescind can do so only if he can substantially return the other party to the status quo. No relief will be afforded if the other party has changed his position in reliance on the contract to the extent that he cannot be restored to his former position.

Bilateral Mistake   The word *bilateral* as used in this context means two-sided, or mutual, mistakes as contrasted with one-sided, or unilateral, mistakes. Both parties to the contract have made a factual assumption that is false.

A bilateral mistake may exist when parties enter into a contract on a mistaken assumption regarding a material fact. The fact concerning which the mistake was made must control the conduct of the party seeking rescission. It must appear that but for the mistake, the agreement would not have been made.

Case: P entered into a contract to sell land to D. Both parties thought the property was zoned for business, and D's sole interest in the property was for use for a retail store. In fact, the property was not so zoned. P seeks to enforce the contract and to require D to purchase the property.

Issue: Does the mutual mistake with regard to zoning justify a rescission of the contract?

Decision: Yes.

Reason: Whether the area was zoned for business was a matter of fact and an important element of the contract. Because both parties were mistaken the contract may be rescinded.

MacKay v. McIntosh, 153 S.E.2d 800 (N.C.) 1967.

This mutual assumption, called *mutual mistake of fact*, arises in two situations. In one the minds of the parties fail to meet, and no contract results. In the other the mistake merely makes the agreement more burdensome for one of the parties and therefore renders it voidable at his option.

Typical of the first type are those cases in which, unknown to either party, the subject matter of the contract has been destroyed prior to the date of the agreement. No contract results because there was no meeting of the minds. There are also cases in which the language used in the contract is clearly subject to two interpretations, and each party construes it differently. For example, assume that there is a sale of floor covering for certain rooms at a lump-sum figure on the assumption by both parties that only a certain number of square feet are involved. If the area is substantially greater than both parties thought to be true, the contract is voidable at instance of the seller.

In the transaction of business, it is customary in many situations to dispose of property about which the contracting parties willingly admit that all the facts are not known. In such instances the property is sold without regard to its quality or characteristics. Such agreements may not be rescinded if it later appears that the property has characteristics that neither of the parties had reason to suspect or if it otherwise differs from their expectations. Under such conditions the property forms the subject matter of the agreement regardless of its nature. For example, A sells B a farm, and shortly thereafter a valuable deposit of ore is discovered on it. The agreement could not be rescinded by the seller on the grounds of mutual mistake.

Unilateral Mistake A contract entered into because of some mistake or error on the part of only one of the contracting parties usually affords no basis for relief to such party. The majority of such mistakes result from carelessness or lack of diligence on the part of the mistaken party and should not, therefore, affect the rights of the other party.

This rule is subject to one well-recognized exception. When a mistake has been made in the calculation or transmission of the figures that form the basis of a contract, and prior to acceptance such mistake is clearly apparent to the offeree who thereupon accepts the mistaken offer, the contract may be avoided by the offeror. Hence a contractor who arrives at or transmits his estimates for a bid on construction work using the wrong figure may be relieved of his contract if the error was so great as to be obvious and therefore apparent to the offeree before the latter's acceptance. Courts usually refuse to allow one party to knowingly take advantage of another's mistake.

Reformation of Written Contracts In most instances a written contract is preceded by negotiations between the parties who agree orally upon the clauses or terms to be set forth in the final written contract. This is certainly the case when the parties contemplate a written statement signed by both as necessary to a binding agreement, that is, the oral agreement was not itself to have binding effect. Of course the parties could intend otherwise. They could regard the oral agreement as binding without any writing, or they could regard the writing as simply a subsequent memorial of their oral agreement.

What is the situation if the written agreement that is finally entered into by the parties contains a mistake—does not conform to what the parties had agreed to orally? Frequently the draftsman or typist may have made an error that was not discovered prior to the signing of the contract, and the party benefiting from the error seeks to hold the other party to the agreement as written. Courts of equity provide a remedy known as *reformation* for such situations.

Case: P entered into a contract to sell real property to D. By mistake, a forty-acre parcel not intended to be a part of the transaction was included in the legal description of the land in the written contract. P sought to have the documents reformed in order to remove the forty-acre tract.

Issue: Is P entitled to reformation?

Decision: Yes.

Reason: Courts will reform contracts and deeds in accordance with the true intention of the parties when their intentions have been frustrated by mutual mistake in reducing the agreement to writing.

Seyden v. Trade, 494 P.2d 1281 (Nev.) 1972.

Reformation is only available where there is clear and positive proof of the drafting error. Courts frequently justify this remedy on the basis that the contract is not being changed—that the written evidence is only being corrected. This problem can be prevented by a careful reading of contracts before they are signed.

Duress and Undue Influence   Equity allows a party to rescind an agreement that was not entered into voluntarily. The lack of free will may take the form of duress or undue influence. A person who has obtained property under such circumstances should not in good conscience be allowed to keep it. A person may lose his free will because of duress—some threat to his person, his family, or property—or it may result from a more subtle pressure whereby one person overpowers the will of another by use of moral or social force as contrasted with physical or economic force. Cases of undue influence frequently arise in situations involving the elderly. In those cases in which the free will is lacking, some courts hold that the minds of the parties did not meet. If a person has free choice, there is no duress even though some pressure may have been exerted upon him. A threat of a lawsuit is not duress which will allow rescission. Under certain circumstances economic pressure may constitute duress.

Case: P corporation was awarded a $6 million contract by the Navy for the production of radar sets. It was a very severe contract that imposed substantial penalties for late deliveries and gave the Navy the right to cancel in case of default by P corporation. P corporation entered into a contract with D corporation whereby the latter agreed to furnish many of the components. After making some deliveries, D corporation refused to deliver any more unless the price was increased. Being unable to get the components elsewhere, P corporation acceded to the demand. Later P sued to have the increased price set aside.

Issue: Did the facts warrant a finding of duress—was the contract voidable?

Decision: Yes.

Reasons: 1. A contract is voidable for duress when it is established that the party making the claim was forced to agree to it by means of a wrongful threat precluding the exercise of free will.

2. The existence of economic duress or business compulsion is demonstrated by proof that immediate possession of needful goods is threatened. It should be noted that a mere threat by one party to breach the contract by not delivering the required items, though wrongful, does not in itself constitute economic duress.

3. It must appear (1) that the threatened party could not obtain the goods from another source of supply; and (2) that the ordinary remedy of an action for breach of contract would not be adequate.

Austin Instrument, Inc. v. Loral Corporation, 272 N.E.2d 533 (N.Y.) 1971.

REVIEW QUESTIONS AND PROBLEMS

1. Why does the law allow minors the right to disaffirm contracts?

2. M, a minor, purchased a motorcycle from the XYZ company for $500 cash. A few days later, the cycle was stolen, and there was no insurance to cover M's loss. M sued XYZ for return of the $500. With what issues of law and fact will the court be faced? Explain.

3. M, a minor, sold a bicycle to B, an adult, who later sold it to C, another adult. May M rescind and recover possession from C? Why?

4. A, a minor, was married and had one child. He entered into an installment contract to buy furniture from B. After making several payments he defaulted, and the furniture was repossessed. A seeks to recover the payments he had made. Should he succeed? Why?

5. While still a minor, M agreed to purchase on an installment plan a set of books from the XYZ company. XYZ shipped the books to M. Three months after M reached the age of majority, M sought to rescind the contract. What result? Discuss.

6. While A was considering whether to purchase B's house, A never asked nor did B ever volunteer any information about the condition of the plumbing. Shortly after A purchased the house, A learned that the underground plumbing system required extensive repairs. A demanded that B pay for the costs, but B refused. What will A have to prove in an action of fraud? Explain fully.

7. A entered into a contract to purchase a motel from B. During the negotiations, B told A that the motel took in a gross of $2,500 every month, and he offered his books for A's inspection. Actually the gross was much less than this; the books reflected this fact. A now seeks to rescind the contract on the basis of the misrepresentation. Should he succeed? Why?

8. Under what circumstances will a written contract be reformed?

9. A was in need of ten tons of steel. He telephoned B and by mistake ordered fifty tons. Later he sought to avoid the contract because of the mistake. Should he succeed? Why?

147

10. A, a contractor, submitted a bid of $50,000 on a project to the XYZ school board. After the opening of the bids, XYZ notified A of acceptance, since A's bid was the lowest. The other bids ranged from $75,000 to $100,000. Soon thereafter, A discovered an error in calculation, and that his bid should have been $80,000. XYZ demanded that A complete the job as originally promised. What would be A's defense in a suit for breach of contract by XYZ? Explain.

11. A, a builder, had a contract with the XYZ company in which XYZ promised to supply A with steel rod for $0.25 per pound. During the period of the contract, XYZ notified A, "Unless you agree to pay $0.35 per pound immediately, we can no longer sell you any steel." Although the particular type of steel was readily available from other suppliers, A agreed to pay the increased price to XYZ. Could A rescind the agreement to pay the additional amount on the basis of duress? Why?

10 ILLEGALITY

Introduction   An additional requirement for a valid contract is that it have a lawful purpose or object. Contracts that do not have a lawful object are illegal and therefore *unenforceable*. As a general rule, the status of an illegal contract is that a court will not entertain a lawsuit involving it. This means that if the illegal contract is executory, neither party may enforce performance by the other. If the contract is executed, the court will not allow recovery of what was given in performance. An illegal contract cannot be ratified by either party, and the parties can do nothing to make it enforceable. Stated simply, in an illegal contract situation the court literally "leaves the parties where it finds them."

A party to an illegal contract cannot recover damages for breach of such contract. If one party has performed, he cannot, generally, recover either the value of his performance or any property or goods transferred to the other. As a result of the rule, one wrongdoer may be enriched at the expense of the other wrongdoer, but the courts will not intercede to rectify this because the purpose is to deter illegal bargains.

There are three basic exceptions to the rule that a person who is a party to an illegal contract will not be granted any relief. First, if a person is within the category of those for whose protection the contract was made illegal, he may obtain back what he has paid or may even be able to enforce the illegal agreement. For example, both federal and state statutes require that a corporation follow certain procedures before securities (stocks and bonds) may be offered for sale to the public. It is illegal to sell such securities without having complied with the legal requirements. One who purchases securities from a corporation that has failed to follow the necessary procedures is allowed to obtain a refund of the purchase price if he desires to do so. The act of one party (the seller) is more illegal than that of the other party (the

149

buyer). Many statutes are designed to protect one party in an illegal transaction, and when this is the case, the protected party is allowed a legal remedy.

A second exception applies when a person is induced by fraud or duress to enter into an illegal agreement. In such cases, the courts do not regard the defrauded or coerced party as being an actual participant in the wrong, and they will, therefore, allow restitution of what he has rendered by way of performance. It has been suggested that the same result would obtain if the party were induced by strong economic pressure to enter into an illegal agreement.

Third, there is a doctrine called *locus poenitentiae* which may provide the remedy of restitution to one who has become a party to an illegal contract. Literally, the phrase means "a place for repentance"; by extension, "an opportunity for changing one's mind." As applied to an illegal contract, it means that within very strict limits, a person who repents before actually having performed any illegal part of the contract may rescind it and obtain restitution of his part performance.

Case: P, the losing party in a wager, sued D, the winner, to recover his bet. P had attempted to cancel the bet before the happening of the event on which the wager was to be decided. A state law allowed suits to recover bets if filed within three months. P's suit was filed nine months after the event.

Issue: Is P entitled to a return of his wager?

Decision: Yes.

Reasons: 1. One may sue at common law and recover his stake in a bet, provided he repudiates the bet before the happening of the event on which the wager was to be decided and gives timely and proper notice thereof to and makes demand on the other gamester or stakeholder.

2. However, once the bet has been determined, the law will not aid a gamester in recovering his money without resorting to the procedures provided by statute.

3. If the bet had not been canceled before the event, the statute of limitations would have prevented recovery, but here the suit was based on the common-law right to cancel a bet and obtain a return of the stake.

Cox v. Lee, 530 S.W.2d 273 (Mo.) 1975.

Contracts Against Public Policy— Generally

A contract or a provision of a contract may be declared to be illegal if it is specifically prohibited by statute, contravenes the rule of the common law, or is contrary to public policy. It is axiomatic that a contract that violates a statute or an ordinance is illegal and void. A contract provision is contrary to public policy if it is injurious to the interests of the public, contravenes some established interest of society, violates the policy or purpose of some statute, or tends to interfere with the public health, safety, morals, or general welfare. While all agreements are subject to the paramount power of the sovereign and to the judicial power to declare contracts illegal, contracts are not to be lightly set aside on the grounds of public policy. Doubts will usually be resolved in favor of legality.

The term *public policy* is vague and variable and changes as our social, economic, and political climates change. As society becomes more complex, courts turn more and more to statutory enactments in search of current public policy. A court's own concept of right and wrong as well as its total philosophy will frequently come into play in answering complex questions of public policy.

Case: D, an attorney, had arranged for P to give expert testimony in a lawsuit. The lawsuit involved the condemnation of property belonging to D's client. It was D's purpose to have the jury value the property as high as possible. D agreed to pay a certain fee to P if the jury verdict placed a value of $200,000 or below and a higher fee if the value were determined to be in excess of $200,000. D did not call upon P to testify and refused to pay the fee when the case was settled.

Issue: Is a contract to pay an expert witness a fee that is based on the outcome of the trial legal?

Decision: No.

Reason: It would be against public policy to enforce such a contract. There is a possibility that such a contract would bias the witness in his testimony.

Laos v. Soble, 503 P.2d 978 (Ariz.) 1972.

There is an endless variety of other contracts that may be against public policy. Examples are wagering agreements; contracts to affect the administration of justice, such as to conceal evidence or suppress a criminal investigation; and contracts to influence legislative or executive action or to interfere with or injure public service. Such contracts are frequently declared illegal by statute and others are held to be illegal as being contrary to public policy. Of course, lobbying is legal as long as it does not amount to bribery or undue influence.

Violations of License Requirements   A contract that calls for the performance of an act or the rendering of a service may be illegal for one of two reasons. The act or service itself may be illegal, and thus any contract involving this act or service is illegal. For example, prostitution is an illegal activity in most states, and contracts to engage in prostitution are illegal per se in such states. Other personal service contracts are not illegal per se but may be illegal if the party performing or contracting to perform the service is not legally entitled to do so. This refers to the fact that a license is required before a person is entitled to perform certain functions for others. For example, doctors, dentists, pharmacist, architects, lawyers, surveyors, real estate brokers, and others rendering specialized professional services must be licensed by the appropriate body before entering into contracts with the general public.

As a general rule, if the service that is rendered requires a license, the party receiving the benefit of the service can successfully refuse to pay for the service on the ground the contract is illegal because the plaintiff has no license. This is true even if the person is licensed in another jurisdiction but not the one in which the services were rendered. For example, a real estate broker licensed in one state cannot perform services in another state, and if he does so, he cannot collect for the services.

Case: D was in charge of a project involving an addition to a hospital in Vermont. D engaged the services of a Massachusetts architectural firm specializing in hospital design. P performed services as an architect and when the construction was completed presented a bill for his architectural fee. D refused to pay. P was licensed as an architect in Massachusetts but not in Vermont.

Issue: Can P recover for architectural services performed in connection with the project in Vermont?

Decision: No.

Reasons: 1. Architectural contracts entered into by persons without proper license are illegal and unenforceable.

2. The underlying policy is one of protecting the citizens of the state from untrained, unqualified, and unauthorized practitioners. It has been applied to many professions and special occupations for similar protective purposes.

Markus and Nocka v. Julian Goodrich Architects, Inc., 250 A.2d 739 (Vt.) 1969.

The practice of law by unauthorized persons is a significant problem. A person who practices law without a license is not only denied the right to a fee but also subject to criminal prosecution in many states, and such activity may also be enjoined. Since the practice of law primarily entails the giving of advice, difficult questions are presented when advice is given by business specialists such as certified public accountants, insurance brokers, bankers, and real estate brokers. Although the line between permissible and impermissible activities of these business specialists is often difficult to draw, it is clear that some of the activities and services that may be performed by the various business specialists do constitute the unauthorized practice of law. For example, the handling of a complicated tax case by an accountant has been held to constitute unauthorized practice of law, and the preparation of a real estate contract of sale by a real estate broker is illegal in most states. Business specialists should be aware that the giving of legal advice and the preparing of legal documents by one not licensed to practice law is illegal. A major danger in doing so is the loss of the right to compensation.

ILLEGALITY BASED ON UNEQUAL BARGAINING POWER

Introduction Many contracts are entered into between parties with unequal bargaining power. In the early law this factor was generally immaterial. The doctrine of caveat emptor was applied, and contracts were enforced according to their terms in the absence of a ground for rescission such as fraud.

Today the basic philosophy of the law has changed substantially. Courts frequently step in on the side of a party with limited bargaining power and declare provisions to be illegal that would not be agreed to if the bargaining power were equal. Many statutes require such a result also. This is especially true when one of the parties is a consumer or a debtor. Today, when the subject matter of a contract involves items of everyday necessity, courts frequently hold that the party with the superior bargaining power is restricted in what contractual provisions it can enforce. The sections that follow illustrate this trend of the law.

Contracts
Disclaiming
Liability A party to a contract frequently includes a clause that provides that the party has no tort liability even if at fault. Such a clause is commonly called an *exculpatory clause*. These disclaimers of liability are not favored by the law and are strictly construed against the party relying on them. They are frequently declared to be illegal by courts as contrary to public policy. Some states have by statute declared these clauses in certain types of contracts such as leases to be illegal and void.

The reasoning behind these statutes and judicial decisions is clear. Absolute freedom of contract exists in a barter situation because of the equal bargaining position of the parties. At the other extreme are the contracts with public utilities, in which there is no equality of bargaining power between the parties because of the existence of a virtual monopoly. The law therefore denies freedom of contract in the monopoly situation. The difficulty is that many contracts involve parties and circumstances that fall between these extremes. Many contracts are entered into between parties with substantially unequal bargaining power. When the subject matter of the contracts involves items of everyday necessity, courts frequently hold that one of the parties is a quasi-public institution and that such institutions are not entitled to complete freedom of contract because freedom of contract is not in the public interest. Thus contracts or parts of the contracts of such institutions may be held illegal whenever the quasi-public institution has taken advantage of its superior bargaining power and drawn a contract, or included a provision in a contract, which in the eyes of the court excessively favors the quasi-public institution to the detriment of the other party and the public. This is especially true when the contract provision is an exculpatory clause.

Case: P rented a trailer and hitch from D rental company in order to haul some household belongings. D attached the trailer and hitch to P's car and advised him that the trailer was ready for travel. While P was driving the car the trailer hitch broke, and as a result P's car and the trailer overturned. It was established that the safety chain on the trailer hitch had not been properly installed. When P sued D, D relied upon a term in the rental contract that said that D had absolutely no responsibility or obligation in the event of an accident.

Issue: Will the disclaimer of liability in the rental contract be enforced?

Decision: No.

Reasons: 1. Contracts for exemption for liability from negligence are not favored by the law. They are strictly construed against the party relying on them.

2. An agreement is against public policy if it is injurious to the interest of the public, contravenes some established interest of society, violates some public statute, or tends to interfere with the public welfare or safety.

3. This provision is contrary to public policy.

Hunter v. American Rentals, Inc., 371 P.2d 131 (Kan.) 1962.

Tickets Disclaiming Liability Tickets purchased for entrance into places of amusement, as evidence of a contract for transportation, or for a service such as repair or parking a car often contain provisions that attempt to limit or to define the rights of the holder of the ticket. It is generally held that the printed matter on the ticket is a part of an offer that is accepted by the holder of the ticket if he is aware of the printed matter even though he does not read it. There are some cases in which the purchaser is presumed to know about the printed matter even though his attention is not called to it at the time the ticket is delivered.

If a ticket is received merely as evidence of ownership and is to be presented later as a means of identification, the provisions on the ticket are not a part of the contract unless the recipient is aware of them or his attention is specifically directed to them at the time the ticket is accepted. Tickets given at checkrooms or repair shops are usually received as a means of identifying the article to be returned rather than as setting forth the terms of a contract. Thus the fine print on such tickets is usually not a part of the offer and acceptance unless communicated.

However, many terms on tickets may be illegal and will not be enforced in any event. The terms are illegal when public policy, as previously noted, would declare such a provision in a formal contract to be illegal. The equality of the bargaining power of the parties and the nature of the product or service are major factors to be considered in determing legality.

It is also noted that printed material often found on the back of contract forms, and occasionally on letterheads, is not generally considered part of any contract set forth on such a form or letterhead unless specific reference is made to it in the body of the contract. The law does not favor secret contract provisions.

Contracts of Adhesion The term *contract of adhesion* was developed in the French civil law. It has been widely used in international law, and in recent years the term has become important in our law of contracts. An adhesion contract is a standardized contract entirely prepared by one party. As a result of the disparity or inequality of bargaining power between the draftsman and the second party, the terms are submitted on a take-it-or-leave-it basis. The standardized provisions are such that they are merely "adhered to," with little choice as a practical matter on the part of the "adherer." If the terms are viewed as unsatisfactory, the party cannot obtain the desired product or service. The opportunity for bargaining and changing terms is usually nonexistent.

Contracts of adhesion are strictly construed against the party drafting them. Such contracts are given special scrutiny by courts to ensure that their terms are not unconscionable. Courts frequently refuse to enforce many of the more onerous or burdensome clauses in contracts of adhesion. They typically find that such clauses are unconscionable. Employment contracts, insurance policies, and leases are frequently held to be contracts of adhesion.

Unconscionable Bargains   As a general proposition, a court of equity will not specifically enforce a contract if its provisions are so harsh, severe, and unfair that the other party would be unduly oppressed. Such contracts are referred to as *unconscionable bargains*. An unconscionable bargain or contract is one that no man in his senses, not under delusion, would make on the one hand, and which no fair and honest man would accept on the other.

Case: P, an oil company, sued D, one of its dealers, to recover possession of a leased service station. The lease and the dealer agreement gave P the power to cancel on ten days' written notice if P believed that D was indulging in practices that tended to impair the quality, good name, goodwill, or reputation of P's product. The same agreements gave D, the dealer, the right to terminate only by notice not less than sixty days prior to the expiration of any yearly period. Failure to give the notice resulted in automatic renewal of the lease.

Issue: Are the contract terms on termination unconscionable?

Decision: Yes.

Reasons: 1. Termination provisions of an agreement involving the sale of goods which, if applied strictly, are so one-sided as to lead to absurd results, will be declared unconscionable.

2. There is imposed on both parties an obligation of good faith and the observance of reasonable commercial standards of fair dealing in the trade.

3. The parties need not be in business forever and the trial court must decide what kind of notice is required under all the circumstances between the parties.

Ashland Oil, Inc. v. Donahue, 223 S.E.2d 433 (W.Va.) 1976.

AGREEMENTS IN RESTRAINT OF TRADE

Introduction   Several federal laws declare that agreements in restraint of trade are illegal. These laws are discussed in Chapter 42 with other aspects of government regulation of business. In the meantime, it should be recognized that price-fixing and other agreements that tend to eliminate competition are generally illegal. For example, an agreement among lawyers that they would not represent each other's clients for five years is illegal. However, some agreements, such as those between a franchiser and its franchisees, are usually found to be legal. They are legal because their effect on competition is minimal compared with the interests of the franchiser in having similarity in all of its franchised operations. Thus, certain exclusive dealing contracts are legal.

Another form of agreement that may be legal even though it is in partial restraint of trade is an agreement not to compete. An agreement by one person not to compete with another is frequently contained in a contract for the sale of a going business. The seller by such a provision agrees not to compete with the buyer. Agreements not to compete are also commonly found in contracts creating a business or a professional practice. Each partner or shareholder in the closely held corporation agrees not to compete with the firm or practice should he leave the business or professional activity. In addition, as a part of their employment contract, many employees agree that they will not compete with their employer upon termination of their employment.

Agreements Not To Complete— General Principles

Agreements not to compete must be a part of another contract. A bare agreement by one party not to compete with another is against public policy. For example, if A threatens to open a business to compete with B and B offers A one thousand dollars to agree that he will not do so, such a contract would be illegal.

However, an agreement that is reasonably necessary for the protection of a purchaser, the remaining members of a business, or an employer will be enforced provided the agreement (1) is reasonable in point of time, (2) is reasonable in the area of restraint, (3) is necessary to protect goodwill, (4) does not place an undue burden on the covenator, and (5) does not violate the public interest. Each agreement is examined by the court to see if it is reasonable to both parties and to the general public. Such factors as uniqueness of product, patents, trade secrets, type of service, employee's contact with customer, and other goodwill factors are significant on the reasonableness issue. In the employment situation, whether or not the employee will become a burden on society, and whether or not the public is being deprived of his skill and so forth, are factors.

The law will look with more favor on these contracts if they involve the sale of a business interest than it will in the case of such a provision included in an employment contract. In fact an agreement not to compete may even be presumed in the case of a sale of business and its goodwill, and the seller must not thereafter directly or by circular solicit business from his old customers, although he may advertise generally. The reason courts are more likely to hold the agreements between a buyer and seller or partners valid as contrasted with employer-employee contracts is that in the former situations there is more equality of bargaining power than in the latter. A seller or a former partner could readily refuse to sign an agreement not to compete, whereas an employee seeking a job might feel obliged to sign almost anything in order to gain employment. An employment contract may actually be a contract of adhesion. In addition, it is evident that there is a goodwill factor involved in the sale of almost any going business and that goodwill as an asset deserves protection, whereas in employee-employer situations it is less evident that the employee is able to create goodwill or take it with him upon termination of his employment.

A few states have by statute or by their constitutions declared agreements to restrict an employee's right to seek other employment to be illegal as a matter of public policy. In most states, if the restrictive covenant is unreasonable, it is illegal and the court leaves the parties where it finds them. In other words, the party who agreed not to compete is allowed to do so. However, if the restriction exceeds what is reasonably necessary, a few courts will reform the contract so as to make the restrictions reasonable.

Case: P corporation was a corporation engaged in franchising individuals and other concerns to operate a business of preparing income tax returns under the corporate name. The corporation entered into a contract with D that provided that if D should terminate the agreement, D would not enter into competition directly or indirectly for five years. After seven years D gave notice to terminate, and he set up his own office. P corporation brought suit and asked the court to order D to refrain from competing.

Issue: Will D be ordered to refrain from competing?

Decision: No.

Reasons: 1. The agreement does not specify any geographical area within which D is not to compete. Accordingly, the agreement was unreasonable as to territorial extent and is not enforceable.

2. Courts are generally less prone to enforce restrictive covenants between an employer and employee than when the restriction is part of the sale of a business.

H & R Block, Inc. v. Lovelace, 493 P.2d 205 (Kan.) 1972.

Restrictive Covenants in Real Estate Transactions A situation comparable to that of the employee's agreement not to compete is that of a restrictive provision in a contract for the sale or lease of real property. The owner of land may wish to prevent the use of this land for any purpose that would be competitive with his own business. Suppose that A owns an entire block, one-half of which is occupied by his appliance store. He may lease the other half of the property to B with a stipulation that B will not operate an appliance store on the land. As long as the vendor or lessor does not desire to have competition on property that he controls, he may avoid such competition by contract. Since other property in the community may be used for competitive purposes, the agreement is binding, although it does to some extent restrain trade. However, a restriction may be unenforceable as an illegal restraint on trade as a result of the Sherman Antitrust Act. It may also be illegal as a result of Federal Trade Commission rulings finding that the restriction is an unfair method of competition. This is discussed further in Chapter 42.

Usury State statutes limit the amount of interest that may be charged upon borrowed money. Any contract by which the lender is to receive more than the maximum interest allowed by the statute is usurious and illegal. In most states, the civil penalty for usury is that the lender is denied the right to collect any interest. Of course, there are also criminal penalties for charging illegal interest.

The law against usury is generally not violated if the seller has a different cash price than credit price. However, a seller cannot disguise interest by calling it something else. If the buyer is charged for making a loan, it is interest regardless of the terminology used in many states.

Case: P purchased a trailer from D on an installment contract. The "time price" was determined by applying a rate schedule to the cash price so that the total payments would substantially exceed the cash price. The plaintiff contended that the difference between the cash price and the time sale price was interest and that it was at a usurious rate.

Issue: Is a time price differential interest?

Decision: Yes.

Reason: This type of transaction is essentially a loan to finance the balance of the cash purchase price. Regardless of the term used, if the result is a charge for the loan of money, the result is interest. If it exceeds the maximum allowed by law, it is usurious.

Lloyd v. Gutgsell, 124 N.W.2d 198 (Neb.) 1963.

The laws in usury are not violated by collection of the legal maximum interest in advance or by adding a service fee that is no larger than reasonably necessary to cover the incidental costs of making the loan—inspection, legal, and recording fees. It is also allowable for a seller to add a finance or carrying charge on long-term credit transactions in addition to the maximum interest rate. Many of these exceptions are created by statute. Other statutes allow special lenders such as pawnshops, small loan companies, or credit unions to charge in excess of the otherwise legal limit. In fact, the exceptions to the maximum interest rate in most states far exceed the situations in which the general rule is applicable. The laws relating to usury were designed to protect debtors from excessive interest; this goal has been thwarted by these exceptions, so that only modest protection is actually available.

The purchase of a note at a discount greater than the maximum interest is not usurious, unless the maker of the note is the person who is discounting it. Thus if A, who is in need of funds, sells to B a $500 note made by C payable in six months for $100, the sale is not usurious, although the gain to B could be very large. A note is considered the same as any other personal property and may be sold for whatever it will bring upon the market.

As long as one lends the money of others, he may charge a commission in addition to the maximum rate. A commission may not be legally charged when one is lending his own funds, even though he has to borrow the money with which to make the loan and expects to sell the paper shortly thereafter.

Interest rates have increased substantially over the past few years. As a result, many states have raised the legal maximum to 10 or 12 percent. Additional statutory exceptions to the general law have also been created. Perhaps the most common relatively new exception concerns loans to a business. Today, in most states, there is no maximum legal rate of interest when the borrower is a business, whether or not it is incorporated. Some states limit this exception to a fixed sum, such as $10,000, but little protection is afforded by such laws. Historically, loans to corporations were exempt in most states, and the extension of this to all business loans is a recognition of the demands of the money market.

Another new trend in the law of usury is that federal laws supersede state laws with regard to federally guaranteed loans, such as FHA mortgage loans. As a result, interest on such loans can exceed the maximum allowed by the states.

REVIEW QUESTIONS AND PROBLEMS

1. Give two examples of illegal contracts.

2. What is an *exculpatory clause?* Why are such clauses used?

3. Is the fine print on a ticket given by a laundry a contract with its customers?

4. What is the legal effect of charging a usurious rate of interest?

5. A lost $9,000 in a card game with B. He brought action against B to recover this amount and asserted that B had used a "marked deck." Should A recover? Why?

6. A, landlord, brought an action to evict B, tenant, from a rented house for nonpayment of rent. B contended that A could not bring action because the premises were uninhabitable in violation of Housing Code regulations. Is B's contention correct? Why?

7. A agreed to ship a quantity of fireworks to B. After B sent A a portion of the purchase price, B learned that state law prohibits this type of sale. Before A sent the fireworks, B notified A of cancellation and asked for the return of the amount previously sent. Is B entitled to a refund? Why?

8. A, a real estate broker, prepared a contract for the sale of land for a buyer and a seller. A state statute made it illegal for brokers to prepare such agreements. What two dangers did A face? Explain.

9. A purchased a refrigerator on an installment basis from the XYZ appliance company. The contract included the following provision: "In the event of default by the buyer, XYZ shall have the right to repossess all merchandise previously delivered to the buyer by XYZ, regardless of whether payment has been made for any item." A could not pay for the refrigerator, and XYZ attempted to repossess both the refrigerator and a washing machine that had previously been delivered and paid for. Is XYZ's action legal? Why?

10. A wanted to locate a retail wine and cheese specialty shop in a shopping mall, which was being developed by the XYZ company. How may A reduce competition by the terms of the lease with the mall? Explain fully.

11 FORM OF THE AGREEMENT

Introduction   As a general rule, contracts may be oral or written or may even result from the conduct of the parties (contracts implied in fact). Except for certain exceptions created by statute, many of which are discussed in this chapter, an oral contract is just as valid and enforceable as a written contract. However, there are obvious advantages to written contracts over oral contracts. For example, it is much easier to establish the existence and terms of a written contract because the contract is its own proof of terms. An attempt may be made to establish the terms of an oral contract by testimony, but the testimony is often conflicting. Moreover, as a general rule, the terms of a written contract cannot be changed by oral testimony that the written contract did not state what the parties intended. This rule is known as the *parol evidence rule*.

Each state has a series of statutes, called the statute of frauds. These generally require that certain contracts must be evidenced by a writing before they are legally enforceable. These statutes have been enacted in recognition of the fact that certain types of contracts are susceptible to fraudulent proofs and perjured testimony.

Another aspect relating to the form of the agreement involves the situation in which an informal agreement is reached with the understanding that the parties will later execute and sign a formal written instrument. This raises the question of whether the informal agreement is binding prior to the time that the document is prepared and signed. The mere fact that a subsequent formal writing was contemplated does not prevent the informal agreement from being enforceable.

162

Case: P was the owner of a vacant commercial building which he wished to rent. After D expressed an interest in leasing the building, the parties agreed upon the terms of a lease. The basic terms of the lease were set forth in a letter signed by both parties. Later D called P to state that he had changed his mind and that he would not sign the lease. D contended that the letter was a preliminary proposal and not a contract. P then sued D for breach of contract.

Issue: Were the parties bound without the execution of a formal lease?

Decision: Yes.

Reasons: 1. It is well settled that parties may effectively bind themselves by an informal memorandum where they agree upon the essential terms of the contract and intend to be bound by the memorandum, even though they contemplate the execution of a more formal document.

2. The signed document was in terms of a bilateral undertaking and contained the necessary terms.

Berg Agency v. Sleepworld-Willingboro, Inc., 346 A.2d 419 (N.J.) 1975.

The Parol Evidence Rule The parol evidence rule prevents the introduction of oral testimony to alter or to vary the terms of a written agreement. The general proposition is that "a writing speaks for itself," and nothing should be considered that is not contained within the four corners of the written agreement. The result is that evidence may not be introduced in a lawsuit that the parties had agreed upon something orally that is different from that contained in the writing.

Case: P purchased a mobile home from D. The contract disclaimed any warranty obligation of D. P claimed that D had orally promised to take care of any problems that might arise with the mobile home.

Issue: Is oral evidence of a warranty admissible if the written contract disclaims the warranty?

Decision: No.

Reason: The evidence contradicts the writing. It does not fall within any of the exceptions to the parol evidence rule.

Hathaway v. Ray's Motor Sales, 247 A.2d 512 (Vt.) 1968.

163

It is important to note that although the parol evidence rule excludes evidence that attacks the terms of a written agreement, there are numerous exceptions to the rule. For example, it is possible to introduce evidence that after the parties entered into the written agreement, they agreed to certain modifications of it or even that they agreed to cancel the contract. Likewise if a contract is so ambiguous that the court is not certain as to what the parties intended, parol evidence may be introduced solely for the purpose of clarifying the ambiguous terms.

THE STATUTE OF FRAUDS

Introduction   The statute of frauds is of ancient English origin. It is designed to prevent fraud by excluding from the courts legal actions on certain specified contracts unless there is written evidence of the agreement signed by the defendant. The statute was enacted in order to protect people from perjured testimony in connection with contracts.

The statute in effect creates a defense to a suit for breach of contract. Except for some cases under the Code to be discussed later, the statute may be used as a defense, even though there is no factual dispute as to the existence of the contract or to its terms. A contract that requires a writing may come into existence at the time of the oral agreement, but it is not enforceable until written evidence of the agreement is available. The agreement is valid in every respect except for the lack of proper evidence of its existence. The statute creates a defense in suits for the breach of executory oral contracts if such contracts are covered by its provisions.

Historically and in modern times, the statute of frauds requires a writing in connection with the following contracts: (1) contracts to be liable for another person's debts; (2) contracts involving real property; (3) agreements that cannot be performed within one year from the date of making; and (4) contracts for the sale of goods when the price exceeds $500. There are also many special statute of frauds provisions. For example, most states by statute require that all life insurance contracts, real estate listing agreements, and promises to pay debts that have been discharged in bankruptcy be in writing. In addition, many statutes provide that any agreement required to be in writing may be modified only by a writing. Such a provision does not bar all oral modifications, but it does bar any modification of an essential element necessary to satisfy the statute of frauds. If the contract as orally modified would violate the statute, the statute is a defense. The sections that follow discuss the modern version of the major statute of frauds revisions.

Promise to Answer for the Debt of Another For the statute to be defense, a promise to answer for the debt of another must be a *secondary* promise. A primary promise is not within the statute and is enforceable even though oral. For example, a promise "sell goods to A, and I will pay for them" is a primary or original promise and enforceable even though oral. An oral promise to pay one's own obligation is not within the statute of frauds.

On the other hand, a promise "sell goods to A; if he doesn't pay you for them, I will" is a secondary promise and must be in writing to be enforceable. Note that in the second situation the primary responsibility to pay is A's, and the other party has agreed to pay only if A doesn't pay.

An original or primary promise can be distinguished from a secondary promise by analyzing the leading object or main purpose of the promisor in making the promise. When the leading object is to become a guarantor of another's debt, the promise is collateral and it is covered by the statute. When the leading object of the promisor is to subserve some interest or purpose of his own, even though it involves the debt of another, the promise is original and it is not within the statute. When the issue arises, the court must determine what object or purpose was sought to be advanced by the promisor.

Case: P's engineering firm sued D, an attorney, to recover for professional services rendered the X corporation, a land developer. D owned 18 percent of the stock of X corporation and was its legal counsel. X corporation also owed D $14,000 in legal fees. In order to encourage P to finish its survey work for X, D had orally promised to pay P's bill.

Issue: Is D liable for the oral promise to pay for the services rendered to X corporation?

Decision: Yes.

Reasons: 1. The promise was not within statute of frauds as a special promise to answer for the debt of another, since the consideration, i.e., continued professional services, was mainly desired for D's personal benefit, in that D's corporation owed him $14,000 for legal services. Continued engineering and surveying services were necessary to secure additional financing, and if the corporation was eventually successful the amount that D would receive would be substantial.

2. Where the consideration for which a new promise is given is beneficial both to the promisor and to the original debtor, the factor that is determinative of whether the statute of frauds applies is whether such consideration is mainly desired for the promisor's benefit or for benefit of

165

the original debtor. In applying the rule, the fact finder must examine all circumstances bearing on the transaction, the relationship of the parties to one another, and endeavor to discern the intent, purpose, and object of the promisor. In undertaking such examination the nature of the consideration will be of great, if not paramount, importance.

3. Under the "original collateral promise" test, where the leading object or main purpose of the promise is to become surety for another's debt, the promise is a collateral one and within the statute of frauds. On the other hand, where the principal purpose is to subserve or promote some interest personal to the promisor, then the promise will be deemed an original one and not controlled by the statute.

Howard M. Schoor Assoc., Inc. v. Holmdel Hts. Con. Co., 343 A.2d 401 (N.J.) 1975.

Contracts Involving Real Property   Contracts involving interests in land have always been considered important by the law; therefore, it is logical that such contracts are covered by the statute of frauds. The statute requires a writing for a contract creating or transferring any interest in land. In addition to contracts involving a sale of an entire interest, the statute is applicable to contracts involving interests for a person's lifetime, called life estates; to mortgages; to easements; and to leases for a period in excess of one year.

The section of the statute under consideration requires a writing in contracts for real property—land and those things affixed thereto. What is the status of such things as standing timber, minerals, and growing crops? Is an oral contract to sell timber a contract involving real estate? The general rule is that these items are real property if the title to them is to pass to the buyer before they are severed from the land; they are personal property if title to them passes subsequently. The Code provides that a contract for the sale of timber, minerals, and the like or for a structure or its materials to be removed from realty is a contract for the sale of goods if they are to be severed by the seller. (2-107) If the buyer is to sever them, the contract affects and involves land and is subject to the real estate provisions of the statute of frauds. The Code also provides that a contract for the sale apart from the land of growing crops is a contract for the sale of goods, whether they are to be severed by the buyer or by the seller. (2-107(2))

The statute of frauds is not applicable to executed contracts. A party who has purchased or sold land under an oral contract cannot obtain a refund of his money or cannot obtain a return deed to his land. The statute of frauds does not allow rescission—it only serves as a defense to a suit for breach of an executory contract. This principle creates a special problem in real estate contracts because many oral

166

contracts involving real estate become partially executed as a result of part payment by the buyer or surrender of possession to the buyer by the seller or both. Since the statute of frauds is a complete defense to an executory oral contract involving real estate and it is no defense to a fully executed contract, what is the status if the contract is partially performed?

The problem of part performance to satisfy the statute of frauds provisions on real estate has two aspects. First, the part performance must establish and point unmistakably and exclusively to the existence of the alleged oral agreement. Part performance eliminates the statute of frauds as a defense in such cases because it eliminates any doubt that the contract was made, and thus the reason for the defense does not exist.

Second, the part performance must be substantial enough to warrant specific performance of the oral agreement. In other words, it must be such that returning the parties to the status quo is not reasonably possible. To illustrate the foregoing, assume that a buyer under an oral contract has paid part of the purchase price. The money can be returned and the statute of frauds would be a defense because even if it was admitted that the oral contract was entered into, there is no equitable reason to enforce the oral agreement. However, when the seller under an oral contract also delivers possession to the buyer, the defense of the statute of frauds becomes more tenuous because returning the parties to the status quo becomes somewhat difficult. When improvements are made by one in possession, a return to the status quo becomes quite difficult if not impossible.

Case: P entered into an oral contract to purchase a farm from D. P went into possession of the farm, made several improvements, tore down an old farmhouse, paid taxes, and made payments on the purchase price. D thereafter refused to deed the farm to P. P sought specific performance of the contract.

Issue: Is the oral contract to sell real property enforceable under these circumstances?

Decision: Yes.

Reasons: 1. The statute of frauds requires a transfer of real property to be in writing, but the statute does not apply when there has been partial or complete performance. Here practically all the terms of the contract had been performed.

2. Here the contract was established from the fact of the buyer's possession, payments, and improvements to the premises.

Brown v. Burnside, 487 P.2d 957 (Idaho) 1972.

From the foregoing, it is clear that the transaction is taken out of the statute if the buyer has taken possession, paid all or part of the price, and made valuable improvements. However, a lesser part performance may also take the contract out of the statute. If the buyer takes possession and pays part of the price, there is good evidence of a contract, and if he also pays taxes and mortgage payments, specific performance may be warranted. Payment of the price, standing alone, is not a basis for specific performance and will not satisfy the statute. If the buyer enters into possession and makes valuable improvements, there is also sufficient part performance to make the contract enforceable and to satisfy the statute.

Contracts Not To Be Performed within One Year A contract is within the statute if by its terms it cannot be performed within one year from the time it is made. The period is measured from the time an oral contract is made to the time when the promised performance is to be completed. Thus an oral agreement to hire a person for two years, or to form and carry on a partnership for ten years, would not be enforceable.

The decisive factor in determining whether a long-term contract comes within the statute is whether performance is *possible* within a year from the date of making. If a contract, according to the intentions of the parties as shown by its terms, may be fully performed within a year from the time it is made, it is not within statute of frauds, even though the time of its performance is uncertain and may probably extend, and in fact does extend, beyond the year.

Case: P entered into an oral contract to furnish D with all the nylon tape that would be used by D in its business. It was agreed that the contract would continue so long as D had requirements for the tape. D sought to terminate the contract and claimed that the contract could not be enforced because it was not in writing.

Issue: Is a contract that provides for continued performance for an indefinite period of time required to be in writing?

Decision: No.

Reasons: 1. Because D's requirements for the tape could have terminated within a year, the statute of frauds does not apply.

168

2. The statute of frauds does not apply to a contract that may, by any possibility, be performed within a year.

Haveg Corporation v. Guyer, 211 A.2d 910 (Del.) 1965.

Even though it is most unlikely or improbable that performance could be rendered within one year, the statute does not apply if there is even a remote possibility that it could. Thus a promise to pay $10,000 "when cars are no longer polluting the air" would be enforceable even though given orally. Moreover, if a contract, otherwise to continue for more than a year, is by its own terms subject to termination within a year, it is not within the prohibition of the statute of frauds.

Nature of the Writing The statute of frauds does not require a formal, written document signed by both parties. All that is required is a note, memorandum, or some form of correspondence evidencing the transaction. It must be signed by the party sought to be bound by the agreement (the defendant). The memorandum need contain only the basic terms of the contract expressed with such certainty that they may be understood without resort to oral evidence.

It thus follows that under the statute one party may be bound by an agreement although the other is not. Only the party who resists performance need sign. Such a result is based on the theory that the oral agreement is legal in all respects, but proper evidence of such an agreement is lacking, and this is furnished when the person sought to be charged with the contract has signed a writing. The moving party (plaintiff) is simply seeking to enforce the contract whose formal existence the other denies. Any kind of note or memorandum that describes the property involved, that sets forth the major terms, and that indicates the parties to the agreement is sufficient. If one memorandum is incomplete, but it is clear that two or more writings relate to the same subject matter, they may be joined to supply the necessary memorandum, providing parol evidence is not required to join them.

The signature may be quite informal and need not necessarily be placed at the close of the document. It may be in the body of the writing or elsewhere so long as it identifies the writing with the signature of the person sought to be held.

Contracts to sell land create special statute of frauds requirements because of the use of legal descriptions. A contract to sell or convey land or a memorandum thereof, within the meaning of the statute of frauds, must contain a land description that is either certain in itself or is capable of being reduced to certainty by reference to something extrinsic to which the contract refers. For example, a sale of one acre out of a ten-acre tract without more would not be a sufficient legal description to satisfy the statute of frauds.

169

THE CODE

Contracts for the Sale of Goods— Generally The Code contains several statute of frauds provisions. The provision applicable to the sale of goods stipulates that, as a general rule, a contract for the sale of goods for the price of $500 or more is not enforceable unless there is some writing sufficient to indicate that a contract for sale has been made. The writing must be signed by the defendant or his authorized agent or broker. (2-201)

The liberal approach of the Code is seen in the Code provision that stipulates that the writing need not contain all material terms of the contract, and errors in stating a term will not affect the fact that the statute of frauds is not a defense. The writing need not indicate which party is the buyer or which is the seller or include the price or time of payment. The only term that must appear is the quantity term, which need not be accurately stated. However, a contract is not enforceable beyond the quantity stated in the writing. Since the requirement is that it be signed by the party to be charged, it need not be signed by a plaintiff who is seeking to enforce it.

Exceptions The Code provisions relating to the sale of goods contain several exceptions to the rule requiring a writing if the contract involves over $500. One exception is limited to transactions between "merchants," and it arises from the business practice of negotiating contracts orally, such as on the telephone. A merchant who contracts orally with another merchant can satisfy the statute of frauds requirement by sending a writing to the other merchant confirming the contract that they made orally. (2-201(2)) This confirmation sent by one merchant to the other will satisfy the statute, *even though it is not signed by the party to be charged*, unless written notice of objection to its contents is given within ten days after it is received. This means that a merchant who has dealt orally with another merchant will have an enforceable contract unless the merchant receiving the writing objects within the ten-day period. Other exceptions are based on partial performance of the contract for the sale of goods. An oral contract is enforceable with respect to goods (1) for which payment has been made or (2) that have been received and accepted. If either of these things has occurred, there would be a clear indication that a contract actually exists, and there should be no need for a writing to establish this fact. Such contracts are enforceable only to the extent of such payment or acceptance of the goods.

Another substitute for a writing under the Code also relates to conduct that in and of itself clearly indicates that a contract has been entered into. If (1) the goods are to be specially manufactured for the buyer, for example, according to the buyer's specifications, and are not suitable for sale to others; (2) the seller has either made a substantial beginning of their manufacture or commitments to obtain the goods; and (3) the circumstances reasonably indicate that the goods are for the buyer, the contract is enforceable without a writing. (2-201(3))

Case: P entered into an oral contract to install asphalt paving on D's property. D refused to pay the amount claimed by P on the ground that he had charged a higher price than he had previously charged. D contended that there was no enforceable contract because the price was over $500 and it was not in writing.

Issue: Is it required that the contract be in writing in order to be enforceable?

Decision: No.

Reason: The goods were considered to be manufactured specially for the buyer and are not suitable for sale to others in the ordinary course of the seller's business. Also this case comes under the exception that if the goods have already been accepted and received then the statute of frauds will not defeat the contract.

Rose Acre Farms Inc. v. L. P. Cavett Company of Indiana, 279 N.E.2d 280 (Ind.) 1972.

The final substitute for a writing is based upon recognition that the required writing is simply a formality—that a contract may very well exist, but no action can be taken to enforce it unless and until the necessary proof of its existence is forthcoming. The contract is simply unenforceable pending such proof. The proof may become available at a later date, and its effect will be retroactive. If the party who is resisting the contract admits its existence in the proper circumstances and surroundings, such admission will substitute for a writing. Thus the Code provides that an oral contract for the sale of goods is enforceable if when legal action is brought to enforce it the defendant admits in the court proceedings that a contract for sale was made. Thus it is quite possible that an admission will be made in the pleadings or testimony that an oral contract was made, and this will satisfy the statutory requirement. (2-201(3))

Case: P sued D to enforce an oral contract for the sale of a mobile home. D defended on the ground that the contract was unenforceable under the statute of frauds. At the trial, D took the stand and on cross-examination admitted to facts which as a matter of law established that a contract was formed.

Issue: Is the contract enforceable?

Decision: Yes.

Reasons: 1. Section 2-201(3) of the Uniform Commercial Code provides that a contract that does not satisfy the requirements of 2-201(1) (written evidence) but is valid in other respects is enforceable if the party against whom enforcement is sought admits in his pleading, testimony, or otherwise in court that a contract for sale was formed.

2. Involuntary admissions in open court are sufficient to obtain enforcement of an otherwise unenforceable contract under the statute of frauds.

Lewis v. Hughes, 346 A.2d 231 (Md.) 1975.

Because the "sale of goods" provision of the statute of frauds is applicable to sales where the price is $500 or more, it must be determined whether a transaction involves more than that amount. In determining whether the price is such as to cause it to fall within the statute, it often becomes necessary to decide how many contracts have been entered into. Thus A orders from B $400 worth of one item to be delivered at once and $200 of another item to be delivered a few weeks later. Either item considered on its own is worth less than $500; both items total over $500. If the parties intended only one contract, the statute of frauds is applicable; however, if two contracts were entered into, no writing is required.

Contracts Involving Personal Property Other Than Goods

The Code has several additional sections that require a writing. A contract for the sale of securities such as stocks and bonds is not enforceable unless (1) there is a signed writing setting forth a stated quantity of described securities at a defined or stated price; (2) delivery of the security has been accepted or payment has been made; (3) within a reasonable time a writing in confirmation of the sale or purchase has been sent and received and the party receiving it has failed to object to it within ten days after receipt; or (4) the party against whom enforcement is sought admits in court that such a contract was made. Note that this relates only to contracts for the sale of securities. (8-319)

Another section provides for contracts for the sale of personal property *other than* goods or securities. Here there is a requirement of a writing if the amount involved exceeds $5,000. Included in this coverage are such things as royalty rights, patent rights, and rights under a bilateral contract. (1-206)

In addition, the Code requires a signed security agreement in the article on secured transactions. This means that when a person, for example, borrows money and gives the lender an interest in his property as security, the debtor (borrower) must sign a security agreement that describes the transaction. (9-203) Such a signed agreement is not required if the secured party (lender) has possession of the property. If he is not in possession, the secured party cannot enforce his security interest unless there is a signed security agreement.

REVIEW QUESTIONS AND PROBLEMS

1. What advantage does a written contract have over an oral contract?

2. During a sales presentation for a swimming pool, a salesman for the XYZ pool company told A that all the construction materials would be removed immediately after completion of the pool. Later, A signed a written contract which did not mention any time for removal of the material. Two weeks after the pool was finished, XYZ still had not cleaned up the area around the pool. If A sued XYZ for breach of contract, in this case the costs of removing the material, what would be a defense of XYZ? Explain.

3. After A and B orally agreed on the terms of a contract for A to buy B's house, they contacted a lawyer to prepare a written contract. A signed the contract, but on the way to the lawyer's office, B changed his mind and decided not to sell. Could A obtain a court order for B to sell to A? Why?

4. A, a beverage company, orally promised B that he would be the exclusive wholesale distributor for A in a certain county. A sought to avoid this promise on the ground that it was oral. What result? Why?

5. A entered into an oral contract to purchase land from B. In reliance upon the oral contract, A passed up an opportunity to purchase other land that would have been suitable for his needs. B refused to sell the property to A, and A sought to enforce the oral contract. What result? Why?

6. On June 15, 1975, G orally promised H that he, G, would work for H as an architect until January 1, 1980, or until the project was completed. On January 1, 1977, G resigned his position and refused to finish the project. H sued G for breach of contract, and G used the statute of frauds as a defense. What result? Why?

7. P contracted to do certain construction work for G, the written contract providing that no additional work was to be done unless agreed to in writing. Later G made several oral requests for added work at specified rates, but after the work was completed, he refused to pay because the requests were not in writing. Is P permitted to recover? Why?

8. A made an oral contract with B whereby A was to convey certain real estate to B for the price of $6,000. In reliance upon the oral agreement, B hauled fertilizer to the farm, piped water to the feedlots, and made cement platforms for feeding livestock. Under these conditions, was the oral agreement enforceable? Explain.

9. X orally sold his wife's house to Y. Y made a down payment, sold his old residence, moved to the new house, and made substantial improvements thereon. Can Y enforce the oral contract? Why?

10. A signed an order form to purchase a new car from the B auto company for $2,500. B company did not sign the form. A made a $25 down payment.

Later B company told A that a mistake had been made and that the price would be $2,675. A sued the B company, which defended on the ground that it had not signed the form. What result? Why?

11. A ordered plastic materials from B, a supplier, by telephone. The price was $800. This was followed by a purchase order enclosed with a letter stating it was being sent in accordance with the telephone conversation. Thereafter B refused to deliver the material and contended that the statute of frauds had not been satisfied. What result? Why?

12 RIGHTS OF THIRD PARTIES

Introduction The discussion to this point has dealt with the law of contracts as applied to the contracting parties. Frequently, persons who were not parties to the contract may have rights and even duties under the contract. There are two basic situations in which the rights and duties of third parties (persons not involved in the original contract) may come into play: (1) when there is an *assignment* of the contract—a party to a contract (assignor) transfers to a third party (assignee) his rights under the contract; or (2) when there is a *third-party beneficiary* contract—one in which a party contracts with another party for the purpose of conferring a benefit upon a third party (beneficiary). In both these situations, the primary question is whether the third party—assignee or beneficiary—can enforce the contract.

ASSIGNMENTS

Terminology and Requirements A bilateral contract creates *rights* for each party and imposes on each corresponding *duties*. With respect to the duties, each is an *obligor* (has an obligation to perform); with respect to rights, each is an *obligee* (entitled to receive the performance of the other). Either party may desire to transfer to another his rights or both his rights and his duties. A party *assigns* his rights and *delegates* his duties. The term *assignment* may mean a transfer of one's rights under a contract, or it may mean a transfer of both his rights and his duties. The person making the transfer is called the *assignor*, and the one receiving the transfer is called the *assignee*.

A person who has duties under a contract cannot relieve himself of those duties by transferring the contract or delegating the duties to

175

another person. If an obligor delegates his duties as well as assigns his rights, he is not thereby relieved of his liability for proper performance if the assignee fails to perform. He continues to be responsible for the ultimate performance.

No particular formality is essential to an assignment. Consideration, although usually present, is not required. As a general proposition, an assignment may be either oral or written, although it is of course desirable to have a written assignment. Some statutes require a writing in certain assignment situations. For example, an assignment of an interest in real property must be in writing in most states. Therefore it is advisable to check the statutes of each state to determine which assignments must be in writing to be enforceable.

Consent Required

The rights under most contracts may be assigned if both parties to the agreement are willing to let this be done. Public policy prevents the assignment of some contract rights, however. For example, many states by statute prohibit or severely limit the assignment of wages under an employment contract. In addition, rights created by the law, such as the right to collect for personal injuries, frequently cannot be assigned.

What, however, is the effect of an assignment when the other (nonassigning) party to the original contract refuses to respect the assignment and insists upon performance by the original party? Most contracts can be assigned without the consent of the other party, but there are certain situations in which a contract may not be assigned over the objection of the other party.

Of the several classes of contracts that may not be transferred without the consent of the other party, the most important are contracts involving personal rights or personal duties. A personal right or duty is one in which special trust and confidence is involved or one in which the skill, knowledge, or experience of one of the parties is important. In such cases the personal acts and qualities of one or both parties form a material, integral part of the contract. For example, a lease contract in which the rent is a percentage of sales is based on the ability of the lessee and would not be assignable without the consent of the lessor. Likewise a contract that grants an exclusive agency would generally not be assignable without consent.

Case: D, a manufacturer of steel products, entered into a contract with X whereby X was the exclusive distributor of D's products in the New England states. Thereafter X assigned this exclusive agency contract to P, but D refused to recognize P as its agent. P sued D for breach of contract.

Issue: Can a contract for exclusive agency be assigned without the approval of both parties?

Decision: No.

Reason: The contract in this case is one requiring a relationship of particular trust and confidence, and such a contract cannot be assigned effectively without the consent of the other party to the contract. The grant of an exclusive agency to sell one's goods presupposes a reliance upon and a confidence in the agent.

Wetherell Bros. Company v. United States Steel Company, 105 F.Supp. 81 (1952).

Some duties that might appear to be personal in nature are not considered so by the courts. For example, a building contractor may delegate responsibility for certain portions of the structure. If the construction is to be done according to agreed specifications, the entire agreement to build is assignable. It is presumed that contractors are able to follow specifications, and because the duties are mechanical in nature, the owner is bound to permit the assignee to build the structure. Of course it is always possible to include in the contract that it may not be assigned without the other party's approval, and such an agreement against assignment will be enforced.

Another example of a contract that is unassignable is one in which an assignment would place an additional burden or risk upon a party, one not contemplated at the time he made the agreement. Such appears to be true of the assignment of the right to purchase merchandise on credit. Most states hold that one who has agreed to purchase goods on credit and has been given the right to do so may not assign his right to purchase the goods to a third party (assignee) because the latter's credit may not be as good as that of the original contracting party—the assignor.

This reasoning is questionable because the seller could hold both the assignor and the assignee responsible. However, the inconvenience to the seller in connection with collecting has influenced most courts to this result. But in contracts where the seller has security for payment such as retention of title to the goods, a mortgage on the goods, or a security interest in the goods, the seller has such substantial protection that the courts have held that the right to purchase on credit is assignable.

Some contracts contain a provision that they are not assignable without consent. Courts usually enforce such a provision, even though it has the effect of restraining transfer of property. Many courts allow

177

an assignment in violation of the agreement. These courts consider the assignment to be a breach of contract for which dollar damages become due. However, many courts in effect specifically enforce the agreement against assignment by holding that an obligor who refuses to perform for the objectionable assignee has no liability.

Case: H entered into a contract with D whereby H acquired the franchise to operate a "Dairy Queen" establishment. The contract specifically provided that the contract and franchise could not be assigned without D's consent. Without obtaining such consent, H assigned the franchise to P. D refused to recognize the assignment, and P sought a declaratory judgment that the provision against assignment was against public policy and unenforceable.

Issue: Will a contractual provision against assignment of a business franchise be enforced?

Decision: Yes.

Reason: The authorities support the proposition that a reasonable provision against assignment will be enforced. Here the restriction was reasonable and necessary to protect the business reputation of D.

Hanigan Wheeler, 504 P.2d 972 (Ariz.) 1972.

Claims for Money   All claims for money due or to become due under existing contracts may be assigned. For example, an automobile dealer may assign to a bank the right to receive money due under contracts for the sale of automobiles on installment contracts. Likewise an employee may assign a portion of his wages to a creditor in order to obtain credit or to satisfy an obligation. There is a trend in the law toward greatly reducing or eliminating the use of wage assignments. For example, the Uniform Consumer Credit Code adopted in several states imposes severe restrictions upon assignments of earnings by employees. A seller cannot take an assignment of earnings for payment of a debt arising out of a consumer credit sale. Lenders are not allowed to take an assignment of earnings for payment of a debt arising out of a consumer loan. The Consumer Credit Code is a part of the trend toward greater consumer and debtor protection.

When a claim for money is assigned, an issue that frequently arises is the liability of the assignor in case the assignee is unable to collect from the debtor-obligor. If the assignee takes the assignment merely as *security* for a debt owing from the assignor to the assignee, it is clear that if the assigned claim is not collected the assignor will still have to pay the debt to the assignee. On the other hand, if the assignee has *purchased* a claim against a third party from the assignor, he would generally have no recourse against the assignor upon default by the debtor-obligor. The purchase price presumably has taken into account the risk of nonpayment by the debtor. However, if the claim is invalid for some reason or if the claim is sold expressly "with recourse," the assignor would be required to reimburse the assignee if the debtor-obligor did not pay.

However, the assignor *warrants* or guarantees that the claim he assigns is a valid legal claim which the debtor-obligor is legally obligated to pay and also guarantees that there are no valid defenses to the claim that has been assigned. If this warranty is breached, that is, if there are valid defenses or if the claim is otherwise invalid, the assignee can go against the assignor if the obligor's refusal is based upon these grounds. The assignor under these circumstances would have to return to the assignee the amount the latter had paid for the claim.

Rights of the Assignee

An assignment is more than a mere authorization or request to the person who owes the money or other duty to pay or to perform for the assignee rather than the assignor. The obligor-debtor *must* pay or perform for the assignee, who now in effect owns the rights under the contract. If there is a valid assignment, the assignee owns the rights and is entitled to receive them. Performance for the original party will not discharge the contract.

Since in an assignment, the assignee receives exactly the same rights that the assignor had, problems arise when there is a defense against the assignor. Because the rights of the assignee are neither better nor worse than those of the assignor, any defense that the third party (obligor) has against the assignor is available against the assignee. For example, A entered into a contract to buy a machine from B and to pay for it in installments. B warranted that the machine had just been overhauled and that it had new valves. B then assigned the contract account receivable to C. In truth the machine had never been overhauled and there were no new parts. Under these circumstances A could assert this breach of warranty against C. A common expression defining the status of the assignee is that he "stands in the shoes" of the assignor.

Case: D, Hudson Supply, owed an open account to Eastern Brick and Tile Co. These accounts were sold and assigned to P. When P sought to collect on the assigned accounts, D refused to pay on the ground that Eastern owed more money to D than D owed Eastern.

Issue: Can a setoff be asserted against the assignee of a money claim?

Decision: Yes.

Reasons: 1. The assignee of a money claim takes only the rights of the assignor. Thus, setoffs available against the assignor may also be asserted against the assignee.

2. Any defense an obligor has against an assignor may be asserted against an assignee.

Hudson Supply & Equipment Company v. Home Factors Corp., 210 A.2d 837 (D.C.) 1965.

Duties of the Assignor An assignor is not relieved of his obligations by the mere delegation of them to an assignee. An assignor is still liable on the original contract if the assignee fails to perform as agreed. (Of course, the assignee in that event would have liability to the assignor for breach of contract.) If a party upon the transfer of a contract to a third person wishes to be released of liability, a legal arrangement known as a novation is required.

The term *novation* is used to describe an agreement whereby an original party to a contract is replaced by a new party. In order that the substitution be effective, it must be agreed to by all three of the parties. The remaining contracting party must agree to accept the new party and at the same time consent to release the withdrawing party. A novation is never presumed. While an express release is not necessary and a novation may be established from the acts and the conduct of the parties, there must be an agreement to accept the third party in place of the original promisor. In addition, the new party must agree to assume the burdens and duties of the retiring party. If all these essentials are present, the withdrawing party is discharged. To illustrate: A purchases an automobile from B, making a small down payment and agreeing to pay the balance of $400 within six months. Finding times somewhat hard, A sells the car to C, who agrees to pay the balance to B. Both parties notify B of this arrangement. As yet no novation is completed because B has not agreed to release A and to look only to C for payment. If B releases A and agrees to look solely to C, A is then discharged from any duty arising under the agreement, and a novation is created.

The term *novation* is also used to describe a new contractual relation between the original parties made with the intent to extinguish a contract already in existence. The new obligation is substituted for the old obligations. Most novations include a new party who is to be obligated, but the term has the dual meaning noted.

Duties of the Assignee The liability of the assignee to perform the duties of the assignor is a much more complicated issue. The liability of the assignee is determined by a careful examination of the transaction to see whether it is an assignment of only the rights under the agreement or whether the duty has also been delegated. This is

180

often difficult to determine when the language used refers only to an "assignment of the contract."

As a general rule, the *mere assignment* of a contract which calls for the performance of affirmative duties by the assignor, with nothing more, does not impose those duties upon the assignee. However, there is a decided trend in such cases to hold that an assignment of an entire contract carries an implied assumption of the liabilities. When the assignee undertakes and agrees to perform the duties as a condition precedent to enforcement of the rights, or has assumed the obligation to perform as part of the contract of assignment, he has liability for failure to perform. To illustrate: If a tenant assigns a lease, the assignee is not liable for future rents if he vacates the property prior to expiration of the period of the lease, unless he expressly assumes the burdens of the lease at the time of the assignment. He is obligated simply to pay the rent for the period of his actual occupancy. To the extent that an assignee accepts the benefits of a contract, he becomes obligated to perform the duties that are related to such benefits.

If the duties have been delegated to the assignee, a failure by the assignee to render the required performance gives rise to a cause of action in favor of the third party (obligee). The obligee can elect to sue either the assignor or the assignee.

Notice   Immediately after the assignment, the assignee should notify the other party, obligor or debtor, of his newly acquired right. This notification is essential for two reasons.

First, in the absence of any notice of the assignment, the obligor is at liberty to perform—pay the debt or do whatever else the contract demands—for the original contracting party, the assignor. In fact he would have no knowledge of the right of anyone else to require performance or payment. Thus the right of the assignee to demand performance can be defeated by his failure to give this notice. As soon as notice of the assignment is given to him the obligor must perform for the assignee, and his payment or performance to the assignor would not relieve him of his obligation to the assignee.

Second, the notice of assignment is also for the protection of innocent third parties. The assignor has the *power*, although not the *right*, to make a second assignment of the same contract. Thus he might dishonestly assign the same contract to two or more people. If notice of the assignment has been given to the obligor, he would then know of his obligation to pay a particular assignee, and any other person contemplating taking an assignment could check with the obligor and would then find out that the contract had already been assigned. A person who considers taking an assignment should therefore always confirm that the right has not previously been assigned. He can do this very easily by simply asking the obligor if an assignment has previously been made. If the obligor has not been notified of a previous assignment, and if the person who is going to take the assignment is aware of none, he can in many states feel free to take the assignment. He should immediately give notice to the obligor that he has in fact taken the assignment. Thus the rule in most states is that the first assignee to give notice to the debtor without knowledge of a prior assignment will prevail over a prior assignee.

Case: A, a contractor, in order to get a construction job was required to put up a performance bond. The purpose of the bond was to assure that A would perform properly and would pay all his bills. D bonding company agreed to write the bond provided A would assign to it (for security) payments under the contract. A did so. Thereafter A borrowed money from P bank and assigned the right to the same payments to the bank. P was the first to notify the owner of its assignment.

Issue: Does P have priority over D?

Decision: Yes.

Reason: The first assignee to give notice to the debtor will prevail over the first assignee in point of time.

Boulevard National Bank of Miami v. Air Metals Industry, 176 So.2d 94 (Fla.) 1965.

Some states, however, hold that the first party to receive an assignment has a prior claim regardless of which one gave notice first. These courts adopt the theory that once an assignment has been made, the assignor has parted with all his interest and has nothing left to transfer to the second assignee.

In all states, however, the party who is injured by reason of the second assignment has a cause of action against the assignor—the assignor has committed a wrongful and dishonest act by making a double assignment.

Assignments under the Code The Code provides that an assignment of "the contract" or of "all my rights under the contract" or an assignment in similar general terms is an assignment of rights, and unless the language or circumstances (as in an assignment for security) indicate the contrary it is also a delegation of performance of the duties of the assignor. (2-210(4)) The acceptance of the assignment by the assignee constitutes a promise by him to perform those duties. Thus, under the Code, if general terms are used, it is implied that the assignee undertakes to perform the duties under the assigned contract.

When the assignor delegates his duties, although the assignor remains liable, the obligee may feel insecure as to the ability of the assignee to perform the delegated duties. The obligee may demand that the assignor furnish him with adequate assurance that the assignee will in fact render proper performance. (2-210(5))

The Code contains provisions that generally approve the assignment of rights and the delegation of duties by buyers and sellers of goods. The duties of either party may be delegated *unless* the parties have agreed otherwise or the nondelegating party has ". . . a substantial interest in having his original promisor perform or control the acts required by the contract." (2-210(1)) Accordingly, a seller can ordinarily delegate to someone else the duty to perform the seller's obligations under the contract. This would occur when no substantial reason exists why the delegated performance would be less satisfactory than the personal performance.

However, the Code also specifically provides that a contract cannot be assigned if the assignment would materially increase the burden or risk imposed upon the nonassigning party or impair his chance of obtaining the performance that he bargained for. (2-210(2))

Some contracts contain a provision that they are not assignable. Under the Code, such a clause is construed to bar only a delegation of duties. (2-210(3)) If a contract contains a prohibition against assignment, this still does not prevent an assignment of the right to receive money payments that are due or to become due under the contract.

CONTRACTS FOR BENEFIT OF THIRD PARTIES

Nature of Such Contracts   Contracts are often made for the express purpose of benefiting some third party who is not a party to the contract. The most typical example of such an agreement is the contract for life insurance. The insured has made a contract with a life insurance company for the purpose of conferring a benefit upon a third party, namely the beneficiary named in the policy.

There are two types of third-party beneficiaries—"donee beneficiaries" and "creditor beneficiaries." Both are entitled to enforce a contract made on their behalf—the promisee has provided that the performance shall go to the beneficiary rather than to himself.

If the promise was obtained by the promisee in order to make a gift to the third party, such party is a donee beneficiary. The life insurance situation is an example of this.

If the promisee has contracted for a promise to pay a debt that he owes to a third party, such third party is a creditor beneficiary—the debtor has arranged to pay his debt by purchasing the promise of another that he will satisfy the obligation. The promisee obtains a benefit because his obligation to his creditor will presumably be satisfied. To illustrate: A borrowed money from B bank to buy a house. He gave the bank a note for the amount borrowed and the note was secured by a mortgage on the home. If A did not keep up his payments, the bank could foreclose the mortgage. Also A is liable for payment of the note. A later sold his home to C, who assumed and agreed to pay the mortgage debt. B bank is a creditor beneficiary of C's promise to pay A's debt.

Legal Requirements A third-party beneficiary is not entitled to enforce a contract unless he can establish that the parties actually intended to make the contract for his benefit. The third party need not be named as a beneficiary in the contract if he can show that he is a member of a group for whose benefit the contract was made.

Case: A university athletic department leased an airplane to fly its football team. The lease provided that the university would furnish liability insurance to cover any deaths or injuries resulting from the operation of the plane. No such insurance was purchased and the plane crashed, killing all on board. (The crash resulted when the plane was twenty-nine hundred pounds in excess of allowable takeoff weight.) The estates of the deceased players sued the university, claiming to be third-party beneficiaries of the contract.

Issue: Were the estates of the passengers entitled to sue on the contract?

Decision: Yes.

Reasons: 1. A person may avail himself of a promise made by a second party to a third party for the benefit of the first party, even though the first party had no knowledge of the contract when it was made.

2. Here the contract provision requiring insurance was for the benefit of the passengers. They could sue for its breach.

Brown v. Wichita State University, 540 P.2d 66 (Kan.) 1975.

If the benefit to the third party is only incidental, the beneficiary cannot sue. For example, an orphanage lost a suit that was based on an agreement between several merchants to close their places of business on Sunday with a provision that each one that remained open was to pay $100 to the orphanage. The court stated that the contract was entered into primarily to benefit the contracting parties and that the orphanage was only indirectly to be a beneficiary. Contracts of guarantee that assure the owner of property that contractors performing construction contracts for him will properly complete the project and pay all bills have been held in many states to benefit the material man and laborers. Thus, if the supplier of lumber and building materials was not paid by the contractor, he could bring legal action against the person who gave the guarantee.

In most states a contract made for the express purpose of benefiting a third party may not be rescinded without the consent of the beneficiary after its terms have been accepted by the beneficiary. The latter has a vested interest in the agreement from the moment it is made and accepted. For example, an insurance company has no right to change the named beneficiary in a life insurance policy without the consent of the beneficiary, unless the life insurance contract gives the insured the right to make this change. Until the third-party beneficiary has either accepted or acted upon provisions of a contract for his benefit, the parties to the contract may abrogate the provisions for the third party's benefit and divest him of the benefits that would otherwise have accrued to him under the contract. Infants, however, are *presumed* to accept a favorable contract upon its execution, and such contract may not be changed so as to deprive an infant of his benefits.

REVIEW QUESTIONS AND PROBLEMS

1. What is the difference between an *assignment* and a *delegation*?

2. What should one do before accepting an assignment? Why?

3. What is meant by the statement, "The assignee stands in the shoes of the assignor"?

4. A, a tenant, had a one-year lease with the XYZ apartments. After two months, A decided to sublet to B. B moved in, and A rented another apartment. B occupied the apartment for only one month and then left town and was never heard from again. Is A liable to XYZ for the unpaid future rent? Why?

5. A sold sponges to B on open account and then assigned the account receivable to C. B rejected the sponges because they were not of proper quality. C seeks to collect from B. Should he succeed? Why?

6. After careful investigation of his financial position A, the owner of an office building, entered into a contract to lease the building to B. B then assigned the contract to C, who prepared a lease for the signature of A. A refused to sign the lease, and C sought specific performance. Was A justified in refusing to sign? Why?

7. X, a contractor, assigned his claim for work being done to Y, a bonding company. Y did not notify the owner of the building for whom X was doing the work. X later assigned the same claim to Z, who did notify the owner of the building. To whom should the owner of the building make payment? Explain.

8. P employed A to work, the latter agreeing that he would not compete with P when he terminated his employment. P sold his business to T and assigned

the employment contract. A quit and began to compete immediately with T. Has T a good cause of action against A? Why?

9. A contracted with B to build a house for B. A assigned the contract to C, who substantially performed the contract but committed several minor breaches. From whom can B collect? Explain.

10. A and B included in their contract for the sale of hardware a clause that prohibited any assignment. After A made delivery to B, A assigned B's unpaid account to C. Is the assignment valid so that B is liable to C? Why?

11. A, an employee of ABC company, was injured when the elevator he was operating fell. ABC had a contract with C, the elevator company, whereby C was to inspect and service the elevator on a regular basis. A contended that C had not properly inspected the elevator and that its omission to do so caused the accident. Was A entitled to the benefits of the contract between ABC and C? Why?

13 PERFORMANCE AND DISCHARGE OF CONTRACTS

Introduction   Many problems can arise during the period of the performance of a contract. One of the parties may refuse to perform or may perform in an unsatisfactory manner. A party may be unable to perform because of circumstances beyond his control, or he may contend that because of changed conditions he should be excused from performing. When a breach of contract occurs through no fault of the parties, the law recognizes such a fact and the party in breach is excused. For example, when performance becomes a literal impossibility, there is no liability for breach of contract. Usually a default or a breach of contract will occur at or after the time when performance was due, but a contract may be breached even prior to the date for performance. This chapter will discuss many of the foregoing problems.

The rights and duties created by a contract continue in force until the contract is discharged. The usual and intended method of discharge is the complete performance by both parties of their obligations under the agreement. When this has been accomplished, the parties are automatically discharged—the contract is completely executed. There are, however, many other ways in which a discharge may be brought about. Discharge may also result from an excuse for nonperformance, mistake, or frustration. In these situations the law provides for a discharge because the intended performance by either or both parties is in some way not in keeping with the situation as it existed or was believed to exist when the parties entered into their agreement. These and other methods of discharge are discussed later in this chapter.

CONDITIONS

Introduction   Those terms of a contract the breach of which justifies rescission are called *conditions*. Conditions may be either *precedent*, *concurrent*, or *subsequent*. A condition subsequent is an event the occurrence of which takes away rights that would otherwise exist. A provision in an insurance policy that takes away the right to recover for a fire loss unless the insured gives notice of the loss within a stated period is an example of a condition subsequent. Failure to give notice within the prescribed time relieves the company from its obligation to pay for the loss.

The word *condition* means an act or event that must take place before a promisor is obligated to render performance. The condition may be an *express condition*, specifically provided for in the contract, or it may be an *implied condition*.

Conditions Precedent

A contract may expressly provide that one party must perform before he obtains the right to performance by the other party.

The other party's performance is a *condition precedent*—a prerequisite to his duty to perform. Because one party must perform before the other is under a duty to do so, it follows that the failure of the first party to perform permits the other to refuse to perform and to cancel the contract or sue for damages. A condition precedent is something that must occur before the other party has a right to immediate performance or before the usual judicial remedies are available.

Not all the terms that impose a duty of performance on a person are of sufficient importance to be conditions precedent. As a general rule, if a provision is relatively insignificant, its performance is not required before recovery may be obtained from the other party. In such cases the party who was to receive performance merely deducts the damages caused by the breach before performing on his part. The basic question presented is: What breaches justify rescission of a contract?

Case: P sought to rescind a contract for the construction of a house to be built by D. D failed to follow certain specifications: (1) bathroom fixtures were white rather than colored, (2) sealdown shingles were used instead of T-lock shingles, (3) only the front was brick instead of an all-brick exterior, and (4) there was a two-inch bow in the foundation.

Issue: Does D's deviation from the specifications justify rescission by P?

Decision: Yes.

Reasons: 1. It is not every breach which gives rise to the right to rescind a contract. In order to warrant rescission of a contract the breach must be material and the failure to perform so substantial as to defeat the object of the parties in making the agreement. Obviously, the variance in the appearance of the bathroom fixtures is not so substantial that it would constitute a material breach of contract.

2. The variance in the shingles and the brick veneer are entirely different matters. We are inclined to agree with plaintiffs that there was a material breach of the contract. Substantial variations such as shown here entitle the purchaser to rescind the contract.

Whiteley v. O'Dell, 548 P.2d 798 (Kan.) 1976.

If, in the foregoing case, the contractor had followed all of the specifications but had completed the work ten days late, rescission would not have been justified. Such a breach is of minor importance. The purchaser would have been required to pay the contract price less any damages sustained because of the delay. Judging whether the breach of a particular provision is so material as to justify rescission is often difficult. If the damage caused by the breach can be readily measured in money, and if the other party receives basically what he was entitled to under the contract, the clause breached is not considered a condition precedent.

Express Conditions The condition may be an *express* condition, specifically provided for in the contract, or it may be *implied*. An express condition is one that is included in a contract and stated to be one that must be strictly performed before the other party's duty to perform arises. The effect of an express condition is to compel the other party to perform properly and on time. The penalty for failure to properly perform such a condition may be the loss of the right to receive payment or to otherwise obtain the return performance. The parties may stipulate that something is important—a condition precedent—even though it would not ordinarily be considered so. In such a case failure to perform exactly as specified would allow the other party to rescind the contract.

Thus a contract may provide that "time is of the essence." This means that performance on or before the date specified is a condition precedent to the duty of the other party to pay or to perform.

It is common in building contracts to provide that the duty of the owner to make final payment on completion of the building is conditional upon the builder's securing an architect's certificate. This is a certification by the owner's architect that the construction is satisfactory and in accordance with the plans and specifications. The furnishing of this architect's certificate would be a condition precedent to the owner's obligation to make the final payment.

189

Implied Conditions　Probably the most common problems of conditions precedent arise when parties have simply entered into a contract and have not mentioned anything about conditions. Often one party has promised to render a certain service or to deliver certain goods, and the other has promised to pay a certain sum for such goods or services. In such a contract the question is presented: Will the law *imply* that the performance by one party is a condition precedent to the duty of the other party to render his performance? Will the latter be required to perform in spite of the other's breach, obtaining relief by deducting his damages caused by the other's breach? If under the contract one party is to perform first in time, that performance is construed to be a condition precedent.

If a provision is important when all of the facts and circumstances are considered, the law will imply that it is a condition precedent. For example, even though the contract does not provide that "time is of the essence" of this agreement, the time of performance may be considered material. Failure to peform on time in such cases will justify rescission.

Case:　On May 14, 1973, P entered into a contract to purchase a motor vehicle from D, an auto dealer, and paid $1,000 down. P informed D that he intended to use the vehicle for camping during the summer. The vehicle was supposed to be delivered during June, but no delivery was made through August. P seeks to cancel the contract and to obtain a refund of the $1,000.

Issue:　Is time of the essence of this agreement (a condition precedent)?

Decision:　Yes.

Reason:　Plaintiff's known intent to use the vehicle for camping during the summer in question made timely performance necessary here, and failure to make delivery was a material breach of contract.

Hedrick v. Goodwin Brothers, Inc., 325 N.E.2d 73 (Ill.App.) 1975.

Substantial Performance of Conditions　Assuming that performance by one party is a condition precedent, the next question is what *degree* of performance is required before the other party is obligated to perform on his part? The general rule is that the conditions must be substantially performed. It is therefore necessary to measure the performance. The general rule is that failure to render full and complete performance will amount to a breach of the constructive condition only if the failure was so significant and important that the other party is deprived of what he bargained for. Stated differently, if the breach is immaterial,

190

there has been substantial performance; if the breach is material, a party is relieved of his obligation to perform.

A number of factors must be taken into account in determining whether a breach is material or is of lesser significance. To illustrate: Assume that R, a retail grocer, contracts to buy from S ten thousand pounds of brand X margarine at sixty-five cents a pound. The contract provides that R is to pay for the margarine within thirty days and S is to send a salesman to display and assist in selling the margarine. If S fails to send a salesman and the margarine does not sell, must R pay for it or may he return it and rescind the contract? In other words, was the provision for sending a salesman a condition precedent to R's duty to pay? Whether the provision is an important one would doubtless depend in part on whether R had previously sold margarine and upon whether this brand was new to the trade. If the brand is a new one and needs special promotion, and if R is a somewhat inexperienced grocer, it seems likely that the breach would be substantial enough to justify rescission.

Several general principles have been applied in determining materiality of a breach: (1) Failure to perform on a specified date will not usually be treated as a material breach, especially if there is some justification for the delay. Delays in payment of money or completion of building contracts are regarded as less significant than delays in shipment of goods. (2) In contracts for the sale of marketable goods, a clause calling for performance within a certain time is usually held to be a condition precedent. In contracts whereby retailers purchase goods that are normally bought and sold in the market, performance by the seller on the date specified is considered quite important. (3) Performance on time can be made a condition precedent by adding a clause such as "time is of the essence of this agreement." (4) The quantitative element of a breach will often determine materiality. Thus if an order calls for 1,000 items and 999 are sent, there would likely be substantial performance; whereas if only 800 had been sent, the breach would be more substantial.

**Concurrent
Conditions**

Many contracts are so drawn that the parties thereto are to act simultaneously as to certain matters. An agreement that calls for a conveyance by A of a certain lot upon payment of $60,000 by B is illustrative of such a situation. The deed is to be delivered at the time payment is made. Those terms of a contract that require both parties to the agreement to perform at the same time are designated *concurrent conditions*. Under the terms of such an agreement, neither party is placed in default until the other has offered to perform. Such offer to perform is called a *tender*, and actual performance is unnecessary to place the other party in default. For this reason B could not successfully sue A for failure to deliver the deed until he had offered to make the payment required.

LEGAL CONCEPTS RELATING TO PERFORMANCE

Tender   A tender in the law of contracts is an offer to perform—to carry out a promise to do something or to pay something. When a person makes a tender, it means that he is ready, willing, and able to perform. The tender is especially significant in those contracts in which both parties are required to perform at the same time. One party can place the other party in default by making a tender of performance without having actually rendered the performance.

The concept of tender is applied not only to concurrent condition situations but also to contract performance in general. Suppose that B and S enter into a contract for the sale of goods; that S, the seller, offers the proper goods at the proper time and place to B, the buyer; and that B refuses to accept the goods. B's refusal of the tender discharges S's obligation, and S can proceed to bring action against B for damages. Also should B subsequently seek to enforce the contract, S's tender and B's rejection would be a defense.

In most contracts, one party or the other is required to tender payment. Such a "tender" requires that there be a bona fide, unconditional offer of payment of the amount of money due, coupled with an actual production of the money or its equivalent. A tender of payment by check is not a valid tender when an objection is made to this medium of payment. However, when a tender is refused for other reasons, one may not later complain about the use of a check as the medium of tender. The purpose of requiring a person to whom a tender is made to specify any objection to the tender or waive it is to allow the debtor to know what the creditor demands so that he may comply with them.

Tenders of payment are often refused for one reason or another. A party may contend that the tender was too late. The creditor may refuse to accept the offer to pay because he believes that the amount tendered is less than the amount of the debt. If it turns out that the tender was proper, the valid tender will have three important legal effects: (1) it stops interest from accruing after the date of the tender; (2) in case the creditor later brings legal action recovering no more than the amount tendered, he must pay the legal costs; and (3) if the debt were secured by a security interest in property belonging to the debtor, this security interest would be extinguished. Thus a tender of payment, although it does not discharge the debt, has important advantages to the person making it.

192

Anticipatory Repudiation   A breach of contract usually occurs when a party fails to perform at the time agreed upon. However, a party may announce his intention not to perform prior to the time of the agreed performance. This is called *anticipatory breach*, or *repudiation*.

Anticipatory breach occurs when one of the parties to a bilateral contract repudiates it either expressly or impliedly. An *express repudiation* of a contract is a clear, positive, unequivocal refusal to perform. An *implied repudiation* results from conduct where the promisor puts it out of his power to perform so as to make substantial performance of his promise impossible. For example, assume that A contracts on June 1, 1977, to sell his store building and to give occupancy to B on July 1, 1978. If A sells the store to X and gives occupancy to him on October 1, 1977, A has clearly repudiated—he has made impossible his own performance. On the other hand, if S, who is under a contract to deliver ten thousand television sets to B on July 1, 1977, announces on January 1, 1977, that a threatened strike casts doubt upon his ability to perform, this would not be a positive and unequivocal repudiation.

When a promisor repudiates a contract, the injured party faces an election of remedies. He can treat the repudiation as an anticipatory breach and immediately seek damages for breach of contract, thereby terminating the contract. He can also treat the repudiation as an empty threat, wait until the time for performance arrives, and exercise his remedies for actual breach if breach does in fact occur at such time. The practical aspects of business will often dictate the course to be followed.

Generally a party may withdraw his repudiation provided he does so before there has been any material change of position by the other party in reliance upon it. The retraction would simply be notice that he would perform the contract after all. Thus the repudiating party's right to reinstate the contract depends upon what action has been taken by the other party.

There are limitations on the application of the doctrine. One is that it does not apply to promises to pay money on or before a specified date. For example, if a promissory note matured on June 1, 1979, a statement by the maker of the note in 1978 that he will not pay it when the maturity date arrives would not give rise to a present cause of action by the holder. Also in order that the right of immediate action for breach can arise, the repudiation must be positive and unequivocal.

Case: P had entered into a contract to purchase two campers from D and had made a deposit of $1,000 as partial payment. P then wired D not to ship the campers. By letter, P later explained the reason for canceling the shipment. Subsequently, P decided not to buy the campers and demanded a return of his $1,000. D refused and P instituted legal action. D contended that the claim was barred by the statute of limitations (three years), since the action was not commenced within three years from the date of the telegram. The suit was within three years from the demand for the return of the down payment.

Issue: Was the instruction not to ship an anticipatory repudiation?

Decision: No.

Reason: The telegram was simply an implication that plaintiff would not perform his part of the contract at that time. Such action is "not the equivalent of a positive and unequivocal refusal to perform" at any time.

McMahon v. Fiberglass Fabricators, Inc., 496 P.2d 616 (Ariz.) 1972.

Divisibility— Installment Contracts

Although many contracts require a single performance by each party and are completely performed at one point of time, others require or permit performance by one or both of the parties in installments over a period of time. The rights and obligations of parties during the period when the contract is being performed frequently depend upon whether the contract is "entire" or "divisible." A contract is said to be divisible if performance by each party is divided into two or more parts *and* performance of each part by one party is the agreed exchange for the corresponding part by the other party. Note that a contract is not divisible simply by virtue of the fact that it is to be performed in installments.

When performance of a contract may take place in installments rather than all at one time, several questions arise: (1) Is the contract divisible on both sides so that the second party is under a duty to perform in part after the first party performs an installment? (2) Does a material breach of any installment justify a rescission of the balance of the agreement? (3) If one party is in default, may he nevertheless recover for the performance rendered prior to default? The parties may specify in their contract whether it is divisible or entire and provide the answers to each of these questions. In the absence of such a specification, certain general principles are applied by the courts. For example, employment contracts are usually interpreted to be divisible, but construction contracts are usually deemed to be entire.

If A employs B to serve as a financial consultant for one year at a salary of $2,000 per month, B would be entitled to $2,000 after one month's service. He would not have to complete a year's service as a condition to payment. Also if B wrongfully resigned after working for one month, he would nevertheless be entitled to his salary. A could, of

194

course, sue B for damages for breach of contract, and if sued by B for his salary, A could counterclaim for damages.

If C contracts with B to build an additional bedroom on D's house for $5,000, the contract might provide for payments to be made by D as the work progresses: $500 upon execution of the contract, $1,000 upon completion of the rough carpentry, $1,000 when the electrical wiring is done, $1,000 upon completion of the plumbing, and $1,500 when the room is completed. If C abandoned the work after completing the rough carpentry, he would not be able to recover for that portion of the work. The breach would be one of the entire contract, and no recovery would be allowed for the partial performance.

EXCUSES FOR NONPERFORMANCE

Introduction   A party to a contract may be relieved from the duty to perform or his liability for breach may be eliminated if he is legally excused from performance of the contract. The usual legal excuses are (1) waiver, (2) prevention of performance, (3) impossibility of performance, and (4) frustration.

Basically a waiver is conduct that shows that a party does not intend to enforce certain provisions of a contract. It is a voluntary relinquishment of a known right. Thus, if a building contract provides for completion on a certain date and the owner grants an extension of six months, he has waived his right to insist upon completion at the earlier date. Waiver occurs when a person who has a right to some performance under a contract surrenders that right. Thus the continued acceptance of late payments over a period of time may constitute a waiver of the right to insist on payment at the right time. This waiver may be withdrawn by notice to the other party, providing the other party is given a reasonable time to perform the condition that was waived.

Many contracts provide that any changes or amendments to the contract must be in writing. However, the parties may waive this provision by words, acts, or conduct.

The prevention of performance by one party to a contract will excuse the nonperformance by the other party. It is obvious that a person may not recover for nonperformance of a contract if he is responsible for the nonperformance. If a party creates a situation that makes it impossible for the other party to perform, the other party is excused. It is an implied condition of every contract that neither party will prevent performance by the other. To illustrate: A had leased a building to B for the operation of an ice cream store. The rent was to be a percentage of the gross income. Thereafter B established another ice cream store a block away and did very little business in the building rented to him by A. B has prevented the normal performance of the contract by carrying on another business that detracted from the profits. A may cancel the lease without liability because B has prevented the performance of the contract.

Impossibility of Performance Actual impossibility of performance is a valid excuse for breach of contract and releases a party from his duty to perform. *Impossibility* is to be distinguished from *additional hardship*. The parties may provide in their contract that the occurrence of additional hardships would excuse performance, but unless they do so additional hardships do not constitute an excuse for breach of contract.

Case: P, a general contractor, had a subcontract with D roofing company. There was a delay in construction because of a labor dispute, and D roofing company claimed that because of the delay it was relieved of its duties to perform.

Issue: Does a labor dispute in a construction project excuse performance by a subcontractor?

Decision: No.

Reason: Labor disputes are foreseeable events, and their occurrence does not excuse a party from his duty to perform. There would be a hardship upon D because of the labor dispute, but this could have been provided for in the contract.

Luria Engineering Company v. Aetna Casualty and Surety Co., 192 N.E.2d 145 (Ill.) 1963.

Many contracts provide that manufacturers, suppliers, or builders shall be relieved from performance in case of fire, strikes, difficulty in obtaining raw materials, or other incidents over which they have no control. Assume that A contracts to sell and deliver five hundred bales of cotton from a certain plantation, delivery from other sources not being contemplated by the contract terms. A actually raises only two hundred bales of cotton and seeks to be relieved from his duty to deliver the balance. Naturally if his inability to deliver has developed because he failed to plant a sufficient acreage or was careless in his planting, cultivation, or harvesting of the crop, A would not be relieved. However, if he planted enough to have produced eight hundred bales under normal conditions, but the weather or other factors were such as to decrease the yield materially below that normally grown, failure to perform would be excused because of the contract provision. Many agricultural states have achieved the same result by statute. Contract clauses and statutes that create an excuse under such circumstances are called "force majeure" clauses.

There are four basic situations in which impossibility of performance is frequently offered as an excuse for nonperformance: (1) performance becomes illegal when a law is passed making such contracts illegal; (2) the death or incapacitating illness of a contracting party when his personal service is required; (3) the destruction of the source from which he has agreed to make delivery; and (4) when an essential element to performance is lacking and both parties had assumed that it did exist. To illustrate number 4: A contracts to build an office building at a certain location. Because of the nature of the soil, it is utterly impossible to build the type of building provided for in the agreement; the agreement must therefore be terminated. The missing element is the proper condition of the soil. In other words, from the very beginning the contract terms could not possibly have been complied with, and in such cases the courts have seen fit to release the contracting party.

If an impossibility of performance becomes apparent only after the agreement has been partly performed, the courts generally allow recovery for the part performance. For example, one coat of paint is applied upon a house, and then the house is destroyed by fire. It is impossible to apply the second coat, and the painter will be allowed to recover for the value of the coat that he did apply.

Frustration   *Frustration* relates to a situation in which actual impossibility is not present, but something happens that prevents the achievement of the object or purpose of the contract. In such cases the courts may find an implied condition that certain developments will excuse performance.

Frustration has the effect of excusing nonperformance and arises whenever there is an intervening event or change of circumstances that is so fundamental as to be entirely beyond that which was contemplated by the parties. Frustration is not impossibility, but it is more than mere hardship. It is an excuse created by law to eliminate liability when a fortuitous occurrence has defeated the reasonable expectations of the parties. It will not be used when the supervening event was foreseeable or assumed as a part of the agreement.

Case: P, a contractor, agreed with D, a city, to construct a golf course for $230,329.88. After P had completed all of the clearing and dirt work, a torrential rainfall of 12.47 inches occurred in a ten-hour period. It will cost $60,000 to restore the golf course to its condition prior to the rain. P seeks to be relieved from the contract. The contract contained provisions that implied that the contractor was to assume all risks relative to ground conditions and the weather.

Issue: Is the contractor relieved of liability by the doctrine of commercial frustration?

Decision: No.

Reasons: 1. The commercial frustration doctrine is set forth in Restatement of Contracts §288 (1932), as follows:

> Where the assumed possibility of a desired object or effect to be attained by either party to a contract forms the basis on which both parties enter into it, and this object or effect is or surely will be frustrated, a promisor who is without fault in causing the frustration, and who is harmed thereby, is discharged from the duty of performing his promise unless a contrary intention appears.

2. A partial frustration by subsequent events is less likely to be held to discharge a contractor from a duty than is total frustration.

3. Thus it follows that P is not entitled to relief under the commercial frustration doctrine because the contract expressed a contrary intent and the doctrine is not applicable in the event of only a partial frustration that only increases the cost of performance.

Pete Smith Co., Inc. v. City of El Dorado, 529 S.W.2d 147 (Ark.) 1975.

OTHER METHODS OF DISCHARGE

Introduction A common method of discharge is mutual cancellation. It is always possible for the parties to an agreement to mutually rescind a contract. As long as the contract is executory on both sides, the parties are free to agree that the contract is terminated. However, if there has been part performance by one of the parties, the agreement to discharge is not enforceable unless it is supported by consideration.

In some situations a contract may be discharged if the written evidence of the agreement is canceled. This would be the case when the obligation is evidenced by a negotiable instrument, such as a promissory note, when the surrender of the note to the person who made it or its cancellation by the holder works a discharge. Any material alteration of the contract by one party without the consent of the other bars a suit on the contract against the nonconsenting party. A discharge in bankruptcy (Chapter 29) will relieve a debtor of his obligation to pay his creditors. The legal doctrine of novation previously discussed in Chapter 12 provides for the substitution of one obligor for another, and therefore the discharge of the one who is replaced. The legal concept of accord and satisfaction discussed in Chapter 8 allows discharge of a contract by performance different from that agreed upon in the contract. The sections that follow discuss some additional methods of discharge.

198

Payment   The obligation of one party to a contract will be to pay the other party for goods sold, services rendered, and the like. There are three questions about payment that affect the matter of discharge: What constitutes payment? What is good evidence that payment has been made and that the obligation has been discharged? When a debtor has several obligations to a creditor, how will a payment be applied?

Certainly the transfer of money constitutes payment, but this is not necessarily the case when the payment is by a negotiable instrument, such as a check or a promissory note. Generally, payment by check or note is a conditional payment and not an absolute discharge of the obligation. If the instrument is paid, the debt is discharged; if it is not so paid, the debt then continues to exist as it did prior to the conditional payment. In the latter situation the creditor can either bring an action to recover on the defaulted instrument or pursue his rights under the original agreement.

A receipt given by the creditor will usually suffice as acceptable evidence of payment and discharge. Such receipt should clearly indicate the amount paid and specify the transaction to which it relates. A canceled check is good evidence of payment, but this evidence is more conclusive when the purpose for which it is given is stated on the check. The drawer of the check may specify on the instrument that the payee by endorsing or cashing it acknowledges full satisfaction of an obligation of the drawer.

Where a debtor owes several obligations to one creditor or has a running account with him that consists of several items, he may specify how any payment is to be applied. The creditor who receives such payment is obligated to follow the debtor's instructions. In the absence of any instructions the creditor may apply the claim against any one of several obligations that are due, or he may credit a portion of the payment against each of the several obligations. Thus the creditor may apply payment against a claim that has been outlawed by the statute of limitations. If the creditor fails to make a particular application prior to the time the issue is raised, the payment will be applied against the debtor's obligations in the order of their maturity. In other words, the oldest in point of time will be credited first.

Mutual debts do not automatically extinguish each other. In order for one debt to constitute payment of another, in whole or in part, there must be an agreement between the creditor and the debtor that the one shall be applied in satisfaction of the other.

Statutes of Limitation   The statutes of limitation prescribe a time limit within which suits must be started after causes of action arise. There are a variety of statutes of limitation in all states, including a special provision under the Code. For example, in some states there is a six-year period for contracts and a two-year period for tort claims.

The purpose of a statute of limitations is to prevent actions from being brought long after the evidence is lost or important witnesses have left or died. A suit for breach of contract must be brought within the prescribed period after the obligation matures or after the cause of action arises. A tort suit must be brought within the prescribed time after the injury.

A voluntary part payment made on a money obligation *tolls* the statute, starting it to run anew. Thus if A owes a debt to B that became due and payable on June 1, 1978 (and assuming a six-year statute of limitations), the claim would be outlawed on June 1, 1984. However, if A made a payment on account on May 1, 1979, the six-year period would commence to run over again, and the claim would then not be outlawed until May 1, 1985.

CHANGES UNDER THE UNIFORM COMMERCIAL CODE

Tender   The Code article that deals with the sale of goods has two provisions relating to tender. Unless the buyer and the seller have otherwise agreed, *tender of payment* by the buyer is a condition to the seller's duty to deliver the goods sold. (2-511(1)) Unless the seller demands payment in legal tender, the buyer is authorized to make payment by check. (2-511(2)) The Code also provides for the manner of a seller's tender of delivery of the goods involved in the contract. The Code requires that the seller make the goods available to the buyer and that he give the buyer reasonable notification that the goods are available for him. (2-503(1)) If the seller gives notice that the goods are available for the buyer and the buyer does not proffer payment, then of course the buyer would be placed in default. *Tender of delivery* is a condition to the buyer's duty to accept the goods. (2-507(1))

Anticipatory   The Code has a special provision relating to anticipatory
Repudiation   repudiation. (2-610) If the seller announces in advance that he will not live up to the contract for the sale of goods, the buyer may "cover" by making other arrangements to purchase the goods that he needs in substitution for those due from the seller. The buyer may recover from the seller as damages the difference between what it cost him to "cover" and the contract price, together with any other damages that he has suffered because of the seller's breach. (2-711(1)) This Code provision makes it possible for a disappointed buyer to make other arrangements to obtain goods and at the same time to recover his damages from the seller.

With regard to waiver, the Code provides that if a buyer retains defective goods without notifying the seller of his objections to the goods, he will have waived his objections based upon these defects. (2-607(3))

Impracticability   The Code makes provision for several situations in which the promised performance in connection with the sale of goods becomes *impracticable*. It is important to note that there is a difference between "impossibility" and "impracticability." The latter may be compared with frustration. The Code provides for relief to a seller who has been unable to deliver the goods under the contract because his inability to perform as agreed has been made impracticable by the happening of the contingency, which the parties had assumed would not occur. (2-615) Thus relief afforded because of impracticability is based upon the fact that the parties to the contract had assumed that if such a contingency occurred, they would be relieved of their duties under the contract.

The Statute of Limitations   For breach of any contract for the sale of personal property, an action must be commenced within four years. The Code also provides that the parties in their agreement may reduce the period of limitation to not less than one year. (2-725(1)) They may not increase the period—four years is the maximum.

A question arises as to when a cause of action accrues so that the statute of limitations commences to run. The Code provides that it accrues when the breach occurs whether or not the party was at the time aware that a breach had occurred. (2-725(2)) Thus it is quite possible that the time may have commenced to run without a party's knowledge.

A breach of warranty occurs when the seller tenders delivery to the buyer—the statute commences to run at that point. However, "where a warranty explicitly extends to future performance of the goods and discovery of the breach must await the time of such performance the cause of action accrues when the breach is or should have been discovered." (2-725(2))

Case: P sued the manufacturer, distributor, and installer of a gas furnace for personal injuries caused by the explosion of the furnace. The furnace was manufactured in 1967 and was installed on February 9, 1968. The injuries were sustained on May 1, 1971, and suit was filed on July 28, 1971. The defendants assented the statute of limitations as a defense. P's suit was predicated upon various theories of product liability.

Issue: Is the statute of limitations a defense?

Decision: No.

Reasons: 1.   Except in topsy-turvy land, you can't die before you are conceived, or be divorced before ever you marry, or harvest a crop never planted, or burn down a house never built, or miss a train running on a nonexistent

201

railroad. For substantially similar reasons, it has always heretofore been accepted, as a sort of legal "axiom," that a statute of limitations does not begin to run against a cause of action before that cause of action exists, i.e., before a judicial remedy is available to the plaintiff.

2. In a cause of action for personal injuries due to a defective product, the statute of limitations begins to run when the injury occurs, not when the product is purchased.

McCroskey v. Bryant Air Conditioning Company, 524 S.W.2d 487 (Tenn.) 1975.

REVIEW QUESTIONS AND PROBLEMS

1. Define *condition precedent, condition subsequent,* and *concurrent conditions.*

2. A contracted to install carpeting in an apartment building being constructed by B. On July 1, the date when A was to have installed the carpeting, B called and informed him that the contract was terminated because A had not performed on time. B then contracted with C to do the work, but C was not able to start work until September because the construction of the apartment had not yet proceeded to the point at which carpeting could be installed. A sued B for breach of contract. Should A prevail? Why?

3. A, a clothing manufacturer, entered into a contract to sell ladies' coats to B, a retailer. The contract called for shipment on August 15. A did not ship the goods until September 28, and they did not arrive until October 12. Upon arrival, B refused to accept or pay for them. A sued for the purchase price. What result? Why?

4. A, a furniture manufacturer, ordered 1,000 drawer bottoms from B. They were manufactured in accordance with the specifications of A. A refused to accept the bottoms on the ground that his furniture factory had in the meantime burned to the ground. B brought action on the contract. Should he succeed? Explain.

5. The CDE company installed and leased to E at his restaurant a burglar-alarm system for five years at a certain rental. CDE was to maintain and repair the system as needed. The state condemned E's property for public use under an urban renewal program. CDE sued for rental falling due thereafter, and E claimed impossibility as a defense. What result? Why?

6. Does payment by check discharge an obligation? Explain.

7. A sold property to B on a contract. The price was $30,000, and B made a down payment of $1,000. B was unable to pay the balance of $29,000, and A brought suit. B contended that he should be discharged because his business had declined, and he did not have nor could he borrow the money. Is this a good defense? Explain.

8. A made a number of purchases from B. A made a payment on account to B, and the question arose as to how B should apply this payment to the various accounts. How should this question be resolved? Explain.

9. Doctor A operated on B for a gall bladder in 1970. In 1978 an X ray revealed that surgical clamps had been left in B's body during the operation. Does the statute of limitations prevent B from bringing an action against the doctor? Why?

10. The XYZ furniture company, as specified in its contract with A, brought a new couch to A's home. A, due to the installation of new carpeting, told the employees of XYZ to return the couch to XYZ's warehouse. The next day, XYZ sold the couch to another customer. Is XYZ liable to A for breach of contract? Why?

11. A borrowed a sum of money from B. According to the contract, A agreed to pay B $50 per month on the first day of each month until the debt was paid. A made the first ten payments on the tenth day of the month, and B never complained. However, soon after A sent the next payment on the tenth, B instituted an action for breach of contract. Does A have a defense? Explain.

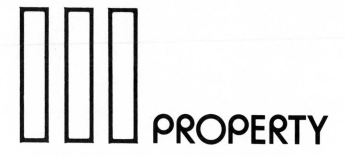

PROPERTY

14 PERSONAL PROPERTY

Introduction   The term *property* is meaningless unless it is associated with people. Some of the terms frequently used in expressing this association are *ownership*, *title*, and *possession*. The word *owner* usually describes someone who possesses all of the rights or interests associated with the thing involved. The word *title* is often used synonymously with *ownership*. Title is also used to signify the method by which ownership is acquired, as by a transfer of title. It may also be used to indicate the evidence by which ownership is established—a written instrument called a title, as for example, a car title. Thus the word *title* has a variety of meanings, depending upon the context in which it is used.

The word *possession* is equally difficult to define accurately. Its meaning is also dependent somewhat on the context in which it is used. Possession implies the concept of physical control by a person over property. While it is physically possible to possess a watch or a ring, it is obviously physically impossible to possess one thousand acres of land in the same manner. Yet the word *possession* as a legal term is used in both instances. Possession describes not only physical control but the power to obtain physical control by legal sanctions, if necessary.

In the early law, property was thought of as a thing that could be touched, possessed, and delivered. As the law of property developed, courts began to recognize that property was more accurately described as the "bundle of rights" a person had in respect to a thing. Today, property is thought of as an object or a thing over which someone exercises legal rights.

Defining property as a "bundle of rights" enables courts and the law to develop a variety of interests in property. A person may possess all of the bundle of rights in relation to a thing, in which case he is the

207

only owner. On the other hand, the bundle of rights may be divided among several people, in which case there is incomplete ownership by any one person. For example, assume that the owner of a tract of land authorizes the local public utility companies to install power and telephone lines through his land. The utility companies are granted what is called an *easement*, which is a property right. As a result, the owner has less than the full bundle of rights and the title is subject to an *encumbrance*.

One other fact of life must be recognized when studying the law of property. There can be no property rights without a government and a legal system to create and enforce them. Private property rights cannot exist without some method of keeping the bundle of rights for the true owner and for restoring these rights to him when deprived of them. It should also be recognized that no one person has a complete bundle of rights, since the law limits private property rights and the use of private property to some extent in the public interest. The owner of land may not use it in violation of the local zoning ordinance. The owner of an automobile may not use it contrary to the law without penalty. Much of our legal system is designed to provide a means of creating, transferring, and limiting the bundle of rights that individuals possess in relation to land, movable objects, or things or intangibles—which we collectively call property.

Classifications   From the standpoint of its physical characteristics, property is classified as either personal property or real property. Land and things affixed to or growing upon the land come under the heading of *real property*. All other property is said to be *personal property*. In many ways, personal property is subject to different treatment under the law than is real property.

Personal property may be classified as either tangible or intangible. The term *tangible personal property* includes objects such as goods. The term *intangible personal property* refers to such things as accounts receivable, goodwill, patents, and trademarks. Intangible personal property has value just as has tangible property, and each can be transferred.

The term *chattel* is used to describe personal property generally. Chattels may also be classified as *chattels real* and *chattels personal*. Chattels real describes an interest in land, such as a leasehold. Chattels personal is applied to movable personal property.

When the term *chattel* is used in connection with intangible personal property, such property is referred to as *chattels personal in action*. A chattel personal in action, or *chose in action* as it is frequently called, is used to describe some thing to which one has a right to possession, but concerning which he may be required to bring some legal action in order ultimately to enjoy possession. For example, a contract right may be said to be a chose in action because a lawsuit may be necessary to obtain the rights under the contract. A negotiable instrument is a common form of chose in action. Although the instrument itself may be said to be property, in reality it is simply evidence of a right to money, and it may be necessary to maintain an action to reduce the money to possession.

The Distinction Between Real and Personal Property

The distinction between real and personal property is of special significance in three situations: (1) in determining the substantive law applicable to a transaction; (2) in matters of inheritance; and (3) in the methods that may be used to transfer the property. The first situation refers to the principles and problems of conflict of laws that arise in connection with various types of property. Conflicts of law problems arise when a legal issue has contact with more than one state.

As a general rule, conflict of laws principles provide the law of the situs—the law of the state where real property is located—determines all legal questions concerning real property. Legal issues concerning conflict of laws relating to personal property are not so easily resolved. Conflict of laws rules may refer to the law of the owner's domicile to resolve some questions and to the law of the state with the most significant contacts with the property to resolve others. The law of the situs of the property is also used to resolve some legal issues. Therefore the description of property as real or personal has a significant impact on the determination of the body of substantive law that is used to decide legal issues concerning the property.

The second situation in which the distinction is important is in matters of inheritance. If a person dies leaving a will, he is said to die testate. His personal property passes to the executor named in the will, to be distributed in accordance with the terms of the will, and his real property passes to the devisees named in the will.

When a person dies without leaving a will, he is said to die intestate, and his property passes in conformity with the laws of "intestate succession." The laws of intestate succession frequently have different provisions for real estate than for personal property. For example, assume that D died leaving W, his widow, and C, a child, as his only heirs at law. A typical intestate statute might provide that the widow is entitled to all personal property but to only one-half the real property of the deceased. In such cases the importance of the distinction between real and personal property is obvious.

The distinction between real and personal property is also significant during the lifetime of the owner in determining the methods by which the property can be transferred. The methods of transferring personal property and real property are substantially different. Formal instruments such as deeds are required to transfer an interest in land, whereas few formalities are required in the case of personal property. A bill of sale may be used in selling personal property, but it is not generally required and does not in any event involve the technicalities of a deed. For example, a motor vehicle transfer may require the delivery of a certificate of title, but, as mentioned above, the transfer of personal property is as a rule quite simply accomplished, whereas formality is required to transfer real property.

METHODS OF ACQUIRING TITLE TO PERSONAL PROPERTY

Introduction Title to personal property may be acquired through any of the following methods: *original possession, transfer, accession,* or *confusion.* Original possession is a method of extremely limited applicability. It may be used to obtain title over things such as wild animals and fish, that are available for appropriation by individuals. Property that is in its native state and over which no one as yet has taken full and complete control belongs to the first person who reduces such property to his exclusive possession. Property once reduced to ownership, but later abandoned, belongs to the first party next taking possession.

In addition to the above, it might be said that property created through mental or physical labor belongs to the creator unless he has agreed to create it for someone else, being induced to do so because of some compensation that has been agreed to by the interested parties. Such items as books, inventions, and trademarks might be included under this heading. This kind of property is usually protected by the government through means of copyrights, patents, and trademarks.

Title by Transfer Personal property may be transferred by sale, gift, will, or operation of law. The law relating to transfer by sale will be discussed in connection with the Uniform Commercial Code in Chapter 19. Transfers by operation of law include such transfers as judicial sales, mortgage foreclosures, and intestate succession.

As a general rule, a transferee receives the rights of the transferor, and a transferee takes no better title than the transferor had. If the transferor of the personal property did not have title to the property, the transferee would not have title either. This is true even though the transferee believes that his transferor has a good title. For example, an innocent purchaser from a thief obtains no title to the property purchased, and no subsequent purchaser stands in any better position. Because the thief had no title or ownership, persons who acquired the property from or through the thief have no title or ownership. However, if the transferor of the property has a voidable title and he sells property to an innocent purchaser, the transferee may obtain good title to the property. For example, assume that X acquires the title to property from Y through fraudulent representations. Y could avoid the transaction with X and obtain a return of his property. However, if X sells the property to Z and Z does not know about X's fraudulent representations, Y cannot disaffirm against Z and Z has good title to the property. This concept of voidable title will be discussed further in Chapter 19, "Sales."

**Title
by Gift** There are three elements of a valid gift—intention to make the gift, delivery, and acceptance of the gift. From a legal standpoint, the element of delivery is the most significant because the law requires an actual physical change in possession of the property, with the owner's consent. However, all elements of a valid gift must be established in the event of a dispute over the ownership of property.

Case: Securities that a mother had purchased with her own funds were registered in the names of the mother and her daughter as joint tenants with the right of survivorship. The purpose of the arrangement was to ensure that the property would go to the daughter upon the mother's death without probate proceedings. The mother had custody of the stock certificates. The daughter sought to claim half the dividends on the stock and sued her mother for them.

Issue: Was there a completed gift of the certificates?

Decision: No.

Reasons: 1. There was a valid delivery. In the case of stock certificates a legal delivery for purposes of making a gift takes place when stock certificates are registered in the name of the donor and the donee as joint tenants.

2. There was no intention to make a present gift. The mother had no intent to give daughter any interest in securities during mother's lifetime but only on death. The daughter, therefore, had no right or interest in the securities.

Kinney v. Ewing, 492 P.2d 636 (N.M.) 1972.

A promise to make a gift is ordinarily not enforceable because no consideration is present to support the promise. However, an executed gift—one accomplished by delivery of the property to the donee—cannot be rescinded except in the case of a gift *causa mortis*—one in contemplation of death. The delivery of the gift can be either actual, constructive, or symbolic, as the situation may demand. Thus, if the property is in storage, the donor could make delivery by giving the donee the warehouse receipt. A donor may also accomplish delivery by giving the donee something that is a token representing the latter's right to the property. For example, delivery of a key to a lockbox given to a person with words indicating an intent to make a gift of the contents may constitute the symbolic delivery of the gift.

It was previously noted that gifts *causa mortis* constitute an exception to the general rule on the finality of completed gifts. A gift *causa mortis* is one in which a person who is, or who believes that he is, facing death makes a gift on the assumption that he is about to die. A person about to embark on a perilous trip or to undergo a serious operation or one who has an apparently incurable and fatal illness might make a gift and deliver the item to the donee on the assumption that he is not long for this world. If he returns safely, the operation is successful, or the illness is miraculously cured, the donor is allowed to revoke the gift and recover the property from the donee.

Accession   *Accession* literally means "adding to." In the law of personal property, accession has two basic meanings. First of all, it refers to the right of an owner to all that his property produces. For example, the owner of a cow is also the owner of each calf born, and the owner of lumber is the owner of a table made from the lumber by another. *Accession* is also the legal term used to signify the acquisition of title to personal property when it is incorporated into other property or joined with other property.

When accession occurs, the issue of who has title is frequently in issue. The general rule is that when the goods of two different owners are united together without the willful misconduct of either party, the title to the resulting product goes to the owner of the major portion of the goods. This rule is based on the principle that personal property permanently added to other property and forming a minor portion of the finished product becomes part of the larger unit. Since title can be in only one party, it is in the owner of the major portion. The owner of the minor portion may recover damages, if his portion were wrongfully taken from him. The law of accession simply prevents the owner of the minor portion from recovering the property itself.

To illustrate the foregoing, assume that X owns some raw materials, and that Y inadvertently uses these materials to manufacture a product. The product belongs to X. If Y also adds some raw materials of his own, the manufactured product belongs to the party who contributed the major portion of the materials. If Y becomes the owner, X is entitled to recover his damages. If X is the owner, Y is not entitled to anything, since he used X's materials.

A similar issue arises when one party repairs goods of another without authority. In such a case the owner is entitled to the goods as repaired irrespective of the value of the repair, unless the repairs can be severed without damaging the original goods.

The law of accession distinguishes between the rights of "innocent" and "willful" trespassers, although both are wrongful. An innocent trespasser to personal property is one who acts through mistake or conduct, less than intentionally wrongful. A willful trespasser cannot obtain title, as against the original owner, under any circumstances.

If the property that is the subject of accession is sold to a good-faith purchaser, the rights and liabilities of the original owner and the third party are the same as those of the original trespasser. A willful trespasser has no title and can convey none. The owner can recover the property without any liability to the third party. If the third party makes improvements or repairs, he has the right to remove his additions if they can be removed without damaging the original goods. An innocent trespasser can convey this right to remove to a good-faith purchaser.

Case: An automobile owned by P was stolen. The thief, T, put in a new motor. T then sold it to a used-car dealer, who sold it to D. D added a sun visor, seat covers, and a gasoline tank.

Issue: May P reclaim the automobile and may P keep the items added?

Decision: P may obtain the automobile, including the motor added by the thief. P may not keep the other items added by D.

Reasons: 1. The owner of stolen personal property is not divested of ownership by the theft. He may reclaim from any purchaser, including a good-faith purchaser. The value added by the thief belongs to the owner.

2. Because D was not a willful wrongdoer, the items D placed on the car belong to him if they can be removed without damage to the car.

Farm Bureau Mut. Automobile Ins. Co. v. Moseley, 90 A.2d 485 (Ill.) 1950.

Confusion Property of such a character that one unit may not be distinguished from another unit and that is usually sold by weight or measure is known as *fungible property*. Grain, hay, logs, wine, oil, and other similar articles afford illustrations of property of this nature. Such property, belonging to various parties, often is mixed by intention of the parties, and occasionally by accident, by unintentional mistake, or by the wrongful misconduct of an owner of some of the goods. Confusion of fungible property belonging to various owners, assuming that no misconduct (confusion by consent, accident, or unintentional mistake) is involved, results in an undivided ownership of the total mass. To illustrate: Grain is stored in a public warehouse by many parties. Each owner holds an undivided interest in the total mass, his particular interest being dependent upon the amount stored by him. Should there be a partial destruction of the total mass, the loss would be divided proportionately.

Confusion of goods that results from the wrongful conduct of one of the parties causes the title to the total mass to pass to the innocent party. If the mixture is divisible, an exception exists, and the wrongdoer, if he is able to show that the resultant mass is equal in value per unit to that of the innocent party, is able to recover his share. Where the new mixture is worth no less per unit than that formerly belonging to the innocent party, the wrongdoer may claim his portion of the new mass by presenting convincing evidence of the amount added by him. If two masses are added together and the wrongdoer can only establish his proportion of one mass, he is only entitled to that proportion of the combined mass.

Case: P owned a three-fourths working interest in an oil and gas lease. He brought this action against D, the owner of the other one-fourth interest, because D had not paid his share of the operating expenses. P owned another lease and had commingled the oil of the two leases. P could not prove the actual source of any of the oil.

Issue: Is D entitled to one-fourth of the oil from his lease or one-fourth of all the commingled oil?

Decision: One-fourth of all oil.

Reason: When commingling of personalty is proven, the party who commingled has the burden of going forward to show the correct proportions. If he does not do so, he bears the loss caused by the confusion.

Troop v. St. Louis Union Trust Co., 166 N.E.2d 116 (Ill.) 1960.

Abandoned and Lost Property Property is said to be abandoned whenever it is discarded by the true owner, who, at that time, has no intention of reclaiming it. Such property belongs to the first individual again reducing it to possession.

Case: P purchased feed mill equipment from D and left the equipment in a metal warehouse building owned by D. From time to time, over a period of years, P removed some of the equipment and then, after a considerable lapse of time, went to the warehouse to pick up the balance. D refused to allow P to take the equipment, and P brought an action in replevin.

Issue: Had P abandoned the equipment?

Decision: Yes.

Reasons: 1. Abandoned property is that to which the owner has voluntarily relinquished all right, title, claim, and possession with the intention of terminating ownership and never reclaiming it.

2. Actual relinquishment accompanied by intent to abandon must be shown. Actual intent to abandon is required, and it is not enough that the owner's act gives others reason to believe that the property has been abandoned.

3. All facts must be considered. Nonuse and lapse of time are facts to be considered.

4. Considering all of the evidence, the court found the intent to abandon had been proven.

Botkin v. Kickapoo, Inc., 505 P.2d 749 (Kan.) 1973.

Property is lost whenever, as a result of negligence, accident, or some other cause, it is found at some place other than that chosen by the owner. Title to lost property continues to rest with the true owner. Until the true owner has been ascertained the finder may keep it, and his title is good as against everyone except the true owner. The rights of the finder are superior to those of the person in charge of the property upon which the lost article is found. Occasionally state statutes provide for newspaper publicity concerning articles that have been found. Under these statutes if the owner cannot be located, the found property reverts to the state or county if its value exceeds an established minimum.

Mislaid or misplaced property is such as is intentionally placed by the owner at a certain spot in such a manner as to indicate that he merely forgot to pick it up. In such a case the presumption is that he will later remember where he left it and return for it. The owner of the premises upon which it is found is entitled to hold such property until the true owner is located. The finder of such property must turn it over to the owner of the premises.

Multiple Ownership   There are three distinct methods by which two or more people may own personal property at the same time: (1) *tenancy in common*, (2) *joint tenancy*, and (3) *community property*. Community property as a method of common ownership is limited to only a few states. Several states have modified the common law

215

characteristics of these forms of ownership, so it is essential that each state law be consulted for the technicalities of these tenancies.

The main distinction between a tenancy in common and a joint tenancy is the effect of death on the tenancy. In the event of the death of a tenant in common, his or her share in the property passes to the executor named in the will or to the administrator of the deceased's estate. If property is held in joint tenancy, the interest of a deceased owner automatically passes to the surviving joint owner. Such property is not subject to probate or to the debts of the deceased joint tenant. Thus joint tenancy with the right of survivorship passes the title of the deceased by operation of law to the survivor or survivors free of the claims of anyone else except for taxes that may be due.

Both joint tenancy and tenancy in common ownership may include two or more persons who may or may not be related. In tenancy in common, the share of the tenants may differ. For example, A may own an undivided two-thirds and B an undivided one-third. In joint tenancy, the interests must not only be equal but they must be created at the same time.

In some states, property acquired after the marriage of either spouse is community property. While there are slight deviations in the approach to community property, such laws usually provide that the husband shall have the management and control of community personal property just as if he were the sole owner. However, he may not transfer more than one-half of it by will, and the other half automatically passes to the surviving spouse on death. The community property laws often provide additional limitations on the disposition of community property real estate. The usual requirement is that the wife must join in any conveyance of real estate, but not personal property.

Case: D, a real estate developer, sold several tracts of land on contract, retaining legal title to the land. D made an arrangement with P whereby D agreed to transfer the real estate contracts to P. Later the plan was changed and P executed. a quitclaim deed to D covering all the land covered by the contracts. P's wife did not join in the deed, and his wife then sought to rescind the quitclaim deed to D on the ground that it violated the community property law in the State of Washington. The determination turned upon the question of whether a vendor's interest in real estate contracts is real or personal property.

Issue: Was it necessary under the community property law of Washington for the wife to join in the transfer?

Decision: No. (Affirmed in favor of defendant.)

Reasons: 1. The right to receive payments under a real estate contract is a chose in action and personal property.

2. The conveyance by the husband of the vendor's interest in the real estate contracts was a transfer of personal property, and the joinder of the wife was not required.

Meltzer v. Wendell-West, 497 P.2d 1348 (Wash.App.) 1972.

Special Aspects of Joint Tenancy   When there is a question as to which form of ownership actually exists in any specific case, the law usually favors property passing by will or intestacy to it passing by right of survivorship. Courts do not find that property is held in joint tenancy with the right of survivorship unless there is a contract between the two co-owners clearly stating that such is the case and that the right of survivorship is to apply. Bank signature cards and stock certificates that use the term *joint tenancy* or "with the right of survivorship" create such a contract, as does the language "as joint tenants and not as tenants in common." In most states the contract must be signed by both parties to be effective. Failure to use the proper language or have a properly executed contract results in a tenancy in common.

Case: The deceased purchased a certificate of deposit from a bank which provided that the ownership was in the deceased and his nephew. The nephew did not know of the joint ownership of the certificate until after his uncle died, and he admitted that he had not signed any signature card. The bank paid the proceeds of the certificate to the nephew, and the executor of the deceased's estate sought to recover the funds.

Issue: Need a signature card be signed by all of the parties in order to create a joint tenancy in a bank certificate of deposit?

Decision: Yes.

Reason: Under the statute a signed agreement is necessary to create rights of survivorship in the deposit.

In re estate of White, 282 N.E.2d 235 (III.) 1972.

Several additional aspects of holding property in joint tenancy frequently result in litigation. First of all, joint tenancy is often used as a substitute for a will. A party wanting to leave property to another on death sometimes puts the property in joint tenancy. As previously noted in the case of *Kinney* v. *Ewing*, a present gift is often not intended. The new joint tenant does not necessarily have the right to share in the income of the property prior to the death of the original owner.

A similar issue arises when one person who may be in ill health or incapacitated adds another person's name to a savings or a checking account in order to allow the latter to pay bills and handle the former's business transactions. The signature card often provides for a joint tenancy. Was a joint tenancy or mere agency intended? Joint tenancy arrangements are frequently challenged successfully on the ground that the right of survivorship was not intended.

Another difficulty involves describing the property held in joint tenancy. Frequently, a contract covering a safety deposit box will provide that it be held in joint tenancy. Does such a contract cover the contents of the box as well? For example, assume that A and B hold a safety deposit box in joint tenancy. The box contains $20,000 in cash. Most courts would hold that the cash was not held in joint tenancy.

Another disadvantage of the joint tenancy arrangement is the ease with which it may be severed or terminated. Each joint tenant has the power to terminate the right of survivorship by a simple transfer or conveyance of his interest to a third party. The severance converts the joint tenancy to a tenancy in common.

Finally, joint tenancy property creates many gift and estate tax problems. The creation of a joint tenancy is generally a taxable gift.

REVIEW QUESTIONS AND PROBLEMS

1. What is the advantage of describing property as a "bundle of rights"?

2. Is it possible for one person to be the absolute owner of an item of property? Explain.

3. Define the following terms: *chose in action, chattel real, chattel personal, intestate succession, gift causa mortis, accession, confusion of goods*, and *fungible goods.*

4. List three situations in which the distinction between real and personal property is important. Give an example of each.

5. What are the elements of a valid gift?

6. Compare the rights of the finder of lost property with the rights of a finder of abandoned property.

7. Compare *tenancy in common, joint tenancy*, and *community property* insofar as the transfer of the property on the death of the owner is concerned.

8. A stole a bicycle belonging to B and sold it to C. C had no knowledge of the theft. Later, the police located the bicycle in C's possession. Who is entitled to the property? Why?

9. While swimming in a pond on X's farm, several boys discovered some money in a watertight jar on the bottom of the pond. X admits it is not his money. Who has the title to the money? Who has the right to possession? Explain.

10. While building a garage on Y's property, X, a workman, found a wallet containing $1,000 buried under about two inches of dirt. Who has title to the $1,000? Who is entitled to possession? Why?

11. A steamboat, owned by the XYZ company and loaded with lead castings, sank in the Mississippi River in 1927. The XYZ company made no effort to locate the boat. In 1961 A located the boat and raised it. Does the XYZ company have any rights against A? Explain.

12. A intentionally took corn belonging to B and distilled it into whiskey. B had the sheriff seize the whiskey, but A contends that the whiskey belongs to him because of the greater value of the whiskey over the corn. Is A correct? Why?

13. A owns some lumber that he fraudulently mixes with lumber owned by B. The quality of the two piles of lumber was entirely different, but circumstances are such that the amount in each pile can no longer be determined. May B retain title to both amounts? Why?

15 BAILMENTS OF PERSONAL PROPERTY

Introduction   Possession of personal property is often temporarily surrendered by the owner to another person. Often the person to whom the goods are delivered may perform some service pertaining to the goods, such as a repair, after which the goods are returned to the owner. On other occasions a person may borrow or rent an article from its owner. Another example of a temporary transfer of possession occurs when the owner causes the goods to be stored in a warehouse.

An agreement whereby possession of personal property is surrendered by the owner with provision for its return at a later time is known as a *bailment*. The owner of the goods is called the *bailor*. The one receiving possession is called the *bailee*.

There are three distinct requirements for a bailment: (1) retention of title by the bailor; (2) possession and temporary control of the property by the bailee; and (3) ultimate possesson to revert to the bailor or to someone designated by the bailor.

Case: P parked his airplane at D's airport for a fee of $15 per month. P tied and locked the aircraft and kept the keys. The aircraft was damaged in high winds. P sued, contending that D was liable as a bailee for the damage to the plane.

Issue: Was the airport operator a bailee?

Decision: No.

Reasons: 1. A "bailment" is the delivery of personal property by one person to another in trust for a specified purpose. There must be a contract, express or implied, that the trust shall be faithfully executed and the property returned or duly accounted for when the special purpose is accomplished or until the bailor reclaims the property.

2. A bailment does not arise in those situations where the owner of the property retains control over the property.

Simons v. First National Bank of Denver, 491 P.2d 602 (Colo.) 1972.

There have been similar decisions involving automobile parking lots. Where the owner of the automobile keeps the keys and the lot attendant has no control over the automobile, most courts hold that there is no bailment, although the cases are in some conflict.

Types of Bailments   Bailments group naturally into three classes: bailments for the benefit of the bailor; bailments for the benefit of the bailee; and bailments for the mutual benefit of both the bailor and the bailee. Typical of the first group are those cases in which the bailor leaves goods in the safekeeping of the bailee without any provision for paying the bailee for caring for the article. Because the bailee is not to use the goods or to be paid in any manner, the bailment is for the exclusive benefit of the bailor.

A bailment for the benefit of the bailee is best illustrated by a loan of some article by the bailor to the bailee without any compensation to the bailor. For example, assume that A borrows B's automobile for a day. The bailment is one for the sole benefit of A, the bailee.

The most common type of bailment is the one in which both parties are to benefit. Contracts for repair, carriage, storage, or pledge of property fall within this class. The bailor receives the benefit of some service; the bailee benefits by the receipt of certain agreed compensation. Thus both parties benefit as a result of the bailment.

Degree of Care Required by Bailees   Provided that proper care has been exercised by the bailee, any loss or damage to the property bailed falls on the bailor. Each type of bailment requires a different degree of care by the bailee. In a bailment for the benefit of the bailor, the bailee is required to exercise only slight care; in one for the benefit of the bailee, extraordinary care is required. A bailment for the mutual benefit of the parties demands ordinary care on the part of the bailee. *Ordinary care* is defined as that care that the average individual usually exercises over his own property.

Case: P left his car in D's parking garage overnight. As was the custom, the key was left in the ignition. During the night an intoxicated sailor stole the car and wrecked it. D's employee had seen an intoxicated man in the garage earlier in the evening.

221

Issue: Was D negligent?

Decision: Yes.

Reasons: 1. Ordinary care means such care as ordinary prudent men exercise in caring for their own property under like circumstances.

2. The trial court was justified in finding that the lack of surveillance at night fell below the standard of reasonable care. Had there been proper observation, the theft could have been prevented.

Althoff v. System Garages, Incorporated, 371 P.2d 48 (Wash.) 1962.

In addition to the duty to exercise due care, the bailee promises to return the property to the bailor undamaged upon termination of the bailment. This promise can be used to create a prima facie case of negligence. To illustrate, assume that a bailor proves delivery of the bailed property in good condition and the failure of the bailee to return it in the same condition or redelivery in bad condition. This evidence establishes a presumption of negligence and entitles the bailor to recover from the bailee. If there is no other evidence, the bailor will win the suit. However, the bailee may rebut this prima facie case by introducing evidence to establish that there was no negligence on its part. In other words, the bailee has the burden of proving that it has used reasonable care and caution after the prima facie case has been established.

Case: P's automobile had been taken to D for repairs. It had been broken into and stripped by unknown parties while it was parked by the bailee in an open, unfenced, well-lighted lot adjacent to D's building. D proved that it was common for automobile repair businesses to follow these procedures.

Issue: Is the bailee liable for the damage to the automobile?

Decision: Yes.

Reasons: 1. When goods delivered to a bailee in good condition can only be redelivered in a damaged condition, a presumption of negligence on the part of the bailee arises.

2. The bailee then has the burden of proving that he was not negligent.

3. The fact that the bailee of an automobile met operational standards followed by others in the community does not, as a matter of law, establish any lack of negligence by the bailee so as to relieve bailee of liability for damage caused to the vehicle by vandals.

Chabot v. William Chevrolet Company, 491 P.2d 612 (Colo.) 1971.

The amount of care demanded of a bailee varies with the nature and value of the article bailed. The care found to be sufficient in the case of a carpenter's tool chest would probably not be ample for a diamond ring worth $10,000. A higher standard of protection is required for valuable articles than for those less valuable.

Degree of Care Required by Bailors

Property leased by a bailor to a bailee (a mutual benefit bailment) must be reasonably fit for the intended purpose. For this reason, it is the duty of the bailor to notify the bailee of all defects in the property leased, of which the bailor might reasonably have been aware. The bailor is responsible for any damage suffered by the bailee as the result of such defects, unless the notice is given. This rule holds true even though the bailor is not aware of the defect if, by the exercise of reasonable diligence, the defect could have been discovered.

If, on the other hand, an article is merely loaned to a bailee—a bailment for the benefit of the bailee—the bailor's duty is to notify the bailee only of known defects. A bailor who fails to give the required notice of a known defect is liable to any person who might be expected to use the defective article as a result of the bailment. For example, employees of the bailee and members of the bailee's family may recover from the bailor for injuries received as a consequence of known defects.

A bailment occurs when personal property is leased. A lease by a merchant dealing in goods of the type involved is similar to a sale of the goods. As a result, the bailor (lessor) makes the same warranties as a seller of goods, and the provisions of the Code are applicable to such bailments. These provisions are discussed in Chapter 21.

Contract Clauses Affecting Liability

Bailees frequently attempt to disclaim liability for damage to the property that may occur while it is in their possession. Such a clause in a contract is known as an *exculpatory clause*. For example, a laundry may seek to disclaim liability for damage to property delivered to it for cleaning by including a statement to that effect on the claim check or receipt given to the customer. An exculpatory clause disclaiming liability for negligence is illegal if the bailee is a quasi-public institution because such contracts are against public policy. This was discussed in detail in Chapter 10.

More and more bailees are being classified as quasi-public businesses because of the inequality of bargaining power between many bailors and their bailees. Not all exculpatory clauses seek to eliminate liability completely; some seek to limit the amount of damages. Contracts limiting the amount of damages are looked upon more favorably than absolute disclaimers because it is fair for both parties to know the value of the property and the risk present. In accordance with this theory, the Uniform Commercial Code provides that damages may be limited by a term in the warehouse receipt or storage agreement limiting the amount of liability in case of loss or damage to the covered property. However, a warehouseman cannot disclaim the obligation of reasonable care by such agreement.

Carriers also attempt to limit their liability. A carrier may not contract its liability for goods damaged in shipment, but it may limit the liability to a stated amount. A carrier may also, where lower rates are granted, relieve itself from the consequences of causes or of conduct over which it has no control.

Because a carrier may limit liability to an agreed valuation, the shipper is limited in his recovery to the value asserted in the bill of lading. The rate charged for transportation will vary with the value of the property shipped. It is for this reason that the agreed valuation is binding.

Rights and Duties of Bailees The bailment agreement governs the rights and duties of the bailee. If the bailee treats the property in a different manner, or uses it for some purpose other than that contemplated by the bailment contract, the bailee becomes liable for any loss or damage to the property. This is true even though the damage can in no sense be attributed to the conduct of the bailee. To illustrate: Let us assume that A stores a car in B's public garage for the winter. B, because of a crowded condition, has the car temporarily moved to another garage without the consent of A. As the result of a tornado, the car is destroyed while at the second location. The loss falls upon B, as B breached the terms of the bailment contract. In a restricted sense, the bailee is guilty of conversion of the bailor's property during the period in which the contract terms are being violated.

The bailee has no right to deny the title of the bailor unless the bailee has yielded possession to one having a better title than the bailor. The bailee has no right to retain possession of the property merely because he is able to prove that the bailor does not have legal title to the goods. In order to defeat the bailor's right to possession, the bailee must show that the property has been turned over to someone having better title.

COMMON CARRIERS AS BAILEES

Definition The law distinguishes a common, or public, carrier from a private carrier. A *common carrier* performs a public service for all, so that it will be liable if it refuses, without excuse, to carry for all who may request service. A *private carrier* is one who undertakes only by special arrangement to transport property. Private carriers are not bound to serve everyone who may request service. A private carrier may advertise and secure as much business as possible without losing the status of a private carrier.

Common carriers are licensed by public bodies such as the Interstate Commerce Commission or the commerce commissions of the various states. They are licensed to serve a designated territory with specified points of departure and destination. Their rates are uniform and a matter of public record in their tariffs. These tariffs usually contain provisions limiting the liability of the carrier. For example, a typical tariff would limit the liability of the carrier to $50 for the luggage or baggage of its passengers. A passenger wishing to collect more than $50 would be required to pay for the extra value.

A common carrier may specialize; that is, it may restrict itself to carrying a particular type of goods, it may specialize in the means of transportation it employs, or limit its services to a specific area. Common carriers do not undertake to carry by any means, any and all property to any place. The area served by the carrier, the types of goods carried, and the methods employed are all set forth in the certificate of public oonvenience and necessity issued by the appropriate regulatory agency.

Care Required of the Common Carrier The contract for carriage of goods constitutes a mutual benefit bailment, but the care required of the carrier greatly exceeds that of the ordinary bailee. A common carrier is an absolute insurer of the safe delivery of the goods to their destination. Proof of delivery to a carrier of a shipment in good condition and its arrival at the destination in a damaged condition creates a prima facie case against the carrier. This rule is subject to only five exceptions. Any loss or damage that results from (1) an act of God, (2) action of an alien enemy, (3) order of public authority, (4) inherent nature of the goods, or (5) misconduct of the shipper must fall upon the shipper. Thus any loss that results from an accident or the willful misconduct of some third party must be borne by the carrier. For example, A, in order to injure a certain railway company, sets fire to several boxcars loaded with freight. Any damage to the goods falls upon the carrier. On the other hand, if lightning, an act of God, had set fire to the cars, the loss would have fallen upon the shipper. However, the defense of an act of God is narrowly construed to include only events that were not foreseeable.

Case: P arranged to have produce shipped on the D railroad to California. The shipment was delayed, and as a result the produce spoiled. D claimed that it would not be liable because the delay was caused by an act of God—unusually heavy rains and flood conditions. When the goods were accepted for shipment, the railroad was aware of the heavy rains and that some of its bridges had been washed out. The train was delayed while D made arrangements to repair the bridges, and the repairs were accomplished.

Issue: Was the loss the result of an act of God so as to relieve the carrier from liability?

Decision: No.

Reason: A rainstorm of unusual duration or intensity is not necessarily a superhuman cause or an act of God. The rainfall in the instant case was not shown to be totally unforeseeable or of greater intensity than other rainfalls in the region, so as to justify being called an "act of God."

Southern Pacific Company v. Loden, 508 P.2d 347 (Ariz.) 1972.

Any damage to goods in shipment that results from the very nature of the goods, from improper crating, or from failure to protect the property must be suffered by the shipper. Thus if a dog dies because his crate was poorly ventilated, the shipper is unable to recover from the carrier. However, it must be kept in mind that the carrier has the burden of proving that it was free from negligence and that the damage falls within one of the exceptions to the rule establishing the carrier's liability as an insurer of the shipment.

Goods may be damaged while in the possession of either the receiving, a connecting, or the delivering carrier. Damages arising while goods were being transported may be recovered by the shipper or the consignee from the delivering carrier. This result is based on a federal statute which relieves shippers and consignees of the impossible burden of proving which specific carrier along the chain of transportation caused the actual damage to the goods. If the shipper files a claim against the original carrier, it in turn may demand restitution from the connecting carriers.

The burden is on the shipper to prove that the goods were in good condition at the time and place of shipment. As previously noted, proof that the goods were in good condition when delivered to the carrier and that they were damaged when delivered by the carrier creates a prima facie case of liability. However, there is no presumption that the goods were in good condition when delivered to the carrier. Actual proof is required.

A common carrier, while not an insurer of passengers, owes the highest degree of care to them. In other words, a common carrier will be liable to passengers for injuries for even slight negligence, but a carrier of passengers is not liable for every injury. For example, a bus company was held not to be liable for injuries received by passengers when an unknown person threw a rock through the bus window. This high duty is not required except on board the carrier. Carriers, however, must exercise ordinary care to persons on its premises.

Case: P was moving to board a train but was not yet actually boarding it. She was injured when she fell. P sued the railroad.

Issue: What standard of care was required by the carrier?

Decision: Ordinary care.

Reason: P was not a passenger and therefore the railroad owed a duty of ordinary care. The highest degree of care is owed only to passengers.

Katmay v. Chicago Transit Authority, 273 N.E.2d 510 (III.) 1971.

**Duration
of the Relation** The liability of the carrier attaches as soon as the goods are delivered. The receipt of the goods is usually acknowledged by a bill of lading, which sets forth the terms and conditions of shipment. The carrier becomes responsible for a carload shipment as soon as the car has been delivered. If the car is loaded while located upon railroad property, the carrier becomes liable at the moment the car is fully loaded.

The extreme degree of care required of the carrier may be terminated before the goods are actually delivered to the consignee. Three views prevail in this country as to when the relationship of the carrier ceases. Some states hold that the duties of the carrier end and those of a warehouseman begin as soon as the local shipment is unloaded from the car into the freight house. Others hold the carrier to strict liability until the consignee has had a reasonable time in which to inspect and remove the shipment. Still other states hold that the consignee is entitled to notice and that he has a reasonable time after notice in which to remove the goods before the liability of the carrier as a carrier is terminated. To illustrate: Let us assume that goods arrive at their destination and are unloaded in the freight house. Before the consignee has had time to take them away the goods are destroyed by fire, although the carrier has exercised ordinary care. Under the first of these views the loss would fall upon the shipper, as at the time of the fire the railway was no longer a carrier but a warehouseman. Under the other two views the loss would fall on the carrier, as the extreme liability had not yet terminated, inasmuch as no time had been given for delivery.

The carload shipment is deemed to be delivered as soon as it is placed on the private track of the consignee or "spotted" at the unloading platform. Any subsequent loss, unless it results from the negligence of the carrier, must fall upon the owner of the goods.

Rates Rates charged by common carriers must be reasonable. Carriers engaged in interstate business are subject to the regulation of the Interstate Commerce Commission, and all tariffs or rate schedules must be filed with the ICC and approved. Almost all the states have commissions for the purpose of establishing rates for intrastate business. These commissions also require tariffs to be filed with them. Any rate either higher or lower than that shown in the approved tariff is illegal. Discriminatory rates by the use of rebates are also forbidden, and the giving or receiving of rebates constitutes a crime.

A carrier may insist upon the payment of the charges at the time it accepts the delivery. Because it has a lien upon the goods as security for the charges, however, it customarily waits until the goods are delivered before collecting. The carrier usually refuses to surrender the goods unless the freight is paid, and, if the freight remains unpaid for a certain period of time, it may advertise the property for sale. Any surplus, above the charges, realized from the sale reverts to the owner of the goods.

Any undue delay on the part of the consignee in removing the goods from the warehouse or the tracks of the railway permits the carrier to add a small additional charge known as *demurrage.*

Innkeepers' Liability Issues similar to those involved with common carriers frequently arise in suits against hotel and motel operators. At common law, an innkeeper was an insurer of the safety of the goods of its guests. This rule came from the amount of control the innkeepers had over such goods as the result of the retention of keys to each room. Because of the ease of access of its employees to each guest room, the law imposed liability as a matter of public policy. There were exceptions to this general rule, however. As exceptions, the innkeeper was not liable for loss caused by an act of God, a public enemy, an act of public authority, the inherent nature of the property, or the fault of the guest.

Most states have enacted statutes pertaining to hotel or motel operators' liability. These statutes usually provide that if the operator maintains a safe or lockbox for guests to deposit valuable property in, then there is no liability if such property is stolen from the room. Such laws usually cover property of "small compass," which includes money, negotiable instruments, jewelry, and precious stones. These laws further require that notice of the availability of the safe be given with notice of the liability limitation.

Case: P, a guest in D's hotel, sued D for $3,685, the value of an allegedly stolen wristwatch. The state statute eliminated the liability of innkeepers on personal property of small compass if a safe or vault was provided for their safekeeping.

Issue: Is a wristwatch covered by the statute?

Decision: Yes.

Reasons: 1. A statute limiting the liability of a hotelkeeper with respect to guests' valuables is in derogation of the common law and strictly construed.

2. A wristwatch valued at $3,685 is valuable property of small compass and subject to the statute.

3. If a guest fails to deposit a valuable wristwatch, the hotelkeeper is relieved of all liability by statute.

Walls v. Cosmopolitan Hotels, Inc., 534 P.2d 1373 (Wash.App.) 1975.

Some states also have laws that limit the maximum liability of hotel and motel operators to a stated amount, such as $500. Others have changed the liability from that of an insurer to that of a bailee of a mutual benefit bailment (ordinary care as the duty). In all states, the liability of the innkeeper is limited to the value of the property. There is no liability for consequential damages that may flow from the loss of the property.

REVIEW QUESTIONS AND PROBLEMS

1. Define a *bailment* and list its elements.

2. What are the three classes of bailments and the duties owed the bailee under each?

3. To what extent may a bailee limit its liability? May a carrier limit its liability? Explain.

4. A left his TV set at B's shop for repairs. The shop had been broken into several times over the past few months, but B did not bother to install any additional burglary protection. During the night, A's set was stolen from B's shop. Can A collect from B for the loss of the set? Why?

5. The XYZ motor company loaned an automobile to A while A's car was being repaired. A parked the car improperly on a busy street, and it was struck by another auto. May the XYZ company recover from A? Why?

6. A purchased construction equipment from the XYZ company. However, because delivery would take over a month, the company loaned A some used equipment. On demand A returned all but one truck, which had been destroyed. May the XYZ company recover the value of the truck from A? Why?

7. Upon registering at the XYZ hotel, A turned his car over to B, the bellhop, and told him to put it on the hotel lot. B did so, but when B went off duty he took the car off the lot, with the permission of the lot attendant, and demolished it. May A recover from the hotel? Why?

8. The XYZ company, duly licensed by the ICC as a motor carrier, delivered some wood shipped by B to A. The wood was watersoaked, although there was no evidence that this resulted from the XYZ company's negligence or fault. May A recover from XYZ? Why?

9. A shipped some mink skins on the XYZ airlines The shipment was hijacked and the skins stolen. May A recover from XYZ? Why?

10. A arranged with the XYZ railroad to ship some orange juice from Florida to New York. The train was delayed, due to a snowstorm, and the juice spoiled. May A recover from XYZ? Why?

11 A common carrier's bill of lading contains a clause relieving it of liability for all loss due to fire of any property in transit. A fire, caused by the negligence of the carrier's agent, destroyed goods in shipment belonging to B. Has B an action against the carrier? Explain.

12. When A checked into the XYZ motel, he noticed a sign on the desk which read, "Our safe is available for your valuables." A's camera was stolen from his room. Is the motel liable? Why?

16 REAL PROPERTY

The Nature of Real Property   The preceding chapter dealt with personal property; the following discussion concerns real property. Real property includes not only land but also things permanently affixed thereto, such as buildings, fences, and trees. The Uniform Commercial Code has special provisions relating to the sale of goods to be severed from the land. Its provisions apply to contracts for the sale of timber, minerals, or other items that are to be severed by the seller. However, transactions involving items to be severed from real estate are subject to any third-party rights as disclosed by realty records.

Sometimes property has characteristics of both personal and real property. Such property is commonly referred to as fixtures. Fixture problems arise in areas such as secured transactions and in other ways that are discussed in the next section.

FIXTURES

Introduction   A *fixture* is an article of personal property that has become attached, annexed, or affixed to real property. It is personal property such as a furnace or an air conditioner that has become part of the real property. The question as to whether or not a given item is a fixture and thus part of the real estate arises in several situations: (1) in determining the value of real estate for tax purposes; (2) in determining whether or not a sale of the real estate included the item of property in question; (3) in determining whether or not the item of property is a part of the security given by a mortgagor of the real estate to a mortgagee; and (4) in determining whether the item belongs to the

231

owner of the building or to the tenant on termination of a lease. Fixture issues also arise under Article 9 of the Uniform Commercial Code in disputes between secured creditors and persons with an interest in the land. The UCC provides that no security interest exists in "goods incorporated into a structure in the manner of lumber, bricks, tile, cement, glass, metal work and the like." A party with a security interest in such goods loses it when the goods are incorporated into the real estate. This topic is discussed further in Chapters 25 and 26.

If property is a fixture: (1) it is included in the value of real estate for tax purposes; (2) it is sold and title to it passes with the real estate; (3) it is a part of the security covered by a mortgage; and (4) it belongs to the landlord owner and not to the tenant on termination of a lease. Of course, the lease itself may govern the rights of the parties to the property and the agreement may be contrary to their general rules.

What Is a Fixture?—Tests Several tests are used by courts in determining whether or not an item of personal property has become a fixture.

Case: D, a sewage equipment company, sold sewage disposal tanks to the owner of some land on which P had a mortgage. A statute provided that security interests in fixtures were invalid against owners of a security interest in the land itself. The tanks are buried eleven feet deep, and their removal would destroy a sewage system of adjacent property, rendering it uninhabitable. The owner of the land defaulted, and D attempted to remove the tanks. P sued D to enjoin their removal.

Issue: Are the tanks fixtures so that they are subject to the real estate mortgage and cannot be removed?

Decision: Yes.

Reasons: 1. Generally, in determining whether personalty is a fixture, so that it merges with the realty, three tests are used: (1) the nature of the annexation to the realty, or the degree of the physical attachment to it; (2) the adaptability of the item to the use or purpose of the realty to which it is attached; and (3) the intention of the parties.

2. Here the tanks were so permanently attached and so adapted to the performance of a necessary function that renders this land and land adjacent to it habitable that tests (1) and (2) dictate a finding for P.

First Fed. S. & L. Assn. of Willoughby v. Smith, 216 N.E.2d 396 (Ohio) 1965.

These three tests are explained more fully in the sections that follow.

the annexation test The common law required the chattel to be "let into" or "united" to the land. The test of annexation alone is inadequate, for many things attached to the soil or buildings are not fixtures and many things not physically attached to the soil or buildings are considered fixtures. For example, articles of furniture substantially fastened but capable of easy removal are not necessarily fixtures. Physical annexation may be only for the purpose of more convenient use. On the other hand, machinery that has been annexed, but detached for repairs or other temporary reason, may still be considered a fixture although severed.

Doors, windows, screens, storm windows, and the like, although readily detachable, are generally considered fixtures because they are an integral part of the building and pertain to its function. The mode and degree of attachment and whether the article can be removed without material injury to the article, building, or land are often important considerations in determining whether the article is a fixture. Electric ranges connected to a building by a plug or vent pipe are not fixtures, but the removal of wainscoting, wood siding, fireplace mantels, and water systems would cause a material injury to the building and land, and these items are therefore fixtures.

the adaptation test Because the annexation test alone is inadequate to determine what is a fixture, the adaptation test has been developed. Adaptation means that the article is used in promoting the purpose for which the land is used. Thus, if an article is placed upon or annexed to land to improve it, make it more valuable, and extend its use, it is a fixture. For example, pipes, pumps, and electric motors for an irrigation system are chattels that may be so adapted as to become fixtures. This test alone is not adequate because rarely is an article attached or placed upon land except to advance the purpose for which the land is to be used.

the intention test Annexation and adaptation as tests to determine whether a chattel has become realty are only part of the more inclusive test of intention. Annexation and adaptation are evidence of an intention to make a chattel a fixture. In addition to annexation and adaptation as evidence of an intention, the following situations and circumstances are also used from which intention is deduced: (a) the kind and character of the article affixed; (b) the purpose and use for which the annexation has been made; and (c) the relation and situation of the parties making the annexation. For example, the relation of landlord and tenant suggests that such items as showcases, acquired and used by the tenant, are not intended to become permanently part of the real property. Such property, called trade fixtures, is an exception to the general rule of fixtures because such items are generally intended to be removed by the tenant at the end of the lease. The general principles previously discussed are not applicable to trade fixtures. Trade fixtures may be removed by the tenant at the end of the lease.

Describing Real Property Real property may be described by using (1) the metes and bounds system, (2) the congressional survey system, and (3) the plat system. The metes and bounds system establishes boundary lines by reference to natural or artificial monuments, that is, to fixed points such as roads, streams, fences, and trees. A metes and bounds description starts with a monument, determines the angle of the line and the distance to the next monument and so forth until the tract is fully enclosed and described. Because surveyors may not always agree, the law of metes and bounds creates an order of precedence. Courses (angles) control over distances, and it is presumed that lines connect the monuments if the angle is wrong. Some metes and bounds descriptions use only courses and distances starting from a known point.

The term *congressional survey* refers to a system of describing land by using a known base line and principal meridians. The base line runs from east to west, and principal meridians run from north to south. Townships are thus located in relation to these lines. For example, a township may be described as 7 North, Range 3 East of the 3rd Principal Meridian. This township is seven townships north of the base line and three east of the third principal meridian.

The townships are then divided into thirty-six sections, each section being one square mile. (There will be fractional sections due to the convergence of the meridians.) With the exception of the fractional sections, each section consists of 640 acres. Parts of the section are described by their locations within it, as the drawing on page 235 illustrates.

A *plat* is a recorded document dividing a tract described by metes and bounds or congressional survey into streets, blocks, and lots. The land may thereafter be described in relation to the recorded plat by simply giving the lot number, block, and subdivision name. For example, Lot 8 in Block 7 of Ben Johnson's Subdivision in the City of Emporia, Kansas, might describe real property located in that municipality.

METHODS OF ACQUISITION

Introduction Title to real property may be acquired in several different ways: (1) by original entry, called title by occupancy; (2) by transfer through a deed from the owner; (3) by judicial sale; (4) by benefit of the period of the statute of limitations, called adverse possession; (5) by will; (6) by descent, under intestacy statutes; and (7) by accretion, as when a river or a lake creates new land by depositing soil. Transfer by will and by intestacy statute is discussed in Chapters 14 and 18.

```
+-------------+-------------+---------------------------+
|             |             |                           |
| W 1/2       | E 1/2       |    NE 1/4                  |
| NW 1/4      | NW 1/4      |    160 acres              |
| 80 acres    | 80 acres    |                           |
|             |             |                           |
+-------------+-------------+---------------------------+
|             |             |                           |
| NW 1/4      |             |    N 1/2                   |
| SW 1/4      |             |    SE 1/4                  |
| 40 acres    |             |    80 acres               |
|             |             |                           |
+-------------+-------------+---------------+---+-------+
|             |             |               | 5 | NE 1/4 of |
|             | SE 1/4      |               | A | SE 1/4 of |
|             | SW 1/4      |               |   | SE 1/4    |
|             | 40 acres    |               |   | 10 acres  |
|             |             |               +---+-----------+
|             |             |               |   20 acres    |
+-------------+-------------+---------------+---------------+
```

Original entry refers to a title obtained from the sovereign. Except in those portions of the United States where the original title to the land was derived from grants that were issued by the king of England and other sovereigns who took possession of the land by conquest, title to all the land in the United States was derived from the United States government. Private individuals who occupied land for the period of time prescribed by federal statute, and met such other conditions as were established by law, acquired title by patent from the federal government.

Transfer by Deed   The title to real property is most commonly transferred by the owner's executing a document called a deed and delivering it to his transferee. A *deed* is generally a formal instrument under seal that is executed and acknowledged in the presence of a notary public. The deeds most generally used are warranty and quitclaim deeds.

A *warranty deed* is one in which the grantor (seller) warrants or guarantees (1) that, at the time of the making of the deed, he has clear title to the land and the right and power to convey it; (2) that the property is free from all encumbrances, except those encumbrances specified; (3) that the grantee and the grantee's heirs or assigns will have the quiet and peaceful enjoyment of the property; and (4) that the grantor will defend on behalf of the grantee the title to the property against all persons who may lawfully claim it.

Case: D conveyed certain realty to P by deed, with a covenant against encumbrances. Running across the property was an irrigation ditch that had been in existence so long that it could not legally be removed. P had inspected the property and had seen the ditch but had concluded that it was abandoned.

Issue: Does a warranty deed with a covenant against encumbrances include a covenant against visible easements such as the ditch?

Decision: Yes.

Reasons: 1. An easement is a burden upon the title conveyed. It diminishes the value of the land and constitutes a breach of the covenant against encumbrances in the deed. This breach occurs regardless of whether or not the grantee had knowledge of its existence or that it was visible and notorious.

2. The intention to exclude an encumbrance should be stated in the deed itself as an exception to the warranties. A resort to oral or other extraneous evidence to negate an easement would violate settled principles of law in regard to deeds.

Jones v. Grow Investment and Mortgage Company, 358 P.2d 909 (Utah) 1961.

There may be circumstances under which a grantor would not wish to make warranties with respect to the title, and under such conditions he may execute a *quitclaim deed.* Such a deed merely transfers all the "right, title, and interest" of the grantor to the grantee. Whatever title the grantor has the grantee receives, but the grantor makes no warranties. A quitclaim deed is used where the interest of the grantor is not clear, as for example, where a deed will clear a defective title. It is also used to eliminate possible conflicting interests where there in fact may be no interest in the grantor.

The statutes of the various states provide the necessary requirements for proper execution of deeds. A deed ordinarily is required to be signed, sealed, acknowledged, and delivered. A deed is not effective until it is delivered to the grantee; that is, placed entirely out of the control of the grantor. This delivery usually occurs by the handing of the instrument to the grantee or his agents. Where property is purchased on an installment contract—and occasionally in other cases—the deed is placed in the hands of a third party to be delivered by him to the grantee upon the happening of some event, usually the final payment by the grantee. Such delivery to a third party is called delivery in *escrow*. An escrow arrangement takes control over the deed entirely out of the hands of the grantor. Only if the conditions are not satisfied is the escrow agent at liberty to return the deed to the grantor.

In order that the owner of real estate may notify all persons of the change in the title to the property, the statutes of the various states provide that deeds shall be recorded in the recording office of the county in which the land is located. Failure to record a deed by a new owner makes it possible for the former owner to convey and pass good title to the property to an innocent third party, although the former owner has no right to do so and would be liable to his first grantee in such a case.

Transfer by Judicial Sale   Title to land may be acquired by a purchaser at a sale conducted by a sheriff or other proper official. Such sale is one made under the jurisdiction of a court having competent authority to order the sale. For example, in order to secure the money to pay a judgment secured against the owner, it may be necessary to sell the property of the defendant. Such a sale is called a *judicial sale*. A *tax sale* is also a public sale of land, owned by a delinquent taxpayer, for the collection of unpaid taxes. The purchaser at such sale acquires a tax title. A mortgage foreclosure sale is a proceeding in equity by which a mortgagee secures, by judicial sale, money to pay the obligation secured by the mortgage. The word *foreclosure* is also applied to the proceedings for enforcing other types of liens, such as mechanic's liens, assessments against realty to pay public improvements, and other statutory liens. The character of title acquired by a purchaser at such judicial sale is determined by state statute.

Title by Adverse Possession   Title to land may be acquired under a principle known as *adverse possession*. Thus a person who enters into actual possession of land and remains thereon openly and notoriously for the period of time prescribed in the statute of limitations, claiming title thereto in denial of, and adversely to, the superior title of another, will at the end of the statutory period acquire legal title.

Case: P, claiming title by adverse possession, sued D, the owner of the record title, to quiet the title to "lot 29." P had received a deed to lots 18 and 28 of a certain subdivision. P thought that she had received a deed to lots 17 and 29. P lived on lot 17 for more than twenty years. She paid the taxes on lot 29 for more than six years and maintained a privy on it for more than ten years. Lot 29 was also used by P's family as a playground.

Issue: Does P have title to lot 29?

Decision: Yes.

Reasons: 1. In order to establish title by adverse possession, the claim must be hostile or adverse, actual, visible, notorious and exclusive, continuous and under claim of ownership.

2. The hostility of a claimant's possession of property claimed by adverse possession is not defeated by a mistaken belief at the time of inception of possession that P was the record owner.

3. The evidence established that all elements of adverse possession were met and P was entitled to clear title to lot 29.

Hankins v. Pontoon Beach Amusement Park, Inc., 328 N.E.2d 714 (Ill.App.) 1975.

Actual knowledge by the true owner that his land is occupied adversely is not essential. However, the possession must be of such a nature as to charge a reasonably diligent legal owner with knowledge of the adverse claim. It has also been held that adverse possession will not run against a municipal corporation or other governmental body.

In many states adverse possession by one with color of title who pays the real estate taxes will ripen into title in a much shorter period than is required for adverse possession without color of title. For example, a state with a 20 year requirement may only require 10 years if there is color of title and payment of the taxes. *Color of title* refers to a defective title, but one that but for the defect would be good title. For example, a mistake in a deed does not convey clear title but does convey color of title. This use of adverse possession is very important in clearing defective titles. Errors can be ignored after the statutory period if there is adverse possession, color of title, and payment of taxes.

Covenants and Conditions Quite often the grantor places restrictions upon the use that may be made of the land conveyed. These restrictions may be contained in the deed, or they may be made applicable to several tracts of land by including them with the plat of a subdivision. Where such restrictions are contained in a plat, they are binding on all subsequent purchasers and they supplement the applicable zoning laws.

Case: Ds owned land in a subdivision and proposed to erect two apartment buildings on it. Ps, residents of the subdivision, brought suit to enjoin the construction of the apartment buildings, since the construction would violate the covenants contained in the plat of the subdivision which restricted buildings to one-story residences. Ds contended that they could construct the apartments because the land had been rezoned for apartment buildings.

Issue: Will a restrictive covenant be enforced if it is more restrictive than the zoning laws?

Decision: Yes.

Reasons: 1. The covenants control because they require a more restrictive use of the land than is required under the applicable zoning requirements.

2. The zoning ordinance, itself, provides that it shall not interfere with any covenants or agreements between the parties, except where the ordinance imposes a *greater* restriction upon the use of buildings or land.

Lidke v. Martin, 500 P.2d 1184 (Colo.) 1972.

The typical restrictions contained in a plat or a deed may, for instance, provide that the land shall be used exclusively for residential purposes, that the style and cost of the residence must meet certain specifications, and that certain portions shall be dedicated to the public for streets and sewers. These restrictions inserted in the deed are covenants or promises on the part of the grantee to observe them and are said to run with the land. Even though the grantee fails to include them in a subsequent deed made by him, any new owner is nevertheless subject to them. They remain indefinitely as restrictions against the use of the land. Such restrictions will not be enforced, however, if conditions have changed substantially since the inception of the covenants.

Most of these covenants are inserted for the benefit of surrounding property and may be enforced by the owners of such property. This is particularly true when the owner of land that is being divided into a subdivision inserts similar restrictions in each deed or in the plat. The owner of any lot that is subject to the restrictions is permitted to enforce the restrictions against the other lot owners located in the same subdivision. However, restrictions in a deed are strictly construed against the party seeking to enforce them. Doubts about restrictions are resolved in favor of freedom of the land from servitude as a matter of public policy.

239

Case: Ps owned land that was restricted against use for any business purpose. They wish to construct an apartment house on the land and asked that the court determine that the deed restriction would not preclude such construction. Ds, who are other landowners in the neighborhood, objected.

Issue: Does the restriction prevent the construction of an apartment house on the land?

Decision: No.

Reasons: 1. The use of Ps' premises for apartment house purposes does not violate the deed restriction against the use of those premises for any business purpose. The plaintiffs' apartment building will be used by its occupant for residential purposes.

2. Restrictions in a deed are to be strictly construed against the party seeking to enforce those restrictions, so that any doubt should be "resolved in favor of the freedom of land from servitude."

Walker v. Gross, 290 N.E.2d 543 (Mass.) 1972.

Occasionally, a convenant is inserted for the personal benefit of the grantor and will not run with the land. If grantee B as part of the consideration covenants to repair a dam on land owned by grantor A, such covenant will not run with the land and will not place a duty upon a subsequent grantee of B. The promise does not touch and concern the land granted from A to B but is only a personal convenant for the benefit of A.

It should be emphasized that covenants and conditions that are designed to discriminate on the grounds of race, creed, color, or national origin are unconstitutional as a denial of equal protection of the laws. Such covenants were common at one time and many are still incorporated in restrictions that accompany plats. When challenged, such restrictions have been held to be unconstitutional; they should today be considered a nullity without a court test case.

Proving Ownership Ownership of real estate is a matter of public record. Every deed, mortgage, judgment, lien, or other transaction that affects the title to real estate must be made a matter of public record in the county in which the real estate is located. Deeds and other documents are usually recorded in the county recorder's office. The records of the probate court furnish the public documents necessary to prove title by will or descent. Divorce proceedings and other judicial

240

proceedings that affect the title to real estate are also part of the public record.

In order to establish title to real estate, it is necessary to examine all the public records that may affect the title. Because it would be difficult for an attorney to examine all the records, businesses have been formed in most states for the express purpose of furnishing the appropriate records for any given parcel of real estate. These companies, known as abstract companies, are usually well-established firms that have maintained tract indexes for many years that they keep current on a daily basis. Upon request these companies prepare an abstract of record that sets forth the history of the parcel in question and all matters that may affect the title. (In states without abstract companies, law offices develop files and records similar to tract indexes, so that a complete search of the original records is not always required.)

The abstract of title is examined by an attorney who furnishes his written opinion concerning the title. The opinion will set forth any defects in the title as well as encumbrances against it. The abstract of title must be brought down to date each time the property is transferred or proof of title is required in order that the chain of title will be complete.

It should be noted that an attorney's opinion on title is just that—an opinion. If the attorney makes a mistake, for example, his opinion states that X has title to Blackacre, when in fact X does not have title to Blackacre, X does not have title. X's only recourse would be a malpractice suit against the attorney.

Because of limited resources, many lawyers are unable to respond in damages to pay losses caused by their mistakes. Therefore the abstract of title and attorney's opinion as the means of protecting owners is in many cases not satisfactory. In addition, there may be title defects that do not appear of record and that the attorney does not cover in his title opinion. For example, an illegitimate child may be an unknown heir with an interest in property, as may be a spouse in a secret marriage. In order to protect owners against such hidden claims and to offset the limited resources of most lawyers, *title insurance* has been developed.

Title insurance is in effect an opinion of the title company instead of the lawyer. The opinion of the title company is backed up to the extent of the face value of the title insurance policy. If the purported owner loses the property, he collects the insurance just as if it were life insurance and the insured had died. Title insurance can cover matters beyond those in a title opinion. It has the financial backing of the issuing company that is financially more secure than any law firm. Modern real estate practice uses abstracts and title policies rather than abstracts and title opinions. Title insurance companies usually maintain their own tract records, thus eliminating the cost of bringing the abstract down to date.

ESTATES IN REAL PROPERTY

Estates in Fee Simple A person who owns the entire estate in real property is said to be an *owner in fee simple*. A fee simple title is that which is usually received by the grantee of a warranty deed. It is the greatest and most complete interest a person may have in real estate. It is the maximum "bundle of rights."

Life Estates An owner of land may create, either by will or by deed, an interest known as a *life estate*. A life estate may be for the life of the grantee or it may be created for the duration of the life of some other designated person. In addition, it may be created until the happening of an event such as the marriage of the life tenant. For example, a husband may convey property to his wife for life or until she remarries. Unless the instrument that creates the life estate places limitations upon it, the interest can be sold or mortgaged like any other interest in real estate. However, the buyer or mortgagee must take into consideration the fact that the life estate may be terminated at any time by the death of the person for whose life it was created.

The life tenant is obligated to use reasonable care to maintain the property in the condition in which it was received, ordinary wear and tear excepted. There is a duty to repair, to pay taxes, and, out of the income received, to pay interest on any mortgage that may have been outstanding at the time the life estate was created. The life tenant has no right to waste the property or to do anything that tends to deplete the value of the property. For instance, a life tenant would have no right to drill for oil, to mine coal, or to cut timber from the land, unless such operations were being conducted at the time the life estate was created. Likewise a life tenant has no duty to make lasting improvements to the property.

Life estates have many tax-savings features. They are widely used in estate planning to reduce both income and death taxes.

Remainders and Reversions After the termination of a life estate, the remaining estate may be given to someone else, or it may go back to the original owner or to his heirs. If the estate is to be given to someone else upon the termination of a life estate, it is called an *estate in remainder*. If it is to go back to the original owner, it is called a *reversion*. If the original owner of the estate is dead, the property reverts to the heirs of the original owner. A remainder or a reversionary interest may be sold, mortgaged, or otherwise disposed of in the same manner as any other interest in real property. Upon the death of the life tenant, the remainder of reversion becomes a fee simple interest once more.

Easements   An *easement* is a right, granted by the grantor to the grantee, to use real property. For example, the grantor may convey to the grantee a right of way over his land, the right to erect a building that may shut off light or air, the right to lay drain tile under the land, or the right to extend wires over the land. If these rights of easement are reserved in the deed conveying the property, or granted by a separate deed, they pass along with the property to the next grantee and are burdens upon the land. An easement may also be made by separate contract—in such a case it is binding only on the immediate parties to the agreement. If such right to use another's land is given orally, it is not an easement but a *license*. The owner of the land may revoke a license at any time unless it has become irrevocable by conduct constituting estoppel. However, an easement given by grant cannot be revoked or taken away, except by deed, as such a right of way is considered a right in real property. An easement, like title to property, may be acquired by *prescription*, which is similar to adverse possession.

Case: D had, for many years, used a lane across P's land for taking cattle to pasture. During this period of time, P had paid taxes on the property in dispute and D had paid P nothing to use the land or for a share of the taxes. P sought to stop D from using the land. D claimed an easement by prescription over the land.

Issue: Did D have an easement over P's land?

Decision: Yes.

Reason: D had used the land for a cattle lane and grazing for more than twenty years. A person can acquire interests in another's land after an adverse use for twenty years. Such an easement is known as an easement by prescription.

Anderson v. Osguthorpe, 504 P.2d 1000 (Utah) 1972.

Multiple Ownership   Multiple ownership of personal property was discussed in Chapter 14. The principles discussed there are generally applicable to real estate also. Real property may be owned by two or more unrelated persons, either as *tenants in common* or as *joint tenants*. The nature of the granting clause in the deed or will by which the title is transferred will determine which form of multiple ownership exists. A joint tenancy can be created only by a specific statement that the grantees shall hold title as joint tenants with the right of

243

survivorship, and not as tenants in common. Without such a clause, the grantees are tenants in common. It should be kept in mind that on death, joint tenancy property passes to the surviving joint tenant. Tenancy in common property passes to one's heirs or pursuant to the will of the deceased tenant in common.

If the grantees are related by marriage and the state law so provides, a conveyance to a husband and wife creates a *tenancy by the entireties.* A tenancy by the entirety in states that authorize such common ownership of real estate can exist only between husband and wife. A conveyance of real estate to a husband and wife in these states is automatically a tenancy by the entirety. Neither tenant can unilaterally sever or end the tenancy. It may only be terminated by divorce, a joint transfer to a third party, or a conveyance by one spouse to the other. The inability of either spouse to terminate the tenancy unilaterally is the primary difference between a joint tenancy and a tenancy by the entireties, as the basic characteristic of each is the right of survivorship. In most states that authorize tenancy by the entireties, not only is there a prohibition on one tenant making a voluntary transfer of his or her share but there are also severe restrictions on the rights of creditors to collect an individual debt of one tenant of the property. For example, assume that H and W own their home as tenants by the entireties. X has a judgment for $10,000 against H alone. In most states, X could not cause a sale of the house to collect the debt. Of course, if X had a judgment against both H and W, he could collect from a judicial sale of the property.

Some states have abolished joint tenancies and tenancies by the entireties. The law has always favored tenancy in common. This favoritism has been seen in cases that resolve doubts about which tenancy was created in favor of tenancy in common. The right of survivorship has often been used to defeat the justifiable expectations of creditors and sometimes results in property passing to other than those intended. Hence, there is pressure to abolish this form of ownership in many states.

Several of the southwestern and western states have what is known as *community property*, having inherited it in part from their French and Spanish ancestors. In these states most property acquired after marriage other than by devise, bequest, or from the proceeds of noncommunity property becomes the joint property of husband and wife. Control of the property is vested primarily in the husband, and he is authorized, in most states, to sell or to mortgage it. The proceeds of the sale or mortgage in turn become community property. Upon the death of one of the parties, title to at least half the community property passes to the survivor. In most of the states the disposition of the remainder may be by will or under the rules of descent.

REVIEW QUESTIONS AND PROBLEMS

1. List the three tests for determining if personal property has become a fixture.

2. List three methods for describing real estate and illustrate each.

3. Name two types of deeds and distinguish the legal effect of each.

4. What is the purpose of an escrow provision in a real estate transaction?

5. Discuss the advantages of a title policy over an attorney's title opinion.

6. Why, in some states, is there pressure to abolish joint tenancies and tenancies by the entireties?

7. Define the following terms: *life estate, remainder, reversion, adverse possession, easement, joint tenancy, tenancy in common, tenancy by the entireties,* and *fee simple.*

8. X leased a building from Y for the operation of a plant and retail outlet for processing and sale of meat. Under the terms of the lease, X could make alterations in the building. X ran pipelines to the street and insulated each room in order to make each room a self-contained refrigerator. X also installed a new false front on the building and put in counters and showcases on the main floor. Which of the improvements could X remove and take with him upon termination of the lease? Explain.

9. X sold a home to Y and gave a warranty deed. Unknown to Y, there were valid unrecorded encumbrances against the property. Does Y have any remedy against X? Explain.

10. While selling his home to B, A discovers that his brother, C, may have a claim against the land. C, independently wealthy, and on good terms with A, wishes to help A sell the house. What method can A use to clear the title? Explain.

11. The XYZ company had an easement for underground cables through A's land duly recorded. A hired B to dig and prepare a foundation for a building on the property. In doing so, B's tractor broke through the XYZ company's cable. B was negligent. May XYZ recover from B? Was the recording of the easement knowledge to all the world? Why?

12. A sold Whiteacre to B, inserting the provision in the deed that "Whiteacre shall not be transferred to any Negro or colored person." B sells Whiteacre to C, a black. May A obtain an injunction forbidding the sale, or in the alternative, damages from B? Why?

13. The owner of two adjoining buildings sold one of them to A. The deed provided that A should have the privilege of passage from the other building to the one that he purchased. Subsequently the owner sold the remaining building to X. X tore down the building and built a new one. Does A have a right of passage in the new building? Why?

14. A purchased a lot in a subdivision that included plat restrictions against mobile homes. Land, which included the subdivision, was rezoned to allow mobile homes. A sold the lot to B, who attempted to set up a mobile home on the lot. May residents of the subdivision enforce the plat restrictions? Why?

15. A willed certain land to W for life, with the remainder to W's minor children. A died, and some time thereafter W leased the property to X coal company, which stripped the land of coal and destroyed it for other useful purposes. Have the children a good cause of action against the coal company? Why?

17 REAL ESTATE TRANSACTIONS

Introduction   Real property is involved in a variety of transactions, such as contracts of sale, contracts for a deed, and leases. There are three distinct interests in land—surface rights, mineral rights, and air rights. Some real estate transactions may involve only one of these rights. For example, a sale or lease of surface rights only may be executed. Such a contract would not affect either the air rights or the mineral rights. Similarly a party may sell or lease part or all of the mineral rights, such as the rights to oil and gas, without it affecting the surface or the air rights. However, unless the instrument transferring the property clearly separates the interests in real property, all three interests are included in a sale or lease.

Real estate contracts are subject to the same general principles of contract law as are other contracts. The chapters on offer and acceptance, consideration, and voidable contracts discussed several special aspects of the law as it relates to contracts involving real estate. There are also special provisions of the statute of frauds relating to real estate contracts. It will be extremely helpful to review these subjects at this time.

THE REAL ESTATE CONTRACT OF SALE

The Offer   The typical contract for sale of real estate originates with an
to Purchase   *offer to purchase* from the buyer to the seller. This offer to purchase is frequently obtained by a real estate broker or an agent. In most states an offer to purchase may be prepared by a real estate broker without the broker's being guilty of unauthorized practice of law. The offer is submitted to the seller for acceptance or rejection.

247

In many cases, this offer upon acceptance is the only contract between the parties. In other cases, if it is accepted, the informal offer and acceptance are then taken to the buyer's or the seller's attorney for preparation of the actual contract. After acceptance of the offer to purchase by the seller, an enforceable contract exists in most states. However, it is desirable to have an attorney prepare a formal contract which will set forth all aspects of the transaction. Real estate brokers cannot legally prepare such contracts in most states, since the preparation would constitute unauthorized practice of law. Real estate brokers may properly prepare offers to purchase but not formal contracts and deeds.

It is not only important that an attorney prepare an actual contract of sale after the offer and acceptance are complete, it is equally important that the other party's attorney review the contract so prepared. Each party to a real estate contract needs the advice of legal counsel for several reasons. First of all, historically, the doctrine of caveat emptor did apply to real estate transactions. While there is a trend developing toward holding that a contractor impliedly warrants new construction to be of workmanlike quality for a short period of time, it is clear that buyers should require that the contract include those express warranties relating to the quality of construction or the condition of the premises actually relied upon. For example, if there is to be a warranty that the premises are free of termites, the contract should so provide.

Second, it should always be recognized that the interests of the seller and the interests of the buyer are in conflict and adversary. For example, a seller is best served by a contract requiring delivery of a quitclaim deed, while a buyer's interests are best served by a contract calling for a warranty deed. It is neither wise nor ethical for one attorney to represent both parties to a real estate transaction because of these conflicts of interest.

Third, several essential provisions are usually omitted from offers to purchase. Among the provisions that may not be found in offers to purchase are those relating to grace periods upon default, the terms of escrow, and forfeiture clauses. These and other provisions are discussed in the following sections.

Terms of the Contract and Escrows   The typical real estate contract of sale describes the property and sets forth the price, the method of payment, and the date of possession. It also contains provisions concerning the prorating of real estate taxes, the assignment of hazard insurance, the selection of an escrow agent, and whether the proof of title will be made by furnishing an abstract or a title insurance policy. The contract may also contain provisions concerning such contingencies as default by the buyer or destruction of the premises.

An escrow provision is desirable because a deed must be delivered during the lifetime of the grantor to be effective. Because it is always possible for the grantor to die between the time of executing the contract and the date of delivery of possession and final payment, the deed is executed concurrently with the contract. The deed is then delivered to a third person known as the escrowee or escrow agent to be delivered to the grantee upon final payment. If the seller-grantor dies in the meantime, the transaction can still be consummated without delay.

Case: H and W had a life estate in a tract of land, and Melford Egan owned the remainder. An agreement between the life tenants and the remainderman provided for a fifty-fifty division of the proceeds of any sale of the property, including a sale to the state in condemnation proceedings. On October 5, 1960, the parties under threat of condemnation executed a contract of sale and deed to the state of Missouri for a sale price of $30,500. The contract and deed were placed in escrow to be held until a check in the amount of the purchase price was received from the state. The check was received November 9, 1960. H and W were killed October 25, 1960, and their estates claim one-half the proceeds. Melford Egan contends that he is entitled to all the proceeds as the remainderman.

Issue: Was the delivery of the deed to the escrow agent effective to pass title to the state so that the life tenants were entitled to one-half the proceeds?

Decision: Yes.

Reasons: 1. Upon final delivery by a depository of a deed deposited in escrow the instrument will be treated as relating back to, and taking effect at the time of, the original deposit in escrow. This shall apply even though one of the parties to the deed dies before the second delivery.

2. The relation of vendor and purchaser exists as soon as a contract for the sale and purchase of land is entered into. Equity regards the purchaser as the owner and the vendor as holding the legal title in trust for him. This equitable principle may be invoked in actions at law, and that even though the purchaser has not been put in possession.

Donnelly v. Robinson, 406 S.W.2d 595 (1966).

An escrow also prevents a claim of a creditor of the seller from interfering with the rights of the purchasers. The escrow in effect transfers title to the purchaser before the transaction is complete.

Case: X entered into an escrow sale agreement to sell certain real estate to Y. On January 15, 1964, an escrow was opened, and on March 2, 1964, the deed to the property was deposited in the escrow. On March 12, 1964, a judgment creditor of X's levied an attachment on the property that was the subject of the sale. The contract provided that the closing date was to be March 17, 1964.

Issue: Had title passed to the purchaser prior to the attachment by the creditor of the seller?

Decision: Yes.

Reasons: 1. The escrow had been opened, the deed executed, and the deed placed in the escrow before the attachment. All the conditions relating to the sale were performed before the attachment. Title passes when all conditions of sale are performed, so the closing date becomes immaterial.

2. When the conditions of the sale had been met, the escrow agent could have been compelled by either or both of the parties to the sale to deliver the deed and the purchase money. Thus ownership had transferred to the buyer before the attachment was levied, and the seller no longer had an interest in the property that was subject to a levy of attachment.

Sturgill v. Industrial Painting Corp. of Nevada, 410 P.2d 759 (Nev.) 1966.

Closing the Transaction   After the execution of the contract and deed, these documents are placed in escrow until the date for delivery of possession and final payment. During the interim period, the buyer's attorney will seek to verify that the seller has marketable title to the property. This may be done by checking the original records, but it will usually be accomplished by use of either an abstract of title or a title report from a title insurance company.

The *title report* is a letter committing the title company to issue a title policy upon payment of the premium. The preliminary commitment serves as a check of the records to date to make sure that the title is clear. If the buyer obtains a loan on the premises, the lender will also want its lawyer to examine the title and to prepare the mortgage documents. In addition, many contracts require the seller to furnish to the buyer a survey of the premises. Some contracts require the seller to prepare an affidavit concerning repairs and improvements to the premises within the applicable time period for mechanic's liens. A *mechanic's lien* is an encumbrance on real estate in favor of a contractor, subcontractor, supplier of materials, or laborer. Such persons are given a lien to ensure that they will be paid for their goods or services which have contributed value to the property by means of either a repair or an improvement. When the premises that are being sold have been constructed recently, an affidavit of the building contractor will be obtained showing what mechanic's liens exist, if any.

At the time of closing the transaction, a closing statement will be prepared showing all sums due the seller and all credits due the buyer.

In the event that a mortgage is being assumed, it would serve as a credit to the buyer. Other credits would include abstract costs, documentary revenue stamps, if required by state law, and taxes and special assessments that are liens. The buyer will pay the net amount due to the seller or to the escrow agent for delivery to the seller, and the escrow agent will deliver the deed to the buyer for recording. At the same time the seller will deliver possession of the premises to the buyer, and the transaction will be completed.

A Contract for a Deed

One special type of real estate contract is generally referred to as a *contract for a deed*. Such a contract is actually a conditional sale of real estate in which the seller retains title to the property, and the buyer makes payments for an extended period of time. The buyer's right to a deed to the property is conditioned on his making all of the payments. Such contracts are sometimes called *installment land contracts*, and they contain the usual provisions found in other real estate contracts. The purchaser has the risk of loss if the improvements are destroyed during the period of the contract.

Case: In October 1954, P contracted to purchase a four-story hotel, together with fixtures, from D. P paid $11,500 down, with installments payable each month, and took possession of the property. In 1957 a fire substantially damaged the premises. P settled with the insurance company for $31,000, though it would cost $107,000 to restore the structure. The parties had a dispute over the contract. P abandoned the building and now asks the return of all funds paid by him under the contract because D cannot deliver the building contracted for.

Issue: Who has the risk of loss during the contract period in an installment contract?

Decision: Buyer.

Reasons: 1. Generally an executory contract for the sale of lands requiring the seller to execute a deed conveying legal title upon payment of the full purchase price works an equitable conversion so as to make the purchaser the equitable owner of the land and the seller the equitable owner of the purchase money. In other words, the court of equity converts the buyer's contract interest from personal property (money) to real estate. It also converts the seller's interest (real estate) to personal property (money).

2. Therefore the purchaser, or equitable owner of the land, takes the benefit of all subsequent increases in value, and necessarily all subsequent decreases in value.

Briz-Ler Corporation v. Weiner, 171 A.2d 65 (Del.) 1961.

The escrow provision is absolutely essential in contracts for a deed because there is usually a period of several years between execution of the contract and delivery of the deed. In such cases payments by the buyer are usually made to the escrow agent, so that at all times the escrow agent is aware of the status of the contract.

Acceleration and Forfeiture Clauses

Two additional clauses in most installment land contracts are of particular significance. One of them is known as the *acceleration clause;* the other is known as the *forfeiture clause.* The acceleration clause allows the seller to declare the full amount of the contract due and payable in the event the buyer fails to make any of the payments or fails to perform any other of the contract's provisions as agreed. The default or forfeiture clause allows the seller, when the buyer is in default, to terminate the contract and to get the deed back from the escrow agent. The net effect of this clause is to allow the seller to keep all payments and improvements made as liquidated damages for breach of contract.

In contracts for a deed where the buyer has made substantial payments or in which he has a substantial equity, it is apparent that forfeiture of the contract might be inequitable. The principles discussed in Chapter 6 that apply to liquidated damages and forfeitures are also applicable to these contracts because courts of equity abhor forfeitures. When the buyer's equity is substantial and forfeiture would be inequitable, a court upon proper application may prohibit the forfeiture. In such cases the court orders the sale of the property and the proceeds distributed to the seller to the extent necessary to pay off the contract, and the balance is paid to the buyer. No general rule can be stated to describe those cases in which a forfeiture will be allowed and those in which it will not. As a part of its equitable jurisdiction, the court will examine all the facts. If the buyer has paid only a small amount, forfeiture usually will be permitted. However, if the buyer has made only a slight default with regard to the amount and time of payment, or the amount of the unpaid purchase price is much less than the value of the property involved, forfeiture will be denied.

Housing Warranties

Historically, the doctrine of caveat emptor has been applied to real estate transactions including the sale of new homes. Buyers have been allowed to rescind purchases on the ground of fraud or misrepresentation, but warranties have been found to exist only when specifically included in the contract of purchase. In other words, historically, the seller of housing did not by the simple act of sale make any warranties as to either the habitability of the structure or the quality of workmanship and materials.

In recent years, several states have changed the law as it relates to the sale of housing. The courts in these states have imposed liability on sellers and builders of housing by use of a variety of theories.

Some courts have held that there is an implied warranty against structural defects similar to the implied warranty of fitness in the sale of personal property. These courts have held that there is no rational basis for differentiating between the sale of a newly constructed house by the builder-vendor and the sale of any other manufactured product. These courts usually have not extended the warranty against structural defects to the case where an individual builds a house himself and later decides to sell it. Casual sales are not included because the warranty arises when the seller is in the business of selling housing.

Case: P purchased a new home from D. D was a subdivider of land who hired contractors to actually build homes. As the homes were completed, D sold them without any warranty. P's house was admittedly structurally defective. P sued D on a theory of implied warranty.

Issue: Is D liable for defective construction when D was the seller-subdivider and not the actual builder?

Decision: Yes.

Reasons: 1. If a seller is in the business of selling houses and the sale is commercial in nature, there is an implied warranty against structural defects in the house.

2. The warranty does not arise in a casual sale by a seller not in the business of selling houses.

3. That the seller did not personally drive the nails is immaterial. The seller was in the business of selling homes.

Bolkum v. Staar, 346 A.2d 210 (Vt.) 1975.

Other courts have created an implied warranty that a home is built and constructed in a reasonably workmanlike manner and that it is fit for its intended purpose—habitation. In one case there was no water supply, and the subdivider-seller was held liable for breach of this warranty. In another case the air-conditioning system did not work properly, and the seller was held to have breached an implied warranty. In some cases the buyer is entitled to damages. If the breach is so great that the home is unfit for habitation, of course rescission is the remedy. In this regard it should be kept in mind that the theory of implied warranty does not impose on the builder an obligation to build a perfect house.

Property

At the present time, Congress is considering legislation that will require all contractors and builders to provide warranties on new construction for periods as long as ten years. In addition, used-home buyers today may purchase insurance against defects. In effect, the seller furnishes the buyer with a warranty contract covering the basic construction and major fixtures such as the furnace or air-conditioning system.

LEASES

Introduction A *lease* is a transfer of possession of real estate from a landlord (lessor) to a tenant (lessee) for a consideration called *rent*. A lease may be oral or written. It may be expressed or simply implied from the facts and circumstances. A lease differs from a mere license, which is a privilege granted by one person to another to use land for some particular purpose. A license is not an interest in the land. A license to the licensee is personal and is not assignable.

Duration A lease may be (1) a tenancy for a stated period, (2) a tenancy from period to period, (3) a tenancy at will, or (4) a tenancy at sufferance. As its name implies, a tenancy for a stated period lasts for the specific time stated in the lease. A lease is required to be in writing by the statute of frauds if the period exceeds one year. The lease for a stated period terminates without notice at the end of the period. It is not affected by the death of either party during the period. A lease of land for a stated period is not terminated by destruction of the improvements during the period unless the lease so provides. However, if a lease covers only the improvements on land, destruction of them creates impossibility of performance.

A tenancy from period to period may be created by the terms of the lease. For example, a lease may run from January 1, 1978, to December 31, 1979, and from year to year thereafter unless terminated by the parties. Many leases from period to period arise when the tenant with the consent of the landlord holds over after the end of a lease for a stated period. When a holdover occurs, the landlord may object and may evict the former tenant as a trespasser. However, the landlord may also elect to treat the tenant as a tenant, in which case the lease continues from period to period, with the period being identical to that of the original lease, not to exceed one year. The one-year limitation results from the language of the statute of frauds. The amount of rent is identical to that of the original lease.

Case: P, a hotel, leased space in the lobby to D. The lease was to expire on February 28, 1971. D did not vacate the premises on February 28 but remained in possession and sent a check in payment of the March rent.

The check was cashed by P. D contended that by cashing the check, the lease was renewed for another year. Upon his refusal to vacate the premises, P brought an action to force D to leave, and the lower court found for P.

Issue: Did the holding over and payment of the rent renew the lease for another year?

Decision: No.

Reason: The receiving and cashing of the March rent check did not create a holdover year-to-year tenancy. The landlord had the right to treat the tenant as a holdover tenant and to permit the terms of the original lease to continue in effect or to consider D a trespasser. The landlord chose the latter and accordingly, as a trespasser, the defendant was ordered to vacate the premises.

Sheraton-Chicago Corporation v. Lewis, 290 N.E.2d 685 (Ill.) 1972.

Leases from year to year or from month to month can only be terminated upon the giving of proper notice. The length of the notice is usually prescribed by state statute. For example, most state statutes require thirty days' notice to terminate a month-to-month lease. Sixty to ninety days is usually required when the lease is year to year. Statutes usually provide the time of the notice, such as on the day the rent is due.

A tenancy at will by definition has no period and can be terminated by either party at any time upon giving the prescribed statutory notice. A few states do not require notice, but if legal action is necessary to obtain possession for the lessor, a time lag will be automatically imposed. A tenancy at sufferance occurs when a tenant holds over without the consent of the landlord. Until the landlord decides to evict him or to allow him to stay, he is a tenant at sufferance.

Rights of Lessees The rights and duties of the parties to the lease are determined by the lease itself and by the statutes of the state in which the property is located. Several rights of lessees are frequently misunderstood. For example, the lessee is entitled to exclusive possession and control of the premises unless the lease provides to the contrary. The landlord has no right to go upon the premises except to collect rent. This means that the owner of an apartment building cannot go into the leased apartments and inspect them unless the lease specifically reserves the right to do so. Of course, at the end of the lease the landlord may retake possession of the premises, and at this time he may inspect for damage. A landlord may also retake possession for purposes of protecting the property, if the tenant abandons the premises.

An important right in many leases of commercial property is the right that the tenant has to remove trade fixtures that he has installed during the lease period. However, the right of removal terminates with the lease, and unremoved fixtures become the property of the lessor.

Another important right of the tenant relates to his corresponding duty of payment. The duty to pay rent is subject to setoffs for violations of the provisions of the lease by the landlord. The duty to pay rent is released in the event of an eviction, actual or constructive. Constructive eviction occurs when the premises become untenantable due to no fault of the tenant or because some act of the landlord deprives the tenant of quiet enjoyment of the premises. For example, assume that X rents a basement apartment. A spring rain floods the apartment and makes it uninhabitable. The tenant has been constructively evicted. He may move out, and his duty to pay rent is released. Failure to vacate the premises is a waiver of constructive eviction grounds, however. A tenant who continues in possession despite grounds for constructive eviction must continue to pay rent unless this duty is relieved by statute.

Case: A tenant in an office building withheld rent because the air-conditioning system did not work at night. The offices were so constructed that outside air ventilation was not possible. The tenant continued to occupy the premises but contended that no rent was due because of the constructive eviction.

Issue: Does the tenant owe the rent?

Decision: Yes.

Reason: A tenant who continues in possession must pay rent. Constructive eviction is a ground for cancellation but it is waived if the tenant continues in possession.

Barash v. Pennsylvania Terminal Real Estate Corporation, 256 N.E.2d 707 (Pa.) 1971.

As a general rule, a tenant has a right to sublease the premises or to assign the lease to a third party without the consent of the lessor. However, many leases contain provisions prohibiting subleases and assignments. Such provisions are strictly construed against the lessor in cases of ambiguity or doubt about the tenant's rights.

In recent years, courts have been called upon to decide if there is an implied warranty of habitability in a lease. (This is similar to the issue of warranties on the sale of new housing and is part of the broadened protection given the consuming public.) Some courts have held in all housing leases that there is an implied warranty of habitability. One court held that the fact that a tenant knew of a substantial number of defects when he rented the premises and that rent was accordingly reduced did not remove the tenant from protection of the warranty. The court reasoned that permitting that type of bargaining would be contrary to public policy and the purpose of the doctrine of implied warranty of habitability. In determining the kinds of defects that will be deemed to constitute a breach of warranty of habitability, several factors are considered. Among the common factors are (1) the violation of any applicable housing code or building or sanitary regulations; (2) whether the nature of the deficiency affects a vital facility; (3) the potential or actual effect upon safety and sanitation; and (4) whether the tenant was in any way responsible for the defect.

Defects in vital portions of the premises which may affect health are more important than defects in extras such as swimming pools or recreational facilities. Defects in the latter are not likely to render the premises uninhabitable. It should also be kept in mind that not all states recognize that there is an implied warranty of habitability in leases. While holding that such a warranty exists is a definite trend in the law, it is not universal.

Case: P, a tenant, sued D, the landlord, to recover rents paid on a house lease. The leased house was in violation of the local building codes. It had inadequate plumbing and was improperly wired, and the windows and doors were not airtight. D admitted the building code violations but contended that there was no warranty that the house would be habitable.

Issue: Does a landlord impliedly warrant that residential premises are habitable?

Decision: No.

Reasons: 1. While several jurisdictions have changed the common law and have imposed an implied warranty of habitability, this state will not do so.

2. As between the landlord and tenant, when there is no fraud, false representations, or deceit, and in the absence of an express warranty or covenant to repair, there is no implied contract that the premises are suitable for or fit for habitation, or for the particular use intended, or that they are safe for use, or that they shall continue fit for the purposes for which they were leased.

3. A landlord does not impliedly warrant that his residential rental premises are fit for human habitation, nor does he warrant that such premises are in compliance with applicable housing codes.

Blackwell v. Del Bosco, 536 P.2d 838 (Colo.App.) 1975.

Rights of Lessors A landlord is entitled to possession of the premises upon termination of the tenancy. If the tenancy is lawfully terminated, the right to possession is absolute. The motive of the landlord in termination is usually immaterial. Of course, a landlord may not discriminate in leasing or termination on the basis of race, color, creed, sex, or national origin.

A landlord is entitled to recover from either the tenant or a third party for injuries to the property. In addition, in many states and by the express terms of many leases, the landlord has a lien for unpaid rent on the personal property of the tenant physically located on the premises. This lien right is exercised in a statutory proceeding known as *distress for rent*. By following the prescribed procedures, the landlord is able to distrain or physically hold personalty on the premises until the rent is paid. If not paid, the tenant's personal property may be sold pursuant to court order. The proceeds of the sale, after deducting court costs, are applied to the rent.

It is common practice for a landlord to require that the tenant deposit a stated sum of money, such as one month's rent, as security for the lease. This security deposit covers nonpayment of rent and possible damage to the premises. Many landlords have been reluctant to return these security deposits, contending in most cases that damages were present requiring repairs. As a result, many tenants have refused to pay the last month's rent, demanding that the security deposit be applied. Such practices by landlords and tenants have created a great deal of animosity and litigation. To alleviate this problem, the legislatures of many states have passed laws governing lease security deposits. Such laws usually require that the landlord pay interest on the deposits, and itemize the cost of any repairs that were made from the deposit. They further require the landlord to return the deposit promptly and prohibit the landlord from using it to repair conditions caused by normal wear and tear. In the event a tenant is required to sue the landlord to recover the deposit, the tenant is entitled to collect attorney's fees. Finally, under these statutes, the tenant usually is not allowed to set off the deposit against the last month's rent.

A tenant is estopped from denying his landlord's title and has a duty to redeliver the premises upon expiration of the lease in the same condition as received, ordinary wear and tear excepted. Unless the lease or a statute provides to the contrary, the lessee has the duty to make ordinary repairs but not to make improvements. Conversely, the landlord is not bound to make repairs unless the lease expressly so provides. Moreover, even if an express covenant to repair has been given the tenant by the landlord, the usual construction is that the covenants of a landlord and a tenant are independent, and therefore a tenant may not treat a landlord's failure to repair as a basis for stopping rent payments.

Liability to Third Persons   Difficult legal questions arise in cases involving the landlord's and tenant's liability for injuries to persons on the premises. As a general rule, a landlord makes no warranty that the premises are safe or suitable for the intended use by the tenant, and third persons are on the premises at their own peril. A landlord does have a duty to give notice of latent defects of which he has knowledge. Some states add unknown defects of which he should have knowledge in the exercise of ordinary care to those actually known for the purpose of this notice rule.

The owner of business property, knowing that business invitees of the lessee will be constantly entering it to transact business, has an increased responsibility. This increased responsibility is known as the "public use" exception to the general rule. The basis of the exception is that the landlord leases premises on which he knows or should know that there are conditions likely to cause injury to persons entering on them, that the purpose for which the premises are leased involve the fact that people will be invited upon the premises as patrons of the tenant, and that the landlord knows or should know that the tenant cannot reasonably be expected to remedy or guard against injury from the defect. Thus a landlord of a business owes a higher duty than does the landlord of essentially private premises. Moreover, landlords of business premises often undertake to care for the common areas. In such cases, reasonable care is owed to all tenants and business visitors.

Many suits against lessors by third persons result from falls on the premises. These falls are often associated with ice and snow or waxed floors. As a general rule, a landlord has no duty to remove ice and snow. The landlord has a duty to use reasonable care, and in the absence of an agreement, most courts hold that this does not require removal of ice and snow. However, if the landlord undertakes to remove snow and ice, he must do so with ordinary care. This includes the duty to take into account dangerous conditions caused by the subsequent thawing and freezing of snow placed near the walkway. This duty to use reasonable care in removing ice and snow has been found to exist by many courts when the lease is a business one. This is part of the "public use" exception previously noted.

Case: P, who leased office space from D, slipped and fell on ice in the parking lot in which he rented space from D. There was no written agreement relative to the landlord's duties.

Issue: Did landlord violate any duty owing to defendant?

Decision: Yes.

259

Reason: In the absence of a statute or agreement the landlord is under a duty to exercise reasonable care to keep the common passageways, approaches, and parking facilities within his control in a reasonably safe condition. It is a jury question as to whether defendants' failure to remove snow and ice constituted a lack of reasonable care in the maintenance of the parking lot.

Kopke v. AAA Warehouse Corporation, 494 P.2d 1307 (Colo.) 1972.

Condominiums A condominium is an individually owned apartment or town house in a multiunit structure, such as an apartment building, or in a complex. It is a method of owning and transferring property that possesses some of the characteristics of a lease and some of a contract of sale. In addition to the individual apartment or townhouse, the owner has an undivided interest in the common areas of the building and land, such as hallways, entrances, yard, and recreation areas. Thus the deed to a condominium covers the housing unit involved and an undivided fractional interest in the common areas. There is usually an organization to operate the common areas, to make repairs, and to make improvements. Each owner of a unit has one vote in the management of this organization. Taxes are usually prorated on the common areas by using the fractional proportion of the undivided interests. Condominiums are of growing importance in metropolitan areas, and a determination of an owner's rights requires a study of not only the law of real property but also the law of business organizations.

There is a distinction between a *condominium* and a *cooperative* insofar as the ownership of real estate is concerned. A cooperative venture may involve an activity such as a retail store or it may involve the ownership and operation of a residential development. If a person buys an interest in a cooperative, he is purchasing a share of a not-for-profit corporation. Strictly speaking, the owner of an interest in a cooperative does not own real estate. He owns personal property—his share of the cooperative. The cooperative would pay taxes and upkeep out of the assessments to its members. A condominium contains multiple units for taxing purposes; the cooperative is a single unit. The same may be said for the financing. Each owner of a condominium may mortgage his or her own portion. In a cooperative if there is financing, there will be only one mortgage. In both the condominium and the cooperative there is a special form of business organization to coordinate the operation of the property.

REVIEW QUESTIONS AND PROBLEMS

1. What three interests in land may be separately transferred?

2. Give three reasons why both parties to a contract for the sale of real estate should obtain legal advice.

3. What is the primary reason for using an escrow agent?

4. What is an *acceleration clause* in a contract for a deed? What is a *forfeiture clause* in a contract for a deed?

5. X, the owner of an apartment building, leased an apartment to Y. During Y's absence X inspected the property to ascertain if Y had alcoholic beverages on the premises. When X confronted Y with some empty beer bottles he had taken from the apartment, Y sued X for trespass. Is X guilty? Explain.

6. Compare a *real estate contract of sale* with a *contract for a deed*.

7. Explain the concept of *equitable conversion*.

8. A as seller and B as buyer executed a contract for the sale of a parcel of real property for $12,000. B paid $4,000 down, and the deed was placed in escrow pending payment of the $8,000 balance by B on March 12, 1963. On March 5 A died. B paid the $8,000 to the escrowee and received the deed on March 12. A's heirs challenge the transaction. What result? Why?

9. X purchased Y's used home. The contract of sale did not mention any warranties as to the condition of the home. One week after the delivery of possession and final payment, the roof began to leak. Is Y liable for the cost of repairs? Why?

10. X executed a contract for the purchase of a commercial building from Y. The contract contained a provision stating that if the payments by X were more than thirty days overdue, Y could declare a default and obtain the deed back from the escrowee. After twelve years of the twenty-year contract, X fell on hard times and made no payments for almost a year. Would a court allow Y to default the contract, cancel the deed, and reacquire possession of the property? Explain.

11. The ABC bank, as a land trustee, held title to Blackacre. A trust agreement had been executed, naming X, Y, and Z as beneficiaries of the trust. W, a judgment creditor of X, seeks to have Blackacre sold at a public sale to satisfy his judgment. May he do so? Why?

18 WILLS, ESTATES, AND TRUSTS

Introduction   Perhaps no problem associated with the ownership of property is of greater significance than the various methods available for disposing of that property on death. While the methods and techniques for distributing property on death have always been of considerable importance, their significance is greatly increased today because of the very substantial death taxes imposed by both federal and state governments. As a result of these death taxes, associated income tax problems, and other related concerns, there has developed an activity commonly referred to as *estate planning*, in which many business specialists are actively engaged.

Lawyers play a key role in estate planning, in drafting the various legal documents and analyzing the legal effect of various ideas that people have as to the disposition of their estates. Life insurance salesmen and banking personnel are also actively engaged in the field of estate planning. Life insurance not only creates estates for many people but is a method used to provide the liquid assets to pay the death taxes and other substantial costs of dying in our society. Numerous techniques for reducing income and death taxes utilize life insurance. The trust departments of banks frequently serve as personal representative of the estate of a deceased as well as trustee of living and testamentary trusts used to accomplish the desired goals of an estate plan. Besides providing management of capital, the professional personal representative possesses special skills and techniques that help the property owner accomplish his goals both during his lifetime and upon his death. In addition to the attorney, the insurance broker, and the trust officer, other professional persons are actively a part of the estate-planning endeavor. The investment broker is frequently asked for advice on his area of specialty, and of course the accountant provides much of the data, income tax information, and tax planning that goes into the development of an estate plan. Since all these business specialists are involved in the estate-planning activity, this chapter discusses some of the general principles of the law of wills, estates, and trusts so that the legal aspects of estate planning will be understood.

Terminology The law of wills and estates has certain terminology that is commonly used by those engaged in estate planning. If a person dies without a will, he or she is said to die *intestate*. When a person dies intestate, his property passes according to the applicable statute on descent and distribution to his heirs or next of kin. These statutes provide that property will in effect pass to the deceased's closest relatives, since the law presumes that this would be the intent of the deceased. For example, a typical statute provides that property of a person dying leaving a spouse and children will pass one-third to the spouse and two-thirds to the children.

A person making a will is generally referred to as the *testator*. The personal representative of a deceased who dies without a will is an *administrator*, while the personal representative of a testator is an *executor*. A *guardian* is the personal representative of a living person known as a *ward*, who is usually a child, while a *conservator* is the personal representative of a living person who is mentally incompetent for reasons other than age.

A gift by will of real estate is usually called a *devise*, while a gift of personal property is called a *bequest*. Devises and bequests are further classified as *specific*, *general*, and *residuary*. A specific legacy, or specific devise, is a gift of particular property so described as to identify it and to distinguish it from all other parts of the deceased's property. A general legacy is one that does not describe any particular property, and it may be satisfied by delivery of any property of the general kind described. For example, a gift of a specified sum of money is a general legacy. A residuary gift is one that includes all the rest of that type of property. For example, a residuary gift of personal property would include all the personal property not included in the specific and general legacies.

WILLS

General A *will* is a document that expresses a person's intention as to
Characteristics the disposition of his or her property on death. However, a will has several additional functions. It designates the personal representative who is to be responsible for settling the affairs of the deceased. A will may make provisions for the appointment of a guardian of the person and a guardian of the estate of a minor child.

Many wills contain provisions relating to the payment of taxes that may be due on the death of the deceased and such matters as whether or not the personal representative should be required to have sureties on the official bond.

While legal provisions vary from state to state, the law generally stipulates that to be valid, a will must be executed by a person possessing testamentary capacity and must be signed either by the testator or by someone in his presence and at his direction. In most states, a will must be attested in the presence of the testator by two or more credible witnesses.

Testamentary capacity does not require a perfect mind or average intelligence. Testamentary capacity first of all requires that the minimum age be met, which in most states is eighteen. The person executing the will must have sufficient mental capacity to comprehend and remember who are the natural objects of his affection, to comprehend the kind and character of his property, and to understand that he or she is engaged in making a will. Less mental capacity is required to execute a will than is required to execute ordinary business transactions and contracts. Since many people at the time of making a will are in poor health, the law recognizes that many testators will not be of perfect mind, and all that is required is a minimum capacity to understand the nature and the plan involved in making the will.

Case: A testator, T, executed a will when he was eighty-four years of age. He died about one and one-half years later, and his will was contested by his brother and six of his nieces. They contended that T was not of sound mind when he made his will. The evidence showed that T had allowed his person and his property to become filthy and that he was an eccentric. In addition, T was often intoxicated, suffered from arteriosclerosis, and had insane delusions about being attacked by Indians.

Issue: Did T possess the requisite mental capacity to make a will?

Decision: Yes.

Reasons: 1. Eccentricity, uncleanliness, slovenliness, neglect of person and clothing, and offensive and disgusting personal habits do not constitute unsoundness of mind.

2. A testator does not have to be absolutely of sound mind and memory in every respect. All that is required is that he have sufficient mental capacity to comprehend and remember who are the natural objects of his bounty, to comprehend the kind and character of his property, and to make a disposition of that property among his relatives according to some plan formed in his mind.

Pendarvis v. Gibb, 159 N.E. 353 (Ill.) 1927.

It should be noted that the testator need not actually sign the will, since many people who are physically incapacitated will not be able to do so. Thus a will may be signed by someone else in the testator's presence and at his direction. It will not be set aside simply by proving that the signature on it is not that of the deceased.

In most states, the testator need not sign in the presence of witnesses if he acknowledges that the instrument is his own and that it bears his signature. The witnesses need not be informed that the document is a will, but only that it is the testator's instrument. The signature aspect of attestation is that the testator watch the witnesses sign, and in most states it is essential that the witnesses testify that the testator watched them sign as attesting witnesses.

A credible witness is one who is competent to testify to support the will. If the witness is an interested party he takes something under the will, then in most states the witness will not be allowed to receive any more property as a result of the will than he would have received had there been no will. In other words, a witness to the will cannot profit or gain any property as a result of the will. He will be required to testify and will lose whatever the will gives him in excess of his intestate share of the deceased's estate.

A will that on its face is properly executed may be challenged on several grounds. With the exception of lack of testamentary capacity, the most frequently cited ground for a will contest is undue influence. This ground for challenging a will is defined as influence that overpowers the mind of the testator and deprives him of his free agency in the execution of the will. It is the equivalent of saying, "This is not my wish, but I must do it." It is more than mere persuasion, for here there is an exercise of independent judgment and deliberation. A presumption of undue influence is often found to exist where there is a fiduciary relationship between a testator and a beneficiary who takes substantial benefits from the will. This is especially true where the beneficiary is a nonrelated dominant party and the testator a dependent party and the will is written or its preparation procured by the beneficiary.

Case: X, an undertaker, served as confidential adviser to Y, the deceased, a woman eighty years of age. X managed all of Y's affairs. At a time when Y's mind was deteriorating, X called in his attorney to draw a will for her. The will left practically all of the estate to X. The will was contested, and the probate court disallowed it on the ground of undue influence.

Issue: Did the conduct of X constitute undue influence?

Decision: Yes.

Reasons: 1. When a confidential or trust relationship exists between a testator and a beneficiary under a will, the law requires the closest scrutiny and most careful examination of all of the circumstances. Here, the facts clearly establish a relationship of trust and confidence and an elderly spinster with a weakened mind.

2. By undue influence is meant influence, in connection with the execution of the will and operating at the time the will is made, amounting to moral coercion, destroying free agency, or importunity which could not be resisted, so that the testator, unable to withstand the influence, or too weak to resist it, was constrained to do that which was not his actual will but against it.

Barton v. Beck Estate, 195 A.2d 63 (Me.) 1963.

Revocation of Wills

A will is said to be *ambulatory*, or not effective until the death of the testator. It may be revoked at any time. Among the common methods of revoking a will are physical destruction, making a will declaring the revocation, a later will that is inconsistent with the prior will, marriage, and divorce. In many states, divorce only revokes the will to the extent of bequests or devises to the former spouse. Marriage revokes a will because it is presumed that the testator would want a different plan of distribution as the result of the marriage. It is therefore important that whenever there is a marriage or a divorce, the law of the state of the domicile be consulted to determine its effect on a prior will.

Most state laws prohibit partial revocation of a will except by a duly signed and attested instrument. Additions, alterations, substitutions, interlineations, and deletions on the face of a will are therefore ineffective, and the will stands as originally executed. The law prohibits partial revocation because of the ease with which such minor changes could be made by third parties even after the death of the person whose will is involved.

In most states, unless a provision is made for a child born after the execution of the will, or unless the will by clear and convincing language indicates that after-born children are to be disinherited, the after-born child takes from the estate whatever he or she would have received had there been no will. A legal adoption has the same effect. This stipulation is based on the assumption that the testator at the time of the execution of the original will would not have considered the after-born child and that a provision would have been intended had the child been considered.

In most states, a will that is in any manner totally revoked can only be revived by the reexecution of the will or by an instrument in writing declaring the revival and executed in the same manner as a new will. To illustrate, assume that a person during his lifetime has executed four wills, each will specifically revoking the former. Assume also that none of these wills has been destroyed and that the testator shortly before his death physically destroyed will No. 4. The question arises as to whether or not will No. 3 is then valid. In most states, the answer is no. Wills are not stacked one on the other so that the revocation of the latest will revives the earlier will. In such a situation, the person would die without a will. A similar problem arises when a person executes a codicil or a minor change to a will. When a codicil is executed and it specifically refers to a former will, it has the effect of bringing the former will down to the date of the codicil, and the will is then construed as of the date of the codicil. A codicil can validate a previously invalid will. It can also validate a will that has been revoked by marriage or divorce.

The Administration of Estates

The statutes of each state specify the steps to be taken by the executor or the administrator in the settlement of an estate. These usually require that a petition be filed informing the court of the death of the deceased, together with a copy of the will, if any, requesting the court to hold a hearing at which time the will will be presented for probate. If the person dies without a will, the petition would be signed by someone entitled under the law to be administrator of the estate. This is usually the closest relative. In either case, every person interested in the estate as a beneficiary under the will, or as an heir or next of kin of the deceased, is entitled to notice of the time and place of the hearing. This notice may be waived by a written document filed with the court.

At the time of the hearing there will be testimony about the death of the deceased, and the attesting witnesses will be called upon to testify about the execution of the will. If it appears to the court that the will was properly executed, it will be admitted to probate and an executor named by the testator will be appointed. If there was no will and the person entitled to administer has so requested, then an administrator will be appointed. The executor or the administrator will then file an oath of office and an appropriate bond to guarantee the faithful discharge of the duties of personal representative. In the case of an administrator, sureties on the bond will be required. In the case of an executor, sureties will be required unless these are waived by the will.

After the executor or the administrator is appointed, there will usually be a notice of publication in an appropriate newspaper informing all creditors that they may file their claims against the estate. In addition, the executor or the administrator will gather up the personal property of the deceased, inventory the same, and file an inventory with the court. Should there be any disputed claims, the court will hold an appropriate hearing and determine which claims, if any, will be paid.

During the period of administration, the personal representative will file the deceased's final income tax returns, the necessary income tax returns for the estate, the federal estate tax return if one is required, and the appropriate state death tax returns. The personal representative will also attempt to collect any sums due the deceased and compromise any claims owing to, or debts owed by, the deceased. At the end of the period of administration, the property remaining after the payment of all debts and taxes will be distributed by the personal representative to the persons entitled to it. If the deceased died intestate, these will be the persons who are determined by the court to be the legal heirs of the deceased as of the date of death.

Substitutes for Wills

Many methods, legal devices, and techniques can serve as a valid substitute for a will. In one sense, the law of intestacy is a substitute for a will because it is in effect a state-made will for people who have not taken the trouble to execute one for themselves. Among the more common substitutes for wills are contracts, including life insurance contracts, trusts, and joint tenancy property.

Life insurance policies name a beneficiary to receive the proceeds on the death of the insured. This beneficiary may be the estate of the insured, in which case the proceeds will pass under the will of the deceased, or if the insured dies without a will, the proceeds will go according to the laws of intestacy. However, the usual arrangement is to name an individual beneficiary and successive beneficiaries in the event the primary beneficiary predeceases the insured. In such a case, the provisions of the will are immaterial, and the life insurance will be paid in accordance with the terms of the policy. This is true even if the will purports to cover life insurance.

Individuals enter into numerous contracts that have the effect of disposing of property on death. Some contracts stipulate the terms of a will or surrender rights to renounce a will or to take an intestate share. Such contracts are known as *antenuptial agreements.*

Case: P and D, the deceased, were engaged to be married. Two days before the marriage, the deceased presented an antenuptial agreement by the terms of which P renounced all claim to the deceased's property on his death in return for the payment of the sum of $1,000. P signed the agreement. Thereafter, D died and P brought suit to cancel the antenuptial agreement. D had not revealed to P the extent of his estate and D was, in fact, a man of considerable wealth.

Issue: Was the antenuptial agreement valid?

Decision: No.

Reasons: 1. Where parties are engaged to be married and then enter into an agreement, a confidential relationship exists and the parties are obligated to reveal the extent and value of their respective estates.

2. Here, the provisions made for the wife were clearly disproportionate to the value and extent of the husband's estate. There is a presumption of concealment under these facts and the burden is cast upon those who would uphold the agreement to show the absence of concealment and that the intended wife had full knowledge of the nature and extent of the husband's property.

Watson v. Watson, 126 N.E.2d 220 (III.) 1955.

In Book VII, "Business Organizations," reference will be made to buy and sell agreements between partners and between the shareholders of closely held corporations. These contracts in effect dispose of the interest of partners and shareholders on death. The contractual agreement will dispose of the property irrespective of any provision in a will in much the same manner as life insurance. Other contracts, including employment contracts and leases, may have a similar effect.

A living trust is another substitute for a will when it contains provisions as to the disposition of property on the death of a life tenant. Since this device is so important and so commonly used, it is discussed more fully in the sections that follow.

In Chapters 14 and 16, the use of joint tenancies as a means of common ownership was discussed. *Joint tenancy* is a substitute for a will because ownership passes to the surviving joint tenant on the death of one joint tenant. It will be recalled that joint tenancy property is unaffected by the will of the deceased and that joint tenancy property is not subject to probate or to the debts of a deceased joint tenant.

TRUSTS

Introduction   While the law recognizes four distinct types of trusts, the term *trust* is generally used to describe an express private trust. The other types of trusts are known as charitable, resulting, and constructive trusts. These will be discussed later.

An *express private trust* is a fiduciary relationship with respect to property, which subjects the person with legal title to property (the trustee) to equitable duties to deal with the property for the benefit of another (the beneficiary). In other words, a *trust* is a fiduciary relationship under which one person, the trustee, holds title to property and deals with it for the benefit of another person known as the *beneficiary*. The most important single aspect of the relationship is its fiduciary character. The trustee is under an absolute obligation to act solely for the benefit of the beneficiary in every aspect of the relationship. Both real and personal property may be held in trust.

A trust may be created by a transfer of property during one's lifetime, or it may be created by a transfer on death. The former is generally called a *living*, or *inter vivos, trust*, while the latter is called a *testamentary trust*. The person creating the trust is usually called the *settlor*, although he is sometimes referred to as the *creator* or the *trustor* in estate-planning literature. The settlor may create the trust by a transfer of property to the trustee, or the settlor may declare himself to be trustee of described property for the benefit of designated beneficiaries.

Consideration is not required to create a trust, and, of course, consideration is rarely present in a testamentary trust. The statute of frauds is applicable to the creation of a trust. Therefore, to be valid, a trust involving real estate requires written evidence of the intention to create the trust and an exact description of the property held in trust. Personal property may be held in a trust that is created orally.

A trust may have several beneficiaries, and their rights may be dependent upon several variable factors. For example, the trustee may be authorized to determine which of the beneficiaries shall receive the income of the trust and how much each shall receive. The right of a trustee to allocate the income of the trust among the beneficiaries is sometimes referred to as a "sprinkling trust" provision. It has the advantage of allowing the trustee with actual knowledge of the needs of the beneficiaries to take those needs into account in the distribution of income. A trust may also have successive beneficiaries. For example, a trust could provide that the income would go to the deceased's spouse for life and on the death of the spouse to their children for life, and on the death of the children to the grandchildren. This would provide the equivalent (in personal property) of a life estate in real estate.

A settlor may be a trustee as well as one of the beneficiaries of a trust. A trustee may be one of the beneficiaries of a trust, but the sole trustee cannot be the sole beneficiary. If the sole trustee is the sole beneficiary of a trust, there is a merger of the legal and equitable interests, causing a termination of the trust by operation of law.

When the settlor is also the trustee and life beneficiary, the trust operates in effect as a will. It is nevertheless valid in most states, even though it is not executed with the formality required of a will.

Case: S created a trust of certain farmland. S was the trustee and the income beneficiary during her lifetime. The trust agreement provided that upon S's death, the income would go to her brother for life, and after his death all interest in the trust would pass to the brother's son. S died without leaving a will, and her nieces contended that they were entitled to a share in the estate. They contended that the trust arrangement was an attempt to make a testamentary disposition of property and that it failed, since it was not executed with the formality required of a will.

Issue: Was the trust agreement valid to dispose of the property on S's death?

Decision: Yes.

Reason: Under the law of Illinois, even though the settlor retains a life estate, the trust is nevertheless valid. Upon the death of the life tenant, the property passes in accordance with the trust instrument.

Conley v. Petersen, 184 N.E.2d 888 (Ill.) 1962.

The Administration of a Trust Since a trust is a fiduciary relationship, the trustee owes a high duty of loyalty to the beneficiary. The trustee is not allowed to individually enter into transactions with the trust. Such contracts or transactions are voidable without regard to fairness, and good faith is no defense. A trustee also has a duty not to delegate his responsibility to another.

Perhaps the most important duty of the trustee is in regard to investments. The trustee has a duty not to commingle trust funds with his individual funds and a duty to earmark and segregate trust property. The trustee has a duty to diversify investments. The trustee's duty to diversify investments is sometimes described as horizontal and vertical. *Horizontal diversity* means that the trustee should diversify his investments geographically and in various industries throughout the country. *Vertical diversity* means that he should diversify by investing in different companies within the same industry.

In the selection of trust investments, it is frequently stated that a trustee must exercise that degree of care that men of prudence and intelligence exercise in the management of their own affairs not in regard to speculation but in regard to the permanent disposition of their funds, considering probable income as well as probable safety of the investment. This is generally known as the *prudent man rule.*

To have the requisite diversification, especially in trusts with relatively small amounts of assets, there have developed in recent years what are known as *common trust funds.* These common trust funds allow a trustee, such as a bank or a trust company that holds several trusts, to invest the funds together to obtain the requisite diversity. The duty not to commingle is not violated because each trust fund has its stated proportion of the total investment.

The trustee has all necessary powers to carry out the duties of trustee. These generally include the power to sell if necessary, to lease, to incur necessary expenses, to settle claims, and to retain investments. A trustee generally has no power to borrow money or to mortgage the trust assets. A trustee is liable to the beneficiary for any loss caused by a breach of trust and for any personal profit made in breach of his duty of loyalty. A trustee who makes improper investments cannot set off the gains on one against the losses on the other. Any gain in an improper investment remains in the trust, and the trustee is required to make up the losses on improper investments.

Termination of Trusts   In the absence of fraud or mistake, a settlor cannot revoke a trust unless he has specifically reserved the power to do so. The same principle applies to modifications of the trust. A trust may be terminated when its purposes have been accomplished or if the trust purpose becomes illegal. A trust may be terminated by the consent of all beneficiaries, providing they are all of legal age and all consent, and providing also that termination will not defeat the purpose for which the trust was created. This latter provision is especially important in the so-called spendthrift trust. If the purpose of the settlor was to conserve the estate of a spendthrift, it cannot be terminated even with the consent of the beneficiaries.

In regard to spendthrift trusts, it should be noted that all trusts are spendthrift trusts to a certain extent. That is, as a general rule a creditor cannot collect a debt of the beneficiary directly from the trust estate if the trust was created by someone other than the beneficiary. One of the purposes of a trust is to protect the beneficiary from the claims of his creditors, and allowing a creditor to collect directly from the trust estate would defeat this purpose. Therefore, with the exception of a few claims, such as alimony, child support, and taxes, the trustee is not obligated to pay over the income or principal of the trust estate to anyone other than the beneficiary. Of course, after the beneficiary has received the income, a creditor may use legal process to collect a claim. The fact that all trusts are spendthrift as to involuntary transfers is a major reason for use of the trust device.

Other Types of Trusts   As previously noted, in addition to the express private trust, the law recognizes charitable trusts, resulting trusts, and constructive trusts. The two latter terms are used to describe trusts created by operation of law. For example, a court of equity will create a constructive trust in order to prevent unjust enrichment, as in the situation where a transfer of property is procured by fraud or violation of some fiduciary duty. Courts of equity also create resulting trusts, or a trust results where the person with legal title is not intended to have it. For example, if a child purchases property in the name of a parent, there is no presumption of a gift and the child may establish that the parent holds title in trust for the child.

The charitable trust is a valuable estate-planning tool. It differs from a private trust in that it can benefit an indefinite group and can have perpetual existence. Among typical charitable purposes for which a trust can be created are the promotion of religion, the promotion of education, the promotion of health, public comfort, and the relief of poverty.

Perhaps the single most important principle in the law of charitable trusts is a doctrine as *cy pres.* The doctrine of cy pres provides that if a particular charitable purpose cannot be carried out in the manner directed by the settlor, the court can carry out the general charitable intention by directing the application of the trust property to another charitable purpose consistent with the general charitable intention. The words *cy pres* mean "as nearly as," and the courts simply choose another charitable purpose that is as nearly like the one selected by the settlor as possible.

Case: The deceased executed a will which provided that all of his estate be used to establish an orphans' home bearing his name to be located in his hometown. It provided that the home be under the control of a Catholic Sisterhood. The Sisterhood declined to serve in this capacity. The bank, as executor of the will and estate, asked the court for instructions as to what should be done in view of the refusal of the Sisterhood to assume this responsibility. The heirs of the deceased contended that the purpose of the trust had failed and that the property should be conveyed to them. Another Catholic charity, which was located in another community and which bore the name of a Catholic cardinal, asked that the property be turned over to it. The trial court ruled that the trust was valid, since it evidenced a general charitable intent and that the *cy pres* principle should be followed.

Issue: Should the cy pres doctrine be applied?

Decision: Yes.

Reasons: 1. This was a charitable gift and where the literal execution of the charity is impossible, impracticable, or inexpedient, the general charitable purpose to devote the property to charitable purposes will be upheld. The cy pres doctrine will be applied and the property will be given to the Cardinal Stritch Home.

2. The general charitable purpose here was to benefit orphans and that is more important than where it is done or in whose name.

First National Bank of Chicago v. Elliott, 92 N.E.2d 66 (Ill.) 1950.

Charitable trusts provide a valuable estate-planning tool, as such gifts are not subject to death taxes. In addition, living gifts to a charitable trust qualify for income tax deduction.

The Role of Trusts in Estate Planning The trust device performs several useful functions as an estate-planning tool. As was previously mentioned, it can be used to protect the property of a spendthrift and to ensure that property continues to produce income in spite of the claims of creditors of a beneficiary. It can also be used to secure professional management advice for the beneficiary and to eliminate the worry, decision making, and so forth, that are involved in handling a person's investments.

The trust device allows decisions to be postponed until all the facts are known. The sprinkling device previously noted, and a trustee's authority to make investments and to sell property under changing conditions, illustrate this principle.

Perhaps the best use of the trust device is in tax planning. The trust allows for the maximum use of such estate-tax-planning devices as the marital deduction. The trust device is also used where the beneficiaries are minors or are suffering from other disabilities and it is desired that someone with legal capacity to contract have title to trust property.

REVIEW QUESTIONS AND PROBLEMS

1. Define the following terms: *will, testator, administrator, executor, guardian, ward, devise, bequest, codicil, trust.*

2. Distinguish between *specific, general,* and *residuary* devises and bequests.

3. What are three functions of a will?

4. B, one of D's sons, signed as a witness to D's will. The will included a bequest to B of $1,000. Upon D's death, it was determined that if D had died intestate, B's share would have amounted to only $500. How much would B receive from D's estate? Why?

5. D executed a will in which she named B as the beneficiary of a ranch. B had been D's foreman for many years and had occupied the same dwelling house at the time of death. Upon D's death, P, D's daughter, sought to invalidate the will on the ground of undue influence. What result? Explain.

6. T, a trustee, was given broad authority by the trust instrument in the administration of the trust. Using trust funds, T made a personal profit from a real estate investment. B, a beneficiary to the trust, sued to recover the profits for the estate. What result? Explain.

7. A, a real estate salesman, induced B to give A money sufficient to purchase 320 acres of land at $20 per acre. The salesman, in fact, purchased the land at $11 per acre and failed to disclose the purchase of additional acreage with the money that B advanced. B sued to obtain title to the additional acreage. What result? Explain.

8. Upon D's death, the personal representative of D found two wills, each containing different dates, in D's safe deposit box. The earlier will had left his entire estate to A, while the later one had left everything to B. The latter will did not specifically revoke the earlier will. Which will, if either, should be admitted to probate? Why?

9. D executed a will and left the original with his sister. Later, D wrote across his copy, "This will is hereby revoked." This was unattested. On D's death, the sister sought to admit the will to probate. What result? Why?

10. D executed a will which contained a specific legacy to A. D later changed his mind and crossed through with a pen the particular provision. D's intention was to leave a larger share to the residuary beneficiaries. Upon D's death, A sued to collect the legacy. What result? Why?

IV UNIFORM COMMERCIAL CODE

19 SALES

Introduction   As discussed in the chapters on contracts, the Code recognizes that many of the principles of general contract law are not desirable in contracts for the sale of goods. Rules and principles of contract law that produce a desirable result in a transaction for the sale or construction of a building or in a contract between an employer and an employee do not necessarily produce a good result in a contract for the purchase and sale of goods. Accordingly, many common-law contract rules have been changed or modified by Article 2 of the Code in order to achieve a commercially desirable result. This chapter will discuss many of the technical aspects of the law as they relate to the sale of goods.

The Code provisions on the sale of goods are also based on two additional assumptions: (1) that the parties should be given the maximum latitude in fixing their own terms, and (2) that the parties will act in "good faith." *Good faith* means honesty in fact in the conduct or transaction. (1-201(19)) In the case of a merchant, "good faith" also includes the observance of reasonable commercial standards of fair dealing in the trade. (2-103(1)(b))

Summary of Code Changes to Law of Contracts   The changes in the law of contracts for the sale of goods were discussed in the chapters on contracts. The chart immediately following contains a summary of these changes and also references to the Code section in which the change is made.

279

SPECIAL RULES FOR CONTRACTS FOR THE SALE OF GOODS

Rule	Code Section

Offer and Acceptance
1. Unilateral offers may be accepted either by a promise to ship or by shipment. — 2-206(1)(b)
2. Firm written offers by *merchants* for three months or less are irrevocable. — 2-205
3. All terms need not be included in negotiations in order for a contract to result. — 2-204
4. Particulars of performance may be left open. — 2-311(1)
5. Failure to reject may constitute an acceptance. — 2-206(1)(b)
6. Variance in terms between offer and acceptance may not be a rejection and may be an acceptance. — 2-207
7. An acceptance may be made by any reasonable means of communication and is effective when deposited. — 2-206(1)(a)
8. Acceptance by performance requires notice within a reasonable time, or the offer may be treated as lapsed. — 2-206(2)
9. To have a contract, the price need not be included. — 2-305

Consideration
1. Consideration is not required to support a modification of a contract for the sale of goods. — 2-209(1)
2. Adding a seal is of no effect. — 2-203

Voidable Contracts
1. A minor may not disaffirm against an innocent third party. — 2-403
2. Rescission is not a bar to a suit for dollar damages. — 2-721

Illegality
1. Unconscionable bargains will not be enforced. — 2-302

Form of the Agreement
1. Statute of Frauds: — 2-201
   a. $500 price for goods.
   b. Written confirmation between merchants.
   c. Memorandum need not include all terms of agreement.
   d. Payment, acceptance, and receipt limited to quantity specified in writing.
   e. Specially manufactured goods.
   f. Admission pleadings or court proceedings that a contract for sale was made.

Rights of Third Parties
1. An assignment of "the contract" or of "rights under the contract" includes a delegation of duties. — 2-210(4)

Performance of Contracts
1. Tender of payment is a condition precedent (rather than a condition concurrent) to a tender of delivery. — 2-511
2. Anticipatory breach may not be withdrawn if the other party gives notice that it is final. — 2-610, 2-611
3. Rules on divisible contracts. — 2-307, 2-612
4. Impracticability of performance in certain cases is an excuse for nonperformance. — 2-614
5. Claims and rights may be waived without consideration. — 2-209

Discharge
1. The statute of limitations is four years, but parties can reduce by mutual agreement to not less than one year. — 2-725

Definitions   Article 2 of the Code is applicable to transactions in "goods."
(2-102) It is not applicable to sales of other types of property
or to other types of contracts. The term *goods* encompasses all things
that are movable, that is, items of personal property (chattels) that are
of a tangible, physical nature. (2-105(1)) The term is broadly
interpreted and even includes such things as electricity.

The definition of goods excludes investment securities, such as
stocks and bonds and negotiable instruments. The limitation of the
coverage to *goods* necessarily excludes sales of real property, contracts
for personal services and those involving intangible personal property.
However, the sale of timber, minerals, or a building that is to be
removed from the land is a sale of goods if these are to be severed by
the seller. (2-107) Growing crops are also included within the definition
of goods, whether they are to be removed by the buyer or the seller.
(2-105(1))

A *sale* consists of the passing of title to goods from the seller to the
buyer for a price. (2-106(1)) The seller is obligated to transfer and
deliver or tender delivery of the goods, and the buyer is obligated to
accept and pay in accordance with the contract. (2-301) In general, the
parties to a contract for sale can agree upon any terms and conditions
that are mutually acceptable.

Special provisions of Article 2 relate to transactions involving a
merchant. A merchant is a person who is in effect a professional
businessman and who holds himself out as having knowledge or skill
peculiar to the practices or goods involved in the transaction.
(2-104(1)) This designation is of great importance and is recognition of
a professional status for a businessman, justifying the application of
different standards to their conduct than to "nonprofessionals." The
courts of some states have held that farmers are merchants when selling
grain and other items raised by them. Other courts have held that
farmers are not merchants, so the application to farmers of the Code
provisions relating to merchants varies from state to state.

Another term used in Article 2 is *future goods*. Future goods are
goods that are not in existence at the time of the agreement or that
have not been "identified"—designated as the specific goods that will be
utilized in the transaction. (2-105(2))

adequate   A concept applicable to both parties in a sales transaction is
assurance   known as *adequate assurance*. Under certain circumstances,
either party may be concerned as to whether or not the other
party will *actually render* the performance due. For example, if a buyer
is in arrears on payments due to the seller on other contracts, the seller
will naturally be concerned about making further deliveries to such a
buyer. Likewise, a buyer who has contracted to purchase goods may
discover that the seller has been delivering faulty goods to other
customers. He will be concerned that the goods that he is to receive

may also be defective. The law recognizes that no one wants to buy a lawsuit and that merely having the right to sue for breach of contract is a somewhat "hollow" remedy. There is need for some protection to be afforded to the party whose reasonable expectation that he will receive due performance is jeopardized.

The Code grants such protection by providing that the contract for sale imposes an obligation on each party that the other's expectation of receiving due performance will not be impaired. (2-609) A party who has reasonable grounds for insecurity as to the other's performance can demand in writing that the other offer convincing proof that he will in fact perform. Having made such demand, he may then suspend his own performance until he receives such assurance. If none is forthcoming within a reasonable time, not to exceed thirty days, he may treat the contract as repudiated. (2-609(2))

BASIC CONTRACT TERMS

Price The parties are privileged to specify in detail the terms of their agreement. Most contracts contain terms relating to the price to be paid, the quantity of goods involved, the time and place for delivery, and the time for payment. Sometimes, however, the parties do not specify all the terms; accordingly, the Code sets forth rules that are applicable in the absence of such specific terms.

The price term of the contract can be left open, with the price to be fixed by later agreement of the parties, or some agreed market standard or other standard may be designated for fixing the price. (2-305) It may even be agreed that the buyer or the seller shall fix the price, in which event he is obligated to exercise good faith in doing so. If the contract is silent on price, or if for some reason the price is not set in accordance with the method agreed upon, it will be determined as a reasonable price at the time of delivery. Thus, if it appears that it is their intention to do so, parties can bind themselves even though the price is not actually agreed upon.

Case: P sued D, an oil company, to recover personal property obtained by D under an alleged option contract. The purported contract gave D the right to purchase the property at P's cost less depreciation to be mutually agreed upon. The parties failed to agree on the amount of depreciation and P claimed that as a result, there was no valid agreement.

Issue: Is the contract binding?

Decision: Yes.

Reasons: 1. The contract was valid even though the price was yet to be determined.

2. Under the circumstances it was the function of the court to determine the method and the amount of reasonable depreciation.

Schmieder v. Standard Oil Co. of Indiana, 230 N.W.2d 732 (Wis.) 1975.

Quantity   The Code also allows flexibility in the quantity term of a sales contract. For example, there may be an agreement to purchase the entire output of the seller, or the quantity may be specified as all that is required by the buyer. To ensure fair dealing between the parties in "output" and "requirements" contracts, the Code provides that if parties express an estimate as to the quantity involved, no quantity that is unreasonably disproportionate to the estimate will be enforced. (2-306) If the parties have not agreed upon an estimate, a quantity that is in keeping with normal or other comparable prior output or requirements is implied.

Delivery   The term *delivery* signifies a transfer of possession of the goods from the seller to the buyer. A seller makes delivery when he physically transfers into the possession of the buyer the actual goods that conform to the requirements of the contract. However, a seller satisfies the requirement that he "transfer and deliver" when he "tenders delivery." (2-507)

A proper tender of delivery requires the seller to make available conforming goods at the buyer's disposition and to give the buyer any notification reasonably necessary to take delivery. (2-503(1)) The seller's tender must be at a reasonable hour, and he must keep the goods available for a reasonable time to enable the buyer to take possession.

Unless the contract provides to the contrary, the place for delivery is the seller's place of business. If the seller has no place of business, it is his residence. (2-308(a)) In a contract for the sale of identified goods that are known to both parties to be at some other place, that place is the place for their delivery. (2-308(a)(b))

Goods are frequently in the possession of a bailee such as a warehouseman. In this event, in order to make delivery, the seller is obligated to either (1) tender a negotiable document of title (warehouse receipt) representing the goods or (2) procure acknowledgment by the bailee (warehouseman) that the buyer is entitled to the goods. (2-503(4)(a))

Unless otherwise agreed, the seller is required to tender the goods in a single delivery rather than in installments over a period of time. The buyer's obligation to pay is not due until such a tender is made. (2-307) In some situations, the seller may not be able to deliver all the goods at once or the buyer may not be able to receive the entire quantity at one time, in which event more than a single delivery is allowed.

**Time
of Performance**   Where the time for performance has not been agreed upon by the parties, the time for shipment or delivery or any other action under a contract shall be a *reasonable* time. (2-309(1)) What a reasonable time is depends upon what constitutes acceptable commercial conduct under all of the circumstances, including the obligation of good faith and reasonable commercial standards of fair dealing in the trade.

A definite time for performance may be found to exist, even though the contract did not express it. Such definite time may be implied from a usage of the trade or course of dealing or performance or from the circumstances of the contract.

Payment is due at the time and place where the buyer is to receive the goods. (2-310) *Receipt of goods* means taking physical possession of them. The buyer is given the opportunity to inspect the goods before paying for them. (2-513(1)) The preliminary inspection by the buyer does not require that the seller surrender possession of the goods. However, when the shipment is C.O.D., the buyer is not entitled to inspect the goods before payment of the price. (2-513(3)(a))

The parties may enter into an open-ended contract that calls for successive performances, such as one thousand barrels of flour per week. If the contract does not state the duration, it will be valid for a reasonable time. Unless otherwise agreed, either party can terminate it any time.

Abbreviations   As a matter of convenience, a number of contract terms are generally expressed as abbreviations. *F.O.B.* (free on board) is the most commonly used. *F.O.B. the place of shipment* means that the seller is obligated to place the goods in possession of a carrier so that they may be shipped to the buyer. *F.O.B. the place of destination* means that the seller is obligated to cause the goods to be delivered to the buyer. (2-319(1)(c)) Thus, "F.O.B. Athens, Georgia," where Athens, Georgia, is the seller's place of business, is a *shipment contract.* "F.O.B. Champaign, Illinois," where Champaign is the place where the buyer is to receive the goods, is a *destination contract.* In such a case, the seller must provide transportation to that place at his own risk and expense. He is responsible for seeing to it that the goods are made available to the buyer at the designated place. (2-319(1)(b))

If the terms of the contract specify *F.O.B. vessel, car, or other vehicle,* in addition, the seller must at his own expense and risk load the goods on board. *F.A.S. vessel* (free alongside) at a named port requires the seller at his own expense and risk to deliver the goods alongside the vessel in the manner usual in the port, or on a dock designated and provided by the buyer. (2-319(2))

C.I.F. means that the price includes, in a lump sum, the cost of the goods and of the insurance and freight to the named destination. (2-320) The seller's obligation is to load the goods, to make provision for payment of the freight, and also to obtain an insurance policy in favor of the buyer. Generally, *C.I.F.* means that the parties will deal in terms of the documents that represent the goods; the seller performs his obligation by tendering to the buyer the proper documents, including a negotiable bill of lading and an invoice of the goods. The buyer is required to make payment against the tender of the required documents. (2-320(4))

Returned Goods   The agreement between the buyer and the seller may be such that the buyer has the privilege of returning the goods that have been delivered to him. If the goods are delivered primarily for use, as in a consumer purchase, the transaction is called a *sale on approval.* If the goods are delivered primarily for resale, it is called a *sale or return.* (2-326(1)) The distinction is an important one because goods delivered "on approval" are not subject to the claims of the buyer's creditors until the buyer has indicated his acceptance of the goods; goods delivered on "sale or return," however, are subject to the claims of the buyer's creditors while such goods are in his possession. (2-326(2)) A delivery of goods on consignment, such as a transaction in which a manufacturer or a wholesaler delivers goods to a retailer who has the privilege of returning any unsold goods, is a "sale or return." The goods in possession of the buyer-consignee are subject to the claims of the buyer's creditors, unless the seller complies with the filing provisions of Article 9 dealing with secured transactions. (2-326(3))

A characteristic of the sale on approval is that risk of loss in the event of theft or destruction of the goods does not pass to the buyer until he accepts the goods. Failure to seasonably notify the seller of his decision to return the goods will be treated as an acceptance. After notification of election to return, the seller must pay the expenses of the return and bear the risk of loss. In contrast, the buyer in a sale or return transaction has the risk of loss in the event of theft or destruction of the goods. (2-327(2))

Case: P company delivered stereo tapes, cartridges, and stereo equipment to D, a service station operator, for resale. P company's salesman had written on the invoice, "Terms 30-60-90. This equipment will be picked up if not sold in 90 days." D's service station was burglarized about two weeks later, and the stereo equipment was stolen.

Issue:	Who must bear the loss resulting from the burglary?
Decision:	D.
Reasons:	1. The transaction was a "sale or return."
	2. Unless otherwise agreed, a transaction whereby goods delivered for resale may be returned to the seller is a sale or return. When a transaction is a sale or return agreement, the risk of loss is the buyer's.

Collier v. B & B Parts Sales, Inc., 471 S.W.2d 151 (Tex.) 1971.

THE TRANSFER OF TITLE TO GOODS

Introduction The concept of title to goods is somewhat nebulous, but it is generally equated with ownership. Issues related to the passage of title are important in the field of taxation and in such areas of the law as wills, trusts, and estates. However, the Code has deemphasized the importance of title, and the location of title at any given time is not usually the controlling factor in determining the rights of the parties on a contract of sale. As a general rule, the rights, obligations, and remedies of the seller, the buyer, and the third parties are determined without regard to title. (2-401) However, the concept of title is still basic to the sales transaction, since by definition a sale involves the passing of title from the seller to the buyer.

The parties can, with few restrictions, determine by their contract the manner in which title to goods passes from the seller to the buyer. They can specify any conditions that must be fulfilled in order for this to happen. However, since the parties to a contract for a sale seldom indicate any intention regarding title or its passage, the Code sets forth specific provisions as to when title shall pass, if the location of title becomes an issue. As a general rule, it provides that title passes to the buyer at the time and place at which the seller completes his performance with reference to the physical delivery of the goods.

Identification to the Contract Title to goods cannot pass until the goods have been *identified* to the contract. (2-401(1)) Identification requires that the seller specify the particular goods involved in the transaction. (2-501(1)) For example, A may contract with B to purchase one hundred mahogany desks of a certain style. B may have several hundred of these desks in his warehouse. Identification takes place when A or B specifies the particular one hundred desks that will be sold to A. There could not, of course, be a present identification of future goods—those not yet in existence or not owned by the seller.

Identification can be made at any time and in any manner "explicitly agreed to" by the parties. (2-501(1)) However, the parties usually do not make provision for identification, in which event the Code rules determine when it has occurred. For example, if the goods that are the subject of the contract were already in existence and identified at the time the parties entered into the contract, identification occurs and title passes at the time and place of contracting. (2-501(1)(a)) If the goods are in a warehouse and the seller delivers the warehouse receipt to the buyer, identification occurs and title passes at the time and place the document of title (warehouse receipt) is delivered. (2-401(3)(a))

Contracts to sell future goods and agricultural items raise more difficult identification problems. As to future goods, the seller provides identification when he ships the goods or marks them as the goods to which the contract refers. (2-501(1)(b)) The requirement is that the seller make an appropriate designation of the specific goods.

Case: Ds were package liquor store operators. They were in the practice of paying for large quantities of liquor in advance in order to take advantage of quantity discounts. Ds would then order out the liquor as they needed it. When Ds learned that a supplier was having financial difficulties, Ds seized a good deal of the undelivered liquor. The supplier then went into bankruptcy. P, the trustee in bankruptcy, claimed that under the arrangement Ds were simply creditors and that Ds did not have title to the liquor.

Issue: Did Ds have title to the liquor so that P could not reclaim it?

Decision: No.

Reason: Title to goods does not pass to the buyer until the goods have been identified to the contract. When the contract calls for the sale of goods from a larger stock, title does not pass to the buyer until the specific goods are separated and set apart for the buyer. The retailers must, therefore, return the liquor to the trustee in bankruptcy.

In re Colonial Distributing Company, 291 F.Supp. 154 (1968).

There are special provisions for agricultural items—crops and animals—because of their nature. When there is a sale of a crop to be grown, identification occurs when the crop is planted. If the sale is of the unborn young of animals, identification takes place when they are conceived. (2-501(c))

Identification occurs and title passes insofar as the specific goods are concerned when the seller completes his performance with respect to the physical delivery of the goods. In a shipment contract where he is to send the goods to the buyer but is not required to deliver them at the destination, title passes at the time and place of shipment. (2-401(2)) On the other hand, if the contract requires that he deliver at the destination, title will not pass until the seller has tendered the goods to the buyer at that point.

If the buyer rejects the goods when tendered to him, title will be revested in the seller. Upon the buyer's refusal to receive or retain the goods, the title automatically returns to the seller, whether the buyer was justified in his action or not. The same result obtains if the buyer has accepted the goods but subsequently revokes his acceptance for a justifiable reason. (2-401(4))

As a means of assurance that the price will be paid before the buyer can obtain title to the goods, a seller may ship or deliver goods to the buyer and reserve title in himself. Under the Code, such an attempted reservation of title does not prevent the title from passing to the buyer. It is limited to the reservation of a security interest in the goods. (2-401(1)) To give protection to the seller, the security interest must be perfected under the provisions of Article 9. This will be discussed in Chapters 25 and 26. Accordingly, a seller who simply reserves a security interest will not have availed himself of protection against the claims of third parties against the property sold unless the law relating to secured transactions is complied with.

**The Title
of Good-Faith
Purchasers**

A purchaser of goods usually acquires at least as good a title as the seller possessed. Moreover, a good-faith purchaser for value may acquire a better title than the seller had if the seller's title was voidable. (2-403) For example, assume that X obtains goods by fraud or pays for them with a check that is later dishonored. X has voidable title to the goods. If X should sell the goods to Y who does not know that X's title was voidable, Y has clear title to the goods. Thus a good-faith purchaser for value has better title than did X, the seller.

Title issues frequently arise when the same goods are sold to more than one buyer. For example, assume that S sells goods to X. X leaves them at S's store with the intention of picking them up later. Before X takes possession, S sells them to Y, a good-faith purchaser. Y has title to the goods because if possession of goods is entrusted to a merchant who deals in goods of that kind, the merchant has the power to transfer all rights of the entrusting owner to a buyer in the ordinary course of business. (2-403(2)(3)) A good-faith purchaser from a merchant in the ordinary course of business acquires good title. This rule is applicable to any delivery of possession to a merchant with the understanding that the merchant is to have possession. Thus the rule applies to consignments and bailments as well as to the cash sale situation. However, the facts of each case must be examined to ensure that the buyer qualified as a good-faith purchaser for value.

Case: P and D were automobile dealers. Both had been using the services of X company for the purpose of selling used cars at auction. P delivered two cars to X company for sale in December. Shortly thereafter D, who was holding uncollected checks from X company in the sum of $30,000, went to X company and exchanged two of the checks totaling $7,460 for the two cars that had been delivered by P. P sought to recover the cars from D. P argued that D did not obtain clear title to the cars.

Issue: Was P entitled to recover the cars from D?

Decision: Yes.

Reasons: 1. D was not a good-faith purchaser for value of the cars.

2. A preexisting debt is not sufficient consideration, and therefore D was not a bona fide purchaser for value.

3. Also D knew or should have known that X company was not the true owner of the automobiles in question.

National Car Rental v. Fox, 500 P.2d 1148 (Ariz.) 1972.

RISK OF LOSS

In Breach of Contract Cases The Code sets forth a number of rules for determining which party to a sales contract must bear the risk of loss in the event of theft, destruction, or damage to the goods during the period of the performance of the contract. The approach is contractual rather than title oriented. Two basic situations are involved: (1) where no breach of contract exists and (2) where one of the parties is in breach. Of course the provisions are only applicable where the contract has not allocated the risk of loss. (2-303)

If the contract has been breached, the loss will be borne by the party who has breached. (2-510(1)) Thus, if the seller has tendered or delivered goods that are "nonconforming," the seller bears the risk of loss for such goods. He remains responsible until such time as he rectifies the nonconformity or the buyer accepts the goods notwithstanding their defects. A buyer has the privilege of revoking his acceptance of the goods under proper circumstances. If he does do so for good cause, the risk of loss is back on the seller to the extent that the buyer's insurance does not cover the loss. In this situation, the seller has the benefit of any insurance carried by the buyer—the party most likely to carry insurance—but any uninsured loss is on the breaching seller.

The loss may occur while the goods are in the seller's control before the risk of loss has passed to the buyer. If the buyer repudiates the sale (breaches the contract) at a time when the seller has identified proper goods to the contract, the seller can impose the risk of loss upon the buyer for a reasonable time. The basic concept of the Code is that the burden of losses should be that of the party who has failed to perform as required by contract.

Where No Breach Exists

There are three distinct situations in risk of loss cases when neither party is in breach. First, the contract may call for shipment of the goods; second, the goods may be the subject of a bailment; and third, the contract may be silent on shipment, and no bailment exists.

shipment

Where the contract between buyer and seller provides for shipment by carrier, the risk of loss passes to the buyer when the goods are delivered to the carrier if it is a shipment contract (F.O.B. shipping point); if it is a destination contract (F.O.B. destination), risk of loss does not pass to the buyer until the goods arrive at the destination and are made available to him so that he can take delivery. (2-509(1)) A shipment contract is one that requires only that the seller make the necessary arrangements for transport, while a destination contract imposes upon the seller the obligation to deliver at a destination. When the parties do not use such symbols as C.I.F., F.A.S., or F.O.B., or otherwise make provision for risk of loss, it is necessary to determine whether a contract does or does not require the seller to deliver at a destination. The presumption is that a contract is one of shipment, not destination, and that the buyer should bear the risk of loss until arrival, unless the seller has either specifically agreed to do so or the circumstances indicate such an obligation.

Case: P, a seller of goods, sued D, the buyer, for their purchase price. The contract contained no F.O.B. terms. After the goods were delivered to the carrier for shipment, they were destroyed. The contract was silent on the risk of loss.

Issue: Who has the risk of loss?

Decision: The buyer.

Reasons: 1. The parties may by their agreement control who has the risk of loss.

2. Under Article 2 of the Code, the "shipment" contract is regarded as the normal one and the "destination" contract as the variant type. The seller is not obligated to deliver at a named destination and bear the concurrent risk of loss until arrival, unless he has specifically agreed so to deliver or the commercial understanding of the terms used by the parties contemplates such delivery.

3. Thus a contract that contains neither an F.O.B. term nor any other term explicitly allocating loss is a shipment contract and the buyer has the risk of loss during shipment.

4. D's argument that the contract provided that the goods be "shipped to" the buyer makes it a shipment contract is rejected. A "ship to" term has no significance in determining whether a contract is a shipment or destination contract for risk of loss purposes.

Eberhard Manufacturing Company v. Brown, 232 N.W.2d 378 (Mich.) 1975.

bailments Often the goods will be in the possession of a bailee such as a warehouse, and the arrangement is for the buyer to take delivery at the warehouse. If the goods are represented by a negotiable document of title, a warehouse receipt for instance, when the seller tenders such document to the buyer, the risk of loss passes to the buyer. Likewise, risk passes to the buyer upon acknowledgment by the bailee that the buyer is entitled to the goods. (2-509(2)) In this situation, it is proper that the buyer assume the risk, as the seller has done all that could be expected to make the goods available to the buyer, who controls the goods at this point. It should be noted that if a nonnegotiable document of title is tendered to the buyer, risk of loss does not pass until the buyer has had a reasonable time to present the document to the bailee. (2-503(4)(b)) A refusal by the bailee to honor the document defeats the tender, and the risk of loss remains with the seller.

other cases In all cases other than shipment and bailment as mentioned above, the passage of risk to the buyer depends upon the status of the seller. If the seller is a merchant, risk of loss will not pass to the buyer until he receives the goods, which means takes physical possession of them. (2-509(3))

A nonmerchant seller transfers the risk by *tendering* the goods. (2-509(3)) A tender of delivery requires that the seller make conforming goods available to the buyer and give him reasonable notice so that he may take delivery. The risk of loss remains with the merchant-seller

291

even though the buyer has paid for the goods in full and has been notified that the goods are at his disposal. Continuation of the risk in this case is justified on the basis that the merchant would be likely to carry insurance on goods within his control, while a buyer would not likely do so until he had actually received the goods.

Case: P, a seller of a mobile home, sued D, the buyer, for the price of the home. After P and D had executed the contract of sale, the mobile home had been stolen from P's lot.

Issue: Did the seller retain the risk of loss after the contract was signed?

Decision: Yes.

Reasons: 1. While a contract of sale may transfer the risk of loss to the buyer before delivery of the goods, such a provision is so unusual that a seller who desires to achieve this result must clearly communicate this intent to the buyer and it must be done in clear and unequivocal language.

2. A seller of a mobile home is a merchant. In a sale by a merchant, the risk of loss passes to the buyer on his receipt of the goods. Receipt of the goods means taking physical possession of them.

3. The risk of loss is not determined by title to the goods but by contract principles. The party who has control of the goods generally bears the loss.

Caudle v. Sherrard Motor Company, 525 S.W.2d 238 (Tex.) 1975.

PERFORMANCE OF THE SALES CONTRACT

Introduction   The law recognizes that each party to a contract for the sale of goods has certain rights and obligations unless the contract legally eliminates them. In addition, the Code has several provisions relating to the remedies of the buyer and the seller in the event of a breach of the contract by the other party.

As a general rule, a seller is obligated to deliver or tender delivery of goods that measure up to the requirements of the contract and to do so at the proper time and at the proper place. The goods and other performance of the seller must "conform" to the contract. (2-106(2))

The seller is required to tender delivery as a condition to the buyer's duty to accept the goods and pay for them. (2-507(1)) Thus the seller has performed when he has made the goods available to the buyer. The buyer in turn must render his performance, which means he must accept the goods and pay for them.

The parties may in their agreement limit or modify the remedies available to each other. The measure of damages may be limited or altered. For example, the agreement may limit the buyer's remedies to return of the goods and repayment of the price or to replacement of the goods or parts.

The parties may limit or exclude consequential damages, and such limitations and exclusions will be enforced if they are not unconscionable. (2-719(3)) A limitation of consequential damages for injury to the person in the case of *consumer goods* is prima facie unconscionable, but limitations where the loss is commercial are not.

These rights and remedies are examined in the sections that follow. Keep in mind that these sections cover sales contracts where the contract is silent on the matter under discussion.

Buyer's Right to Inspect and to Reject The buyer has a right before payment or acceptance to inspect the goods at any reasonable time and place and in any reasonable manner. (2-513(1)) The place for the inspection is determined by the nature of the contract. If the seller is to send the goods to the buyer, the inspection may be postponed until after arrival of the goods.

If the contract provides for delivery C.O.D., the buyer must pay prior to inspection. Likewise payment must be made prior to inspection if the contract calls for payment against documents of title. (2-513(3)) When the buyer is required to make payment prior to inspection, such payment does not impair his right to pursue remedies if subsequent inspection reveals defects. (2-512)

The buyer must pay the expenses of inspection, but he can recover his expenses from the seller if the inspection reveals that the goods are nonconforming and the buyer accordingly rejects them. (2-513(2))

If the goods or the tender of delivery fails to conform to the contract, the buyer has the right to reject them. Several options are available. The buyer may reject the whole, or he may accept either the whole or any commercial unit or units and reject the rest. (2-601) A *commercial unit* is one that is generally regarded as a single whole for purposes of sale, and that would be impaired in value if divided. (2-105(6)) The buyer, when he accepts nonconforming goods, does not impair his right of recourse against the seller. Provided he notifies the seller of the breach within a reasonable time, he may still pursue his remedy for damages for breach of contract even though he accepts the goods.

The right to reject defective or nonconforming goods is dependent on the buyer's taking action within a reasonable time after the goods are tendered or delivered to him. If the buyer rejects, he must seasonably notify the seller of this fact, and his failing to do so would render the rejection ineffective and constitute an acceptance. (2-602(1)) If the buyer continues in possession of defective goods for an unreasonable time, he forfeits his right to reject them.

A buyer who rejects the goods after taking physical possession of them is required to hold the goods with reasonable care, at the seller's disposition, for a time sufficient for the seller to remove them. (2-602(2)(b)) Somewhat greater obligations are imposed upon a merchant-buyer who rejects goods that have been delivered to him. (2-603) The merchant is under a duty to follow the seller's reasonable instructions as to the disposition of the goods. If the seller does not furnish instructions as to the disposition of the rejected goods, the merchant-buyer must make reasonable efforts to sell them for the seller's account if they are perishable or if they threaten to decline in value speedily. If not the latter, the buyer has three options. He may store the rejected goods for the seller's account; he may reship them to the seller; or he may resell them for the seller's account. (2-604)

The requirement of seasonable notice of rejection is very important. Without such notice, the rejection is ineffective. (2-602(1)) As a general rule, a notice of rejection may simply state that the goods are not conforming, without particular specification of the defects relied upon by the buyer. If, however, the defect could have been corrected by the seller had he been given particularized notice, then the failure to particularize will take away from the buyer the right to rely upon that defect as a breach justifying a rejection. (2-605(1)(a)) Therefore, a buyer should always give detailed information relative to the reason for the rejection.

In transactions between merchants, the merchant-seller is entitled to require that he be furnished a full and final written statement of all the defects. If the statement is not forthcoming after a written request for it, the buyer may not rely upon such defects to justify his rejection or to establish that a breach has occurred. (2-605(1)(b))

**Buyer's Right
to Revoke
an Acceptance**
The buyer has *accepted* goods (1) if after a reasonable opportunity to inspect them, he indicates to the seller that the goods are conforming or that he will take or retain them in spite of their nonconformity, (2) if he has failed to make an effective rejection of the goods, or (3) if he does any act inconsistent with the seller's ownership. (2-606)

The buyer may revoke his acceptance under certain circumstances. In many instances, the buyer will have accepted nonconforming goods because (1) the defects were not immediately discoverable, or (2) the buyer reasonably assumed that the seller would correct by substituting goods that did conform. In either of these events, the buyer has the privilege of "revoking his acceptance" by notifying the seller of this fact. (2-608(1)) Such revocation must take place within a reasonable time after the buyer has discovered, or should have discovered, the reason for revocation. (2-608(2)) If a buyer revokes his acceptance, he is then placed in the same position with reference to the goods as if he had rejected them in the first instance. (2-608(3)) He has a security interest in the goods for the payments made.

In addition, the buyer is entitled to damages just as if no acceptance had occurred.

Case: P, a cash buyer of a mobile home, sued D, the seller, for damages for breach of contract. The home was delivered on June 7, 1973, but P was not given the keys for three weeks. When P finally gained access, he found that the windows and doors would not shut tightly, the floors were buckled, and the rafters were warped. When it rained, the floors flooded and the water caused an electrical failure. P occupied the mobile home for three months before moving out. D claimed that the right to cure the defects still existed.

Issue: Is P entitled to revoke the acceptance?

Decision: Yes.

Reasons: 1. A buyer, including those who pay cash, is entitled to a reasonable time after the goods are delivered to inspect them and to reject them if they do not comply with the contract. Cash payment does not waive this right.

2. The fact that P stayed in the home for three months does not eliminate his right to revoke the acceptance. P could assume that D would cure the defects and the revocation could be based on the failure to cure the defects.

3. A buyer who revokes an acceptance has the same rights as if they had been originally rejected. These rights include so much of the price as has been paid plus incidental and consequential damages.

4. D originally had a right to cure the defects. However, when D's employee told P that he did not know how long it would take, this right was lost. The right to cure defects requires a conforming tender within a reasonable time.

Davis v. Colonial Mobile Homes, 220 S.E.2d 802 (N.C.) 1975.

Buyer's Remedies— Generally When the seller fails to perform properly, a number of remedies are available to the aggrieved buyer. Most of these involve the collection of dollar damages, with the amount being dependent on the remedy used. The basic remedies available to the aggrieved buyer are (1) to cancel the contract, (2) to "cover" and collect damages, (3) to collect damages for nondelivery of the goods or for delivery of nonconforming goods, and (4) to enforce the contract and obtain the goods from the seller.

The remedy of cancellation does not prevent a suit for damages. (2-106(4)) The remedy of cancellation in the sale of goods is the same as in other contracts. A material breach of contract by one party justifies rescission or cancellation by the other.

Damages When the Buyer Covers

The buyer who has not received the goods he bargained for may *cover*—arrange to purchase the goods he needs from some other source in substitution for those due from the seller. (2-712) This is a practical remedy, as the buyer must often proceed without delay in order to obtain goods needed by him for his own use or for resale to others. The only limitation is that he must act reasonably and in good faith in arranging for the cover. (2-712(1))

He may recover from the seller the difference between what he paid for the substitute goods and the contract price. (2-712(2)) In addition, he may recover any incidental and consequential damages sustained. *Incidental damages* are defined as those that are reasonably incurred in connection with handling rejected goods, and "commercially reasonable charges, expenses or commissions in connection with effecting cover and any other reasonable expense incident to the delay or other breach." (2-715(1)) *Consequential damages* include "any loss resulting from general or particular requirements and needs of which the seller at the time of contracting had reason to know and which could not reasonably be prevented by cover or otherwise." (2-715(2)) The buyer is obligated to keep his damages to a minimum by making an appropriate cover insofar as his right to any consequential damages is concerned.

The cover remedy has the advantage of providing certainty as to the amount of the buyer's damages. The difference between the contract price and the price paid by the buyer for substitute goods can be readily determined. While the buyer must act reasonably and in good faith, he need not prove that he obtained the goods at the cheapest price available.

Damages— Other Cases

The aggrieved buyer who did not receive any goods from the seller or who received nonconforming goods is not *required* to cover; instead, he may bring an action for damages. (2-712(3)) The measure of damages for nondelivery or repudiation is the difference between the *market price at the time when the buyer learned of the breach* and the contract price. (2-713) The buyer is also entitled to any incidental or consequential damages sustained. The damages to which a buyer is entitled consist of "the loss resulting in the ordinary course of events from the seller's breach as determined in any manner which is reasonable." (2-714(1)) For example, in a purchase for resale, it would be appropriate to measure the buyer's damage upon nondelivery as the difference between the contract price and the price at which the goods were to be resold. In other words, the damages equal the difference between the contract price and the fair market value of the goods.

In addition to collecting damages from the seller, an aggrieved buyer may deduct the damages resulting from any breach of contract from any part of the price still due under the same contract. (2-717) The buyer may determine what his damages are, and he may withhold this amount when he pays the seller. He is required to give notice to the seller of his intention to deduct. Where the buyer's damages are established by the cover price, the amount would be clear-cut. In other instances the seller might question the amount of the deduction, and this dispute would have to be resolved between the parties or by a court.

It is to be noted that the damages may be deducted only as against the price due under the same contract. Accordingly, a buyer could not deduct damages for goods under one contract from the price due under other contracts from the same seller.

Buyer's Right to the Goods Under proper circumstances, the buyer has rights in and to the goods. The remedy of specific performance is available (1) when the goods are unique and (2) when other circumstances make it equitable that the seller render the required performance. (2-716(1)) To obtain specific performance, the buyer must have been unable to cover. While the Code does not define "unique," it is fair to assume that it would encompass output and requirement contracts in which the goods were not readily or practically available from other sources.

Case: P entered into a contract to purchase 4,000 tons of cryolite, a chemical used in the production of aluminum, from D. When D did not deliver the chemical, P brought a suit for specific performance. P contended that it was not able to readily purchase the chemical from any other source.

Issue: Is P entitled to the remedy of specific performance?

Decision: Yes.

Reason: One of the factors to be taken into account in determining whether specific performance will be allowed is the ability of the plaintiff to "cover." Here P has demonstrated that he would not be able to cover, and he is therefore entitled to specific performance.

Kaiser Trading Company v. Associated Metals and Minerals Corp., 321 F.Supp. 923 (1970).

Another remedy that enables the buyer to reach the goods in the hands of the seller is the statutory remedy of replevin. *Replevin* is an action to recover the goods that one person wrongfully withholds from another. A buyer has the right to replevin goods from the seller if the goods have been *identified* to the contract and the buyer is unable to effect cover after making a reasonable effort to do so. (2-716(3))

A related remedy that also reaches the goods in the hands of the seller is the buyer's right to recover them if the seller becomes insolvent. (2-502) The right exists only if (1) the buyer has a "special property" in the goods, that is, existing goods have been identified to the contract, and (2) the seller becomes insolvent within ten days after he received the first installment payment from the buyer. Absent such factors, the buyer is relegated to the position of a general creditor of the seller. It is apparent that if the buyer can recover the goods, he is in a much better position than he would be as a general creditor, particularly if he had paid a substantial amount of the purchase price. To exercise this remedy, the buyer must make and keep good a tender of any unpaid portion of the price.

THE SELLER'S RIGHTS AND REMEDIES

Introduction   The Code establishes certain rights and remedies for sellers just as it does for buyers. One of the most significant rights is to "cure" a defective performance. A seller has several alternative courses of action when a buyer breaches the contract. The seller may cancel the contract if the buyer's breach is material. Under certain circumstances, a seller may withhold delivery if it has not been made or may stop delivery if the goods are in transit. A seller also has the right to resell the goods and recover damages or to simply recover damages for the buyer's failure to accept the goods. Finally, the seller may under certain circumstances file suit to recover the price of the goods. The remedies of the seller are cumulative and not exclusive. The technical aspects of "cure" and of these remedies are discussed in the sections that follow.

Cure   If upon inspecting the goods the buyer finds that they do not conform to the contract, he may reject them providing he acts fairly in doing so. If the rejection is for a relatively minor deviation from the contract requirements, the seller must be given an opportunity to correct the defective performance. This is called *cure*. The seller may accomplish this by notifying the buyer of his intention to cure and then tendering proper or conforming goods if the time for performance has not expired. If the time for performance has expired, the seller, if he has reasonable grounds to believe that the goods will be acceptable in spite of the nonconformity, will be granted further time to substitute goods that are in accordance with the contract. The main purpose of this rule allowing cure is to protect the seller from being forced into a breach by a surprise rejection at the last moment by the buyer. The seller, in order to take advantage of this privilege, must notify the buyer of his intention to cure.

Right to Reclaim Goods on Buyer's Insolvency If a seller discovers that a buyer on credit is insolvent, the seller will want to withhold delivery, or if delivery is in process, to stop it before it is completed. A buyer is insolvent "who either has ceased to pay his debts in the ordinary course of business or cannot pay his debts as they become due or is insolvent within the meaning of the federal bankruptcy law." (1-201(23))

A seller, upon discovering that a buyer is insolvent, may refuse to make any further deliveries except for cash, and he may demand that payment be made for all goods theretofore delivered under the contract. (2-702(1)) If goods are en route to the buyer, they may be stopped in transit and recovered from the carrier. (2-705) If they are in a warehouse or other place of storage awaiting delivery to the buyer, the seller may stop delivery by the bailee. Thus the seller can protect his interests by retaining or reclaiming the goods prior to the time they come into the possession of the insolvent buyer.

This right to reclaim the goods on the buyer's insolvency includes situations in which the goods have come into the buyer's possession. If the buyer has received goods on credit while he is insolvent, the seller can reclaim the goods by making a demand for them within ten days after their receipt by the buyer. (2-702(2)) By receiving the goods the buyer has, in effect, made a representation that he is solvent and able to pay for them. If the buyer has made a written misrepresentation of solvency within the three-month period before the goods were delivered to him, and the seller has justifiably relied on the writing, the ten-day limitation period during which the seller can reclaim the goods from the insolvent buyer does not apply. (2-702(2))

Case: P, a carpet company, sold carpeting to D on credit. Six weeks later P discovered that D was insolvent, and P reclaimed the carpeting. Thereafter D filed a petition in bankruptcy. D had submitted to P a year-old financial statement which was inaccurate. D's trustee contended that P had not acted within the time limits in reclaiming the goods from the insolvent buyer.

Issue: Did P act within the time limits of the Code in reclaiming the goods?

Decision: Yes.

Reasons: 1. A seller has a three-month period within which to recover goods from an insolvent buyer if the buyer had made false statements in writing about his financial condition.

2. The three-month time was said to begin on the date that the financial statement was presented to the seller, so that a written statement presented six weeks before credit was extended would qualify.

In re Bel Air Carpets, 452 F.2d 1210 (1971).

The importance to a seller of the privilege of reclaiming goods or stopping them in transit should be obvious. If the insolvent buyer is adjudicated a bankrupt, the goods will become a part of the bankrupt estate and will be sold by the trustee in bankruptcy for the benefit of *all* the creditors of the buyer. If the seller is able to reclaim the goods, his loss will be kept to a minimum.

Right to Reclaim Goods-- Buyer Not Insolvent The right to stop goods in transit or to withhold delivery is not restricted to the insolvency situation. Where the buyer has (1) wrongfully rejected a tender of goods, (2) revoked his acceptance, (3) failed to make a payment due on or before delivery, or (4) repudiated with respect to either a part of the goods or the whole contract, the seller can also reclaim the goods. This right extends to any goods directly affected by the breach.

To exercise his right to stop delivery by a carrier, the seller must give proper and timely notice to such carrier so that there is reasonable time to follow the instructions given. (2-705(3)) Once the goods have been received by the buyer, or a bailee has acknowledged that he holds the goods for the buyer, the right of stoppage is at an end. Only in the case of insolvency (2-705(2)) can the seller reclaim the goods after they are in the buyer's possession.

The right to stop delivery to a solvent buyer is restricted to carload, truckload, planeload, or larger shipments. This restriction is designed to ease the burden on carriers which could develop if the right to stop for reasons other than insolvency applied to all small shipments. The seller who is shipping to a buyer of doubtful credit can always send the goods C.O.D. and thus preclude the necessity for stopping in transit. Of course, the seller must exercise care in availing himself of this remedy, as improper stoppage is a breach by the seller and would subject him to an action for damages by the buyer.

Right to Resell the Goods The seller who is in possession of goods at the time of the buyer's breach has the right to resell the goods. (2-706) If part of the goods has been delivered, he can resell the undelivered portion. In this way the seller can quickly realize at least some of the

300

amount due from the buyer. He also has a claim against the buyer for the difference between the resale price and the price that the buyer had agreed to pay. The resale remedy thus affords a practical method and course of action for the seller who has possession of goods that were intended for a breaching buyer.

Frequently, a buyer will breach or repudiate the contract prior to the time that goods have been identified to the contract. This does not defeat the seller's right to resell the goods. The seller may proceed to identify goods to the contract (2-704(1)(a)) and then use his remedy of resale. If the goods are unfinished, the seller may use his remedy of resale if he can show that the unfinished goods were intended for the particular contract. (2-704(1)(b))

The seller is also given other choices of action when the goods are in process at the time he learns of the breach. He may (1) complete the manufacture and identify the goods to the contract, or (2) resell the unfinished goods for scrap or salvage value, or (3) take any other reasonable action in connection with the goods. (2-704(2)) The only requirement is that the seller use reasonable commercial judgment in determining which course of action he will take in order to mitigate his damages. Presumably he would take into consideration such factors as the extent to which the manufacture had been completed and the resalability of the goods if he elected to complete the manufacture. Thus the law allows the seller to proceed in a commercially reasonable manner in order to protect his interests.

When the seller elects to use his remedy of resale, the resale may be either a private sale or a public (auction) sale. (2-706(2)) It must be identified as one relating to the broken contract. If the resale is private, the seller must give the buyer reasonable notification of his intention to resell. (2-706(3)) If the resale is public, the seller must give the buyer reasonable notice of the time and place so that he can bid or can obtain the attendance of other bidders. With goods that are perishable or threaten to speedily decline in value, the notice is not required. The seller is permitted to buy at a public sale or resale. The prime requirement is that the sale be conducted in a commercially reasonable manner. (2-706(2))

It is to be noted that the resale could conceivably bring a higher price than that provided for in the contract. In such case, the seller is not accountable to the buyer for any profit. (2-706(6))

Right to Collect Damages   In many situations, resale would not be an appropriate or satisfactory remedy. The seller may elect to bring an action for damages if the buyer refuses to accept the goods or repudiates the contract. (2-708) The measure of damages is the difference between the market price at the place for tender and the unpaid contract price, plus incidental damages. (2-708) Incidental damages include expenses reasonably incurred as the result of the buyer's breach. (2-710)

In most situations, this measure of damages would not be adequate to restore the seller to as good a position as would have been accomplished by performance by the buyer because of the lost sale. Under such circumstances, the measure of damages includes the profit that the seller would have made from full performance by the buyer (2-708(2)) as well as incidental damages. In computing profit, the reasonable overhead of the seller may be taken into account. The measure of damages recognizes that a seller suffers a loss, even though he may ultimately resell for the same amount that he would have received from the buyer. He has lost a sale and the profit on the sale.

**Right to
Collect the
Purchase Price**

When the buyer fails to pay the price as it becomes due, the seller may sue for the contract price of the goods if (1) the goods were accepted by the buyer, (2) the goods were lost or damaged within a commercially reasonable time after the risk of loss passed to the buyer, or (3) the goods were identified to the contract and the seller was unable to sell them at a reasonable price, or the circumstances indicated that the effort to do so would be unavailing. (2-709) Thus an action for the price is generally limited to those situations in which the buyer has accepted the goods, the goods were destroyed after risk of loss passed to the buyer, or the resale remedy is not practicable. In other cases, the suit for dollar damages would be used. (2-709(3))

If the seller sues for the price, the goods involved are, of course, held by the seller on behalf of the buyer; they become in effect the buyer's goods. After the seller obtains a judgment against the buyer, the seller may still resell the goods at any time prior to collection of the judgment, but he must apply the proceeds toward satisfaction of the judgment. Payment of the balance due on the judgment entitles the buyer to any goods not resold. (2-709(2))

REVIEW QUESTIONS AND PROBLEMS

1. What are *goods?*

2. What is a *merchant?* Why is it important to determine whether a person has merchant status?

3. In a sales contract, if nothing is said about delivery, where will delivery take place?

4. A of Eugene, Oregon, entered into a contract to purchase magnesium flares from B, whose plant is in Elgin, Illinois. The contract called for delivery "F.O.B. Eugene." While the flares were en route a bolt of lightning struck the car, and the flares were destroyed. Who must bear the loss? Why?

5. A, a Georgia merchant, ordered goods from B, a supplier in Ohio. The contract did not specify any F.O.B. term, nor did it provide for allocation in the event of loss of the goods. After B delivered the goods to a carrier, the goods were destroyed. Is A still liable to B for the purchase price? Explain.

6. A, a fruit grower, entered into a contract to sell fruit to B, a food processor. The contract did not contain a specified price. Is the contract enforceable? Why?

7. A purchased a color television set from B, a dealer. When it was installed, the color was not clear, and B, who came to A's home, said that it would be necessary to take it to his shop to repair it. A refused to allow this and demanded that the set be replaced immediately by another new one. Is he entitled to this? Explain.

8. A entered into a contract to purchase fruit from B. Several months prior to the delivery date, A announced that he would not take the fruit. B did not attempt to resell the fruit until after the delivery date specified in the contract. Is B entitled to recover damages from A? Why?

9. A contracted to sell cosmetics to B. A refused to perform, and B brought suit for specific performance on the ground that the goods were purchased at closeout prices and that they could not be otherwise obtained at the agreed price. Has B selected the correct remedy? Explain.

10. A, a clothing manufacturer, had a contract to purchase all his wool cloth requirements from B. B repudiated the contract. Can A require B to abide by the terms of the contract? Why?

11. A sold goods to B under a contract that required B to pick up the goods at A's place of business and that allowed B thirty days in which to pay for the goods. When B came to get the goods, A refused to let B have them unless he paid cash. Under what circumstances would A's conduct be justified? Explain.

20 WARRANTIES AND PRODUCT LIABILITY

Introduction   The word *warranty* as used in the law of sales of goods describes the obligation of the seller with respect to the goods that have been sold. As a general rule, a seller is responsible for transferring to the buyer a good title and goods that are of the proper quality and free from defects. He may also be responsible for the proper functioning of the article sold and for its suitability to the needs of the buyer. Thus a warranty may extend not only to the present condition of goods but also to the performance that is to be expected of them.

A seller may make a variety of statements about the goods. It is necessary to evaluate these to determine which statements are warranties and which do not impose legal responsibility because they are merely sales talk.

A warranty made by a seller is an integral part of the contract. If the warranty is breached and the buyer notifies the seller of the breach within a reasonable time, the buyer may bring an action for breach of warranty. A breach of warranty may also result in injuries to the buyer or to third persons. Thus the law relating to warranties has tort aspects also.

The obligation of a seller of goods to the buyer has been subject to reevaluation in recent years. In the early law, the parties were usually in fairly equal bargaining positions, and the law did not regard the seller as having any substantial obligation to the buyer. *Caveat emptor* ("let the buyer beware") was the philosophy of the early law of sales.

As the nature of the sales transaction changed, the need for more protection to the buyer was recognized. *Caveat emptor* was gradually replaced by *caveat venditor* ("let the seller beware"). The law took the position that if the goods were defective, the seller should be held responsible. As the law changed to *caveat venditor*, various tort and contract theories developed which imposed liability for injuries caused by defective products. These theories are discussed in this chapter.

The Code has several provisions relating to warranties. It draws a distinction between express warranties made by a seller and those implied from the transaction. The Code classifies warranties as (1) express warranties, (2) implied warranties, and (3) warranties of title. When the seller is a merchant, special treatment is sometimes afforded to the warranty. A new federal law on warranties is discussed in Chapter 28 with other aspects of consumer protection.

WARRANTIES

**Express
Warranties**
An *express warranty* is one that is made as a part of the contract for sale and becomes a part of the basis of the bargain between the buyer and the seller. (2-313(1)(a)) Such a warranty, as distinguished from an implied warranty, is part of the contract because it has been included as part of the individual bargain. To create an express warranty, the seller does not have to use formal words such as "warrant" or "guarantee," nor must he have the specific intention to make a warranty. (2-313(3)) For example, a label on a bag of insecticide stated that it was developed especially to control rootworms. There was an express warranty that the insecticide was effective to control the rootworm.

An express warranty comes into existence by virtue of any *affirmation of fact or promise* made by the seller to the buyer which relates to the goods and becomes part of the basis of their bargain. (2-313(1)(a)) These statements by the seller create an express warranty that the goods will conform to his affirmation or promise. Any statement of fact or even of opinion, if it becomes a part of the basis of the bargain, is an express warranty.

Case: P sued D, manufacturer, to recover for injuries. P was hit on the head by a golf ball following a practice swing with a golf-training device. D's catalog stated that the device was a "completely equipped backyard driving range." The label on the shipping carton and on the cover of the instruction booklet urged players to "drive the ball with full power." They also stated: "Completely safe—Ball will not hit player."

Issue: Is D liable for breach of an express warranty?

Decision: Yes.

Reasons: 1. A seller's statements whether of fact or opinion that become a part of the basis of the bargain constitute express warranties. The buyer need not prove reliance on the statement.

2. The statements here were more than mere puffing. They were factual descriptions of the characteristics of the product and express warranties.

Hauter v. Zogarts, 534 P.2d 377 (Cal.) 1975.

Most statements of opinion such as to the value of the goods do not give rise to an express warranty. As a general rule, a buyer is not justified in relying upon mere opinions and they are not usually a part of the basis of the bargain. However, expressions of opinion by a seller are part of the basis of the bargain in some situations. For example, the opinion of an expert with regard to the value of a gem might be considered as justifying the reliance of the buyer, and thus the opinion becomes part of the basis of the bargain.

Statements are warranties if they can properly be considered as terms of the agreement ultimately reached by the parties. The seller makes warranties in order to induce the sale of goods, and for this reason, warranties are regarded as essential parts of the contract. It should be remembered that warranties made after the sale of goods has been consummated are binding without any new consideration. (2-209)

An express warranty may be made in a variety of ways. One of these is for the seller to specifically make a factual statement about the goods, such as "this engine will produce 500 horsepower" or "this fabric is 100 percent nylon." This factual statement may be on the label to the goods or in a catalog or other sales promotion material. Another is for him to make a direct promise with respect to the goods, such as "this grass seed is free from weeds." Generally, words that are descriptive of the product are warranties that the goods will conform to the description. (2-313(1)(b)) Descriptions may also be in the form of diagrams, pictures, blueprints, and the like. Technical specifications of the product would constitute warranties if they were part of the basis for the bargain. An express warranty can also be based on the instructions of the seller in how to use the product.

There is a federal law relating to express warranties. It will be discussed in Chapter 28, which deals with consumer protection.

The Implied Warranty of Merchantability *Implied warranties* come into being as a matter of law, without any bargaining, and as an integral part of the normal sales transaction. Express warranties are negotiated aspects of the bargain between seller and buyer; implied warranties are legally present, unless clearly disclaimed or negated. Implied warranties exist even if a seller is unable to discover the defect involved or unable to cure it if it can be ascertained. Liability for breach of warranty is not based on fault but on the public policy of protecting the buyer of goods.

306

A warranty that the goods shall be merchantable is implied in a contract for sale if the seller is a merchant who deals in goods of the kind involved in the contract. It is not enough that the defendant sold the goods. The seller-defendant must have been a merchant with respect to the goods. A person making an isolated sale is not a merchant. This important warranty imposes a very substantial obligation upon the merchant-seller. For goods to be merchantable, they must at least be such as

a. Pass without without objection in the trade under the contract description; and
b. In the case of fungible goods, are of fair average quality within the description; and
c. Are fit for for the ordinary purposes for which such goods are used; and
d. Run, within the variations permitted by the agreement, of even kind, quality and quantity within each unit and among all units involved; and
e. Are adequately contained, packaged, and labeled as the agreement may require; and
f. Conform to the promises or affirmations of fact made on the container or lable if any. (2-314)

It will be noted that the foregoing standards provide the basic acceptable standards of merchantability. Fungible goods (subsection *b*) are those usually sold by weight or measure, such as grain or flour. The term "fair average quality" generally relates to agricultural bulk commodities and means that they are within the middle range of quality under the description. Fitness for ordinary purposes (subsection *c*) is not limited to use by the immediate buyer. If a person is buying for resale, the buyer is entitled to protection, and the goods must be honestly resalable by him. They must be of such nature that they are acceptable in the ordinary market without objection. Subsection *e* is applicable only if the nature of the goods and of the transaction require a certain type of container, package, or label. Where there is a container or label and there is a representation thereon, the buyer is entitled to protection under subsection *f* so that he will not be in the position of reselling or using goods delivered under false representations appearing on the package or container. He obtains this protection, even though the contract did not require either the labeling or the representation.

The implied warranty of merchantability imposes a very broad responsibility upon the merchant-seller to furnish goods that are at least of average quality within the industry. In any given line of business, the word *merchantable* may have a meaning somewhat different from the Code definition, and the parties by their course of dealing may indicate a special meaning for the term.

One purpose of this warranty is to require sellers to provide goods that are reasonably safe for their ordinary intended use. While the law does not require accident-proof products, it does require products that are reasonably safe for the purposes for which they were intended when such products are placed in the stream of commerce.

Liability for breach of the warranty of merchantability extends to direct economic loss as well as to personal injuries and to property damage. (Product liability based on this theory is discussed more fully later in this chapter.) Direct economic loss includes damages based on insufficient product value. In other words, the buyer is entitled to collect the difference in value between what was received and the value the product would have had if it had been of merchantable quality. Direct economic loss also includes the cost of replacement goods and the cost of repairs. These damages need not be established with mathematical certainty, but a reasonable degree of certainty and accuracy is required so that the damages are not based on speculation.

**The Warranty
of Fitness for
a Particular
Purpose**
Under the warranty of merchantability, the goods must be fit for the *ordinary purposes* for which such goods are used. An implied warranty of fitness for a *particular purpose* is created if, at the time of contracting, the seller has reason to know any particular purpose for which the buyer requires the goods and that the buyer is relying on the seller's skill or judgment to select or furnish suitable goods. (2-315) This means that the seller must in these circumstances select goods that will in fact accomplish the purpose for which they are being purchased.

Case: P, a fertilizer manufacturer, entered into a contract to buy sacks for his fertilizer from D, a bag-manufacturing company. P informed D of the chemical nature of the fertilizer and how the sacks of fertilizer would be stored. D then manufactured the sacks and placed the name of P on the bags. When the bags were exposed to the weather, the colors ran and the bags took on a shopworn appearance. P sued D for damages.

Issue: Was there an implied warranty that the bags would be fit for the purpose to which they were put?

Decision: Yes.

Reason: A manufacturer-seller of an article for a particular purpose impliedly warrants that such article will be reasonably fit for the purpose for which it is intended to be used if the buyer communicates to the manufacturer-seller the specific purpose for which he wants the article.

Southwest Distributors Inc. v. Allied Paper Bag Corp., 384 S.W.2d 838 (Mo.) 1964.

The implied warranty of fitness applies to both merchants and nonmerchants but would normally apply only to the former, since a nonmerchant would not ordinarily possess the required skill or judgment. The buyer need not specifically state that he has a particular purpose in mind or that he is placing reliance upon the seller's judgment if the circumstances are such that the seller has reason to realize the purpose intended or that the buyer is relying on him. However, the buyer must actually rely upon the seller's skill or judgment in selecting or furnishing suitable goods in order for the warranty to apply. Both issues are questions of fact for a jury.

There is a difference between merchantability and fitness for a particular purpose, although both may be included in the same contract. The particular purpose involves a specific use by the buyer; whereas the ordinary use as expressed in the concept of merchantability means the use that would ordinarily be made of the goods. Thus an appliance such as a dishwasher could be of merchantable quality because it could ordinarily be used to wash dishes but might not be fit for a particular purpose because it would not be suited for the dishwashing needs of a restaurant.

Breach of the warranty of fitness for a particular purpose may result in disaffirmance of the contract. If the product causes an injury including economic loss, it may also result in a suit for dollar damages. This also will be discussed further as a part of product liability later in this chapter.

The Warranty of Title

The *warranty of title* is treated as a separate implied warranty under the Code. Since the concept of title is intangible and is often overlooked by the buyer, the law ensures such a warranty by including it in the sale as a matter of law.

A seller warrants that he is conveying good title to the buyer and that he has the right to sell the goods. He further warrants that there are no encumbrances or liens against the property sold and that no other person can claim a security interest in them. (2-312) In effect the seller impliedly guarantees to the buyer that he will be able to enjoy the use of the goods free from the claims of any third party. Of course, property may be sold to a buyer who has full knowledge of liens or encumbrances, and he may buy such property subject to such claims. In this event there would not be a breach of warranty of title. The purchase price would, however, reflect that he was obtaining something less than complete title.

Warranty of title can be excluded or modified only by specific language or by circumstances that make it clear that the seller is not vouching for the title. (2-312(2)) Judicial sales and sales by executors of estates would not imply that the seller guarantees the title. Also a seller could directly inform the buyer that he is selling only the interest that he has and that the buyer takes it subject to all encumbrances.

A seller who is a merchant regularly dealing in goods of the kind that are the subject of the sale makes an additional warranty. He warrants that the goods are free of the rightful claim of any third person by way of infringement of such person's interests—that the goods sold do not, for example, infringe upon a patent. But a buyer may furnish to the seller specifications for the construction of an article, and this may result in the infringement of a patent. Not only does the seller not warrant against such infringement but the buyer must protect the seller from any claims arising out of such infringement. (2-312(3))

**Disclaimers
of Warranties**
A seller will often seek to avoid or restrict warranty liability. The Code provisions on exclusion or modification of warranties are designed to protect the buyer from unexpected and unfair disclaimers.

During the course of the dealings between the buyer and the seller, there may be both statements or conduct relating to the creation of an express warranty and statements or conduct tending to negate or limit such warranties. To the extent that it is reasonable, the two different kinds of statements or conduct shall be construed as consistent with each other. (2-316(1)) Negation or limitation is inoperative to the extent that such construction is unreasonable. In other words, if the express warranty and the attempt to negate warranties cannot be construed as consistent, the warranty predominates. The seller may have given the buyer an express warranty and may then have included in the contract a provision that purports to exclude "all warranties express or implied." The disclaimer in such a case will not be given effect, and the express warranty will be enforceable.

Implied warranties can be excluded if the seller makes it clear that the buyer will not have the benefit of such warranties. To exclude or modify the implied warranty of merchantability, the word *merchantability* must be used. (2-316(2)) If the disclaimer is included in a written contract, it must be set forth in a conspicuous manner. The disclaimer clause of the contract should be in type of a larger size or different color of ink or indentation so that it will be brought to the buyer's attention. It has been held that a disclaimer will not be effective if it is set forth in the same type and color as the rest of the contract.

To exclude or modify any implied warranty of fitness for a particular purpose, the exclusion must not only be conspicuous but also be set forth in writing. Such a statement as "there are no warranties which extend beyond the description on the face hereof" is sufficient to exclude the implied warranty of fitness for a particular purpose. (2-316(2)) The exclusionary clause should be set forth in type that will set it apart from the balance of the contract.

Case: P, the buyer of a tractor and backhoe, sued D, the seller, for breach of express warranties and for breach of the implied warranties of merchantability and of fitness for a particular purpose. The sales contract above the buyer's signature contained the following:

> The equipment covered hereby is sold subject only to the applicable manufacturer's standard printed warranty, if any, in effect at the date hereof, receipt of a copy of which is hereby acknowledged, and no other warranties, express or implied, including without limitation, the implied warranties of <u>merchantability and fitness for a particular purpose shall apply.</u>

The type size used in the foregoing was slightly larger than the rest of the contract, but it was not in boldface type.

Issue: Was the disclaimer effective to negate the express and implied warranties?

Decision: No.

Reasons: 1. The exclusion of the implied warranty of merchantability if in writing must be conspicuous.

2. The exclusion of the implied warranty of fitness for a particular purpose must be in writing and conspicuous.

3. The word *conspicuous* means that it must be so written that a reasonable person against whom it is to operate ought to have noticed it.

4 The Code provisions on exclusion of warranties were intended to protect the buyer from the situation where a salesman's "pitch," advertising brochure, or large print in the contract giveth, and the disclaimer clause, in the fine print, taketh away.

5. A valid disclaimer must be prominently set forth in large bold print in such a position as to compel notice. This one did not.

Dorman v. International Harvester Company, 120 Cal. Rptr. 516 (1975).

The Code also provides for other circumstances in which implied warranties may be wholly or partially excluded. The seller may inform the buyer that he is selling goods "as is," "with all faults," or use other language that calls the buyer's attention to the exclusion and makes it plain to him that the sale involves no implied warranty. (2-316(3)(a)) The implied warranty of merchantability may be excluded by oral agreement or by the *parties'* course of performance. The Code does not guarantee every buyer a good deal.

The buyer's examination of the goods, or a sample, or a model is also significant in determining the existence of implied warranties. If, before entering into the contract, he has examined the goods, sample, or model as fully as he desired, there is no implied warranty as to defects that an examination ought to have revealed to him.

311

(2-316(3)(b)) If the seller has *demanded* that the buyer examine the goods fully and the buyer refuses to do so, there would be no implied warranty as to those defects that a careful examination would have revealed. By making the demand, the seller is giving notice to the buyer that the buyer is assuming the risk with regard to defects that an examination ought to reveal.

Extent of the Warranties

Historically, suits for breach of warranty required "privity of contract," or a contractual connection between the parties. Lack of privity of contract was a complete defense to the suit.

There are two aspects to privity of contract requirements. These are sometimes described as horizontal and vertical. The *horizontal* privity issue is, To whom does the warranty extend? Does it run only in favor of the actual purchaser, or does it extend to others who may use or be affected by the product? The *vertical* privity issue is, Against whom can action be brought for breach of warranty? Can the party sue only the seller, or will direct action lie against wholesalers, manufacturers, producers, and growers?

When privity of contracts is required, only the actual buyer can collect for breach of warranty, and he can collect only from the actual seller. A seller who is liable may recover from his seller. Thus the requirement of privity of contract prevents many suits for breach of warranty where privity does not exist. It also encourages multiple lawsuits over the same product.

It is not surprising that the law has generally abandoned strict privity of contract requirements. It has done so by statute and also on a case-by-case basis. The Code is silent on the vertical issue. A special provision on the horizontal issue provides that express and implied warranties extend to any person who is in the family or household of the buyer or who is a guest in his home, if it is reasonable to expect that such a person would use, consume, or be affected by the goods. (2-318) It should be noted that this does not extend to employees of the buyer. They are not family or guests in the home. The Code leaves the final development of the law of warranties beyond this statement to the courts. The extent of warranties will be discussed further in the sections that follow. However, privity of contract has been abolished as a defense in most states.

Case: P purchased a contaminated cheeseburger from a vending machine where he worked. P suffered acute food poisoning when he ate the cheeseburger. P sued D, the baking company that baked the bun, for breach of the warranty of merchantability. D moved to dismiss for lack of privity of contract.

Issue: Is lack of privity of contract a defense to a breach of implied warranty?

Decision: No.

Reasons: 1. For many years West Virginians suffering injuries as the result of defective products have been unable to recover against defendant manufacturers, wholesalers, or retailers for breach of warranty unless they stood in privity of contract with the defendant. At the same time West Virginia manufacturers, wholesalers, and retailers selling products nationally have been exposed to extensive liability for defective products manufactured in this State and sold elsewhere because the majority of American jurisdictions have abolished privity as a requirement in warranty actions.

2. In order to correct the situation referred to in #1 above and to bring the state in line with the rest of the country, the requirement of privity is abolished.

Dawson v. Canteen Corp., 212 S.E.2d 82 (W.Va.) 1975.

PRODUCT LIABILITY

Introduction   One of the consequences of manufacturing or selling a product is the responsibility to a consumer or user if the product is defective and causes injury to a person or property. This liability is generally referred to as *product liability*. The subject of product liability involves several legal theories. A suit for dollar damages for injuries caused by a product may be predicated on the theory of (1) negligence, (2) misrepresentation, (3) breach of warranty, either express or implied, or (4) strict liability.

Product liability cases may be brought against manufacturers, sellers, or anyone in the chain of sale. Such cases may be brought by the buyer, by another user of the product, or by some third party whose only connection with the product is the sustaining of an injury caused by it.

Since the Code is silent on the vertical aspects of privity, the law has developed on a case-by-case basis. The trend of the law on product liability is clearly in the direction of extending greater protection to consumers. A manufacturer has an obligation to the public to put on the market a product that is safe to use and free from defects. A manufacturer is presumed to know of the defects in its products and is therefore in bad faith in selling defective products. The consumer is entitled to protection from injuries. In furtherance of these policies, some cases have imposed liability when the facts indicate that the product was not defective but that the injury was caused by the way in

313

which the product was used. Product liability has been imposed because of defects in design as well as defects in manufacture. For example, a manufacturer of power lawnmowers was held liable to a person whose hand was injured when he reached under the machine to remove a rock that had obstructed the blades. The ruling of the court was that the company was negligent in failing to install a guard that would have made it impossible to put a hand in the blade compartment.

Negligence   In order to recover on a negligence theory, the plaintiff has to establish that the defendant failed to exercise reasonable care in manufacturing the product. Contributory negligence on the part of the plaintiff is a bar to a recovery. Privity of contract is not required, since it is not a contract action.

An action based on negligence can be maintained not only by the person who purchased the defective product but also by any person who suffered an injury on account of a defect in the product. Thus, in the case of an automobile with defective brakes, it is reasonably foreseeable that other persons would be placed in jeopardy if the brakes failed, and they can sue on a negligence theory. The Restatement of Torts (Second), Section 395, states the rule as follows:

> A manufacturer who fails to exercise reasonable care in the manufacture of a chattel which, unless carefully made, he should recognize as involving an unreasonable risk of causing physical harm to those who use it for a purpose for which the manufacturer should expect it to be used and to those whom he should expect to be endangered by its probable use, is subject to liability for physical harm caused to them by its lawful use in a manner and for a purpose for which it is supplied.

Misrepresentation   If the seller has advertised the product through newspapers, magazines, television, or otherwise and in so doing made misrepresentations with regard to the character or quality of the product, tort liability may be imposed on him.

For example, a manufacturer may advertise that a certain shampoo contains no harmful ingredients and is perfectly safe to use even by people with tender skin. If someone uses the shampoo and suffers a skin ailment as a result thereof, he would be entitled to recover. The Restatement of Torts (Second), Section 402B, summarizes the liability of a seller for misrepresentation as follows:

> One engaged in the business of selling chattels who, by advertising, labels, or otherwise, makes to the public a misrepresentation of a material fact concerning the character or quality of a chattel sold by him is subject to liability for physical harm to a consumer of the chattel caused by justifiable reliance upon the misrepresentation, even though

a. It is not made fraudulently or negligently, and

b. The consumer has not bought the chattel from or entered into any contractual relation with the seller.

The rationale of the Restatement position is that a great deal of what the consumer knows about a product comes to him through the various media, and sellers should be held responsible and accountable for misrepresentations made to the public.

Breach of Warranty Liability

An action based upon a defective product can be based on a breach of either the implied warranty of merchantability or the implied warranty of fitness for a particular purpose.

Case: P, a farmer, had contracted to grow sweet corn for processing and freezing for the A canning company. Before planting, he consulted with D, who sold herbicides. D recommended a product manufactured by X chemical company. Following this recommendation, P applied the product. Thereafter his corn crop was noted to be stunted, twisted, and infested with parasites.

Issue: 1. Was the seller (D) liable in damages to P?

2. Was the manufacturer (X chemical company) liable in damages to P?

Decision: Yes, on both questions.

Reasons: 1. D is responsible because there was an implied warranty of fitness for a particular purpose. P had communicated to D his need for a herbicide to control weeds on his farmland.

2. X chemical company is liable in spite of disclaimers because it had represented that the product was compatible with corn when it had no real knowledge on that score as to corn in the area where P farmed.

Dobias v. Western Farmers Association, 491 P.2d 1346 (Wash.) 1971.

As previously noted, the privity requirement in cases of personal injuries caused by defective products has been generally eliminated. The early cases that abandoned the privity requirement involved personal injury and sickness caused by food and drugs. The law took the position that as a matter of social policy, a packer, grower, or manufacturer of a product consumed by human beings should be liable if that product caused injury.

Various courts have used different justifications to eliminate the privity requirement in cases involving products other than food and drugs. Some have employed the *dangerous instrumentality* theory in nonfood cases. These courts said that privity was not required in such cases because food was inherently dangerous, and therefore if another product was inherently dangerous, the same rationale would be applied, and privity of contract would not be required. Other courts stated that "warranties run with goods" in much the same way that a warranty involving the title to land runs with the land. A warranty is an invisible appendage that is a part of the goods, and as such, it belongs to anyone who is affected by the goods.

Today, in almost every state, actions can be maintained for breach of either implied warranty without privity of contract. An action based upon such breach, being a contract action, does not require proof of negligence on the part of the manufacturer or seller. The injured plaintiff must only prove that the product was defective and that such defect was the proximate cause of his injury.

Strict Liability   The latest development in product liability is a natural extension of the demise of privity of contract. Known as the theory of *strict liability*, this tort theory imposes liability whenever an injury is caused by a defective product that is unreasonably or inherently dangerous. It is not enough in most cases that the product be defective—it must also be unreasonably dangerous.

A cause of action in strict liability requires proof that the defendant sold the product in a defective condition unreasonably dangerous to the user or consumer, that it reached the plaintiff without a change of condition, and that the product caused an injury to the plaintiff. The test as to whether or not a defect is unreasonably dangerous depends upon the reasonable expectations of the ordinary consumer. If the average consumer would reasonably anticipate the dangerous condition of a product and fully appreciate the risk, it is not unreasonably dangerous. In strict liability cases, there are no issues on disclaimer of warranties, there is no inconsistency with express warranties, and knowledge of defect need not be proved. Of course, privity of contract is not required.

The theory is applicable whether the product is new or used because the gist of the tort is that the product is unreasonably dangerous. The theory imposes liability on manufacturers and designers as well as on the seller of the goods. In almost every state, the liability extends not only to users and consumers but also to bystanders such as pedestrians.

Case: P, while shopping in a grocery store, was injured when a bottle of pop exploded. P sued D, the bottler, for her personal injuries. D contended that it had no liability because the doctrine of strict liability does not extend to bystanders.

Issue: Is D liable?

Decision: Yes.

Reasons: 1. The rule of strict product liability in tort applies to any person engaged in the business of supplying products for use or consumption, including any manufacturer of such product and any wholesaler, retail dealer, distributor, or other middleman.

2. The rule of strict product liability in tort extends not only to users and consumers but also to bystanders whose injury from the defective product is reasonably foreseeable.

3. The risk of personal injury and property damage will be minimized by charging the costs of injuries against the manufacturer who can procure liability insurance and distribute its expense among the public as a cost of doing business. Since the risk of harm from defective products exists for mere bystanders and passersby as well as for the purchaser or user, there is no substantial reason for protecting one class of persons and not the other.

4. The result does not give the bystander a "free ride." When products and consumers are considered in the aggregate, bystanders, as a class, purchase most of the same products to which they are exposed as bystanders. Thus, as a class, they indirectly subsidize the liability of the manufacturer, middleman, and retailer and in this sense do pay for the insurance policy tied to the product.

Embs v. Pepsi-Cola Bot. Co. of Lexington, 528 S.W.2d 703 (Ky.) 1975.

Strict liability is not synonymous with *absolute liability*. There must be proof that some dangerous defect caused the injury. In addition, a plaintiff must prove that the product was being used in the manner reasonably anticipated by the seller or manufacturer. There need be no proof of negligence, but contributory negligence may be a defense in certain cases. For example, failure to heed a warning with regard to the product will bar a recovery.

The theory of strict liability has been applied to leases of goods as well as to sales. The potential liability extends to all commercial suppliers of goods. Strict liability has been applied both to personal injuries and to damage to the property of the user or consumer. Some courts, however, have refused to extend it to property damage. Most courts have refused to extend it to allow recovery for economic loss.

Strict liability may be imposed upon a seller of goods manufactured by a *third person*, if the seller fails to give proper warning that a product is or is likely to be dangerous or if he fails to exercise reasonable care to inform buyers of the danger or to otherwise protect them against it. A similar duty to give warning applies to the manufacturer. For example, a warning must be placed on a container or label if a product is explosive, poisonous, and so forth. Some cases

317

extend the liability to the manufacturer of a component part of a product that fails. For example, the manufacturer of the jet engine as well as the manufacturer of the airplane may be liable to the victims of a plane that crashes due to mechanical failure of the engine.

The potential liability under all theories of product liability is usually covered by product liability insurance. In recent years, the cost of product liability insurance has skyrocketed. It has become a significant cost item in many products with a high exposure to product liability suits.

REVIEW QUESTIONS AND PROBLEMS

1. What is meant by a *warranty*?

2. What is the meaning of *merchantability?*

3. Under what circumstances does the warranty of fitness for a particular purpose come into play?

4. Can warranties be disclaimed? How?

5. A was considering the purchase of a used crane from B. The crane was demonstrated to A but did not do any actual lifting in the demonstration. A decided to purchase the crane and was assured that it would lift thirty tons. If the crane were not capable of lifting thirty tons, would A have a cause of action against B? Why?

6. A sold skins to B with knowledge that B would make leather jackets from them. Nothing was said about warranties. Has A made any warranties to B? Explain.

7. A was pallbearer at a funeral. The casket handle he was holding broke and caused the casket to fall and injure him. A brought action against the funeral parlor and the manufacturer of the casket. Upon what basis could A obtain recovery? Explain.

8. A purchased a new stereo set marked "As Is" from the XYZ electronics company during a special sale. Two days later, the stero failed to operate. Will XYZ be required to repair the set? Why?

9. A operated a restaurant. He purchased clams from B. C, a customer at A's restaurant, ordered clams, ate them, and claimed that he had contracted hepatitis. Does C have a cause of action against A? Against B? Why?

10. The XYZ cosmetic company included the following warning on a can of hair spray: "Danger—Avoid spraying into eyes." While spraying her hair, A allowed some of the contents to get into her eyes. A sued XYZ for personal injuries using various theories of product liability. Discuss the possible results of this case.

11. A, a scuba diver, purchased an underwater depth gauge from B, a retailer of diving equipment. Upon surfacing from his first dive with the new gauge, A suffered injury due to the bends. The injury was caused by A's staying at a certain depth too long. It was later determined that the gauge would cause the diver to believe that he was not as deep as he actually was. Can A recover actual damages from B? Why?

21 INTRODUCTION TO COMMERCIAL PAPER

Introduction The term *commercial paper* is used to describe certain types of negotiable instruments. The adjective *negotiable* means that the written contract is able to move freely through the financial community as a substitute for money.

Commercial paper may be divided into two basic types of instruments—notes and drafts. A *note* is a promise to pay money. A *draft* is an order directed to some other person to pay money. (3-102(b)(c)) A *check* is a typical draft, since it is an order on a bank to pay money.

Commercial paper serves two basic functions. It is a substitute for money and it is a credit device. For example, if A buys goods from B and pays with a check, the check is a substitute for money. If A pays with a sixty-day note, it is a credit device. B may sell the note and receive money for it.

The Concept of Negotiability Negotiable instruments developed because of the commercial need for something that would be readily acceptable in lieu of money and would accordingly be readily transferable in trade or commerce. This requires that substantial protection and assurance of payment be given to any person to whom the paper might be transferred. To accomplish this, it is necessary to insulate the transferee from most of the defenses that a primary party, such as the maker of a note, might have against the payee. The purpose of the negotiability trait is to prevent the primary party from asserting defenses to the instrument against the person to whom the paper was transferred.

To accomplish the foregoing, Article 3 of the Code provides that a person to whom commercial paper is negotiated takes it free of

319

personal defenses of the maker or drawer. This basic theory of negotiability can be further explained by noting the difference between the *assignment* of a contract and the negotiation of a negotiable instrument. For example, assume that A owes B $100 from A. Assume also that A has a defense in the nature of a counterclaim against B because the goods sold were defective. The right that C purchased from B would be subject to A's defense of failure of consideration. C, the assignee, would secure no better right against A than the original right held by B, the assignor. Therefore, C could not collect $100 from A.

In the example given above, if the evidence of the debt is not a simple contract for money but a negotiable promissory note given by A to B and it is properly negotiated to C, C is in a superior position to that which he occupied when he was an assignee. Assuming that C is a "holder in due course," C has a better title because he is free of the personal defenses that are available against B, the original party to the paper. Therefore, A cannot use the defense of failure of consideration against C, and C can collect the $100.

Transfer of the instrument free of personal defenses is the very essence of negotiability. Three requirements must be met before a holder is free from personal defenses. First, the instrument must be negotiable, that is, it must comply with the statutory formalities and language requirements. An instrument that does not qualify is nonnegotiable, and any transfer is an assignment subject to defenses. Second, the instrument must be properly *negotiated* to the transferee. Third, the party to whom negotiable commercial paper is negotiated must be a *holder in due course* or have the rights of a holder in due course. Each of these concepts is discussed in the text chapters.

The defenses that cannot be asserted against a holder in due course are called *personal defenses*. *Real defenses*, on the other hand, may be asserted against anyone, including a holder in due course. Real defenses are matters that go to the very existence of the instruments. Personal defenses such as failure of consideration involve less serious matters and usually relate to the transaction out of which it arose.

**Kinds of
Commercial
Paper**   Article 3 of the Code, Commercial Paper, is restricted in its coverage to the draft, the check, the certificate of deposit, and the note. A *draft* is an order upon another person to pay money; a *check* is a draft drawn on a bank. A *certificate of deposit* is a type of savings account wherein the bank agrees to repay the sum with interest at a specified time. A *note* is a promise to pay other than a certificate of deposit. (3-104(2))

A note is two-party paper, as is a certificate of deposit. The parties to a note are the *maker*, who promises to pay, and the *payee*, to whom the promise is made. The draft and the check are three-party instruments. A draft presupposes a debtor-creditor relationship between the *drawer* and the *drawee* or some other obligation on the part of the drawee in favor of the drawer. The drawee is the debtor; the drawer is the creditor. The drawer-creditor orders the drawee-debtor to pay money to a third party who is the *payee*. The mere execution of the draft does not obligate the drawee on the paper. The drawee's liability on the paper arises when it formally *accepts* the obligation to pay in writing upon the draft itself. By accepting, the drawee becomes primarily liable on the paper. (3-410(1)) Thereafter, the drawee is called an *acceptor*, and its liability is similar to the liability of the maker of a promissory note.

A check drawn by a bank upon itself is a *cashier's* check. A *certified* check is a check that has been "accepted" by the drawee bank. Certification is discussed further in the next section. *Traveler's* checks are like cashier's checks in that the financial institution issuing such instruments is both the drawer and the drawee. Such instruments are negotiable when they have been completed by the identifying signature. A *bank draft* is a banker's check; that is, it is a check drawn by one bank on another bank, payable on demand. Such drafts are often used in the check collection process and are called "remittance instruments" in this connection.

Certified Checks

Either the drawer or the holder of a check may present it to the drawee bank for certification. The bank will stamp "certified" on the check, and an official of the bank will sign it and date it. By certifying, the bank assumes responsibility for payment and sets aside funds from its customer's account to cover the check.

Certification may or may not change the legal liability of the parties upon the instrument. When the *drawer* has a check certified, such a certification merely acts as additional security and does not relieve the drawer of any liability. On the other hand, when the *holder* of a check secures certification by the drawee bank, he thereby accepts the bank as the only party liable thereon. Such an act discharges the drawer and all prior indorsers from liability. (3-411(1)) The effect of such certification is similar to a payment by the bank and redeposit by the holder.

The refusal of a bank to certify a check at the request of a holder is not a dishonor of the instrument. The bank owes the depositor a duty to pay but not necessarily the duty to certify checks that are drawn on it, unless there is a previous agreement to certify. (3-411(2)) A drawer cannot stop payment on a check after the bank has certified it.

Ambiguous Terms and Rules of Construction In view of the millions of negotiable instruments that are made and drawn daily, it is to be expected that a certain number of them will be ambiguously worded. Accordingly, the Code provides a number of rules to be applied in interpreting negotiable instruments.

Some instruments are drawn in such a manner that it is doubtful whether the instrument is a draft or a note. For example, it may be directed to a third person but contain a promise to pay rather than an order to pay. The holder may treat it as either a draft or a note and present it for payment to either the person who signed it or the apparent drawee. Where a draft is drawn on the drawer, it is treated as a note. (3-119(a))

An instrument may contain handwritten terms, typewritten terms, or printed terms. Where there are discrepancies in the instrument, handwritten terms control typewritten and printed terms, and typewritten terms control printed terms. (3-118(b))

There may also be a conflict between the words and the figures of an instrument. Thus a check may have the words "fifty dollars" and the figures "$500." The words control, and the check would be for fifty dollars. However, if the words are ambiguous, the figures will control. (3-118(c)) For example, in a check with the words "Five seventy five dollars" and the figures "$5.75," the figures will control. In some cases, the ambiguity may arise from the context of the words.

If two or more persons sign an instrument as maker, acceptor, drawer, or indorser as part of the same transaction, they are jointly and severally liable unless the instrument otherwise specifies. This means that the full amount of the obligation could be collected from any one of them or that all of them might be joined in a single action. Joint and several liability is imposed even though the instrument contains such words as "I promise to pay." (3-118(e))

BANK DEPOSITS AND COLLECTIONS

Terminology The check is the most common form of commercial paper. Article 4 of the Code—Bank Deposits and Collections—provides uniform rules to govern the collection of checks. These rules govern the relationship of banks with each other and with depositors in the collection and payment of *items.*

The following terminology of Article 4 is significant, especially with regard to the designation of the various banks in the collection process:

a. "Depositary bank" means the first bank to which an item is transferred for collection even though it is also the payor bank;

b. "Payor bank" means a bank by which an item is payable as drawn or accepted;

c. "Intermediary bank" means any bank to which an item is transferred in course of collection except the depositary or payor bank;

d. "Collection bank" means any bank handling the item for collection except the payor bank;

e. "Presenting bank" means any bank presenting an item except a payor bank;

f. "Remitting bank" means any payor or intermediary bank remitting for an item. (4-105)

Timing is important in the check collection process. Many of the technical rules of law refer to a *banking day*, which is defined as "that part of any day on which a bank is open to the public for carrying on substantially all of its banking functions." (4-104(c)) A bank is permitted to establish a cutoff hour of 2 P.M. or later so that the bank may have an opportunity to process items, prove balances, and make the necessary entries to determine its position for the day. If an item is received after the cutoff hour—if one be fixed—or after the close of the banking day, it may be treated as having been received at the opening of the next banking day. (4-107) The term *midnight deadline* with respect to a bank means midnight on its next banking day following the banking day on which the bank receives the check or notice with regard to it. (4-104(1)(h))

Another important term is *clearing house*, which means an association of banks that engages in the clearing or settling of accounts between banks in connection with checks. (4-104(1)(d))

**The Collection
Process**   The collection process begins when the customer deposits a check to his account. The account is provisionally credited by the bank. The check then passes through the collecting banks, each of which provisionally credits the account of the prior bank. When the check reaches the payor (drawee) bank, that bank debits the drawer's account.

If the payor bank honors the check, the settlement is final. Transactions prior to this final settlement by the payor bank are called "provisional settlements" because until final settlement, it is not known whether the check is "good." If the payor bank dishonors the check, each provisional settlement is *revoked*, and the depositary bank which had given its provisional credit to the customer for the deposit cancels it. The dishonored check is then returned to the customer.

When a bank has received a check for collection, it has the duty to use ordinary care in performing its collection operations. Failure of the collecting bank to use ordinary care in handling a check subjects the bank to liability to the depositor for any loss or damage sustained.

To act seasonably, a bank is generally required to take proper action before the midnight deadline following the receipt of a check, a notice, or a payment. Thus, if a collecting bank receives a check on Monday and presents it or forwards it to the next collecting bank any time prior to midnight Tuesday, it has acted seasonably.

If a check has been dishonored, as in the case of an "N.S.F." (not sufficient funds) check, each of the collecting banks must return the item or send notification of the facts by its midnight deadline. The right to charge back by the depositary bank is not affected by the fact that the depositor may have drawn against the provisional credit.

A depositor does not have the right to draw against uncollected funds. Accordingly, he is not entitled to draw against an item payable by another bank until the provisional settlement which his depositary bank has received becomes final. (4-213(4)(a))

Where the deposit is an item *on which the depositary bank is itself the payor* ("on us" items), the credit becomes final on the opening of the second banking day following receipt of the item. (4-213(4)(b))

A customer who deposits an item for collection should indorse it, but quite frequently a customer overlooks doing so. The depositary bank may supply the missing indorsement. If the bank states on the item that it was deposited by a customer or credited to his account, such a statement is effective as the customer's indorsement. This is a practical rule intended to speed up the collection process by making it unnecessary to return to the depositor any items he may have failed to indorse. (4-205)

Collection from the Payor Bank

An item may be presented to a payor bank for payment over the counter. If the bank pays the item, it may not later collect back the payments if its customer has insufficient funds on deposit. (4-213)

Case: D indorsed and presented a $2,500 check to the teller of P bank on which it was drawn. P's teller paid D the $2,500. The next day P discovered that the drawer of the check had insufficient funds to cover it. P then sued D to recover the $2,500 paid to D on the check.

Issue: Is P entitled to recollect its payment?

Decision: No.

Reasons: 1. An item is finally paid by a payor bank when the bank pays the item in cash. If paid by mistake, it is the bank's error and the bank's loss.

2. An indorser has no liability to a drawee bank. If a drawee bank dishonors a check, it has suffered no loss.

3. A presenter of a check does not make a warranty that the drawer has sufficient funds to cover the check.

4. A payment in the ordinary course of business of a check by a bank on which it is drawn under the mistaken belief that the drawer has funds in the bank is not such a payment under a mistake of fact as will permit the bank to recover the money so paid from the recipient of such payment. To permit the bank to repudiate the payment would destroy the certainty which must pertain to commercial transactions if they are to remain useful to the business public. Otherwise no one would ever know when he can safely receive payment of a check.

Kirby v. First & Merchants Nat. Bank, 168 S.E.2d 273 (Va.) 1969.

Most items will be presented through a clearinghouse or by mail. If the payor bank makes a provisional settlement for them on the banking day they are received, it has until its midnight deadline on the following day to decide whether or not the item is good. Within this time the bank may revoke the settlement and return the item or, if this is not possible, send written notice of nonpayment. (4-212)

Another problem relates to the *order of payment checks.* There is no priority as among checks drawn on a particular account and presented to a bank on any particular day. The checks and other items may be accepted, paid, certified, or charged to the indicated account of its customer in any order convenient to the bank. (4-303(2))

Stop Payments A customer has the right to stop payment on checks drawn on his account. To be effective, a stop payment order must be "received at such time and in such manner as to afford the bank a reasonable opportunity to act on it prior to an action by the bank with respect to the item. . . ." (4-403) If a check has been certified, the depositor cannot stop payment. An oral stop payment order is binding on the bank for only fourteen days. A written stop payment order is effective for only six months. (4-404)

A bank that honors a check upon which payment has been stopped is liable to the drawer of the check for any loss suffered because of the failure to obey the stop order. The burden is on the customer to establish the amount of loss. It may be that the customer cannot establish any loss. Thus, if the drawer did not have a valid reason to stop payment, he cannot collect from a bank that fails to obey the stop payment order. (4-403(3)) The bank cannot by agreement disclaim its responsibility for its failure to obey stop payment orders. (4-103(1)) Thus a form signed by a customer agreeing not to hold the bank responsible for failure to pay could not be enforced.

Because of the concept of negotiability previously noted, a stop order on a check gives the drawer only limited protection. If the check is negotiated by the payee to a holder in due course, such person can require payment of the amount of the check notwithstanding the stop order.

Case: D equipment company bought equipment from X and gave him a check drawn upon Y bank in payment. It was understood that the equipment would be delivered the following day. When it was not delivered, D stopped payment on the check. X attempted to cash the check at Y bank, but payment was refused. X then took the check to his own bank, P bank, which cashed it for him. When the check was sent to Y bank, that bank refused to honor it because of the stop order. P bank seeks to collect the amount of the check from D equipment company.

Issue: Does the stop order protect D equipment company against the claim of the bank?

Decision: No.

Reasons: 1. The bank was a holder in due course and had no reason to know of the stop order.

2. If a check gets into the hands of a holder in due course, the drawer will be liable to such person notwithstanding the stop payment order.

Suit & Wells Equipment Co., Inc. v. Citizens National Bank of Southern Maryland, 282 A.2d 109 (Md.) 1971.

THE RELATIONSHIP BETWEEN A BANK AND ITS CUSTOMERS

Rights and Duties of Banks The legal relationship between a bank and its depositors is that of debtor and creditor. If the depositor is a borrower of the bank, the reverse relationship (creditor-debtor) also exists between the bank and its customers. This dual relationship provides the bank with a prompt and easy method of protecting itself in the event of a depositor's default or pending insolvency. A bank can "seize" bank deposits under its right of setoff if it becomes necessary to do so to protect its account receivable.

Case: P, a grain elevator, sued D bank for wrongful dishonor of its checks. P owed D $272,000 on certain promissory notes; $190,000 was owed on short-term notes and the balance was due on long-term notes. These notes were secured by mortgage and security agreements.

P, in negotiating a new loan, told D's officers that it lost $22,000 during the last year and that its checking account was overdrawn by $35,000. It sought to borrow $50,000. The loan was turned down, and P's elevator closed for two days. D bank then set off P's $71,000 checking account balance against its loans and returned all of P's checks when presented for payment.

Issue: Is D liable for not honoring P's checks and for seizing the checking account?

Decision: No.

Reasons: 1. A bank may set off as general deposit against a depositor's debts. Here the notes allowed acceleration of the due dates if the bank in good faith felt insecure.

2. Here the bank's acceleration was in good faith in its belief that it was insecure.

Farmers Co-op El., Inc., Duncombe v. State Bank, 236 N.W.2d 674 (Iowa) 1975.

A bank is under a duty to honor checks drawn by its customer when there are sufficient funds in his account to cover the checks. Even if there are insufficient funds, the bank may honor the checks even though this creates an overdraft. The customer is indebted to the bank for the overdraft and impliedly promises to reimburse the bank. (4-401(1))

If a bank wrongfully dishonors a check, it is liable in damages to its customer for damages proximately caused by the wrongful dishonor. When the dishonor occurs by mistake, as distinguished from a malicious or willful dishonor, liability is limited to the *actual damages* proved. (4-402) Actual damages includes damages for arrest or prosecution of the customer and for any other *consequential damages* proximately caused by the wrongful dishonor. The Code rejects early common-law decisions that held that if the dishonored item were drawn by a merchant, he was defamed in his business because of the reflection on his credit. Accordingly, a merchant cannot recover damages on the basis of defamation, and he is limited to actual damages.

If a bank in good faith pays a raised check, it can only charge the account of its customer the original amount of the check. (4-401(2)(a)) However, if a person signs his name to an incomplete check and it is thereafter completed, presented to the drawee bank, and paid, the bank can charge the customer's account for the full amount of such check if it pays in good faith and does not know that the completion was improper. (4-401(2)(b))

A bank is not *obligated* to pay a check that is over six months old. The bank, however, is entitled to pay a check that has been outstanding more than six months and may charge it to the customer's account. (4-404(1))

The death of a customer does not revoke the bank's authority to pay checks until the bank knows of the death and has a reasonable opportunity to act on it. The same rule applies to an adjudication of incompetency. (4-405)

Even though the bank knows of the death of its customer, it *may* pay or certify checks for a period of ten days after the date of his death. This is intended to permit holders of checks drawn and issued shortly before death to cash them without the necessity of filing a claim in probate. This is subject to the proviso that a stop order may be made by a relative or other person who claims an interest in the account. (4-405(2))

Rights and Duties of Depositors

Banks make available to their customers a statement of account. Canceled checks are returned with the bank statements. Within a reasonable time after they are received by the customer, he is under a duty to examine them for forgeries and for raised checks. The bank does not have the right to charge an account with forged checks, but the customer's failure to examine and to notify will prevent him from asserting the forgery (or alteration) against the bank if the bank can establish that it suffered a loss because of this failure. For example, the bank may be able to prove that a prompt notification would have enabled the bank to recover from the forger. (4-406(2))

Case: A and B were partners. They maintained a bank account in D bank. One of their employees, without their knowledge or consent, wrote checks on the partnership bank account and forged the names of A and B. D bank honored these checks and charged the partnership account. Sometime later A and B discovered the forgeries and sought to recover from the bank. The bank claimed that A and B were negligent in that they received most of the canceled checks and did not discover the forgeries for several months.

Issue: Can A and B recover from the bank?

Decision: No.

Reason: Under the Code a customer of a bank is precluded from asserting a forgery against a bank when he has failed to exercise reasonable care.

Terry v. Puget Sound National Bank, 492 P.2d 534 (Wash.) 1972.

The Code does not specify the period of time within which the customer must report forgeries or alterations. However, it does specify a time limit if the same wrongdoer commits successive forgeries or alterations. In such cases, the customer's failure to examine and to notify within a period not to exceed fourteen days after the first item and statement were available to him will bar him from objecting to the forgeries or alterations of subsequent checks by the same person paid by the bank in good faith. (4-406(2)) This rule is intended to prevent the wrongdoer from having the opportunity to repeat his misdeeds. However, if the customer can establish that the bank itself was negligent or failed to observe reasonable commercial standards in paying a forged or altered item, the bank cannot avail itself of a defense based upon the customer's failure to promptly examine and report. (3-306(3)) Thus, if both parties are "at fault," the bank is liable because its fault prevents it from asserting the fault of the other party.

Case: The checking account of a church in the D bank required the signature of two church officers. One of the officers had forged the signature of the other and had cashed fifty checks in this fashion. The court ordered that the bank return the money to the church. The bank argued that the church was negligent in not requiring a better accounting and that in any event the church had not examined its returned checks.

Issue: Is a bank necessarily relieved of liability for paying forged checks if the customer does not make a timely examination of returned checks?

Decision: No.

Reasons: 1. The bank will be liable if it is guilty of negligence in paying the items even though the depositor fails to make a timely examination of returned checks. In this case the bank should have been alerted that something was wrong because all the checks were payable to the order of the forger personally and all bore the indorsement of a race track.

2. If both parties are negligent, the bank must bear the loss.

Jackson v. First National Bank of Memphis, 403 S.W.2d 109 (Tenn.) 1966.

A customer is precluded from asserting a forged signature or alteration on a check after one year from the time the check and statement were made available to him, even though the bank was negligent. Forged indorsements must be reported within three years. (4-406(4)) If a payor bank, as a matter of policy or public relations, waives its defense of tardy notification by its customer, it cannot thereafter hold the collecting bank or any prior party for the forgery. (4-406(5))

REVIEW QUESTIONS AND PROBLEMS

1. What are the two basic kinds of negotiable instruments?

2. Explain the difference between *negotiation* and *assignment.*

3. What is the advantage of having a check certified?

4. A check contained the words "One hundred dollars," but the amount of "$10.00" also appeared on the face of the instrument. What is the amount of liability of the drawer? Explain.

5. A, the payee of a check, presented it for payment to a drive-in teller of the XYZ bank, the drawee. The teller paid the check and later discovered that there were not sufficient funds in the drawer's account. May XYZ recover the amount of the check from A? Why?

6. A, drawer, sent a check to B, payee, as payment for some goods. After inspecting the goods, it was A's opinion that B had breached the contract of sale. A then executed a stop payment order on the check to the XYZ bank, drawee. XYZ paid the check in spite of the order. Is XYZ automatically liable to A for the amount of the check? Why?

7. A, a depositor with the XYZ bank, failed to make payment to XYZ according to the terms of a loan from XYZ to A. XYZ seized funds in A's checking account to satisfy the loan balance. Was this action legal? Explain.

8. By mistake, the XYZ bank failed to honor a check drawn on A's account. A, a prominent businessman, became outraged when he had to ask the payee to redeposit the check. A sued XYZ for damages due to the embarrassment. What result? Explain.

9. A thief broke into A's car and carefully removed a check from A's checkbook. A did not notice the theft. The thief forged A's name and was successful in cashing the check at A's bank, XYZ. Will XYZ bank be liable to A? Why?

10. Smith introduced himself to Brown as "Professor Weinstein," a noted psychologist, and claimed to be raising funds for a study of juvenile delinquency. Brown drew a check for $10,000 payable to the order of "Professor Weinstein." Smith (alias Weinstein) indorsed the check in the name of Weinstein and cashed it at a bank. Is the bank liable to Brown? Why?

22 COMMERCIAL PAPER: CREATION AND TRANSFER

Introduction The concept of negotiability was introduced in Chapter 21. It was noted that a holder in due course of a negotiable instrument is not subject to personal defenses that may be asserted by prior parties to the instrument. This chapter and the next one examine this legal principle in detail. They will be concerned with the following four questions (Chapter 22 with questions 1 and 2, Chapter 23 with questions 3 and 4):

1. What legal requirements must be met if an instrument is to qualify for the special treatment afforded negotiable instruments?
2. What distinguishes a transfer by assignment from one by a negotiation?
3. What requirements must be met for a holder to qualify as a holder in due course?
4. Which defenses are personal defenses and which are real defenses?

THE REQUIREMENTS OF NEGOTIABILITY

Generally The negotiability of an instrument is determined by the terms written on the face of the instrument. The Code (Article 3) provides that in order for an instrument to be negotiable, it must satisfy four basic requirements. The instrument must (a) be signed by the maker or drawer; (b) contain an unconditional promise or order to pay a sum certain in money; (c) be payable on demand or at a definite time; and (d) be payable to order or to bearer. (3-104(1))

A negotiable note must contain a *promise* to pay. A draft must contain an *order* to pay. The mere acknowledgment of a debt in writing does not create negotiable paper. The simplest form of an instrument that merely acknowledges a debt is an IOU. Though such a written memorandum is sufficient to evidence and create a valid enforceable instrument upon which recovery may be had, it is not negotiable.

The Promise or Order Must Be Unconditional

Negotiable instruments serve as a substitute for money and as a basis for short-term credit. If these purposes are to be served, it is essential that the instruments be readily and freely transferable. Conditional promises or orders would defeat these purposes because it would be necessary for every transferee to make a determination with regard to whether or not the condition had been performed. Therefore the law requires that the promise or order be unconditional. If the promise or order is a conditional one, the instrument is not negotiable.

The question whether or not the promise or order is conditional arises when the instrument contains language in addition to the promise or order to pay money. The promise or order is conditional if the instrument provides that payment is controlled by or is subject to the terms of some other agreement. Clearly, a promise or order is conditional where payment is *subject* to the terms of another contract. Negotiability is also destroyed if reference to another writing would be necessary in order to determine the exact nature of the promise or order. (3-105(2)(a))

Case: D executed a note and purchase-money mortgage to X. X negotiated the note to P. The note contained the following stipulation:

This note with interest is secured by a mortgage on real estate, of even date herewith, made by the maker hereof in favor of the said payee, . . . The terms of said mortgage are by this reference made a part hereof.

When P sued D to collect the note and to foreclose the mortgage, D alleged that X was guilty of fraud. P claimed to be a holder in due course and not subject to the defense.

Issue: Is the note negotiable so that P is a holder in due course?

Decision: No.

Reasons: 1. The note, incorporating by reference the terms of the mortgage, did not contain an unconditional promise to pay. It was therefore not negotiable and P could not be a holder in due course.

2. Mere reference to a note being secured by mortgage is a common commercial practice and such reference in itself does not impede the negotiability of the note. There is, however, a significant difference in a

note stating that it is "secured by a mortgage" and one that provides, "the terms of said mortgage are by this reference made a part hereof." In the former instance the note merely refers to a separate agreement which does not impede its negotiability, while in the latter instance the note is rendered nonnegotiable.

Holly Hill Acres, Ltd. v. Charter Bk. of Gainesville, 314 So.2d 209 (Fla.App.) 1975.

As noted in the preceding case, a mere *reference* to some other contract or agreement does not condition the promise or order and does not impair negotiability. For example, many instruments will contain a statement indicating that collateral has been given. Such a statement, including the provisions relating to the rights of the payee or holder in the collateral, does not affect negotiability. (3-112(1)(b)(c)) Statements of the consideration for which the instrument was given and statements of the transaction out of which the instrument arose are simply informative and do not affect negotiability.

A statement that an instrument is to be paid only out of a particular fund imposes a condition. (3-105(1)(b)) Such an instrument does not carry the general personal credit of the maker or drawer. There are two exceptions to the foregoing rule. First, an instrument issued by a government is not deemed nonnegotiable simply because payment is restricted to a particular fund. (3-105(2)(a)) Second, an instrument issued by or on behalf of a partnership, unincorporated association, trust, or estate may be negotiable, although it is limited to payment out of their entire assets. (3-105(2)(b))

Sum Certain in Money   An instrument, to be negotiable, must be payable in money. Instruments payable in chattels, such as grain or metals, are not negotiable. *Money* is defined as "medium of exchange authorized or adopted by a domestic or foreign government as a part of its currency." (3-107(1)) If the sum payable is stated in foreign currency, the instrument may be satisfied by payment of the dollar equivalent.

The language used in creating commercial paper must be certain with respect to the amount of money promised or ordered to be paid. (3-106) If the principal sum to be paid is definite, negotiability is not affected by the fact that it is to be paid with interest, in installments, or with cost of collection and attorney's fees in case payment shall not be made at maturity. (3-106(1))

Case: D was the maker of a note. The note provided that in the event of nonpayment when due and if legal action were instituted, D would pay a reasonable sum as attorney's fees to the holder of the note.

Issue: Is the instrument negotiable?

Decision: Yes.

Reasons: 1. Negotiable instruments may provide for charging the maker with the costs of collection, including attorney's fees. The purpose of this provision is to be of aid in insuring the holder the full proceeds of the note.

2. If at any point of time during the term of the paper its full value can be ascertained, the requirement that the sum must be certain is satisfied.

3. The obligation to pay costs and attorney's fees is part of the security contract, separate and distinct from the primary promise to pay money and does not, therefore, affect the requirement as to a sum certain.

Young v. Northern Terminals, Inc., 290 A.2d 186 (Vt.) 1972.

The certainty of amount is not affected if the instrument specifies different rates of interest before and after default; nor is the certainty affected by a provision for a stated discount for early payment or an additional charge if payment is made after the date fixed. Likewise a penalty charge for early payment does not affect negotiability. (3-105(b)(c))

THE TIME OF PAYMENT MUST BE CERTAIN

As a substitute for money, negotiable instruments would be of little value if the holder were unable to determine at what time he could demand payment. It is necessary, therefore, that there be certainty as to the time of payment. A negotiable instrument must be payable on demand or at a "definite time." (3-108), (3-109)

Demand Paper   An instrument is payable on demand when it so states, when payable at sight or on presentation, or *when no time of payment is stated.* (3-108) In general, the words *payable on demand* are used in notes and the words *at sight* in drafts. If nothing is said about the due date, the instrument is demand paper.

A check is a good illustration of a demand instrument. The characteristic of demand paper is that the holder of such paper can require payment at any time by making a demand upon the person who is obligated on the paper.

Payable at a Definite Time   The requirement of a definite time is in keeping with the necessity for certainty in instruments. If an instrument is payable only upon an act or event, the time of whose occurrence is uncertain, it is not payable at a definite time even though the act or event has occurred. (3-109(2))

334

Case: P sued D to collect for a loan origination fee. The alleged promissory note provided that it was due and payable when D obtained and accepted a loan commitment. This had not occurred.

Issue: Is the note negotiable?

Decision: No.

Reasons: 1. To be negotiable, a note must be payable on demand or at a definite time.

2. An instrument which by its terms is otherwise payable only upon an act or event uncertain as to time of occurrence is not payable at a definite time even though the act or event has occurred.

3. The note here was not payable on demand or at a definite time. It was payable upon acceptance of a loan commitment.

Barton v. Scott Hudgens Realty & Mortg., 222 S.E.2d 126 (Ga.) 1975.

The requirement of certainty as to the time of payment is satisfied if it is payable on or before a specified date. Thus an instrument payable on June 1, 1979, is payable at a definite time, as is one payable "on or before" June 1, 1979. In the latter situation the obligor on the instrument has the privilege of making payment prior to June 1, 1979, but is not required to pay it until the specified date. An instrument payable at a fixed period after a stated date, or at a fixed period after sight, is payable at a definite time. (3-109(1)(a)(b)) The expressions "one year after date" or "sixty days after sight" are definite as to time.

Acceleration Clauses Instruments frequently contain a provision known as an *acceleration clause*. An acceleration clause hastens or accelerates the maturity date of an instrument. Accelerating provisions may be of many different kinds. One kind, for example, provides that in case of default in payment, the entire note shall become due and payable. Another kind gives the holder an option to declare the instrument due and payable when he feels insecure with respect to ultimate payment. An instrument payable at a definite time subject to *any acceleration* is still negotiable. (3-109(1)(c))

If the acceleration provision permits the holder to declare the instrument due when he feels insecure, the holder must act in good faith in the honest belief that the likelihood of payment is impaired. The presumption is that the holder has acted in good faith, placing the burden on the obligor-payor to show that such act was not in good faith. (1-208)

335

Case: P was the payee of a note of which D was the maker. The note provided that P could demand payment at any time he should feel himself insecure as to D's ability to pay. D's business was faced with new competition and lost money for a year. Thereafter P told D that he deemed himself insecure and demanded payment. When payment was not forthcoming, P sued on the note. D contended that there was no reason for P to feel insecure.

Issue: Is P entitled to accelerate the due date?

Decision: Yes.

Reasons: 1. The Code provides that the term "when he deems himself insecure" means that he shall have the power to accelerate payment of a note if he in good faith believes that the prospect of payment is impaired.

2. The court found that P had acted in good faith because of D's business problems.

Van Horn v. Van de Wol, Inc., 497 P.2d 252 (Wash.) 1972.

THE MAGIC WORDS OF NEGOTIABILITY

Introduction The *words of negotiability* express the intention to create negotiable paper. The usual words of negotiability are *order* and *bearer.* (3-110), (3-111) When these words are used, the maker or drawer has in effect stated that the instrument may be negotiated to another party. When the word *bearer* is used, it means that payment will be made to anyone who *bears* or possesses it. When the word *order* is used, it means that it will be paid to the designated payee or to anyone that such payee may order it paid to.

Other words of equivalent meaning may be used, but to ensure negotiability it is preferable to use the conventional words. If the instrument is not payable to "order" or to "bearer," it is not negotiable and all defenses are available in suits on the instrument.

Case: P sued D to recover on two promissory notes. The notes stated: "Buyer agrees to pay to Seller. . . ." D attempted to assert several personal defenses to the note. P claimed to be a holder in due course.

Issue: Is P a holder in due course of a negotiable instrument?

Decision: No.

Reasons: 1. To be a negotiable instrument, the writing must be payable to order or to bearer. The notes sued on were payable "to seller" and, therefore, were not negotiable instruments.

336

2. There can be no holder or holder in due course of an instrument that is not negotiable. The transferee of such an instrument is an assignee.

3. P is subject to all defenses.

Locke v. Aetna Acceptance Corporation, 309 So.2d 43 (Fla.App.) 1975.

Order Paper

If the terms of an instrument provide that it is payable to the order of a person or to him or his order, the instrument is *order* paper. (3-100(1)) For example, "Pay to the order of John Doe" or "Pay to John Doe or order" creates order paper.

Ordinarily, an instrument will be payable to a payee who is not a maker or drawer or drawee. However, an instrument may be drawn payable to order of the maker or drawer. (3-110(1)(a)(b)(c)) An instrument in which the maker and the payee are the same person will have to be indorsed by the maker as payee before negotiation.

An instrument may be payable to the order of two or more payees together, such as "A and B," or in the alternative, such as "A or B." An instrument payable to "A and B" must be indorsed by both. One payable to the order of "A or B" may be negotiated by either. (3-116)

Case: A check in settlement of accounts was drawn payable to the order of X *and* the Y concrete company. The check, indorsed only by Y, was deposited in Y's bank. When the check was presented for payment to D bank, it refused payment because of the missing indorsement of X.

Issue: Was D bank justified in refusing to honor the check?

Decision: Yes.

Reason: Because the check was made payable to the order of two payees, the signatures of both payees were required for negotiation.

Clinger v. Continental National Bank, 503 P.2d 363 (Colo.) 1972.

An instrument may be payable to the order of an estate, a trust, or a fund. Such instruments are payable to the order of the representative of such estate, trust, or fund. (3-110(1)(e)) An instrument payable to the order of a partnership or an unincorporated association such as a labor union is payable to such partnership or association. It may be indorsed by any person authorized by the partnership or association. (3-110(1)(g))

Bearer Paper

The basic characteristic of bearer paper as distinguished from order paper is that it can be negotiated by delivery without indorsement. An instrument is payable to bearer when created if it is payable (1) to bearer or to the order of bearer (as distinguished from the order of a specified person or bearer), (2) to a specified person or bearer (notice that it is not to *the order of* a specified person or bearer), or (3) to "cash" or "the order of cash." (3-111)

While bearer paper may be negotiated without indorsement, the person to whom it is transferred will often require an indorsement. The reason for this is that an indorser has a greater liability than one who negotiates without indorsement. Also, the problem of identifying the person who negotiated the paper is much easier. This becomes important if the instrument is dishonored.

**Incomplete
Instruments**
A person may sign an instrument that is incomplete in that it lacks one or more of the necessary elements of a complete instrument. Thus, a paper signed by the maker or drawer, in which the payee's name or the amount is omitted, is incomplete.

An incomplete instrument cannot be enforced until it is completed. (3-115(1)) If the blanks are subsequently filled in by any person in accordance with the authority or instructions given by the party who signed the incomplete instrument, it is then effective as completed. A person might, for example, leave blank signed checks with an employee with instructions to complete the checks as to amounts and payee in payment of invoices as goods are delivered. When the employee completes the checks in accordance with these instructions, they are perfectly valid.

A date is not required for an instrument to be negotiable. However, if a date is necessary to ascertain maturity ("payable sixty days from date"), an undated instrument is an incomplete instrument. The date may be inserted by a holder. If an instrument is payable on demand or at a fixed period after the date, the date that is put on the instrument controls even though it is antedated or postdated. (3-114(2))

If the completion of the blanks is not in conformity with the signer's authority, the unauthorized completion is treated as a material alteration of the instrument, (3-115(2)), but a holder in due course can enforce the instrument as completed. The loss is placed upon the person who signed the incomplete paper because he made wrongful completion possible. A person not a holder in due course is subject to the defense of improper completion.

TRANSFER AND NEGOTIATION

Introduction
The rights that a person has in an instrument may be transferred by either "negotiation" or "assignment." The transfer of an instrument by assignment vests in the transferee such rights as the transferor has. *Negotiation* is defined as a specific type of transfer by means of which the transferee becomes a holder. A *holder* who qualifies

as a holder in due course will be free of personal defenses and thus have rights superior to those of his transferor.

There are two methods of negotiating an instrument so that the transferee will become a holder. If the instrument is payable to bearer, it may be negotiated by delivery alone; if it is order paper, indorsement and delivery are required. (3-202(1))

The indorsement to be effective as negotiation must convey the entire instrument or any unpaid balance due on the instrument. If it purports to be of less, it will be effective only as a partial assignment. (3-202(3)) For example, an indorsement "Pay to A one-half of this instrument" would not be a negotiation, and A's position would be that of an assignee.

The indorser may add to his indorsement words of assignment, condition, waiver, guarantee, or limitation or disclaimer of liability and the like. The indorsement is nevertheless effective as an indorsement. (3-202(4))

It sometimes happens that an order instrument, or one that is specially indorsed, is transferred without indorsement. Thus a purchaser may pay for an instrument in advance of the time when it is delivered to him, and the seller either inadvertently or fraudulently may fail to indorse the paper. Of course, an indorsement would be necessary for negotiation. If the transferee has given value for the instrument, and if there was no contrary agreement between the parties, the transferee can demand an indorsement. (3-201(3)) The negotiation is not effective until the indorsement is given. The transferee is not a holder and cannot qualify as a holder in due course until such indorsement is obtained.

Kinds of Indorsements

Indorsements are either *special* or *blank*. These are the ordinary indorsements used in negotiating paper. If other terms are added which condition the indorsement, it is also a *restrictive* indorsement. A restrictive indorsement restricts the indorsee's use of the paper. Also, the indorser may *limit* or qualify his liability as an indorser by adding such words as "without recourse." This qualified indorsement has the effect of relieving the indorser of his contractual liability as an indorser—that he will pay if the primary obligor refuses to do so. A qualified indorsement will also be a blank or a special indorsement. These indorsements are discussed in the sections that follow.

Blank Indorsements

A blank indorsement consists simply of the indorser's name written on the instrument. If an instrument drawn payable to order is indorsed in blank, it becomes bearer paper. (3-204(2)) For example, if a check on its face payable to the order of Henry Smith is indorsed in blank, it is bearer paper. As such it can be negotiated by mere delivery, and a thief or finder could by such delivery pass title to the instrument.

Special Indorsements A special indorsement specifies the person to whom or to whose order it makes the instrument payable. When an instrument is specially indorsed, it becomes payable to the *order of* the special indorsee and requires his indorsement for further negotiation. Thus an indorsement "Pay to John Jones" or "Pay to the order of John Jones" is a special indorsement and requires the further indorsement by John Jones for negotiation. If a bearer instrument is indorsed specially, it requires further indorsement by the indorsee. This is true if the instrument was originally bearer paper or if it became bearer paper as the result of a blank indorsement. In other words, the last indorsement determines whether the instrument is order paper or bearer paper. (3-204)

The holder of an instrument may convert a blank indorsement into a special indorsement by writing above the blank indorser's signature any contract consistent with the character of the indorsement. (3-204(3)) Thus, Richard Roe, to whom an instrument has been indorsed in blank by John Doe, could write above Doe's signature "Pay to Richard Roe." The paper would now require Roe's indorsement for further negotiation.

Restrictive Indorsements A person who indorses an instrument may impose certain restrictions upon his indorsement, that is, the indorser may protect or preserve certain rights in the paper and limit the rights of the indorsee. There are four types of restrictive indorsements. A restrictive indorsement may be one that is conditional, such as "Pay John Doe if Generator XK-711 arrives by June 1, 1979," or it may purport to prohibit further transfer of the instrument, such as "Pay to John Doe only." (3-205(a)(b)) A restrictive indorsement is often used when a check is deposited in a bank for collection. Thus the indorsements "For Collection," "For Deposit Only," and "Pay any Bank" are restrictive. (3-205(c)) The fourth type is an indorsement in which the indorser stipulates that it is for the benefit or use of the indorser or some other person, such as "Pay John Doe in trust for Richard Roe." (3-205(d))

A restrictive indorsement does not prevent further transfer or negotiation of the instrument. (3-206(1)) Thus an instrument indorsed "Pay to John Doe only" could be negotiated by John Doe in the same manner as if it had been indorsed "Pay to John Doe."

The effect of restrictive indorsements is substantially limited as applied to banks that are involved in the process of deposit and collection of instruments. An intermediary bank or a payor bank that is not a depository bank can disregard any restrictive indorsement except that of the bank's immediate transferor. This limitation does not affect whatever rights the restrictive indorser may have against the bank of deposit or his rights against parties outside the bank collection process. (3-206(2)) Except for an intermediary bank, any transferee under a conditional indorsement, or an indorsement for collection and the like, must pay or apply any value given by him consistently with the indorsement, and to the extent that he does so he becomes a holder for value. (3-206(3))

Where the indorsement is for the benefit of the indorser or another person, such as "Pay to John Doe in trust for Richard Roe," only the first taker is required to act consistently with the restrictive indorsement. (3-206(4)) John Doe has the obligation to use the instrument or the proceeds from it for the benefit of Richard Roe. John Doe could negotiate the instrument to John Smith, who could qualify as a holder in due course and ignore the restriction. Of course, if the instrument was transferred in violation of Doe's fiduciary duty, as where Doe transferred it to Roe in payment of a debt that he personally owed to Roe, the latter would not be a holder in due course. (3-304(2))

REVIEW QUESTIONS AND PROBLEMS

1. What are the requirements of a negotiable instrument?

2. Whan A purchased a new home, A executed a note, which was secured by a mortgage to B. The note contained the following clause: "This note is secured by a mortgage." B sold the note to C. Could C be a holder in due course? Why?

3. A note contained a provision: "This note is payable from the proceeds of the sale of the Douglas building." Is the note negotiable? Explain.

4. Would an instrument payable in "ten ounces of gold" be negotiable? Explain.

5. A executed a note payable to B, which was due "as soon as B shall deliver to A fifty gallons of fuel oil." B transferred the note to C. After the delivery of the oil, could C be a holder in due course? Why?

6. M executed a note to P in the sum of $500. The note did not contain words of negotiability. Can P recover on the note from M? If P transferred the note to X, could X recover from M? Why?

7. A note provides: "Payable on January 1, 1978, or sooner in the event that the AB partnership is dissolved." Is the note negotiable? Why?

8. A issued a check payable to the order of B, who lost the instrument without indorsing it. Could a finder negotiate the check? Why?

9. A, the payee of a check, indorsed it in blank. The check was subsequently stolen. A informed the drawer, B, of the theft and asked for a replacement check. Should B replace it? Explain.

10. A executed a promissory note payable to the order of B. B indorsed it in blank and delivered it to C. C wrote on the back of the note, above B's signature, "Pay to C." Is the paper now order paper or bearer paper? Explain.

COMMERCIAL PAPER: HOLDERS IN DUE COURSE AND DEFENSES

23

Introduction   If an instrument is rightfully in possession of a third party, the third party may be an *assignee*, a *transferee*, a *holder*, or a *holder in due course*. If the instrument is a simple contract as contrasted with a negotiable instrument, the party in possession is an assignee. Likewise, if the instrument is negotiable but if it has not been properly negotiated (delivery only of order paper), the party in possession is a transferee with the status of an assignee. If the instrument is negotiable and if it has been properly negotiated, the person in possession is a holder. If certain special requirements are met, the holder may qualify as a holder in due course.

A *holder* is a person in possession of a negotiable instrument payable to him or to his order or to bearer. (1-201(20)) Thus either the original payee or a third party may qualify as a holder. A holder of an instrument may transfer or negotiate it. A holder may discharge an instrument and may enforce payment in his own name. (3-301) A thief or finder may qualify as a holder of a bearer instrument. A holder who does not qualify as a holder in due course is in a position equivalent to that of an assignee of a simple contract, in that he cannot enforce payment in the event that a defense to the instrument legally exists.

A *holder in due course* is a holder who, because he meets certain requirements, is given a special status and a preferred position in the event that there is a claim or a defense to the instrument. (3-302) If there is no claim or defense to the instrument, it is immaterial whether the party seeking to enforce it is a holder or a holder in due course. A holder in due course can enforce payment, notwithstanding the presence of a personal defense to the instrument. (As previously noted, defenses fall into two categories—personal and real.) Even a holder in due course will not be able to enforce the instrument in the event that a real defense is asserted.

343

*Commercial
Paper:
Holders in
Due Course
and Defenses*

Issues as to whether or not a given party is a holder in due course usually arise when the party seeks to collect on the instrument. However, occasionally a party is sued on a negligence theory for losses incurred in transactions involving an instrument. If the defendant in such a negligence case can establish that he is or was a holder in due course, liability can be avoided. Thus a holder in due course is free of claims and is not subject to defenses.

THE REQUIREMENTS TO BE A HOLDER IN DUE COURSE

Generally   To qualify as a holder in due course, a holder must have taken the instrument for value and in good faith. In addition, he must not have notice that the instrument is overdue, that it has been dishonored, or that any other person has a claim to it or a defense against it. (3-302(1))

A payee may be a holder in due course (3-302(1)) if all of the requirements are met. Since a holder in due course is only free of personal defenses of parties with whom he has not dealt, any situation that allows a payee to be a holder in due course would be unusual.

When an instrument is acquired in a manner other than through the usual channels of negotiation or transfer, the holder will not be a holder in due course. Thus, if an instrument is obtained by an executor in taking over an estate, is purchased at a judicial sale, is obtained through legal process by an attaching creditor, or is acquired as a transaction not in the regular course of business, the party acquiring it is not a holder in due course. (3-302(3))

Value   A holder must have given value for an instrument in order to qualify as a holder in due course. Thus a person to whom an instrument was transferred as a gift would not qualify as a holder in due course. *Value* does not have the same meaning as *consideration* in the law of contracts. A mere promise is consideration, but it is not value. As long as a promise is executory, the value requirement to be a holder in due course has not been met. (3-303)

Case: D issued commercial paper to S. S indorsed and delivered it to P, a lawyer, as a retainer for legal services to be performed. D has defense of fraud and seeks to assert the defense against P. P claims to be a holder in due course.

Issue: Does P qualify as a holder in due course?

Decision: No.

Reason: P did not pay value. He had simply promised to perform services in the future—this is not present value.

Korzenik v. Supreme Radio, 197 N.E.2d 702 (Mass.) 1964.

While a mere promise is not value, if the promise to pay is negotiable in form, it does constitute value. (3-303(c)) For example, a drawer who issues his check in payment for a negotiable note that he is purchasing from the holder becomes a holder for value even before his check is cashed.

A holder who takes an instrument in payment of an existing debt is a holder for value. (3-303(b)) Thus, if A owed B $500 on a past-due account and transferred a negotiable instrument to B in payment of such account, B would qualify as a holder for value.

A purchaser of a limited interest in paper can be a holder in due course only to the extent of the interest purchased. (3-302(4)) For example, if a negotiable instrument is transferred as collateral for a loan, the transferee may be a holder in due course, but only to the extent of the debt which is secured by the pledge of the instrument.

A person who purchases an instrument for less than its *face value* can be a holder in due course to the full amount of the instrument. For example, A is the payee of a note for $1,000. He may discount the note and indorse it to B for $800. B has nevertheless paid value and is entitled to collect the full $1,000.

Good Faith   In addition, a holder must take the instrument in good faith in order to qualify as a holder in due course. (3-304) *Good faith* is defined as "honesty in fact in the conduct or transaction concerned." (1-201(19)) If a person takes an instrument under circumstances that clearly establish the fact that there is a defense to the instrument, he does not take it in good faith. However, failure to follow accepted business practices or to act reasonably by commercial standards does not establish lack of good faith.

Historically, the good-faith requirement was often challenged by consumers when consumer paper was immediately transferred by a seller to a bank. If the bank qualified as a holder in due course, the consumer would have to pay even though the goods were defective. Consumers would contend that the close relationship between the seller and its bank constituted lack of good faith. This issue has been eliminated for all practical purposes today by a 1976 Federal Trade Commission ruling which allows consumers to use all defenses when sued on consumer paper.

This FTC rule will be discussed in detail in Chapter 28, which deals with consumer protection. However, it should be kept in mind that as a practical matter it prevents the use of the holder in due course concept when the maker or drawer is a consumer.

Without Notice   Closely related to good faith is the requirement that the transferee must not have notice of any claim or defense to the instrument and that he not have notice either that the instrument is overdue or that it has been dishonored. (3-304) A person has notice of a fact if he has actual knowledge of it, has received notification of it, or—from the facts and circumstances known to him—has "reason to know" that it exists. (1-201(25)) The law generally provides that a person has reason to know a fact if he has information from which a person of ordinary intelligence (or of the intelligence of the person involved if it is above the ordinary) will conclude that the fact exists, or there is such a strong probability that it exists that a person exercising reasonable care will assume that it exists.

Certain irregularities on the face of an instrument put a purchaser on notice that there may be a claim or defense to the instrument. For example, if there is visible evidence of forgery or alteration, a purchaser is put on notice of a claim or defense. (3-304(1)(a))

Case: D was approached at his home by a salesman who prevailed upon him to purchase a food plan. The price was $100, and D signed a note for that amount. Some time later he received a payment book from P finance company showing the amount due on the note to be $843.48. The note had been indorsed to D by the food-plan company. It had been erased, and the figures that were in ink had been typed over in the larger amount. P sued D on the note.

Issue: Is P a holder in due course?

Decision: No.

Reason: The alterations were "obvious to the naked eye." A purchaser has notice of a defense if the instrument bears visible evidence of alteration.

Nationwide Acceptance Corporation v. Henne, 194 So.2d 434 (La.) 1967.

If an instrument is incomplete in some important respect at the time it is purchased, notice is imparted. (3-304(1)(a)) Blanks in an instrument that do not relate to material terms do not impart notice. Knowledge that blanks in an instrument have been completed after it was issued does not give notice of a claim or defense. However, if the purchaser has notice that the completion was improper, he is not a holder in due course. (3-304(4)(d))

Actual knowledge that a defense exists or that it has been dishonored usually prohibits the status of a holder in due course. However, there are situations in which knowledge of certain facts does *not* of itself give the purchaser notice of a defense or claim. Knowledge

345

that an instrument is antedated or postdated does not prevent a holder from taking in due course. (3-304(4)(a)) Knowledge of a separate contract is not notice. While a defense will arise if the contract is not performed, such knowledge does not prevent him from becoming a holder in due course. Of course, if the purchaser is aware that the contract has been breached or repudiated, he will not qualify as a holder in due course.

Actual notice to prevent a party from being a holder in due course must be received at such time and in such manner as to give a reasonable opportunity to act on it. (3-304(6)) For example, a notice received by the president of a bank one minute before the bank's teller cashes a check is not effective to prevent the bank from becoming a holder in due course.

**Before
Overdue** To be a holder in due course, a purchaser of an instrument must take it without notice that it is overdue. (3-302(1)(c)) A purchaser of overdue paper is charged with knowledge that some defense may exist.

A purchaser has notice that an instrument is overdue if he has reason to know that any part of the principal amount is overdue. (3-304(3)(a)) However, past-due interest does not impart notice to the holder. (3-304(4)(f))

Demand paper poses a special problem, since it does not have a fixed date of maturity. A purchaser of demand paper cannot be a holder in due course if he has reason to know that he is taking it after a demand has been made, or if he takes it more than a reasonable length of time after its issue. (3-304(3)(c)) What is a reasonable or an unreasonable time is determined on the basis of a number of factors—the kind of instrument, the customs and usages of the trade or business, and the particular facts and circumstances involved. In the case of a check, a reasonable time is presumed to be thirty days. (3-304(3)(c)) The thirty-day period is a presumption rather than an absolute rule.

**Holder from
a Holder
in Due Course** A transferee may have the rights of a holder in due course even though the requirements to be a holder in due course are not met. Because a transferee obtains the rights of the transferor, a person who derives title through a holder in due course has the rights and privileges of a holder in due course. (3-201(1)) This is referred to as the "shelter provision." The shelter concept advances the marketability of commercial paper.

Case: D executed a note in payment for a trailer. The seller indorsed and delivered the note to X bank. When D defaulted, X as a gift assigned its interest in the note to P, a charity. When P sued D, D sought to assert the defense of fraud.

Issue: Is P subject to the personal defense of fraud?

Decision: No.

Reasons: 1. Transfer of an instrument vests in the transferee such rights as the transferor had.

2. The transfer of rights is not limited to transfers for value. An instrument may be transferred by gift. In such a case, the donee acquires the rights of the donor.

3. Since the X bank was a holder in due course, P acquired the rights of a holder in due course and P is not subject to personal defenses.

Canyonville Bible Academy v. Lobemaster, 247 N.E.2d 623 (Ill. App.) 1969.

The shelter provision is subject, however, to the limitation that a person who formerly held the paper cannot improve his position by later reacquiring it from a holder in due course. If a former holder was himself a party to any fraud or illegality affecting the instrument, or if he had notice of a defense or claim against it as a prior holder, he cannot claim the rights of a holder in due course by taking from a later holder in due course.

DEFENSES

Introduction   A holder in due course takes commercial paper free from the *personal* defenses of the parties to the paper.(3-305) One who is not a holder in due course or who does not have the rights of one under the shelter provision is subject to such defenses. However, all transferees including holders in due course are subject to what are referred to as *real* defenses.

In general, real defenses are those that relate to the existence of any obligation on the part of the person who asserts them. The most obvious real defense is the forgery of the signature of the maker of the note or the drawer of a check. The person whose signature was forged has not entered into any contract, and he has an absolute defense even against a holder in due course.

The Code specifies which defenses are real and which are personal. The following chart indicates various defenses and their usual status.

347

Personal Defenses	*Real Defenses*
1. Lack or failure of consideration	1. Unauthorized signature
2. Nonperformance of a condition precedent	2. Material alteration
3. Nondelivery, conditional delivery, or delivery for a special purpose	3. Infancy, if it is a defense to a simple contract
4. Payment	4. Lack of capacity
5. Slight duress	5. Extreme duress
6. Fraud in the inducement	6. Fraud in the inception
7. Theft by the holder or one through whom he holds	7. Illegality
8. Violation of a restrictive indorsement	8. Discharge in bankruptcy
9. Unauthorized completion	9. Discharge of which the holder has notice
10. Other defenses to a simple contract	
11. Any real defense where the party was negligent	

Most of these defenses are self-explanatory. Many of them are discussed with the materials on contracts. However, a few aspects will be discussed in the following sections.

Real Defenses The real defense of unauthorized signature includes forgeries and signatures by agents without authority. (3-404(1)) It applies to indorsements as well as to the signature creating the instrument.

The most common example of a material alteration is the "raising" of a check. (3-407) For example, a check drawn in the amount of $50 might be raised by alteration to $500. Such alteration is a real defense to the extent of the alteration. A subsequent holder in due course could enforce the check only in the amount of its original sum—$50. As will be discussed in the next chapter, a material alteration of an instrument operates to discharge it. A basic change in the contract without the permission of its creator will cancel it.

The defense of lack of capacity is a real defense if the state law so provides. If it is a defense to a simple contract, it is a real defense. (3-305(2)(a)) The same is true for all forms of illegality. If a contract is merely voidable, the defense is personal. If the contract is void or unenforceable, the defense is a real one. For example, if state law provides that usurious contracts are null and void, usury is a real defense.

Personal Defenses A distinction exists between fraud in the *inducement* and fraud in the *inception* or *execution*. The former pertains to the consideration for which an instrument is given. The primary party intended to create an instrument but was fraudulently induced to do so. Such a defense is personal and is not available against a holder in

349

*Commercial
Paper:
Holders in
Due Course
and Defenses*

due course. Fraud in the *inception* exists where a negotiable instrument is procured from a party when circumstances are such that the party does not know that he is giving a negotiable instrument. Fraud in the inception is a real defense. (3-305(2)(c)) The theory is that since the party primarily to be bound has no intention of creating an instrument, none is created. Such fraud is rare because persons are usually charged with knowledge of what they sign.

Case: P purchased an aluminum-siding installation for his home upon the false representation that he would receive a $100 credit for every other job contracted in the area. Without reading the forms, P signed notes and mortgages. They were transferred to a finance company. P sought to have the notes and mortgages canceled.

Issue: Is the defense of fraud in the inception available to P?

Decision: No.

Reasons: 1. For the real defense of fraud in the execution to exist, there must be excusable ignorance. The party must not only have been in ignorance, but must also have had no reasonable opportunity to obtain knowledge. In determining what is a reasonable opportunity all relevant factors are to be taken into account, including the age and sex of the party; his intelligence, education and business experience; his ability to read or to understand English, the representations made to him and his reason to rely on them or to have confidence in the person making them; the presence or absence of any third person who might read or explain the instrument to him, or any other possibility of obtaining independent information; and the apparent necessity, or lack of it, for acting without delay.

2. The reliance upon the representations of a complete stranger was not reasonable. P was of sufficient age, intelligence, education, and business experience to know better.

3. The signing of papers without reading them is negligence, and this precludes P from asserting the defense of fraud in the inception.

Burchett v. Allied Concord Financial Corp., 396 P.2d 186 (N.M.) 1964.

Bearer paper may be negotiated by a finder or even a thief. Acquisition of title through a thief is only a personal defense. This can always be prevented by converting bearer paper to order paper.

The concept of a material alteration includes the completion of an incomplete instrument otherwise than as it was authorized. A holder in due course is not subject to the defense of unauthorized completion of an incomplete instrument. (3-407(3)) In this instance the defense is personal. The person who left the blank space must bear the risk of wrongful completion as against such a holder.

Negligence of a party will reduce a real defense to a personal defense. (3-406) Negligent conduct is frequently present in situations of fraud and material alteration. Thus one who writes a check and leaves a large, blank space in front of the amount of the check renders it easier for a wrongdoer to raise the check and constitutes negligence, reducing the defense to a personal one.

Case: P, a husband whose wife (W) had signed a check, sued D, the bank on which it was drawn. X had repaired a lightning rod for W. She owed $1.26. W handed her checkbook to X to fill out the check in payment. He wrote it in such a way that the figures were to the far right-hand side so that there was space to add 684 to the left. The words were written close to the word "dollars" so that there was space to add "Six Thousand Eight Hundred Forty" ahead of it. D honored the check for $6,841.26.

Issue: Is the alteration a real or personal defense?

Decision: Personal.

Reasons: 1. W was negligent in allowing the check to be prepared in the manner that it could be easily raised.

2. The loss would not have occurred except for W's negligence.

Williams v. Montana National Bank of Bozeman, 534 P.2d 1247 (Mont.) 1975.

REVIEW QUESTIONS AND PROBLEMS

1. What is the advantage of being a holder in due course?

2. What are the requirements to be a holder in due course?

3. What is the "shelter provision"?

4. A, the payee of a note for $500, indorsed the note to B upon payment of $100. May B qualify as a holder in due course? Explain.

5. A drew a check to the order of B. B indorsed it to C in payment of an existing indebtedness that B owed to C. A stopped payment on the check before C deposited it. A seeks to assert his defense, which is failure of consideration, against C. Should he succeed? Why?

6. A gave B a check in the amount of $500 in payment for linoleum installed in A's home. The check was dishonored, and B brought action to recover on the check. A contended that the linoleum was not satisfactory. The trial judge instructed the jury that the check was not subject to any defenses arising from claimed breaches of the contract. Was this instruction correct? Explain.

7. A executed a note payable to the order of B, which was due January 1, 1978. After that date, B negotiated the note to C. Is C subject to personal defenses of A? Why?

351

*Commercial
Paper:
Holders in
Due Course
and Defenses*

8. After A lost his checkbook, he immediately notified his bank of the loss. A finder forged A's name to a check and B cashed it. Under what circumstances is B entitled to payment? Explain.

9. A issued a $100 check to the order of B, who altered the amount to $1,000 and negotiated it to C. C paid value and had no notice of the alteration. A's bank dishonored the check due to insufficient funds. To what extent, if any, is A liable to C? Explain.

10. A and B entered into a contract in which B agreed to clean A's house. B told A, "Give me $25 in advance so that I may buy my supplies." A didn't trust B, so A wrote B a check. When B did not return as promised, A stopped payment on the check. Meanwhile B transferred the check to a merchant, C, who gave B some goods in exchange for the check. C had no knowledge of the agreement between A and B. A's bank refused to cash the check for C. Is A liable to C? Why?

24 COMMERCIAL PAPER: LIABILITY OF PARTIES

Introduction   The preceding chapters were primarily concerned with the rights of holders and holders in due course. In those discussions it was usually assumed that the party being sued had liability unless there was a valid defense that could be asserted against the plaintiff. In this chapter the issues arise in the opposite factual situation. It is assumed in most of this chapter that there is no valid defense to be asserted. The issues involved go to the basic question of the liability of the defendent in the absence of a defense.

Liability in a transaction involving commercial paper may be predicated either on the instrument itself or on the underlying contract. No person is liable on the instrument itself unless his signature appears thereon, but the signature may be affixed by a duly authorized agent. (3-401(1)) Persons whose signatures appear on instruments may have different types of liability, depending on their status. This chapter will discuss the liability of various parties to commercial paper transactions. The liability is, unless indicated otherwise, predicated on the instrument itself and on the rules of the Code relating to commercial paper.

Liability   A person's liability on commercial paper usually results from his
Based on   signature on the instrument. The signature may be affixed as a
Signatures   maker or drawer on the face of the instrument. It may also be on the back of the instrument as an indorsement.

The general principles of the law of agency are applicable to commercial paper. A principal is bound by the duly authorized acts of his agent. If the agent is not authorized to sign, the principal is not bound. An agent who fails to bind his principal because of failure to

352

name him or due to lack of authority will usually be personally liable to third parties.

An agent is personally liable if he fails to show his representative capacity. (3-403(2)(a)) This occurs if the agent signs his own name without indicating either the name of his principal or the fact that he is signing in a representative capacity. (3-403(2)(a)) However, an agent can relieve himself of liability to the person to whom he issued the paper by proving that such party knew that he was acting only as an agent for his principal. (3-403(2)(b))

Case: P, a supplier of a corporation, sued D, the corporate president, to collect three checks drawn on the corporate account which had insufficient funds. The checks bore the printed name of the corporation in the upper-left-hand corner. There were no words before, after, above, or below D's signature in the lower-right-hand corner.

Issue: Is D personally liable on the checks?

Decision: Yes.

Reasons: 1. The drafts do not show prima facie that D signed in a representative capacity. Although the corporate name is on the checks, there is nothing preceding or following D's signature to show that he was signing in a representative capacity.

2. D is personally liable under 3-403(b)(2) of the Code unless there is a different agreement between the parties. No such agreement was proven here.

Griffin v. Ellinger, 530 S.W.2d 329 (Tex.) 1975.

Another issue concerning signatures relates to the capacity in which the signature is affixed. The liability of primary parties such as makers of notes is different from the liability of secondary parties such as indorsers. The capacity of a signature may be ambiguous because of its physical location or because of the language used.

The capacity in which a person signs is usually obvious because of the location of the signature. For example, makers and drawers usually sign in the lower-right-hand corner of an instrument, and indorsers sign on the back of an instrument. In the case of a drawee, he normally would place his signature of acceptance on the face of the instrument, but his signature on the back would clearly indicate that he was signing as an acceptor unless he could establish otherwise. In those situations in which the signature does not reveal the nature of the obligation of the party who signs, the signature is an indorsement. (3-402)

LIABILITY BASED ON STATUS

Classifications: Primary and Secondary   For the purposes of liability, the Code divides the parties to commercial paper into two groups—primary parties and secondary parties. The *primary parties* are the makers of notes and the acceptors of drafts. These parties have incurred a definite obligation to pay and are the parties who, in the normal course of events, will *actually* pay the instrument.

The *secondary parties* are drawers of drafts and checks, and indorsers of any instrument. These parties do not expect to pay the instrument but assume rather that the primary parties will fulfill their obligations. The drawer and indorsers expect that the acceptor will pay the draft. The indorsers of a note expect that the maker will pay when the note matures.

Drawers and indorsers have a responsibility to pay if the primary parties do not, *provided* that certain conditions precedent are satisfied. The drawer and the indorser are, in effect, saying that they will pay if the primary party—acceptor or maker—does not, but only if the party entitled to payment has made a proper demand upon the primary party, and due notice of the primary party's dishonor of the instrument has then been given to them. (3-413(2)), (3-414(1))

Liability of the Maker and the Acceptor   A primary party engages that he will pay the instrument according to terms. The maker thus assumes an obligation to pay the note as it was worded at the time he executed it. The acceptor assumes responsibility for the draft as it was worded when he gave his acceptance. (3-413(1))

The maker of a note is obligated to pay the instrument according to its terms. Of course, if a maker signs an incomplete note, it can be enforced as completed against him by a holder in due course. The maker admits as against all subsequent parties the existence of the payee and his capacity to indorse. (3-413(2))

The drawee of a check or draft is not liable on the instrument until acceptance. Upon acceptance, the acceptor becomes primarily liable. The usual method of acceptance for a check is to have it certified. An acceptance must be in writing on the draft and signed by the drawee-acceptor. (3-410(1)) Acceptance is usually made by the drawee's writing or stamping the word "Accepted," with his name and the date, across the face of the instrument. An acceptance makes the drawee-acceptor the primary obligor; the drawer and all indorsers are secondary parties.

A party presenting a draft for acceptance is entitled to an *unqualified acceptance* by the drawee. Thus, when the drawee offers an acceptance that in any manner varies or changes the direct order to pay

354

or accept, the holder may refuse the acceptance. (3-412(1)) The paper is dishonored, and upon notice of dishonor or protest, the holder may hold all prior parties on the paper back to and including the drawer.

Liability of Banks in Cases of Forgery   A special problem exists in connection with forgeries insofar as banks are concerned. Checks presented to drawee banks for payment may bear forged signatures of drawers or forged indorsements. If the drawer's signature was forged, the bank that honors the check has not followed the order of the drawer and cannot charge his account. (3-418) If charged, it must be recredited. Likewise, the bank will have to make restitution to the party whose name was forged on the check as an indorsement. (3-419(1)(c)) In either case, the loss initially is that of the bank that pays the instrument bearing the forgery.

In the case of a forged drawer's signature, the drawee bank as a general rule cannot collect the payment back from the party who received it. The bank has the signature of the drawer on file and is charged with knowledge of the forgery. This general rule is subject to the exception that if the party receiving the payment is the forger or dealt with the forger and was negligent in doing so, the drawee may recover the payment. Thus, if a collecting bank was negligent, the drawee bank that paid on a forged drawer's signature could recover from the collecting bank.

A drawee who pays on a forged indorsement has greater rights in seeking to recover the payment than does the drawee who pays on a forged drawer's signature. In the case of a forged indorsement, the drawee has no way of knowing about the forgery, and thus it can collect from the person to whom payment was made who in turn can collect from all prior parties back to the forger.

Impostors: Fictitious Payees   A situation similar to forgery arises when an instrument is made payable to a fictitious person or to an impostor. The drawer's signature is genuine, but the instrument is indorsed in the fictitious name or the name of the person who is being impersonated. In the impostor situation, one person poses as someone else and induces the drawer to issue a check payable to the order of the person who is being impersonated. The imposter then signs the name of the person being impersonated. In such situations the indorsement by the imposter is effective, and the loss falls on the drawer rather than on the person who took the check or the bank that honored it. (3-405(1)(a))

The loss falls upon the drawer because the check was indorsed by the actual person whom the drawer intended to indorse it. If the check is

355

intended for the party named but is diverted and forged by an employee, the "impostor rule" is not applicable.

A typical situation of a fictitious payee is one in which a dishonest employee is either authorized to sign his employer's name to checks or draws checks that he presents to his employer for the latter's signature. Thus the employee may draw payroll checks or checks payable to persons with whom the employer would be expected to do business. He either signs the checks or obtains his employer's signature and then cashes the checks indorsing the name of the payee. If he is in charge of the company's books, he is able to manipulate the books when the canceled checks are returned and may thus avoid detection. The Code imposes this loss on the employer—the dishonest employee can effectively indorse in the payee's name. (3-405(1)(c)

Case: A was employed by P brokerage company. He devised a scheme to defraud his employer by issuing fraudulent orders to sell customers' securities. When P company issued a check to the customer whose stock had been sold, A would obtain the check, forge the customer's indorsement, and pocket the money. When the fraud was discovered, P sought to recover its losses from the D bank upon whom the checks were drawn.

Issue: Is D liable for honoring the checks on a forged indorsement?

Decision: No.

Reasons: 1. Although A did not deal directly with the person who wrote the check, he did initiate the transaction that a check be drawn and he knew that the payee was not to have any interest in it.

2. The Code protects the drawee bank under these circumstances by providing that the indorsement by the employee is effective.

New Amsterdam Casualty Co. v. First Pennsylvania Banking and Trust Co., 451 F.2d 892 (1971).

THE LIABILITY OF SECONDARY PARTIES

Drawers The drawer engages that upon *dishonor* of the draft and any necessary notice of dishonor or protest he will pay the amount of the draft to the holder or to any indorser who takes it up. (3-413(2)) In effect, the drawer assumes a conditional liability on the instrument— that he will pay if the instrument is dishonored and he is properly notified of this fact. The party who draws a draft or check, like one who makes a note or accepts a draft, admits as against all subsequent parties the existence of the payee and his then capacity to indorse. (3-413(3))

Indorsers   Indorsers of checks, drafts, or notes have two kinds of secondary liability. First, they are liable on their *contract* of indorsement. (3-414(1)) If an unqualified indorsement (blank or special) is given, the indorser agrees to pay if the primary party does not. This liability can be disclaimed by a qualified indorsement "without recourse." By indorsing "without recourse" the indorser is in effect saying, "I do not guarantee that the primary party will pay."

The contractual liability of the unqualified indorser is conditional in that the indorser obligates himself to pay only if (1) the instrument is properly presented to the primary party, (2) the instrument is dishonored, and (3) notice of dishonor is given to him. This obligation runs to subsequent parties. It is discussed further in subsequent chapters.

Second, an indorser has unconditional liability. This unconditional liability is based on breach of warranty. An indorser makes warranties with reference to the instrument that is transferred. (3-417(2)) He warrants that he has good title to the instrument, that all signatures are genuine or authorized, that the instrument has not been materially altered, and that no defense of any party is good against him. He also warrants that he does not have knowledge of any insolvency proceedings with respect to any of the parties involved. (3-417(2)(e))

The warranties are made whether the transfer is by delivery only, by qualified indorsement (without recourse), or by unqualified indorsement.

Case: D, a used-car dealer, sold P bank a note and an installment sale contract allegedly received in connection with the sale of a car. The note was indorsed "without recourse." The signatures on the note and contract were forgeries. D claims that he has no responsibility because of his indorsement "without recourse."

Issue: Does an indorsement "without recourse" relieve the indorser of all liability?

Decision: No.

Reasons: 1. The transferor of an instrument warrants that all signatures are genuine or authorized. This is true regardless of the fact that the endorsement is "without recourse."

2. D has liability for breaching this warranty.

The Union National Bank v. Mobella, 40 Erie Co., J. 45 (Pa.) 1959.

It is important to note that liability is automatic if any of the warranties are breached. The indorser and transferor by delivery must make good without regard to the performance of any conditions precedent, such as presentment or notice of dishonor.

Transferors Without Indorsement All secondary parties have unconditional liability because this liability is based on a theory of breach of warranty. Technically speaking, the party who presents an instrument for payment and signs it is not an indorser. The signature is a receipt for the payment. However, the person who presents the instrument warrants that no indorsements are forged, that so far as he knows the signature of the maker or drawer is genuine, and that it has not been materially altered. (3-417(1)) Thus the person who pays or accepts will have recourse against the presenting party if the warranties are breached. There is no warranty that the drawer has sufficient funds on deposit to cover a check. If a drawee pays a check when the drawer has insufficient funds on deposit, the party presenting the check is not liable for breach of warranty. The warranty with regard to the drawer's signature is not absolute—it is only that the warrantor has no knowledge that such signature is forged or unauthorized.

A transferor without an indorsement (bearer paper) also makes warranties to the transferee. They are the same warranties as a qualified indorser makes. These differ from the warranties of an unqualified indorser in only one particular way. The qualified indorser's warranty about defenses is simply that he has no *knowledge* of any defense. (3-417(3)) In the case of delivery of bearer paper without indorsement, the warranties run only to the immediate transferee, whereas the indorser's warranties extend to subsequent holders. (3-417(2))

Accommodation Parties and Guarantors One who signs an instrument for the purpose of lending his name and credit to another party to an instrument is an "accommodation" party. (3-415(1)) His function is that of a surety. He may sign as an indorser, maker, or acceptor or as a comaker or coacceptor. The accommodation party is liable in the capacity in which he signed. (3-415(2)) As an indorser, he does not indorse for the purpose of transferring the paper but rather to lend security to it.

There is some significance to the surety status of an accommodation party. In some situations he is entitled to be discharged under the general law and may exercise this right against one who is not a holder in due course. (3-415(3)) He is not liable to the party accommodated, and if he is required to pay, he can obtain reimbursement from such party. (3-415(5))

The liability of an accommodation party arises without express words. A guarantor's liability is based on words of guaranty. For example, if the words "Payment guaranteed" or their equivalent are added to a signature, the signer engages that if the instrument is not paid when due, he will pay it *without previous resort by the holder to other parties on the paper*. (3-416(1)) If the words "Collection guaranteed" are added to a signature, the signer becomes liable only after the holder has reduced his claim against the maker or acceptor to judgment and execution has been returned unsatisfied, or after the maker or acceptor has become insolvent or it is otherwise apparent that it is useless to proceed against him. (3-416(2))

A guarantor waives the conditions precedent of presentment, notice of dishonor, and protest. The words of guarantee do not affect the indorsement as a means of transferring the instrument but impose upon such indorser the liability of a comaker. (3-416(5))

CONDITIONAL LIABILITY

Introduction The term *conditional liability* is used to describe the secondary liability that results from the status of parties as drawers or unqualified indorsers. The adjective *conditional* refers to the fact that certain conditions precedent must be fulfilled to establish liability. (3-501) The conditions precedent are *presentment, dishonor, notice of dishonor*, and in some instances *protest.* Presentment is a demand for acceptance or payment, and such demand will be made by the holder upon the maker, acceptor, or drawee. (3-504(1)) There may be two or more makers, acceptors, or drawees, in which event the presentment can be made to any one of them. (3-504(3)(a))

The importance of exact compliance with the conditions precedent cannot be overemphasized. Failure to comply will result in the discharge of the secondary parties.

Presentment— Presentment is a demand made upon a maker or drawee.
Generally (3-504(1)) In the case of a note, it is a demand for payment made by the holder upon the maker. In the case of a draft, it may be either a demand for acceptance or a demand for payment.

The drawee of a draft is not bound upon the instrument as a primary party until acceptance. The holder will usually wait until maturity and present his draft to the drawee for payment, but he may present it to the drawee for acceptance before maturity in order to give credit to the instrument during the period of its term. The drawee is under no legal duty to the holder to accept; but is he refuses, the draft is dishonored by nonacceptance. A right of recourse arises immediately against the drawer and the indorsers, and no presentment for payment is necessary.

In most instances it is not necessary to present an instrument for *acceptance.* Presentment for *payment* alone is usually sufficient, but *presentment for acceptance must be made in order to charge the drawer and indorsers of a draft* in a few cases. For example, if the date of payment depends upon presentment as where the draft is payable after sight, presentment is required in order to determine the maturity date of the instrument. (3-501(1)(a)) Failure to make a proper presentment for payment results in the complete discharge of an indorser. (3-501(1)(b)) A limited discharge is accorded to drawers and to the acceptor of a draft payable at a bank or to the maker of a note payable at a bank. Such parties are discharged to the extent that the failure to make a proper presentment caused them a loss.

Presentment—
How and Where

Presentment may be made by personally contacting the primary party and making a demand for acceptance or payment.

Presentment may be made by mail or through a clearinghouse. (3-504(2)(a)(b)) Presentment by mail is effective when received. If the instrument specifies the place of acceptance or payment, presentment may be made at such place. If no place is specified, presentment may be made at the place of business of the party to accept or to pay. Presentment is excused if neither the party to accept or pay nor anyone authorized to act for him is present or accessible at such place. (3-504(2)(c)) It is required that a draft accepted or a note made payable at a bank in the United States must be presented at such bank. (3-504(4))

The party to whom presentment is made may without dishonor require the exhibition of the instrument at the proper place. He may also require the reasonable identification of the person making presentment and evidence of authority to make it if made for another.

If the primary party does not avail himself of these rights, the presentment is perfectly valid no matter how the presentment is made or where it is made. If he does require proper presentment, a failure to comply invalidates the presentment and the instrument is not dishonored. The requirement of identification of the presenting party applies to bearer paper as well as order paper. (3-505)

Presentment—
When

In general, an instrument must be presented for payment on the day of maturity. The presentment must be made at a reasonable hour, and if at a bank, during banking hours.

When an instrument is payable on demand, it must be presented or negotiated within a reasonable time after such secondary party became liable, for example, after his indorsement. (3-503(1)(e)) Thus, in the case of a demand note, an indorser would be discharged if presentment were not made within a reasonable time after he indorsed the note.

Note that presentment within a "reasonable time" is required in those situations when a definite maturity date is not included in the instrument, that is, sight and demand instruments. A reasonable time for presentment is determined by the nature of the instrument, any usage of banking or trade, and the facts of the particular case. (3-503(2))

With respect to the liability of the drawer of a check, a reasonable time within which to present for payment or to initiate bank collection is presumed to be thirty days after date or issue, whichever is later. (3-504(2)(a)) As to an indorser's liability, the presumed reasonable time is seven days after his indorsement. (3-504(2)(b))

Thus the drawer must "back up" a check for a longer period than an indorser, but the drawer having issued the check is not being imposed upon by the requirement that he keep funds on hand for thirty days to cover it. Thirty days is also the period after which a purchaser has notice of the staleness of a check. But an indorser is in a different position and is entitled to notice promptly, so that he may take adequate steps to protect himself against his transferor and prior parties if the check is dishonored. The drawer of a check is protected as to funds on deposit by Federal Deposit Insurance.

Dishonor The party who presents an instrument is entitled to have the instrument paid or accepted. If the party to whom the instrument is presented refuses to pay or accept, the instrument is dishonored. (3-507(1)) The presenting party then has recourse against indorsers or other secondary parties, provided proper notice of dishonor is given.

When a draft is presented to the drawee for *acceptance*, the drawee, may wish to ascertain some facts from the drawer. As a result, the law allows the drawee to defer acceptance until the close of the next business day following presentment. The holder who presents the draft for *acceptance* is seeking the drawee's obligation on the paper and will not receive payment until a later date. For this reason, the Code permits a longer period of time within which to accept a draft than is allowed when the draft is presented for payment. When an instrument is presented for payment, the party to whom presentment is made is allowed a reasonable time to examine the instrument to determine whether the instrument is properly payable, but payment must be made in any event on the same day that it is presented and before the close of business on that day. (3-506(2))

Notice of When an instrument has been dishonored on proper present-
Dishonor ment, the holder must give prompt notice of the dishonor in order to have a right of recourse against unqualified indorsers. (3-507(2)) Failure to give prompt and proper notice of dishonor results in the discharge of indorsers. Notice of dishonor should also be given to the drawer. However, the failure to do so discharges the drawer only to the extent that he has suffered a loss because of the failure of the holder to give proper notice. (3-502(1)) This would occur if the bank failed in the interim.

Generally, notice is given to secondary parties by the holder or by an indorser who has received such notice. Any party who may be compelled to pay the instrument may notify any party who may be liable on it. (3-508(1))

Except for banks, notice must be given before midnight of the third business day after dishonor. (3-508(2)) In the case of a person who has received notice of dishonor and wishes to notify other parties, notice must be given by him before midnight of the third business day after receipt of the notice of dishonor.

In the case of banks, any necessary notice must be given before the bank's "midnight deadline" —before midnight of the next banking day following the day on which a bank receives the item or notice of dishonor. (3-508(2))

Case: D received a check drawn on P bank. D indorsed the check and received payment from his bank. That bank sent the check for collection to P bank and the check was honored. Several days later, P discovered that the drawer of the check did not have an account and that it had mistakenly charged the check to another of its customers. P then sought to recover from D as an indorser. D contended that the check had not been dishonored within the time allowed by law.

Issue: Is D liable as an indorser?

Decision: No.

Reasons: 1. Unless excused . . . notice of any dishonor is necessary to charge any indorser.
2. Any necessary notice must be given by a bank before its midnight deadline . . . that is, "midnight on its next banking day following the banking day on which it receives the relevant item."
3. Where without excuse any necessary presentment or notice of dishonor is delayed beyond the time when it is due, any indorser is discharged.
4. Here there was no excuse. P made a mistake and must suffer the loss.

Samples v. Trust Co. of Georgia, 165 S.E. 2d 325 (Ga.) 1968.

Notice may be given in any reasonable manner, which would include oral notice, notice by telephone, and notice by mail. Such notice must identify the dishonored instrument and state that it has been dishonored. Written notice is effective when sent even though it is not received, assuming proper address and postage. (3-508(4))

Proper notice preceded by any necessary presentment and dishonor imposes liability upon secondary parties to whom such notice of dishonor is given. Proper notice operates for the benefit of all parties who have rights on the instrument against the party notified. (3-508(8)) Thus it is only necessary to notify a party once for his liability to be fixed. For example, assume that if A, B, C, and D are indorsers in that order, and the holder gives notice only to A and C. C will not be required to give additional notice to A, and if D is compelled to pay, he would have recourse against A. B and D are discharged if they are not notified by the holder or one of the indorsers. This result follows because indorsers are in general liable in the order of their indorsement. An indorser who is required to pay can recover from an indorser prior to him. But each indorser is entitled to notice of dishonor in order that he can take appropriate steps to pass the responsibility on to those prior to him on the paper.

Protest Protest is a certificate that sets forth that an instrument was presented for payment or acceptance, that is was dishonored, and the reasons, if any, given for refusal to accept or pay. (3-509) It is a formal method for satisfying the conditions precedent. It is required only for drafts that are drawn or payable outside the United States. The protest requirement is in conformity with foreign law in this respect. In other cases, protest is optional with the holder. Protest serves as evidence both that presentment was made and that notice of dishonor was given. It creates a presumption that the conditions precedent were satisfied.

Excuses for Failure to Perform Conditions Precedent An unexcused delay in making any *necessary* presentment or in giving notice of dishonor discharges parties who are entitled to performance of the conditions precedent. Indorsers are completely discharged by such delay, and drawers, makers of notes payable at a bank, and acceptors of drafts payable at a bank are discharged to the extent of any loss caused by the delay. (3-502)

Delay in making presentment, in giving notice of dishonor, or in making protest is excused when the holder has acted with reasonable diligence, and the delay is not due to any fault of the holder. He must, however, comply with these conditions or attempt to do so as soon as the cause of the delay ceases to exist. (3-511(1))

Case: P bank forwarded two checks to D bank for collection. D bank failed to give notice of dishonor by its midnight deadline. D claims to be excused because of a computer breakdown. Section 4-108 of the Code excuses delays by banks if caused by "emergency conditions or other circumstances beyond the control of the bank provided it exercises such diligence as the circumstances require."

Issue: Is D excused from giving proper notice of dishonor?

Decision: Yes.

Reasons: 1. The computer malfunction constituted both an emergency condition and a circumstance beyond the control of the bank, and the bank acted with diligence.

2. A computer failure qualifies for the application of the section excusing delays.

Port City State Bank v. American Nat. Bank, Lawton, Okla., 486 F.2d 196 (1973).

The performance of the conditions precedent is entirely excused if the party to be charged has *waived* the condition. When such waiver is stated on the face of the instrument, it is binding on all parties; when it is written above the signature of the indorser, it binds him only. (3-511(6)) Most promissory notes contain such a waiver.

The performance of the conditions precedent is also excused if the party to be charged has himself dishonored the instrument or has countermanded payment or otherwise has no reason to expect or right to require that the instrument be accepted or paid. (3-511(2)(b)) For example, if a drawer of a check has stopped payment on the check, the drawer is not in a position to complain about slow presentment or any lack of notice of dishonor.

Discharge   The liability of various parties may be discharged in a variety of ways. (3-601) Many of these have been previously noted. For example, certification of a check at the request of a holder discharges all prior parties. (3-411) Any ground for discharging a simple contract also discharges commercial paper. (3-601(2))

Payment usually discharges a party's liability. This is true even if the payor has knowledge of the claim of another person. Payment does not operate to discharge liability if the payor acts in bad faith and pays one who acquired the instrument by theft. Payment is also no defense if paid in violation of a restrictive indorsement. (3-603)

A holder may discharge any party by intentionally canceling the instrument or by striking out or otherwise eliminating a party's signature. The surrender of the instrument to a party will also discharge that party. (3-605)

If a holder agrees not to sue one party or agrees to release collateral, then all parties with rights against such party or against the collateral are discharged from liability. This assumes that there is no express reservation of rights by the holder and that the party claiming discharge did not consent to the holder's actions. (3-606)

When an instrument is reacquired by a prior party, he may cancel all intervening indorsements. In this event, all parties whose indorsements are canceled are discharged. (3-208)

An alteration of an instrument that is both fraudulent and material discharges any party whose liability is affected by the alteration. Of course this is not true if the alteration is agreed to or if the party seeking to impose liability is a holder in due course. (3-407) In fact no discharge is effective against a holder in due course unless he has notice of the discharge when he takes the instrument. (3-602)

REVIEW QUESTIONS AND PROBLEMS

1. A cashed a payroll check drawn by D company at the XYZ supermarket. The check was returned to XYZ because of insufficient funds. May XYZ recover the amount of the check from A? Why?

2. A, the holder of a note, indorses it to B "Without recourse." The maker of the note had filed a petition in bankruptcy prior to the indorsement. Can B hold A responsible for the payment of the note? Why?

3. M, the bookkeeper for X corporation, prepared payroll checks to the order of persons not on the payroll. The checks were presented to the company's treasurer, who signed them as a matter of course. M indorsed the checks in the name of the purported payees and cashed the checks at various stores. The checks were honored by the drawee bank. X corporation seeks to recover from the stores that cashed the checks and from the drawee bank. How would you decide this case? Discuss fully.

4. H holds a note that, unknown to him, has been forged. He, by an indorsement "Without recourse," indorses it to A, a holder in due course. It is presented and payment is refused. A desires to hold H liable on his indorsement. May he do so? Why?

5. What is an *accommodation party*? Explain.

6. A indorsed a note to B, who presented it to the maker. The note was dishonored. B lost A's address and found it several weeks later. B then mailed A written notice of the dishonor. Is A liable to B? Why?

7. A is the holder of a draft drawn by X on Y. A presents the draft to Y for acceptance, and Y refuses to accept. What should A do to protect his rights? May he wait until the bill matures before taking any action? Why?

8. Why could it be considered dangerous to sign as a witness to the maker's signature on a promissory note? Explain.

9. A, the treasurer of a club, signed a check and delivered it to B, payee. The check included the club name, but there was nothing to indicate the capacity by which A signed. The check was dishonored by the club's bank due to insufficient funds. Could A be held personally liable? Explain.

10. A gave B, one of A's employees, a "blank check" and told B to fill in the amount when B was to purchase some goods for A. B wrote in $5,000 and transferred the check to a holder in due course, C. Will A be liable to C for $5,000? Why?

25 SECURED TRANSACTIONS: BASIC CONCEPTS

Introduction   A *secured transaction* is one in which a borrower or a buyer gives security to a lender or seller that an obligation will be satisfied. Secured transactions occur at all levels of commerce. For example, manufacturers finance raw materials, retailers and wholesalers finance inventory, and consumers finance their purchases by giving their creditors security in the form of personal property. These transactions take many forms, but they are all secured transactions under Article 9 of the Code.

The simplest form of secured transaction is a *pledge*. In a pledge transaction, a borrower gives the physical possession of his property to a lender as security for a loan. If the loan is not repaid, the lender can sell the property in order to satisfy the debt. Stocks and bonds are frequently used as collateral in pledge transactions. However, in many transactions the pledge is not satisfactory as a security arrangement because it requires that the possession must be delivered to the creditor. Therefore security devices that allow the debtor to retain the possession and use of the property were developed. In the early law these devices were covered by different statutes and separate rules of law. Among the common terms used to describe such security arrangements were chattel mortgages, conditional sales contracts, trust receipts, factor's liens, and assignment of accounts receivable. These terms continue to be used even though they have been replaced by a single security device under the Code: the *security interest*. Whatever name is used, the purpose of the secured transaction is to give a creditor an interest in the debtor's personal property which the creditor can use to obtain satisfaction of the debt in the event of nonpayment. Such personal property is called *collateral*. (9-105(1)(c))

366

Article 9 as originally written is not the law in very many states today. Nonuniform amendments to forty-seven of the fifty-four sections of Article 9 have been adopted by various states. Some sections of Article 9 have been amended by as many as thirty states. As a result, in 1972 a new official text and comments were published. Several states have adopted the Revised Article 9 of the Code and most others are considering it. Therefore, as this chapter and Chapter 26 are studied, it should be kept in mind that the law in this area is in a state of flux. The statutes of each state must be carefully examined not only to see if the revision has been adopted but also to see which of the many amendments to the original Code are applicable. It must be understood that Article 9 is correctly described as the "Un-Uniform Commercial Code." We will indicate some of the areas of major change in the Revised Article 9 in the sections that follow.

The Scope of Article 9

Although Article 9 deals primarily with secured transactions, it also covers outright sales of certain types of property, such as accounts receivable. (9-102(1)(b)) Thus a sale of the accounts receivable of a business must comply with the Code requirements to the same extent as would be the case if the accounts were used as security for a loan.

Case: X, a contractor, sold his accounts receivable, including progress payments on a construction job, to D bank. The bank did not file a financing statement. Thereafter the government filed a tax lien against X for unpaid payroll taxes. The government claims priority to the progress payments.

Issue: Which claimant has priority?

Decision: The government.

Reason: The Code requires that the assignee of accounts receivable record its interest to protect it from the claims of third parties. The Code subordinates the rights of a secured party to claims of creditors if there is not a proper filing.

United States v. Trigg, 465 F.2d 1264 (1972).

Except for sales, such as those of accounts receivable, the main test to be applied in determining whether a given transaction falls within the purview of Article 9 is whether it was intended to have effect as security. Every transaction with such intent is covered. (9-102(1)(a))

For example, a lease with option to buy may be considered a security transaction rather than a lease if the necessary intent is present.

Certain credit transactions are expressly excluded from Article 9 coverage. (9-104) The exclusions in general are transactions that are not basically of a commercial character, such as landlord's liens, a wage assignment, or a transfer of an insurance policy. One important exclusion is liens given by state law for services and materials—for example, the artisan's lien given to a person who repairs a car.

Terminology   A *security interest* is an interest in personal property or fixtures that secures either payment of money or performance of an obligation. (1-201(37)) The reference to *fixtures* is included because personal property is often attached to real property, in which event it is called a fixture. (9-102(1)) The security interest is the interest that the creditor has in property belonging to the debtor.

The security interest comes into being when the debtor and the creditor enter into what is called a *security agreement*. (9-105(h)) The property in which a security interest is given is called *collateral*. (9-105(c)) The parties to the security agreement are the *debtor*, who owes the obligation and is giving the security, and the *secured party*, who is the lender, seller, or other person in whose favor there is a security interest. (9-105(d)(i)) Thus the typical transaction involves an agreement between a debtor and a secured party (security agreement) whereby the debtor agrees to give to the secured party a security interest in the debtor's collateral.

Before a security interest is effective between the parties, it must *attach* to the collateral, (9-204); and before it is effective to give priority over the rights of third parties, the security interest must be *perfected*. (9-301) Attachment is the means whereby the secured party acquires rights in the collateral; perfection is the method whereby the secured party is given priority over claims of third parties. Perfection usually occurs by the filing of a *financing* statement.

CLASSIFICATIONS OF COLLATERAL

Introduction   Collateral may be classified according to its physical makeup into (1) tangible, physical property or goods, (2) purely intangible property, such as an account receivable, and (3) property that has physical existence, such as a negotiable instrument, but is simply representative of a contractual obligation. Each type of collateral presents its own peculiar problems, and the framework of Article 9 is structured on the peculiarities of each type. There may be a security interest not only in the collateral itself but also in the proceeds of the sale of the collateral.(9-306(1)) The method of perfecting the security interest depends upon the classification of the collateral.

Goods as Collateral Four classifications of goods are established: consumer goods, equipment, inventory, and farm products. In determining the classification of any particular item of goods, it is necessary to take into account not only the physical attributes but also the status of the debtor who is either buying the property or using it as security for a loan and the use the debtor will make of the goods. Keep in mind that the classification will determine the place of filing to perfect the security interest against third parties. It may also affect the rights of the debtor on default.

consumer goods Goods fall into this classification if they are used or bought primarily for personal, family, or household purposes. (9-109(1))

equipment Goods that are used or bought for use primarily in a business, in farming, in a profession, or by a nonprofit organization or government agency fall within this category. (9-109(2)) The category is something of a "catchall," so that goods that otherwise defy classification are treated as equipment. Since equipment often becomes attached to realty so as to constitute a "fixture," the discussion on fixtures later is especially significant for this classification of goods.

inventory Inventory consists of goods that are held by a person for sale or lease or are to be furnished under a contract of service. They may be raw materials, work in process, completed goods, or material used or consumed in a business. (9-109(4)) The basic test to be applied in determining whether goods are inventory is whether they are held for immediate or ultimate sale or lease. A security interest in inventory automatically covers after-acquired inventory.

farm products This category includes crops and livestock, supplies used or produced in farming operations, the products of crops or livestock in their unmanufactured state (e.g., ginned cotton, wool, milk, and eggs)—provided that such items are in the possession of a debtor who is engaged in farming operations. (9-109(3)) Farm products are *not* equipment or inventory.

The proper classification of goods is determined on the basis of their nature and the intended use to be made of them by the debtor. For example, a television set in a dealer's warehouse is inventory to the dealer. When the set is sold and delivered to a consumer-customer, it becomes a consumer good. If an identical set were sold on the same terms to the owner of a tavern to be used for entertaining his customers, the set would be equipment in the hands of the tavern owner. The secured party cannot rely on the classification furnished by the debtor. All facts must be analyzed to ensure proper classification and proper filing of the financing statement.

Case: A bankrupt purchased a truck from an automobile dealer and executed a promissory note and a separate security agreement-financing statement. In that statement he warranted, by checking a box thereon, that the pickup was to be used primarily "In Business." The dealer assigned the note and the purchase-money security interest to the bank for value. In reliance on the "In Business" designation, the bank filed the security agreement in Oklahoma County.

The trustee in bankruptcy contends that the truck was actually consumer goods and, therefore, the financing statement had to be filed in Tulsa County, the county of the debtor's residence. As a result, there is no valid security interest because of improper filing.

Issue: Can a creditor rely on the debtor's designation to classify the goods?

Decision: No.

Reasons: 1. Goods under the Code are classified into four categories: consumer goods, equipment, farm products, and inventory. The classes are mutually exclusive, and the goods cannot be in two categories at the same time as to the same person.

2. The perfection of a security interest by filing requires the determination of the proper county in which to file. If the collateral is classified as consumer goods, the proper county in which to file is the county of the debtor's residence, in this case Tulsa County. If business equipment, the security agreement is to be filed with the county clerk of Oklahoma County.

3. The principal use to which the property is put is considered determinative—not what the debtor says. Further, in bankruptcy situations courts independently inquire into the classification and filing of collateral. A creditor in doubt about the proper classification of collateral should file in all possible counties where filing might be required.

In re McClain, 447 F.2d 241 (1971).

Other Types of Collateral Another type of collateral is that which is represented by a writing. Included within this classification are documents of title, such as bills of lading and warehouse receipts (1-201(15)); "chattel paper," which is evidence of a debt (9-105(b)); and instruments such as a negotiable instrument, or a security, such as stocks and bonds. (9-105(g)) These "writings" may also serve as collateral and may be the subject of a security interest.

Finally, there is a type of collateral that is intangible in that it simply represents a right to receive money without any writing. The most common example of this would be an account receivable that may be nothing more than a bookkeeping entry in the seller's books. It does represent a right to receive money, however, and this right may be used as collateral.

CREATION OF THE SECURITY INTEREST

The Security Agreement   The basic instrument in a secured transaction is the *security agreement*. (9-105(h)) The security agreement must be in writing, unless the security arrangement is a possessory one and the secured party is in possession of the collateral. (9-203(1)) The only other formal requirement is that the agreement be signed by the debtor and that it contain a description of the collateral sufficient to reasonably identify it.

Case: P sold office furniture to X real estate company. To secure the sale, the parties entered into a security agreement. The security agreement stated that the collateral is "furniture as per attached listing." No listing was attached, nor was any listing included in the financing statement. X real estate company sold the furniture to Y real estate company.

Issue: Does P have a security interest in the furniture?

Decision: No.

Reason: The Code requires (1) that the security agreement contain a description of the collateral and (2) that the description reasonably identifies what is described. The security agreement in question does not meet these criteria.

J.K. Gill Co. v. Fireside Realty, Inc., 499 P.2d 813 (Or.) 1972.

The security agreement will usually contain many other provisions. The forms in general use include a statement of the amount of the obligation and the terms of repayment, the debtor's duties in respect to the collateral, such as insuring it, and the rights of the secured party on default. In general, the parties can include such terms and provisions as they may deem appropriate to their particular transaction.

Attachment   A security interest is not enforceable between the debtor and the secured party until it attaches to the collateral. A security interest attaches to collateral when three events have occurred: (1) the debtor must have rights in the collateral, (2) the secured party must have given value, and (3) there must be an agreement between the debtor and the secured party. (9-204(1)) They may occur in any order. For example, a security agreement may be executed and the secured party may give value—e.g., loan money to the debtor before the debtor acquires rights in the collateral. "Attachment" is the legal term used to describe the phenomenon whereby the secured party acquires rights in the collateral.

371

Value for purpose of attachment is defined somewhat differently than it is in commercial paper. Basically, value means that a secured party has furnished to the debtor any consideration sufficient to support a simple contract. (1-201(44)) For example, a bank loans $10,000 to a merchant and takes a security interest in his inventory; the loan of money constitutes the value.

The third requirement for attachment is that the debtor have *rights in the collateral.* A debtor has no right (1) in crops, until they are planted or otherwise become growing crops, or in the young of livestock until they are conceived; (2) in fish until they are caught; (3) in oil, gas, or minerals until they are extracted; (4) in timber until it is cut. (9-204(2)) A debtor has no rights in an account until it comes into existence—until goods have been sold there could not be an account receivable. Although a merchant could enter into an agreement to assign future accounts to a secured party, the latter's security interest could not *attach* until the accounts actually came into existence.

Case: The Grain Merchants, in order to finance their business of buying and selling feed and grain, entered into a security agreement with the D bank. D was given a security interest in accounts receivable including those in the future. The Grain Merchants became insolvent and ceased doing business. D proceeded to collect the accounts receivable. Shortly thereafter Grain Merchants filed a petition in bankruptcy. P, the trustee in bankruptcy, claimed the amounts collected by D.

Issue: Does D's security interest in after-acquired accounts receivable prevail over a trustee in bankruptcy?

Decision: Yes.

Reason: As soon as the account receivable comes into existence it is subject to the security interest. A secured creditor who has filed a financing statement covering after-acquired collateral is entitled to priority over a subsequent lien creditor.

Grain Merchants of Indiana v. Union Bank and Savings Co., 408 F.2d 209 (1961).

The security agreement may provide that property acquired by the debtor at any later time shall also secure the obligation covered by the security agreement. This means that if such a clause were included in the security agreement, *after-acquired property* property of the debtor would be additional security for the secured party—i.e., as soon as the debtor acquires rights in other property, a security interest would attach to such property in favor of the secured party. (9-204(3)) The subject of after-acquired property security interests is discussed in more detail in the next chapter.

PERFECTION OF THE SECURITY INTEREST

In General The security agreement creates the security interest in the debtor's collateral as between the secured party and the debtor, provided that the security interest has attached to the collateral. This is not sufficient, however, to give the secured party priority over other persons who may claim an interest in the collateral. Such claims could arise in a variety of circumstances. The debtor's other creditors might seek to have the collateral sold to satisfy their claims. The debtor might give a security interest in the same collateral to another person, or the debtor might sell the collateral to another person. Another possibility is that the debtor might become bankrupt, and the trustee might seek to include the collateral as an asset of the bankrupt estate.

To have priority in the above situations and thus obtain the maximum protection from the security interest, the secured party must "perfect" the security interest. (9-303(1)) The concept of perfection usually entails giving notice to third persons that the secured party has a security interest in the debtor's collateral. If such notice is given, persons dealing with the debtor are made aware that his property is encumbered, and they can take this into account in their dealings with the debtor.

A secured party who has a perfected security interest in collateral still does not always have complete protection. For example, if the collateral is inventory, a buyer in the ordinary course of business will obtain good title to goods free and clear of any security interest. (9-307) For example, A, a retailer, has financed his inventory of television sets with X bank and has given the bank a security interest. He now sells one of the television sets to B who buys it in the ordinary course of business. B takes the set free of even a perfected security interest on the part of X bank. This rule does not apply, however, to good-faith purchasers of farm products.

An issue is sometimes presented as to whether or not a buyer is a purchaser in the ordinary course of business.

Case: P sold a car to Brown on an installment contract and retained a security interest. The contract was assigned to a New York bank. Brown drove the car to another state and sold it to D, a car dealer. Brown failed to make payments on the contract, and the car was repossessed by P. D claimed that he was entitled to keep the car free of any security interest.

Issue:	Did D, the purchaser of the car, qualify as a buyer in the ordinary course of business?
Decision:	No.
Reasons:	1. This was not a sale in the ordinary course because Brown was not a dealer and the sale was not from inventory.
	2. The defendant was not a buyer in the ordinary course of business as he was a dealer rather than a consumer.

Al Maroone Ford, Inc. v. Manheim Auto Auction, Inc., 208 A.2d 290 (Pa.) 1965.

Perfection by Possession The simplest way to give notice of a security interest is for the secured party to take possession of the collateral. (9-305) For example, the delivery of pledged property is the means of perfecting a security interest in it. The possession of the collateral by the secured party gives notice of his security interest—hence no public filing is required. As noted previously, the possessory security interest does not require a written security agreement either.

Possession is the required method of perfection of a security interest in instruments. It is the optional method in the case of collateral consisting of goods, negotiable documents of title, and chattel paper. (9-305) However, possession is the only method whereby complete protection in documents and chattel paper can be obtained. (9-308)

Perfection by Filing A second method of perfection and the most usual one is for the secured party to file a "financing statement" in the proper public office designated for that purpose. (9-401) This has the effect of giving notice that the debtor and the secured party have made an arrangement for secured financing. Any person interested can determine from the public records that the debtor may have encumbered his property, and if he desires more explicit information he can contact the debtor for further details.

Perfection by Attachment The third method of perfection is known as perfection by attachment. It is accomplished simply by the attachment of the security interest without any further action being required. This method of perfection is limited to transactions involving installment sales to consumers and to sales of farm equipment having a purchase price of $2,500 or less. (9-302(c)(d)) The Revised Article 9 eliminates

374

farm equipment from perfection by attachment because the effect of the law had been to make farm equipment unacceptable as collateral to many lenders. The transaction must be a purchase-money security interest, one that is related to the purchase of goods. In such transactions the secured party obtains a perfected security interest without filing a financing statement.

Case: P sold a television set and tape player to a customer on a conditional sale contract designated a purchase-money security agreement. On the day of the purchase, the customer pledged the items to D (a pawnbroker) as security for a loan. P did not file any financing statement.

Issue: Which creditor has priority?

Decision: The seller.

Reasons: 1. The property was consumer goods. Filing is not required to perfect a purchase-money security interest in consumer goods. P's security interest was perfected when the contract was signed and the goods were delivered.

2. A purchase-money security interest in collateral other than inventory has priority over a conflicting security interest in the same collateral if the purchase-money security interest is perfected at the time the debtor receives possession of the collateral or within ten days thereafter.

3. D was not a buyer in the ordinary course of business because the debtor-seller was not a person in the business of selling goods of that kind.

Kimbrell's Furniture Company, Inc. v. Friedman, 198 S.E.2d 803 (S.C.) 1973.

The protection afforded the secured party with this type of perfection is limited. He is protected against the claims of creditors of the debtor and from others to whom the farmer or consumer debtor may give a security interest in the collateral, but he is *not* protected against the rights of a good-faith purchaser from the debtor. (9-307(2)) For example, if another consumer buys the collateral from the debtor-consumer without knowledge of the security interest, the purchaser will take the collateral free of the security interest. (9-307(2)) The secured party can obtain protection against this risk by filing a financing statement.

Several factors must be taken into account in determining which of the three methods of perfection is appropriate in any given transaction: (1) the kind of collateral in which a security interest was created, (2) the use the debtor intends to make of the collateral, and (3) the status of the debtor in relation to the secured party.

The Financing Statement Although a security interest may be perfected by taking possession of the collateral or by attachment in some cases, the most important method of perfection is by filing a financing statement. The financing statement must be distinguished from the *security agreement.* It is a document signed by both the debtor and the secured party that contains a description of the collateral and indicates that the debtor and the secured party have entered into a security agreement. (9-402) Simple forms are available that contain room for additional provisions as agreed upon by the parties, but this basic information is all that is required. If crops or fixtures constitute the collateral, then the financing statement must include a description of the real estate concerned. (9-402)

A financing statement is not a substitute for a security agreement. A security agreement may be filed as a financing statement if it contains the required information and is signed by both parties, but the converse is not true. However, filing the security agreement would make public certain information that the parties might prefer to have remain confidential, and for this reason there will usually be a separate financing statement.

The purpose of filing is to give notice that the secured party who filed it may have a security interest in the described collateral. A person searching the records therefore obtains minimal information, and further inquiry from the parties to the financing statement is required to obtain more complete information. A procedure is established for such disclosure by the secured party at the request of the debtor. (9-208)

The financing statement may provide a maturity or expiration date, but more often it is silent on this point. In the absence of such date, the filing is effective for a period of five years, subject to being renewed by the filing of a continuation statement signed by the secured party. (9-403(2)) If so renewed, it continues the effectiveness of the original statement for another five years.

The presence in the records of a financing statement constitutes a burden upon the debtor, since it reveals to all persons with whom he may be dealing that his property is or may be subject to the claims of others. Therefore, the Code provides for the filing of a *termination statement* to clear the record when the secured party is no longer entitled to a security interest. The secured party is required by law to furnish the termination statement.

Filing a financing statement is *required* in order to perfect a nonpossessory security interest in most secured transactions. However, filing is not required in the case of an assignment of accounts or contract rights where assignments to the same assignee are not a significant part of the outstanding accounts or contract rights of the assignor. (9-302(1)(e)) These isolated transactions are exempt.

The Code allows the various states three alternative methods in regard to the place where the financing statement is to be filed. A state may choose a central filing system, a local filing system, or a combination. (9-401) A central filing system means that all filing is in the state capital except for fixtures, which are filed locally. Local filing means that filing is at the county level. Most states have enacted dual filing systems. The usual system requires local filing for fixtures, local filing for farm-related collateral and consumer goods, and central filing for other collateral such as inventory and equipment.

The Code makes special provisions for goods that have a certificate of title. The filing requirements of the Code do not apply, and the usual method of indicating a security interest is to have it noted on the certificate of title. (9-302(3))

REVIEW QUESTIONS AND PROBLEMS

1. Is an artisan's lien covered by Article 9? Explain.

2. If a creditor is in doubt as to which place to file a financing statement, what should he do? Explain.

3. A, a retailer, had a large amount of outstanding accounts receivable. He needed cash to pay his expenses. How might he raise the necessary cash? Discuss.

4. A owned an expensive diamond ring. He entered into an agreement with B whereby he borrowed $1,000 from B and handed over the ring as security for the debt. Must B file a financing statement in order to perfect his security interest in the ring? Why?

5. A bank had a security interest in a machine that B was building for C. Does the bank have a security interest in the contract right that B has against C when the machine is ultimately delivered to C? Why?

6. What is the difference between a *security agreement* and a *financing statement*?

7. A loaned B $500 to enable him to purchase a color TV set. A and B entered into a security agreement whereby A was given a security interest in the set. A wishes to know whether or not he should file a financing statement. Advise him.

8. A sold a TV set to a dentist for the waiting room in the dentist's office. What should A do to perfect a security interest in the set? Why?

9. A is negotiating with B to furnish financing for B's retail business. What should he do in order to determine the status of B's assets? Why?

10. A is aranging with B to finance B's business. It will be a secured financing plan, and A will have a security interest in inventory, equipment, and accounts receivable belonging to B. What provisions should A require for inclusion in the security agreement? In the financing statement? Explain.

11. A has a financing arrangement with B and has given B a security interest in his inventory of goods. B files in bankruptcy. What are A's rights? Explain.

12. Assume that you are considering loaning money to A and to taking a security interest in property belonging to A. What steps would you take in order to have assurance that your security interest will not be inferior to that of other creditors? Explain.

26 SECURED TRANSACTIONS: TECHNICAL ASPECTS

Introduction Many technical aspects in the law of secured transactions result in a substantial amount of Article 9 litigation. The adoption of the Revised Article 9 and its clarifying language will no doubt eliminate much of the confusion that exists relative to some of these technical provisions. However, many highly technical rules of law will remain, and creditors should carefully comply with the statute if the desired security interests are to be obtained.

One of the more important technical aspects of the Code, commonly referred to as the "floating lien," is discussed in this chapter, along with purchase-money security interests, the rules of law that determine priority among conflicting claims, and the rights of the parties upon default. The discussion will be based on the original Article 9 except where the Revised Article 9 is specifically mentioned.

The "Floating Lien" The security agreement may provide that property acquired in the future by the debtor will also constitute collateral. The agreement may also provide that future advances to the debtor will be covered by the security agreement. (9-204) A secured party may have a security interest in the debtor's assets even though the debtor has the freedom to use or to dispose of the collateral. For example, a secured party who is financing a retailer can maintain a security interest in the debtor's constantly changing inventory. It can also have a security interest in the proceeds of the sale of inventory in the debtor's ordinary course of business. The amount of credit may vary from time to time.

378

The secured party's security interest is protected against the claims of third parties by virtue of the public notice that such financing arrangement has been made. The amount of the debt and the actual collateral can be constantly changing if the security agreement is so worded as to include after-acquired property and future advances of money. This sort of arrangement has the effect of tying up most of the assets of a debtor by the secured party. This possibility is considered to be acceptable with regard to business financing but is restricted insofar as consumers and farmers are concerned. The after-acquired clauses covering farm crops must be limited to crops that become such within one year of the security agreement. In addition, the Code limits after-acquired clauses on consumer goods to goods obtained within ten days after the secured party gives value. (9-204(4))

Proceeds The passing of the security interest from goods to the proceeds of the sale is an important part of the "floating lien" concept. A debtor may sell or otherwise dispose of the collateral. In such event, the secured party may have an interest in the "identifiable proceeds." The proceeds may be "cash proceeds" or "noncash proceeds," such as an account receivable. (9-306(1))

Two different factual situations may arise. A debtor may have the authority to dispose of the collateral, as in the case of a sale of inventory. A debtor may also dispose of the collateral without authority to do so. In either situation, the secured party has an interest in the *proceeds.* In the former he loses his security interest in the *collateral* that is sold in the ordinary course of business. (9-307) In the latter he retains a security interest in the collateral and thus has a security interest in *both* the collateral *and* the proceeds. (9-306)

The financing statement may provide for a security interest in proceeds, in which event no further filing is required. (9-306(33)) If (1) the financing statement did *not* cover proceeds or (2) the security interest was perfected by possession or attachment, a perfected security interest in proceeds continues for ten days. At the end of the ten-day period, the interest in the proceeds ends unless the secured party has filed a financing statement covering proceeds *within* the ten-day period.

Special provisions relate to the secured party's interest in proceeds if the debtor becomes involved in bankruptcy or other insolvency proceedings. (9-306(4)). In general, the secured party is entitled to reclaim from the trustee in bankruptcy proceeds that can be identified as relating to the original collateral. If the proceeds are no longer identifiable because they have been commingled or deposited in an account, the secured party nonetheless has a perfected security interest in an amount up to the proceeds received by the debtor within ten days prior to the commencement of the bankruptcy proceedings.

PRIORITIES

Introduction Collateral is frequently the subject of conflicting claims. Two or more persons may claim a security interest in the same collateral or a person may claim that he has a better right to the collateral than does the secured party. There are many ways in which conflicting claims to collateral may arise. Some of the more important are (1) when the debtor gives more than one security interest in the same collateral; (2) when a trustee in bankruptcy claims the collateral in connection with bankruptcy proceedings involving the debtor; (3) when the debtor sells the collateral to a good-faith purchaser who is not aware of the security interest; (4) when the collateral becomes attached to real property so that it is a fixture; (5) when it becomes attached to personal property that belongs to another or in which another has security interest; (6) when it has been repaired or improved by the services or materials of another; (7) when it has been processed, as when raw material in which there is security interest is converted into a finished product; and (8) when the government or some other creditor claims a lien on the property. In all of the foregoing situations as well as many others, it becomes necessary to sort out the conflicting interests and determine a priority among them.

Generally, a secured party who has not perfected his security interest has only a very limited protection against third parties. He only has priority over persons who acquire the property with *knowledge* of his interest or become lien creditors with such knowledge. (9-301)

The Code rules on priorities are based on the nature of the collateral, its intended use, and the relationship of the parties. For example, a buyer in the ordinary course of business takes free of a security interest in the seller's inventory even though the security interest has been perfected. (9-307) To illustrate, assume that A, a retailer, has financed his inventory of television sets with X bank and has given the bank a security interest. He now sells one of the television sets to B who buys it in the ordinary course of business. B takes the set free of even a perfected security interest on the part of X bank. This rule does not apply, however, to good-faith purchasers of farm products.

Case: D advanced money to a farmer. Subsequently, the FHA loaned money to the farmer and obtained a security interest in his crop. The farmer then gave D a part of his crop in satisfaction of his obligation to D. D then sold the crop. The FHA claimed the right to the money that D received upon the sale of the crop. D claimed that it was entitled, as a good-faith purchaser, to retain the money.

Issue: Will a good-faith purchaser from a debtor prevail over the holder of a perfected security interest in farm products?

Decision: No.

Reason: Although in many situtations a good-faith purchaser in the ordinary course of business will prevail over the holder of a perfected security interest, such protection is not afforded to a person who buys farm products from a farmer.

United States v. McCleskey Mills, Inc., 409 F.2d 1216 (1969).

First to File As a general rule, if the conflicting interests in the same collateral are both perfected by filing, the *first* to *file* will prevail, even though the other interest attached first, and whether it attached before or after filing. Unless both are perfected by filing, the *first* to be *perfected* will have priority regardless of which one attached first. If neither of the security interests is perfected, priority will be given to the first to attach. (9-312(5))

Case: P sued D to determine which of them had priority in the collateral of X, a debtor of both parties. P, who had financed X for a long time, obtained a financing statement covering X's inventory and equipment. This was filed on June 5, 1972. P gave no value at that time, and no security agreement was entered into. On March 5, 1973, P and X signed a security agreement, and P loaned X money.
However, on June 1, 1972, D had loaned X a sum of money and had entered into a security agreement covering the same collateral. D filed a financing statement on June 27, 1972.

Issue: Which party has priority in the collateral?

Decision: P.

Reasons: 1. Both parties have perfected security interests which were perfected by filing.

2. If both interests are perfected by filing, the order of filing determines priority and P filed first.

3. D's security interest was perfected first because perfection required attachment to the collateral as well as filing. Attachment requires an agreement to that effect plus value must be given. D was perfected on June 27, 1972. P was perfected on March 5, 1973.

381

4.   Notwithstanding that D was the first to perfect, P wins because the law gives priority to the first to file. It does so in order to protect the filing system.

Enterprises Now v. Citizens & Southern Dev., 218 S.E.2d 309 (Ga.) 1975.

Purchase-Money Security Interests   A purchase-money security interest arises in either of two situations: (1) a seller of goods retains a security interest in the goods as collateral to secure payment of the purchase price, or (2) a person advances money to enable the debtor to acquire the collateral. (9-107) The secured party who has a purchase-money security interest enjoys a preferred status in some situations. (9-312(3))

This preferred status is very important when the debtor has given another secured party a security interest in after-acquired property. For example, assume that X, a retailer, has given the Y bank a security interest in his inventory with an after-acquired clause covering subsequent inventory purchases. Z, a manufacturer of goods, can defeat the claim of the Y bank to subsequent inventory purchases from Z if the proper steps are taken. Z, who is going to furnish inventory on a purchase-money basis, can notify the prior secured party that he has or expects to obtain a purchase-money security interest in inventory. The notice must be given prior to the time that X obtains possession of the goods and must set forth the type of collateral that will be involved. If such notice is given, Z, the secured party who furnishes the inventory, has priority, provided its interest is perfected at the time the debtor receives the collateral. (9-312(3))

Case: P, a manufacturer of appliances, entered into a security agreement covering all of X's inventory in the fall of 1970. A financing statement was filed on November 27, 1970. On November 24, 1970, X entered into another security agreement with D bank covering all of X's inventory as collateral. D filed its financing statement on December 9, 1970.

X later became bankrupt. P's claim was for $23,682.30. However, X's inventory of P's products was only $12,974.96, and $10,707.34 of them had been sold by X without payment to P. D took over all of X's inventory and repaid P the $12,974.96. P sues for the $10,707.34, claiming an interest in all of the inventory and not just in what it manufactured.

Issue: Is P entitled to priority in the other inventory items?

Decision: Yes.

Reasons: 1.   P was clearly the prior secured creditor. The security interest was the total inventory and not simply P's own manufactured products.

382

2. D could have protected itself by complying with the purchase-money security interest procedures relating to inventory.

Borg-Warner Accept. Corp. v. First Nat. Bank, 238 N.W.2d 612 (Minn.) 1976.

For collateral other than inventory, a purchase-money security interest is superior to conflicting security interests in the same collateral, provided the purchase-money security interest is perfected at the time the debtor receives the collateral or within ten days thereafter. (9-312(4)) Thus, prior notice to other secured parties is not required in cases of equipment if the security interest is perfected within ten days. The prior notice requirement is limited to inventory.

A secured party with a purchase-money security interest is given a special status for ten days after the debtor receives the property. Of course, the secured party must file within the ten-day period. The protection during such period is limited. It gives priority only over the rights of (1) transferees in bulk from the debtor and (2) lien creditors to the extent that such rights arise between the time the purchase-money security interest attaches and the time of filing. (9-301(2)) It is to be noted that the secured party is *not* protected against (1) a sale by the debtor to another party or (2) a secured transaction wherein the collateral is given as security for a loan during the period prior to filing.

It should be remembered that purchase-money security interests in consumer goods and farm equipment may be perfected by attachment if the purchase price is under $2,500. (Farm equipment is eliminated under the revised Code.) As noted, the purchase-money security interest in consumer goods and farm equipment will be inferior to the rights of another consumer or farmer purchaser from the debtor.

Proceeds More than one interest may exist in the same proceeds. For example, a merchant whose inventory is financed under a security agreement with a secured party may sell items from inventory to a customer on an installment sale contract. Such contract (chattel paper) is now the collateral in place of the item sold, since it is the proceeds derived from the sale. If the secured party does not take possession of the chattel paper, the debtor could sell the paper to a third party, and a question would arise as to the right to the paper as between the secured party and the third party. If the third party gave new value and took the paper in the ordinary course of his business, he will prevail. This is true even though the purchaser of the chattel paper knew that it was subject to a security interest. (9-308)

The situation is different if the secured party's interest in the chattel paper is not based upon its status as proceeds of the sale of inventory. If the chattel paper itself was the original collateral, a transferee will not prevail over the secured party if he had knowledge of

the prior security interest. Thus, if the secured party under these circumstances entrusts the paper to the debtor for collection purposes, the
wrongful disposition by the debtor will not subordinate the interest of
the secured party. (9-308)

It is to be noted that the secured party who allows the debtor to
have possession of the paper could stamp or designate on the paper that
it has been assigned or sold. In this way he could impart knowledge of
his interest and prevent the conflict from arising.

Returned or Repossessed Goods

Conflicting claims to collateral may arise when a debtor who
sells an item from inventory receives in return either chattel
paper or an account receivable, and the goods are subsequently
reacquired. The debtor may have reacquired the goods under
several circumstances. The buyer may have returned them because of
his dissatisfaction; the seller may have repossessed them because of a
default by the buyer; or the seller may have stopped the goods in
transit upon discovery of the buyer's insolvency. In any event, the
goods are now again in the possession of the debtor. There may be
conflict between the inventory secured party and the transferee of the
chattel paper or account receivable related to the returned goods.

The original security interest of the inventory secured party
attaches to the returned or repossessed goods. The security interest in
the goods continues to be perfected provided it has not lapsed or
terminated. As between the inventory secured party and the transferee
of the chattel paper, the person holding the chattel paper has priority.
This is not the result if an account receivable was transferred; then the
transferee of the account is subordinate to the party having a security
interest in inventory with respect to goods that were returned or
repossessed. (9-306(5))

Fixtures— Original Article 9

Goods that are collateral for a security agreement may be
attached to real property, in which event such goods are
fixtures (9-313(1)) This raises a question of priority as between
the secured party and one who has a security interest in the real
property—e.g., one who has a mortgage upon the real property. An
example of a fixture would be a heating system installed in a building.
Article 9 does not determine the circumstances under which goods
become fixtures, but it does provide rules for determining priorities
when a fixture is involved.

A security interest that attaches to goods before they become
fixtures has priority if it is *perfected* before they become fixtures.
(9-313(2)) Even if it is not perfected, it will have priority over prior
mortgages because of the value added to the real estate. It will be
inferior to subsequent purchasers or mortgagees because they persum-

ably bought or loaned on the value of the property including the fixtures. (9-313(3))

The secured party who has priority is entitled, upon default, to remove the fixtures. He is required to reimburse any encumbrancer or owner other than the debtor for the cost of repair of any physical damage caused by the removal. (9-313(5))

As noted previously, filing is required to perfect a security interest in fixtures regardless of the classification of the goods as consumer goods, farm equipment, and so forth. The filing should be done in the office where real estate mortgages are filed or recorded.

Fixtures—Revised Article 9

No portion of Article 9 has been more criticized than the provisions relating to fixtures. The original Code failed to recognize many principles of real estate law relating to competing interests in land and the relative priority of such interests. The Revised Code attempts to correct these errors.

The Revised Code does make it clear that building materials are not fixtures. (9-313(2)) It recognizes three categories of goods: (1) those that retain their chattel character and are not a part of the real estate, (2) building materials that lose their chattel character entirely and are a part of the real estate, and (3) an intermediate class which becomes a part of the real estate for some purposes but which may be a part of a secured transaction. The third category is *fixtures.*

The Revised Code uses the term *fixture filing* to require filing where a mortgage on real estate would be filed. The financing statement for fixture filing (1) must show that it covers fixtures, (2) must recite that it is to be filed in the real estate records, (3) must describe the real estate, and (4) if the debtor does not own the real estate, must show the name of the record owner.

The Revised Code allows a mortgage to describe fixtures in the mortgage and thus treat the mortgage as a financing statement. In such cases the mortgage is exempt from the five-year limitation on financing statements.

Under the Revised Code, a purchase-money security interest in a fixture prevails over a prior encumbrance on the land if the security interest was perfected by fixture filing before the goods became fixtures or within ten days thereafter. However, a security interest in fixtures added as a part of new construction is subordinate to the construction mortgage or to a "take-out" mortgage replacing it recorded before the goods became fixtures. This later provision recognizes the priority of a construction loan.

The Revised Code also has a special rule relating to readily removable fixtures, such as office machines or appliances. (9-313(4)(c)) A perfected security interest in such fixtures has priority without filing where the security interest is otherwise properly perfected prior to the installation of the fixture. There are other special aspects of the Revised Code relating to fixtures which must be consulted in those states that have enacted it. (9-313)

Accessions Goods, in addition to being affixed to real estate, may become installed in or affixed to other goods. The goods so installed or affixed are called "accessions." In general, a perfected security interest that attaches to goods *before* they become accessions has priority as to such goods over a security interest in the whole and subsequent purchasers of the whole. (9-314(1)) A security interest may attach to goods after they have become joined with other goods. The secured party has the same priorities as those stated above, but his security interest will prevail over another security interest in the whole only if the holder of the security interest in the whole has consented in writing to the security interest. (9-314(2)) As in the case of fixtures, the secured party can upon default remove his collateral from the whole, but he must make payment for the cost of repair of any physical damage caused by removal. (9-314(4))

Commingled and Processed Goods In a manufacturing process several items, including raw materials and components, each of which may be subject to different security interests, combine to make a finished product. The security to which the financing party is entitled will ultimately be the product that results from the combination of the materials in which he has a security interest. If a security interest in the raw materials was perfected, in the security interest continues in the product if the identity of the goods is lost, or the original financing statement provided for a security interest that covered the "product." (9-315(1)) In a situation in which component parts are assembled into a machine, the secured party would generally have a choice of either (1) claiming a security interest in the machine or (2) claiming an interest in a component part as provided for security interests in accessions. (9-314(1)) If he stipulates "product," he cannot claim an accession. Where more than one security interest exists in the product, the secured parties share in the product in proportion to the costs of their materials used. (9-315(2))

Liens on Goods The common-law lien on goods which is allowed for repair, improvement, storage, or transportation is superior to a perfected security interest as long as the lien claimant retains possession of the property. Statutory liens also have such priority unless the statute expressly subordinates them. Even though a lien is second in point of time, it will be granted priority over a perfected security

386

interest in the goods, unless the statute creating the lien provides that it is subordinate. (9-310) The reason for this is that the service rendered by the lienholder has added to or protected the value of the property.

Case: X, the owner of a motor vehicle, left it with D for extensive repair. D's repair bill was $1,152.38. Earlier, X had entered into a security agreement with P bank to secure a loan. The unpaid balance of the loan was $2,846.29. The automobile was sold to satisfy these claims, but the sale price was insufficient to pay both.

Issue: Which party has priority?

Decision: The possessory lienholder (repairman).

Reasons: 1. A mechanic in possession of a motor vehicle is entitled to priority over a prior secured creditor under the Code.

2. When a person in the ordinary course of his business furnishes services or materials with respect to goods subject to a security interest, a lien upon goods in the possession of such person given by statute or rule of law for such materials or services takes priority over a perfected security interest *unless the lien is statutory and the statute expressly provides otherwise.*

Krueger v. Texas State Bank, 328 S.W.2d 121 (Tex.) 1975.

RIGHTS AND REMEDIES OF THE SECURED PARTY

Before Default   As a result of the law and the security agreement, the secured party has certain rights in the collateral. If the secured party is in possession of the collateral, there are also certain duties imposed. For example, the secured party in possession is required to exercise reasonable care of it.

Unless the security agreement provides otherwise: (1) any reasonable expenses related to the collateral are chargeable to the debtor; (2) the risk of accidental loss or damage is on the debtor to the extent that it is not covered by insurance; and (3) the secured party is entitled to hold as additional security any increase or profits received from the collateral. (9-207(2))

In most situations the collateral will remain in the possession of the debtor. He may be given wide latitude in using, commingling, or disposing of the property without thereby rendering the security interest invalid or fraudulent against creditors.

Usually, the financing statement will state only that a secured party may have a security interest in specified types of collateral owned by the debtor. Nothing is said about either the amount of the secured debt or the particular assets covered. The debtor, for various reasons, may need a detailed statement as to both the present amount of the obligation and the collateral that is covered. The Code provides that the secured party is obligated to furnish such information when so requested by the debtor. (9-208)

After Default When the debtor is in default, the secured party is given several remedies. These remedies, as well as the protection afforded the debtor in connection with the default procedures, are determined by the security agreement and the rules set forth in the Code. The Code contains limitations designed to protect not only the defaulting debtor but also other creditors of the debtor. The basic remedies of the secured party on default are to repossess the collateral and to dispose of it. (9-504)

If the secured party is already in possession of the collateral, he is of course entitled to retain possession. If he does not have possession, he has the right to take possession. The secured party can simply take possession of the collateral without any judicial process if he can do so without "breaching the peace." (9-503) If he meets with resistance in his effort to repossess, he can, of course, obtain judicial assistance in accomplishing it. The security agreement may require the debtor after default to gather the collateral together and voluntarily make it available to the secured party at a place designated by the secured party. (9-503)

If the collateral is accounts, chattel paper, contract rights, instruments, or general intangibles, the secured party can simply proceed to collect whatever may become due on the collateral. For example, he may direct the person who owes the account receivable to make payment directly to the secured party.

The secured party has broad powers to dispose of the collateral in order to obtain satisfaction of the obligation. (9-504) He may sell the goods at either a public or a private sale so long as he does so in a commercially reasonable manner. (9-504(3))

There are many limitations on private sales because the secured party may attempt to take unfair advantage of the debtor in such cases. The requirement of a "commercially reasonable manner" is strictly followed.

Case: P, a furniture manufacturer, sold furniture to D on credit secured by a security agreement. When D did not pay as agreed, P repossessed the furniture. P contacted one possible buyer to resell the items but failed to do so. P then sold to himself at a private sale and sued D for a deficiency of $7,000. D contends that he is entitled to credit for the full value of the repossessed goods because the private sale was improper.

Issue: Was the private sale a proper method for determining the deficiency?

Decision: No.

Reasons: 1. Every aspect of the dispostion of collateral at a private sale must be commercially reasonable.

2. A secured party may only buy at a private sale if the collateral is of a type commonly sold in a recognized market or is of a type which is the subject of widely distributed price quotations.

3. For a private sale to the secured party, the collateral must be such that its value can be readily ascertained.

Luxurest Furn. Mfg. Co. v. Furniture, Etc., 209 S.E.2d 63 (Ga.) 1974.

In general, the secured party is required to notify the debtor of the time and place of any public sale or of the time after which a private sale is to be made. (9-504(3)) The notification is not required where (1) the collateral is perishable or threatens to decline speedily in value, or (2) it is of a type "customarily sold on a recognized market." (9-504(3)) Notice must also be sent (except in the case of consumer goods) to any other person who has filed a financing statement covering the same collateral and who is known to have a security interest in the collateral. The secured party may buy at public sale if he so desires. (9-504(3))

The person who buys the collateral at a sale thereof receives it free of the security interest under which the sale was made and free, also, of any subordinate security interest. (9-504(4)) Thus the good-faith purchaser at a disposition sale receives substantial assurance that he will be protected in his purchase. After the sale has been made, the proceeds of the sale will be distributed and applied as follows: (1) the expenses of the secured party in connection with the repossession and sale; (2) the satisfaction of the debt owing to the secured party; (3) satisfaction of the indebtedness owing to persons who have a subordinate security interest in the collateral; and (4) if any surplus remains after the satisfaction of all the above, the secured party shall account for it to the debtor. (9-504(1)) The debtor is liable for any deficiency if the sale does not produce enough to satisfy all the above charges. (9-504(2)) This is true only if the sale is proper in all respects.

Case: On September 1, 1970, D executed a $12,500 purchase-money security agreement on a 1962 tractor in favor of P. D paid $370 and defaulted. Four months later, P repossessed and sold the tractor for $2,500. P sued D for the deficiency of $9,945 including interest. D contended that he received no notice of the default sale. P had posted a notice of the sale on the courthouse door but had made no other effort to notify D.

Issue: Is P entitled to collect deficiency?

Decision: No.

Reasons: 1. Collateral may be sold at public or private sale. Every aspect of the disposition must be commercially reasonable.

2. A public sale is presumed to be commercially reasonable. However, posting of a notice at the courthouse is not a commercially reasonable notice. D is entitled to notice by registered mail at least five days prior to the sale.

3. P's failure to give notice and to dispose of the collateral in a commercially reasonable manner precludes or limits his right to a deficiency judgment. In some states, it is an absolute bar. In others, there is a presumption in such cases that the collateral was worth at least the amount of the debt and the burden is on P to prove it was not.

Hodges v. Norton, 223 S.E.2d 848 (N.C.) 1976.

Acceptance in Discharge The secured party may prefer to simply keep the collateral in satisfaction of the obligation rather than dispose of it. He is entitled to make such a proposition in writing and send it to the debtor. (9-505(2)) Except in the case of consumer goods, the proposal must also be sent to all persons who have filed a financing statement covering the collateral or who are known to have a security interest in it. Within prescribed time limits, the debtor, a secured party entitled to receive notification, or any other secured party can object in writing to the proposal, in which event the collateral would have to be sold. If no such notice is forthcoming, the matter is closed and the secured party can retain the collateral in satisfaction. (9-504(2))

Special provisions relate to consumer transactions. Disposition of the goods is *compulsory*, and a sale must be made within ninety days after possession is taken if, in the case of (1) a purchase-money security interest in consumer goods, 60 percent of the cash price has been paid; or (2) a security interest based upon a loan against consumer goods, 60 percent of the loan has been repaid. The consumer can, however, waive this right by signing a statement to that effect after default. (9-504(1)) These rules exist because there will presumably be a surplus in the event of a sale and the debtor is entitled to it promptly.

The Debtor's Rights Except for the ninety-day period for consumer goods, the secured party is not required to make disposition of the repossessed goods within any time limits. The debtor has the right to redeem the property until such time as (1) the property has been sold or contracted to be sold, or (2) the obligation has been satisfied by the retention of the property. He must, as a condition to redemption, tender the full amount of the obligation secured by the collateral, plus the expenses incurred by the secured party in connection with the collateral, and if so provided in the agreement, attorney's fees and legal expenses. (9-506)

If the secured party fails to comply with the provisions of the Code relating to default, a court may order disposition or restrain disposition as the situation requires. If the sale has already taken place, the secured party is liable for any loss resulting from his noncompliance and may lose his right to recover any deficiency. If the collateral is consumer goods, the consumer-debtor is entitled to recover from the secured party an amount not less than (1) the credit service charge plus 10 percent of the principal amount of the debt or (2) the time-price differential plus 10 percent of the cash price. (9-507(1)) Thus the secured party who forecloses a security interest in consumer goods must be very careful to comply with the law as it relates to the sale of them.

Revised Article 9   Some of the provisions contained in the Revised Article 9 have been previously noted. Attachment as a means of perfecting an interest in farm equipment has been eliminated. Fixture filing under Article 9 is a most significant new development. Since this revision is likely to become the law in most states in the near future, its provisions have been included in the Appendix containing the Uniform Commercial Code.

Many of the revisions of Article 9 clarify the Code provisions and its relationship with other articles. One of the major clarifications is in the language relating to perfection of interests in multiple-state transactions. (9-103) The basic rule is that the controlling law on perfection of security interests is the state where the collateral is when the last event occurs necessary for perfection. There are certain exceptions to this rule. For example, in the case of a purchase money security interest where the parties intend to remove the collateral to another jurisdiction within 30 days, the law of the new jurisdiction covers the initial perfection provided the goods are taken to the other jurisdiction within 30 days. In addition, if the collateral is covered by a certificate of title, perfection is controlled by the certificate of title rather than by the law of the state where the security interest is attached. A security interest that is perfected by notation on the certificate continues until the certificate is surrendered. If the vehicle is reregistered in another state, the security interest is valid for four months following removal. To be valid for longer than four months reregistration is required.

The law also clarifies the consignment situation by providing that a consignor must give notice to prior inventory secured parties the same as if the transaction were a sale. (9-114) The Revised Article 9 has clarified and changed the law somewhat relating to termination statements. Under the revision, termination statements must be filed in the case of consumer goods even without a demand for such statements by the consumer. Since many consumers will not realize the significance of the termination statement, the law requires the filing. (9-404)

REVIEW QUESTIONS AND PROBLEMS

1. In what situations do conflicts arise between secured parties who claim a security interest in the same collateral?

2. Does the holder of an unperfected security interest have any protection? Explain.

3. What is the difference between *accession* and *fixture?*

4. A, a merchant, and the XYZ bank entered into a security agreement which provided XYZ with a security interest in A's inventory. A sold the inventory and deposited the proceeds in a bank account. One week later, A filed a bankruptcy petition. Is XYZ entitled to obtain the amount of the proceeds from the trustee in bankruptcy? Why?

5. A purchased an automobile and gave his note for $1,400 in payment. Shortly thereafter he went to the office of the finance company, said that he did not want the car, and authorized the company to sell it. The finance company sold the car for $750 to a used-car dealer and now seeks to recover the balance due on the note. A claims that the $750 selling price was not reasonable and that he should not be required to pay the balance. Is A's contention correct? Why?

6. The A bank had a perfected security interest in B's property. C, a creditor of B, obtained a judgment against him. Both the A bank and C are seeking to obtain possession of the property. Who prevails? Why?

7. X sold goods to Y and has a security interest in Y's inventory. The security agreement provides for a security interest in after-acquired property. Y is now negotiating for the purchase of additional inventory items from Z and wishes to give Z a security interest in the new inventory. Z is concerned over the status of his security interest if he sells goods to Y. Advise Z as to the proper course of action.

8. R, a retail automobile dealer, at times borrowed money from the X company and the Y company, each of whom had filed the necessary financing statement, X company being the first to file. Thereafter on October 1, R borrowed $10,000 from Y company and used four cars as security. He later borrowed $8,000 from X company and used the same cars as security. R is now insolvent, and X company took possession of the cars. Which company, X or Y, has priority? Why?

9. A, a furniture dealer, by a valid security agreement retained a security interest in a $750 sofa sold to B on credit. No financing statement was filed. B in turn sold the sofa to C. If A is not paid, may he repossess the sofa?

10. K piano company sold pianos to R, a retail dealer, and retained security interest in the pianos. R sold one of the pianos to X for cash but did not account to the K company for the proceeds of the sale. K company had filed a financing statement. It claims to be entitled to possession of the piano. Can K recover the piano from X? Why?

V CREDITORS AND DEBTOR/ CONSUMERS

27 LAWS ASSISTING CREDITORS

Introduction The materials on contracts and the Uniform Commercial Code dealt with many aspects of the law that are of substantial significance to creditors. Suits for breach of contract and the collection methods provided to enforce judgments based on such suits are basic legal procedures available to creditors. The secured transaction as discussed in the preceding two chapters is a very significant method used by creditors to ensure payment of debts.

In this chapter we will be concerned with several additional aspects of the law that are of substantial significance to creditors. Real estate mortgages, suretyship, and various forms of liens will be discussed.

REAL ESTATE MORTGAGES

Introduction A *real estate mortgage* is an interest in real property that is created for the purpose of securing a debt. A mortgage is not a debt—only security for a debt. The owner of the land that is being used as security for the debt is called the *mortgagor;* the party to whom the security interest in the real estate is conveyed is called the *mortgagee.*

Technical Aspects A mortgage states that the property is conveyed to the mortgagee, subject to the conditions set forth in the mortgage. It is executed with all the formalities of a deed. The contract between the parties with respect to the loan need not be included in the mortgage but may be set forth in a separate document.

In order that the mortgagee may give notice to third parties that he has an interest in the real estate, it is necessary that the mortgage be

397

recorded in the county where the real estate is situated. Recording serves to notify subsequent parties of the lien or encumbrance of the mortgage.

An instrument known as a *deed of trust* may be used as a substitute for a mortgage. The property is conveyed to a trustee to hold in trust for the benefit of the noteholders. If the debt is paid at the time required by the contract, the trustee reconveys the property to the borrower, or releases the lien. If there is a default in payment, the trustee forecloses the trust deed and applies the proceeds to the payment of the debt secured. An important feature of the deed of trust is that the note secured by it can be freely negotiated separate and apart from the deed of trust.

Property that one does not own cannot be mortgaged, but a mortgage may be so drawn as to cover property to be acquired in the future. A mortgage of such property creates no lien at the time of its execution. However, the lien exists at the time the property is acquired by the mortgagor. If the mortgage is properly recorded, the lien has priority over all rights of others that arise or are created after the recording of the mortgage.

A mortgage may also be given prior to the time when the money is advanced to the mortgagor. Such a mortgage is usually called a *mortgage to secure future advances*. When the mortgagee advances the money, the mortgage is a valid lien as of the date when the mortgage was recorded.

When a mortgage is given as a part or the whole of the purchase price of land, it is known as a *purchase-money mortgage*. In many jurisdictions, a deficiency decree obtained upon the foreclosure of a purchase-money mortgage will not be enforced.

Rights and Duties of the Parties

The mortgagor is usually personally liable for the mortgage debt because he makes a note, a bond, or other contract that evidences the debt secured by the mortgage. When there is more than one mortgagor, all of them need not sign the note nor be liable on the underlying obligation. In such a case the property is given as security for the debt, but only those signing the note or incurring the obligation have personal liability.

Payment of the mortgage debt terminates the mortgage. Upon payment, the mortgagor is entitled to a release or satisfaction of the mortgage. This release should be recorded in order to clear the title to the land.

The mortgagor is entitled to retain possession of the real estate during the period of the mortgage unless a different arrangement is provided for in the mortgage. The mortgagor may not use the property in such a manner as to reduce materially its value.

Any parcel of real estate may be subject to more than one encumbrance. For example, the owner may execute more than one mortgage. In addition, mortgaged land may be subject to a lien for property taxes. As a general rule, the first recorded mortgage in point of time has priority over any subsequently recorded mortgage. Taxes usually have priority over mortgages.

A mortgagee has a right to pay off any superior mortgage in order to protect his security. He can charge the amount so paid to the mortgagor. Likewise he may pay taxes or special assessments that are a lien on the land and recover the sum so expended.

Unless modified by statute, a mortgagee has the right to collect any deficiency upon foreclosure from the mortgagor or any transferee who assumes and agrees to pay the mortgage debt. For example, A, the mortgagee, owns a mortgage that is security for an indebtedness of $10,000 against B's land. If on foreclosure and sale of the land the sum of only $7,000 is raised, A may obtain a deficiency judgment against B for $3,000.

**Transfer
of Mortgaged
Property**
The mortgagor may sell, will, or give away the mortgaged property, subject to the rights of the mortgagee. A grantee of mortgaged property is not personally liable for the mortgage debt unless he impliedly or expressly assumes and agrees to pay the mortgage debt. A purchase "subject to" the mortgage is usually considered not to be an assumption of the mortgage.

If the grantee assumes and agrees to pay the mortgage, he becomes primarily liable for the debt and for any deficiency upon foreclosure. The assumption by the grantee of a debt secured by a mortgage does not relieve the mortgagor of his obligation to the mortgagee, unless he is released from his indebtedness. Such a release must comply with all the requirements for a novation. In the absence of a novation, the original mortgagor is a surety.

**Mortgage
Foreclosures**
If the mortgagor fails to perform as agreed, the mortgagee may foreclose for the purpose of collecting the indebtedness. The statutes of the various states specify the procedure by which mortgages are foreclosed.

The usual method of foreclosing a mortgage is a proceeding in a court of equity. If the mortgagor is in default, the court will authorize the sale of all the land at public auction. Following the sale, the purchaser receives a deed to the land. The funds received from the sale are used to pay court costs, the mortgage indebtedness, and inferior liens in the order of their priority. If any surplus remains, it is paid to the former owner of the property.

Foreclosure of a second mortgage (one that is second in time to another) is made subject to all superior liens. For example, foreclosure of a second mortgage does not affect a first mortgage. The buyer at the foreclosure sale takes title, and the first mortgage remains a lien on the property. All inferior liens are cut off by foreclosure. For example, a foreclosure of a first mortgage would eliminate the rights of the second.

The statutes in many states provide a period of time after the sale within which the mortgagor or other persons having an interest are entitled to redeem the property. Where such statutes are in force, the purchaser is not entitled to a deed until after the expiration of the period within which redemption may be made. The purchaser may request that the court appoint a receiver and order the mortgagor to pay rent during the redemption period. The purchaser is entitled to the net rent during this period.

In some states there are some nonjudicial methods of foreclosure. These allow the mortgagee to personally sell the property or to take title to it. These are of little importance today.

**Mortgagor's
Right to Redeem**
The mortgagor may, within a specified period of time after a foreclosure sale, redeem the real estate so sold. To do so, he must pay to the court for the benefit of the purchaser at the foreclosure sale the sum of money, with interest and costs, for which the premises were sold. The period of time allowed for redemption varies from state to state. The redemption price usually includes the value of any repairs made by the purchaser during the period of his possession.

Case: A court fixed the amount that the mortgagor must pay the purchaser of property sold after foreclosure in order to redeem the property at $9,081.35. Of this sum, $3,202.66 was for repairs that the purchaser made to the property. However, of the $3,202.66, $350.00 was the value of purchaser's personal services in supervising and helping make the improvements.

Issue: Should the redemption price include these repairs?

Decision: Yes.

Reason: It is a proper charge because they added to the value of the improvements, and necessarily to the property.

Ladd v. Parmer, 178 So.2d 829 (Ala.) 1965.

SURETYSHIP

Introduction   Suretyship is a method of providing security for a creditor which does not involve an interest in property. In suretyship, the security for the creditor is provided by a third person's promise to be responsible for the debtor's obligation.

In the law of suretyship, the person who borrows money or assumes direct responsibility to perform is called the *principal* or *principal debtor.* The party who promises to be liable for the principal's obligation is called the *surety.* The party entitled to performance or payment is customarily called the *creditor.*

Suretyship most often results from an express contract in which the surety agrees that he may be called upon to pay or to perform in case the principal defaults. Like other contracts, the contract of suretyship requires consideration. In the majority of instances, the consideration that supports the surety's promise is the same as that received by the principal. Some sureties are compensated, others are not. Most compensated sureties are bonding and insurance corporations.

One major difference in the treatment afforded compensated as contrasted with uncompensated sureties is in the interpretation of the contract. Ambiguous provisions of surety agreements are construed in favor of the unpaid surety and against the creditor. Ambiguous provisions of surety agreements involving compensated sureties are resolved against the surety.

Liability   The surety is liable to the creditor as soon as the principal
of Sureties   defaults. The creditor need not exhaust his remedies against the principal before looking to the surety.

When there is more than one surety on an obligation, the liability of the sureties is described as joint and several. This means that the creditor may sue them jointly for the debt or he may sue each surety separately for the total debt. If the sureties are sued jointly, the entire judgment against them can be collected from one debtor just as if the debtor had been sued separately.

Whenever two or more sureties become secondarily liable for the same obligation of the principal, they become cosureties. There is an implied contract between cosureties that they will share any loss equally. So long as the balance of a claim remains unpaid, a cosurety has no right to contribution unless he has paid more than his share of the claim, and then only to the extent of the excess. This he may recover from any cosurety unless it compels the latter to pay more than his full share.

The liability of a surety may be released and the surety discharged upon the happening of several events. Among these are changes in the

401

contract terms, extension of the time of payment, payment of the obligation, and any other act that materially prejudices the rights of the surety.

Effect of an Extention of the Time of Payment Debtors frequently seek an extension of time for payment from the creditor. In cases in which the debt is secured by a promise of a surety, the creditor should be careful not to enter into a contract to extend the time for performance without the surety's consent. As a general rule, a binding contract between the principal and the creditor that definitely extends the time within which performance may be demanded, releases the unpaid surety.

Case: S, the son of D, wanted to buy some furniture. P, the seller, required that D guarantee the debt as a condition of the sale. D cosigned the note and security agreement. Later when S was in default on his payments, P agreed to extend the time of the payments and to reduce the amount of each weekly payment. D did not agree to the extension and did not sign the new contract.

Issue: Was D released of his liability?

Decision: Yes.

Reasons: 1. D is a classic example of a nonprofessional surety: a mother who seeks to help her twenty-two-year-old son to acquire furniture. Suretyship law throws up many defenses around such a person.

2. An extension agreement constitutes a material alteration of the original obligation, discharging the surety. Under such circumstances, injury to the surety is presumed.

Wexler v. McLucas, 121 Cal. Rptr. 453 (1973).

An extension agreement will also release the compensated surety if the compensated surety can show actual injury as a result of the extension agreement. Injury is shown when the ability of the principal to perform has perceptibly weakend during the period of extension.

To release a surety, the extension agreement must be a binding enforceable contract. As such, it must be for a definite time and must be supported by consideration. Mere indulgence upon the part of the creditor or passively permitting the debtor to take more time than the contract calls for does not release the surety. In such cases the surety is in no sense injured by such conduct because he is free at any time to perform and immediately start suit against the principal.

An extension agreement that stipulates that it does not release the surety or that all rights are retained against the surety does not release the surety. Such an extension agreement affects only the creditor. It does not bind the surety. He is free at any time to complete performance for the principal and immediately to sue him for damages suffered.

**Additional
Aspects of
the Surety's
Liability**
Any material change in the terms of the contract between the principal and the creditor, without the consent of the surety, discharges him. Inasmuch as the basic contract governs the surety's liability, any change in its terms must be assented to by him. Likewise the creditor's failure to comply with the terms of the contract of suretyship will result in the discharge of the surety.

A discharge of the principal debtor, unless agreed to by the surety, also releases the surety. This rule is subject to those exceptions existing in the case of an extension of time; that is, the surety is not released if the principal debtor is discharged with reservation of rights against the surety, or if the surety is protected by securities or is a paid surety and is not injured.

Although discharge is the most important defense available to a surety, there are others. As a general rule, any defense available to the principal is available to the surety. This means that if the principal debtor has a defense to its obligation to the creditor, then the surety can use this defense if the creditor seeks to collect from the surety. This general rule is subject to three exceptions—infancy of the principal, bankruptcy, and the statute of limitations. Infancy and bankruptcy are not available to the surety as a defense because the surety is employed in the first instance to protect the creditor against the inability of the debtor to perform. The statute of limitations available to the principal may not be used by the surety because each has his own period after which he is no longer liable to the creditor.

Forgery of the principal's signature is a defense for the surety, but forgery of a cosurety's signature is not a defense. Forgery of the principal's signature means that there is no principal obligation.

**Rights of
Sureties**
A surety is entitled to be reimbursed by the principal. The surety also has the right to compel the principal to perform in the first instance. Naturally, this right has little value where the principal is financially unable to make payment or to take such other action as his contract requires.

The surety who fully performs the obligation of his principal is subrogated to the creditor's rights against the principal. The surety who pays his principal's debt becomes entitled to any security that the principal has placed with the creditor to secure that particular debt.

MECHANIC'S LIEN LAWS

Introduction   Mechanic's lien laws provide for the filing of liens upon real estate where such real estate has been improved. Their purpose is to protect the laborer and materialman in the event of nonpayment of their accounts by the owner or the contractor. The laws of the states vary slightly in the protection accorded and the procedure required to obtain it. For this reason, the laws of the state in which the property is located should be consulted.

The persons entitled to a lien include those who (1) deliver material, fixtures, apparatus, machinery, forms, or form work to be used in repairing, altering, or constructing a building upon the premises; (2) fill, sod, or do landscape work in connection with the premises; (3) act as architect, engineer, or superintendent during the construction of a building; or (4) furnish labor for repairing, altering, or constructing a building.

Any contract between the owner and another that has for its purpose the improvement of real estate gives rise to a lien on the land. Anyone who furnishes labor, materials, or apparatus to subcontractors also has a lien.

As a general rule, the mechanic's lien is superior to any mortgage because presumably the value of the improvements has increased the value of the property to the extent of the liens. Consequently, the value of the property remaining as security under the mortgage after satisfying the mechanic's lien is as great as it was prior to the improvement that resulted in the lien.

Perfection   A contractor has a lien as soon as the contract to repair or to
of Mechanic's   improve the real estate is entered into. A supplier of materials
Liens   has a lien as soon as the materials are furnished. A laborer has a lien when the work is performed. The statutes relating to mechanic's liens provide for the method of perfecting these mechanic's liens and for the time period during which they may be perfected.

The usual scheme of mechanic's lien laws is to provide a relatively long period, such as two or three years, during which time a contractor may file a mechanic's lien and proceed to enforce it against the property interest of the party with whom he contracted. This time period is relatively long because the obligation is known to the owner, and he is in no way prejudiced if the lien is not promptly filed.

However, a much shorter time period is set for subcontractors, laborers, and materialmen to file their mechanic's liens. The owner of the premises may not know the source of materials and may not know the names of all persons performing services on the premises. To this extent the liens of subcontractors, materialmen, and workers may be secret and the owner may pay the wrong person. Therefore the time period in which the statutory procedures must be followed is relatively short, such as sixty to ninety days.

If the property is sold or mortgaged, the existence of any mechanic's lien often would be unknown to the purchaser or mortgagee. For this reason, the statutes on mechanic's liens usually specify the same short period of time for the perfection of the mechanic's lien—whether by a contractor, subcontractor, materialman, or laborer. Under these statutory provisions, a mechanic's lien that could be enforced against the property interest of the original contracting owner cannot be enforced against the property interest of the new owner or mortgagee after the expiration of the prescribed statutory period.

Thus, during the relatively short statutory period, a mechanic's lien is good against innocent third parties even though it has not been properly perfected. For this reason, a purchaser of real estate should always ascertain if any repairs or improvements have been made to the premises within the time period for filing mechanic's liens. If it is determined that repairs or improvements have been made, the procedures outlined in the next section should be followed.

The usual procedure is that the party seeking to perfect a mechanic's lien files or records a notice of lien in the office of the county in which deeds are recorded. A copy of the notice is sent to the owner of record and to the party contracting for the repair or improvement. This notice must be filed within the prescribed statutory period. The law then requires a suit to foreclose the lien and that it be commenced within an additionally prescribed period.

If a contractor, subcontractor, supplier of material, or laborer fails to file his notice of lien within the appropriate prescribed time period or fails to commence suit within the additional period, the lien is lost.

Case: A materialman did not file his notice of mechanic's lien until more than sixty days after his last performance. The owner of the premises had not obtained from the contractor a sworn list of suppliers as required by the mechanic's lien statute but had paid the total contract amount to the contractor.

Issue: May the materialman collect from the property owner?

Decision: No.

Reasons: 1. Strict compliance with the mechanic's lien statute is a condition precedent to recovery. The law required filing a notice of lien within sixty days of the completion of the work.

2. The fact that the owner was potentially liable for failure to obtain the list of suppliers was immaterial. The suppliers must themselves comply with the law.

Hill Behan Lumber Company v. Marchese, 275 N.E.2d 451 (Ill.) 1971.

Protecting Against Mechanic's Liens Mechanic's lien statutes usually provide that an owner is not liable for more than the contract price if he follows the procedures outlined in the law. These usually require that the owner prior to payment obtain from the contractor a sworn statement setting forth all the creditors and the amounts due, or to become due, to each of them. It is then the duty of the owner to retain sufficient funds at all times to pay the amounts indicated by the sworn statements. In addition, if any liens have been filed by the subcontractors, it is the owner's duty to retain sufficient money to pay them. He is at liberty to pay any balance to the contractor. If the amount owed is insufficient to pay all the creditors, they share proportionately.

An owner has a right to rely upon the truthfulness of the sworn statement of the contractor. If the contractor misstates the facts and obtains a sum greater than that to which he is entitled, the loss falls upon the subcontractors who dealt with him rather than upon the owner. Under such circumstances, the subcontractors may look only to the contractor to make good their deficit. Payments made by the owner, without first obtaining a sworn statement, may not be used to defeat the claims of subcontractors, materialmen, and laborers. Before making any payment, it is the duty of the owner to require the sworn statement and to withhold the amount necessary to pay the claims indicated.

The owner may also protect himself by obtaining waivers of the contractor's lien and of the liens of subcontractors, suppliers, and laborers. In a few states a waiver of the lien by the contractor is also a waiver of the lien of the subcontractors, as they derive their rights through those of the contractor. However, in most states lien waivers must be obtained from all persons furnishing labor or materials.

Artisan's Liens An *artisan's lien* is a security interest in personal property in favor of one who has performed services on the personal property, usually in the form of a repair. From a very early date the common law permitted one who expended labor or material upon the personal property of another to retain possession of such property as security for compensation.

Case: P sought to attach goods of D that were in possession of a third party, who had packaged the goods. The third party claimed an artisan's lien.

Issue: Does a writ of attachment have priority over an artisan's lien?

Decision: No.

406

Beck v. Nutrodynamics, Inc., 186 A.2d 715 (N.J.) 1962.

At common law, the artisan's lien arose when the task was completed. It was not assignable because it was personal. The lien did not arise where the parties had agreed to extend credit. The lien also existed in favor of public warehousemen and common carriers of goods entrusted to their care. It has been extended by statute to cover all cases of storage or repair in most states.

The artisan's lien is usually superior to other prior liens of record or the claim of a party with a security interest in the goods. Because it is based on possession, voluntary surrender of possession terminates the lien, unless the surrender is only temporary, with an agreement that the property will be returned. Even in such case, if the rights of a third party arise while the lienholder is not in possession of the property, the lien is lost. Surrender of part of the goods will not affect the lien on the remaining goods. Surrender of possession will not terminate the lien if a notice of lien is recorded in accordance with state lien and recording statutes.

At common law, the lienholder retained the property until a judgment was obtained, at which time he levied execution on the property. Modern statutes permit the lienholder to foreclose, and the property is sold to satisfy the claim. Such statutes usually require notice to the owner prior to the sale. Any surplus proceeds after the claim is satisfied are paid to the owner of the property.

Bulk Transfers   Article 6 of the Uniform Commercial Code is concerned with bulk transfers. A *bulk transfer* occurs when a business or a substantial portion of it is sold. The sale of a business usually includes such assets as inventory, equipment, furniture, and fixtures. Creditors presumably extend credit on the strength of these assets. The sale of them jeopardizes the ability of the creditor to collect. The law attempts to remedy this situation by imposing certain requirements on debtors and those who purchase businesses from them if the sale is to pass title to the property free of the claims of creditors of the seller.

As between the parties, a contract of sale of a business is valid without compliance with Article 6. However, if the statutory requirements are not met, the property in the hands of the purchaser is subject to the claim of the seller's creditors.

Article 6 is not limited to sale of an entire business. It covers sales of less than an entire business if (1) the sale is in bulk and not in the ordinary course of business; (2) the sale is of the major part of the materials, supplies, merchandise, or other inventory; and (3) the seller's principal business is the sale of merchandise from stock. Ordinarily a manufacturing concern is not covered by the law. It would be covered if it maintained a retail outlet that it was selling. Enterprises that manufacture what they sell, certain bakeries for example, would be covered. Enterprises whose principal business is the sale of services rather than merchandise are not subject to the provisions of Article 6.

In addition to a sale of inventory, Article 6 is applicable to transfers of a substantial part of the equipment of a business if such a transfer is made in connection with a bulk transfer of inventory. A sale of just the equipment is not subject to the law.

requirements   Basically, Article 6 imposes two requirements: (1) a scheduling of the property and a listing of the creditors of the seller and (2) a notification of the proposed sale to the seller's creditors. Unless an optional provision of the Code is enacted, the law does not require that the proceeds of any sale be paid to the creditors.

It is the duty of the *transferee* (the person who is buying the property) to obtain from the transferor a schedule of the property transferred and a sworn list of the transferor's creditors, including their addresses and the amount owed to each. The transferee can rely on the accuracy of this listing.

Case: P, a trustee in bankruptcy, sued D for $13,052.50, the value of merchandise purchased by D from the bankrupt. D did not require the bankrupt to furnish a list of his existing creditors before the sale was consummated. D did not give notice to the creditors of the transferor as required by the bulk transfer provision of the Code. D contended that the transaction was an "arms-length" deal with a fair price and that the bulk transfer law does not create personal liability on the transferee.

Issue: Is a transferee personally liable to the extent of the value of the property purchased when the UCC bulk transfer provisions are not complied with?

Decision: Yes.

Reason: A creditor has a right to rely on property as security for a debt. If the transferee fails to require compliance and is not personally liable, the creditor would lose all security for his debt.

Darby v. Ewing's Home Furnishings, 278 F.Supp. 917 (1967).

The transferee must keep the list of creditors showing the amounts due for six months. It must also be kept available for creditors who may desire to inspect it.

The transferee must then give notice personally or by registered mail to all persons on the list of creditors and all other persons known to the transferee to assert claims against the transferor. The notice must be given at least ten days before the transferee takes possession of the goods or pays for them (whichever happens first) and must contain the following information: (1) that a bulk transfer is about to be made; (2) the names and business addresses of both transferor and transferee; (3) whether the debts of the creditors are to be paid in full as a result of the transaction and, if so, the address to which the creditors should send their bills. If no provision is made for payment in full of the creditors, the notice must contain the following additional information: (1) estimated total of transferor's debts; (2) location and description of property to be transferred;(3) address where creditor's list and property schedule may be inspected; (4) whether the transfer is in payment of or security for a debt owing to transferee and, if so, the amount of the debt; (5) whether the transfer is a sale for new consideration and, if so, the amount of the consideration and the time and place of payment.

If the required procedure has been followed, the transferor's creditors will have had ample opportunity to take any necessary steps to protect their interests. Such steps might include the levying of execution against the property, obtaining a writ of attachment or a temporary injunction to stop the sale. If the Code procedures have not been followed, the transfer is ineffective as to the creditors, and they may use any appropriate remedy to collect the debt from the property. The creditors must act within six months after the transferee took possession unless the transfer was concealed, in which case they must act within six months after they learn of the transfer. A purchaser who buys for value and in good faith from the transferee obtains the property free of objection based on noncompliance with the Code.

auctions Article 6 is applicable to bulk sales by auction. The auctioneer is required to obtain a list of creditors and of the property to be sold. (All persons who direct, control, or are responsible for the auction are collectively called the *auctioneer.*) The auctioneer is also required to give ten days' notice of sale to all persons on the list of creditors. Failure to do so makes the auctioneer liable, up to but not exceeding the proceeds of the auction, to the creditors as a class.

REVIEW QUESTIONS AND PROBLEMS

1. Is it possible to have a mortgage without a debt? Explain.

2. Must a prospective buyer "qualify" with the existing mortgage company before the seller will be allowed to sell to a buyer who assumes the mortgage. Explain.

3. A executed a purchase mortgage to B at the time A bought a new home. B failed to record the mortgage in compliance with the state recording act. Later,

A sold the house to C. Does the property continue to serve as collateral for A's debt to B? Explain.

4. When A financed a new home through the XYZ company, A signed a note and a mortgage for $40,000. Several years later, A sold the home to C, who agreed to pay the mortgage payments. C did not pay, and XYZ instituted a foreclosure action. Should A be concerned? Why?

5. Discuss the different treatment given by law to a *compensated surety* as distinguished from an *uncompensated surety.*

6. At the time A purchased a new home, A's attorney examined the recorded documents affecting interests in the property. No mechanic's liens were revealed. A short time after A bought the home, B, a roofer, demanded payment for a roof installed prior to A's purchase. Could B have any rights against A's property? Why?

7. C company loaned J company $68,000, $59,280 of the amount being guaranteed in writing by W and his wife. As security for the guaranty, they pledged a note for $59,280 owing to them as joint tenants by X. The $68,000 debt fell due, and in settlement a new note for a lesser amount and a different rate of interest was given C company by J company. W guaranteed the new debt and repledged the $59,280 note as security, his wife not joining in the guaranty or pledge. J company is again in default, and C company proposes to use the $59,280 note as a means of collection. W's wife claims one-half of it because she did not join in the pledging. Was her original pledge still good? Why?

8. B repaired A's automobile and installed a new engine. He wished to retain a lien on the car for parts and labor. How can he accomplish this? Explain.

9. G held a security interest in a certain automobile. The owner of the car took it to H's garage for repairs. The owner paid neither G nor H, and H is now in possession of the car. G seeks to obtain possession of the car from H. Will he succeed? Why?

10. X owned a shoe store and purchased his stock from the ABC shoe co. X was approximately a year behind in paying for his stock. ABC is contemplating suit to recover the funds. X's only property is the shoe store and its stock. The president of ABC learns that X is about to sell the store and its stock to Y at a rather substantial loss. May ABC bring an action for injunction? What steps must X and Y follow in the sale? Explain.

28 LAWS ASSISTING DEBTORS AND CONSUMERS

Introduction   The preceding chapter discussed several laws that were designed to assist creditors in the collection of debts. There are also numerous laws that have as their avowed purpose the protection of debtors and consumers. Many such laws and legal principles have already been discussed. For example, the law relating to usury was covered with the materials on illegal agreements, and the Code provision on unconscionable bargains was discussed as a part of the law as it relates to the sale of goods. This chapter will be concerned with additional efforts to aid debtors and consumers. Most of the materials are based on new statutes, and therefore this chapter includes fewer cases.

This period is sometimes referred to as the era of consumer protection because so many laws have been enacted at both the state and national levels to aid consumers. Courts have also been active in extending protection to consumers. The demise of privity of contract in the breach of warranty cases is an example of judicial consumer protection.

The law has been aiding the consumer-debtor for several reasons. Consumers and debtors frequently have unequal bargaining power with sellers and creditors. Many of them are financially unsophisticated and easily deceived. Frequently they lack the information to make intelligent decisions. Therefore, much of the consumer movement has been directed at providing all of the relevant information so that borrowers and purchasers will be able to make reasonably intelligent decisions in the marketplace.

Exemptions   Typical of state laws protecting debtors are those exempting property from debts. In most states, the exemption statutes include both real and personal property. The real property exemption is

411

usually called the *homestead exemption.* It provides that upon the sale of the family home to satisfy a judgment debt, a certain amount of the sale price shall be paid to the judgment debtor to be his property free of the debt. For example, assume a homestead exemption of $5,000 and that the family home is sold for $26,000 at public auction to satisfy a judgment for $10,000. Assume also that the house was mortgaged for $15,000. The creditor will collect $6,000 ($26,000– $5,000 – $15,000), leaving the judgment unsatisfied to the extent of the $4,000. Of course, the judgment creditor could collect the balance from other nonexempt property, if any.

The reason for the homestead exemption is to provide sufficient funds to the debtor for another home. Public policy favors the debtor and his family's having a home rather than the creditor's being able to collect his entire debt. In some states, the homestead exemption is not available to debtors who do not have a family, thus evidencing the policy of protecting the family.

Statutes in most states also exempt a certain amount of personal property. These usually include wearing apparel and other personal possessions, such as family pictures, books, Bible, and a specified dollar value of other items.

**Garnishment
Limitations** By statute, the various states and the federal government limit the amount of disposable earnings of an employee that may be used to pay the judgment creditors (garnishment). For example, the federal law, which is a part of the Consumer Credit Protection Act, provides that for an individual, the maximum part of the total disposable earnings subject to garnishment in any week *may not* exceed the *lesser* of

1. Twenty-five percent of the disposable earnings for that week, or
2. The amount by which the disposable earnings for that week exceed thirty times the federal minimum hourly wage prescribed by the Fair Labor Standards Act.

Disposable earnings means earnings after deductions for income taxes and social security taxes.

Case: P, the trustee in bankruptcy, sued D, the bankrupt, for an order directing the bankrupt to turn over an income tax refund upon its receipt to the trustee. D claimed that 75 percent of the refund was exempt under the Consumer Credit Protection Act's limitation on garnishment of wages.

Issue: Is an income tax refund "disposable earnings" within the exemption?

Decision: No.

Reasons: 1. The Consumer Protection Act was not intended to alter the clear purpose of the bankruptcy which is to assemble the debtor's assets for the benefit of creditors.

2. A major purpose of the Consumer Protection Act is to prevent bankruptcies by limiting harsh garnishment laws which often cause them.

3. "Disposable earnings" are limited to periodic payments of compensation. They do pertain to every asset that is traceable to compensation.

Kokoszka v. Belford, 94 S.Ct. 2431 (1974).

The federal law does not preempt the field of garnishment or affect any state law. Many state laws exempt larger amounts than does the federal law, and the net effect of the federal law is to exempt the larger amount that either provides. Both the state and the federal law illustrate a public policy against using a wage earner's income to pay judgment debts.

Many employers in the past have discharged employees who were the subject of garnishment proceedings; the federal law has prohibited this practice in situations involving only one garnishment proceeding. The federal law covers all employers and prohibits discharge because of one garnishment proceeding.

Elimination of the Holder in Due Course Concept   Historically, the holder in due course concept was predicated on the premise that personal defenses should not be used against a holder in due course because of the need for commercial paper to move freely through the business community as "a courier without luggage" and as the equivalent of money. Today consumer advocates argue that protection of the consumer is more important than the reasons for the holder in due course concept and that all defenses should always be available to the consumer-debtor.

Before considering the recent developments in the law relating to the availability of defenses, it should be noted that defenses may be "cut off" in two basic ways. A holder in due course of a negotiable instrument takes free of personal defenses. In addition, many contracts specifically provide that if the contract is assigned, the consumer agrees that he will not assert any defense against the assignee. Such provisions not only give the assignee the rights of a holder in due course of a negotiable instrument but purport to eliminate real defenses as well.

A number of states have enacted statutes that prohibit the use of clauses that cut off defenses. If such clauses are used, they will not be enforced. Several states have enacted the Uniform Consumer Credit Code, which provides two alternative approaches to the problem. A

413

state legislature can select the one it considers best suited to the needs of the state.

One alternative simply provides that the consumer can assert all claims and defenses against the assignee of any paper that he signed. This gives maximum protection to the consumer. The other alternative provides that the assignee can give written notice of the assignment to the debtor. The consumer is then given the right to assert defenses for three months. After the three-month period, the assignee is free of any defense and the debtor's only remedy is against the seller.

These state efforts were not universal. Therefore, in 1976 the Federal Trade Commission, acting under its authority to prohibit unfair or deceptive methods of competition, adopted a rule that prohibits the use of the holder in due course concept against consumers. It also provides that a clause purporting to cut off defenses is an unfair method of competition and illegal.

The FTC rule is designed to eliminate substantial abuses which were often inflicted upon the purchaser of consumer goods. Under the holder in due course concept, consumers were often required to pay for defective merchandise and even for merchandise not received. Since consumer paper was usually sold to a bank or other financial institution, the purchaser of the paper would qualify as a holder in due course. As such, it would be able to collect, and the consumer was left to fight it out with the seller when a problem arose.

The FTC rule is applicable to any sale or lease of goods or services to consumers in commerce. In such a transaction, it is an unfair or deceptive act or practice for a seller to receive a credit contract that does not contain the following provision in at least 10-point bold type:

NOTICE
ANY HOLDER OF THIS CONSUMER CREDIT
CONTRACT IS SUBJECT TO ALL CLAIMS AND
DEFENSES WHICH THE DEBTOR COULD ASSERT
AGAINST THE SELLER OF GOODS OR SERVICES
OBTAINED PURSUANT HERETO OR WITH THE
PROCEEDS HEREOF.

Thus the holder could not be a holder in due course because the holder agrees to be subject to all defenses.

To prevent sellers from sending buyers directly to the lender and thus circumventing the law, the rule has a special provision relating to lending institutions. It declares that it is an unfair or deceptive practice for a seller to accept in payment the proceeds of a purchase-money loan unless the following is included in the loan agreement in 10-point bold type:

For the purpose of the foregoing rule, a purchase-money loan exists if the seller refers the consumer to the creditor or is affiliated with the creditor by common control, contract, or business arrangement. This means that if the lending institution regularly does business with the seller or has an understanding that its customers may obtain financing, the provision must be included in the loan contract. Again, it provides that all defenses are available to the consumer.

As a result of the FTC rule, if a consumer-purchaser or buyer has any defense against the seller, it may assert that defense against the bank or other financial institution that seeks to collect the debt. Thus, banks and other financial institutions must make sure that the seller stands behind the products sold. In addition, they must only deal with responsible parties on a recourse basis if losses are to be avoided.

The full effect of the FTC rule is not yet known. Sellers of defective merchandise where customers constantly complain will probably lose their sources of credit. Financial institutions will be much more careful in buying consumer paper. Almost all transfers will be with recourse. Violators of the rule are subject to a $10,000-per-day fine, so compliance ought to be easily obtained.

Federal Consumer Warranty Act To provide consumers with adequate information about express warranties and to prevent deceptive warranties, Congress has enacted a federal law on warranties (Moss-Magnusen Act). The law and the Federal Trade Commission rules adopted under it are applicable to all express warranties if the product sold for over $15.

The first requirement of the law is that a warrantor of a consumer product, by means of a written warranty, shall fully and conspicuously disclose in simple and readily understood language the terms and conditions of such warranty. The law and the rules then specify what must be included. For example, a written warranty among other things must include a statement of what the warrantor will do in the event of a defect or breach of warranty, at whose expense, and for what period of time. It must also tell the consumer what he must do and what expenses he must bear. The law does not require that a warranty be given or that, if given, that it be in writing. If one is given, it must include the items provided by law and be in simple and readily understood language.

415

The law also requires that each warranty be labeled "full" or "limited." A "full" warranty must indicate its duration. Products covered by a "full" warranty must be repaired or replaced by the seller without charge and within a reasonable time in the event there is a defect. A purchaser of a limited warranty is put on notice to find out the limits of the warranty.

To assist the consumer in making an intelligent purchase decision, sellers are required to make all information about the warranties available prior to the sale. This information must be clearly and conspicuously displayed in close connection with the warranted product.

A significant aspect of the federal law deals with informal dispute mechanisms for the resolution of consumer disputes. The law does not require such mechanisms, but it strongly encourages sellers to use them. If a seller establishes a procedure for an independent or government entity to resolve disputes with its buyers, the consumer must resort to the procedure before filing suit against the seller. Consumers are given access to these informal dispute procedures free of charge.

Under the federal law, a warrantor may not impose any limitation on the duration of any implied warranty. Any warrantor may not exclude or limit consequential damages for breach of any warranty unless the exclusion or limitation conspicuously appears on the face of the warranty. Finally, no supplier may disclaim or modify any implied warranty if there is a written warranty or if at the time of sale or within ninety days the supplier enters into a service contract with the buyer. This latter restriction does not prevent a seller from limiting the time period of a written warranty. The time period of the warranty must also be set forth in clear and unmistakable language on the face of the warranty. The law also authorizes class-action suits for damages for breach of warranty if at least one hundred persons are affected. This could be of substantial help to consumers.

Some persons question whether it is possible to write a warranty in simple and readily understandable language. It will take several years of working with the new law before all its ramifications are known. However, as a result of the new law, many sellers have eliminated their warranties or have opted for the limited warranty. A few companies, rather than become involved with all the law's requirements, have taken away their warranty in its entirety. Warranties are more detailed and their language is changed substantially.

**Consumer Credit
Protection Act**
In 1969 the federal Consumer Credit Protection Act was enacted. It is commonly known as the Truth-in-Lending Act.

This law gives protection both to people who buy property on credit and to people who borrow money. Its terms and provisions apply not only to those who lend money or sell on credit in the ordinary course of business but also to anyone who arranges for the extension of credit. Truth-in-lending applies only to natural persons who borrow money or obtain credit for personal, family, household, or agricultural purposes. If a purchaser or borrower is other than a natural person (e.g., a corporation or partnership), or if the purchase or loan is for business rather than, for example, household use, the law is not applicable. It covers real estate credit transactions as well as personal property transactions. In the latter case, it is not applicable if the loan or purchase exceeds $25,000.

The law does not apply to a credit sale by one consumer to another consumer. Typical of transactions covered are installment loans and sales, short-term notes, real estate loans, home improvement loans, and farm loans.

Case: P purchased magazines from D's door-to-door salesman. The contract covered four magazines for five years. P paid $3.95 down and owed a balance of $118.50. The contract did not recite the total purchase price or the amount unpaid, and it made no reference to finance charges. P defaulted, and D sent her two collection letters. P filed suit, alleging a violation of the Truth-in-Lending Act, asking for the statutory penalty of twice the finance charge but not less than $100 and attorney's fees.

Issue: Is the transaction subject to the Truth-in-Lending Law?

Decision: Yes.

Reasons: 1. Regulation 2 of the Federal Reserve Board provides that disclosure is necessary whenever credit is offered to a consumer "for which either a finance charge is or may be imposed or which pursuant to an agreement, is or may be payable in more than four installments."

2. The four-installment rule was designed to prevent circumvention of the objectives of the law by burying the cost of credit in the price of the goods.

3. The Truth-in-Lending Act reflects a transition in congressional policy from a philosophy of let-the-buyer-beware to one of let-the-seller-disclose. By erecting a barrier between the seller and the prospective purchaser in the form of hard facts, Congress expressly sought "to . . . avoid the uninformed use of credit."

Mourning v. Family Publications Service, Inc., 93 S.Ct. 1652 (1973).

The Federal Reserve Board was given responsibility to develop regulations to implement the purpose of the law. For this reason, most of the procedures developed to implement the law are based on the regulations of the Federal Reserve Board, and like all rules of administrative agencies, they are periodically changed. Because of this, businesses subject to the law should make sure that they comply with the current regulations.

The purpose or goals of the Truth-in-Lending Act consist of disclosing certain figures to a prospective purchaser or borrower so that he may shop for credit. The theory is that he may then obtain disclosure statements from several dealers or financers, compare them, and determine whether or not he wishes to go ahead with his purchase or loan. But whether this works in practice is subject to debate.

The goals of the Truth-in-Lending Act are expected to be accomplished by the use of disclosure statements. A copy of the disclosure statement is given to the borrower, and the original is retained by the lender for two years or until the debt is paid, whichever is longer. Separate disclosure statements are required for each transaction including refinancing. These statements inform the borrower of the amount financed, the finance charge, and the annual percentage rate. They also disclose the amount of each payment and the number of payments. It is important to realize that the annual percentage rate generally will not be the same as the interest rate. One important reason for this difference is that the annual percentage rate is based upon the finance charge, and the finance charge includes all charges imposed by the creditor, only one of which is interest. For example, the finance charge may include the cost of credit reports, credit life insurance, health insurance, appraisals, and so forth.

Any creditor subject to the law who fails to make the required disclosure may be sued by the debtor within one year from the date of the violation for *twice the amount of the finance charge*. This may not be less than $100 or more than $1,000. If the creditor has made an incorrect disclosure, he must, within fifteen days after discovering the error, notify the debtor and make whatever adjustments are necessary to ensure that the debtor will not be required to pay a finance charge in excess of the amount of the percentage rate actually disclosed. If he is to avoid the penalty, the creditor must discover the error and give notice to the debtor before notification by the debtor or before the debtor institutes action against him.

Uniform Consumer Credit Code

The Commissioners on Uniform State Laws have prepared a Uniform Consumer Credit Code (UCCC) designed to accomplish many of the same purposes as the federal Truth-in-Lending Act.

The UCCC also attempts to protect consumers by utilizing the technique of full disclosure of all pertinent facts about the credit transaction to buyers. Where enacted, it is applicable to practically every transaction involving credit.

This credit code does not fix the actual rates of interest to be charged but does set maximums that may be charged in credit transactions. It has provisions relating to delinquency charges, service charges, deferral charges, and revolving charge accounts.

In addition to regulating the cost of credit, the UCCC prohibits certain types of agreements. For example, it prohibits the use of multiple agreements to obtain higher interest. Since the law authorizes higher charges for smaller purchases, a total higher interest would be possible by use of multiple transactions. It also prohibits "balloon" payments by providing that if any scheduled payment is more than twice as large as the average payments, the buyer has the right to refinance the balloon payment without penalty on terms no less favorable than the original terms. The balloon payment provision is not applicable to a sale for agricultural purposes or one pursuant to a revolving charge account.

The UCCC prohibits debtors from assigning their earnings as part of a credit sale. It also prohibits referral sales schemes in which the buyer is given credit on a purchase for furnishing the names of other purchasers.

One major part of the UCCC deals with home solicitation sales. The home solicitation sale rules cover goods other than farm equipment involving a personal solicitation at the residence of the buyer. Under the act, a buyer has the right to cancel a home solicitation sale until midnight of the third business day after the day the buyer signed the agreement or the offer to purchase. Written notice of cancellation must be given, and notification is effective when deposited in the mail. The law also requires that the written agreement in a home sale conspicuously inform the buyer of his right to cancel. When such a sale is canceled, the seller must refund any payment made by the buyer within ten days. However, the seller may retain, as a cancellation fee, an amount not to exceed 5 percent of the cash price or the down payment, whichever is less.

Violations of the UCCC may be punished criminally. In addition, debtors are relieved of their obligation to pay the finance charge, and they are entitled to recover up to three times the finance charge actually paid from creditors who violate the law. Of course debtors are not obligated to pay charges in excess of those allowable by the act. If a debtor entitled to a refund is refused a refund, the debtor is entitled to recover the total amount of the credit service charge or ten times the excess charge, whichever is greater. If the excess charge was in deliberate violation of the act, the penalty may be recovered even if the excess has been repaid.

Credit Card Protection   Most credit card contracts provide that defenses that may be available against the seller cannot be asserted against the credit card company. Such contracts continue to be valid. The FTC rule changing the holder in due course concept does not cover credit cards.

The large number of credit cards in existence and their widespread use creates difficult problems. Credit cards are easily lost or stolen. Lost or stolen cards are often used for unauthorized purchases, resulting in a loss to (1) the business that dealt with the wrong person, or (2) the credit card company (which may be the same as number 1, as for example an oil company's gasoline credit card), or (3) the actual cardholder.

The law favors limiting the cardholder's loss. As part of the federal Turth-in-Lending Act, Congress included provisions that limit the cardholder's liability to fifty dollars. The law also prohibits the issuance of credit cards except upon application therefor. Thus no liability for unauthorized purchases would be present if the card was unsolicited.

Other provisions of the law require that companies issuing credit cards provide a simple method of notification that a card has been lost or stolen. The cardholder must be informed of his rights and obligations in connection with the card and its use. Also, the card issuer must provide a method whereby the user can be identified as the person authorized to use it.

The net result is to shift the burden of unauthorized use of a credit card from the cardholder to the issuer of the card. Although the cardholder may still be liable for unauthorized use to a limited extent, he does have a practical means of protecting himself by notifying the company promptly of any loss or theft.

CREDIT REPORTING AND COLLECTION PRACTICES

Introduction   In recent years the federal government has enacted several laws relating to the granting of credit. The Fair Credit Reporting Act is aimed at eliminating abuses in the system of credit reporting. The Fair Credit Billing Act imposes duties on creditors when debtors complain about errors in billing. There is also a federal law that prohibits discrimination on the basis of age, race, color, religion, national origin, sex, or marital status in extending credit. In addition, there are numerous federal laws relating to the credit aspects of real estate transactions.

Fair Credit Reporting Act   This law is not designed to prevent credit reporting. Its purpose is to prevent abuses in the system of credit reports which may result from inaccurate information in a report. It is also designed to prevent the undue invasion of individual privacy in the

420

collection and dissemination of information about a person's credit record. The act is applicable to anyone who prepares or uses a credit report in connection with (1) the extending of credit, (2) the sale of insurance, or (3) the hiring or discharge of an employee. It covers credit reports on consumers but not those on businesses.

The law covers two situations. First of all, it covers cases in which an individual is rejected for credit, insurance, or employment because of an adverse credit report. When this occurs, the individual has (1) the right to be told the name of the reporting agency, (2) the right to require the agency to reveal the information given in the report, and (3) the right to correct the information or at least give the consumer's version of the facts in dispute.

This law has one important limitation. A report containing information solely as to transactions or experiences between the consumer and the person making the report is not a "consumer report." For example, assume that a bank is asked for information about the credit experience of the bank and one of its customers. If it reports only as to its own experiences, the report is not covered by the act. The law only covers credit-reporting agencies that obtain information from several sources, compile it, and furnish it to potential creditors.

Many businesses can avoid being a credit-reporting agency, but most businesses will be subject to the "user" provisions of this law. The "user" provision requires that consumers seeking credit be informed if their application is denied because of an adverse credit report. They must be informed of the source of the report and of the fact that they are entitled to make a written request within sixty days as to the nature of the information received. The information in the report may then be used to challenge the accuracy of the report.

The second situation covered by this law involves "investigative consumer reports." A consumer is entitled to be informed when an "investigative consumer report" is being made. Upon request, he is entitled to be informed as to (1) the nature and scope of the investigation, (2) the kind of information that has been placed in the credit-reporting agency's file, and (3) the name of anyone to whom the report has been sent. He also has the right to require a consumer-reporting agency to reinvestigate any material that he finds to be inaccurate in his file and the right to have removed from his file any inaccurate material or material that cannot be verified by the reporting agency. If there is a dispute as to the accuracy, the consumer has the right to place a one-hundred-word statement in his file setting forth his position with regard to the disputed matter. This statement must be included in all future agency reports that contain the material in dispute.

In addition, the consumer has the right to require that obsolete information included in the consumer report be removed from the file. Included are bankruptcies that occurred more than fourteen years prior to the report; lawsuits and judgments that antedate the report by more than seven years or until the statute of limitations has expired, whichever is longer; and, in general, adverse items of entered information that antedate the report by more than seven years.

Fair Credit Billing Act This 1974 law requires that a creditor must take certain steps if a debtor within sixty days of the receipt of a bill complains that the billing is in error. First of all, the creditor is required to acknowledge the notice within thirty days. Second, the creditor within two billing cycles and within not more than ninety days must either (1) correct the error or (2) send a written statement of clarification to the debtor.

The act further provides that a creditor operating an open-end credit plan may not until explanation of the complaint or its correction curtail, restrict, or close the debtor's account. In addition, the law prohibits a creditor from reporting or threatening to report the debtor to a credit-rating organization. Violation of either of these provisions results in a forfeiture of the right to collect the amount stated in the billing.

The law also contains several provisions relating to the accounting practices of creditors. For example, prompt posting of all payments is required to prevent the application of additional finance charges. Creditors of revolving charge accounts cannot charge finance charges on a new purchase unless a statement including the billing and finance charge is rendered at least fourteen days prior to the date the finance charge can be avoided by paying the amount of the original bill.

The law also contains some restrictions on credit card issuers and their business practices. For example, issuers of credit cards may not prohibit sellers who honor these cards from offering discounts for cash or immediate payment by check.

Other Aspects of Consumer Protection The proceding sections have discussed several of the important new laws and legal principles that give substantial protection to consumers and especially to debtor-consumers. There are other proposed laws or changes in existing laws that are designed to give even more protection. Some of these have been enacted in a few states, and others are being developed by courts and legislatures at this time. For example, the Uniform Deceptive Trade Practices Act has been adopted by seven states. This act removes restrictions on common-law tort actions for deceptive business practices. It recognizes a cause of action for financial loss as a result of misleading identification of a business or goods or as a result of false or deceptive advertising. It also

422

recognizes common-law liability to a competitor because of false or deceptive advertising.

Among the types of conduct considered unfair and deceptive are the following: (1) advertising goods or services without intent to sell them as advertised, (2) misrepresenting the character, extent, volume, or nature of the business, (3) advertising secondhand, used, defective, blemished, or rejected merchandise without disclosure of those facts, (4) selling unassembled items without disclosure of that fact, (5) selling merchandise marked "made in U.S.A." when it is manufactured elsewhere.

The Uniform Deceptive Trade Practices Act also attempts to prevent one person from passing off his goods or services as those of another. It includes within the concept of deceptive trade practice conduct that causes confusion or misunderstanding about the goods or the seller. In addition to allowing suits for dollar damages, this act authorizes courts to enjoin such conduct.

There is a definite trend in many states toward allowing class-action suits on behalf of consumers. Most consumers cannot afford to sue because their complaints do not involve a sufficient amount of money to warrant the retention of an attorney. However, the class-action suits, which allow one plaintiff to sue on behalf of all persons similarly situated, make such suits worthwhile. Legislation has been introduced in many states authorizing class-action suits on behalf of consumers. In addition, many states have created consumer protection agencies which are authorized to take legal action on behalf of consumers.

Case: Thirty-seven plaintiffs joined in a legal action on behalf of themselves and two hundred others who had purchased frozen food and freezers from the defendant. It was claimed that the salesmen employed by the defendant had made misrepresentations to the purchasers in order to induce them to buy. The defendant claimed that there could not be a class action based upon fraud and misrepresentation.

Issue: Will a class action be allowed?

Decision: Yes.

Reason: In the usual consumer fraud situation, the same scheme is used to defraud all the consumers. All of them rely upon the same misrepresentation. Thus, where there is proof of misrepresentation to one of the plaintiffs, this is representative of misrepresentations made to others and all may be joined in one suit.

Vasquez v. Superior Court, 484 P.2d 964 (Cal.) 1971.

REVIEW QUESTIONS AND PROBLEMS

1. What is the reason for the recent trend toward "consumerism"?

2. What is a "class action" suit?

3. What is the basic purpose of the Truth-in-Lending law?

4. What is meant by *garnishment*?

5. What restrictions have been placed upon a creditor's right to garnish wages?

6. What right does a consumer have to cancel a purchase made from a door-to-door salesman?

7. When A purchased a new car in 1977 he made a promissory note payable to B, dealer. B transferred the note to the XYZ bank, which provided most of B's financing. B later failed to honor its warranty with A. Is A under a duty to make car payments to XYZ? Why?

8. The XYZ company issued a credit card to A. A's card was stolen and A immediately notified XYZ. The thief used A's card for motel and gasoline purchases for two months. Does A or XYZ suffer the loss? Explain.

9. Why is it unlikely that a person will receive an unsolicited credit card in the mail? Explain.

10. A was rejected for life insurance on the basis of a report from an independent credit agency. What are A's rights concerning the report? Why?

11. The XYZ company mailed A a bill that was erroneous. A promptly mailed a letter to XYZ which called attention to the error. XYZ continued to send faulty statements of A's account and did not reply to A's complaint. What is A's liability? Why?

29 BANKRUPTCY

Introduction   The law of bankruptcy is concerned with the problems that arise when a person, firm, or corporation is unable to satisfy obligations due to creditors. It provides various methods for relieving debtors of their debts or postponing the time of payment, and for protecting some of the rights of the creditors.

Bankruptcy proceedings are based on federal law and are conducted in the federal courts. They may be voluntary (started by the debtor) or involuntary (started by the creditors). The law of bankruptcy is designed to accomplish several purposes. Historically, the major purpose was to provide a method of applying a debtor's assets in an equitable distribution among his creditors. The major purpose today is to relieve honest debtors of the weight of oppressive indebtedness in order that they may start afresh, free of their former obligations. This purpose recognizes that misfortune and poor judgment often create a situation in which a debtor will never be able to discharge his debts by his own efforts. Public policy dictates that such debtors should be able to obtain a fresh start not only in their personal lives but in business as well.

Today more and more people are using voluntary bankruptcy proceedings to rid themselves of their debts. Although divorce, medical bills, and unemployment can be causative factors, easy credit and poor financial management of personal affairs are more often involved. A significant portion of the public do not know how to use credit. After it mounts to such levels that repayment is difficult if not impossible, bankruptcy provides a relatively easy solution to the financial problem.

As bankruptcy proceedings have involved more and more people, the stigma of using it as a solution to financial problems has tended to fade away. Many middle-class persons who have gone through bank-

425

ruptcy have suffered little loss of social status. Moreover, their credit rating often actually improves because they no longer owe the debts and they are not permitted to file bankruptcy again for six years. As the result of state laws declaring that certain property is exempt from the proceedings, bankruptcy has frequently meant little or no change in the life-style of the bankrupt. Today bankrupts are not outcasts. They are persons who have been granted a new financial start unburdened by the heavy weight of their former debts.

Bankruptcy Proceedings

Bankruptcy proceedings are relatively simple. A petition is filed (by the debtor if voluntary and by the creditors if involuntary) with the federal district court. A filing fee is required of all petitioners, although it may be paid in installments over a six-month period.

Case: K, an indigent, filed a voluntary petition in bankruptcy. K did not pay the required $50 filing fee within the six-month period allowed. The court refused to grant a discharge. K contended that the court's refusal constituted an unconstitutional denial of due process and equal protection of the law.

Issue: Is the payment of the filing fee a valid condition precedent to obtaining a discharge in bankruptcy?

Decision: Yes.

Reasons: 1. There is no common-law right to proceed in bankruptcy without the payment of filing fees.

2. The filing fee requirement is not a denial of due process because the right to a discharge in bankruptcy is not a fundamental right nor is it a constitutional right. It is not akin to free speech or similar rights.

3. The filing fee requirement has a rational basis. Bankruptcy is not the only conceivable relief available to bankrupts.

United States v. Kras, 93 S. Ct. 631 (1973).

The filing of voluntary petition in bankruptcy constitutes a judicial finding that the debtor is a bankrupt. The petition contains essentially four items—a list of creditors, secured and unsecured; a list of property or assets; a list of property claimed by the debtor to be exempt; and a statement of affairs of the bankrupt. The petition is filed on official forms designated by the Supreme Court for that purpose. Great care must be exercised in the completion of these forms. Concealing assets is a crime under the bankruptcy laws, as is the willful making of a false oath. The schedules are sworn to, and knowingly supplying false information is the making of a false oath.

Involuntary petitions are filed by creditors to have the debtor adjudged a bankrupt. The special aspects of involuntary bankruptcy are discussed in the next section, but it is noted here that the petition filed by the creditors must allege, among other things, that the debtor has committed an act of bankruptcy. The debtor answers the petition, and if adjudged a bankrupt by the court, the debtor will be required to complete the same schedules as the debtor in a voluntary proceeding.

After the adjudication of the debtor as a bankrupt, which is the formal decision by which jurisdiction over the debtor's property is obtained, the proceedings in voluntary and involuntary bankruptcy are identical. The court notifies each creditor of the proceeding, of the date by which all claims are to be filed, and of the date of a meeting of the creditors with the debtor.

If upon the filing of the petition it appears to the court that it is necessary to have control over the debtor's property prior to the first meeting of creditors, the judge may appoint a receiver. A *receiver* is a temporary officer designated to take charge of property and to care for it to prevent waste and loss. Receivers are usually appointed to operate a business until the first meeting of creditors can be conducted.

At this first meeting, a *trustee in bankruptcy* is elected by the creditors, unless the bankrupt's estate has "no assets." A majority in number and amount of claims held by those present at the meeting is necessary for election. The trustee takes title to all nonexempt property, both real and personal, owned by the bankrupt at the time the petition was filed. It becomes his duty to dispose of the property as best he can, under the supervision of the court, for the benefit of creditors. Property received by the bankrupt after the filing of the petition belongs to his new estate. However, all devises, bequests, or inheritances received within six months thereafter belong to the trustee.

Case: A bankrupt wage earner had accrued but unpaid vacation pay. The trustee sought to collect these wages.

Issue: Is accrued vacation pay property that passes to the trustee?

Decision: No.

Reason: The wage-earning bankrupt who must take a vacation without pay or forgo a vacation altogether cannot be said to have achieved the "new opportunity in life and the clear field for future effort, unhampered by the pressure and discouragement of pre-existing debt," which it was the purpose of the statute to provide.

Lines v. Frederick, 91 S.Ct. 113 (1970).

At a meeting of creditors, the debtor may be examined by the creditors to ascertain if property has been omitted from the list of assets, if property has been conveyed in defraud of creditors, and about other matters that may affect the right of the debtor to have his obligations discharged. In many voluntary bankruptcies after this meeting of creditors, the proceedings are essentially over. This is true in "no asset" cases because there is no property to be sold and nothing to be used to pay creditors. The only issues remaining are possible grounds for denying a discharge. If there are nonexempt assets, the trustee in bankruptcy will take control of them, sell them for cash, pay all expenses, and use the balance to pay dividends to creditors in accordance with the rules on claims and priority discussed later in the chapter.

Bankruptcy Jurisdiction

Any person, firm, or corporation may become a *voluntary* bankrupt, with five exceptions. Railway, banking, insurance, and municipal corporations, and building and loan associations may not become voluntary bankrupts. This does not mean that such organizations may not become insolvent—only that their debts may not be discharged in bankruptcy proceedings. There are special laws relating to the liquidation of such organizations, and all of them are subject to the jurisdiction of some administrative agency, such as the Interstate Commerce Commission.

Any natural person, except a farmer or wage earner, any partnership and any moneyed business or commercial corporation, except the five previously mentioned, may be adjudged an *involuntary* bankrupt for proper cause. Thus three groups are exempt from involuntary bankruptcy—farmers, wage earners, and nonbusiness corporations.

A *farmer* is defined as anyone engaged in the tillage of the soil, raising poultry or livestock and their products, or operating a dairy. If he spends most of his time on the farm and expects to derive most of his income from it, he is deemed a farmer although he is incidentally engaged in other enterprises. A *wage earner*, for the purpose of involuntary bankruptcy, is one who works for another at a rate of pay of $1,500 a year or less. A worker who earns over $1,500 per year is not exempt from involuntary bankruptcy.

Involuntary bankruptcy proceedings require that the debtor's liabilities equal at least $1,000 if an individual, and $5,000 if a corporation. If twelve or more creditors exist, at least three of them must sign the petition; if there are fewer than twelve creditors, only one need sign. The petitioning creditors as a group must also own definite unsecured claims totaling $500 or more. Relatives, persons holding fully secured claims, and other biased creditors are not counted in determining the number of creditors required to sign the petition.

Acts of Bankruptcy The purpose of involuntary bankruptcy is to force an equitable distribution of an insolvent debtor's assets. Mere insolvency affords no basis for a petition in involuntary bankruptcy. Unless a debtor has committed some act that indicates an intention to abuse his creditors or to prefer certain creditors, or has done something that shows a willingness to have his assets distributed, he may not be adjudged an involuntary bankrupt. An act of bankruptcy must have been committed within four months of the filing of the petition.

Acts of bankruptcy consist of a debtor's having

1. Made a transfer of his property with intent to defraud creditors
2. Made a preferential transfer of his property
3. Failed to have a lien against his property discharged within thirty days after it was filed
4. Made a general assignment for the benefit of creditors
5. A receiver appointed, voluntarily or involuntarily, to take charge of his property because of insolvency or inability to pay debts as they mature
6. Admitted in writing his inability to pay his debts and his willingness to be adjudged a bankrupt

Attention is called to the fact that the second, third, and fifth acts require insolvency. The first, fourth, and sixth acts do not require it. However, solvency at the time the petition is filed is a good defense to the first act of bankruptcy, and proof of solvency will cause a denial of the creditor's petition. Insolvency, where required, refers to the financial condition at the time the act is committed. Except for the fifth act, *insolvency*, as used in bankruptcy, refers only to the situation in which the debtor's assets, valued on the basis of a voluntary sale, fail to equal his liabilities. It differs from involvency in the equity sense, which means that a debtor is unable to pay his debts in the ordinary course of business. In accounting terms, *insolvency* in the equity sense means that current liabilities exceed current assets. Insolvency in the bankruptcy sense means that total liabilities exceed total assets. By definition, the fifth act encompasses both concepts of insolvency, but the others use the "balance sheet" test.

The petition in involuntary bankruptcy must be filed within four months of the commission of one of the acts of bankruptcy. Transfers of property are frequently not fully effective as to third parties until a document is recorded and made a matter of public record. For example, a conveyance of real estate is not complete until the deed is recorded. Whenever recording is required, the four-month period is calculated from the date of recording and not from the date of the transfer.

429

CLAIMS

Introduction The claims of some creditors are not allowed to share in the bankrupt estate. The term *provable claim* is used to describe those claims that are entitled to share in the estate. The term *dividend* describes payments by the trustee to creditors. A *dischargeable claim* is one that will be barred to the extent that it is not paid in the proceedings. It must be distinguished from claims that survive as a binding obligation of the debtor after the proceedings are over.

Before a claim is dischargeable, it must meet the statutory requirements to qualify as a provable claim. Claims that are not provable are not dischargeable. However, it should not be overlooked that the mere fact that a claim qualified as provable does not necessarily mean that it is also dischargeable. Some debts continue after the conclusion of the bankruptcy proceedings.

Provable Claims To qualify as a provable claim, the claim must be filed by the creditor within six months of the date first set by the referee for the first meeting of creditors. However, claims of the United States and claims of persons under a disability, such as infants and insane persons without guardians, are not subject to this requirement. In the latter case an additional six months is granted for filing the claim.

To qualify as provable, the claim must be liquidated or certain in amount. Among the typical claims that are not liquidated are those involving contracts in dispute, tort claims, and claims of secured creditors where the security may be of lesser value than the amount of the claim. If a suit on a contract is pending at the time of the petition, the claim may be made certain by agreement with the trustee as to the amount of damages, or by judicial decision either in the court in which the suit is pending or by proof before the court. The claim must still be filed within the six-month period. A claim of a secured creditor will be allowed to the extent that the claim exceeds the security. This amount can be determined by selling the security or by compromise or by litigation with the trustee.

Most provable claims are fixed liabilities based on judgments or instruments in writing such as commercial paper. All judgments, including those arising in tort, are provable. Claims may also be based on open accounts and on any contract, express or implied, including anticipatory breach of executory contracts.

If the breach of contract action is for the breach of an unexpired lease, the claim is limited to one year's future rent plus unpaid accrued rent. Thus landlords' claims are limited to the rent due to the date of surrender of possession plus one year, provided the lease runs for that period.

430

Claims based on intentional tort are not provable unless they have been made certain by contract or judgment prior to the petition in bankruptcy. However, claims based on a theory of negligence are provable if the injured party has instituted suit prior to the filing of bankruptcy proceedings. To illustrate this distinction, assume that A has sued B for an intentional tort, such as assault and battery, and that the case has not proceeded to judgment when B files a petition in bankruptcy. A cannot file a claim and will not share in B's bankrupt estate. However, the claim is not discharged and may be enforced against any new assets B may acquire. On the other hand, if A's cause of action is based on negligence, A is entitled to share in the estate, and his claim is discharged. If A has not filed his negligence suit, the claim is not provable and is not discharged by the proceedings.

Other provable claims that are exceptions to the general principle of certainty are workmen's compensation awards based on injuries, sickness, or death occurring prior to the adjudication of bankruptcy; claims for costs in suits started against the bankrupt or in cases started by him and abandoned by the trustee; and tax claims.

Claims That Are Not Discharged

Provable claims are generally dischargeable. However, discharge may be denied either because of the nature of the claim or because of conduct of the debtor. The debtor's conduct that may result in a denial of discharge may occur before the proceedings are commenced or during the proceedings.

Among provable claims that are not discharged because of the nature of the claim are (1) claims for taxes due any governmental body within three years preceding bankruptcy; (2) debts created by fraud, embezzlement, misappropriation, or defalcation of a debtor acting in any fiduciary capacity; (3) alimony and child support; (4) liability resulting from willful or malicious torts: (5) wages earned within three months of filing the petition in bankruptcy; (6) liabilities for property or money obtained under false pretenses or by fraudulent representations; and (7) claims for money of an employee that had been retained by his employer to secure the faithful performance of the employment contract.

While most of the above are self-explanatory, a few additional aspects need to be noted. While debts for taxes owing for more than three years are dischargeable, the discharge does not affect any tax lien. The alimony and child support exception does not include liability between spouses created by property settlement agreements unrelated to support.

A judgment based on an intentional tort is not dischargeable even though it is a provable claim. However, a claim based on the tort of simple negligence is both provable and dischargeable.

A difficult issue is presented when the theory of the lawsuit lies between simple negligence on the one hand and a clearly intentional tort on the other. Such lawsuits proceed on a theory known as *willful and wanton misconduct*. Modern cases tend to hold that judgments based on willful and wanton misconduct are not dischargeable.

Case: D's car, while traveling at a high rate of speed, struck P's car. D had been drinking. P obtained a judgment against D, and D filed bankruptcy. P contended that the judgment could not be discharged.

Issue: Was D's conduct "willful and wanton," so as to preclude discharge in bankruptcy?

Decision: Yes.

Reason: D's conduct was "willful and wanton," and such conduct supplies the requisite intent on the part of D to constitute a willful tort.

Perrett v. Johnson, 175 So.2d 497 (Miss.) 1965.

As previously noted, it is the duty of the bankrupt to file a schedule of all creditors and the amount due each. Notice of the proceedings is then given each creditor in order that he may attend the meetings of creditors and file claims. The claim of any creditor who is not listed or who does not learn of the proceedings in time to file his claim is not discharged. The bankrupt, under such circumstances, remains liable. In the case of nonlisted creditors, the burden of proof to establish that the creditor had knowledge of the proceedings in time to file a claim rests with the bankrupt. Proof of actual knowledge is required, and although such knowledge is often present, care should be taken to list all creditors so that all claims will unquestionably be discharged. In certain cases the schedules may be amended to correct errors.

Bankrupts Who Are Not Discharged   A discharge in bankruptcy is a privilege and not a right. Therefore, in addition to providing that certain *claims* are not discharged, the act lists seven grounds for denying a *bankrupt* a discharge. These grounds must be specifically set forth by a creditor as an objection to discharge and must be proven to the satisfaction of the court at a hearing on the objection. When a discharge is denied, the assets are distributed among the creditors, but the debtor remains liable for the unpaid portion of all claims. The act provides that discharge will be denied if the bankrupt has (1) committed a crime under the Bankruptcy Act; (2) failed to keep or preserve records, from which his financial condition and business transactions might be ascertained; (3) while engaged in business obtained money, property, or credit by making a materially false statement in writing respecting his financial condition or the financial condition of the business; (4) within twelve months immediately preceding the filing of the petition in bankruptcy, transferred, removed, destroyed, or concealed any of his property, with intent to hinder, delay, or defraud his creditors; (5) within six years prior to bankruptcy been granted a discharge; (6) refused to obey any lawful order or to answer any material question approved by the court; and (7) failed to explain satisfactorily any losses of assets or deficiency of assets to meet his liabilities.

Case: Branch made false statements under oath to obtain a loan. Thereafter in subsequent bankruptcy proceedings a creditor objected to his discharge.

Issue: Are false financial statements by a businessman a grounds for denying discharge?

Decision: Yes.

Reason: The Bankruptcy Act was intended to protect only honest debtors. False financial statements are a ground for denying discharge to businessmen.

Branch v. Mills & Lupton Supply Company, 348 F.2d 901 (1965).

Any of the circumstances mentioned may be set up by a creditor as a bar to a discharge, or they may be set up by the trustee when he has been authorized to do so by the creditors. Furthermore, if any creditor can show reasonable cause for believing that the bankrupt has done any of the things mentioned, the burden shifts to the bankrupt to show that he has not committed an act that will bar discharge.

It should be remembered that the third ground for barring the discharge is limited to businessmen. Persons not in business who furnish false financial statements to obtain property or credit may nevertheless be discharged. Such false statements will not bar discharge but will prevent discharge of the debt that arose out of the transaction in which the fraudulent financial statement was submitted. Therefore, a false financial statement by a businessman is a complete bar to a discharge, but a false financial statement by a person not engaged in business is only a bar to discharge of the debt involved.

Payment of Claims Creditors are either *secured* or *unsecured*. Because the trustee's title to property is only the title previously held by the bankrupt, any valid lien or security interest against the property continues after bankruptcy. The secured creditor can collect the debt by enforcing his security interest. If the total value of the property securing the secured creditor is greater than the debt, the trustee may pay off the debt and then use the property to satisfy the unsecured creditors. A secured creditor who forecloses his security interest without accepting the property in full satisfaction is an unsecured creditor to the extent of any deficiency.

The law relating to priority of claims is concerned with the order in which unsecured creditors are paid. Unsecured creditors are paid dividends from any assets remaining after secured creditors have exercised their rights. The law creates six classes of unsecured creditors and directs that each class be paid in full before anything is paid to the next class. If funds are insufficient to pay in full any particular class of creditors, the funds available for such group are distributed in proportion to the amount of each claim; and all classes falling lower in the list receive no payment. For example, if the assets are not sufficient for paying in full the claims of wage earners amounting to $600 per person and earned within the previous three months, the wage earners would share proportionately the amount available, but the claims for taxes and general creditors would not share. The order of priority of the classes of unsecured creditors is as follows:

1. Cost of preserving and administering the bankrupt estate. This includes such items as court costs, receiver, trustee and attorney's fees, and appraisal fees. It also includes rent of property occupied by the receiver or trustee during the administration of the bankrupt's estate.

2. Claims of wage earners not exceeding $600 to each claimant, provided the wages have accrued within the three months preceding bankruptcy. Wage earners include workmen, clerks, servants, and salesmen. These people were dependent on the bankrupt for their support and are thus preferred. Claims in excess of $600 are treated as a sixth-class claim, as are wages before the three-month period.

3. Claims for money expended in defending suits against or setting aside arrangements of the bankrupt debtor.

4. Claims for taxes. The priority accorded to taxes in the distribution of bankrupt estates applies to those taxes that became legally due and owing within three years preceding bankruptcy. Other taxes are a sixth-class claim.

5. Claims for rent granted priority by state statute and any claims allowed priority by federal law. Many of the claims held by the federal government have been given priority under this provision. The law restricts the priority for rent to not more than three months' rent owing at the time of bankruptcy and further restricts this priority to rent accruing for actual use of the premises. This priority is given because of the limitations imposed on landlords' liens under the statute.

6. Claims of general creditors.

Property that is exempt is not used to pay dividends. Property is
exempt from the bankrupt estate if an exemption is provided by either
the laws of the United States or the laws of the state of the bankrupt's
domicile. The whole subject of exemptions was discussed in Chapter
28.

The debtor is required to prepare a list of property claimed to be
exempt. Failure to claim the exemptions or to list property may result
in the use of property otherwise exempt to pay the creditors.

VOIDABLE TRANSFERS

Grounds A trustee in bankruptcy may bring suit to avoid transfers of
property by the debtor on several grounds. First, the trustee
may do so on any ground that could have been used by the debtor to
obtain a return of his property. Since the trustee has stepped into the
debtor's shoes, grounds such as fraud, mutual mistake, and lack of
capacity may be used by the trustee to obtain a return of property.

Second, a trustee may avoid a transfer that constitutes a preference
by the debtor for one or more creditors over others. Preferences are
discussed in the next section.

Third, the trustee may avoid any judicial lien (judgment) or judicial
sale that is obtained or conducted within four months of the filing of
the bankruptcy petition if the lien or sale was obtained or conducted
while the debtor was insolvent. The reasons for not allowing liens to be
treated as valid secured claims if perfected within four months
immediately preceding the filing of the petition in bankruptcy are the
same as those for allowing the recovery of payments or transfers that
constitute preferences.

Fourth, the trustee may set aside any transfer made by the debtor,
or any obligation incurred by the debtor, that is fraudulent under either
federal or state law.

Besides having several grounds for avoiding a transfer of property,
the trustee has several statuses in which to act. The trustee has the
rights and powers of a judgment creditor. The trustee has these rights
whether or not any judgment creditor actually exists.

The trustee also has the status of a lien creditor with a lien on all of
the bankrupt's property, whether or not a lien creditor actually exists.
Thus the trustee may avoid any transfer of property made by the
debtor that any creditor would have been able to avoid under any state
law.

Preferences One of the goals of bankruptcy proceedings is to provide an
equitable distribution of a debtor's property among his creditors. As one judge said, "A creditor who dips his hand in a pot which he
knows will not go round must return what he receives so that all may

share." Therefore the trustee in bankruptcy is allowed to recover payments that constitute a preference of one creditor over another.

To constitute a recoverable preference, the payment must have been made (1) by an insolvent debtor; (2) to a creditor for, or on account of, a prior debt; (3) within four months of the filing of the bankruptcy petition; and (4) to a creditor who, at the time of the payment, knew, or had cause to believe, that he was obtaining a greater percentage of his claim than other creditors could recover. The term *payment* includes transfers of property. The distinction between a transfer that constitutes the second act of bankruptcy and one that constitutes a recoverable preference is found in the fourth requirement for a recoverable preference. A payment or transfer may be an act of bankruptcy, but it may not be a recoverable preference if the creditor does not know that he is being preferred. Knowledge that the debtor is insolvent will establish the knowledge that the creditor is being preferred.

Case: P, a trustee in bankruptcy, sued D to recover an alleged preference. D had collected its debt by garnisheeing the bank account of the bankrupt. At the time of the garnishment, D's attorney was told by the bankrupt's attorney that such action would force the bankrupt out of business and that bankruptcy proceedings were imminent. Five days later, the petition in bankruptcy was filed. D claimed that it did not know that the bankrupt was insolvent.

Issue: Was the collection in the garnishment proceeding a recoverable preference?

Decision: Yes.

Reasons: 1. A preference is a transfer of any property of a debtor to a creditor while the debtor is insolvent and within four months before the filing ... the effect of which enables the creditor to obtain a greater percentage of his debt than other creditors of the same class.

2. A preference may be avoided if the creditor receiving it has at the time when the transfer is made reasonable cause to believe that the debtor is insolvent.

3. A person is not insolvent because he cannot meet his currently accruing obligations. The test of insolvency is the excess of debts over assets at a fair valuation or the balance sheet test.

4. D had reasonable cause to believe that the bankrupt was insolvent because of the statements made to its attorney. Therefore, the collection by garnishment was a recoverable preference. D knew or should have known that it was being preferred.

Saperstein v. Holland, McGill, & Pasker, 496 P.2d 896 (Utah) 1972.

Recoverable preferences include not only payments of money but also the transfer of property as payment of, or as security for, a prior indebtedness. A mortgage or pledge may be set aside as readily as payment, providing it is received by the creditor with knowledge of the debtor's insolvency. Such pledge or mortgage can be avoided, however, only if it was received within the immediate four months prior to the filing of the petition in bankruptcy and was obtained as security for a previous debt. In the case of the mortgage, the four-month period dates from the recording of the mortgage rather than from its signing. In the case of a security agreement covering after-acquired property, it is the date of filing that controls and not the date of the receipt of the property.

Case: B, a bankrupt, gave D a security interest in its inventory. The financing statement was filed August 5, 1971. Later B became insolvent, and on November 15, 1971, D seized B's inventory. On January 26, 1972, B filed its voluntary petition in bankruptcy. P, the trustee, sued D to recover the value of the inventory.

Issue: Was the foreclosure of the security interest a preferential transfer?

Decision: No.

Reasons: 1. If a security interest is perfected more than four months prior to the initiation of bankruptcy proceedings, the secured party's interest prevails over any claim by the trustee in the collateral covered by the security agreement.

2. This is equally true of security agreements that cover after-acquired property even though the rights in such property attach within four months of bankruptcy.

3. When a security interest covering after-acquired property is perfected by filing prior to the four months before bankruptcy, the secured party prevails over the trustee in bankruptcy as to property thereafter acquired by the debtor.

Fliegel v. Associates Capital Co. of Delaware, Inc., 537 P.2d 1144 (Or.) 1975.

Payment of a fully secured claim does not constitute a preference and, therefore, may not be recovered. Transfers of property for a present consideration may not be set aside because there is a corresponding asset for the new liability. For example, a mortgage given to secure a contemporaneous loan is valid, although the mortgagee took the security with knowledge of the debtor's insolvency. An insolvent debtor has a right to attempt to extricate himself, as far as possible, from his financial difficulty.

Any debtor of a bankrupt may set off against the amount he owes the bankrupt estate any sum that the estate owes him. To the extent of his setoff, he becomes a preferred creditor, but he is legally entitled to this preference. For example, a bank that has loaned a bankrupt $2,000, and happens to have $1,500 of the bankrupt's on deposit at the time of bankruptcy, is a preferred creditor to the extent of the deposit. It may seize the deposit under its right of setoff.

Fraudulent Conveyances

A transfer of property by a bankrupt debtor may be fraudulent under either federal or state law. The trustee may proceed under either to set aside a fraudulent conveyance. Under federal law, a fraudulent conveyance is a transfer within one year of the filing of the petition, with the intent, actual or implied, to hinder, delay, or defraud creditors. Under state law, the period may be longer and is usually within the range of two to five years.

An actual intent to hinder, delay, or defraud creditors may be present. If so, the trustee will be successful in setting aside the conveyance. The intent to hinder, delay, or defraud creditors may also be implied. Such is the case when the debtor is insolvent and makes a transfer for less than a full and adequate consideration. The intent will also be implied when the transfer results in insolvency. *Implied intent* means that the law conclusively supplies such intent regardless of the actual intent of the debtor. A conveyance of property to a relative or a friend is a typical situation in which the intent will be implied.

If the debtor is in business, the intent to defraud will be implied where the transfer is without fair consideration, if it leaves the businessman with an unreasonably small amount of capital, even though he may still be solvent. Whether or not the remaining capital is unreasonably small is a question of fact.

Fraudulent intent sufficient to avoid a transfer without fair consideration may be implied from the state of mind of the debtor at the time of the transfer. For example, assume that A is about to enter business and that he plans to incur debts in the business. Because of A's concern that he may be unable to meet these potential obligations, he transfers all his property to his wife without consideration. Such a transfer may be set aside as fraudulent, and the requisite intent is supplied by the factual situation at the time of the transfer and the state of mind of the transferor. The actual financial condition of the debtor in such a case is not controlling but does shed some light on the intent factor and state of mind of the debtor.

Other Bankruptcy Proceedings

The previous sections have discussed ordinary bankruptcies. The Bankruptcy Act also contains provisions that are for the purpose of debtor relief rather than the liquidation of assets. These debtor relief provisions are designed to assist debtors by developing some plan to enable them to pay their debts in full. Most plans involve an extension of time for payment and such other relief as cancellation of executory contracts and determination of the priorities of claims so that the pressure by creditors is alleviated. In addition to aiding the debtor, arrangement and reorganization provisions also aid the majority of creditors by allowing them to work with the debtor in attempting to straighten out his affairs.

Arrangements to delay the payment of debts and reorganization plans of corporations must be approved by the court and by a stipulated percentage of the creditors who are affected by the plans. Secured creditors are not affected by extension arrangements and wage earner plans.

Wage earner plans are available to persons who desire to work out a means to pay off unsecured creditors over a period of time in lieu of filing an ordinary petition in bankruptcy. A *wage earner* is a person whose principal income is derived from wages, salary, or commissions. Such a plan enables a person having financial problems and being pressed by his creditors to work out a long-range program to pay off his debts. The debtor submits his future earnings to the supervision and control of the court for the purpose of carrying out the approved plan. If the plan is not carried out, the wage earner may be entitled to convert it to straight bankruptcy. Unfortunately, many wage earner plans are converted to regular bankruptcy before much of the indebtedness is paid.

REVIEW QUESTIONS AND PROBLEMS

1. What is the major purpose of the law of bankruptcy?

2. To what extent does a discharge in bankruptcy cause harm to the debtor's credit rating? Explain.

3. Define the following terms: *provable claims, dividend, preference, fraudulent transfer, wage earner, voidable transfer.*

4. A is insolvent. His assets are $50,000 in value, and his liabilities are $100,000. State whether the following transactions (1) would justify the filing of a petition in involuntary bankruptcy by his other creditor. If so, (2) would they be recoverable preferences?

    a. A paid creditor X in full on an open account.

    b. A gave creditor Y a mortgage on part of A's property.

    c. A paid creditor Z in full a debt secured by a mortgage on property owned by A.

    d. A borrowed $10,000 from creditor R and gave a mortgage on A's property to secure a loan.

5. A was able to prove in court that B committed libel against A with malice, which resulted in a judgment against B. B later filed a petition for bankruptcy. Will a discharge in bankruptcy relieve B from his debt to A? Why?

6. A petition in involuntary bankruptcy was filed against K on November 29. On November 30, K sold to M $16,000 in accounts receivable for $15,600, M

knowing of the petition in bankruptcy. K used these funds to meet payroll and taxes. On December 10, K was adjudicated a bankrupt, and the trustee sought to obtain the return of the accounts. The court allowed the trustee to recover. Was this decision sound? Why?

7. A staged a fireworks display at which B was injured due to A's negligence. B sued A and obtained a judgment against him. Before B could collect, A deeded all his real property to his wife. Under what circumstances can B collect from the real estate? Explain.

8. The ABC company had outstanding liabilities of $250,000 and assets of $300,000. However, at the insistence of its three major creditors, the company made a general assignment of its property for the benefit of creditors. Is this an act of bankruptcy? Why?

9. X, a Russian immigrant, ran a one-man shoe store. He kept his papers, what there were of them, on a nail on the wall. The business made about $6,500 per year, mostly in cash trade. X filed a voluntary petition in bankruptcy, and Y, a creditor, objected to his discharge. What result? Why?

10. At the time the XYZ company sold merchandise to A, a retailer, XYZ filed a financing statement that covered after-acquired property. Three days before A instituted a bankruptcy proceeding, XYZ obtained possession of property covered by the security agreement. Must XYZ return the inventory to the trustee in bankruptcy? Why?

VI AGENCY AND EMPLOYMENT

30 INTRODUCTION TO AGENCY AND EMPLOYMENT

AGENCY

Introduction The term *agency* is used to describe the legal relationship that exists when one person acts on behalf of and under the control of another person. The person who acts for another is called an *agent.* The person for whom he acts and who controls the agent is called a *principal.* Traditionally, issues of agency law arise when the agent has attempted to enter into a contract on behalf of his principal. However, the law of agency includes several aspects of the law of torts. Although tort litigation usually uses the terms *master* and *servant* rather than principal and agent, both relationships are encompassed within the broad legal classification of agency law.

The principles of agency law are essential for the conduct of business transactions. A corporation, as a legal entity, can function only through agents. The law of partnership is to a large degree a special application of agency principles to that particular form of business organization. It is not surprising, therefore, that a substantial number of agency issues are involved in litigation. Case law provides us with most of the principles applicable to the law of agency.

Agency issues are usually discussed within a framework of three parties: the principal (P), the agent (A), and the third party (T), with whom A contracts or against whom A commits a tort while in P's service. The following examples illustrate the problems and issues involved in the law of agency.

1. T v. P. Third party sues principal for breach of a contract that T entered into with A or for damages because of a tort committed by A.

443

2. T v. A. Third party sues agent personally for breach of the contract entered into by the agent or for committing a tort.

3. P v. T. Principal sues third party for breach of a contract that A entered into with T for P.

4. A v. T. Agent sues third party for some loss suffered by A. For example, the loss of a commission due to T's interference with a contract.

5. P v. A. Principal sues agent for loss caused by latter's failure to follow his duties, such as to obey instructions.

6. A v. P. Agent sues principal for injuries suffered in course of employment, for wrongful discharge, or for sums due for services or advancements.

Agency Terminology An agent may act on behalf of a designated principal, in which case the latter is called a *disclosed principal.* If the agent purports to act for himself and keeps his agency a secret, the principal is called an *undisclosed principal.* A third term, *partially disclosed principal,* is used to describe the situation in which the agent acknowledges that he is acting for a principal but does not disclose his identity.

Some persons who perform services for others are known as *independent contractors.* A person may contract for the services of another in such a way as to have full and complete control over the details and manner in which the work will be conducted, or he may simply contract for a certain end result. If the agreement provides merely that the second party is to accomplish a certain result and that he has full control over the manner and methods to be pursued in bringing about the result, he is deemed an independent contractor. The party contracting with an independent contractor and receiving the benefit of his service is usually called a *proprietor.* A proprietor is generally not responsible to third parties for the independent contractor's actions, either in contract or in tort. On the other hand, if the second party places his services at the disposal of the first in such a manner that the action of the second is generally controlled by the former, an agency relation is established.

Classification of Agents Agents are frequently classified by the functions they perform and by the rights and powers they possess. Two common terms are *broker* and *factor.* A *broker* is an agent with special and limited authority to procure a customer in order that the owner can effect a sale or exchange of property. For example, a real estate broker has authority to find a buyer for another's real estate. The real estate remains under the control of the owner. A *factor* is a person who has possession and control of another's personal property, such as goods, and is authorized to sell such property. A factor has a property interest and may sell the property in his own name, whereas a broker may not.

Agents are also classified as *general* or *special* agents. A *general* agent has much broader authority than does a special agent. Some cases define a general agent as one authorized to conduct a series of transactions involving a continuity of service, whereas a *special* agent conducts a single transaction or a series of transactions without continuity of service.

**Capacity
of Parties** It is generally stated that anyone who may act for himself may act through an agent. To this rule there is one well-recognized exception. An infant may enter into a contract, and so long as he does not disaffirm, the agreement is binding. However, there is considerable authority to the effect that any appointment of an agent by an infant is void and not merely voidable. Under this view any agreement entered into by such an agent would be ineffective, and an attempted disaffirmance by the minor would be superfluous. Many recent cases hold, however, that a contract of the agent on behalf of a minor principal is voidable only and is subject to rescission or ratification by the minor the same as if the minor had personally entered into the contract.

An infant may act as an agent for an adult, and agreements he makes for his principal while acting within his authority are binding on the principal. Although the infant agent has a right to terminate his contract of agency at his will, as long as he continues in the employment his acts within the scope of the authority conferred upon him become those of his principal.

**Formal
Requirements** As a general rule, no particular formalities are required to create an agency. The appointment may be either written or oral, and the relationship may be expressed or implied.

There are, however, two situations in which formalities are required. First, when the purpose of the agency can be exercised only by the signing of a formal document, the agency must be created in writing. When a formal instrument is used for conferring authority upon the agent, he is said to possess a *power of attorney*. The agent is called an *attorney in fact* to distinguish him from an *attorney at law*, the term used to describe lawyers. A power of attorney may be general, giving the agent authority to act in all respects as the principal could act, or it may be special, granting to the agent only restricted authority. A power of attorney is customarily executed before a notary public.

Second, the statute of frauds in the majority of the states requires that any agent who is given power to sell or to convey any interest in or concerning real estate must obtain such power by a written authorization from the principal.

Case: P sued D for specific performance of a real estate contract. P had contracted to purchase land owned jointly by D and his sister. The sister signed the contract individually and as agent for D. D had not authorized the contract but had orally agreed to its terms. D later refused to go along with the sale and asserted the statute of frauds as a defense.

Issue: Is the statute of frauds a defense?

Decision: Yes.

Reason: The statute of frauds requires all authorizations of persons to sell or convey any real estate to be in writing. Here the sister's authority was oral.

Dineff v. Wernecke, 190 N.E.2d 308 (Ill.) 1963.

In most states the law does not require a written agreement to contract with an ordinary real estate broker. The function of the broker is merely to find a buyer with whom the seller is willing to contract. Normally he has no authority to enter into a binding contract to convey the property. However, in many states a "listing agreement" is required to be in writing by special statute. If not, the real estate broker is not entitled to a commission.

Case: P, a real estate broker, found a ready, willing, and able buyer for D's real estate. D sold the real estate to the purchaser found by P but refused to pay P the commission orally agreed to. The state had a law that required that all listing agreements be in writing.

Issue: Is P entitled to the commission?

Decision: No.

Reasons: 1. The purpose of the law requiring a listing agreement to be in writing is similar to that of the statute of frauds, which is to prevent a party from being compelled by oral and perhaps false testimony to be held responsible for a contract he claims he never made.

2. To recover a real estate sales commission, the broker must establish that sellers had entered into a contract with the broker to sell their

property for a commission, and the only legitimate evidence of such an agreement is a written listing agreement containing all ingredients expressly mandated by law.

Green Mountain Realty, Inc. v. Fish, 336 A.2d 187 (Vt.) 1975.

When an agent signs a simple contract or commercial paper, he should execute it in such a fashion as to clearly indicate his representative capacity. If the signature fails to indicate the actual relationship of the parties and fails to identify the party intended to be bound, the agent may be personally liable on the instrument. Many states permit the use of oral evidence to show the intention of the agent and the third party when the signature is ambiguous—the agent is allowed to offer proof that it was not intended that he assume personal responsibility. The Code contains express provisions on the liability of an agent who signs commercial paper. These were discussed in Chapter 24. Also, in contracts in general the agent may be liable if he fails to clearly indicate his representative capacity. If he does so indicate, liability may be avoided.

TERMINATION OF AGENCY RELATIONSHIPS

Introduction Two basic issues are involved with the subject of termination of an agency relationship. First, what acts or facts are sufficient to terminate the authority of the agent insofar as the immediate parties are concerned? Second, what is required to terminate the agent's authority insofar as third parties are concerned? The latter question recognizes that an agent may continue to have the *power* to bind the principal but not the *right* to do so. The methods of termination are usually divided into termination by act of the parties and termination by operation of law. The discussion in the sections that follow is limited to termination of the agency relationship and is not applicable to employment generally.

It should be recognized that termination of the employer-employee relationship will frequently be subject to the terms of an applicable collective bargaining agreement. In addition, public policy considerations may deny the employers the right to terminate the employment relationship with impunity. Public policy preventing termination of employment is found in the provisions of the civil rights laws relating to hiring, firing, promotion, and tenure of the employment. Courts in recent years have added other grounds for imposing liability on employers for wrongful discharge even if the employment relationship is one described as at will. Liability has been imposed for discharges that resulted from (1) refusing to give perjured testimony, (2) resisting sexual advances, and (3) serving on a jury.

447

Case: P, an employee of D, was called for jury duty. D wrote a letter to the court asking that P be excused. P told the court that she would like to serve. P, after serving three days on a jury received a notice from D that her employment was terminated. P then sued D in tort for the wrongful termination of her employment.

Issue: Is an employer liable for discharging an employee for a socially undesirable motive?

Decision: Yes.

Reasons: 1. Generally, in the absence of a contract or legislation to the contrary, an employer can discharge an employee at any time and for any cause and an employee can quit at any time for any cause. Such a termination by the employer or the employee is not a breach of contract and ordinarily does not create a tortious cause of action.

2. However, there are instances in which the employer's reason or motive for discharging the employee harms or interferes with an important interest of the community and therefore justifies compensation to the employee.

3. The jury system and jury duty are high on the scale of American institutions and citizen obligations. If employers are permitted to discharge employees with impunity for fulfilling these obligations, the system will be adversely affected. The will of the community would be threatened. Therefore the discharge is tortious.

Nees v. Hocks, 536 P.2d 512 (Or.) 1975.

By Act of the Parties Termination by act of the parties includes termination by force of their agreement or by the act of one or both of the parties.

An example of the former is an agency that is created to continue for a definite period of time. It ceases, by virtue of the terms of the agreement, at the expiration of the stipulated period. If the parties consent to the continuation of the relationship beyond such period, the courts imply the formation of a new contract of employment. The new agreement contains the same terms as the old one and continues for a like period of time, except that no implied contract can run longer than one year because of the statute of frauds.

Another example is an agency created to accomplish a certain purpose, which automatically ends with the completion of the task assigned. In such case third parties are not entitled to notice of the termination. Furthermore when it is possible for one of several agents to perform the task, such as selling certain real estate, it is held that performance by the first party terminates the authority of the other agents without notice of termination being required.

Many, if not most, agency contracts do not provide for the duration of the agreement. A contract for permanent employment, not supported by any consideration other than the performance of duties and payment of wages, is a contract for an indefinite period and terminable at the will of either party at any time.

Some agency agreements purport to be for a definite period, but on close examination are actually terminable at will.

Case: Suit was brought for improper termination of a contract of employment. Ps were employed by D under a contract that said it would remain in effect for a period of twelve months, and would be automatically renewed for twelve-month terms, "unless sooner terminated." Ps were discharged before the completion of the first twelve-month period.

Issue: Did D have the right to terminate the contract before the end of the first twelve-month term?

Decision: Yes.

Reason: An employment contract for a stated term that is expressly terminable by either party upon notice is valid and is in effect an agency terminable at will. The phrase "unless sooner terminated" refers to the original twelve-month period as well as to the additional periods.

Brekken v. Reader's Digest Special Products, Inc., 353 F.2d 505 (1965).

Any contract may be terminated by mutual agreement; therefore, the agency relationship may be canceled in this manner. Furthermore, as a general rule, either party to the agreement has full *power* to terminate it whenever he desires, although he possesses no *right* to do so. Wrongful termination of the agency by either party subjects him to a suit for damages by the other party. An exercise of the power without the right is a wrongful termination.

**Wrongful
Termination**
As a general rule and subject to the exceptions previously noted, an employment that continues at the will of the parties may be rightfully terminated by either party at any time. Termination is not a breach of contract, but tort liability may be injured if public policy demands it. On the other hand, if the employer wrongfully terminates a contract that was to continue for an agreed period, there is liability for damages for breach of contract. Of course if the agent is discharged for cause, such as for the failure to follow instructions, he may not recover damages from the employer.

The employee whose employment has been wrongfully cut short is entitled to recover compensation for work done before his dismissal and an additional sum for damages. Most states permit him to bring an action either immediately following the breach, in which event he recovers prospective damages, or after the period has expired, in which event he recovers the damages actually sustained. In the latter case, as a general rule he is compelled to deduct from the compensation called for in the agreement the amount that he has been able to earn during the interim. Some agreements contain exceptions to this rule, and courts sometimes create exceptions. For example, if an employee is not supposed to work full time, earnings would not be deducted.

Case: P was employed by D to serve as its president. The employment contract was for three years and provided that P's services as president could be terminated by the employer, but if this happened the employee could remain available as a consultant at the same salary. D removed P as president, and P filed suit for the balance due under the contract. D claims that any earnings of P must be offset against the salary.

Issue: Is P entitled to the full salary for the balance of the contract period?

Decision: Yes.

Reasons: 1. A contract of employment for a definite term may not be terminated before the expiration of such term except for cause or by mutual agreement unless the right to do so is reserved in the contract.

2. A wrongfully discharged employee may not sit idly by and must make a reasonable effort to secure other work, and any income from such work may be offset against the damages sought. However, an exception to this rule is recognized where the wrongfully discharged employee is not required to devote his entire time to work under the contract.

3. P could have earned other income and still have been available as a consultant.

Rochester Capital Leasing Corp. v. McCracken, 2965 N.E.2d 375 (Ind.) 1973.

As noted in the foregoing case, a wrongfully discharged employee is under a duty to exercise reasonable diligence in finding other work of like character. Idleness is not encouraged by the law. However, apparently this rule does not require him to seek employment in a new locality or to accept work of a different kind or more menial character. The duty is to find work of like kind, provided it is available in the particular locality.

Termination by Law Certain acts are held by law to terminate the agency. Among these are death, insanity, bankruptcy of either of the parties, or destruction of the subject matter of the agency. Bankruptcy has such an effect only in case it affects the subject matter of the agency.

It is said of such cases that the agency is immediately terminated and that no notice need be given to either the agent or the third parties. However, with reference to insanity, unless the principal has been publicly adjudged insane, it is believed that an agent's contracts are binding on the principal unless the third party is aware of the mental illness, especially where the contract is beneficial to the insane principal's estate.

Agency Coupled with an Interest As a general rule, any agency contract may be terminated at any time by either party. As previously noted, the power to terminate exists even though the right to do so may not. If the power is exercised wrongfully, there is liability. Agency contracts are not specifically enforceable against the principal because of the lack of mutuality in the remedy. Because the principal could not require the agent to work (involuntary servitude), the agency cannot, as a general rule, compel the principal to continue the agency.

Case: P, a doctor, had organized D hospital and had been appointed medical and surgical director under an "irrevocable" ten-year contract. Before the expiration of the term, a controversy arose in the board of directors. They sought to discharge P, who then brought suit to enjoin his discharge.

Issue: Can P be discharged?

Decision: Yes.

Reasons: 1. Personal service contracts are generally not specifically enforceable.

2. A principal may revoke an agency, subject to the right of the agent to damages. This is so because of the lack of mutuality of enforcement. Should specific enforcement be granted for the employee, the agent could still resign at any time, and the employer would be remediless except for damages (involuntary servitude). Since the employer is limited to damages, so is the employee.

Sarokhan v. Fair Lawn Memorial Hospital, Inc., 199 A.2d 52 (N.J.) 1964.

To the general rule, however, there is one well-recognized exception known as *an agency coupled with an interest.* The term describes the relationship that exists when the agent has an actual beneficial interest

451

in the property that is the subject matter of the agency. For example, a mortgage that contains a provision naming the mortgagee as agent to sell the property in the event of default creates an agency coupled with an interest in property. An agency coupled with an interest in property cannot be terminated unilaterally by the principal and is not terminated by events (such as death or bankruptcy of the principal) that otherwise terminate agencies by operation of law. The net effect is that an agency coupled with an interest in property cannot be terminated without the consent of the agent.

An agency coupled with an interest in property must be distinguished from *an agency coupled with an obligation.* This latter term describes the situation in which the agency is created as a source of reimbursement to the agent. For example, an agent who is given the right to sell a certain automobile and to apply the proceeds on a claim against the principal is an agency coupled with an obligation. Such an agency is a hybrid between the usual agency and the agency coupled with an interest in property. The agency coupled with an obligation cannot unilaterally be terminated by the principal, but death or bankruptcy of the principal will terminate the agency by operation of law.

Under either type of agency, it should be clear that the interest in the subject matter must be greater than the mere expectation of profits to be realized or in the proceeds to be derived from the sale of the property. The interest must be in the property itself. For example, a real estate broker is not an agent coupled with an interest, even though he expects a commission from the proceeds of the sale. Likewise a principal who has appointed an agent to sell certain goods on commission has the power to terminate the agency at any time, although such conduct might constitute a breach of the agreement.

**Notice in
Event of
Termination**
Termination of the agency, as explained above, may take place by act of the parties or by operation of law. If the parties by their own action have terminated the agency, it is the duty of the principal to notify all third parties who have learned of the existence of the agency of its termination. Without such notice, the agent would still possess apparent authority to act for his principal. Those persons entitled to such notice may be divided into two groups: (1) those who have previously relied upon the agency by dealing with the agent; and (2) those who have never previously dealt with the agent, but who nevertheless have learned of the agency. The principal's duty to the first class can be satisfied only by the actual receipt of notice of the termination by the third party. The principal satisfies his duty to the second group by giving public notice, such as newspaper publicity, in the location involved. If any one of the second group does not actually learn of the termination and deals with the former agent,

there is no cause of action against the principal because of the public notice.

Where the agency is terminated by death, insanity, or bankruptcy, no duty to notify third parties is placed upon the principal. Such matters receive publicity through newspapers, official records, and otherwise, and third parties normally become aware of the termination without the necessity for additional notification.

THE EMPLOYMENT RELATIONSHIP

Introduction Although the law of agency has developed primarily from decided cases, the law as it affects most aspects of the employment relationship is statutory. The statutes are society's means of controlling such matters as the standard of living of workers, working conditions, and equal job opportunity for all.

Among the statutes that regulate employment are the federal statutes that regulate labor-management relations and especially collective bargaining. These statutes, the judicial decisions interpreting them, and the actions of the administrative agency that enforces and administers them are the subject matter of Chapter 34.

In addition to labor laws relating to union activity, there are both federal and state statutes that regulate wages, hours, and working conditions. The Fair Labor Standards Act controls such matters as minimum wages, hours, and the records to be kept by employers. State laws control such matters as child labor, safety devices, workmen's compensation, unemployment compensation, and fair employment practices. It must be recognized that many of the rights and duties of both employers and employees are determined by these statutes and the administrative agencies operating pursuant to them. The businessman must be familiar with these statutes and the regulations related to them and must comply with those applicable to his business.

**Discrimination
in Employment** Many cities, most states, and the federal government have enacted statutes designed to prevent discrimination in hiring, promotion, pay, or layoffs because of race, color, creed, sex, national origin, or age. These statutes have modified the basic common-law concept that an employer had a free choice in selecting his employees and, in the absence of a contract, a free choice in discharging them. They have been enacted as a part of the general philosophy of government that all persons should have equality of opportunity. These statutes frequently contain criminal sanctions and authorize civil suits for damages.

The basic federal law or equal employment opportunity was enacted in 1964. The Civil Rights Act of 1964, as now amended, covers all employers with fifteen or more employees, labor unions with fifteen or more members, labor unions that operate a hiring hall, and employment agencies. This 1972 amendment extended coverage to state and local governments and to educational institutions with respect to persons whose work involves educational activities.

The types of employer action in which discrimination is prohibited include discharge; refusal to hire; compensation; and terms, conditions, or privileges of employment.

A federal administrative agency known as the Equal Employment Opportunity Commission has the primary responsibility for enforcing the act. The EEOC is composed of five members, not more than three of whom may be members of the same political party. In the course of its investigations, the commission has broad authority to examine and copy evidence, require the production of documentary evidence, hold hearings, and subpoena and examine witnesses under oath.

By a 1972 amendment, the EEOC has the power to file a civil suit in court and to represent a person charging a violation of the act. However, it must first exhaust efforts to conciliate the claim. The remedies available in such an action include reinstatement with back pay for the victim of an illegal discrimination and injunctions against future violations of the law.

The federal law seeks to preserve state and local employment practice laws. Where an alleged violation of federal law, if true, is violative of a state or local law, the commission may not act until sixty days after the proceedings, if any, have been commenced under that law. Similarly, the commission must notify the appropriate officials and defer all action until the local authority has had, in general, at least sixty days to resolve the matter. In either case, the sixty-day waiting requirement is dispensed with if the local proceeding is terminated before that time.

tests Practices involving recruiting, hiring, and promotion of employees are often charged with being discriminatory and in violation of the law. For example, the courts have held that the use of a standardized general intelligence test in selecting and placing personnel is prohibited as being discriminatory on the basis of race. Tests neutral on their face, and even neutral in terms of intent, cannot be maintained if they operate to "freeze" the status quo of prior discriminatory employment practices. If an employment practice cannot be shown to be related to job performance, the practice is prohibited. The Civil Rights Act proscribes not only overt discrimination but also practices that are fair in form but discriminatory in operation. As a result, job tests have been dropped by many companies because of the difficulty of proving that all questions are validly related to job performance.

seniority   Bona fide seniority systems are often used to select persons to be laid off in the event an employer is reducing its labor force. They are also used to provide the basis for many promotions. As a result of seniority, the last hired are usually the first fired. Decisions based on seniority have been challenged as violating the laws relating to equal employment opportunity. The challenges arose when recently hired members of minority groups were laid off during periods of economic downturn.

While the law to be applied when seniority systems conflict with equal employment opportunity is still developing, certain principles are emerging. If a company has not discriminated in its employment practices since the adoption of the Civil Rights Act, its seniority system for purpose of layoff is probably valid. However, promotions cannot be awarded on the basis of seniority if the effect is to lock minorities into less desirable jobs and to legally carry forward the effects of past discrimination. In addition, the law requires that employees be given retroactive seniority if they have been discriminated against and denied equal employment opportunity since 1964. In addition to retroactive seniority to the date of the original employment application, minority employees are entitled to back pay and to priority consideration for vacancies when discrimination in violation of statute is proven.

sex discrimination   Discrimination based on sex is a major area of equal employment opportunity litigation. Historically, states had enacted many laws designed to protect women. For example, many states by statute prohibited the employment of women in certain occupations, such as those that require lifting heavy objects. Others barred women from working during the night or working more than a given number of hours per week or day. Under EEOC guidelines and court decisions, such statutes are not a defense to a charge of illegal sex discrimination. Other EEOC guidelines forbid (1) classifying jobs as male or female by employers and (2) advertising in help-wanted columns that are designated male or female, unless sex is a bona fide job qualification. Courts construe this exception narrowly. No bona fide occupational qualification was found to exist where there was (1) a rule requiring airline stewardesses to be single, (2) a policy of hiring only females as flight cabin attendants, (3) a rule against hiring females with preschool-age children, and (4) a telephone company policy against hiring females as switchmen because of the alleged heavy lifting involved in the job. For sex to be a valid job qualification, it must be demonstrably relevant to job performance. Very few jobs meet this test.

There is also a federal law that requires that women be paid wages equivalent to those paid men for equivalent work (or vice versa).

455

Executive personnel are exempt from the Equal Pay Act. Another federal law prohibits discrimination based on age. This law applies to persons between forty and sixty-five years of age. Thus, if persons over forty are just as qualified as younger workers to handle their jobs, they usually must be kept.

The desire to eliminate the adverse effects of past discrimination prompted most governmental bodies and many private employers to adopt policies and practices described as affirmative action programs. These affirmative action programs usually established goals for hiring and promoting members of minority groups. These goals were to be accomplished by active recruitment programs and by giving priority to minorities. Members of such groups were to be given priority when there were fewer of them working in a given job category than one would reasonably expect there should be, considering their availability.

Affirmative action programs and similar efforts have resulted in charges of reverse discrimination by white males. Courts have recently held that the law prohibits discrimination of any kind and that overt attempts to favor minorities are also illegal. Double standards in selection and promotion policies are illegal today. The law is trying to achieve equality of opportunity without discrimination against either the majority of persons or the members of minority groups.

REVIEW QUESTIONS AND PROBLEMS

1. Define the following terms introduced in this chapter: *agent*, *principal*, *undisclosed principal*, and *independent contractor*.

2. Distinguish and compare a *broker* and a *factor*.

3. M, a minor, appoints S, a stockbroker, as his agent to buy and sell stock. M deposits $10,000 with S. The investments are later worth $3,000. Can M recover the other $7,000 from S? Why?

4. What is a power of attorney? Give an illustration of a situation in which it would be used.

5. List the six situations in which agency issues may be litigated. Give an example of each.

6. What subjects are regulated by the Fair Labor Standards Act?

7. List various acts or events that will terminate the agency relationship.

8. Define the term *agency coupled with an interest* and give an example of such an agency relationship.

9. What responsibility does an employee who is wrongfully discharged from a job have to seek a new job? Explain.

10. List the classes of persons who are entitled to notice of termination of an agency relationship and indicate the type of notice each is entitled to.

11. P, the owner of a drive-in grocery store, signed an exclusive-listing agreement with A, a licensed real estate broker. After three months P leased the store to T and revoked A's authority. Does A have any remedy against P? Why?

12. For many years, a posh metropolitan restaurant maintained a policy of hiring only men among its fifty waiters. A woman applied for a job as a waitress and was turned down solely because of her sex. Explain the assistance available to her from the federal government.

13. A, a real estate agent, was authorized by P to sell several lots at a specified price. A was to receive a 5 percent commission on each lot sold. Before any lots were sold, P revoked the authorization. Was A's authority irrevocable as a power coupled with an interest? Why?

14. A was employed by P to manage a farm. A lived in a house on the land and took care of all the details of running the farm. Customarily A hired T to bale and hay in a certain field. Unknown to T, P revoked A's authority, though A continued to live in the house. A gave T permission to cut the hay "as usual." Is P liable to T? Why?

15. X managed a store owned by his brother, Y, and for several years made purchases from Z of clothing and other goods for the store. Z customarily extended credit for these purchases. After an argument Y revoked X's authority. X then purchased from Z on credit a large order of goods similar to those sold in the store. May Z recover from Y? Why?

16. P engaged A to operate a retail lumber business in the latter's name. A sold merchandise to T on credit. Later P notified T that A's agency was terminated and directed T to pay the debt to P. T disregarded instructions and paid the obligation to A, who failed to account to P. May P collect from T? Why?

17. A gave two real estate brokers, X and Y, simple listings on his house. X found a ready, willing, and able buyer one day, and before A could notify the other broker, Y, Y also found a buyer. Is Y entitled to a commission? Why?

18. A, a buyer for the X department store, was discharged. Y had never sold to A but knew that A was X's buyer. After A was discharged, an article about his changing jobs was in the newspaper, but Y did not read it. If A purchases goods on credit from Y, charging them to X, is X liable therefor? Why?

19. What types of employers are covered by the Civil Rights Act of 1964, as amended?

20. What is the purpose of the Civil Rights Act of 1964?

21. What federal agency has the primary responsibility for enforcing the Civil Rights Act of 1964?

22. What is the criterion by which employment practices are determined to be legal?

31 AGENCY AND THE LAW OF CONTRACTS

Introduction The law of agency is essentially concerned with issues of contractual liability. Because corporations act only through agents and because partners in a partnership are agents of the partnership, a substantial portion of all contracts entered into by businesses are entered into by agents on behalf of principals. Whenever a contract is entered into by an agent, issues as to the liability of the various parties may arise. For example, is the agent personally liable on the contract? Is the principal bound? Can the principal enforce the agreement against the third party? This chapter will discuss these issues and others that frequently arise out of contracts entered into by agents on behalf of principals.

THE LIABILITY OF AGENTS

Based on the Contract As a general rule, an agent is not personally liable on contracts into which he has entered on behalf of his disclosed principal. The liability is solely that of the principal. To this rule there are three well-recognized exceptions. First, if the agent carelessly executes a written agreement, he may fail to bind his principal and incur personal liability. For example, an agent who signs a negotiable instrument for his principal but fails to execute it in the principal's name by naming himself as agent or otherwise fails to show his representative capacity is personally liable.

Second, the third party may request the agent to be personally bound on the contract. This may be due to lack of confidence in the financial ability of the principal, because the agent's credit rating is superior to that of the principal, or some other personal reason. When the agent voluntarily assumes the burden of performance in his personal capacity, he is liable in the event of nonperformance by his principal.

Third, if the agent does not disclose his agency or name his principal, he binds himself and becomes subject to all liabilities, express and implied, created by the contract and transaction, in the same manner as if he were the principal. If an agent wishes to avoid personal liability, the duty is upon the agent to disclose the agency. There is no duty on the third party to discover the agency.

An agent who purports to be a principal is liable as a principal. The fact that the agent is known to be a commission merchant, auctioneer, or other professional agent is immaterial. He must disclose not only that he is an agent but the identity of his principal if the agent is not to have personal liability. Any agent for an undisclosed or partially disclosed principal assumes personal liability on the contract into which he enters.

Based on Breach of Warranty

An agent's liability may be implied from the circumstances as well as being the direct result of the contract. Liability in such situations is usually said to be implied and to arise from the breach of an implied warranty. There are two basic warranties that are used to imply liability: the warranty of authority and the warranty that the principal is competent.

As a general rule, an agent impliedly warrants to third parties that he possesses power to affect the contractual relations of his principal. If in any particular transaction the agent fails to possess this power, the agent violates this implied warranty, and he is liable to third parties for the damages resulting from his failure to bind the principal. The agent may or may not be aware of this lack of authority, and he may honestly believe that he possesses the requisite authority. Awareness of lack of authority and honesty is immaterial. If an agent exceeds his authority, he is liable to the third parties for the breach of the warranty of authority.

Case: D was an agent of X, a broker. D contacted P and told P that X had certain land for sale and that if P found a buyer, P would be paid 40 percent of the commission. D had not consulted X about the arrangement. P sued D for the 40 percent of the commission on the sale.

Issue: Is the agent personally liable on the contract?

Decision: Yes.

Reasons: 1. An agent representing authority which exceeds his actual authority is personally responsible and liable to the party to whom he makes such an unauthorized representation if the other party justifiably relies upon the representation.

2. A person who purports to make a contract, conveyance, or representation on behalf of another who has full capacity but whom he has no power to bind, thereby becomes subject to liability to the other party thereto upon an implied warranty of authority, unless he has manifested that he does not make such warranty or the other party knows that the agent is not so authorized.

Glendale Realty, Inc. v. Johnson, 495 P.2d 1375 (Wash. App.) 1972.

Every agent who deals with third parties warrants that his principal is capable of being bound. Consequently, an agent who acts for a minor or a corporation not yet formed may find himself liable for the nonperformance of his principal. The same rule enables the third party to recover from the agent when his principal is an unincorporated association, such as a club, lodge, or other informal group. An unincorporated association is not a legal entity separate and apart from its members. In most states it cannot sue or be sued in the name it uses, but all members must be joined in a suit involving the unincorporated group. When an agent purports to bind such an organization, a breach of the warranty results because there is no entity capable of being bound. However, if the third party is fully informed that the principal is an unincorporated organization and he agrees to look entirely to it for performance, the agent is not liable.

The warranty that an agent has a competent principal must be qualified in one respect. An agent is not liable when, unknown to him, his agency has been cut short by the death of the principal. Death of the principal terminates an agency. Because death is usually accompanied by sufficient publicity to reach third parties, the facts are equally available to both parties, and no breach of warranty arises.

THE LIABILITY OF DISCLOSED PRINCIPALS

Introduction   A principal is liable on all contracts properly executed and entered into by an agent possessing actual or apparent authority to enter into the contract, provided that the third party knows that the agent is contracting for the principal. A principal is also liable on unauthorized contracts entered into by a purported agent, if the principal with knowledge of all the facts ratifies or affirms that he is bound by the contract. Therefore, a principal is not liable upon a contract that he has not actually or apparently authorized and has not ratified. The burden of proving the requisite authority or ratification is on the party dealing with the agent; the principal does not have the burden of proving lack of authority or lack of ratification. The agent's authority can come only from the principal. The agent by words or conduct cannot create his own authority unless the words or conduct are consented to or ratified by the principal. In addition, one who deals with an agent, knowing that he has exceeded his authority, does so at his peril.

**Actual
Authority**

Actual authority is that authority that a principal confers upon the agent or unintentionally by want of ordinary care allows the agent to believe himself to possess. Actual authority includes express authority and implied authority. The term *express authority* describes the authority explicitly given to the agent by the principal. *Implied authority* is used to describe authority that is necessarily incidental to the express authority or that arises because of business custom and usage or prior practices of the parties. Implied authority is sometimes referred to as *incidental authority;* it is required or reasonably necessary in order to carry out the purpose for which the agency was created.

Implied authority based on custom and usage varies from one locality to another and among different kinds of businesses. To illustrate: P appoints A as his agent to sell a certain used automobile for $900. As an incident to his authority to sell, A has authority to enter into a written contract with the purchaser and to sign P's name to the contract. Whether he has implied or incidental authority to sell on credit instead of cash or to warrant the condition of the car sold depends upon local custom. If it is customary for other agents in this locality to make warranties or sell on credit, this agent and the third party with whom he deals may assume he possesses such authority in the absence of knowledge to the contrary. Custom, in effect, creates a presumption of authority.

Implied authority must be distinguished from *apparent* or *ostensible authority* which is authority predicated on the theory of estoppel. This latter type of authority is discussed in the next section.

Implied authority cannot be derived from the words or conduct of the agent. A third person dealing with a known agent may not act negligently in regard to the extent of the agent's authority or blindly trust his statements in such regard but must use reasonable diligence and prudence in ascertaining whether the agent is acting within the scope of his authority. Similarly, if persons who deal with a purported agent desire to hold the principal liable on the contract, they must ascertain not only the fact of the agency but the nature and extent of the agent's authority. Should either the existence of the agency or the nature and extent of the authority be disputed, the burden of proof regarding these matters is upon the third party.

All agents, even presidents of corporations, have limitations on their authority. Authority is not readily implied. For example, possession of goods by one not engaged in the business of selling such goods does not create the implication of authority to sell. Authority to sell does not necessarily include the authority to extend credit, although custom may create such authority. The officers of a corporation must have actual authority to enter into transactions that are not in the ordinary course of the business of the corporation. For this reason, persons purchasing real estate from a corporation usually require a resolution of the board of directors specifically authorizing the sale.

Case: P sued D, a farming corporation, for specific performance of a contract for sale of some farmland. The contract had been signed by the president of the corporation. The board of directors had authorized the president to discuss the sale of the land but had not authorized the sale. The contract covered 35 percent of the corporate assets.

Issue: Is the corporation bound on the contract signed by its president?

Decision: No.

Reasons: 1. A president of a corporation is empowered to transact without special authority from the board of directors, all acts of ordinary nature which are incident to his office by usage or necessity.

2. A president does not have actual authority to sell 35 percent of a corporation's farmland unless the articles of incorporation give such authority or the board specifically authorized the sale.

3. There is no apparent authority for the president of a farming corporation to sell its land. Such a transaction is not in the usual course of business.

Willsey v. W. C. Porter Farms Company, 522 S.W.2d (Mo.) 1975.

**Apparent or
Ostensible
Authority**
The terms *apparent authority* and *ostensible authority* are synonymous. They describe the authority a principal, intentionally or by want of ordinary care, causes or allows a third person to believe the agent to possess. Liability of the principal for the ostensible agent's acts rests on the doctrine of estoppel. The estoppel is created by some conduct of the principal that leads the third party to believe that a person is his agent or that an actual agent possesses the requisite authority. This conduct must be known to and justifiably relied upon by the third party to his injury or damage. The injury or

damage may be a change of position, and the facts relied upon must be such that a reasonably prudent person would believe that the authority of the agency existed. Thus three usual essential elements of an estoppel—conduct, reliance, and injury—are required to create apparent authority.

theory The theory of apparent or ostensible authority is that if a principal by his words or conduct has led others to believe that he has conferred authority upon an agent he cannot be heard to assert, as against third persons who have relied thereon in good faith, that he did not intend to confer such power. The acts may include words, oral or written, or may be limited to conduct that reasonably interpreted by a third person causes that person to believe that the principal consents to have the act done on his behalf by the purported agent. Apparent authority requires more than the mere appearance of authority. The facts must be such that a person exercising ordinary prudence, acting in good faith, and conversant with business practices would be misled thereby. An agent's apparent authority to do an act for a principal must be based on the principal's words or conduct and cannot be based on anything the agent himself has said or done. An agent cannot unilaterally create his own apparent authority.

Case: Patterson and Jensen formed the P corporation. They opened a bank account at D bank with a signature card bearing both names. A corporate resolution required checks be paid only if signed by both. Patterson then spoke to the bank officials, saying he was desirous of changing the arrangements so that he might write checks alone because Jensen was in Las Vegas, several hundred miles away. The bank officials told him to change the signature card and to obtain a new corporate resolution. He did not do so but cashed two checks signed by his own name only, which D honored. Patterson absconded with the funds. D defends on the ground that Patterson had ostensible authority to change the signature card.

Issue: Was there such ostensible authority?

Decision: No.

Reasons: 1. Ostensible authority is grounded on the conduct of the principal that reasonably causes others to believe that the "agent" possesses authority.

2. Here the express conduct of the principal corporation was that such authority was not possessed by Patterson and there was no reliance on any act by the corporation.

Movie Films, Inc. v. First Security Bank of Utah, 447 P.2d 38 (Utah) 1968.

Apparent authority may be the basis for liability when the purported agent is in fact not an agent. It also may be the legal basis for finding that an actual agent possesses authority beyond that actually conferred. In other words, apparent authority may exist in one not an agent or it may expand the authority of an actual agent.

examples An agency by estoppel or additional authority by estoppel may arise from a course of dealing on the part of an agent, which is constantly ratified by the principal, or it may result from a person's holding himself out as an agent without any dissent on the part of the purported principal under conditions where the principal owed a duty to speak. To illustrate: Upon several occasions A indorses his principal's name to checks and has them cashed at the bank. The principal has never given the agent such authority, but no protest is lodged with the bank until the agent appropriates to his own use the proceeds from one of the checks. The principal then attempts to recover from the bank. By approval of the agent's previous unauthorized action, the principal has led the bank to reasonably assume that the agent possesses authority to indorse checks.

Perhaps the most common situation in which apparent authority is found to exist occurs when the actual authority is terminated but notice of this fact is not given to those entitled to receive it. Cancellation of actual authority does not terminate the apparent authority which was created by prior transactions (see Chapter 30).

Case: P was a former partner in a law firm. The firm had deposited checks in D bank by using a rubber stamp to indorse them. P withdrew from the firm, but he did not notify the bank that use of the stamp was no longer authorized. The law firm deposited a check payable to P in the D bank by using the stamp. The bank knew that P was no longer a partner. P sued D bank for the amount of the check.

Issue: Did the law firm have authority to indorse the check for P?

Decision: Yes.

Reasons: 1. An indorsement of a check may be made by an agent and the agent's authority may be actual, implied, or apparent.

2. Here there was apparent authority for use of the stamp in lieu of a signature. It arose from the former practice of using the stamp and the lack of notice that the authority was canceled.

Keane v. Pan American Bank, 309 So.2d 579 (Fla.App.) 1975.

Ratification by Principals   As previously noted, a principal may become bound on an unauthorized contract by ratifying it. Ratification is an express or implied adoption or confirmation, with knowledge of all material matters, by one person of a contract performed in his behalf by another who at that time assumed to act as his agent but lacked authority to do so. It is similar to ratification by an adult of a contract made while a minor. Ratification relates back to and is the equivalent of authority at the commencement of the act or time of the contract. It is the affirmance of a contract already made. It cures the defect of lack of authority and creates the relation of principal and agent.

capacity required   Various conditions must exist before a ratification will be effective to bring about a contractual relation between the principal and the third party. First, because ratification relates back to the time of the contract, ratification can be effective only when both the principal and the agent were capable of contracting at the time the contract was executed and are still capable at the time of ratification. For this reason, a corporation may not ratify contracts made by its promoters on the corporation's behalf before the corporation was formed. For the corporation to be bound by such agreements, a novation or an assumption of liability by the corporation must occur.

acting as agent   Second, an agent's act may be ratified only when he holds himself out as acting for the one who is alleged to have approved the unauthorized agreement. In other words, the agent must have professed to act as an agent. A person who professes to act for himself and who makes a contract in his own name does nothing that can be ratified, even though he intends at the time to let another have the benefit of his agreement.

Case: One of several owners of a parcel of real estate granted an option to X to buy the land. The party granting the option claimed to be the sole owner and did not purport to be the agent of anyone. The other owners refused to go along with the sale. The option consideration had benefited all the owners in that it had been used to pay expenses connected with the land.

Issue: Is the option binding on all owners? (Has there been a ratification?)

Decision: No.

Reasons: 1. The owner granting the option could not have been an agent of the other owners because an agent's authority to bind his principal on a contract to sell real estate must be in writing according to the statute of frauds.

465

2. The doctrine of ratification does not apply to an act claimed to have been ratified by a principal unless the original act was done by one who purported to act as an agent for a principal. Here he claimed to be the sole owner.

Pettit v. Vogt, 495 P.2d 395 (Okla.) 1972.

The above case established that an undisclosed principal may not ratify an unauthorized contract and hold the third party to it. In addition, the undisclosed principal cannot be held liable by the third party on the contract. However, it should be noted that an undisclosed principal who receives the benefits of a contract is liable in quasi contract for the benefits actually received and retained. To allow him to keep the benefits would be a form of unjust enrichment.

full knowledge Third, as a general rule, ratification does not bind the principal unless he acts with full knowledge of all the material facts attending negotiation and execution of the contract. Of course when there is express ratification and the principal acts without any apparent desire to know or to learn the facts, he may not later defend himself on the ground that he was unaware of all the material facts. When, however, ratification is to be implied from the conduct of the principal, he must act with knowledge of all important details.

The law is almost always concerned with mutuality of obligation. One party should not be bound to a contract if the other party is not also bound. Therefore, the law recognizes that the third party may withdraw from an unauthorized contract entered into by an agent at any time before it is ratified by the principal. If the third party were not allowed to withdraw, the unique situation in which one party is bound and the other is not would exist. However, it must be kept in mind that ratification does not require notice to the third party. As soon as conduct constituting ratification has been indulged in by the principal, the third party loses his right to withdraw.

Conduct Constituting Ratification Ratification may be either express or implied. Any conduct that definitely indicates an intention on the part of the principal to adopt the transaction will constitute ratification. It may take the form of words of approval to the agent, a promise to perform, or actual performance, such as delivery of the product called for in the agreement. Accepting the benefits of the contract or basing a suit on the validity of an agreement clearly amounts to ratification.

The issue of whether or not ratification has occurred is a question to be decided by the jury. Among the facts to be considered by the jury are the relationship of the parties, prior conduct, circumstances pertaining to the transaction, and the action or inaction of the alleged principal upon learning of the contract. Inaction or silence by the

466

principal creates difficulty in determining if ratification has occurred. Failure to speak may mislead the third party, and courts frequently find that a duty to speak exists where silence will mislead. Silence and inaction by the party to be charged as a principal, or failure to dissent and speak up when ordinary human conduct and fair play would normally call for some negative assertion within a reasonable time, tends to justify the inference that the principal acquiesced in the course of events and accepted the contract as his own. Acceptance and retention of the fruits of the contract with full knowledge of the material facts of the transaction is probably the most certain evidence of implied ratification. As soon as a principal learns of an unauthorized act by his agent, he should promptly repudiate it if he is to avoid liability on the theory of ratification.

At this point it should be mentioned that an unauthorized act may not be ratified in part and rejected in part. The principal cannot accept the benefits of the contract and refuse to assume its obligations. Because of this rule, a principal, by accepting the benefits of an authorized agreement, ratifies the means used in procuring the agreement, unless within a reasonable time after learning the actual facts he takes steps to return, so far as possible, the benefits he has received. Therefore, if an unauthorized agent commits fraud in procuring a contract, acceptance of the benefits ratifies not only the contract but the fraudulent acts as well, and the principal is liable for the fraud.

THE LIABILITY OF UNDISCLOSED PRINCIPALS

Introduction   For various reasons, a principal may desire to hide his identity. To achieve this secrecy, he will direct an agent to enter into all contracts in the agent's own name, leaving the third party either unaware of the existence of the principal (undisclosed principal) or unaware of the principal's *identity* (partially disclosed principal). The law relating to partially disclosed principals is the same as that relating to undisclosed principals, and they are treated together here. Such agreements are always entered into on the strength of the agent's credit, and the agent is liable thereon until such a time as the third party elects to hold the principal. The third party, upon learning of the principal's existence or identity, may elect to enforce the contract against the principal rather than against the agent. The undisclosed principal is responsible for all contracts entered into by the agent within the scope of the agent's actual authority, and he may be sued when his existence becomes known. Being unknown, the principal could not have created any apparent authority, consequently his liability is limited to actual authority—that which is expressly given and that which may be implied as incidental thereto.

Effect of a Settlement on Liability   In the preceding section it was stated that the third party, after learning of a previously undisclosed principal's interest in a transaction, might elect to look to the principal rather than to the agent for performance. Suppose, however, that the undisclosed principal supplied the agent with money to purchase the goods, but the agent purchased on credit and appropriated the money. In such a case the principal would be relieved of all responsibility. The same result obtains when the undisclosed principal *settles* with the agent after the contract is made and the goods are received, but before disclosure to the third party. Any bona fide settlement between principal and agent before disclosure releases the principal. A settlement cannot have this effect, however, when it is made after the third party has learned of the existence of the principal, and the principal is aware that his identity is known. The settlement rule is based on equitable principle. It is fair to the third party in that it gives him all the protection he originally bargained for, and it is fair to the principal in that it protects him against a second demand for payment.

Effect of an Election on Liability   Election means choice, and a choice becomes possible only when the third party learns of the existence and identity of the principal. If a settlement has taken place previously, no election is possible because only the agent then has liability. When there has been no settlement, the third party, when he learns of the existence of a previously undisclosed principal, may look either to the agent or to the principal for performance. However, if the third party elects to hold the principal liable, the agent is released. Similarly, if the third party elects to hold the agent, the previously undisclosed but now disclosed principal is released. It is simple to state that an election to hold one party releases the other from liability, but it is sometimes difficult to know when an election has occurred. However, it is clear that conduct by the third party that precedes the disclosure of the principal cannot constitute an election. Because of this rule, it has been held that an unsatisfied judgment obtained against the agent before disclosure of the principal will not bar a later action against the principal.

After disclosure, the third party may evidence his election by obtaining a judgment against one of the parties or by making an express declaration of his intention to hold one party and not the other. It has been held that sending a bill to one of the parties does not indicate an election. Most states also hold that the receipt of a negotiable instrument from either principal or agent does not show an election. The mere starting of a suit has been held insufficient to constitute an election, but if the case proceeds to judgment against either the agent or the principal, election has taken place although the judgment remains unpaid.

468

THE LIABILITY OF PRINCIPALS—SPECIAL SITUATIONS

Introduction   Many special problems arise in the law of agency as it relates to contractual liability and authority of agents. Some of these problems are founded on the relationship of the parties. For example, a spouse is generally liable for the contracts of the other spouse when such contracts involve family necessities. In most states this liability is statutory. Others involve special factual situations. For example, an existing emergency that necessitates immediate action adds sufficiently to the agent's powers to enable him to meet the situation. However, if time permits and the principal is available, any proposed remedy for the difficulty must be submitted to the principal for approval. It is only when the principal is not available that the powers of the agent are extended. Furthermore, the agent receives no power greater than that sufficient to solve the difficulty.

Frequently, the liability of the principal is dependent upon whether the agent is as a matter of fact a general agent or a special agent. If the agency is general, limitations imposed upon the usual and ordinary powers of the general agent do not prevent the principal from being liable to third parties where the agent acts in violation of such limitations, unless the attention of the third parties has been drawn to them. In other words, the third party, having established that a general agency exists and having determined in a general way the limits of the authority, is not bound to explore for unexpected and unusual restrictions. He is justified in assuming, in the absence of contrary information, that the agent possesses the powers that like agents customarily have. On the other hand, if the proof is only of a special or limited agency, any action in excess of the actual authority would not bind the principal. The authority for a special agent is strictly construed, and if the agent exceeds his authority, the principal is not bound.

To illustrate the foregoing, assume an instruction to a sales agent not to sell to a certain individual or not to sell to him on credit, when credit sales are customary. Such a limitation cannot affect the validity of a contract made with this individual, unless the latter was aware of the limitation at the time the contract was made. The principal, by appointing an agent normally possessed of certain authority, is estopped to set up the limitation as a defense, unless the limitation is made known to the third party prior to the making of the contract.

There are other issues directly related to the authority possessed by an agent. For example, a common problem involves whether or not notice to an agent or knowledge possessed by him is imputed to the principal. Some of these questions are covered by statutes. For example, civil practice statutes contain provisions on service of a summons on an agent. They specify who may be an agent for the

469

service of process and in effect provide that notice to such agents constitutes notice to the principal. The general principle relating to notice and to some of the other special issues of authority are discussed in the sections that follow.

Notice to Agents Notice to or knowledge acquired by an agent while acting within the scope of his authority binds the principal. This is based on the theory that the agent is the principal's other self, and, therefore, what the agent knows, the principal knows. However, it must be recognized that while *knowledge* possessed by an agent is *notice* to the principal, the principal may not have actual knowledge of the particular fact at all. Knowledge acquired by an agent acting outside the scope of his authority is not effective notice unless the party relying thereon has reasonable ground to believe that the agent is acting within the scope of his authority (similar to apparent authority). To illustrate assume that an agent who is acquiring property for his principal has knowledge of certain unrecorded liens against the property. The principal purchases the property subject to those liens. Equal knowledge possessed by another agent who did not represent the principal in the particular transaction, and who did not obtain the knowledge on behalf of his principal, is not imputed to the principal.

A question exists as to whether or not notice acquired by an agent before he became such can bind the principal. One view is that notice acquired by a person before the creation of the agency is notice to the principal who later hires the person as his agent. There is considerable authority to the contrary.

Notice or knowledge received by an agent under circumstances where the agent would not be presumed to communicate the information to the principal does not bind the principal. This is an exception to the general rule that will be observed in cases when the agent is acting in his own behalf and adversely to the principal or when the agent is under a duty to some third party not to disclose the information. Furthermore, notice to the agent, combined with collusion or fraud between him and the third party that would defeat the purpose of the notice, would not bind the principal.

As a general rule, an agent or person ostensibly in charge of a place of business has apparent authority to accept notices in relation to the business. In addition, an employee in charge of the receipt of mail may accept written notifications.

Agent's Power to Appoint Subagents Agents are usually selected because of their personal qualifications. Owing to these elements of trust and confidence, a general rule has developed that an agent may not delegate his duty to someone else and clothe the latter with authority to bind the principal. An exception has arisen to this rule in those cases in which the acts of the agent are purely ministerial or mechanical. An act that requires no discretion and is purely mechanical may be delegated by the agent to a third party. Such a delegation does not make the third party the agent of the principal or give him any action against the principal for compensation unless the agent was impliedly authorized to obtain this assistance. The acts of such third party become in reality the acts of the agent and bind the principal, if they are within the authority given to the agent. Acts that involve the exercise of skill, discretion, or judgment may not be delegated without permission from the principal.

An agent may, under certain circumstances, have the actual or implied authority to appoint other agents for the principal, in which case they become true employees of the principal and are entitled to be compensated by him. Such a power on the part of the agent is not often implied, but if the situation is such that the major power conferred cannot be exercised without the aid of other agents, the agent is authorized to hire such help as is required. Thus, a manager placed in charge of a branch store may be presumed to possess authority to hire the necessary personnel the size of the business demands.

The Financial Powers of Agents

An agent who delivers goods sold for cash has the implied authority to collect all payments due at the time of delivery. A salesman taking orders calling for a down payment has implied authority to accept the down payment. However, salesmen by the very nature of their jobs have no implied authority to receive payments on account, and any authority to do so must be expressly given or be implied from custom. Thus, a person in his capacity as salesclerk in a store has authority to collect any payments made at the time of sale but no authority to receive payments on account. A payment to a sales agent without authority to collect that is not delivered to the principal may be collected by the principal either from the agent or from the party who paid the agent.

Possession of a statement of account on the billhead of the principal or in the principal's handwriting does not create implied or apparent authority to collect a debt. Payment to an agent without authority to collect does not discharge the debt.

Authority to collect gives the agent no authority to accept anything other than money in payment. Unless expressly authorized, he is not empowered to accept negotiable notes or property in settlement of an indebtedness. It is customary for an agent to accept checks as conditional payment. Under such circumstances, the debt is not paid unless the check is honored. If the check is not paid, the creditor-principal is free to bring suit on the contract which gave rise to the indebtedness or to sue on the check, at his option.

A general agent placed in charge of a business has implied or apparent authority to purchase for cash or on credit. The implied authority is based on the nature of his position and on the fact that the public rightly concludes that a corporation or an individual acting through another person has given him the power and authority that naturally and properly belong to the character in which the agent is held out.

Authority to borrow money is not easily implied. Such authority must be expressly granted or qualify as incidental authority to the express authority, or the principal will not be bound. The authority to borrow should always be confirmed with the principal.

Case: D owned a men's clothing store. Her father from time to time did business in D's name. A checking account in P bank had been opened by D, with a power of attorney given to the father "to sign and indorse checks, notes and drafts . . . and transact all business." D's father borrowed money from P bank.

Issue: Did the power of attorney give the father the power to borrow money?

Decision: No.

Reasons: 1. The power of attorney does not expressly authorize the power to borrow money. It will be strictly construed against the party supplying the instrument—the bank.

2. The power to borrow money will be found only if (1) it is directly granted; (2) it is indispensable to the execution of the powers actually granted; or (3) the agent has apparent authority to do so, as by a long course of similar dealing.

Bank of America, Nat. Trust & Sav. Ass'n v. Horowytz, 248 A.2d 446 (N.J.) 1968.

THE LIABILITY OF THIRD PARTIES

To Principals A disclosed principal may enforce any contract made by an authorized agent for the former's benefit. This right applies to all contracts in which the principal is the real party in interest, including contracts that are made in the agent's name. Furthermore, if a contract is made for the benefit of a disclosed principal by an agent acting outside the scope of his authority, the principal is still entitled to performance, provided the contract is properly ratified before withdrawal by the third party.

An undisclosed principal is entitled to performance by third parties of all assignable contracts made for his benefit by an authorized agent. It is no defense for the third party to say that he had not entered into a contract with the principal.

Case: P and D were competitors in business. P wished to purchase a certain type of asphalt block from D but doubted whether D would sell the blocks to him. P engaged Booth to make the purchase. Booth did so, never disclosing the existence of P as principal or his agency. The blocks were not of merchantable quality. P sued D, who defended on the ground that had he known with whom he was dealing, he would have refused to sell.

Issue: Can P enforce the contract?

Decision: Yes.

Reason: An undisclosed principal may sue on a contract made by an agent. Either the agent or the principal could enforce the contract.

Kelly Asphalt Block Co. v. Barber Asphalt Paving Co., 105 N.E.88 (N.Y.) 1914.

If a contract is one that involves the skill or confidence of the agent and is one that would not have been entered into without this skill or confidence, its performance may not be demanded by the undisclosed principal. This is because the contract would not be assignable, since personal rights and duties are not transferable without consent of the other party.

As a general rule, the undisclosed principal takes over the contract subject to all defenses that the third party could have established against the agent. For example, if the third party contracts to buy from such an agent and has a right of setoff against the agent, he has this same right of setoff against the undisclosed principal. He may also pay the agent prior to discovery of the principal, and such payment will discharge his liability.

To Agents   Normally the agent possesses no right to bring suit on contracts made by him for the benefit of his principal because he has no interest in the cause of action. Where the agent binds himself to the third party, either intentionally or ineptly by a failure properly to express himself, he may, however, maintain an action. An agent of an undisclosed principal is liable on the contract and may sue in his own name in the event of nonperformance by the third party. Thus either the agent or the undisclosed principal might bring suit, but in case of a dispute, the right of the previously undisclosed principal is superior.

Custom has long sanctioned an action by the agent based upon a contract in which he is interested because of anticipated commissions. As a result, a factor may institute an action in his own name to recover for goods sold. He may also recover against a railroad for delay in the shipment of goods sold or to be sold.

473

Similarly, an agent who has been vested with title to commercial paper may sue the maker thereof. The same is true of any claim held by the principal that he definitely places with the agent for collection and suit, where such is necessary. In all cases of this character, the agent retains the proceeds as a trust fund for his principal.

REVIEW QUESTIONS AND PROBLEMS

1. Define the following terms: *warranty of authority*, *apparent authority*, *express authority*, *incidental authority*, *implied authority*, *ostensible authority*, *ratification*, and *undisclosed principal.*

2. P, the owner of a boat, asked A to sell it for him. P told A not to sell the boat to anyone without first obtaining P's permission. T contacted P and inquired about purchase of the boat. P told T, "You will have to talk with A, my agent." A sold the boat to T without asking P's permission. Is P bound on the contract? Why?

3. A entered into a contract with T for the purchase of goods. A informed T that A was acting as an agent, but he did not reveal the identity of the principal, P. P failed to honor the contract. Is P liable to T? What if T obtained a judgment against A only, discovered that A could not pay, and then sued P? Explain.

4. P, the owner of a grocery store chain, hires A to manage one store. P tells A to stock the store himself. Assume that P tells A:
   a. "Be sure to buy soup."
   b. "Don't buy soup."
   c. Nothing about soup.
A then proceeds to buy forty cases of soup from T. In which situation(s), if any, is P liable to T? Why?

5. T enters a private parking lot owned by P. A, P's parking-lot attendant, tells T, "Give the keys to Joe. He will park it for you." Joe, unknown to T, was not P's employee, and A had no actual authority to obtain assistance in his work. Joe steals T's car and demolishes it. May T recover from P? Why?

6. X purchased an insurance policy on his own life. He paid the premiums directly to the insurance agent, Y. Y appropriated the premiums to his own use. X died. May the beneficiaries recover from the insurance company? Explain.

7. X gave Y a power of attorney to "do and perform all and every act which I may do, including mortgaging my property." Y sold X's property to Z. X brought an action against Z for return of the property. May X recover? Why?

8. For two years, A had acted as P's collection agent. P later revoked A's authority to receive payments from customers; however, neither A nor P informed the customers of the termination of authority. X, one of P's customers, made payment to A, who failed to turn the payment over to P. Is X liable to P? Why?

9. A, thinking he had authority to do so, signed P's name to a contract whereby T was to drill an oil well for $7,000. Later A and T learned P had not given A authority to do so. Is A liable if the contract was signed "P per A"? Why?

10. A was authorized by P to purchase bowling alley equipment on credit. He told the seller he was acting as an agent but was not at liberty to disclose his principal's name. The bill remains unpaid, and P is now disclosed. May the seller recover of A? Why?

11. A was the purchasing agent of P for the purpose of buying poultry and farm produce. In all his transactions with the farmers, A acted as the principal and purchased on the strength of his own credit. A failed to pay for some of the produce purchased. The farmers, having ascertained that P was the true principal, seek to hold him. May they do so? Suppose P had previously settled with A? Explain.

32 AGENCY AND THE LAW OF TORTS

Introduction   The fundamental principles of tort liability in the law of agency, which are discussed in this chapter, can be summarized as follows:

1. Agents, servants, and independent contractors are personally liable for their own torts.
2. Agents, servants, and independent contractors are not liable for the torts of their employers.
3. A master is liable under a doctrine known as *respondeat superior* for the torts of his servant if the servant is acting within the scope of his employment.
4. A principal is liable for the torts of an agent who is also a servant in the performance of his duties if the agent is acting within the scope of his employment.
5. A principal, proprietor, employer, or contractee (each of these terms is sometimes used) is not as a general rule liable for the torts of an independent contractor.
6. Injured employees may have rights against their employers as well as against third parties who cause their injuries.

In the foregoing list, numbers 3 and 4 actually express the same basic concept. The terms *master* and *servant* are technically more accurate than the terms *principal* and *agent* in describing the parties when tort liability is discussed. Courts nevertheless frequently describe the parties as "principal" and "agent." However, a principal is liable for torts of only those agents who are subject to that kind of control that

476

establishes the master-servant relationship. For the purpose of tort liability, a servant is a person who is employed with or without pay to perform personal services for another in his affairs, and who, in respect to the physical movements in the performance of such service, is subject to the master's right or power of control. A person who renders services for another but retains control over the manner of rendering such services is not a servant but an independent contractor.

The amount of control present will also determine tort liability when other legal relationships exist. For example, the extent of control determines the liability of a franchiser for the torts of a franchisee because the presence of control creates the agency relationship.

Case: P, a motel guest, slipped and fell on water draining from an air-conditioning unit. P sued D, the franchiser of the motel system. The motel was owned by a corporation which operated as D's franchisee and licensee. Ds name was used in the operation. In addition, D designed the motel, sold the franchisee the equipment, furnishings, and supplies, and trained its employees. D received a license fee plus fifteen cents per room per day from the operator.

Issue: Is the franchisor liable for the torts of its franchisee?

Decision: No.

Reasons: 1. The fact that an agreement is a franchise contract does not insulate the parties from an agency relationship. If a franchise contract so "regulates the activities of the franchisee" as to vest the franchiser with control within the definition of agency, the agency relationship arises even though the parties as a part of the agreement expressly deny it.

2. Whether the power to regulate granted by a franchise contract constitutes control sufficient to establish an agency relationship depends on the nature and the extent of the power defined in the contract.

3. A franchise agreement which permitted the licensee to use the licensor's trade name on motel, which was intended to achieve a system-wide standardization of business identity, uniformity of commercial service, and optimum public goodwill for benefit of both the contracting parties, and which empowers the licensor to regulate architectural style of buildings and type and style of furnishings and equipment but which gives the licensor no power to control daily maintenance of the premises, does not create a principal-agent or master-servant relationship.

4. The regulatory provisions of the franchise contract do not constitute control within the definition of agency.

Murphy v. Holiday Inns, Inc., 219 S.E.2d 874 (Va.) 1975.

Tort Liability of Agents and Servants Every person who commits a tort is personally liable to the individual whose person or property is injured or damaged by the wrongful act. One is not relieved of tort liability by establishing that the tortious act was committed under the direction of someone else or in the course of employment by another. The fact that the employer or principal may be held liable does not in any way relieve the servant or agent from liability. The agent's or servant's liability is joint and several with the liability of the principal. Of course, the converse is not true. An agent, servant, or independent contractor is not liable for the torts of the principal, master, or employer.

In the event that A commits a tort against T, T can bring action against A or against P, or T can sue A and P jointly. Assume that T sues and collects from P, as is typically the case, because P's financial standing is usually better than A's. Can P upon paying the judgment recover his loss from A? The answer is yes if the tort arose from A's negligence and there was no contributing fault on P's part. As will be discussed more fully in Chapter 33, a servant is liable for his own misconduct either to others or to his employer.

Suits by masters against servants for indemnity are not common for several reasons. First, the servant's financial condition frequently does not warrant suit. Second, the employer knows of the risk of negligence by his employees and covers this risk with insurance. If indemnity were a common occurrence, the ultimate loss would almost always fall on employees or workmen. If this situation developed, it would have an adverse effect on employee morale and would make labor-management relations much more difficult. Therefore, few employers seek to enforce the right to collect losses from employees. However, in a few recent cases, some courts have allowed the insurance carrier of the employer to sue the employee under its right of subrogation. If such suits become common, it is likely that legislation will be enacted to eliminate the insurance carrier's claim against the negligent employee on the ground that such suits are against public policy.

Just as P may have a right to reimbursement or indemnity from A, under certain situations A may successfully maintain an action for reimbursement or indemnity against P. Such is the case when A commits a tort in conformity with instructions given to him by P, without knowledge that his conduct is tortious. For example, P, a retail appliance dealer, instructs A to repossess a TV set from T who had purchased it on an installment contract. P informs A that T is in arrears in his payments. Actually, T is current in his payments, and a bookkeeping error had been made by P. In accordance with his instructions and over protest from T, A makes the repossession. A *has* committed a tort, but P must indemnify him and satisfy T's claim against A, if T elects to collect from A.

TORT LIABILITY OF PRINCIPALS AND MASTERS

Respondeat Superior A master is liable to third persons for the torts committed by his servants *within the scope of their employment* and in prosecution of the master's business. This concept, frequently known as *respondeat superior* (let the master respond), imposes vicarious liability on employers as a matter of public policy. Although negligence of the servant is the usual basis of liability, the doctrine of *respondeat superior* is also applicable to intentional torts, such as trespass, assault, libel, and fraud, which are committed by a servant acting within the scope of his employment. It is applicable even though the master did not direct the willful act or assent to it.

This vicarious liability imposed on masters, which makes them pay for wrongs they have not actually committed, is not based on logic and reason but on business and social policy. The theory is that the master is in a better position to pay for the wrong than is the servant. This concept is sometimes referred to as the "deep pocket" theory. The business policy theory is that injuries to persons and property are hazards of doing business, the cost of which the business should bear rather than have the loss borne by the innocent victim of the tort or society as a whole.

Scope of Employment There are two major difficulties in applying the doctrine of *respondeat superior*. The first involves the issue as to whether the party at fault is a servant as contrasted with an independent contractor. The tort liability of one engaging an independent contractor for the acts of an independent contractor is discussed later in this chapter, but it must be noted that as a general rule the doctrine of *respondeat superior* is not applicable to this relationship.

The second problem is whether the servant *is acting within the scope of his employment* at the time of the commission of the tort. The agent or servant may have detoured from his employment and gone off on a frolic of his own. The law of frolics and detours is covered in a later section. In addition, the facts may establish that the control of the master on the servant's employment has ended. If the servant is no longer acting within the scope of his employment and on his master's business, but is acting solely on his own behalf, there obviously can be no liability.

Case: X, an oil field employee, had a work schedule consisting of seven days on and seven days off. On the seventh day of work he traveled 30 miles by boat and then drove his automobile 150 miles to his home. X was paid for oil field work and for boat travel time, but his pay stopped the moment he disembarked. While homeward bound in his automobile, X struck a car and killed a motorist. Her estate sued D, X's employer, for wrongful death.

Issue: Is an employer liable for the torts of its employees while the employee is on his way to or from his employment?

Decision: No.

Reasons: 1. An employer is liable for the torts of its employees if at the time the employee (servant) is in the exercise of the functions in which they are employed.

2. The tortious conduct was not so closely connected to the employment as to be regarded as a risk of harm fairly attributable to the employer's business.

3. The act of going home is purely personal to the employee and is extraneous to the employer's interests.

Boudreaux v. Yancey, 319 So.2d 806 (La.App.) 1975.

As a general rule, the master cannot avoid liability by showing that he has instructed the servant not to do the particular act complained of. When a servant disobeys the instructions of his master, the fact of disobedience alone does not insulate the master from liability. In addition, the master is not released by evidence that the servant was not doing the work his master had instructed him to do, when the servant had misunderstood the instruction. As long as the servant is attempting to further his master's business, the master is liable.

Expanding Vicarious Liability In recent years the law has been expanding the concept of vicarious liability, even to acts of persons who are not employees. A person engaged in some endeavor gratuitously may still be a "servant" within scope of master-servant doctrine. The two key elements for determination of whether a gratuitous undertaking is a part of master-servant relationship are (1) whether the actor has submitted himself to the directions and to the control of the one for whom the service is done, and (2) whether the primary purpose of the underlying act was to serve another. If so, the "master" is liable for the torts of the unpaid "servant."

Most of the expansion of the application of *respondeat superior* and vicarious liability has been by statute. Liability for automobile accidents has been a major area of expansion. Some states have adopted what is known as the "family car doctrine." Under it, if the car is generally made available for family use, any member of the family is presumed to be an agent of the parent-owner when using the family car

480

for his or her convenience or pleasure. The presumption may be rebutted, however. Other states have gone further and provided that anyone driving a car with the permission of the owner is the owner's agent, and the owner has vicarious liability to persons injured by the driver. The family purpose doctrine may extend to nonfamily members under some circumstances.

Case: D, the owner of a family purpose automobile, allowed his minor son to drive the car. The son permitted a friend to drive, and a collision occurred injuring P. P sued D. D contended that there was no liability because of no master-servant relationship.

Issue: Was the operator of the automobile an agent of the owner?

Decision: Yes.

Reasons: 1. The test, with regard to liability of an owner under the "family purpose car doctrine," is whether the car was being operated in the scope of the owner's business. The family purpose car doctrine is but an extension of the principal-agent relationship.

2. A master is responsible for the tortious acts of his servant, done in the master's business, and within the scope of his employment, though the master disapproves, forbids, or is ignorant of a particular act.

3. If a family purpose automobile is being operated for the pleasure of some member of the owner's family, the owner is liable for the acts of the driver, though the driver is a third person.

Dixon v. Phillips, 217 S.E.2d 331 (Ga.) 1975.

Frolics and Detours

Respondeat superior requires that the agent or servant be *acting within the scope of his employment* at the time of the commission of the tort. The law imposes liability on the master only when the master's business is being carried on or where the wrongful act was authorized or ratified. The master's liability does not arise when the servant steps aside from his employment to commit the tort or does the wrongful act to accomplish some purpose of his own. If the tort is activated by a purpose to serve the master or principal, then he is liable. Otherwise he is not. Although the scope of employment is considerably broader than explicitly authorized acts of the employee, it does not extend to cases in which the servant has stepped aside from his employment to commit a tort which the master neither directed in fact nor could be supposed, from the nature of the servant's employment, to have authorized or expected the servant to do.

It is not possible to state a simple test to determine if the tort is committed within the scope of the employment. However, factors that are considered in determining the scope of employment include the nature of the employment; the right of control, "not only as to the result to be accomplished but also as to the means to be used"; the ownership of the instrumentality such as an automobile; whether the instrumentality was furnished by the employer; whether the use was authorized; and the time of the occurrence. Most courts inquire into the intent of the servant and the extent of deviation from expected conduct involved in the tort. The issue is usually one of fact and is left to the jury. Each case in effect depends upon its own special set of circumstances.

A servant is not acting within the scope of his employment if he is on a "frolic" of his own. The deviation may sometimes be described as a "detour," in which case, a problem is presented as to the point at which the detour ends and the course of employment resumes. Another difficult situation is presented when the servant combines his own business with that of his master. As a general rule, this fact does not relieve the master of liability. The doctrine of *respondeat superior* has been extended to create liability for negligence of strangers while assisting a servant in carrying out the master's business, where the authority to obtain assistance is given or is required as in the case of an emergency.

Intentional or willful torts are not as likely to occur within the scope of the servant's employment as are those predicated upon a negligence theory. If the willful misconduct of the servant has nothing to do with his master's business and is animated entirely by hatred or a feeling of ill will toward the third party, the master is not liable. The master is also not liable if the employee's act has no reasonable connection with his employment.

Case: D employed X as a security guard at one of its grocery stores. While shopping at another store and while not on duty, X assaulted P, a customer of D. P had touched X with a grocery cart while both were in a checkout line. P sued D for his personal injuries.

Issue: Is D liable?

Decision: No.

Reasons: 1. The doctrine of *respondeat superior* arises from the principle that the liability of the master for tortious acts of a servant rests at last upon the existence of authority, that the act must have been done in the course of employment which the master has authorized, and that, unless such authority can be shown, there is no liability.

2. The conduct of a servant is within the scope of employment only during the period that has a reasonable connection with an authorized period, and only in the authorized area or in a locality not unreasonably distant from it.

3. The test for determining whether an act of a servant was performed within the scope of employment is whether servant was advancing his master's interest in doing what he did at the time he did it. The issue is a question of fact for the jury.

4. Here X was shopping for his personal use and the doctrine of *respondeat superior* does not apply.

Rusnack v. Giant Food, Inc., 337 A.2d 445 (Md.) 1975.

Tort Suits—
Procedures
As previously noted, the law of torts in most states, unlike the law of contracts, allows joinder of the master and servant as defendants in one cause of action or permits them to be sued separately. Although the plaintiff is limited to one recovery, the master and servant are jointly and severally liable. The party may collect from either or both in any proportion until the judgment is paid in full. If the servant is sued first and a judgment is obtained that is not satisfied, such a suit is not a bar to a subsequent suit against the master, but the amount of the judgment against the servant fixes the maximum limit of potential liability against the master.

If the servant is found to be free of liability, either in a separate suit or as a codefendant with the master, then the suit against the master on the basis of *respondeat superior* will fail. The master's liability is predicated upon the fault of the servant, and if the servant is found to be free of fault, the master has no liability as a matter of law.

Independent
Contractors
An *independent contractor* is a person performing a service for one who employs him under an arrangement by which the person engaged has the power to control the details of the work being performed. Because the performance is within the control of such person, he is not a servant and his only responsibility is to accomplish the result contracted for. To illustrate: A contracts to build a boat for P at a cost of $4,000 and according to certain specifications. In such a case it is clear that A is an independent contractor, with the completed boat as the result. However, had P engaged A by the day to assist in building the boat under P's supervision and at P's direction, the master-servant relationship would have resulted. As previously discussed, it should be kept in mind that an agent with authority to represent his principal contractually will, at the same time, be either a servant or an independent contractor for the purpose of tort liability.

The distinction between servants and independent contractors is important because, as a general rule, the doctrine of *respondeat superior* and the concept of vicarious liability in tort are not applicable to independent contractors. There is no tort liability, as a general rule, because the theories that justify liability on the master for the servant's tort are not present when the person engaged to do the work is not a servant. There is also no liability imputed to one who controls certain activities of persons not employed by him.

Case: P, a patient, sued Ds, a doctor and a hospital, for damages for injuries resulting when a nurse negligently injected a drug intravenously instead of intramuscularly.

Issue: Are hospitals and doctors liable for the negligence of nurses?

Decision: Hospitals, yes; doctors, no.

Reasons: 1. A nurse is not an agent or servant of a doctor, and her negligence cannot be imputed to him under the doctrine of *respondeat superior.*

2. Nurses are employees subject to the control of their hospital employers, and as such the doctrine of *respondeat superior* applies.

Moore v. Guthrie Hospital, Inc., 403 F.2d 366 (1968).

The hallmark of a master-servant relationship is that the master not only controls the result of the work but has the right to direct the manner in which the work shall be accomplished; the distinguishing feature of an independent contractee-contractor relationship is that the person engaged in the work has exclusive control of the manner of performing it, being responsible only for the result and not the means. In ascertaining whether a person is a servant or an independent contractor, the basic inquiry is whether such person is subject to the alleged employer's control or right to control with respect to his physical conduct in the performance of services for which he was engaged. Whether the relationship is master-servant or proprietor-independent contractor is usually a question of fact for the jury.

Case: X, a "commission" salesman in the floor-covering department of D, a department store, had worked in the same position for nineteen years. X had received fringe benefits of insurance, profit sharing, and paid vacations His hours of work were determined by the store. X was involved in an auto accident with P while returning to his home for lunch after leaving a prospective customer's house. P sued D.

Issue: Is the department store liable to P?

Decision: Yes.

Reasons: 1. Whether or not the salesman was an agent or an independent contractor is a question of fact for the jury, as is the issue of scope of employment.

2. If X was engaged in activity that served his own purposes, but at the same time served the business of his employer to any appreciable extent, X would be acting within the scope of his employment at the time of the accident.

3. The general test in determining the existence of the master-servant relationship is the right to direct and control the conduct of the alleged servant at the time the negligent act occurred, and the phrase "right to control" is used, not in a specific sense but in a general sense. It refers only to the right, and not the exercise, of control over the servant, especially where work is such as not to demand a great deal of supervision.

Gibbs v. Miller, 283 N.E.2d 592 (Ind.) 1972.

Since it is generally understood that one is not liable for the torts of an independent contractor, contracts frequently provide that the relationship is that of independent contractor and not master-servant. Such a provision is not binding on third parties, and the contract cannot be used to protect the contracting parties from the actual relationship as shown by the facts.

Exceptions to Independent Contractor Rule
The rule of insulation from liability in the independent contractor situation is subject to several well-recognized exceptions. The most common of these is where the work involved is inherently dangerous to the public, such as blasting with dynamite. The basis of this exception is that it would be contrary to public policy to allow one engaged in such an activity to avoid his liability by selecting an independent contractor rather than a servant to do the work.

Another exception to insulation from vicarious liability exists where the work being done is illegal. An employer cannot insulate himself from liability by hiring an independent contractor to perform a task that is wrongful. Another common exception involves employees' duties that are considered to be nondelegable. In the law of contracts, it was noted that personal rights and personal duties could not be transferred without consent of the other party. Many statutes impose strict duties on parties such as common carriers and innkeepers. If an attempt is made to delegate these duties to an independent contractor, it is clear that the employer upon whom the duty is imposed has liability for the torts of the independent contractor. Finally, an employer is liable for the torts of an independent contractor if the tort is ratified. For example, if an independent contractor wrongfully repossesses an automobile and the one hiring him refuses to return it on demand, the tort has been ratified and both parties have liability.

Tort liability is also imposed where the employer is himself at fault, as when he negligently selects the employee. This is true whether the party performing the work is a servant or an independent contractor. For example, assume that X, a person with known propensities for violence, including a criminal record for assaults, is employed. X assaults a customer of his employer. There is liability even though X may be an independent contractor. There would also be liability even though X went beyond the scope of his employment. Liability exists because of the negligence of the party hiring X.

INJURIES TO EMPLOYEES

Introduction An employer owes certain duties to his employees. These include the duty (1) to warn employees of the hazards of their employment, (2) to supervise their activities, (3) to furnish a reasonably safe place to work, and (4) to furnish reasonably safe instrumentalities with which to work. What is reasonable for the purposes of these rules depends on all the facts and circumstances of each case. For example, what is a reasonably safe place to work can depend upon the age and ability of the worker as well as the condition of the premises. It may be negligent to furnish a minor with, or to fail to supervise a minor in the operation of, a certain instrumentality when to take the same action with a grown man or an experienced employee would not constitute negligence.

At common law, the employer who breached these duties to his employees was liable in tort for the injuries received by the employees. The employer was not an insurer of his employee's safety, but liability was based on negligence. However, the employee in his tort action was confronted with overcoming three defenses available to the employer, one or more of which frequently barred recovery. The first of these defenses was that the employee was *contributorily negligent*. If the employee was even partially at fault, this defense was successful even though the majority of the fault was the employer's. Second, if the injury was caused by some other employee, the *fellow servant* doctrine excused the employer and limited recovery to a suit against the other employee who was at fault. Finally, in many jobs that by their very nature involved some risk of injury, the doctrine of *assumption of risk* would allow the employer to avoid liability.

The common-law rules resulted for the most part in imposing on employees the burdens that resulted from accidental injuries, occupational diseases, and even death. Through the legislative process, society has rather uniformly determined that this result is undesirable as a matter of public policy. Statutes known as *workmen's compensation* have been enacted in all the states. These laws impose liability without fault (eliminate the defenses) on most employers for injuries, occupational diseases, and death of their employees.

**Workmen's
Compensation**

Workmen's compensation laws vary a great deal from state to state as to the covered industries and employees, the nature of the injuries or diseases that are compensable, and the rates of compensation. In spite of the wide variances in the laws of the states in this area, certain general observations can be made.

State workmen's compensation statutes provide a system of paying for death, illness, or injury that arises out of and in the course of the employment. The three defenses the employer had at common law are eliminated. The employers are strictly liable without fault.

Most state statutes exclude certain types of employment from their coverage. Generally, domestic and agricultural employees are not covered. In the majority of states, the statutes are compulsory. In some states, employers may elect to be subject to lawsuits by employees or their survivors for accidental injuries or death. In such cases, the plaintiff must prove that the death or injury resulted proximately from the negligence of the employer. But the plaintiff is not subject to the common-law defenses. In addition, there is no statutory limit to the amount of damages recoverable.

The workmen's compensation acts give covered employees the right to certain cash payments for their loss of income. In the event of an employee's death, benefits are provided for his widow and minor children. The amount of such awards is usually subject to a stated maximum and is based upon the wages of the employee and the number of dependents. If the employee suffers disability, most states provide compensation both for injuries that are scheduled in the statute and for those that are nonscheduled. As an example of the former, a worker who loses a hand might be awarded one hundred weeks of compensation at a specified sum, such as $75 per week. A person who is totally and permanently disabled will receive a pension for life. Compensation for nonscheduled losses would include such items as the earning power the employee lost due to his injury. For example, an injured employee receives weekly payments during the period he is unable to work as a result of the injury. In addition to the above payments, all statutes provide payment of all medical expenses.

In some states, the employers have a choice of covering their risk with insurance or of being self-insured (i.e., paying all claims directly) if they can demonstrate their capability to do so. In other states, employers pay into a state fund used to compensate workers entitled to benefits. In these states, the amounts of the payments are based on the size of the payroll and the experience of the employer in having claims filed.

While the right to workmen's compensation benefits is given without regard to fault of either the employer or the employee, employers are not always liable. The tests for determining whether an employee is entitled to workmen's compensation are simply: (1) "Was the injury accidental?" and (2) "Did the injury arise out of and in the course of the employment?" Since workmen's compensation laws are remedial in nature, they have been very liberally construed. In recent years the courts have tended to expand coverage and the scope of the employer's liability. It has been held that heart attacks as well as other common ailments where the employee had either a preexisting disease or a physical condition likely to lead to the disease were compensable as "accidental injuries." Likewise, the courts have been more and more liberal in upholding awards that have been challenged on the ground that the injury did not arise out of and in the course of the employment.

Case: A traveling salesman died as result of suffocation when his head caught between two metal slats of bed headboard in a rooming house in which he was staying overnight while on business for his employer. The deceased's blood alcohol content was .19 percent at the time of death. The hearing officer found that his intoxication was not such that he was in a deep alcoholic stupor.

Issue: Did the salesman's death arise out of and in the course of his employment?

Decision: Yes.

Reason: Intoxication is not a sufficient basis to deny benefits unless it is to such an extent that it amounts to an abandonment of employment. The overnight stay was an act necessarily incidental to his work as a traveling employee, and therefore his death arose out of and in the course of employment.

Peterson v. Industrial Commission, 490 P.2d 870 (Ariz.) 1971.

The system of separate and varying state workmen's compensation laws as they exist today has been subject to much criticism. The laws have been attacked as inadequate because of their restrictive coverage and limited benefits. Not all types of employment or occupational risks are covered. Many states exempt businesses that do not employ a certain minimum number of workers. Much criticism has also been leveled at the quality of administration of most workmen's compensation programs. The weaknesses in the present laws, and the fact that there are wide variations in the workmen's compensation acts (as well as case law) from state to state, have led to suggestions that workmen's compensation be modernized and reformed to better meet the social needs of today and that it be made uniform from state to state. Some have proposed a Federal Workmen's Compensation Act which would replace the state ones.

**Claims Against
Third-Party
Wrongdoers**

Irrespective of workmen's compensation, an employee injured by the commission of a tort by some third person has a cause of action against and a right to collect from the third-party wrongdoer. However, the employer is entitled to recover any workmen's compensation payments paid to the employee from the sum that the employee recovers from the wrongful third party. Employers are not entitled to sue third parties for lost profits as a result of injuries to their employees.

Three rather unusual tort situations have a direct relation to the employment contract. First, any third party who maliciously or wrongfully influences a principal to terminate an agent's employment thereby commits a tort. The wrongful third party must compensate the agent for any damages that result from such conduct. Second, any third person who wrongfully interferes with the prospective economic advantage of an agent has liability to the agent for the loss sustained. Third, any person who influences another to breach a contract in which the agent is interested thereby renders himself liable to the agent as well as to the principal. To illustrate: The agent has sold goods to T upon which he is entitled to a commission. Anyone who causes T to refuse to carry out the agreement thereby damages the agent and is correspondingly liable.

REVIEW QUESTIONS AND PROBLEMS

1. Explain the reasoning behind the doctrine of *respondeat superior.*

2. Which party, the master or the servant, has the ultimate liability for torts that are the servant's rather than the master's fault? Explain.

3. A, a salesman for the XYZ company, drove his personal car to a sales convention. XYZ reimbursed A for his expenses of the convention. On the way home from the convention, A's negligent driving resulted in injury to B. Is XYZ liable to B? Why?

4. A, as a favor to B, agreed to make a delivery to one of B's customers. A was not an employee of B. On the way to make the delivery, A ran a red light and caused injury to C. Is B liable to C? Why?

5. The *Daily Bugle* customarily dropped several bundles of newspapers at a certain corner where X, a newsboy, picked them up. X then folded the newspapers, throwing the bundling wire on the sidewalk. Y tripped over the wire, injuring himself. Assuming that X is an independent contractor, may Y recover from the *Daily Bugle?* Why?

6. X, a salesman for the Z company, stopped at a hotel while on a business trip. After an argument X hit Y, the bellboy, with his fist and injured him. When told of the injury Z exclaims "I'm glad you hit him. I would have hit him again." May Y hold Z liable? Explain.

7. A, a doctor, was employed at a regular salary by the QRS shipping lines to serve aboard ship and treat passengers. A treated B, a passenger, and B died as a result of A's negligence. May B's heirs recover from QRS? Explain.

8. X, an employee of the ABC company, was put in charge of a construction project in the desert. One day after working hours X was returning in his car with drinking water for the crew when he negligently injured Y. The ABC company had not told him to procure drinking water, but none was available at the job site. May Y recover from ABC? Explain.

9. A, a mechanic for XYZ airlines, decided to fly with B on a test run of a new plane. Due to the negligence of B the plane crashed on takeoff, and A was injured. May A recover from XYZ? Explain.

10. M, driving a gasoline truck, negligently ran into and killed Z. M was driving the truck for his brother, a distributor of T oil and gas products. The contract with T company provided that the truck carry the words *"T Company"* in certain places, that it be used for delivery of T company products to designated filling stations, and that the driver, in collecting for deliveries made, sign the receipt in the name of T company. For these services M's brother received a commission. When sued by Z's executor for wrongful death, T company claimed that M's brother was an independent contractor rather than an agent. What result? Explain.

11. A was employed by D as a laundry-route salesman. He was furnished a truck and uniform. After his usual working hours, A used his personal car to make a delivery he had forgotten to make before returning D's truck. While making the delivery, A negligently injured P. P sues D. What result? Why?

12. A, an employee of the XYZ company, went to work even though he had injured his leg in a fall at his home. While at work, the weakened leg caused a fall that resulted in injury to A's back. Is A entitled to workmen's compensation? Why?

33 DUTIES OF AGENTS AND PRINCIPALS

Introduction The nature and extent of the duties imposed upon agents and servants are governed largely by the contract of employment. In addition to the duties expressly designated, certain others are implied by the fiduciary nature of the relationship and by the legal effects on the principal of actions or omissions by the agent. The usual implied duties are (1) to be loyal to his principal; (2) to obey all reasonable instructions; (3) not to be negligent; (4) to account for all money or property received for the benefit of the principal; and (5) to inform the principal of all facts that materially affect the subject matter of the agency. As will be more fully discussed in the sections that follow, these implied duties are essential to the employer-employee relationship. There is a correlation between these implied duties and the legal principles relating to liability of the parties previously discussed.

Duty of Loyalty An agent stands in a fiduciary relationship to his principal and thus has a duty of undivided loyalty to the principal. Because of the duty of loyalty, it is held that he should undertake no business venture that competes or interferes in any manner with the business of his employer nor make any contract for himself when he should have made it for his principal. The same rule forbids a sales agent to sell or lease his principal's property to himself unless the principal assents to the sale or lease. The rule also prevents a purchasing agent or other person standing in a fiduciary relationship from entering into contracts with himself on behalf of his principal.

Case: P was an executive of D corporation in charge of sales. P induced the corporation to enter into a contract to purchase twenty thousand turkeys from him at a fixed price over a period of three years. P had encouraged management to pay turkey growers a premium price so that they would grow turkeys the year round. D corporation did not carry out the contract because of financial difficulties. P contended that he could sell to the corporation because his job was not directly involved in purchasing.

Issue: Was there a fiduciary relationship between P and D?

Decision: Yes.

Reasons: 1. The evidence clearly showed that the plaintiff was not limited to his duties as a sales manager but also had responsibilities as a member of the total management group. Also, there was evidence to the effect that the plaintiff had an unfair advantage in the negotiation of the contract.

2. When a confidential trust relationship exists, the burden rests upon the dominant confidant to exercise the utmost good faith and undivided loyalty. The existence of such responsibilities upon the part of the confidant will warrant the interposition of equity to scrupulously examine every transaction and set it aside if there is an unfair advantage in favor of the person in whom the confidence is reposed.

Williams v. Pilgrim Turkey Packers, Inc., 503 P.2d 710 (Or.) 1972.

Transactions violating the duty of loyalty may always be rescinded by the principal, if he so desires, despite the fact that the agent acted for the best interests of his principal and the contract was as favorable as could be obtained elsewhere. The general rule is applied without favor in order that every possible motive or incentive for unfaithfulness may be removed.

In addition to the remedy of rescission, a principal is entitled to treat any profit realized by the agent in violation of this duty as belonging to the principal. Such profits include rebates, bonuses, commissions, or divisions of profits received by an agent for dealing with a particular third party. Here again the contracts may have been favorable to the employer, but the result is the same because the agent should not be tempted to abuse the confidence reposed in him. The principal may also collect from the agent a sum equal to any damages sustained as the result of the breach of the duty of loyalty. In addition, persons who are not fiduciaries are liable for breach of the fiduciary duty if they collude with a disloyal agent.

An agent may deal with himself only if he obtains the permission of the principal. In any case in which the agent obtains the consent of the principal to deal with himself, the agent must disclose fully all facts that materially influence the situation. In such a case, the agent and principal do not deal "at arm's length," and the circumstances demand the utmost good faith on the part of the agent.

The duty of loyalty denies a broker the right to represent both the seller and the buyer in the same transaction unless both have been informed of his dual relationship. His desire to earn the commission is apt to cause him to disregard the best interests of one of his principals. Either party who is without knowledge of the dual representation may rescind the agreement, and the agent is not entitled to any fee or commission.

Case: A real estate agent acted as agent for both parties and received a commission from both. The purchasers had no knowledge of the dual agency, but the sellers did know of it.

Issue: Can the purchasers rescind the contract of purchase?

Decision: Yes.

Reason: An agent for one party to a transaction cannot act for the other party without the consent of both principals. When an agent assumes to act in such a dual capacity without such assent, the transaction is voidable as a matter of public policy. Loyalty is the most important duty that an agent owes to his principal.

Taborsky v. Mathews, 121 So.2d 61 (Fla.) 1960.

Confidential Information The duty of loyalty demands that information of a confidential character acquired while in the service of the principal shall not be used by the agent to advance his interests in opposition to those of the principal. This confidential information is usually called a *trade secret.* Trade secrets include plans, processes, tools, mechanisms, compounds, and informational data used in business operations. They are known only to the owner of the business and to such limited other persons in whom it may be necessary to confide. An employer seeking to prevent the disclosure or use of trade secrets or information must demonstrate that he pursued an active course of conduct designed to inform his employees that such secrets and information were to remain confidential. An issue to be determined in all cases involving trade secrets is whether the information sought to be protected is, in fact and in law, confidential. The result in each case depends on the conduct of the parties and the nature of the information.

An employee who learns of secret processes or formulas or comes into possession of lists of customers may not use this information to the detriment of his employer. Former employees may not use such information in a competing business regardless of whether the trade secrets were copied or memorized. The fact that a trade secret is spied out does not make it any less a secret, nor does the fact that a product is on the market amount to a divulgence or abandonment of the secrets connected with the product. The employer may obtain an injunction to prevent their use. Such use is a form of unfair competition. The rule relating to trade secrets is applied with equal severity whether the agent acts before or after he severs his connection with the principal.

Knowledge that is important but that does not amount to a trade secret may be used, although it affects the agent's former employer injuriously. That which by experience has become a part of a former employee's general knowledge cannot and ought not be enjoined from further and different uses. For this reason, there is nothing to hinder a person who has made the acquaintance of his employer's customers from later circularising those whom he can remember. His acquaintanceship is part of his acquired skill. The employer may protect himself in the later case by a clause in the employment agreement to the effect that the employee will not compete with the employer or work for a competitor for a limited period of time after his employment is terminated.

Duty to Obey Instructions

It is the duty of an agent to obey all instructions issued by his principal as long as they refer to duties contemplated by the contract of employment. Burdens not required by the agreement cannot be indiscriminately imposed by the employer, and any material change in an employee's duties may constitute breach of the employment contract.

Case: P sued D for breach of an alleged employment contract. P had sold D a test-publishing business. D had in turn employed P in an executive and supervisory role to head its test book division. Later D put others in charge of P and relegated him to writing test questions. P refused to take orders from those placed above him in the organization. D discharged P for insubordination.

Issue: Does a material change in duties constitute a breach of contract sufficient to justify a refusal to perform them?

Decision: Yes.

Reasons: 1. If an employee is engaged to fill a particular position, any material changes in his duties, or significant reduction in rank, constitutes a breach of contract.

2. Acts done by an employee in defense of his contract rights, or in assertion of an agreed status or function in an enterprise, are not insubordination.

3. While P could be discharged for nonperformance or misperformance, he could not be reduced to a rank or responsibility beneath that defined by the agreement. Nor could he be put into a state of "deep-freeze" until he was provoked into such gross disobedience of "orders" that a discharge for insubordination would be plausible.

Rudman v. Cowles Communications, Inc., 280 N.E.2d 867 (N.Y.) 1972.

An instruction may not be regarded lightly merely because it departs from the usual procedure and seems fanciful and impractical to the employee. It is not his business to question the procedure outlined by his superior. Any loss that results while he is pursuing any other course makes him absolutely liable to the principal for any resulting loss.

Furthermore, an instruction of the principal does not become improper merely because the motive is bad. He may be well aware of the agent's distaste for certain tasks, yet, if those tasks are such as may be called for under the employment agreement, it becomes the agent's duty to perform them. Failure to perform often results in proper grounds for his discharge.

This obligation on the part of the agent to follow carefully his principal's orders applies to an agent who acts gratuitously as well as to one who receives pay for his services. Although the former is under no duty to perform, even though he has promised to do so, if he undertakes to carry out his commission, he must follow explicitly the instructions received.

Closely allied to the duty to follow instructions is the duty to remain within the scope of the authority conferred. Because of the doctrine of estoppel, it often becomes possible for an agent to exceed his authority and still bind his principal. In case of such a violation of his contract, the employee becomes responsible for any resulting loss. He is in this instance failing to follow the instructions set forth in his contract with his employer. These instructions, as well as those issued later by the principal, must be fully complied with.

Case: An agent of an insurance company had been instructed not to issue coverage on boats more than three years old or worth more than $5,000, without a condition survey. He issued a policy on a boat that was thirteen years old and insured for $5,000, without a survey. The insurance company filed a claim against its agent.

Issue: Must the agent indemnify the principal?

Decision: Yes.

495

Reason: An agent owes to his principal the obligation of high fidelity. He may not proceed without or beyond his authority, particularly where he has been forbidden to act, and if he does so and his actions cause loss to his principal, the agent is fully accountable to the principal. The agent also owes a duty of obedience to his principal.

Crawford v. DeMicco, 216 So.2d 769 (Fla.) 1968.

Occasionally, circumstances arise that nullify instructions previously given. Because of the new conditions, the old instructions would, if followed, practically destroy the purpose of the agency. Whenever such an emergency arises, it becomes the duty of the agent, provided the principal is not available, to exercise his best judgment in meeting the situation.

An instruction to do an illegal or immoral act or an act that will impair the security or position of the agent may be disregarded. To illustrate: A factor has a lien on goods in his possession for all money advanced to his principal. An order from the principal to return the goods or to sell them on credit could be disregarded until such time as all advances had been paid.

Duty Not To Be Negligent   As was discussed in Chapter 32, the doctrine of *respondeat superior* imposes liability upon a principal or master for the torts of an agent or servant acting within the scope of his employment. The agent or servant is primarily liable, and the principal or master is secondarily liable.

It is an implied condition of employment contracts, if not otherwise expressed, that the employee has a duty to act in good faith and to exercise reasonable care and diligence in performing his tasks. Failure to do so is a breach of the employment contract. Therefore, if the employer has liability to third persons due to the employee's acts or omissions of negligence and the application of the doctrine of *respondeat superior*, the employer may recover his loss from the employee. This right may be transferred by the doctrine of subrogation to the liability insurance carrier of the employer.

Duty to Account   Money or property entrusted to the agent must be accounted for to the principal. Because of this fact, the agent is required to keep proper records showing receipts and expenditures in order that a complete accounting may be rendered. Any money collected by an agent for his principal should not be mingled with funds of the former. If they are deposited in a bank, they should be kept in a separate account and so designated that a trust is apparent. Otherwise any loss resulting from an insolvent bank must be borne by the agent.

The principal may follow any funds misappropriated by the agent until they fall into the hands of a third party. Even then the principal may follow the proceeds and impress a trust upon them, so long as they have not reached an innocent third party. Furthermore, if such proceeds can be shown to have increased the estate of the agent, a trust may be imposed upon the agent's estate to that extent.

Duty to
Give Notice
Chapter 31 noted that knowledge acquired by an agent within the scope of his authority binds the principal, or more succinctly, knowledge of an agent is notice to the principal. Therefore the law imposes on the agent the duty to inform his principal of all facts that affect the subject matter of the agency and that are obtained within the scope of the employment. The rule requiring full disclosure of all material facts that might affect the principal is equally applicable to gratuitous and to compensated agents.

This rule extends beyond the duty to inform the principal of conflicting interests of third parties or possible violations of the duty of loyalty in a particular transaction. It imposes upon the agent a duty to give his principal all information that materially affects the interest of the principal. For example, knowledge of facts that may have greatly advanced the value of property placed with an agent for sale must be communicated before property is sold at a price previously established by the principal.

DUTIES OF PRINCIPALS

Duty to
Compensate
in General
The agent is entitled to be compensated for his services in accordance with the terms of his contract of employment. If no definite compensation has been agreed upon, there arises a duty to pay the reasonable value of such services. Whenever the party performing the services is a stranger to the employer, the obligation to compensate exists. However, when relatives are working for one another and no express agreement has been formulated, the courts are likely to infer that the services so rendered should be considered gratuitous. This question frequently arises in claims against an estate for the value of care given the deceased prior to his death by a relative. Following this rule, the claims are usually denied in the absence of an express contract to pay for the care.

If the contract is silent on the amount of compensation, the reasonable value will be the customary rate in the community, if any. If no customary rate is available, opinion evidence is received in determining the value of the services.

Many employment contracts include provisions for paying a percentage of profits to a key employee. In the absence of a detailed enumeration in the employment contract of the items to be considered in determining net income, it will be computed in accordance with generally accepted accounting principles, taking into consideration past custom and practice in the operation of the employer's business. It is assumed that the methods of determining net income will be consistent and that no substantial changes will be made in the methods of accounting without the mutual agreement of the parties. The employer cannot unilaterally change the accounting methods, nor can the employee require a change in order to effect an increase in his earnings.

**Duty to
Compensate Real
Estate Brokers**
The right of a real estate broker or agent to a commission is frequently the subject of litigation. In the absence of an express agreement, the real estate broker earns a commission in either of two situations. First, he will be entitled to it if he finds a buyer who is ready, willing, and able to meet the terms outlined by the seller in the listing agreement. The owner cannot deprive the agent of a commission by refusing to deal with the prospective purchaser or by withdrawing the property from sale. The owner cannot relieve himself of the duty to pay the commission by terminating the agency and later contracting directly with the broker's prospect. The fee is earned if it is shown that the broker was the inducing cause of the sale.

The commission is also earned if the owner contracts with the purchaser (whether or not the price is less than the listed price), even though it later develops that the buyer is unable to meet the terms of the contract. The contract is conclusive evidence that the broker found a ready, willing, and able buyer. The seller assumes the risk of performance upon executing the contract with the buyer presented by the broker. This is true even if the law allows the buyer to avoid liability, as for example, where the property is destroyed. However, if a prospective purchaser conditions his obligation to purchase on an approval of credit or approval of a loan, he is not a ready, willing, and able buyer until such approval. If it is not forthcoming, the broker is not entitled to a commission.

The broker's commission is contingent on payment by the purchaser when his contract of employment so states. An owner who lists property with several brokers is obligated to pay the first one to find a satisfactory purchaser, at which time the agency of other brokers is automatically terminated, assuming a simple listing.

**types of
listings**
There are three distinct types of real estate listings—placing of property with real estate brokers for sale. First is the simple listing of the property for sale on the terms set forth by the seller, in which case the listing may be with several brokers and the

right to withdraw or terminate the relationship at any time is reserved by the seller. Under such circumstances, the seller pays the commission to the first broker who finds a buyer. The owner is free to sell on his own behalf without a commission. The second type consists of an exclusive listing, which usually gives to the broker the exclusive right to find a buyer for an agreed period of time. In this case the seller is not free to list the property with other brokers, and a sale through other brokers would be a violation of the contract of listing, although the seller himself is free to find a buyer of his own. The right of an owner to sell his own property is an implicit condition of every contract of agency with a real estate broker unless negatived. Third is the listing by which the broker is given an exclusive right to sell. In this case even the seller is not free to find a buyer of his own choosing. If the seller does sell on his own behalf, he is obliged to pay a commission to the broker holding an exclusive right-to-sell listing.

Case: D entered into an exclusive right-to-sell real estate listing agreement with P, a broker. P advertised D's property, but D found X and sold the property to him. It was undisputed that P was not the "procuring cause" of the sale.

Issue: Is P entitled to a commission?

Decision: Yes.

Reasons: 1. A real estate broker with an "exclusive right-to-sell listing" is entitled to a commission if the broker renders the services required by the contract and if the property is sold during the period of the agreement regardless of by whom.

2. A broker must be the procuring cause of the sale under a simple listing and under an exclusive agency to sell, but not under an "exclusive agency with the sole right-to-sell" contract.

Wade v. Austin, 524 S.W.2d 79 (Tex.) 1975.

In recent years, there has developed what is known as a "multiple-listing agreement." This is a method of listing property with several brokers simultaneously. These brokers belong to an organization, the members of which share listings and divide the commissions. For example, a typical commission would be split, 60 percent to the selling broker, 30 percent to the listing broker, and 10 percent to the organization for operating expenses. These multiple-listing groups give homeowners the advantage of increased exposure to potential buyers. In return for this advantage, most multiple-listing agreements are of the exclusive right-to-sell type.

The right to a real estate commission is subject to statutory limitations in several states. Some of these require a written contract, and most require a license before a person may engage in this activity. Some courts have gone so far as to hold that a broker selling property in a state in which he is licensed is not entitled to a fee if the buyer is found or the sale completed in another state. Strict adherence to the licensing statutes is usually required. A broker may forfeit his right to compensation by improper conduct, breach of the duty of loyalty, or lack of good faith.

A real estate broker is a fiduciary, and his actions must be for the sole benefit of his principal. This requires disclosure to the owner of all matters that are material and that may affect the actions of the principal. A real estate agent must exercise diligence to effect a sale to the best advantage of the principal—that is, on the best terms and at the best price possible. Unfortunately, many brokers and agents frequently work for the potential buyer to some degree.

Duty to Compensate Sales Representatives

Salesmen who sell merchandise on a commission basis are confronted by problems similar to those of the broker, unless their employment contract is specific in its details. Let us assume that X company appoints A as its exclusive sales representative in a certain territory on a commission basis and that the employer is engaged in producing and selling electrical equipment. T, a businessman in the area involved, sends a large order for merchandise directly to the home office of X company. Is A entitled to a commission on the sale? It is generally held that such a salesman is entitled to a commission only on sales solicited and induced by him, unless his contract of employment gives him greater rights.

The salesman usually earns his commission as soon as an order from a responsible buyer is obtained, unless his contract of employment makes payment contingent upon delivery of the goods or collection of the sale's price. If payment is made dependent upon performance by the purchaser, the employer cannot deny the salesman his commission by terminating the agency prior to collection of the account. When the buyer ultimately pays for the goods, the seller is obligated to pay the commission.

An agent who receives a weekly or monthly advance against future commissions is not obligated to return the advance if commissions equal thereto are not earned. The advance, in the absence of a specific agreement, is considered by the courts as a minimum salary.

Duty to Reimburse and to Indemnify A servant is entitled to indemnity for certain tort losses. They are limited to factual situations in which the servant is not at fault and his liability results from following the instructions of the master. An agent or a servant is justified in presuming that instructions given by the principal are such as he lawfully has a right to give, and that performance resulting from such instructions will not injuriously affect third parties. Where this is not the case, and the agent incurs a liability to some third party because of trespass or conversion, the principal must indemnify the agent against loss. There will ordinarily be no indemnification for losses incurred in negligence actions because the servant's own conduct is involved. The indemnification is usually of the master by the servant in tort situations. However, if the agent or servant is sued for actions within the course of employment, the agent or servant is entitled to be reimbursed for attorney's fees and court costs incurred if the principal does not furnish them in the first instance.

Case: P, a newspaper reporter, sued D, his former employer and a newspaper publisher, seeking to recover the attorney's fees and court costs incurred in the defense of a libel action. P had been sued as the result of an article written by P for D's newspaper. P had won the libel case.

Issue: Must D indemnify P for his legal expenses?

Decision: Yes.

Reasons: 1. In this state [California] an employer is required by statute to defend or indemnify an employee who is sued by a third person for conduct in the course and within the scope of his employment.

2. The obligation of the employer to defend or indemnify the employee is not determined by whether the third person's suit was brought in good faith. If the employee was required to defend the suit solely because of acts that he performed within the scope of his employment, there is a right of indemnity.

3. P is entitled to his court costs and attorney's fees.

Douglas v. Los Angeles Herald-Examiner, 123 Cal. Rptr. 683 (1975).

An agent has a general right to reimbursement for money expended on behalf of his principal. It must appear that the money was reasonably spent and that its expenditure was not necessitated by the misconduct or negligence of the agent. It is the duty of the principal to make performance by the agent possible whenever the latter has entered into a contract in his own name for the former's benefit. The undisclosed principal must fully protect his agent by making the funds available to perform the contract as agreed.

REVIEW QUESTIONS AND PROBLEMS

1. List the five implied duties of agents to their principals.

2. Is the principal-agent relationship fiduciary in character? Explain.

3. Must an agent obey all instructions? Explain.

4. A told B that A would find a renter for B's property at a rent of $500 per month and that A would manage the building for $100 per month. B agreed. A rented the property to C at a rate of $550 per month. A kept the $50 difference when he collected the rent. May B recover the extra profits from A? Why?

5. X, while delivering goods for Y, negligently ran into a train, damaging Y's automobile. May Y recover from X? Why?

6. X, a widow, owned a small "country store." Y, her son, managed the store. Although she had no proof because Y's books were very confused, X suspected that Y was stealing funds. May X compel Y to give an accounting? Explain.

7. A, at B's instruction, repossessed C's car. B had no right to repossess the car. A seeks to join B in the suit and attempts to impose any liability on B, which he, A, may have to C. May he do so? Why?

8. P company was engaged in a wholesale business supplying goods to hospitals and novelty stores. A, its manager, while still working for P company, agreed with a salesman of the company and a third party to enter a competing business and arranged to handle two lines for which the P company previously held the exclusive agency. A quit and entered the competing business, but P company seeks to enjoin it from operation. What result? Why?

9. P employed A as manager of his business and authorized him to buy such supplies and merchandise as were needed. Being a member of CO-OP, A purchased all his supplies through it. At the end of the year, he received a personal dividend of $900 because of the purchases. Is he entitled to retain it? Assume that he purchased the supplies as advantageously as he could have at any other place. Explain.

10. B, appointed to sell merchandise in a certain area for S, was to receive a commission of 2 percent on all sales. He received a weekly advance of $750 for ten weeks, but his commissions averaged only $40 a week. Does he owe S the $350 difference? Why?

11. T contacted A, an employee of P, and told A that he would like to sell an item to P. In the event of a sale, T would pay A a commission. T instructed A not to reveal to P that the item was worth $20,000 so that T could ask a higher price. A succeeded in getting P to buy the item for $25,000, and A was paid $5,000 for his efforts. Can P recover the $5,000? If so, from whom? Explain.

12. A listed his house with B, a broker, under a contract that gave B the exclusive right to sell. During the period of the agreement, A sold the house to a friend. A refused to pay B any commission because B did not produce the buyer. Is B entitled to a commission? Why?

34 LABOR-MANAGEMENT RELATIONS

Introduction   Labor law is an important part of any study of the employer-employee relationship. Labor law is concerned with all aspects of collective bargaining as well as with the internal operation of labor unions. Labor law is developed not only by statutes and judicial decisions but also by the rules, regulations, and decisions of the National Labor Relations Board and the Department of Labor.

Labor law is better understood if its goals are recognized and understood. The primary goal of those laws relating to collective bargaining may be simply stated: it is to create equality of bargaining power between management and labor so that they will be able to settle their differences on mutually satisfactory terms consistent with the public interest. Some statutory provisions are designed to equalize the bargaining power of management with labor or vice versa. Other statutory provisions are designed to protect the public interest in the collective bargaining process. The sections that follow will briefly review the various laws that have been enacted to accomplish the goal of equalizing the bargaining power of labor and management.

LABOR LAWS PRIOR TO THE WAGNER ACT

Clayton Act   The Clayton Act of 1914 contained two provisions relating to labor relations. The first attempted to prohibit federal courts from issuing injunctions to prohibit strikes and picketing in disputes over terms or conditions of employment. The second provision provided that the antitrust laws were not applicable to labor unions or their members in carrying out union activities. Prior to the existence of the Clayton Act, the Sherman Antitrust Act was sometimes applied by courts to the activities of those in the labor movement. The Clayton Act provision exempting labor activities followed.

Railway Labor Act   In 1926 Congress enacted the Railway Labor Act. Its purpose was to encourage collective bargaining in the railroad industry so that labor disputes would not interrupt the transportation of goods in interstate commerce. The act was later extended to airlines, and it is now applicable to both forms of transportation. The Railway Labor Act created a National Mediation Board whose duty it is to designate the bargaining representative for any given group of employees in the railway or air transport industries. The act also declared that certain labor practices, such as refusing to bargain collectively, were federal crimes.

When the parties under the jurisdiction of the National Mediation Board cannot reach a collective bargaining agreement, it is the function of the board to attempt mediation of their differences. If mediation fails, the board encourages voluntary arbitration. If the parties refuse to arbitrate and the dispute is likely to be a substantial interruption of interstate commerce, the board informs the president, who may then appoint a special emergency board. This emergency board investigates the dispute and publishes its findings of fact and recommendations for its resolution. During the period of investigation and for thirty days after the report is made public, neither management nor labor can unilaterally change the condition out of which the dispute arose, such as by striking or discharging workers. The parties have no duty to agree to the special board's recommended solution. Thus if no new agreement is reached after the thirty-day waiting period, lockouts, strikes, and other actions by the parties are once again legal.

The procedures of the Railway Labor Act sometimes fail to resolve major disputes in transportation. Such failures may result in special action by the president or the Congress. The transportation industry's labor problems have such a potential for irreparable damage to the public that legislative solutions may be required.

The procedures discussed above apply to assisting employers and unions to arrive at a collective bargaining agreement; they do not apply to issues concerning the interpretation of existing contracts. Such issues in transportation must be submitted to compulsory arbitration.

Norris-LaGuardia Act   In 1932 the Norris-LaGuardia Act was enacted by Congress. Prior to its enactment, management could rather effectively prevent union activity by going to court and obtaining an injunction against a strike or against picketing. The Norris-LaGuardia Act encouraged collective bargaining by limiting the jurisdiction of federal courts in enjoining union activity. Federal courts may not issue an injunction to stop an employee or a union from engaging in lawful union activities such as striking and picketing.

It should be recognized that although Norris-LaGuardia greatly restricts the use of injunctions in labor disputes, it does not prohibit them altogether. The power of state courts to issue injunctions was not affected by Norris-LaGuardia. Moreover, an injunction may still be issued by a federal court if an unlawful act is about to be committed that will result in irreparable damage to the party seeking the injunction.

The second major provision of the Norris-LaGuardia Act was to make "yellow dog" contracts (those forbidding union membership) unenforceable. Because of this provision, it is illegal for an employer to have his employees agree that they will not join or form a union.

Although Norris-LaGuardia attempted to establish a climate in which employees would be free to organize and bargain collectively through a union without interference or coercion on the part of employers, it did nothing to impose any duty on management to deal with or even recognize unions. As a result, it did little to encourage growth of collective bargaining.

THE WAGNER ACT

Introduction In 1935 Congress passed the National Labor Relations Act, commonly called the Wagner Act. Noting that employees individually did not possess bargaining power equal to that of their employers, the Wagner Act stated that its policy was to protect by law the right of employees to organize and bargain collectively in order to encourage the "friendly adjustment of industrial disputes." This policy was to be accomplished by creating for employees equality in their bargaining position with that of employers. In summary, the Wagner Act:

1. Created an administrative agency, the National Labor Relations Board (NLRB), to administer the act. The NLRB was given broad powers.
2. Authorized the NLRB to conduct union certification elections and to certify the union that was to represent any given group of workers.
3. Outlawed certain conduct by employers that generally had had the effect of preventing or at least discouraging union activity. These prohibited acts are known as *unfair labor practices*. The NLRB was authorized to enter corrective orders when unfair labor practices had been committed. Unfair labor practices by management will be discussed further later in this chapter.

It must be kept in mind that the Wagner Act does not cover all workers. Among those exempt from its coverage are employees of the federal and state governments, political subdivisions of the states, nonprofit hospitals, and persons subject to the Railway Labor Act. Also excluded are independent contractors, individuals employed as agricultural laborers or as domestic servants in a home, and those employed by their spouse or a parent.

Taft-Hartley Amendment The Wagner Act provided a climate for rapid union growth. By the end of World War II many people believed that the power and influence of unions was greater than that of management. Although prior to the Wagner Act employers had superior bargaining power, by 1946 many persons felt the pendulum had shifted and the unions with their power of nationwide, crippling strikes had greater bargaining power. It was clear that no one company had equal bargaining power with a union that represented all employees in an industry. Moreover, nationwide strikes were having a substantial adverse effect on an important third party—the public.

In 1947 Congress attempted once again to equalize the bargaining power of management and labor. It did so by passing an amendment to the Wagner Act. This amendment is usually referred to as the Taft-Hartley Act. The Taft-Hartley amendment of the Wagner Act contained the following important provisions:

1. It provided that certain practices by unions were unfair labor practices. The Wagner Act had been one-sided. It had provided that certain practices by management were unfair to labor, but it had contained no provisions about improper activities by unions. The Taft-Hartley amendment added the other side to the coin and equalized bargaining power by declaring that certain activities by unions were improper. (These unfair labor practices are discussed more fully in subsequent sections.)

2. Recognizing the important interest of the public and the adverse effect on the country as a whole of nationwide strikes, Taft-Hartley contained a so-called eighty-day cooling-off period provision. This provision in effect allows the President, acting with an emergency board and through the federal courts, to obtain an injunction to stop a strike or lockout. The injunction to prevent the strike is good for eighty days when the strike or lockout may imperil the national health or safety.

3. It created the Federal Mediation and Conciliation Service to assist in the settlement of labor disputes. This federal agency is of special importance in strikes that threaten to have a serious impact on the national economy.

4. It outlawed the *closed* shop—one in which a person must be a union member as a condition of employment. Taft-Hartley did allow a *union* shop—one in which a worker must join the union after being employed at least thirty days. However, Section 14(b) authorized

states to enact state right-to-work laws. State right-to-work laws may prohibit union shops. Thus Taft-Hartley gave employees some freedom of choice in union membership.

Eighty-day Cooling-off Period The eighty-day cooling-off provisions of Taft-Hartley are extremely important. They may be used in any strike under the jurisdiction of the Wagner Act—almost any industry except transportation. The provisions come into play whenever the President is of the opinion that a strike or lockout will, if permitted to occur or to continue, imperil the national health or safety. The President then appoints a board of inquiry to obtain facts about the strike. The board makes a study of the strike and reports back to the President. If the board finds that the national health or safety is indeed affected by the strike, then the President, through the Attorney General, goes to the Federal District Court for an injunction ordering the union to suspend the strike (or company to suspend the lockout) for eighty days. During the eighty-day period, the Federal Mediation Service works with the two parties to try to achieve an agreement. If no agreement is reached during the eighty-day period, the Presidential board holds new hearings and receives the company's final offer. The members of the union are then allowed to vote on this final proposal of the company. If they vote for the new proposal, the dispute is over. If they vote against the proposal, the workers may again be called out on strike. At this point the strike may continue indefinitely until the disagreement causing it is resolved by collective bargaining, unless of course there is additional legislation by Congress to solve the problem. Experience has shown that most disputes are settled during the eighty-day period. The injunction provided for in the Taft-Hartley Act may not be used for all strikes but is limited to "national emergency" strikes. These must involve national defense or key industries or must have a substantial effect on the economy.

UNFAIR LABOR PRACTICES BY EMPLOYERS

Introduction The Wagner Act provided that five practices by employers were unfair to labor:

1. Interference with efforts of employees to form, join, or assist labor organizations, or to engage in concerted activities for mutual aid or protection.
2. Domination of a labor organization or contribution of financial or other support to it.
3. Discrimination in hire or tenure of employees for reason of union affiliation.

507

4. Discrimination against employees for filing charges or giving testimony under the act.

5. Refusal to bargain collectively with a duly designated representative of the employees.

Interference with Union Activity The unfair labor practice of interfering with the rights of workers to form or to join a union prevents any practice that might discourage union activity. It is intended to guarantee to workers the right to organize and to bargain collectively. It prohibits threats by employers to fire those involved in an attempt to organize employees or to cut back on employee benefits if they succeed in unionizing. It also prohibits the conferral of benefits on workers if the benefits are used by management to discourage union activity.

Case: A union was seeking to organize a plant, and an NLRB election was pending. During the period immediately prior to the election, the company informed the employees that their "floating holiday" in 1959 would fall on December 26 and that there would be an additional "floating holiday" in 1960. Six days after the board called for the election, the company held a dinner for employees at which an officer told the employees that they could decide whether the extra day of vacation in 1960 would be a "floating holiday" or would be taken on their birthdays.

Issue: Does the Wagner Act prohibit the conferral of benefits where the employer's purpose is to affect the outcome of an election?

Decision: Yes.

Reasons: 1. The broad purpose of Section 8(a)(1) is to establish "the right of employees to organize for mutual aid without employer interference." It prohibits not only intrusive threats and promises but also conduct immediately favorable to employees that is undertaken with the express purpose of impinging upon their freedom of choice for or against unionization and is reasonably calculated to have that effect.

2. The action of employees with respect to the choice of their bargaining agents may be induced by favors bestowed by the employer as well as by his threats or domination. The danger inherent in well-timed increases in benefits is the suggestion of a fist inside the velvet glove.

NLRB v. Exchange Parts Co., 375 U.S. 405 (1964).

Numerous complaints have been filed against employers contending that certain practices were designed to discourage union activity. The decision on these complaints usually requires a look at the state of mind of the employer at the time of the act in question. A review of past NLRB decisions reveals that the law is liberally interpreted and applied to give maximum effect to the purpose of the act—the encouragement of collective bargaining and the encouragement of union activity.

Although both parties are entitled to freedom of speech during a campaign to organize workers, management especially must be very careful in what it says. It must make sure that its statements do not contain threats of reprisal if a union is voted in or promises of benefits if the union is rejected. Coercive statements are an unfair labor practice that may result in the election being set aside. For example, a union organizer told the workers that the union would obtain higher wages for the workers. The company responded, "If the union comes in, the wages may go up but they may also go down." This was a coercive statement because it contained an implied threat and therefore it was an unfair labor practice.

A significant penalty for an unfair labor practice is to have an election set aside and a new election ordered. If the climate is such that the activity engaged in will likely affect a new election, the NLRB has on occasion certified a union that lost the election in order to carry out the policy of encouraging collective bargaining.

Other Unfair Labor Practices— Employers

It is also an unfair labor practice for an employer to dominate a labor organization or contribute financial or other support to it. The law views the relationship of employer and employee in the collective bargaining process to be adversary in character. The union must be independent of the employer. If two unions are seeking to organize workers, the law requires the employer to be neutral. An employer who takes sides is guilty of an unfair labor practice. Under this provision, a company cannot even give the union a place to meet. Company unions are out.

The third unfair labor practice listed in the Wagner Act prohibits discrimination in the hiring or tenure of employees for reason of union affiliation. Under this section, an employer may neither discharge nor refuse to hire an employee either to *encourage* or to *discourage* membership in any labor organization. Nor may he discriminate in regard to any term or condition of employment for such purposes.

Case: A union went out on strike against an employer. The employer sought to hire replacement workers, and to encourage them to apply, the company gave the new workers "super-seniority." This "super-seniority" was twenty years' additional seniority insofar as future layoffs were concerned. As a result of this offer, not only did the company hire new workers but many of them were former employees who resigned from the union.

Issue: Is the granting of super-seniority a form of discrimination against union members and thus an unfair labor practice?

Decision: Yes.

Reasons: 1. Super-seniority is a form of discrimination extending far beyond the employer's right to replace striking workers. Here the subjective intent of the employer was to destroy the union and to discourage the worker from further union activity.

2. There was also a desire to penalize union members who were on strike. The stated business purpose was not valid in light of the actual motive of the employer.

NLRB v. Erie Resistor Corp., 373 U.S. 221 (1963).

A fourth unfair labor practice by management is discriminating against employees for filing charges or giving testimony under the Wagner Act. This unfair labor practice protects employees from being discharged or from other reprisals by their employers because they have sought to enforce their rights under the law. It protects the NLRB's channels of information by preventing an employer's intimidation of complainants and witnesses.

In cases alleging retaliation for filing charges or giving testimony, the employer will frequently contend that action was taken against the employee for some reason other than his filing charges or giving testimony. Thus, most often these cases boil down to a question of proof of what motivated the employer in pursuing his course of action. If the employer can convince the NLRB that the employee was discharged because of misconduct, low production, personnel cutbacks necessitated by economic conditions, or other legitimate considerations, there is no unfair labor practice.

The Wagner Act as originally passed required employers to bargain collectively with unions. In other words, it was an unfair labor practice for management to refuse to bargain collectively with a duly certified union. The requirement to bargain collectively will be discussed later in this chapter.

Unfair Labor Practices by Unions The Taft-Hartley amendment to the Wagner Act declared that certain conduct or activities by labor unions were unfair labor practices and thus illegal. The Landrum-Griffin amendment added two additional unfair labor practices by unions to the list. Today, unfair labor practices by unions include the following:

1. Restraining or coercing an employee to join a union or an employer in selecting his representatives to bargain with the union.

510

2. Causing or attempting to cause the employer to discriminate against an employee who is not a union member, unless there is a legal union-shop agreement in effect. (This outlawed the closed shop, but it allows a union shop unless there is a state right-to-work law.)

3. Refusing to bargain with the employer if it is the NLRB-designated representative of his employees.

4. Striking, picketing, and engaging in secondary boycotts for illegal purposes.

5. Charging new members excessive or discriminatory initiation fees where there is a union-shop agreement.

6. Causing an employer to pay for work not performed (featherbedding).

7. Picketing to require an employer to recognize or bargain with a union that is not currently certified as representing his employees.

8. Agreeing with an employer to engage in a secondary boycott.

Illustrations of Illegal Union Activity　The first unfair labor practice includes both misconduct by unions directed toward employees and misconduct directed toward employers. Most allegations of unfair labor practices filed against unions are brought under this provision.

It is illegal for a union to restrain or coerce employees in the exercise of their right to bargain collectively, just as it is an unfair labor practice by employers to interfere with the same rights. Employees also are guaranteed the right to refrain from union activities unless required by a legal union shop agreement in force between their employer and a labor organization.

Mass picketing, threats of physical violence aimed at employees or their families, and blocking of entrances to plants to physically bar employees from going in, have all been held to be unfair union labor practices.

The words *restrain* and *coerce* have the same meaning when used in reference to union activity as they do when used in reference to activities by employers. The test is whether the words or conduct by the union are reasonably likely to have deprived the employees of a free choice. The intent is to ensure that the decision of the employees as to whether or not to be represented by a union in bargaining and also the choice of that representative is arrived at freely, without coercion.

Case:　The NLRB conducted a union certification election for D's employees at the request of P union. Prior to the election, "recognition slips" were circulated among the employees. An employee who signed the slip before the election would become a member of the union automatically and would not have to pay an "initiation fee" if the union was voted in. Those who had not signed a recognition slip would have to pay the fee, or fine as it was sometimes called. The union won the election, and the company seeks to set the election aside.

Issue: Is the waiver of the initiation fee grounds for setting aside the election?

Decision: Yes.

Reasons: 1. Whatever his true intentions, an employee who signs a recognition slip prior to an election is indicating to other workers that he supports the union. His outward manifestation of support must often serve as a useful campaign tool in the union's hands to convince other employees to vote for the union, if only because many employees respect their co-workers' views on the unionization issue. By permitting the union to offer to waive an initiation fee for those employees signing a recognition slip prior to the election, the Board allows the union to buy endorsements and paint a false portrait of employee support during its election campaign. We do not believe that the policy of fair elections permits endorsements, whether for or against the union, to be bought and sold in this fashion.

2. Any procedure requiring a "fair" election must honor the right of those who oppose a union as well as those who favor it. The Act is wholly neutral when it comes to that basic choice. By § 7 of the Act employees have the right not only to "form, join, or assist" unions but also the right "to refrain from any or all of such activities."

NLRB v. Savair Manufacturing Company, 94 S.Ct. 495 (1973).

One of the unfair labor practices previously listed concerns the union's applying what are called secondary pressures against an employer. A secondary pressure may take the form of a strike or a boycott or an attempt to encourage a strike or a boycott. Secondary pressures are those whose purpose it is to force an employer to cease using or dealing in the products of another. For example, it is illegal to strike against employer A for the purpose of forcing him to cease doing business with employer B. Similarly, it is unlawful for a union to boycott employer A because employer A uses or deals in the goods of employer B.

"Featherbedding" is another example of an unfair labor practice by unions. Featherbedding occurs when an employer is required to pay for work not performed. It should be understood that "make work" provisions of union contracts are not illegal featherbedding. This provision of Taft-Hartley is not violated as long as some services are performed, even if they are of little or no actual value to the employer.

Organizational picketing to force the recognition of an uncertified union is illegal:

1. When the employer has lawfully recognized another union as the collective bargaining representative of his employees.
2. When a valid representation election has been conducted by the NLRB within the past twelve months.
3. When the picketing has been conducted for a reasonable time, not in excess of thirty days, without a petition for a representation election being filed with the NLRB.

Such organizational picketing is an unfair labor practice because of the policy of the law to encourage NLRB-conducted elections. The NLRB election procedures are reinforced, and unions that represent only a minority of employees are prevented from continuing a jurisdictional dispute with the union representing the majority of workers.

"Hot-cargo" contracts are unfair labor practices and illegal insofar as both parties to the contract are concerned. A hot-cargo contract is one in which the parties (employer and union) agree that the employer will not handle, use, sell, or transport products of another business involved in a labor dispute. In other words, the product of the company involved in a labor dispute becomes "hot," and other companies agree with their union that they will not be involved with such products.

**The Requirement
to Bargain
Collectively**
As previously noted, it is an unfair labor practice for either the employer or the union to refuse to bargain collectively with each other. The term "to bargain collectively" means to bargain in good faith. Although the parties need not agree with each other's demands, such conduct as the failure to make counterproposals may be evidence of bad faith. Employers and unions must approach the bargaining table with a fair and open mind and sincere purpose to find a basis of agreement. Refusing to meet at reasonable times with representatives of the other party, refusing to reduce agreements to writing, and designating persons with no authority to negotiate as representatives at meetings are examples of conduct that constitute this unfair labor practice.

Another issue is also present in the requirement that the parties bargain collectively. This issue, simply stated, is: about what? Must the employer bargain with the union on all management decisions in which the union or the employees are interested? Are there subjects and issues upon which management is allowed to act unilaterally? The law requires or compels bargaining on issues concerned with wages, hours, and other terms and conditions of employment.

Thus management decisions affecting labor fall into two categories, those that concern *mandatory* or *compulsory* bargaining issues, and those that involve *voluntary* or *permissive* bargaining issues. Classifications must be made on a case-by-case basis. For example, a question relating to fringe benefits such as a pension plan is a compulsory bargaining issue because it is concerned with wages.

Case: A company operated a manufacturing plant. A union represented the company's maintenance employees. The agreement with the union was about to expire, and the company informed the union that after a study it had decided to engage an independent contractor to perform these maintenance services. The company expressed the view that in the light of its decision, negotiation of a new contract would be pointless. At the termination of the contract the employment of the maintenance workers was ended, and a subcontractor's employees began doing this work.

Issue: Is the subcontracting of maintenance work a compulsory bargaining issue?

Decision: Yes.

Reasons: 1. The National Labor Relations Act does not say that the employer and employees are bound to confer upon any subject that interests either of them; the specification of wages, hours, and other terms and conditions of employment defines a limited category of issues subject to compulsory bargaining.

2. Those management decisions that are fundamental to the basic direction of a corporate enterprise but that impinge only indirectly upon employment security are not compulsory bargaining issues.

3. Because it is a widespread industrial practice to include the subject of contracting-out within the collective bargaining process, contracting-out work performed by members of the bargaining unit is a condition of employment.

Fibreboard Paper Products Corp. v. NLRB, 379 U.S. 203 (1964).

Courts tend to defer to the special expertise of the NLRB in classifying collective bargaining subjects, especially in the area of "terms or conditions of employment." Among the issues that have been held to be compulsory bargaining issues are merit-pay increases, incentive-pay plans, bonuses, paid vacations and holidays, proposals for effective arbitration and grievance procedures, and no-strike and no-lockout clauses.

Typical of issues that do not involve compulsory bargaining matters are the price of the employer's product, loading and unloading procedures, and the operation of a cafeteria by an independent contractor.

514

It should be reemphasized that neither the employer nor the union is required to make concessions to the other concerning a mandatory subject of bargaining. The law only demands that each negotiate such matters in good faith with the other before making a decision and taking unilateral action. If the parties fail to reach an agreement after discussing these problems, each may take steps that are against the wishes and best interests of the other party. For example, the employer may refuse to grant a wage increase requested by the union, and the union is free to strike.

Landrum-Griffin Act After the enactment of Taft-Hartley, Congress turned its attention to the internal operations of labor unions. Hearings before congressional committees in the 1950s revealed widespread corruption, lack of democratic procedures, and domination of labor unions by elements thought to be undesirable. As a result, Congress in 1959 enacted the Landrum-Griffin Amendment to the Wagner Act.

In order to eliminate internal corruption and to guarantee that the "rank and file" union members had control of their union, Landrum-Griffin contained a "Bill of Rights" of union members. These protected rights are:

1. To nominate candidates, to vote in elections, to attend membership meetings, and to have a voice in business transactions, subject to reasonable union rules and regulations.
2. To have free expression in union meetings, business discussions, and conventions subject to reasonable rules and regulations.
3. To vote on an increase of dues or fees.
4. To sue and testify against the union.
5. To receive written, specific charges; to be given a reasonable time for defense; and to be accorded a full and fair hearing before any disciplinary action is taken by the union against them.
6. To be given a copy of the collective bargaining agreement that they work under, upon request.

Landrum-Griffin contains provisions relating to reports that must be filed with the secretary of labor. The purpose of these reports is to reveal practices detrimental to union members. For example, each union must adopt a constitution and bylaws and file them with the secretary of labor. In addition, unions must keep the Department of Labor informed as to:

1. The name and address of the union office and the place where records are kept.

2. The names and titles of officers.
3. The amount of initiation fees required.
4. The amount of dues charged.
5. A detailed statement of procedures for (*a*) qualification for office, (*b*) levying fees, (*c*) insurance plans, (*d*) disbursement of funds, (*e*) audits, (*f*) selection of officers, (*g*) removal of officers, (*h*) determining bargaining demands, (*i*) fines, (*j*) approval of contracts, (*k*) calling strikes, and (*l*) issuance of work permits.

In addition, yearly financial reports must be filed that indicate:

1. Assets and liabilities
2. Receipts and sources of funds
3. Salaries of officers
4. Loans to members greater than $250
5. Loans to business enterprises
6. Other disbursements

A major focus of Landrum-Griffin is on union elections. The law requires that elections be held at minimum regular intervals to promote democracy. National unions must hold elections at least every five years, locals every three years, and intermediate bodies every four years. Elections must be by secret ballot of members or of delegates who were chosen by secret ballot of members.

REVIEW QUESTIONS AND PROBLEMS

1. Define the following terms: *unfair labor practice, eighty-day cooling off period, union shop, closed shop, hot-cargo contract, secondary boycott, mandatory bargaining issue,* and *voluntary bargaining issue.*

2. What was the effect of the Clayton Act on labor-management relations?

3. What was the purpose of the Norris-LaGuardia Act? Does it prohibit all injunctions in labor disputes?

4. Briefly state the reasons for passage of the Taft-Hartley Act.

5. A group of employees of the XYZ company, seeking to become the exclusive bargaining agent for all employees of XYZ, decided to organize. While the election was pending, XYZ allowed the group to use the company's photocopy machine and in-house mail system for solicitation purposes. A union also seeking to represent the employees filed an unfair labor practice charge to stop these practices. What result? Why?

6. Union members employed by the XYZ manufacturing company were dissatisfied with their salary schedule. C was one of XYZ's largest customers. The union threw up a picket line in front of C's store in protest of C's business relationship with XYZ. Is this activity legal? Why?

7. An employer, during a strike, tells the strikers that if they are replaced, they will "lose forever their right to reemployment by this company." Is this an unfair labor practice? Explain.

8. Two unions were seeking recognition from the NLRB. The employer wrote a letter to the workers advising them that if he were voting he would vote for union X over union Y. Is this an unfair labor practice? Explain.

9. An employer posted a "no-solicitation rule" that prohibited anyone from soliciting workers to join a union on company premises. The rule also prohibited solicitation at the coffee shop across the street from the plant. Is this an unfair labor practice? Explain.

10. A company fired employees for "poor workmanship." These five were the leaders in an attempt to unionize the shop. No other employees were fired. Are they entitled to reinstatement? Explain.

11. Two unions were arguing over which should assemble and dismantle certain machinery. One of the unions threw up a picket line and the rest of the workers on the job refused to cross the picket line. Is the picketing union guilty of an unfair labor practice? Explain.

12. On the day an election is to be held to determine whether or not A's employees will organize and become members of a labor union, A grants all employees a bonus of $100. Is A guilty of an unfair labor practice?

VII BUSINESS ORGANIZATIONS

CHOOSING THE FORM OF BUSINESS ORGANIZATION

35

Introduction Business organizations may operate under a variety of legal forms. The common ones are sole proprietorships, partnerships, limited partnerships, and corporations. There are also some specialized organizations, such as professional service corporations, that are authorized by statute so that doctors, lawyers, dentists, and other professional persons are able to obtain the tax advantages of corporations.

This chapter will examine the various forms of organization and the factors that influence the actual selection of a particular form. The factors involved in this selection are applicable to all businesses from the smallest to the largest, but the relative influence of the various factors varies greatly depending on the size of the business. As a practical matter, the very large business must be incorporated because that is the only method that can bring a large number of owners and investors together for an extended period of time.

The difficulty of deciding which is the best form of organization to select is most often encountered in the closely held business. Taxation is usually the most significant factor. Although a detailed discussion of the tax laws is beyond the scope of this text, some of the general principles of taxation will be presented in order to illustrate the influence taxation brings to bear in choosing between diverse organizational forms.

General Partnerships Partnerships developed logically in the law merchant, and the common law of partnerships has been codified in the Uniform Partnership Act. A partnership is an association of two or more persons to carry on as co-owners a business for profit. It is the result of an agreement.

521

This form of organization has many advantages: (1) since it is a matter of contract between individuals to which the state is not a party, it is easily formed; (2) the costs of formation are minimal; (3) it is not a taxable entity; (4) each owner, as a general rule, has an equal voice in management; (5) it may operate in more than one state without being required to comply with many legal formalities; and (6) partnerships are generally subject to less regulation and less governmental supervision than corporations. The fact that a partnership is not a taxable entity does not mean that partnership income is tax free. A partnership files an information return allocating its income among the partners, and each partner pays income tax on the portion allocated to him.

Several aspects of partnerships may be considered disadvantageous in many cases. First, as a personal matter, only a limited number of people may own such a business. Second, a partnership is dissolved any time a member ceases to be a partner either by withdrawal or by death. Although dissolution is the subject matter of Chapter 38, it should be observed here that the perpetual existence of a corporation is often a distinct advantage as compared to easily dissolvable partnerships.

Third, the liability of a partner is unlimited as contrasted with the limited liability of a shareholder. The unlimited liability of a partner is applicable to both contract and tort claims. Fourth, since a partner is taxed on his share of the profits of a partnership, whether distributed to him or not, a partner may be required to pay income tax on money that is not received. This burden is an important consideration in a new business that is reinvesting its profits for expansion. A partner in such a business would have to have an independent means of paying the taxes on such income.

Limited Partnerships A limited partnership, just as other partnerships, comes into existence by virtue of an agreement. However, a limited partnership is like a corporation in that it is authorized by statute, and the liability of one or more of the partners, but not of all, is limited to the amount of capital contributed at the time of the creation of the partnership. This latter characteristic supplies the name for this type of business organization, which is in effect a hybrid between the partnership and the corporation.

A limited partnership may be formed by two or more persons, having one or more general partners and one or more limited partners. To create a limited partnership under the Uniform Limited Partnership Act, the parties must sign and swear to a certificate containing among other matters the following information: the name of the partnership; the character of the business; its location; the name and place of residence of each member; those who are to be the general and those who are to be the limited partners; the term for which the partnership is to exist; the amount of cash or the agreed value of property to be contributed by each partner; and the share of profit or compensation each limited partner shall receive.

The certificate must be recorded in the county where the partnership has its principal place of business, and a copy must be filed in every community where it conducts business or has a representative office. In addition, most states require notice by newspaper publication. In the event of any change in the facts contained in the certificate as filed, such as a change in the name of the partnership, the capital, or other matters, a new certificate must be filed. If such a certificate is not filed and the partnership continues, the limited partners immediately become liable as general partners.

The statutes of most states require the partnership to conduct its business in a firm name that does not include the name of any of the limited partners or the word *company*. Some states specify that the word *limited* shall be added.

A limited partner is not liable beyond his contribution to creditors of the partnership in the pursuit of the partnership business, unless the limited partner participates in the management and control of the business. Participation in management makes the limited partner a general partner with unlimited liability.

This unlimited liability cannot be avoided by use of a corporation as the general partner if the limited partners are in control of the corporate general partner.

Case: A limited partnership was formed with a corporation as the general partner. The limited partners were officers and directors of the corporation. P, a creditor of the limited partnership, sought to collect a partnership debt from the limited partners individually. The law provides that a limited partner who takes part in the control of a business is liable as a general partner.

Issue: Can the personal liability that attaches to a limited partner when he takes part in control of the business be evaded by acting through a corporation?

Decision: No.

Reasons: 1. Strict compliance with the limited partnership statute is required if limited partners are to avoid liability as general partners.

2. An exception to the rule that corporate officers are insulated from personal liability arising from their activities or those of a corporation exists where the corporate fiction is used to circumvent a statute.

3. The limited partners effectively controlled the business in their individual capacities. Their personal liability cannot be avoided by the corporate fiction.

4. A limited partner need not hold himself out as a general partner for liability to attach. The liability is statutory and not based on any theory of estoppel.

Delaney v. Fidelity Lease Limited, 526 S.W.2d 543 (Tex.) 1975.

A limited partnership cannot be dissolved voluntarily before the time for its termination as stated in the certificate without the filing and publication of a notice of the dissolution. Upon dissolution, the distribution of the assets of the firm is prescribed by statute. As a general rule, the law gives priority to limited partners over general partners after all creditors are paid.

The limited partnership as a tax shelter is of special value in many new businesses and especially in real estate ventures such as shopping centers and apartment complexes. It gives the investor limited liability and the operators control of the venture. It allows the maximum use of the tax advantages of accelerated depreciation and the investment credit. Accelerated depreciation usually results in a tax loss in early years, which can be immediately deducted by the limited partner. However, there is usually a positive cash flow, notwithstanding the tax loss. Thus a limited partner may be able to receive income and at the same time a loss for tax purposes. When such ventures start to show a taxable gain, the limited partnership is often dissolved and a corporation formed or the venture is sold.

The obvious disadvantage in a limited partnership is the fact that the limited partner cannot participate in management without a change of status to that of a general partner. However, a limited partner does have a right to inspect the books of the business, to receive an accounting, and to engage in activities that are of an advisory nature and do not amount to control of the business.

Case: Ds were limited partners in a real estate venture. After the business was in financial difficulty, the limited partners had two meetings with the general partners to discuss the problems of the venture. In addition, one limited partner visited the construction site and "obnoxiously" complained of the way the work was being conducted.

Issue: Do these actions constitute taking part in the control of the business so as to make the limited partners liable as general partners?

Decision: No.

Reasons: 1. It is well established that just because a man is a limited partner in an enterprise, he is not by reason of that status precluded from continuing to

524

have an interest in the affairs of the partnership, from giving advice and suggestions to the general partner or his nominees, and from interesting himself in specific aspects of the business.

2. Such casual advice as the limited partners may have given in this case can hardly be said to be interference in day-to-day management. Certainly common sense dictates that in times of severe financial crisis all partners in such an enterprise, limited or general, will become actively interested in any effort to keep the enterprise afloat, and many abnormal problems will arise that are not under any stretch of the imagination mere day-to-day matters of managing the partnership business.

3. It would be unreasonable to hold that a limited partner may not advise with the general partner and may not visit the partnership business, especially in times of severe financial crisis.

Trans-Am Builders, Inc. v. Woods Mill Ltd., 210 S.E.2d 866 (64) 1974.

The Business Corporation

The corporation comes into existence when the state issues the corporate charter. A corporation is a legal entity that usually has perpetual existence. The liability of the owners is limited to their investment, unless there is a successful "piercing of the corporate veil." (See Chapter 39 for a further discussion of "piercing the corporate veil.")

Case: A corporation leased real property and purchased certain items of merchandise on credit from P. The corporation failed financially, and P contended that the corporate structure was a sham. P sought to hold D, the sole stockholder, personally liable.

Issue: Is a shareholder personally liable for the debts of a corporation?

Decision: No.

Reason: Being a stockholder in a debtor corporation does not under the law make a stockholder liable for the debts and obligations of the corporation. A corporation is a statutory entity that is regarded as having an existence and personality distinct from that of its stockholders even though the stock is owned by a single individual.

Shaw v. Bailey-McCune Company, 355 P.2d 321 (Utah) 1960.

A corporation, as a general rule, is a taxable entity paying a tax on its net profits. In addition, dividends paid to stockholders are also taxable, giving rise to the frequently made observation that corporate income is subject to double taxation. The accuracy of this observation will be discussed later.

The advantages of the corporate form of organization may be briefly summarized as follows: (1) it is the only method that will raise substantial capital from a large number of investors; (2) the investors have limited liability; (3) the organization can have perpetual existence; (4) it is possible for control to be vested in those with a minority of the investment by using such techniques as nonvoting or preferred stock; (5) ownership may be divided into many separate and unequal shares; (6) the investors, notwithstanding their status as owners, may also be employees entitled to such benefits as workmen's compensation; (7) certain laws such as those relating to usury are not applicable to corporations; and (8) the tax laws have several provisions that are favorable to corporations.

Among the frequently cited disadvantages of the corporate form of organization are (1) the cost of forming and maintaining the corporate form with its rather formal procedures; (2) expenditures such as license fees and franchise taxes that are assessed against corporations but not against partnerships; (3) the double taxation of corporate income and the frequently higher rates; (4) the requirement that it must be qualified to do business in all states where it is conducting intrastate commerce; (5) the fact that corporations are subject to more regulation by government at all levels than other forms; and (6) that a corporation must use an attorney in litigation, whereas a layman can proceed on his own behalf.

Case: The credit manager of a corporation brought suit against D in a small claims court without the assistance of an attorney. Judgment was entered, and garnishment proceedings commenced. D then brought suit to enjoin the proceedings because the association proceeded without an attorney in the original suit.

Issue: May a corporation commence legal proceedings without an attorney?

Decision: No.

Reasons: 1. Although a corporation is a "person," which can maintain an action in a small claims court, it does not follow that any officer or employee of such corporation can properly institute such an action by appearing in behalf of the corporation. Corporations are different in that respect from natural persons.

2. A corporation cannot practice law and must have a licensed attorney representing it in court matters. A natural person may represent himself and present his own case to the court although he is not a licensed

attorney. A corporation is not a natural person. It is an artificial entity created by law, and as such it can neither practice law nor appear or act in person.

Tuttle v. Hi-Land Dairyman's Association, 350 P.2d 619 (Utah) 1960.

taxation   The fact that taxation was listed as both an advantage and a disadvantage of the corporate form illustrates the overwhelming importance of the tax factor in choosing this particular form of organization. The corporate tax law provisions that have most encouraged incorporation are those relating to qualified profit-sharing and pension plans. These provisions allow a corporation to deduct from taxable income its payments under qualified plans up to 25 percent of its payroll. These payments are invested, and the earnings are not subject to taxation when earned. No income tax is paid until the recipients receive payments after retirement. To illustrate the advantages of such plans, assumes that A, B, and C are shareholders and employees of the ABC company. Assume also that the company has five additional employees and that the net income of the company is $100,000. If ABC company pays $20,000 under qualified plans, the income tax reduction is $9,600 (assuming a 48 percent rate). The net cost of the payment to the company is $10,400. The $20,000 is credited to the accounts of the employees by a formula based on wages and years of service. Assume that the amounts credited to A, B, and C total $12,000. This gives them an initial net gain of $1,600 and a tax-free investment. In addition, the employees received substantial benefits and security. A, B, and C as well as the other employees will receive their savings upon retirement at a time when their tax rates will be lower and exemptions increased. Such plans have given impetus to the incorporation of hundreds of thousands of small businesses and professional practices.

Other advantages of the tax laws to corporations are (1) health insurance payments are fully deductible and are not subject to the limitations applicable to individuals; (2) deferred compensation plans may be adopted; (3) earnings up to $25,000 are currently taxed at a rate of 20 percent, and the next $25,000 of earnings are currently taxed at the rate of 22 percent, both of which are often lower than the individual investor's tax rate; (4) income that is needed in the business is not taxed to a person who does not receive it; (5) accumulated income can be taken out as a capital gain on dissolution; (6) the corporation may provide life insurance for its employees as a deductible expense; and (7) medical expenses in excess of health insurance coverage may be paid on behalf of employees as a deductible expense.

The corporate form is frequently at a disadvantage from a tax standpoint because of the double taxation aspect and because the 48

527

percent rate often exceeds the individual rate of the owners of the business. In addition, some states impose a higher tax on corporate income than on individual income. There are also many taxes that are imposed on corporations but not on individuals or partnerships.

avoidance of double taxation In connection with the double taxation of corporate income, it should be noted that certain techniques may be used to avoid, in part, the double taxation of corporate income. First of all, reasonable salaries paid to corporate employees may be deducted in computing the taxable income of the business. Thus, in a closely held corporation, in which all or most shareholders are officers or employees, this technique can be used to avoid double taxation of much of the corporate income. However, the Internal Revenue Code disallows a deduction for excessive or unreasonable compensation, and unreasonable payments to shareholder employees are taxable as dividends. Therefore the determination of the reasonableness of corporate salaries is an ever-present tax problem in the closely held corporation that employs shareholders.

Second, the capital structure of a corporation may include both common stock and interest-bearing loans from shareholders. For example, assume that a company needs $200,000 to commence business. If $200,000 of stock is purchased, there will be no expense to be deducted. However, assume that $100,000 worth of stock is purchased and $100,000 is loaned to the company at 8 percent interest. In this case $8,000 of interest each year is deductible as an expense of the company, and thus subject to only one tax as interest income to the owners. Just as in the case of salaries, the Internal Revenue Code contains a counteracting rule relating to corporations that are undercapitalized. If the corporation is undercapitalized, interest payments will be treated as dividends and disallowed as deductible expenses.

The third technique for avoiding double taxation, at least in part, is simply not to pay dividends and to accumulate the earnings. After the earnings have been accumulated, the shareholders can sell their stock or dissolve the corporation. In both situations the difference between the original investment and the amount received is given capital gains treatment. Here again we have tax laws designed to counteract the above technique. There is a special income tax imposed on "excessive accumulated earnings" in addition to the normal tax and rules relating to collapsible corporations.

Finally, there is a special provision in the Internal Revenue Code that allows small, closely held business corporations to be treated similarly to partnerships for income tax purposes. These corporations, known as Sub-Chapter S corporations, are discussed more fully in the next section.

The Sub-Chapter S Corporation The limited partnership is a hybrid between a corporation and a partnership in the area of liability. A similar hybrid known as a tax-option or Sub-Chapter S corporation exists in the tax area of the law. Such corporations have the advantage of the corporate form without the double taxation of income.

The tax-option corporation is one that elects to be taxed in a manner similar to that of partnerships—that is, to file an information return allocating income among the shareholders for immediate reporting regardless of dividend distributions, thus avoiding any tax on the part of the corporation.

Sub-Chapter S corporations cannot have more than ten shareholders to begin with. After it is in existence for 5 years, it may have up to fifteen shareholders, each of whom must sign the election to be taxed in the manner similar to a partnership. Corporations with more than 20 percent of their income from rents, interest, dividends, or royalties do not qualify. There are many technical rules of tax law involved in Sub-Chapter S corporations, but as a rule of thumb this method of taxation has distinct advantages for a business operating at a loss because the loss is shared and immediately deductible on the returns of the shareholders. It is also advantageous for businesses capable of paying out net profits as earned. In the latter case the corporate tax is avoided. If net profits must be retained in the business, Sub-Chapter S tax treatment is disadvantageous because income tax is paid on earnings not received. There is also a danger of double taxation to the individual because undistributed earnings that have been taxed once are taxed again in the event of the death of a shareholder. However, the tax laws relating to pension plans reduce the advantages of such corporations. They have equal status with partnerships and sole proprietorships for pension and profit-sharing plan purposes. This status is discussed more fully in the next section.

The Professional Service Association Traditionally, professional services, such as those of a doctor, lawyer, or dentist, could only be performed by an individual and could not be performed by a corporation because the relationship of doctor and patient or attorney and client was considered a highly personal one. The impersonal corporate entity could not render the personal services involved.

The tax advantages of profit-sharing and pension plans previously discussed in connection with corporations are not available to private persons and partnerships to the same extent that they are available to corporations. An individual proprietor or partner is limited to a deduction of 15 percent of income or $7,500, whichever is lesser, under what is usually referred to as *H.R. 10*, or *Keogh*, pension plan provision. Therefore, professional persons often desire to incorporate or to form a professional association in order to obtain the greater tax advantages of corporate pension and profit-sharing plans. To make this possible, every state has enacted statutes authorizing professional associations. These associations are legal entities similar to corporations, and they are allowed deductions for payments to qualified pension and profit-sharing plans equal to those of business corporations. To illustrate the advantages of a professional corporation or association, assume that a doctor has a net income of $100,000. If he is unincorporated, he may pay $7,500 into a retirement plan. However, if he incorporates his practice, he may pay $25,000 into a qualified pension (10 percent, or $10,000) and profit-sharing (15 percent, or $15,000) plan. Of this $25,000, one-half, or $12,500 is in federal tax savings, since his income would be taxed at the 50 percent rate. The earnings of the $25,000 invested are tax free until retirement. In addition, he can deduct health insurance premiums, pay additional personal medical expenses as a deductible expense, and provide up to $50,000 of life insurance with tax-free dollars. The cost of these savings is whatever is paid into the plan to cover his employees.

While the foregoing illustration may not be typical of all professional persons, there is obviously great impetus in the law for the formation of professional associations. Today, there are thousands of professional corporations. They can be identified by the letters *S.C.* (Service Corporation), *P.C.* (Professional Corporation), or *Inc.* (Incorporated), or by the word *company* in the name of the professional firm.

**Making
the Decision** The business with substantial capitalization will be a corporation for the reasons previously noted. If the business is to be owned and operated by relatively few persons, the decision as to the form of organization involves a consideration of the factors previously discussed, the most significant of which are (1) taxation, (2) liability, (3) control, (4) continuity, and (5) legal capacity. *Legal capacity* is the power of the business to sue and to be sued in its own name and the power to own and dispose of property as well as to enter into contracts in its own name.

In evaluating the impact of taxation, an accountant or attorney will look at the projected profits or losses of the business, the ability to distribute earnings, and the tax brackets of the individuals involved as owners. A computation of the estimated total tax burden under the various forms of organization will be made. The results will be considered along with the other factors in making the decision as to the form of business organization to be used.

The generalization that partners have unlimited liability and stockholders limited liability must be qualified in the case of a closely held business A small closely held corporation with limited assets and capital will find it difficult to obtain credit on the strength of its own credit standing alone, and as a practical matter the shareholders will usually be required to add their own individual liability as security for the debts. For example, if the XYZ company seeks a loan at a local bank, the bank will require the owners X, Y, and Z to personally guarantee repayment of the loan. This is not to say that closely held corporations do not have some degree of limited liability. The investors in those types of businesses are protected with limited liability for contractlike obligations that are imposed as a matter of law (such as taxes) and for debts resulting from torts that are committed by company employees while engaged in company business.

If the tax aspects dictate a partnership and limited liability is desired by some investors, the limited partnership will be considered.

Issues of liability are not restricted to the investors in the business or to financial liability. Corporation law has developed several instances in which the directors and officers of the corporation will have liability to shareholders or to the corporation for acts or omission by such directors or officers in their official capacity. These matters will be discussed more fully in Chapter 39.

The significance of the law relating to control will be apparent in the discussions on formation and operation of partnerships and corporations in the chapters that follow. The desire of one or more individuals to control the business is a major factor in selecting the form, and the control issues are second only to taxation in importance.

The table on page 533 summarizes the factors that are considered in choosing a form of organization.

REVIEW QUESTIONS AND PROBLEMS

1. List the advantages and disadvantages of the partnership form of business organization.

2. List the advantages and disadvantages of the corporate form of business organization.

3. List four techniques for avoiding double taxation of corporate income and give an example of each.

4. List those characteristics of a limited partnership that are similar to (a) those of a general partnership and (b) those of a corporation.

5. What are the legal restrictions on a corporation electing to be taxed under Sub-Chapter S of the Internal Revenue Code?

6. A, the owner of an automobile dealership, and B signed and recorded a limited partnership agreement in which A was the general partner, and B the limited partner. B contributed $10,000 and worked, under A's control, as manager of the service department. C, a creditor of the partnership, obtained a judgment for $25,000 against the partnership. This amount exceeded the partnership's assets and A's personal assets combined. May C reach B's personal assets? Why?

7. A, B, and C organized an auto repair business as a limited partnership. Their agreement stated that A and B were general partners and that C was a limited partner. The agreement expressly provided that " . . . under no circumstances would C be liable for any negligent acts of A or B." When the business began to experience financial difficulty, C began to participate in decisions concerning methods of attracting new customers. X brought his car in for repairs, and A installed brakes in a negligent manner which resulted in injury to X. Could C be personally liable to X? Discuss.

8. John Doe and Richard Roe wish to enter the camping equipment manufacturing business. Assume that each of the following facts exists. In each case, which type of business association would be most advantageous? Explain.

a. Doe is an expert in the field of camping gear production and sale but has no funds. Roe knows nothing about such production but is willing to contribute all necesary capital.

b. Camping gear production requires large amounts of capital, much more than Doe and Roe can raise personally or together, yet they wish to control the business.

c. Some phases of production and sale are rather dangerous, and a relatively large number of tort judgments may be anticipated.

d. Sales will take place on a nationwide basis.

e. Doe and Roe are both sixty-five years old. No profits are expected for at least five years, and interruption of the business before that time will make it a total loss.

f. Several other persons wish to put funds into the business but are unwilling to assume personal liability.

g. The anticipated earnings over cost, at least for the first few years, will be approximately $70,000. Doe and Roe wish to draw salaries of $25,000 each; they also want a hospitalization and retirement plan, all to be paid from these earnings.

h. A loss is expected for the first three years, due to the initial capital outlay and the difficulty in entering the market.

9. A and B practiced dentistry together as a partnership. Their individual net income exceeded $100,000, and each invested large sums in real estate and stocks. Should the dentists consider another form of business organization? Explain.

Comparison of the Characteristics of Business Organizations

Characteristics	Corporations		Partnerships	
	General	Sub-Chapter S	General	Limited
1. Method of creation	Charter issued by state	Same + file agreement with IRS	Created by agreement of the parties	Same + file statutory form in public office
2. Liability of members	Shareholders have limited liability	Same	Partners have unlimited liability	General partners—unlimited liability; limited partners—limited liability
3. Duration	May be perpetual	Same	Termination by death, agreement, bankruptcy, or withdrawal of a partner	The term provided in the certificate
4. Transferability of interest	Generally freely transferable, subject to limits of contracts between shareholders	Same	Not transferable	General partner—not transferable; limited partner—transferable
5. Management	Shareholders elect directors, who set policy	Same	All partners in absence of agreement have equal voice	General partners have equal voice; limited partners have no voice
6. Taxation	Income taxed to corp; dividends taxed to shareholders	Net income taxed to shareholders whether distributed or not	Not a taxable entity—net income taxed to partners whether distributed or not	Same
7. Legal entity for progress of a. Suit in firm name b. Owning property in firm name c. Bankruptcy d. Limiting liability	Is a legal entity in all states, for all purposes	Same	By modern law is an entity for a. Yes b. Yes c. Yes d. No	Same
8. Transact business in other states	Must qualify to do business and obtain certificate of authority	Same	No limitation	Copy of certificate must be filed in all counties where doing business
9. Organization fee, annual license fee, and annual reports	All required	Same	None	None
10. Modification of amendment of articles	Must obtain state approval	Same	No requirement	Must file changes
11. Agency	A shareholder is not an agent of the corporation	Same	Each partner is both a principal and an agent of his copartners	Limited partners are not principals or agents; general partners are the same as in general partnership

36 FORMATION OF PARTNERSHIPS

Introduction   A *partnership* is defined as an association of two or more persons to carry on as co-owners of a business for profit. It is the result of an agreement between competent parties to place their money, property, or labor in a business and to divide the profits and losses. Each partner is personally liable for the debts of the partnership.

Case: P, a seller of goods, sued D, an alleged partner, for the balance due on merchandise shipped to the partnership. When P extended credit, it did not know that D was a partner The credit was extended to the partnership without the seller's even knowing the names of the partners.

Issue: Is D liable as a partner?

Decision: Yes.

Reason: Persons who join together in a business or venture for a common benefit each contributing property, money, or services to the business or venture having a community of interest in any profits are "partners." A partner is personally liable for the debts of the partnership. The fact that the seller may have sold goods to a partnership in ignorance of the fact that D was a partner does not prevent the seller's recovery for the goods sold.

Johnson v. Plastex Company, 500 So.2d 596 (Okla.) 1972.

Express partnership agreements may be either oral or written, but such agreements should be reduced to writing and be carefully

534

prepared. The provisions usually contained in articles of partnership will be discussed later in this chapter.

Issues concerning the existence of a partnership may arise between the parties or between the alleged partnership and third parties. The legal issues in these two situations are substantially different. When the issue is between the alleged partners, it is essentially a question of intention. When the issue concerns liability to a third person, the question involves not only intention as to the actual existence of the partnership but issues of estoppel as well.

Implied Partnerships   As between the parties, the intention to create a partnership may be expressed or it may be implied from the conduct of the parties. The basic question is whether the parties intend a relationship that includes the essential elements of a partnership, not whether they intend to be partners.

If the essential elements of a partnership are present, the mere fact that the parties do not think they are becoming partners is immaterial. If the parties agree upon an arrangement that is a partnership in fact, it is immaterial whether they call it something else or that they declare that they are not partners. On the other hand, the mere fact that the parties themselves call the relation a partnership will not make it so, if they have not, by their contract, agreed upon an arrangement that by the law is a partnership in fact.

Case: The state unemployment commission sought to collect unemployment taxes from D. D owned and operated a barber shop. D entered into "partnership agreements" with two barbers, which provided (1) that D would furnish the shop and equipment, (2) for a division of the income of each barber, (3) that D would make all business policies and that his decisions would be final, and (4) the hours and days of work for each barber.

Issue: Were the two barbers partners?

Decision: No.

Reasons: 1. The mere existence of an agreement labeled "partnership" agreement and the characterization of signatories as "partners" does not conclusively prove the existence of a partnership. Rather, the intention of the parties, as explained by the wording of the agreement, is paramount.

2. A partnership is defined as an association of two or more persons to carry on as co-owners of a business for profit. As co-owners of a business, partners have an equal right in the decision-making process. But this right may be abrogated by agreement of the parties without destroying the

partnership concept, provided other partnership elements are present, which they are not here.

3. Co-owners carry on "a business for profit." The phrase has been interpreted to mean that partners share in the profits and the losses of the business. The intent to divide the profits is an indispensable requisite of partnership. Paragraph three of the agreement declares that each partner shall share in the income of the business. There is no sharing of the profits, and as the agreement is drafted, there are no profits. Merely sharing the gross returns does not establish a partnership. Nor is the sharing of profits prima facie evidence of a partnership where the profits received are in payment of wages. The failure to share profits, therefore, is fatal to the partnership concept here.

Chaiken v. Employment Security Commission, 274 A.2d 707 (Del.Super.) 1970.

The essential attributes of a partnership are a common interest in the business and management and a share in the profits and losses. However, if there is a sharing of profits, a partnership may be found to exist even though there is no sharing of losses.

The presence of a common interest in property and management is not enough to establish a partnership by implication. Also an agreement to share the gross returns of a business, sometimes called gross profits, does not of itself prove an intention to form a partnership. However, the Uniform Partnership Act provides that the receipt by a person of a share of the real or net profits in a business is *prima facie* evidence that he is a partner in the business.

Case: P sued H and R for the unpaid balance due for grain delivered. H owned two trucks, and it was agreed that H would furnish the trucks and R the labor in hauling grain. The profits from the operation were to be divided equally. R was to keep books on the transactions and to pay all expenses of the operation. R kept the bank account in his own name and wrote all checks. H denied the existence of a partnership or that he was to bear any losses occurring in the operation.

Issue: Were the parties partners?

Decision: Yes.

Reasons: 1. Sharing the profits of a business venture where one furnishes capital and the other labor constitutes prima facie evidence of the existence of a partnership. Although an agreement to share profits in such a venture is not conclusive proof of the existence of a partnership, it raises a

536

presumption of partnership. If such presumption is not overcome by other evidence tending to prove that, in fact, the parties intended there to be no partnership, such prima facie proof of the existence of a partnership becomes conclusive.

2. Parties "entering into agreements and transactions which by the law of the land constitute them partners, whatever they may please to say or think about it, or by whatever name they may choose to call it," will be held to be partners. There was substantial evidence tending to prove that H and R were partners, and the determination of that question was for the jury.

Troy Grain & Fuel Co. v. Rolston et al., 227 S.W.2d 66 (Mo.) 1950.

The presumption that a partnership exists by reason of sharing net profits is not conclusive and may be overcome by evidence that the share in the profits is received for some other purpose such as payment of a debt by installments, wages, rent, annuity to a widow of a deceased partner, interest on a loan, or as payment for goodwill by installments. For example, bonuses are frequently paid as percentage of profit, and such a payment does not make the employee a partner.

Partnership by Estoppel Insofar as third persons are concerned, partnership liability may be predicated upon the legal theory of estoppel. Where a person by words, spoken or written, or by conduct, represents himself or consents to another's representing him to another to be a partner in an existing partnership, such person is not a partner but is liable to any party to whom such representation has been made. If the representation is made in a public manner either personally or with consent of the apparent partner, the apparent partner is liable if credit is extended to the partnership, even if the creditor did not actually know of the representation. This is an exception to the usual estoppel requirement of actual reliance. This liability, created by estoppel, does not arise, however, unless the third party gives credit to the firm in reliance upon such representation.

Case: P sued D for goods sold to D's son, who ran a clothing store in some extra space in a building owned by D. The father and son were not partners, but D joined the son in signing letters ordering supplies for the clothing business. D also signed a note at the bank with the son, and D was aware that a Dun and Bradstreet report showing common ownership of the business had been prepared. The trial court found that the father and son were not partners, but that D was liable to P, on a theory of estoppel.

Issue: Was D estopped from asserting that he was not a partner with his son?

537

Decision: Yes.

Reasons: 1. D should not be allowed to escape the consequences of holding out his credit to suppliers, and then withdraw it when it appears that the business would fail and he might become liable.

2. The father's conduct did lead P to believe that D was a partner, and in reliance upon this belief, credit was extended to the son. D is therefore liable the same as if he were in fact a partner.

Phillip VanHeusen, Inc. v. Korn, 400 P.2d 549 (Kan.) 1969.

Liability based on estoppel is similar to that of a principal based on the apparent authority of an agent or an ostensible agent. If a person not a partner holds himself out to be a partner and all members of the firm consent to it, a partnership obligation results.

The courts are not in accord as to whether a person is under a duty to affirmatively disclaim a reputed partnership where the representation of partnership was not made by or with the consent of the person sought to be charged as a partner. Some court cases hold that if a person is held out as a partner and he knows it, he should be chargeable as a partner unless he takes reasonable steps to give notice that he is not, in fact, a partner. Other cases indicate that there is no duty to deny false representations of partnership where the ostensible partner did not participate in making the misrepresentation.

THE PARTNERSHIP AGREEMENT

Introduction   The partnership agreement, usually called the *articles of partnership*, will vary from business to business. Among the subjects usually contained in such agreements are the following: the names of the partners and of the partnership; its purpose and duration; the capital contributions of each partner; the method of sharing profits and losses; the effect of advances; the salaries, if any, to be paid the partners; the method of accounting and the fiscal year; the rights and liabilities of the parties upon the death or withdrawal of a partner; and the procedures to be followed upon dissolution.

The Uniform Partnership Act or other partnership statute is a part of the agreement as if it had actually been written into the contract or made part of its stipulations. The sections that follow discuss some of the more important provisions of partnership agreement and indicate the effect of the Uniform Act on the agreement.

Profit and Loss Provision   Unless the agreement is to the contrary, each partner has a right to share equally in the profits of the enterprise, and each partner is under a duty to contribute equally to the losses. Capital contributed to the firm is a liability owing by the firm to the contributing partners. If, on dissolution, there are not sufficient assets to repay each partner his capital, such amount is considered as a loss and must be met like any other loss of the partnership. For example, a partnership is composed of A, B, and C. A contributed $20,000, B contributed $10,000, and C contributed $4,000. The firm is dissolved, and upon the payment of firm debts there remains only $10,000 of firm assets. Because the total contribution to captial was $34,000, the operating loss is $24,000. This loss must be borne equally by A, B, and C, so that the loss for each is $8,000. This means that A is entitled to be reimbursed to the extent of his $20,000 contribution less $8,000, his share of the loss, or net of $12,000. B is entitled to $10,000, less $8,000, or $2,000. Because C has contributed only $4,000, he must now contribute to the firm an additional $4,000 in order that his loss will equal $8,000. The additional $4,000 contributed by C, plus the $10,000 remaining, will now be distributed so that A will receive $12,000 and B $2,000.

Occasionally, articles of copartnership specify the manner in which profits are to be divided, but neglect to mention possible losses. In such cases the losses are borne in the same proportion that profits are to be shared. In the event that losses occur when one of the partners is insolvent and his share of the loss exceeds the amount owed him for advances and capital, the excess must be shared by the other partners. They share this unusual loss, with respect to each other, in the same ratio that they share profits.

Thus in the above example if C is insolvent, A and B would each bear an additional $2,000 loss.

In addition to the right to be repaid his contributions, whether by way of capital or advances to the partnership property, the partnership must indemnify every partner in respect of payments made and personal liabilities reasonably incurred by him in the ordinary and proper conduct of its business, or for the preservation of its business or property.

Partnership Capital Provision   Partnership capital consists of the total credits to the capital accounts of the various partners, provided the credits are for permanent investments in the business. Such capital represents that amount that the partnership is obligated to return to the partners at the time of dissolution, and it can be varied only with the consent of all the partners. Undivided profits that are permitted by some of the partners to accumulate in the business do not become part of the capital. They, like temporary advances by firm members, are subject to withdrawal at any time unless the agreement provides to the contrary.

The amount that each partner is to contribute to the firm, as well as the credit he is to receive for assets contributed, is entirely dependent upon the partnership agreement.

A person may become a partner without a capital contribution. For example, he may contribute services to balance the capital investment of the other partners. Such a partner, however, has no capital to be returned at the time of liquidation. Only those who receive credit for capital investments—which may include goodwill, patent rights, and so forth, if agreed upon—are entitled to the return of capital when dissolution occurs.

If the investment is in a form other than money, the property no longer belongs to the contributing partner. He has vested the firm with title and he has no greater equity in the property than any other party. At dissolution he recovers only the amount allowed to him for the property invested.

Provisions Relating to Partnership Property

It is obvious that a partnership may use its own property, the property of the individual partners, or the property of some third person. It frequently becomes important, especially on dissolution and where claims of firm creditors are involved, to ascertain exactly what property constitutes partnership property in order to ascertain the rights of partners and firm creditors to specific property.

As a general rule, the agreement of the parties will determine what property is properly classified as partnership property. In the absence of an express agreement, what constitutes partnership property is ascertained from the conduct of the parties and from the purpose for and the way in which property is used in the pursuit of the business.

The Uniform Partnership Act provides that all property specifically brought into partnership or acquired by it is partnership property. Therefore, unless a contrary intention appears, property acquired with partnership funds is partnership property. In other words, there is a presumption that property acquired with partnership funds is partnership property, but this presumption is rebuttable.

Case: While P's husband was in the penitentiary, he received letters from D, his brother, urging him and his family to move to Minnesota and enter into a partnership for building and operating a tourist camp. The family moved to Minnesota, and the husband constructed buildings and operated the camp for a number of years The land on which the camp was built was purchased by D in his own name and paid for with money from the earnings of the camp. P's husband died, and P sought a court order declaring that the camp was partnership operation and that her deceased husband had a one-half interest in the land. The lower court ruled that there was a partnership and that the real property was a partnership asset.

Issue: Was the land partnership property?

Decision: Yes.

Reasons: 1. All of the facts taken together clearly indicate an intention of the parties to enter into a partnership. There was an intent by the parties to combine their property, labor, and skill as co-owners of a business for a joint profit.

2. Unless the contrary intention appears, property acquired with partnership funds is partnership property. The mere fact that the title was taken in D's name does not prevent it from being partnership property.

Cyrus v. Cyrus, 64 N.W.2d 538 (1954).

Because a partnership has the right to acquire, own, and dispose of personal property in the firm name, legal documents affecting the title to partnership personal property may be executed in the firm name by any partner. The Uniform Partnership Act also treats a partnership as a legal entity for the purposes of title to real estate that may be held in the firm name. Title so acquired can be conveyed in the partnership name. Where title to real property is in the partnership name, any partner may convey title to such property by a conveyance executed in the partnership name. To be effective, such a conveyance must be within the terms of the partnership agreement or within the pursuit of the partnership business.

Name Provision   Because a partnership is created by the agreement of the parties, they select the name to be used. This right of selection is subject to two limitations by statute in many states. First, a partnership may not use the word *company* or other language that would imply the existence of a corporation. Second, if the name is other than that of the partners, they must comply with an assumed name statute that requires the giving of public notice as to the actual identity of the partners. Failure to comply with this assumed name statute may result in the partnership's being denied access to the courts to sue its debtors, or it may result in criminal actions being brought against those operating under the assumed name.

Case: A partnership known as "Stein Properties" brought suit in its firm name against a trustee on a deposit receipt contract. The partnership had not complied with the state's fictitious name statute. The defendant moved to dismiss the suit, contending that the partnership could not sue because of its failure to comply with the state statute.

Issue: Will the suit be dismissed?

541

Decision: Yes.

Reasons: 1. It is unlawful for a partnership to engage in business under a fictitious name unless the name is registered with the clerk of the court in the county of its principal place of business.

2. The penalty for the failure to comply with this law is that neither the business nor the members may maintain suit in any court of this state as a plaintiff until this law is complied with.

3. "Stein Properties" is a fictitious name because it does not reasonably reveal the names of the partners.

4. However, the failure to comply with the statute does not prevent the trial court from taking jurisdiction of the cause, but it does act as an inhibition against allowing the plaintiffs to prosecute their complaint until the requirements of the statute are met.

Aronovitz v. Stein Properties, 322 So.2d 74 (Fla.App.) 1975.

The firm name is an asset of the firm, and as such it may also be sold, assigned, or disposed of in any manner upon which the parties agree. In connection with the firm name, it should be recognized that the firm can sue and be sued in its firm name in most states and can go through bankruptcy as a firm. It should be kept in mind that if a partnership is sued in its firm name, a judgment binds only partnership assets. It does not bind the individual assets of the partners. To the extent that a firm is able to sue and be sued in its firm name and to the extent previously discussed relating to the ownership of property, a partnership is a legal entity. It is not a legal entity to the same extent as a corporation, however.

Provisions Relating to Goodwill Goodwill, which is usually transferred with the name, is based upon the justifiable expectation of the continued patronage of old customers and the probable patronage of new customers resulting from good reputation, satisfied customers, established location, and past advertising. Goodwill is usually considered in an evaluation of the assets of the business, and it is capable of being sold and transferred. Upon dissolution caused by the death of one of the partners, it must be accounted for by the surviving partner to the legal representative of the deceased partner, unless otherwise agreed upon in a buy and sell agreement.

When goodwill and the firm name are sold, an agreement not to compete is usually part of the sales agreement. Such an agreement may be implied but should be a part of the buy and sell provisions.

542

Buy and Sell Provisions As part of the partnership agreement, the partners should provide for the contingency of death or withdrawal of a partner. This contingency is covered by a buy and sell agreement. It is imperative that the terms of the buy and sell provisions be agreed upon before either party knows whether he is a buyer or a seller. Agreement after the status of the parties becomes known is extremely difficult, and many times additional problems may arise upon the death or withdrawal of a partner, which may result in litigation and economic loss to all concerned. Many of these problems can be avoided by providing a method whereby the surviving partner purchases the interest of the deceased partner, or the remaining partner purchases the interest of the withdrawing partner. The means for determining the price to be paid for such interest is provided. The time and method of payment are usually stipulated also. The buy and sell agreement should specify whether a partner has an option to purchase the interest or has a duty to do so.

It is common for partners to provide for life insurance on each other's lives. In the event of a partner's death, proceeds of the insurance are utilized to purchase the deceased partner's interest. Premiums on such life insurance are not deductible for tax purposes but are usually treated as an expense for accounting purposes. There are a variety of methods for holding title to the insurance. It may be individually owned or business owned. The provisions of the policy should be carefully integrated into the partnership agreement; each partner's estate plan should also properly consider the ramifications of this insurance and of the buy and sell agreement.

REVIEW QUESTIONS AND PROBLEMS

1. List four situations in which a person may receive a percentage of the profits without a presumption being made that he is a partner.

2. List the usual provisions found in partnership agreements.

3 Give reasons for including buy and sell provisions in partnership agreements.

4. A and B, both attorneys, agreed to share office space and other overhead expense, but they did not agree to form a partnership. The sign in front of their office and in their common letterhead read "A and B, Attorneys at Law." With the use of this stationery, A purchased some office equipment from C. B did not join in the contract in any way. A could not pay for the equipment. Could B be liable to C? Discuss.

5. A and B operated a business together as partners but had no written partnership agreement. With his own funds, B frequently purchased paintings and other art objects as decorations for their business reception area. When B died, the personal representative of his estate sought to obtain the objects as

exclusive estate property. B argued that he owned a one-half interest in the objects. Who should prevail? Discuss.

6. A and B formed a partnership to do kitchen-remodeling work pursuant to an oral agreement. It was agreed that A was to invest $10,000 and manage the business affairs; B, who would invest $1,000, was to work as job superintendent and manage the work. Profits were to be split fifty-fifty, but possible losses were not discussed. The business proved unprofitable, and A brought action for contribution from B. May he recover?

7. A and B as partners rented a cannery for one season. They entered into a contract with P, a broker, whereby it was agreed to label all products with P's label, to allow P the exclusive right to sell their entire output, and to pay him 5 percent of gross sales. P guaranteed the cannery a supply of cans and other material and promised to advance money for operating expenses and payroll. For this advance P was to receive as "extra compensation" one-half of the net profits of the cannery for the season. P also had the right to control wages and the payroll for the cannery. Is P a partner? Why?

8. M wished to purchase a tract of land, plat it, and sell the lots. He needed capital, and P loaned him $6,000. M gave P a note, and it was understood that when the lots were sold the proceeds would first be used to pay the $6,000 to P. Any profits above the $6,000 would be divided equally. Was there a partnership? Why?

9. A and B formed a partnership, and A contributed an unpatented invention. He later took out the patent in his own name Upon dissolution of the partnership, to whom does the patent belong? Why?

10. A and B, partners, owned the Sunshine Sporting Goods business and had complied with the appropriate state fictitious name law. A creditor of the company, C, obtained a judgment against Sunshine Sporting Goods only. Are A and B liable personally? Explain.

11. A and B are partners. A dies, and B continues the business in his own name. In accounting for the firm assets, he refuses to make any allowance for goodwill. May the executrix of A's estate recover an additional sum for the goodwill of the business? Give a definition of *goodwill*.

12. X and Y operated an automobile agency as partners for over twenty years. At the outset they had prepared a written agreement containing the provision that in the event of either partner's death, the surviving partner would purchase the deceased partner's share for $40,000. X died, and Y tendered the $40,000. X's executor refused to sell on the basis that $40,000 was insufficient. The executor contends that Y is required to proffer the amount of X's share of capital and accumulated profits. Should Y succeed in an action for specific performance against the executor? Why?

37 OPERATING THE PARTNERSHIP

Introduction The operation of a partnership is governed by the provisions of the partnership agreement and by the applicable statutory law, which in most states is the Uniform Partnership Act. Thus the rights, duties, and powers of partners are both expressed (those in the agreement) and implied (those created by law). Many of the expressed rights, duties, and powers were discussed in the preceding chapter, which covered the typical subjects found in the partnership agreement. Those that are implied will be discussed in this chapter, along with some additional observations about the partnership agreement as it affects operations. Throughout the discussion it should be kept in mind that a partner is essentially an agent for the other partners and that the general principles of the law of agency are applicable.

Before examining the rights, duties, and powers of partners, certain terminology should be understood. A *silent partner* in a general partnership is one that does not participate in management. It should be kept in mind that all limited partners in a limited partnership are silent. A *secret partner* is unknown to third parties. He may advise management and actually participate in decisions, but his interest is not known to third parties. A *dormant partner* is both secret and silent.

THE RIGHTS OF PARTNERS

Right to Participate in Management All partners have equal rights in the management and conduct of the firm business. The partners may, however, by agreement place the management within the control of one or more partners. The right to an equal voice in the management and conduct of the business is not determined by the share that each partner has invested in the business.

In regard to ordinary matters arising in the conduct of the partnership business, the opinion of the majority of the partners is controlling. If the firm consists of only two persons, and they are unable to agree, and the articles of partnership make no provision for the settlement of disputes, dissolution is the only remedy. The partnership agreement usually provides for some form of arbitration of deadlocks between partners in order to avoid dissolution.

The majority cannot, however, without the consent of the minority, change the essential nature of the business by altering the partnership agreement or by reducing or increasing the capital of the partners; embark upon a new business; or admit new members to the firm.

Certain acts other than those enumerated above require the unanimous consent of the partners in order to bind the firm, namely: (1) assigning the firm property to a trustee for the benefit of creditors; (2) authorizing a confession of judgment; (3) disposing of the goodwill of the business; (4) submitting a partnership agreement to arbitration; and (5) doing any act that would make impossible the conduct of the partnership business.

Right To Be Compensated for Services It is the duty of each partner, in the absence of an agreement to the contrary, to give his entire time, skill, and energy to the pursuit of the partnership affairs. No partner is entitled to payment for services rendered in the conduct of the partnership business unless an agreement to that effect has been expressed or may be implied from the conduct of the partners.

Case: P sued Ds, his partners, for the reasonable value of services rendered. The parties were partners in the ownership and operation of a fishing vessel. P had perfected a new type of net for catching sharks and contended that he was entitled to compensation for the time and effort expended in constructing the shark nets. P had informed his partners that he was busy getting the nets ready and that it would "be lots of work to fix" them. P did not inform Ds of what the work actually entailed or that he expected any compensation for it.

Issue: Is P entitled to compensation?

Decision: No.

Reason: There was no factual basis for any agreement express or implied to pay compensation. One partner is not entitled to extra compensation from the partnership in the absence of an express or an implied agreement therefor.

Waggen v. Gerde et ux., 36 Wash.2d 563 (1950).

Often one of the partners does not desire to participate in the management of the business. The partnership agreement in such case usually provides that the active partners receive a salary for their services in addition to their share in the profits. A surviving partner is entitled to reasonable compensation for his services in winding up the partnership affairs, unless he is guilty of misconduct in winding up the affairs.

Right to Interest Contributions to capital are not entitled to draw interest unless they are not repaid when the repayment should be made. The partner's share in the profits constitutes the earnings upon his capital investment. In the absence of an express provision for the payment of interest, it is presumed that interest will be paid only on advances above the amount originally contributed as capital. Advances in excess of the prescribed capital, even though credited to the capital account of the contributing partners, are entitled to draw interest from the date of the advance.

Unwithdrawn profits remaining in the firm are not entitled to draw interest. Such unwithdrawn profits are not considered advances or loans by the mere fact that they are left with the firm. However, custom, usage, and circumstances may show an intention to treat such unwithdrawn profits as loans to the firm.

**Right to
Information
and to Inspection
of Books** Every partner is entitled to full and complete information concerning the conduct of the business. A partner has the right to inspect the books of the partnership to secure such information. The partnership agreement usually contains provisions relative to the records that the business will maintain. Each partner is under a duty to give the person responsible for keeping the records whatever information is necessary to carry on the business efficiently and effectively. It is the duty of the person keeping the records to allow each partner access to them. No partner has a right to remove the records from the agreed-upon location without the consent of the other partners. Each partner is entitled to inspect the records and make copies therefrom, provided he does not make such inspection for fraudulent purposes.

**Right to an
Accounting** The partners' proportionate share of the partnership assets or profits, when not determined by a voluntary settlement of the parties, may be ascertained in a suit for an accounting. Such suits are equitable in nature, and in states that still distinguish between suits at law and suits in equity, such actions must be filed in the court of equity.

Because partners ordinarily have equal access to the partnership records, there is usually no need for formal accountings to determine partnership interests. A suit for an accounting is not permitted for settling incidental matters or disputes between the partners. However, if a dispute is of such grievous nature as to make impossible the continued existence of the partnership, a suit for an accounting is allowed.

In all cases a partner is entitled to an accounting upon the dissolution of the firm. In addition, he has a right to a formal accounting without a dissolution of the firm in situations such as where one partner has been denied access to the books.

Property Rights A partner is a co-owner with his partners of partnership property. Subject to any agreement between the partners, a partner has an equal right among his partners to possess partnership property for partnership purposes. He has no right to possess partnership property for other purposes without the consent of the other partners.

A partner has a right that the property shall be used in the pursuit of the partnership business and to pay firm creditors. A partner does not own any specific item of the partnership property. He therefore has no right in specific partnership property that is transferable by him. A partner has no right to use the firm property in satisfaction of his personal debts, and he has no interest in specific partnership property that can be levied upon by his personal creditors.

When a partner dies, his interest in specific partnership property passes to the surviving partner or partners, who have the duty of winding up the affairs of the partnership in accordance with the partnership agreement and the applicable laws. When the winding-up process is complete, the estate of the deceased partner will be paid whatever sum the estate is entitled to according to law and the partnership agreement. The surviving partner may sell the property, real and personal, of the partnership in connection with winding up the business in order to obtain the cash to pay the estate of the deceased partner.

A partner's interest *in the firm* consists of his rights to share in the profits that are earned and, after dissolution and liquidation, to the return of his capital and such profits as have not been distributed previously. This assumes, of course, that his capital has not been absorbed or impaired by losses.

A partner may assign his interest in or his right to share in the profits of the partnership. Such an assignment will not of itself work a dissolution of the firm. The assignee is not entitled to participate in the management of the business. The only right of the assignee is to receive the profits to which the assignor would otherwise have been entitled and, in the event of dissolution, to receive his assignor's interest.

A partner's interest in the partnership cannot be levied upon by his separate creditors and sold at public sale. A judgment creditor of a partner must proceed by obtaining a "charging order" from the court. This order charges the interest of the debtor partner with the unsatisfied amount of the judgment debt. The court will ordinarily appoint a receiver who will receive the partner's share of the profits and any other money due or to fall due to him in respect of the partnership and apply the same upon the judgment. Likewise, the court may order that the interest charged be sold. Neither the charging order nor the sale of the interest will cause a dissolution of the firm, unless the partnership is one that is terminable at will. (See Chapter 38, page 557.)

THE DUTIES AND POWERS OF PARTNERS

Duties in General A partnership is a fiduciary relationship. Each partner owes the duty of undivided loyalty to the other. Therefore every partner must account to the partnership for any benefit, and hold as a trustee for it any profits gained by him without consent of the other partners. This duty also rests upon representatives of deceased partners engaged in the liquidation of the affairs of the partnership.

The partnership relation is a personal one, and each partner is under duty to exercise good faith and to consider the mutual welfare of all the partners in his conduct of the business. If one partner attempts to secure an advantage over the others, he thereby breaches the partnership relation, and he must account for all benefits that he obtains. This includes transactions with partners and with others.

Case: The parties were partners in an oil and gas investment firm which acquired oil and gas leases. D was the managing partner. While the agreement was in effect, D learned of an "Indonesian" oil deal and acquired 10 percent of it for himself. When P learned of the deal, he demanded the right to contribute his share and to participate in the venture. D refused, and P brought suit to establish that D's investment actually belonged to the partnership.

Issue: Is the investment partnerships property?

Decision: Yes.

Reasons: 1 The "Indonesian" venture fell within the nature of the partnership business. Moreover, the partnership was financially able to participate.

2. As managing partner, D owed to his copartners one of the highest fiduciary duties recognized in the law—the duty of loyalty. The rule of undivided loyalty is relentless and supreme.

Huffington v. Upchurch, 532 S.W.2d 576 (Tex.) 1976.

Power to Contract A partner is an agent of the partnership for the purpose of its business. The general laws of agency are applicable to all partnerships. Each partner has the authority to bind the partnership with contractual liability whenever the partner is apparently carrying on, in the usual way, the business of the partnership. An act of a partner that is not apparently for the carrying on of the business of the partnership in the usual way does not bind the partnership unless authorized by the other partners.

Case: A, B, and C were partners operating a business that manufactured packing crates and other wood products. The partnership had purchased a tract of timber and were using it to supply their lumber needs. A, the managing partner, entered into a contract to sell lumber to P and received payment therefor. The lumber was never delivered to P, and A did not account to the partnership for the money received.

Issue: Is the partnership liable on the contract to sell lumber?

Decision: No.

Reasons: 1. A partner is a general agent of the firm but only for the purpose of carrying on the business of the partnership. Any sale by a partner to be valid must be in furtherance of the partnership business, within the scope of the business or such as third persons may reasonably conclude, from all the circumstances, to be embraced within it.

2. Sales made by a partner in a trading firm are not viewed with the same strictness as in nontrading firms such as here involved because in trading firms sales are usually within the scope of the business, while in nontrading firms they are exceptional and only incidental to the main business.

3. Here one of the partners acted in a matter beyond both the real and apparent scope of the business and beyond the real or apparent scope of the agency. The partnership was not in the business of selling lumber.

Bole v. Lyle et al., 287 S.W.2d 931 (Tenn.) 1956.

The rules of agency relating to authority, ratification, and secret limitations on the authority of a partner are applicable to partnerships, but the extent of implied authority is generally greater for partners than for ordinary agents. Each partner has implied power to do all acts necessary for carrying on the business of the partnership. The nature and scope of the business and what is usual in the particular business determine the extent of the implied powers. Among the common implied powers are the following: to compromise, adjust, and settle claims or debts owed by or to the partnership; to sell goods in the

550

regular course of business and to make warranties; to buy property within the scope of the business for cash or upon credit; to buy insurance; to hire employees; to make admissions against interest; to enter into contracts within the scope of firm; and to receive notices. In a trading partnership, a partner has the implied authority to borrow funds and to pledge the assets of the firm. Some of these implied duties are discussed more fully in the sections that follow.

Power to Impose Tort Liability   A partner has the power to impose tort liability through the doctrine of *respondeat superior*. The law imposes tort liability upon a partnership for all wrongful acts or omissions of any partner acting in the ordinary course of the partnership and for its benefit.

Case: D and H were partners doing business as Dan's Used Cars. While driving home in a car that was part of the inventory of the business, H injured P. P sued the partnership. Neither of the partners owned a personal automobile, but both, whenever they desired, drove partnership automobiles with dealer license plates.

Issue: Is the partnership liable?

Decision: Yes.

Reasons: 1. A partnership is bound by a partner's wrongful act if done within the scope of the partnership's business. The question as to whether or not a particular act is within the scope of the partnership's business, and is for its benefit, is for the jury.

2. A partner is similar to an agent except that a partner is also a principal, and control and authorization to do things are within his power to exercise.

3. Here (1) the car involved was for sale by the firm at any time or place; (2) H was on call and often conducted business while using the firm's autos; (3) use of firm's transportation was considered not only convenient but essential by the partners; and (4) H often conducted the firm's business from his home.

Phillips v. Cook, 210 A.2d 743 (Md.) 1965.

If a partnership has liablity because of a tort of a partner, the firm has the right to collect its losses from the partner at fault. In effect, a partnership that is liable in tort to a third person has a right of indemnity against the partner at fault. Likewise, if the injured third party collects directly from the partner at fault, the partner cannot seek contribution from his copartners.

Case: P, a patient, sued D, a physician, for medical malpractice. D was a partner in a medical partnership. D sought contributions from his partners, contending that his negligence, if any, occurred in the course of the partnership's business.

Issue: Is D entitled to contributions from his copartners?

Decision: No.

Reasons: 1. P could have sued all partners and the partnership. All would have had liability if D was negligent because that doctrine of *respondeat superior* is applicable to partnerships.

2. However, if P only sues D, D may not seek contribution because D's wrong caused the damage. The partners are only constructively negligent, and D's negligence was actual.

Flynn v. Reaves, 218 S.E.2d 661 (Ga.) 1975.

Powers over Property
Each partner has implied authority to sell to good faith purchasers personal property that is held for the purpose of resale and to execute such documents as are necessary to effect a transfer of title thereof. Of course, if his authority in this connection has been limited and such fact is known to the purchaser, the transfer of title will be ineffective or voidable. A partner has no power to sell the fixtures and equipment used in the business unless he has been duly authorized. Such acts are not a regular feature of the business, and a prospective purchaser of such property should make certain that the particular partner has been given authority to sell. The power to sell, where it is present, gives also the power to make warranties as normally accompany similar sales.

The right to sell firm real property is to be inferred only if the firm is engaged in the real estate business. In other cases there is no right to sell and convey realty, except where such sale has been authorized by a partnership agreement. In most states, a deed by one partner without authority is not binding on the firm, but it does convey the individual interest of the parties executing and delivering the deed. This conveyance, however, is subject to the rights of creditors of the partnership.

Under the Uniform Partnership Act, title to real property may be taken in the firm name as a "tenancy in partnership," and any member of the firm has power to execute a deed thereto by signing the firm name. In such a case, what is the effect of a wrongful transfer of real estate that has been acquired for use in the business and not for resale? The conveyance may be set aside by the other partners because the purchaser should have known that one partner has no power to sell real estate without the approval of the others. However, if the first purchaser has resold and conveyed the property to an innocent third party, the latter takes good title.

If the title to firm property is not held in the firm name but is held in the names of one or more of the partners, a conveyance by those in whose names the title is held passes good title, unless the purchaser knows or should know that title was held for the firm. There is nothing in the record title in such a situation to call the buyer's attention to the fact that the firm has an interest in the property.

The power to mortgage or pledge firm property is primarily dependent upon the power to borrow money and bind the firm. A partner with authority to borrow may, as an incident to that power, give the security normally demanded for similar loans. Because no one partner, without the consent of the others, has the power to commit an act that will destroy or terminate the business, the power to give a mortgage on the entire stock of merchandise and fixtures of a business is usually denied. Such a mortgage would make it possible, upon default, to liquidate the firm's assets and thus destroy its business. Subject to this limitation, the power to borrow carries the power to pledge or mortgage.

Financial Powers To determine the limit of a partner's financial powers, partnerships are divided into two general classes—trading and nontrading partnerships. A *trading partnership* is one that has for its primary purpose the buying and selling of merchandise. In such a trading firm, each partner has an implied power to borrow money and to extend the credit of the firm, in the usual course of business, by signing negotiable paper.

Case: S and B were partners in the automobile business under the name of Greenwood Sales and Service. B borrowed $6,000 from P and gave a partnership note in return. B borrowed the money to make his initial capital contribution to the partnership.

Issue: Is the partnership liable on the note?

Decision: Yes.

Reasons: 1. Greenwood Sales and Service was a trading or commercial partnership. A partner is an agent of the firm for the purpose of the partnership business and may bind all partners by their acts within the scope of such business. It is of no consequence whether the partner is acting in good faith with his copartners or not, provided the act is within the scope of the partnership's business and professedly for the firm, and third persons are acting in good faith.

2. A partner in a trading partnership has the power to execute negotiable instruments.

Holloway v. Smith et al., 197 Va. 334 (1955).

A *nontrading partnership* is one that does not buy and sell commodities but has for its primary purpose the production of commodities or is organized for the purpose of selling services—for example, professional partnerships in law, medicine, or accounting. In such partnerships a partner's powers are more limited, and a partner does not have implied power to borrow money or to bind the firm on negotiable paper. However, where the act is within the scope of the partnership business, a member of a nontrading partnership may bind the firm by the exercise of implied authority just as a partner in a trading partnership may.

Notice and Admissions Each partner has implied authority to receive notice for all the other partners concerning matters within the pursuit of the partnership business. Knowledge, held by any partner in his mind but not revealed to the other partners, is notice to the partnership. Knowledge of one partner is legally the knowledge of all partners, providing that the facts became known or were knowledge obtained within the scope of the partnership business. A partner has a duty to communicate knowledge to the other partners in the absence of fraud on the partnership by the partner having such knowledge.

Admissions or representations pertaining to the conduct of the partnership business and made by a partner may be used as evidence against the partnership.

REVIEW QUESTIONS AND PROBLEMS

1. Define the following terms: *silent partner, secret partner, dormant partner, trading partnership*, and *tenancy in partnership*.

2. When is a partner entitled to be paid interest on funds used by the partnership?

3. List situations in which a partner is entitled to an accounting in a court of equity.

4. Compare the power to bind the firm of a partner in a trading partnership with that of a partner in a nontrading partnership.

5. A, a partner of the XYZ firm, was indebted to B for a personal loan. A defaulted on the loan, and B learned that A had insufficient personal assets to satisfy the debt. May A's interest in partnership property be levied upon by B? Explain.

6. A was a partner in the ABC roofing firm. While the other partners were on vacation, A negligently made repairs to X's roof, which resulted in damage to X's carpet. X obtained a judgment against the partnership. Is the firm entitled to reimbursement from A? If X had chosen to proceed against A only, would the partnership be responsible for a contribution to A? Explain.

7. A and B operated a law firm as partners. A personality conflict arose, and they agreed to dissolve the partnership. Each individually would continue in practice. After dissolution, A took most of the client files with him without B's knowledge or consent. Does B have a remedy? Why?

8. A trained several horses for other persons, including a horse owned by A and B as partners. A gratuitously loaned one of the stalls assigned to the partnership at a racetrack to C to groom a horse. Sometime thereafter, A told C that this stall was needed for an additional horse. An argument ensued; it ended with A attacking C with a pitchfork, seriously injuring him. May C recover from B? Why?

9. A and B have been partners for a number of years. Upon A's death, B spent considerable time in winding up the partnership affairs. Is he legally entitled to compensation for his services? Why?

10. A and B are partners in a retail clothing business. Being short of funds in the business A, without the consent or knowledge of B, borrowed $500 from C and signed a security agreement. Is the partnership property subject to the debt? Why?

11. X, a partner in an accountancy firm, borrowed $10,000 in the firm name and used the proceeds to pay an individual debt. Is the firm liable for the debt? Why?

38 DISSOLUTION OF PARTNERSHIPS

Introduction   The term *dissolution* is used to describe the legal destruction of the partnership relationship. Dissolution occurs whenever any partner ceases to be a member of the firm or whenever a new partner is admitted to the firm. That dissolution of a partnership is not the same as a termination will be discussed more fully later.

Dissolutions will occur without violation of the partnership agreement: (1) at the end of the stipulated term or particular undertaking specified in the agreement; (2) by the express will of any partner when no definite term or particular undertaking is specified; (3) by the agreement of all the partners; or (4) by the expulsion, in good faith, of any partner from the business, in accordance with such a power conferred by the partnership agreement.

Case: An insurance agency partnership was created by oral agreement. There was no agreement as to how long the partnership would continue. One partner, without consulting the others, removed all the records of the partnership and went into business on his own using the partnership name.

Issue: Was the dissolution by one partner wrongful so that he owed damages to the other partners?

Decision: No.

Reason: Inasmuch as the oral agreement did not specify the life of the partnership, it was at the will of the partners. In a partnership at will, any partner may lawfully dissolve the firm at any time.

Johnson v. Kennedy, 214 N.E.2d 276 (Mass.) 1966.

556

To dissolve a partnership at will, the partner seeking dissolution must give notice of the fact to the other partner or partners. No particular form of notice is required. In addition, notice of dissolution will be implied from circumstances inconsistent with the continuation of the partnership. For example, a partner whose services are essential leaves the community. This is an act of and notice of dissolution.

Expulsion of a partner is a breach of the partnership agreement unless the agreement confers the power of explusion upon a majority of the partners. For example, assume that A, B, and C are partners. A and B cannot expel C unless that power is specifically granted in the agreement. However, if there is no power to expel, partners may seek judicial dissolution if one partner is guilty of violating the partnership agreement (see the next section). To illustrate, assume that C in the above case was not devoting his time to the business as required by the partnership agreement. A and B could seek a judicial dissolution on these grounds, although they could not expel C.

Dissolution may also occur in violation of the partnership agreement. Although the agreement stipulates the length of time the partnership is to last, dissolution is always possible because the relationship is essentially a mutual agency not capable of specific performance. Therefore each partner has the *power*, but not the *right*, to revoke the relationship. In the event of wrongful dissolution, the wrongdoer is liable for damages.

Dissolution by Operation of Law

If during the period of the partnership events occur that make it impossible or illegal for the partnership to continue, it will be dissolved by operation of law. Such events or conditions are: death or bankruptcy of one of the partners, or a change in the law that makes the continuance of the business illegal.

A partnership is a personal relationship existing by reason of contract. Therefore, when one of the partners dies, the partnership is dissolved. However, it is not terminated on dissolution but continues for the purpose of winding up the partnership's affairs. The process of winding up is, in most states, the exclusive obligation and right of the surviving partner or partners. The executor or administrator of the deceased partner has no right to participate in or interfere with the winding-up processes. The only right of the personal representative of a deceased partner is to demand an accounting upon completion of the winding up of the partnership's affairs. As a general rule, the estate of the deceased partner is not bound on contracts entered into by the surviving partners if the contracts are unconnected with the winding up of the affairs of the partnership. This is discussed more fully later in this chapter.

The bankruptcy of a partner will dissolve the partnership because the control of his property passes to the trustee in bankruptcy for the benefit of the creditors. The mere insolvency of a partner will not be sufficient to justify a dissolution. The bankruptcy of the firm itself is a cause for dissolution, as is also a valid assignment of all the firm assets for the benefit of creditors. A judicial sale of a charging order obtained by a judgment creditor may cause dissolution of a partnership terminable at will.

Case: P, a judgment creditor of X, a partner in the D partnership, applied to the court for an order charging the partnership interest of X with the judgment. After the charging order was issued, X's interest in the partnership was sold at public sale pursuant to court order. P purchased the interest at the sale. P then filed a petition to dissolve the partnership. The partnership was one terminable at will.

Issue: May a purchaser of a charging order against a partnership terminable at will obtain dissolution of the partnership?

Decision: Yes

Reasons: 1. The law authorizes a sale of a partner's interest subject to a charging order.

2. The purchaser of the interest has the right to apply for dissolution if the partnership is terminable at will.

Gates Rubber Co. v. Williford, 530 S.W.2d 11 (Mo.) 1975.

Dissolution by Court Decree When a partnership by its agreement is to be continued for a term of years, circumstances may arise that might make the continued existence of the firm impossible and unprofitable. Therefore, upon the application of one of the partners to a court of equity, the partnership may be dissolved. The following are the circumstances and situations in which a court of equity may order dissolution:

1. Total incapacity of a partner to conduct business and to perform the duties required under the contract for partnership.
2. A declaration by judicial process that a partner is insane.
3. Willful and persistent commitment of breach of the partnership agreement, misappropriation of funds, or commitment of fraudulent acts.
4. A partnership that was entered into by reason of fraud may be dissolved on the application of an innocent party.
5. Gross misconduct and neglect or breach of duty by a partner to such an extent that it is impossible to carry out the purposes of the

partnership agreement. The court will not interfere and grant a decree of dissolution for mere discourtesy, temporary inconvenience, differences of opinion, or errors in judgment. The misconduct must be of such gross nature that the continued operation of the business would be unprofitable.

Case: P and D were partners in the farming and livestock business. They became involved in a series of arguments over matters of a trivial nature, such as about walking across the lawn, the amount of cream furnished P, the pounding on a house being remodeled while D's children were asleep, and other similar incidents. P brought suit to dissolve the partnership.

Issue: Will a court order dissolution?

Decision: No.

Reasons: 1. The harsh remedy of dissolution is unnecessary because the business may still be conducted successfully. Differences and discord should be settled by the partners themselves by the application of mutual forbearance rather than by bills in equity for dissolution. Equity is not a referee of partnership quarrels.

2. A going and prosperous business will not be dissolved merely because of friction among the partners. A court will not interfere to determine which contending faction is more "at fault."

Lunn v. Kaiser, 72 N.W.2d 312 (S.D.) 1955.

Effect of Dissolution on Powers of Partners Upon dissolution, a partnership is not terminated. The process of winding up involves the liquidation of the partnership assets so that cash may be available to pay creditors and to make a distribution to the partners. When the agreement provides for continuation and purchase of a deceased partner's interest, the technical dissolution is followed by valuation and payment, and the new firm immediately commences business.

As a general rule, dissolution terminates the actual authority of any partner to act for the partnership except so far as may be necessary to wind up partnership affairs, to liquidate the assets of the firm in an orderly manner, or to complete transactions begun but not then finished.

Case: T and E formed a partnership and purchased coal from P. They executed a purchase-money mortgage on the unmined coal to secure the purchase price. Thereafter, T withdrew from the partnership. T did not inform any of the partnership creditors of his withdrawal. E kept up the payments on the mortgage for some time but then defaulted, and P brought suit against both T and E as partners. Service of process was made on E's private secretary at E's law office. Neither T nor E answered or appeared in the proceedings, and a judgment was entered against the partners. T thereafter petitioned the court to set aside the sheriff's sale on the ground that he hadn't properly been served with process. T claimed that service on the secretary of E did not constitute service upon the partnership, which had already been dissolved.

Issue: Can service of process be made on an employee of a partnership after the partnership has been dissolved?

Decision: Yes.

Reasons: 1. Dissolution of a partnership does not terminate it. The dissolution of a partnership is the change in the relation of the partners caused by any partner ceasing to be associated in the carrying on, as distinguished from the winding up, of the business. Even after dissolution, a partnership is not terminated but continues to exist until the winding up of partnership affairs is completed, and the authority remains to act for the partnership in winding up partnership affairs and completing transactions begun but not yet finished at the time of dissolution.

2. In general a dissolution operates only with respect to future transactions; as to everything past, the partnership continues until all preexisting matters are terminated. The dissolution does not destroy the authority of a partner to act for his former associates in matters in which they still have a common interest and are under a common liability. There is no reason, therefore, why the statute authorizing a judgment against a partnership by service upon one partner should not be just as effective and applicable during the period subsequent to dissolution but prior to termination of the partnership as it is during the period before dissolution.

3. The partnership continues to exist for the purpose of satisfying its obligation to P.

North Star Coal Company v. Eddy, 277 A.2d 154 (Pa.) 1971.

Dissolution of a partnership terminates the actual authority of a partner to bind the partnership except for transactions connected with winding up the business. However, insofar as third persons who had dealings with the firm are concerned, apparent authority still exists until notice of termination is given.

This apparent authority means that one partner of a dissolved partnership binds the firm on contracts unconnected with winding up the firm's affairs. When he does so, issues arise as to whether or not the new obligations may be met with partnership funds or whether the contracting partner is entitled to contribution toward payment of the debt or obligation from the other partners.

The resolution of these issues depends upon the cause of the dissolution. If the dissolution is caused by (1) the act of a partner, (2) bankruptcy of the partnership, or (3) the death of a partner, each partner is liable for his share of any liability incurred on behalf of the firm after dissolution, just as if there had been no dissolution, unless the partner incurring the liability had knowledge of the dissolution. In these situations, where knowledge of the dissolution is present, the partner incurring the liability is solely responsible and he cannot require his fellow partners to share the burden of his unauthorized act. If the dissolution is not caused by the act, bankruptcy, or death of a partner but by some event such as a court decree, no partner has authority to act and therefore no right to contribution from other partners for liabilities incurred after dissolution.

When dissolution results from the death of a partner, title to partnership property remains in the surviving partner or partners for purposes of winding up and liquidation. Both real and personal property is, through the survivors, thus made available to a firm's creditors. All realty is treated as though it were personal property; it is sold, and the surviving partners finally account, usually in cash, to the personal representative of the deceased partner for the latter's share in the proceeds of liquidation.

Rights of Partners after Dissolution

When the dissolution is caused in any way other than the breach of the partnership agreement, each partner, as against his copartners or their assignees, has a right to insist that all the partnership assets be used first to pay firm debts. After firm obligations are paid, remaining assets are used to return capital contributions and then to provide for a distribution of profits. All the partners, except those who have caused a wrongful dissolution of the firm, have the right to participate in the winding up of the business. The majority selects the method and procedures to be followed in the liquidation. The assets are turned into cash unless all agree to distribute them in kind.

If a partnership that is to continue for a fixed period is dissolved by the wrongful withdrawal of one partner, the remaining members may continue as partners under the same firm name for the balance of the agreed term of the partnership. They are required to settle with the withdrawing partner for his interest in the partnership, however. The remaining partners are required to compensate the withdrawing partner, but they are allowed to subtract from the amount due in cash the damages caused by his wrongful withdrawal. In the calculation of his share, the goodwill of the business is not taken into consideration.

Upon dissolution, it is the duty of the remaining partner or partners to wind up the affairs. If they fail to do so and instead continue the business, they have liability to the withdrawing partner, his assignee, or personal representative for use of partnership assets. The liability may include interest if the value of the former partner's portion of the partnership can be ascertained. It may also include liability for a share of postdissolution profits. This liability arises because the business is continuing to use the assets of all of the former partners.

Just as a partner whose property is used to earn postdissolution profits is entitled to share in such profits, one who continues the partnership business after dissolution and contributes substantial labor and management services thereto is entitled to compensation for that share of the profits attributable to such services. A partner who withdraws from a partnership has no interest in profits that are attributable to labor and management services of continuing partners and which are earned after dissolution and before final accounting. Therefore, in determining profits attributable to use of a withdrawing partner's right in the property of dissolved partnership, a court is entitled to make an equitable allowance for services of partners who continue the partnership business.

It is often difficult to accurately value the interest of a withdrawing or deceased partner when the business continues. The buy and sell provisions will control the method for establishing the value of the interest as of the date of dissolution. However, it should be recognized that mathematical certainty is impossible when valuing a withdrawing partner's interest in a dissolved partnership.

Effect of Dissolution on Third Parties Dissolution of a partnership terminates the authority of the partners to create liability, but it does not discharge any existing liability of any partner. An agreement between the partners themselves that one or more of the partners will assume the partnership liabilities and that a withdrawing partner will not have any liability is ineffective insofar as third parties are concerned. However, a partner may be discharged from any existing liability by an agreement to that effect with the creditors.

When firm assets are insufficient to pay firm debts, the individual property of partners, including the estate of a deceased partner, is subject to the claims of third parties for all debts created while the partnership existed.

Notice on Dissolution After dissolution, two categories of parties are entitled to notice of the dissolution. First of all, firm creditors, including all former creditors, are entitled to actual notice of the dissolution. Transactions entered into after dissolution without such notice continue to bind withdrawing partners and the estate of deceased partners.

However, if proper notice is given, former partners are not liable for contracts unconnected with winding up the partnership's affairs. The giving of actual notice eliminates the apparent authority to bind the former firm and its partners.

Case: A partnership was in the process of dissolution, with one partner buying out the other. P, who had been doing business with the partnership for some time, was notified of the dissolution. Thereafter P extended credit to the buying partner. Upon default, P sued the selling partner.

Issue: Is the selling partner liable on the debt incurred after notice was given?

Decision: No.

Reason: Knowledge that a partnership is in the process of being dissolved is sufficient to preclude recovery from a partner by one thereafter extending credit. However, a partnership continues, notwithstanding formal dissolution, as to third persons without notice, and particularly one who has been dealing with the partnership.

Direct Sellers Association v. McBrayer, 492 P.2d 727 (Ariz.) 1972.

Notice of dissolution is required whether the dissolution is caused by an act of the parties or by operation of law, except where a partner becomes bankrupt or the continuation of the business becomes illegal. Therefore, upon death of a partner, the personal representative should give immediate notice of the death and dissolution in order to avoid further liability.

The second category of parties entitled to notice of dissolution consists of persons who knew about the partnership but who were not creditors. Where the dissolution is caused by an act of the parties, the partners will continue to be liable to all such parties unless public notice of such dissolution is given. Notice by publication in a newspaper in the community where the business has been transacted is sufficient public notice.

Where a partner has not actively engaged in the conduct of the partnership business, and creditors have not learned that he was a partner and have not extended credit to the firm on the faith of such partner, there is no duty to give notice to either of the groups mentioned above.

New Partners and New Firms A person admitted as a partner into an existing partnership is liable to the extent of his capital contribution for all obligations incurred before his admission. The new partner is not personally liable for such obligations, and the creditors of the old firm can look only to the firm assets and to the members of the old firm.

If a business is continued without liquidation of the partnership affairs, creditors of the first, or dissolved, partnership are also creditors of the partnership continuing the business. Likewise, if the partners assign all their interest to a former partner or a third person, who continues the business without liquidation of the partnership affairs, creditors of the dissolved partnership are also creditors of the person continuing the business.

Distributions on Dissolution

solvent partnerships

Upon the dissolution of a solvent partnership and a winding up of its business, an accounting is had to determine its assets and liabilities. Before the partners are entitled to participate in any of the assets, whether such partners are owed money by the firm or not, all firm creditors other than partners are entitled to be paid. After firm creditors are paid, the assets of the partnership are distributed among the partners as follows:

1. Each partner who has made advances to the firm, or has incurred liability for or on behalf of the firm, is entitled to be reimbursed.
2. Each partner is then entitled to the return of the capital that he has contributed to the firm.
3. Any balance is distributed as profits in accordance with the partnership agreement.

In many partnerships, one partner contributes capital and the other partner contributes labor. In such cases, the partner contributing labor has nothing to be returned in step number 2 above. Of course, the original agreement could place a value on such labor, but unless it does so, only the partner who actually contributes cash or other property will be repaid in step number 2.

insolvent partnerships

When the firm is insolvent, and a court of equity is responsible for making the distribution of the assets of the partnership, the assets are distributed in accordance with a rule known as "marshaling of assets."

Persons entering into a partnership agreement impliedly agree that the partnership assets shall be used for the payment of the firm debts before the payment of any individual debts of the partners. Consequently, a court of equity, in distributing firm assets, will give priority to firm creditors in firm assets as against the separate creditors of the individual partners. It will give priority to private creditors of individual partners in the separate assets of the partners as against firm creditors. Each class of creditors is not permitted to use the fund belonging to the other until the claims of the other have been satisfied. Because the firm creditors have available two funds out of which to seek payment—firm assets and the individual assets of the partners—and individual creditors of the partners have only one fund, the personal assets of the partners, equity compels the firm creditors to exhaust firm assets before having recourse to the partners' individual assets.

Case: P and D ran a sawmill and cotton gin business as partners. D had made a loan to the partnership, secured by a deed of trust on partnership property and on the home and farms of P. P seeks to enjoin the foreclosure of the deed of trust until a partnership accounting is had, alleging that partnership assets will discharge all debts.

Issue: Should such an injunction be issued?

Decision: Yes.

Reasons: 1. Generally, when a partnership is dissolved, each partner has the right to have partnership property applied to the discharge of partnership liabilities. The surplus, if any, is then paid to the partners proportionately. The equity of an individual creditor of a partner is subordinate to such right.

2. Only after the partnership assets have been applied may individual assets be reached by creditors. A partner has the right to have partnership property used to pay partnership debts in order to avoid personal liability on the debts.

Casey et al. v. Grantham et al., 239 N.C. 121 (1954).

The doctrine of marshaling of assets does not apply, however, if a partner conceals his existence and permits the other member of the firm to deal with the public as the sole owner of the business. Under these circumstances, the dormant partner by his conduct has led the creditors of the active partner to rely upon firm assets as the separate property of the active partner, and by reason of his conduct, the dormant partner is estopped from demanding an application of the equity rule that firm assets shall be used to pay firm creditors in priority, and individual assets to pay individual creditors. Thus the firm assets must be shared equally with firm creditors and the individual creditors of the active partner. In such a case, because the firm assets may not be sufficient to pay all the firm debts when depleted by payments to individual creditors, there may be unpaid firm creditors, and dormant partners will be personally liable. Because the firm creditor's right to firm property rests upon the partners' right that firm assets be used to pay firm debts, the conduct that estops a dormant partner also denies the creditors such a preference. Futhermore, the creditors who relied upon the assets in the hands of the sole active partner cannot claim a preference when later they learn such assets were partnership assets.

Just as the individual creditors are limited to individual assets, firm creditors are limited to firm assets. Therefore, firm creditors are not entitled to payment out of the individual assets of the partners until the individual creditors have been paid. This rule applies even though the firm creditors may at the same time be individual creditors of a member of the firm. There are two main exceptions to this general rule: (1) Where there are no firm assets and no living solvent partners. The rule for the limit of firm creditors to firm assets applies only where there are firm assets. If no firm assets or no living solvent partner exists, the firm creditors may share equally with the individual creditors in the distribution of the individual estates of the partners. (2) If a partner has fraudulently converted the firm assets to his own use, it follows that the firm creditors will be entitled to share equally with individual creditors in such partner's individual assets.

The doctrine of marshaling of assets is not applicable to tort claims under the Uniform Partnership Act. Partners are individually liable in tort for the acts of the firm, its agent and servants. The liability is joint and several. Thus the injured party may sue the partners individually or as a partnership. The firm assets need not be first used to collect a judgment, and direct action may be taken against individual assets.

REVIEW QUESTIONS AND PROBLEMS

1. What is the distinction between *dissolution* and *termination* of a partnership?

2. List four situations in which a court may decree dissolution of a partnership.

3. What groups of persons are entitled to notice of dissolution of a partnership? Indicate the type of notice to which each is entitled.

4. Explain the doctrine of marshaling of assets and indicate two situations in which it will not be followed.

5. A, B, and C were partners in an accounting firm. Their partnership agreement did not expressly grant the power of a majority to expel any partner. A and B decided that they should carry on the business without C, who proved to be lazy and inefficient in producing revenue. How should A and B proceed in removing C? Explain.

6. When A and B began their retail store as a partnership, each executed the same note to the C bank. Later the partnership was dissolved, but B continued to operate the store. A started a different business by himself. B was unable to pay the note, and C bank sued A and B but obtained service only on B. Is the subsequent judgment binding on A? Why?

7. During the period of their partnership, A and B incurred an obligation to a supplier, C. A and B later chose to admit D as an equal partner upon the payment by D of $5,000. The partnership was unable to pay C, and C sued the partnership and the individual partners. To what extent, if any, is D liable? Explain.

8. A and B formed a partnership to operate a restaurant. A contributed a building and fixtures worth $8,500, and B contributed $3,000 cash. A obtained a dissolution of the firm on account of B's wrongful withholding of A's share of the profits in the amount of $5,500. After dissolution, but before final judgment on the accounting and termination of the partnership, A formed another partnership with X and Y that made a profit operating the restaurant. Is B entitled to a share therein? Why?

9. A, B, and C, architects, were in partnership. D, a consulting engineer, did considerable work for the firm in the past and was always paid promptly. A, the senior member of the firm, decided to withdraw from the partnership and retire. The partners executed an indemnity agreement, whereby a new partnership of B and C was formed, and in which the new firm expressly assumed all debts of the old partnership. D was given express notice of A's withdrawal. Without A's services, the firm began to falter and was unable to meet D's bill. A debt in the amount of $5,000 remained from the old partnership, and a new debt of $15,000 was accrued by the new firm. How much may D collect from A? Why?

10. A, B, and C are partners, and by the terms of the agreement the partnership is to continue for a period of five years. At the end of the third year, prevailing conditions indicate that the firm cannot continue to operate except at a loss. B and C refuse to quit, and A files a bill to obtain an order for dissolution. Should he succeed? Why?

11. A, B, and C are partners under an agreement whereby the firm is to continue in business for ten years. A causes a wrongful dissolution of the partnership and demands his interest therein. May he demand that firm assets be liquidated? Is there any asset in which he is not entitled to share? Why?

39 FORMATION OF CORPORATIONS

Introduction Corporations may be classified in a variety of ways. Public corporations may be contrasted with private corporations. Corporations for profit, or business corporations, are distinguished from not-for-profit corporations. Each state classifies corporations doing business within that state as foreign or domestic to denote the state where incorporation took place. Moreover, each state has a variety of statutes relating to such specialized corporations as cooperatives, church and religious corporations, and fraternal organizations. In this chapter and those that follow, we are primarily concerned with the private business corporation.

The statutes relating to business corporations vary from state to state, yet they are quite similar. For our discussion, the basic principles of the Model Business Corporation Act will be used as the basic statute. This model act, prepared by the Commissioners on Uniform State Laws, has been adopted by a few states in total. Many other states have enacted many of its provisions. Thus it is a major influence on the law of corporations throughout the country. However, it is necessary to check one's own state statute relating to corporations in order to be adequately advised on any particular issue.

A corporation is an artificial intangible person or being created by the law. It is a method by which individual persons are united into a new legal entity. For this new legal entity, they select a common name and the purposes that it is to accomplish. As a legal entity separate and apart from the persons who had it created, the corporate existence is not affected by the death, incapacity, or bankruptcy of any of the persons involved in its creation or in its operation. As a legal entity, a corporation is able to own property and to sue or be sued in its own name in the same manner as a natural person. A corporation is also a person for purposes of both tort and criminal law. As an impersonal entity, it can act only through agents and servants, but the corporation is subject to the doctrine of *respondeat superior* and may be punished for certain criminal acts of its agents or servants.

Procedure for Incorporation   The law prescribes the steps to be taken for the creation of the corporation. Most corporate laws provide that a specified number of adult persons, usually not less than three, may file an application for a charter. The application contains the names and addresses of the incorporators, the name of the proposed corporation, the object for which it is to be formed, its proposed duration, the location of its registered office, the name of its registered agent, and information about the stock of the corporation. The information that must be supplied about the corporate stock must include (1) whether there will be preferred stock or only common stock; (2) the stated or par value of the stock, if any (if the stock has no stated value, then it is called no-par stock); (3) the number of shares of stock that will be authorized; and (4) the number of shares of stock that will actually be issued.

Some states also require the names and addresses of the subscribers to the stock and the amount subscribed and paid in by each. Most applications usually indicate whether the stock is to be paid for in cash or in property.

The application, signed by all the incorporators, is forwarded to a state official, usually the secretary of state. If the application is in order, the official then issues a charter. Upon receipt of the charter, it is filed by the incorporators in the proper recording office. The receipt of the charter and its filing are the operative facts that bring the corporation into existence and give it authority and power to operate.

After the charter has been received and filed, the incorporators and all others who have agreed to purchase stock meet and elect a board of directors. They may also approve the bylaws of the corporation if the applicable law so provides. In most instances the bylaws are approved by the board and not by the shareholders. The board of directors that has been elected then meets, approves the bylaws, elects the officers, calls for the payment of the subscription price for the stock, and makes whatever decisions are necessary to commence business.

The Bylaws   A *bylaw* is a rule for governing and managing the affairs of the corporation that is binding upon all shareholders. The provisions of the bylaws are not binding on third parties unless the third parties have knowledge of them. The bylaws contain provisions establishing the corporate seal and the form of the stock certificate to be used. They also contain provisions providing for the number of officers and directors, the method of electing them and removing them from office, as well as the enumeration of their duties. They also specify the time and place of the meetings of the directors and the shareholders. Together with the articles of incorporation and the applicable statute, the bylaws provide the rules for operating the corporation. Failure to follow the bylaws constitutes a breach of the fiduciary duties of a director or officer.

Disregarding the Corporate Entity   One of the basic advantages of the corporate form of business organization is the limitation of shareholder liability. Corporations are formed for the express purpose of limiting one's risk to the amount of his investment in the stock. Sometimes suits are brought to hold the shareholders personally liable for an obligation of a corporation. Such suits attempt to "pierce the corporate veil" and ask the court to look behind the corporate entity and take action as though no entity separate from the members existed. However, the corporate entity may not be disregarded simply because all the stock is owned by the members of a family or by one person, or by another corporation.

Case: P sued D to repossess seven hearses. P is a wholly owned subsidiary of X company. D has a valid counterclaim against X company. D seeks to set off its counterclaim against X company in the suit brought by P.

Issue: Can D assert against P, a subsidiary corporation, a counterclaim that it has against P's parent corporation?

Decision: No.

Reasons: 1. A corporation is an entity separate from its shareholders and from other corporations with which it may be associated.

2. A holding company is not as a general rule liable on the contracts of its subsidiary corporations.

Divco-Wayne Sales Fin. Corp. v. Martin Vehicle Sales, 195 N.E.2d 287 (Ill.) 1963.

In certain situations the corporate entity is often disregarded. First, if the use of the corporation is to defraud or to avoid an otherwise valid obligation, the court may handle the problem as though no corporation existed. To illustrate, let us assume that A and B sold a certain business and agreed not to compete with the buyer for a given number of years. Desirous of reentering business, in violation of the contract term, they **organize a corporation, becoming the principal stockholders and** managers. The buyer may have the corporation enjoined from competing with him as effectively as he could have enjoined A and B from establishing a competing business. Second, if the corporate device is used to evade a statute, the corporate entity may be disregarded. For example, if a state law provides that a person may not hold more than one liquor license at a time, this law cannot be circumvented by forming multiple corporations. The attempt to evade the statute would justify "piercing the corporate veil."

Finally, the corporate entity is sometimes disregarded when a court determines that the ends of justice require "piercing the corporate veil." Today, courts may treat an individual and a corporation as identical where unusual facts and the conduct of the parties are such that the distinct corporate entity ought to be disregarded.

Case: P obtained a judgment against the X corporation. D was the sole shareholder of X corporation. After the judgment was obtained by P, D caused the corporation to be dissolved. D paid off all the debts of the corporation except P's judgment and kept all the corporate assets. P seeks to collect the judgment from D personally.

Issue: Does justice require that the corporation and D be treated as identical?

Decision: Yes.

Reasons: 1. The doctrine that a corporation is a legal entity existing separate and apart from the persons composing it is a legal theory introduced for purposes of convenience and to subserve the ends of justice. The concept cannot, therefore, be extended to a point beyond its reason and policy, and when invoked in support of an end subversive of this policy, will be disregarded by the courts. Thus, in an appropriate case and in furtherance of the ends of justice, a corporation and the individual or individuals owning all its stock and assets will be treated as identical.

2. It is basic that a corporation is a distinct and separate entity from the individuals who compose it as stockholders or who manage it as directors or officers. This is not a rule cast in concrete but rather courts have always looked to substance over form. In a proper case, when the corporate form is being used to evade personal responsibility, courts have not been hesitant to disregard the corporate form and to impose liability on the person controlling the corporation and subverting it to his personal use by the conduct of its business in a manner to make it merely his instrumentality.

3. Here the corporation was a fictional shield employed by D to avoid personal responsibility. D's actions denigrate the purpose of limited liability, that purpose being to encourage the investment of risk capital.

4. While each case is decided on its own facts, here the facts require that the parties be treated as identical in order to prevent injustice and inequitable consequences. After the dissolution, there were no assets from which P could collect. The purpose of the dissolution was to avoid the judgment. A corporation dissolved to avoid creditors is no more a separate entity than one formed to defraud them.

Cohen v. Williams, 318 So.2d 279 (Ala.) 1975.

Domestic and Foreign Corporations

A corporation organized under the laws of a particular state or country is called, within that particular state or country, a "domestic corporation." When such a corporation does business within another state or country, it is called a "foreign corporation" in such state or country.

Domestic corporations become qualified to do business upon receipt and recording of their charter. Foreign corporations doing intrastate business must "qualify" to do business in each state in which they are doing such business. This qualification is evidenced by a certificate of authority to do business from such state. Failure to qualify usually results in a denial of access to the courts as a plaintiff and to possible criminal penalties. The penalty of denial of access to the courts has the net effect of preventing foreign corporations from conducting business because the corporation's contracts are not enforceable by suit.

Most state statutes require foreign corporations to qualify to do business by filing a copy of their articles with the secretary of state. As a part of the qualification procedures, they are also required to appoint an agent upon whom service of process may be served, to pay license fees, to designate and maintain an office in the state, and to keep books and records.

The term *doing business* is not reducible to an exact and certain definition. State statutes frequently do not define the term. The Model Business Corporation Act defines the term to mean that a foreign corporation is *doing business* when "some part of its business substantial and continuous in character and not merely casual or occasional" is transacted within a state. It also states that a foreign corporation is not required to obtain a license to do business by reason of the fact that (1) it is in the mail-order business and receives orders from a state that are accepted and filled by shipment from without the state, and (2) it uses salesmen within a state to obtain orders that are only accepted and approved from without the state. However, a foreign corporation is required to obtain a license if the orders are accepted or filled from within the state or if any sale, repair, or replacement is made from stock physically present within the state in which the order is obtained.

572

POWERS OF CORPORATIONS

Introduction   The application for a charter includes a statement of the powers desired by the corporation. These are usually stated in quite broad language. A corporation has only such powers as are conferred upon it by the state that creates it. The charter, together with the statute under which it is issued, sets forth the express powers of the corporation. In addition, all powers reasonably necessary to carry out the expressed powers are implied.

Case: D corporation gave one of its employees the option to purchase 40,000 shares at $3 per share, the market price at that time. The employee exercised the option when the market price had risen to $8 per share. P, a shareholder of D, contends the action was invalid because the power to grant options was not expressly granted in the Business Corporation Act.

Issue: Did the corporation have authority to grant the option?

Decision: Yes.

Reason: The power to so grant may be implied from the power of corporations to make employment contracts, and the power to do anything necessary or convenient to effectuate such granted powers.

Elward v. Peabody Coal Co. et al., 9 Ill.App.2d 234 (1956).

The following general powers are ordinarily granted to the corporation by statute: (1) to have perpetual existence; (2) to sue and be sued; (3) to have a corporate name and corporate seal; (4) to own, use, convey, and deal in both real and personal property; (5) to borrow and lend money other than to officers and directors; (6) to purchase, own, and dispose of securities; (7) to enter into contracts of every kind; (8) to make charitable contributions; (9) to pay pensions and establish pension plans; and (10) all powers necessary or convenient to effect any of the other purposes. Some of these powers will be discussed more fully in the sections that follow.

Power to Acquire   Treasury stock is a corporation's own stock which has been
Treasury Stock   legally issued, fully paid for, and reacquired by gift or purchase but has not been formally canceled in accordance with a formal procedure specified by the state law. A corporation is restricted from acquiring its own stock because it might effect a reduction of its capital to the detriment of creditors and other stockholders. In most states a

573

corporation is permitted to purchase treasury stock only out of accumulated profits or surplus. This retains an investment in the corporation by stockholders equivalent to the original capital as a protective cushion for creditors in case subsequent losses develop.

A corporation that has issued preferred stock has the power to redeem such stock where there is no injury to or objection by creditors. Here again many of the states require the preferred stock to be redeemed out of surplus or demand that authority to reduce the capital stock be obtained from the state.

Ultra Vires Any acts of a corporation that are beyond the authority, express or implied, given to it by the state are said to be *ultra vires* acts—"beyond the authority." If a corporation performs acts or enters into contracts to perform acts that are *ultra vires*, the state creating such a corporation may forfeit its charter for misuse of its corporate authority. The extent of the misuse is controlling in determining whether the state will take away its franchise or merely enjoin the corporation from further *ultra vires* conduct.

Although third parties have no right to object to the *ultra vires* acts of a corporation, a stockholder may bring court action to enjoin a corporation from performing an *ultra vires* contract. In addition, the corporation may recover from the directors who approved the *ultra vires* contracts any losses or damages sustained because of the *ultra vires* venture. When they exceed corporate powers, the directors may become personally liable for resulting losses.

At common law a corporation had no liability on contracts beyond its corporate powers because the corporation has capacity only to do those things expressly authorized within its charter or that were incidental thereto. However, most modern statutes, including the Model Business Corporation Act, provide that all *ultra vires* contracts are enforceable. Neither party to such a contract may use *ultra vires* as a defense. *Ultra vires* conduct on the part of the corporation may be enjoined by the state or any shareholder as previously noted, but otherwise contracts previously made are binding whether they be wholly executory, partially executed, or fully performed.

Case: D, a religious corporation, leased liquor-dispensing equipment from P. When D defaulted on the lease, P filed suit for the rental. D asserted *ultra vires* as a defense.

Issue: Is *ultra vires* a defense?

Decision: No.

Reasons: 1. Incapacity or lack of power on the part of a corporation does not make a lease invalid and the defense of *ultra vires* is not available.

2. The Business Corporation Code abolishes the doctrine of *ultra vires* as a means of avoiding a transaction which a corporation later claims is beyond its capacity or power, and limits the assertion of the defense to three enumerated instances not applicable here.

Free Baptist Church v. Southeastern Bev. Co., Inc., 218 S.E.2d 169 (Ga.) 1975.

OTHER ASPECTS OF CORPORATE FORMATION

Promoters A *promoter*, as the name implies, is one who promotes the corporation and assists in bringing it into existence. One or more promoters will be involved in making application for the charter, holding the first meeting of shareholders, entering into preincorporation subscription agreements, and engaging in other activities necessary to bring the corporation into existence. Promoters are responsible for compliance with the applicable blue-sky laws (statutes relating to the sale of securities), including the preparation of a prospectus if required.

Many of these activities involve the incurring of contractual obligations or debts. For example, the preparation of the application for a charter usually requires the assistance of a lawyer, and it must be accompanied by the required filing fee. Legal questions as to who has liability for these obligations and debts frequently arise. Is the promoter liable? Is the corporation after formation liable? Are both liable?

Certain general principles of contract and agency law prevent simple answers to these questions. First of all, a promoter is not an agent prior to incorporation because there is no principal. A party who purports to act as an agent for a nonexistent principal is generally liable as a principal. Second, the corporation technically cannot ratify the contracts of promoters because ratification requires capacity to contract both at the time of the contract and at the time of the ratification.

To avoid the difficulties caused by these legal theories, the law has used various fictions to create an obligation on the part of the corporation and to provide a means to eliminate liability on the part of promoters. The parties frequently do not intend the promoter to be liable on a preincorporation contract. A promoter may avoid personal liability by informing the other party that he does not intend to be liable and that he is acting in the name of and solely on the credit of a corporation to be formed. A promoter should make sure that contracts entered into by him on behalf of the proposed corporation are so worded as to relieve him from personal liability. Failure to do so means that the promoter is personally liable on such contracts.

Case: P sued D to recover a broker's commission. D was a promoter of a corporation to be formed. P knew that D was a promoter and that the corporation was not yet formed. The corporation was subsequently formed, but it failed to pay P the commission.

Issue: Is the promoter personally liable for the commission?

Decision: Yes.

Reasons: 1. As a general rule, the promoter of a corporation is personally liable on the contracts entered into on behalf of the corporation he is organizing.

2. On the other hand, if the contract is on behalf of the corporation and the person with whom the contract is made agrees to look to the corporation alone for responsibility, the promoter incurs no personal liability. . . . This exception applies where a promoter contracts in the name of a corporation which is to be formed later and does not intend to be liable on it, and the other party knows that the corporation has not been formed and that the promoter does not intend to be liable.

3. The later formation of a corporation and its adoption of contracts made by its promoters does not release or free the promoters from their liability.

Vodopich v. Collier County Developers, Inc., 319 So.2d 43 (Fla.App.) 1975.

Corporations are liable on contracts made by promoters if they accept the benefit of such contracts. A promise made after incorporation by the directors to pay for the expenses and services of promoters is binding and supported by sufficient consideration, on the theory of services previously rendered. Corporations are liable by implication for the necessary expenses and services incurred by the promoters in bringing them into existence because such expenses and services accrue, or inure, to the benefit of the corporation. Finally, it should be noted that some states have by statute provided that corporations are liable for the reasonable expenses incurred by promoters.

Promoters occupy a fiduciary relationship toward the prospective corporation and have no right, therefore, to secure any benefit or advantage over the corporation itself or over other stockholders because of their position as promoters. A promoter cannot purchase property and then sell it to the corporation at an advance, nor has he a right to receive a commission from a third party for the sale of property to the corporation. In general, however, he may sell property acquired by him prior to the time he started promoting the corporation, provided he sells it to an unbiased board of directors after full disclosure of all pertinent facts.

576

Stock Subscriptions A preincorporation stock subscription is an agreement to purchase stock in a corporation. It is a binding agreement (a subscriber cannot revoke his subscription) created among the subscribers for stock in a corporation to be formed. The subscription is usually drafted in such a manner as to create a contract. Some states by statute have provided that a preincorporation subscription constitutes a binding, irrevocable offer to the corporation, by reason of the mutual promises of the parties. The offer is usually limited to a specified period of time, such as six months.

Certain conditions are inherent in the subscription contract. The subscriber will not be liable unless the corporation is completely organized; the full amount of the capital stock subscribed; and the purpose, articles, and bylaws of the corporation are as originally stated and relied upon by the subscriber. Conditions, express or implied, are often waived by the subscriber if, with knowledge of the nonperformance, he participates in stockholders' meetings, pays part or all of his subscription, or acts as an officer or director of the corporation.

A subscription to stock of a corporation already in existence is a contract between the subscriber and the corporation. Such a contract may come into existence by reason of an offer either made by the corporation and accepted by the subscriber or made by the subscriber and accepted by the corporation. If the corporation opens subscription books and advertises its stock, it is seeking for an offer to be made by the subscriber. The corporation may, however, make a general offer to the public, which may be accepted by the subscriber in accordance with the terms of the general offer.

Corporate Name One of the provisions in the application for a corporate charter is the proposed name of the corporation. In order that persons dealing with a business will know that it is a corporation and that the investors therefore have limited liability, the law requires that the corporate name include one of the following words or end with an abbreviation of them: *corporation, company, incorporated,* or *limited.* In addition, a corporate name must not be the same as or deceptively similar to the name of any domestic corporation or that of a foreign corporation authorized to do business in the state to which the application is made.

Case: P, Legal Aid Services, Inc., brought suit to enjoin D, American Legal Aid, Inc., from using the term "Legal Aid" as a part of its name. The trial court entered judgment in favor of P after finding that the names were deceptively similar and that P was incorporated first.

577

Issue: Should D be enjoined from using the words "Legal Aid" in its transactions and name?

Decision: Yes.

Reasons: 1. What degree of resemblance or similarity between the names of the two companies will warrant the interference of the court is not capable of exact definition. It is and must be a matter to be determined from the facts and circumstances accompanying each particular case.

2. A court of equity may grant injunctive relief against a defendant corporation wrongfully using a name similar to a plaintiff corporation's name, particularly where hardship or damage to defendant is not great. The defendant may under the Corporation Act by a comparatively simple process change its name.

3. There was considerable evidence that many people were confused about the two corporations and that many people believed that they were in some way connected.

American Legal Aid, Inc. v. Legal Aid Services, Inc., 503 P.2d 1201 (Wyo.) 1972.

Most states have procedures for reserving a corporate name for a limited period. Inquiry is usually made as to the availability of a name, and if it is available it is reserved while the articles are being prepared. The name may be changed by charter amendment at any time without affecting corporate contracts or title to corporate property in any way.

Corporate Buy and Sell Agreement
The importance of a buy and sell agreement between partners was previously discussed. Frequently, a buy and sell agreement between shareholders in a closely held corporation is also desirable. It is equally as important to have a means of getting money out of a business as it is to have a means of getting money into the business.

Shareholder buy and sell provisions should be worked out before any shareholder knows whether he is a buyer or a seller. Although withdrawal from active participation will not effect a dissolution, it can have the serious effect of precipitating a lawsuit, or a shareholder may continue to participate in management when he does not desire to do so. Frequently, a withdrawing shareholder will be forced to sell his stock for less than it is worth because a buy and sell agreement was not worked out in advance.

Corporate buy and sell provisions are similar to those in a partnership, except the corporation as an entity is frequently a party to them. Many contracts provide that before a shareholder can sell his

578

stock to an outsider, it must first be offered to the corporation. Some contracts also require that it be offered to other shareholders. Such rights of first refusal are legal.

Corporations may buy life insurance on the life of an officer-shareholder and use the proceeds to buy stock. Stock redemptions on the death of a shareholder are an integral part of estate planning, and the various alternatives and plans to redeem such stock should be carefully studied at the time the corporation is formed.

THE BLUE-SKY LAWS

Introduction Government at both the federal and state levels is actively involved in the regulation of the sale of securities. Numerous statutes have been enacted not only to protect the investing public but to impose liability on anyone assisting in the sale of securities in violation of the law. These laws are commonly known as Blue-Sky laws because of their avowed purpose of preventing one person from selling another a patch of blue sky.

The responsibility for administering the federal securities law is vested in an independent regulatory agency, the Securities and Exchange Commission. The SEC exercises vast quasi-legislative and quasi-judicial powers. To prevent fraudulent sales of securities, the agency has adopted rules and regulations relating to financial and other information, which must be included in the documents filed with the commission as well as those given to potential investors. It also regulates the various stock exchanges, utility holding companies, investment trusts, and investment advisers.

Because the objective of the securities laws is to protect innocent persons from investing their money in speculative enterprises over which they have little or no control, the laws are paternalistic in character and are liberally construed to protect the investing public. The securities laws therefore cover not only stocks and bonds but every kind of investment in which one person invests money and looks to others for the success of the venture. Thus the term *security* is broadly defined to include any investment in which a person turns his money or property over to another to manage for profit.

Securities Act of 1933 The Securities Act of 1933 is a disclosure law. It requires that securities subject to its provisions be registered and that a prospectus be supplied to each investor. The function of the prospectus is to provide the investor with sufficient facts including financial information about the issuer to enable the prospective buyer to make an intelligent investment decision.

The application of the law is limited to transactions in which a security is sold to the general public. Private sales are exempt.

In determining whether or not a sale is public or private the SEC will examine (1) the number of offerees, (2) their knowledge about the company in which they are investing, (3) the relationship between the offeror and offeree, (4) whether the security comes to rest in the hands of the offeree or is resold, and (5) the amount of advertising involved. At one time, a sale to fewer than twenty-five persons was not a public sale. While the SEC does not always follow it, the twenty-five-persons figure is still a good rule of thumb.

The law also exempts certain securities from the registration and prospectus requirement. Securities such as those of banks which are regulated by other governmental agencies fall into this category. In addition, sales wholly in intrastate commerce as contrasted with interstate commerce are exempt. The intrastate exemption covers securities that are offered and sold only to persons who reside within the state of incorporation. If the sale is to a resident with the intention that it will be resold to a nonresident, the intrastate exemption is lost.

Liability under the 1933 Act The 1933 Securities Act imposes both civil and criminal liability for violation of its provisions. The criminal liability is for fraud in *any* offer or sale of securities. Fraud in the sale of an exempt security is still a criminal violation if the mail is used or if an instrumentality of interstate commerce has been used.

The civil liability provisions relating to registration statements impose liability on the following persons in favor of purchasers of securities:

a. Every person who signed the registration statement
b. Every director of the corporation or partner in the partnership issuing the security
c. Every person who with his consent is named in the registration statement as about to become a director or partner
d. Every accountant, engineer, or appraiser who assists in the preparation of the registration statement or its certification
e. Every underwriter

For purposes of civil liability in connection with a registration statement, it is imposed if the registration statement (1) contains untrue statements of material facts, (2) omits material facts required by statute or regulation, and (3) omits information that if not given makes the facts stated misleading. This latter situation describes the factual situation of a statement containing a half-truth which has the net effect of misleading the reader.

The law contains a separate provision relating to liability arising in connection with prospectuses and communications. It imposes liability on any person who sells or offers to sell a security without complying with the legal requirements relating to the furnishing of a proper prospectus. It also imposes liability on anyone who sells a security by use of a prospectus or an oral statement that includes untrue information or omits a material fact necessary so that the statements made will not be misleading.

Securities Exchange Act of 1934

The 1934 act, as the title implies, is concerned with security exchanges and with the trading of securities after the primary offering stage. In addition to creating the SEC, the 1934 act contains provisions regulating the various stock exchanges. It regulates brokers and dealers in securities and contains numerous provisions relating to such matters as proxy solicitation and insider transactions.

The Securities Exchange Act prohibits the sale of a security on a national exchange unless a registration is effective for the security. Issuers of registered securities are required to file periodic reports with the SEC. The insider transaction provisions require that insiders report all of their transactions to the SEC. Directors, officers, and owners of 10 percent or more of any class of security in any company are insiders. The penalty for violating the insider transactions law is the forfeiture to the issuer of any profit from a purchase or sale within any period of less than six months.

Liability under the 1934 Act

Two major statutory provisions impose liability under the 1934 Securities Exchange Act. These are Section 18 and Section 10b.

Section 18 of the act imposes liability for common-law fraud in favor of both purchasers and sellers. Plaintiffs under this section must prove scienter, reliance on the false or misleading statement, and damage. It is a defense that the person sued acted in good faith and without knowledge that the statement was false and misleading. There is no liability under Section 18 for simple negligence.

Most of the litigation under the 1934 act is brought under Section 10b and Rule 10b-5 of the SEC. These provisions are concerned with manipulative and deceptive devices and contrivances. Rule 10b-5 declares that it is unlawful to use the mails or any instrumentality of interstate commerce or any national securities exchange to defraud *any person* in connection with the *purchase or sale* of any security. This section and the rules promulgated under it provide a private remedy for defrauded investors against "any person" who indulges in fraudulent practices in connection with the purchase or sale of securities. Defendants in these cases have tended to fall into four general categories: (1) insiders, (2) broker-dealers, (3) corporations whose stock is purchased or sold by plaintiffs, and (4) those who "aid and abet" or conspire with a party who falls into one of the first three categories. Accountants are an example of those who may fall into the fourth category. Silence may constitute aiding and abetting. While there is no general duty on all persons who have knowledge of improper activities to report them, a duty to disclose may arise in the face of a special relationship or set of circumstances, such as an accountant certifying financial statements.

The application of Rule 10b-5 is not limited to securities subject to the act. It applies to all sales of any security. The rule requires that those standing in a fiduciary relationship disclose all material facts before entering into transactions. This means that an officer, a director, or a controlling shareholder has a duty to disclose all material facts. Failure to do so is a violation and in effect fraudulent.

REVIEW QUESTIONS AND PROBLEMS

1. What are the sources of the powers of a corporation?

2. What are the steps required in forming a corporation? In qualifying it to do business in a foreign state?

3. List the typical subjects covered in the bylaws of a corporation.

4. Give three examples of situations in which courts will "pierce the corporate veil."

5. What is the main limitation on a corporation's acquisition of treasury stock? Explain the reason for this limitation.

6. A is the sole stockholder of the A company, a corporation engaged in construction work. A has complete control over the business and manages all operations; all profits flow to A; and the company is undercapitalized. As president of A company, A makes a contract for the purchase of building supplies and subsequently fails to pay. May A be held personally liable? Why?

7. The ABC country club, inc., had a bylaw requiring ten days' notice of any special stockholders' meeting. X, president of the country club, had made a contract with Y to purchase land for use as a golf course, subject to acceptance by the shareholders. Seven days before the meeting was to be held, X sent notice of the special meeting to consider the contract. At that meeting the contract was accepted. The country club later refused to purchase, setting up the invalidity of the acceptance as a defense. May Y obtain specific performance? Why?

8. A, an air traffic specialist, contracted with B, a promoter for the proposed XYZ air line corporation, to provide advice and management for the corporation. He performed his part of the contract, but upon incorporation, the board of directors of XYZ refused to pay. May A recover from the company? From the promoter? Why?

9. Who can challenge an *ultra vires* act of a corporation? Under what circumstances? Explain.

10. The XYZ corporation was formed, according to its charter, "to engage exclusively in the sale of automobiles." Officers of XYZ entered into a contract to lease an auto to A. Since some shareholders objected to this agreement, XYZ refused to lease to A, and A sued XYZ for breach of contract. May the corporation defend on the ground of ultra vires? Why?

11. D, a director of the XYZ corporation, participated in a board decision to expand business operations in the near future. In anticipation that XYZ's financial status would improve as a result of this decision, D purchased stock from S, a shareholder, who had no knowledge of the board's action. The market value of the stock rose immediately after the decision was announced. Could D be liable to S for any profits made from this transaction? Why?

40 OPERATING THE CORPORATION

Introduction   The preceding chapter was concerned with the legal aspects of forming a corporation. Many of the legal principles that were discussed there are also applicable to the operation of a corporate entity. For example, many bylaw provisions are directly concerned with operations. Some of the subjects dealt with in this chapter, such as stock and the rights of shareholders, have a bearing on formation problems. Therefore the discussion in the preceding chapter and the materials in this chapter should be considered complementary.

Three distinct groups participate in the management of a corporation. The *shareholders* or *stockholders* (the words are synonymous) comprise the basic governing body. Shareholders exercise their control by electing the *board of directors*, by approving the bylaws, and by voting on such matters as merger, consolidation, or dissolution. The board of directors is the policy-making group, and in addition has the responsibility for electing the *officers* who carry out the policies. The duties and powers of the shareholders, the board of directors, and the various officers are regulated by statute, by the bylaws of the corporation, and by corporate resolutions passed by the board of directors.

Case: P, a former employee of D corporation, sued for back wages. X, the company president, had orally given P a raise of $200 per month which had not been paid. D contended that X had no authority to agree to the wage increase.

Issue: Is a company president authorized to grant employees raises?

Decision: Yes.

Reasons: 1. The president of a corporation is not invested with actual or apparent authority to bind his company by contract merely because of his position, but rather to bind the company, the president must be authorized by the statutes of the state, terms of the bylaws, or by appropriate action taken by the directors.

2. A corporate bylaw providing that the president "shall be the chief administrative officer of the corporation" and that he "shall have the power and authority to execute bonds, mortgages, and other contracts with the corporation in the ordinary course of business of the company" clothes the corporation's president with authority to grant raises to employees.

Ennis Business Forms, Inc. v. Todd, 523 S.W.2d 83 (Tex.) 1975.

SHAREHOLDERS

Fiduciary Aspects   The law as it relates to close corporations is somewhat different from the law as it relates to publicly held corporations. The latter term describes corporations with many shareholders, none of whom owns a majority of the stock. A *close corporation* is one in which management and ownership are substantially identical to the extent that it is unrealistic to believe that the judgment of the directors will be independent of that of the shareholders.

The shareholders in a close corporation owe one another substantially the same fiduciary duty in the operation of the enterprise that partners owe to one another. They must discharge their management and shareholder responsibilities in conformity with the strict good-faith standard, and they may not act out of avarice, expediency, or self-interest in derogation of their loyalty to other shareholders and to the corporation. This good-faith standard which shareholders in a close corporation must observe is in contrast to the relationship of the shareholders in a publicly held corporation. As a general rule, there is no fiduciary relationship between shareholders in publicly held corporations. One owner of stock listed on the New York Stock Exchange owes no duty to other owners of the same stock unless of course the shareholder is also an insider subject to SEC regulation.

The duty of the majority shareholder or shareholders in a close corporation to the minority shareholders is often involved in litigation when the majority interest is sold. In any transaction where control of a corporation is material, the controlling majority shareholders must exercise good faith and fairness from the viewpoint of the corporation. For example, assume that a controlling shareholder learns facts that

585

would lead a prudent person to believe that a potential buyer might loot the corporation of its assets to pay for the shares. Such a majority shareholder has a duty to conduct a reasonable investigation and not to sell if it is reasonable to believe that the minority interest will be adversely affected.

Meetings Action by the shareholders normally binds the corporation only when taken in a regular, or properly called, special meeting after such notice as is required by the bylaws or statute has been given. However, it is generally conceded—and most states so provide by statute—that action approved informally by all *shareholders* will bind the corporation. If there is less than unanimous approval, informal action is not possible.

notice Notice of a special meeting must include a statement concerning the matters to be acted upon at the meeting, and any action taken on other matters will be ineffective. If unusual action, such as a sale of corporate assets, is to be taken at the regular annual meeting, notice of the meeting must call specific attention to that fact; but otherwise any business may be transacted at the annual meeting.

Failure to give proper notice of a meeting generally invalidates the action taken at the meeting. A stockholder who, having failed to receive notice, attends and participates in a meeting is said to waive the notice by his presence.

quorum A quorum of shareholders must be present in person or by proxy (a *proxy* is the authority to vote another's stock) in order to transact business. A *quorum* is usually a majority of the voting shares outstanding, unless some statute or the bylaws provide for a larger or smaller percentage. Affirmative action is approved by majority vote of the shares represented at a meeting, provided a quorum exists. There are certain unusual matters, such as merger or sale of all corporate assets, that at common law requires unanimous vote. Today statutes usually provide that such action can be taken by vote of two-thirds or three-fourths of the shareholders. Many of these statutes also provide that the dissenting shareholders have the right to surrender their shares and receive their fair value if they disapprove of the action taken. These matters are discussed in the next chapter.

purposes In large publicly held corporations, the annual meeting of shareholders serves a variety of purposes. Management has usually solicited enough proxies in advance to control any vote that is taken. In other words, the outcome of any vote to be taken is a certainty prior to the meeting. Nevertheless, many shareholders attend such meetings in order to question management on a variety of issues and to "lobby" for certain policies. Management expends a substantial effort in preparing to answer questions at the meeting. In recent years, many activists have raised a number of social and political issues at annual meetings. In addition, corporations have been challenged on certain policy decisions, and some have been required to submit certain issues to the shareholders during the proxy solicitation. For example, some corporations have had their activities in Rhodesia and South Africa challenged. Other issues raised at these annual meetings or in proxy material include minority representation (women, blacks, etc.) on the board of directors, military contracts, political contributions, and environmental pollution.

The annual meeting of shareholders of large corporations is also used by management as a public relations opportunity. Management is able to educate the shareholders on company accomplishments as well as its problems.

Since a large corporation is not designed to be a working example of participatory democracy, many people are urging that the practice of holding an annual meeting be eliminated and that all issues of genuine concern to a substantial number of shareholders be submitted to them by written ballot. Since it is assumed that shareholders who are dissatisfied with management can sell their stock, the annual meeting for the publicly listed corporation may be dispensed with in the years to come.

Voting   The statutes of the various states and the charters issued under their authority prescribe the matters on which shareholders are entitled to vote. Shareholders are usually entitled to vote on the election of directors; on such major policy issues as mergers and consolidations and on dissolution; and, in some instances, on a change in the bylaws.

As a general rule, every shareholder is entitled to as many votes as he owns shares of stock. The shareholder whose name appears upon the corporate records is usually designated by the bylaws as the person entitled to vote. The owners of preferred stock, depending on their contract with the corporation, may or may not be entitled to vote. Some jurisdictions also authorize nonvoting common stock.

The statutes of some states provide for cumulative voting in the election of directors. In cumulative voting, a shareholder may cast as many votes for one board candidate as there are board members to be filled, multiplied by the number of his shares of stock, or he may distribute this same number of votes among the candidates as he sees fit. For example, a shareholder owning one hundred shares of stock has three hundred votes if three directors are to be elected. He may cast all three hundred votes for one candidate, or they may be spread among the candidates.

A shareholder is entitled to vote only by virtue of his ownership of the stock. A shareholder may specifically authorize another to vote his stock. This authorization is made by power of attorney and must specifically state that the agent of the shareholder has power to vote his principal's stock. This method of voting is called *voting by proxy*. It is a personal relationship and may be revoked at any time by the shareholder before the authority is exercised. The laws relative to principal and agent control this relationship.

A shareholder, unlike a director, is permitted to vote on a matter in which he has a personal interest. Although in certain respects he represents the corporate welfare in his voting, in most respects he votes in such a manner as he thinks will best serve his interest. The majority of shareholders may not take action, however, that is clearly detrimental to the corporation and minority interest.

Rights of Shareholders— In General   A shareholder has the following rights usually created by statute and reiterated in the bylaws: (1) the right to inspect the books and papers of the corporation; (2) the right to attend shareholders' meetings and to vote for directors and on certain other matters, such as dissolution or merger; (3) the right to share in the profits when a dividend is declared; (4) the preemptive right; and (5) the right to bring a shareholder's derivative suit. In some states a shareholder has the additional right of cumulative voting previously discussed.

The right to inspect the books and papers is limited to good-faith inspections for proper and honest purposes at the proper time and the proper place. A *proper purpose* is one that seeks to protect the interest of the corporation as well as the interest of the shareholder seeking the information. The inspection must be made with a justifiable motive and not through idle curiosity or for vexatious purposes. The business hours of the corporation are the reasonable and proper hours in which a stockholder is entitled to inspect the books.

In some states, a shareholder who is refused access to the books and records is entitled to damages as provided by statute. For example, a typical statute provides that a shareholder who is denied the right to inspect books and records is entitled to damages equal to 10 percent of the value of the stock owned.

The right to inspect includes contracts and correspondence as well as books and records. These statutes are given a broad and liberal interpretation. The right extends even to confidential records such as those relating to bank loans.

Case: P, a bank, brought a declaratory judgment action against three of its shareholders to determine the bank's obligation to permit inspection of the bank's books and records by the shareholders. P contended that such inspection would invade the private and confidential relationships between the bank and its customers.

Issue: Do bank shareholders have the right to inspect the books and records of the bank?

Decision: Yes.

Reasons: 1. Generally, inspection rights of shareholders of a bank are the same as those of shareholders of other corporations. The statute is liberally construed.

2. A shareholder's statutory right of inspection can only be exercised at reasonable and proper times so as not to interfere with the conduct of the business. It must not be exercised from idle curiosity or for improper or unlawful purposes; in all other respects the statutory right is absolute.

3. The purpose of the statute providing shareholders with a right to inspect a corporation's books and records is to protect small and minority shareholders against the mismanagement and faithlessness of their agents and officers. The inspection right covers books and records, including documents, contracts, and papers, but not secret research or the results of technical investigations.

Bank of Heflin v. Miles, 318 So.2d 697 (Ala.) 1975.

Preemptive Right

The original application for a charter specifies the amount of stock the corporation will be authorized to issue. It also specifies the amount that will be issued without further notice to the state. The amount of authorized stock and the amount of issued stock are used to compute the license fees and franchise taxes due to the state of incorporation. These amounts cannot be increased or exceeded without the authority of the state.

The shareholders may authorize an increase in the authorized capital stock. Such action may not be taken by the directors. An increase in the authorized capital stock is an amendment to the corporate charter which requires state approval.

The board of directors may authorize the sale of unissued capital stock when the amount previously issued is less than that which is authorized. This does not require an amendment to the charter. All that is required in such a case is that the state be informed of the additional issue of the stock so that the correct taxes may be collected.

When an increase in the capital stock has been properly authorized, the existing shareholders have a prior right against third parties to subscribe to the increased capital stock. This right is called the shareholder's *preemptive right*. It is based upon the shareholder's right to protect and maintain his proportionate control and interest in the corporation.

589

The preemptive right may be limited or waived by contract and by provisions in the charter or bylaws of the corporation in most states. In many states it is not applicable to treasury stock.

The preemptive right is applicable to new authorizations of stock. It is generally not applicable to new issues of stock previously authorized. However, if the new issue of an original authorization takes place a long time after the original issue, many states provide that the preemptive right exists. Most states approve the issuance of stock to employees under stock option plans without regard to the preemptive right.

Derivative Suits

A shareholder cannot maintain an *action at law* for injuries to the corporation because the corporation is a legal entity and by law has a right to bring a suit in its own name. Any cause of action based on conduct injurious to the corporation accrues in the first instance to the corporation. Nor can a shareholder bring a suit at law against the directors or other officers of the corporation for negligence, waste, and mismanagement in the conduct of the corporate business. The right to sue for injuries to the corporation rests strictly with the corporation itself.

A shareholder may, however, bring a *suit in equity* known as a shareholder's *derivative suit* to enjoin the officers of a corporation from entering into *ultra vires* contracts or from doing anything that would impair the corporate assets. Likewise the shareholder has a right to bring suit for dollar damages on behalf of the corporation if the officers are acting outside the scope of their authority, are guilty of negligent conduct, or are engaging in fraudulent transactions in such a way as to be injurious to the corporation itself.

Before a shareholder may bring a derivative suit, he must show that he has done everything possible to secure action by the managing officers and directors and that they have refused to act. If the action involves a lawsuit, there must be a demand to sue or it must be apparent that a demand would be futile under the circumstances. Any judgment received in such an action is paid to the corporation. The shareholder who initiates the action is permitted, however, to recover the expenses involved in the suit.

Mere dissatisfaction with the management of the corporation will not justify a derivative suit. In the law of corporations, it is fundamental that the majority shareholders control the policies and decisions of the corporation. Every shareholder impliedly agrees that he will be bound by the acts and decisions of a majority of the shareholders or by the agents of the corporation duly chosen by such majority. Courts will not undertake to control the business of a corporation, although it may be seen that better decisions might be made and the business more successful if other methods were pursued.

The majority of shares of stock are permitted to control the business of a corporation in their discretion, when not in violation of its charter, or some public law, or corruptly, oppressively, and fraudulently subversive of the rights and interests of the corporation or of a shareholder. This principle will be discussed further in the next chapter with the materials on the right of a shareholder to have the corporation dissolved.

DIRECTORS

**Qualifications
and Powers**
A director of a corporation is elected by the shareholders. The duties of directors ordinarily consist of attending meetings, exercising judgment on propositions brought before the board, and voting. A director has no power to issue orders to any officer or employee, nor can he institute policies by himself, or command or veto any other action by the board.

It is not essential that directors hold stock in the corporation. Because they are to supervise the business activities, select key employees, and plan for the future development of the enterprise, they are presumably elected because of their business ability.

The directors have power to take such actions as are necessary or proper to conduct the ordinary business activities of the company. They may not amend the charter, approve a merger, or bring about a consolidation with another corporation without the approval of the shareholders.

Meetings
The bylaws usually provide for the number of directors. In most cases not less than three directors are required. Because the board of directors must act as a unit, it is usually necessary that it assemble at board meetings. The bylaws usually provide for the method of calling directors' meetings and for the time and place of meeting. A record is usually kept of the activities of the board of directors, and the evidence of the exercise of its powers is usually stated in resolutions kept in the corporate record book. A majority of the members of the board of directors is necessary to constitute a quorum. Special meetings are proper only when all directors are notified or are present at the meeting. Directors may not vote by proxy, having been selected as agents because of their personal qualifications.

Modern statutes make informal action possible by a board of directors (usually by telephone), provided the action taken is subsequently reduced to writing and signed by all of the directors. This gives a board the flexibility and capability to make decisions when needed without delay. Failure to have unanimous approval of such informal action or to give proper notice is fatal to actions attempted by the board of directors.

Case: D corporation, by a resolution of its board of directors, granted P a pension that would be paid upon the death of her husband, X. X had been chairman of D's board at the time of the resolution. Later, after a marital dispute, X wrote a letter to the corporation requesting that the pension for his wife be canceled. At a special meeting of the board of directors attended by five of the seven directors, a resolution was passed rescinding P's pension. X was not given notice of the meeting and did not attend. P brought suit, contending that the pension had not been properly rescinded.

Issue: Was the action taken at the special meeting valid?

Decision: No.

Reason: 1. As a general rule, directors may bind a corporation only when they act at a legal meeting of the board.

2. As to special meetings of the board of directors of a corporation, the general rule is that such a meeting held without notice to some or any of the directors and in their absence is illegal, and action taken at such a meeting, although by a majority of the directors, is invalid absent ratification or estoppel.

3. The notice requirement may be waived by a director either prior or subsequent to the special meeting, provided such waiver is in writing.

4. Additionally, any action which may properly be taken at a meeting of a board of directors of a corporation may be effected and is binding without a meeting, if a consent in writing setting forth the action so taken is signed by each and every member of the board and filed with the secretary of the corporation.

5. All directors must be given notice of a special meeting. The rationale is that "each member of a corporate body has the right of consultation with the others, and has the right to be heard upon all questions considered, and it is presumed that if the absent members had been present they might have dissented, and their arguments might have convinced the majority of the unwisdom of their proposed action and thus have produced a different result."

Stone v. American Lacquer Solvents Co., 345 A.2d 174 (Pa.) 1975.

Compensation In the absence of a stipulation in the charter or bylaws or resolution of the shareholders, directors receive no compensation for their services as such. Such compensation is usually provided for, however. Directors who are appointed as officers of the corporation should have their salaries fixed at a meeting of the shareholders or in the bylaws. Because directors are not supposed to vote on any matter in which they have a personal interest, director-officers of small corporations usually vote on salaries for each other but not their own, and the action to determine salaries should be ratified by the shareholders in order to ensure the validity of the employment contracts.

Liabilities of Directors The directors of a corporation may have personal liability both in tort and in contract. While their liability is usually to the corporation, it may extend to shareholders and to third parties as well. It should be noted that officers of corporations also may have personal liability, and the principles herein discussed are applicable to officers as well as to directors.

The liability of corporate officers and directors is frequently expressly provided by statute. However, liability, such as for tortious conduct, is predicated upon basic common-law principles. For example, a director who participates in fraudulent conduct by the corporation has personal liability to the third party on the usual common-law tort theories just as does any other agent or servant. Moreover, the director need not personally commit fraud. He is liable if he sanctions or approves it.

While directors and officers frequently have personal tort liability to third persons, they do not have personal liability to third persons for negligent management of the corporation. This liability of directors is only to the corporation.

Case: P held a corporate note secured by a chattel mortgage and by a mortgage on real property. The note was not paid and a foreclosure suit was instituted. The foreclosure sale did not bring enough to satisfy the obligation. P brought action against Ds, the officers and directors of the corporation, alleging that they had mismanaged the corporate business. The lower court ruled that P, as a creditor, had no standing to sue Ds on a theory of negligence.

Issue: Do creditors of a corporation have a claim against officers and directors for *negligent* mismanagement of its affairs?

Decision: No.

Reasons: 1. Directors or officers may be liable to the corporation or shareholders for mismanagement of the business of the corporation or waste of its assets; but they are not liable to its creditors for mere mismanagement or waste of assets constituting a wrong or breach of duty as to the corporation.

2. A creditor of a corporation may not maintain a personal action at law against the officers or directors of a corporation who have, by their

mismanagement or negligence, committed a wrong against the corporation to the consequent damage of the creditor. The reason given for the rule is the entire lack of privity between the parties.

3. The duty to exercise diligence and care is one owed to the corporation, and it is elementary law that one person cannot maintain an action against another for a wrong to a third person which injures him only incidentally.

Equitable Life & Casualty Insurance Co. v. Inland Printing Co., 454 P.2d 162 (Utah) 1971.

fiduciary duties Directors and officers are said to stand in a fiduciary relation to the corporation. A director occupies a position of trust and confidence with respect to the corporation and cannot, by reason of his position, directly or indirectly derive any personal benefits that are not enjoyed by the corporation or the shareholders. All secret profits obtained by a director in the pursuit of the corporate business must be accounted for to the corporation. For example, if a corporate director acquires property for himself which he knew the corporation desired, there is a breach of the director's fiduciary relation to the corporation. The corporation in such case may obtain the property.

A director may contract with the corporation, but he is subject to the same limitations as an agent is in dealing with his principal. He is required to disclose his interest in all contracts, and the director or officer has the burden of establishing the fairness of the transaction, to volunteer all pertinent information regarding the subject matter involved.

At common law, a director was forbidden to vote as a director on any matter in which he had a personal interest. Even though his vote was not necessary to carry the proposition considered, most courts regarded any action taken as a result of that vote voidable. Some states have altered this view by statute. They allow directors to vote on such matters after a full disclosure of all facts and provide that the transaction is not voidable if a majority of the disinterested directors vote in its favor. However, if an officer or director does not obtain approval of the transaction by disinterested directors, the contract is voidable as a breach of the fiduciary relationship irrespective of fairness or lack of bad faith.

Case: D, while a director, general manager, and treasurer of P corporation, sold to himself certain boats and engines from the corporation's inventory. At the time of the sale, D was aware that he was going to be discharged shortly. P corporation brought suit to have the sale of the boats and engines set aside.

594

Issue: Was the transaction voidable at the option of P?

Decision: Yes.

Reasons: 1. Any corporation may contract for any lawful purpose with a director (1) if the contract is entered into in good faith, (2) if it is approved or ratified by vote of the holders of a majority in interest of its stock or by a majority vote at any meeting of its board of directors excluding any vote by the contracting director, and (3) if the contracting director shall not be necessary for a quorum at the meeting for this purpose. A contract made in compliance with these three shall be voidable by the corporation only in case it would be voidable if made with a stranger.

2. An officer of a corporation stands in a fiduciary relationship toward its stockholders, and his position in relation to that group is analogous to that of trustee and beneficiary of a trust. Such a relationship is one of trust and confidence and imposes the duty on the fiduciary to act with the utmost good faith.

3. Where one standing in a fiduciary relationship deals with himself, the transaction does not acquire validity because the price is fair.

4. The transaction may be set aside by the corporation because of the mere relationship of the parties, and "without regard to whether the corporation has been injured, or the contract is fair or unfair, or the officer has acted in good faith or in bad faith. . . ."

Point Trap Company v. Manchester, 199 A.2d 592 (R.I.) 1969.

Directors are personally liable to the corporation when they willfully misuse their power and misapply the funds of the corporation. There are many instances of liability imposed on directors and officers by statute. For example, they are liable for antitrust violations, discrimination in employment, and for actions contrary to other laws regulating business activity. They are also personally liable when they issue stock as fully paid when it is not paid in full or when dividends are declared without the requisite retained earnings. Directors are required to perform the duties of their office in a reasonable manner and in good faith.

standard of care   The standard of care required of directors cannot be exactly defined. It is generally held that directors are bound to exercise that degree of care that men of prudence exercise in the management of their own affairs. The standard of care varies with the size and type of the corporation. In large corporations many duties must be delegated, thus intimate knowledge of details by the directors

595

is not possible. In corporations invested with a public interest—such as insurance companies, banks, building and loan associations, and public utilities—rigid supervision and specific obligations are imposed upon directors. If a director fails to exercise the requisite degree of care and skill, the corporation will have a right of action against him for resulting losses. When directors by their negligent misconduct involve the corporation in an *ultra vires* transaction that causes a loss, the directors may be liable to the corporation. They are not liable, however, for accidents and mistakes of judgment or for losses, if they have acted in good faith and have exercised ordinary care, skill, and diligence. The corporation must pay the expense of defending unfounded claims against officers and directors.

The liability of directors is to the corporation. This liability may be enforced by a shareholder's derivative suit if the corporation upon demand fails or refuses to sue the director. As previously noted, the liability of a director may not be enforced by creditors, however.

In recent years there has been a dramatic increase in the number of lawsuits filed against directors and officers of publicly held corporations. These lawsuits have been filed by dissenting shareholders, public interest groups, and government regulators. Many of the lawsuits result from the failure of directors to prevent activities such as bribery of foreign officials and illegal political contributions.

It has been a corporate practice in most large corporations to purchase liability insurance coverage for directors. Because of the increased number of suits, the cost of this insurance is soaring. Directors have been held liable for such diverse acts as improvident investments, improper expenditures of corporate funds, and violations of civil rights laws.

CORPORATE STOCK

Introduction   A certificate of stock is written evidence of the ownership of a certain number of shares of stock of a corporation. It shows upon its face the character of the interest and the method by which it may be transferred. The certificate is the physical evidence that the corporation recognizes a certain person as being a shareholder with rights in the corporation. These rights are primarily three in number: the right to share in profits, the right to participate indirectly in the control of the corporation, and the right to receive a portion of the assets at time of dissolution. A share of stock is representative of an investment made in the corporation, but it gives the holder no right to share in the active management of the business. The general rules of law applicable to personal property are applicable to stock.

The term *stock* must be distinguished from the term *bond*. A bond, unlike stock, is an obligation of the corporation to pay a certain sum of money in the future at a specified rate of interest. It is comparable to a promissory note of which the corporation is the maker. Corporate bonds are often secured by a mortgage on the assets of the corporation, but many corporate bonds, called *debentures*, do not have such security. A bondholder is a creditor of the corporation, whereas a shareholder is an owner of the corporation. A shareholder has a right to receive dividends if they are declared by the board of directors and to participate in the assets of the corporation after all creditors have been paid. A bondholder has no right to vote or to participate in the management and control of a corporation unless, upon insolvency, such rights are given by contract. A shareholder, in the absence of contractual limitations, has a right to participate in management to the extent of electing the directors and voting on such matters as dissolution.

Kinds of Stock *Common stock* is the simplest type of corporate stock. It entitles the owner to share in the control, profits, and assets of the corporation in proportion to the amount of common stock held. Such a shareholder has no advantage, priority, or preference over any other class of shareholders unless otherwise specified as to any particular class.

Preferred stock is stock that has a prior claim to dividends, or to assets on dissolution, over other classes of stock. The most important right given to a preferred shareholder is the right to receive a certain specified dividend, even though the earnings are not sufficient to pay a like dividend to common shareholders.

The statutes of most states provide that a corporation may issue stock with *no par value*. The value of no-par stock is determined by its sale price in the open market or by the price set by the directors as a "stated value." Shareholders, creditors of the corporation, and the public are not misled or prejudiced by this type of stock, because there is no holding out that the stock has any particular face value. All persons dealing in such stock are put on notice that they should investigate the corporation's assets and its financial condition. Stock with no par value represents its proportionate part of the total assets of the corporation.

A *stock warrant* is a certificate that gives to the holder thereof the right to subscribe for and purchase a given number of shares of stock in a corporation at a stated price. It is usually issued in connection with the sale of other shares of stock or of bonds, although the law of some states permits the issuance of stock warrants entirely separate and apart from the sale of other securities. Warrants are transferable. The option to purchase contained in the warrant may or may not be limited as to time or otherwise conditioned. Warrants have value and can readily be sold on the market in the same fashion as other securities.

Watered stock is stock that has been issued as fully paid, when in fact its full par value has not been paid in money, property, or services. The original owner of watered stock has liability for the unpaid portion of its stated value. For example, if X receives one thousand shares of $1 par value stock in exchange for property with only $200, X would owe the corporation $800. This could be collected by the corporation or by a creditor in the case of insolvency of the corporation.

The liability for watered stock arises because the capital stock of a corporation represents the total par value of all the shares of the corporation (plus the stated value of no-par stock). The public, including corporate creditors, has a right to assume that the capital stock issued has been paid for in full. The corporation in effect represents that assets have been received in payment equal in amount to its issued capital stock. If stock is issued in excess of the actual assets in money value received for it by the corporation, there is watered stock.

Treasury stock is that which has been issued by the corporation for value and returned by gift or purchase to the corporation. It may be sold at any price including below par, and the proceeds returned to the treasury of the corporation for working capital. It differs from stock originally issued below par, in that the purchaser is not liable for the difference between par and the sale price. It may be sold at any price the company sees fit to charge.

Dividends Although a shareholder has a right to share in dividends when declared, whether or not a dividend is declared is within the discretion of the board of directors. Shareholders are not entitled to the payment of a dividend simply because earned surplus exists. The board of directors, at its discretion, may see fit to continue the profits in the business for the purpose of expansion. A board of directors, however, must act reasonably and in good faith. Where fraud or a gross abuse of discretion is shown and there are profits out of which dividends may be declared, the shareholders may compel the board of directors to declare dividends. It must be clear, however, that the board of directors has illegally, wantonly, and without justification refused to declare a dividend before there is a right to interfere by asking a court to order the payment of dividends.

When a cash dividend is declared, it becomes a debt of the corporation. It will be paid to the person whose name appears on the corporate stock records as the owner of the share on the record date as of which the dividend is payable. This is known as the *ex-dividend date*. A *cash dividend*, once its declaration has been made public, may not be rescinded. A declaration of dividends is proper so long as it does not impair the capital stock. Any declaration, however, that reduces the net assets of the corporation below the outstanding capital stock is illegal.

Dividends are permissible only after provision has been made for all expenses, including depreciation. In those industries with wasting or depleting assets, such as mines and oil wells, it is not necessary to allow for the depletion before declaring dividends.

Directors are personally liable to creditors for dividends improperly declared. In most states, shareholders who receive such dividends may be compelled to return them.

A *stock dividend* is a transfer of retained earnings to capital and is used where the earnings are required for growth of the business. Stock dividends of the issuing company are not taxable income to shareholders. A *stock split* differs from a *stock dividend* in that in the former there is no transfer of surplus to capital but only a reduction in par value and an increase in the number of shares.

Right to Transfer Stock   The right to transfer freely one's share in the ownership of the business is inherent in corporations. It is one of the features of corporate life that distinguishes it from a partnership. However, shareholders of "close" corporations often attempt by agreement or bylaw to limit the group of potential purchasers. A corporate bylaw that provides that the shares of stock can be transferred only to the corporation or to those approved by the board of directors is unenforceable. It places too severe a restraint upon the alienation of property. Society is best protected when property may be transferred freely. However, an agreement or bylaw approved by all shareholders to the effect that no transfer of stock shall be made until it has first been offered to the other shareholders or to the corporation is generally enforced. Notice of the bylaw or agreement should be set forth in the stock certificate because an innocent purchaser without notice of the restriction on alienation receives ownership free from the restriction.

In a close corporation, sometimes the buy and sell agreements between shareholders go even further than a right of first refusal. They may provide for such matters as salary continuation in the event of death or disability, and the amount of dividends to be paid in the future. Some agreements even commit the shareholders to vote for certain persons in the election of directors. Such agreements are valid in closely held corporations, providing the duration of the agreement is not so long as to be contrary to public policy and providing the agreement does not adversely affect minority interests in the corporation. These agreements are used by the majority owners to ensure the election of the desired board of directors. Corporations are governed by the republican principle that the whole are bound by lawful acts of the majority. It is not against public policy or dishonest for shareholders to contract for the purpose of control.

Transfer of Stock and Other Investment Securities A share of stock is personal property, and the owner has the right to transfer it just as he may transfer any other personal property. A share of stock is generally transferred by an endorsement and the delivery of the certificate of stock. A share may be transferred or assigned by a bill of sale or by any other method that will pass title to a chose in action or other intangible property. Whenever a share of stock is sold and a new stock certificate issued, the name of the new owner is entered on the stock records of the corporation. In a small corporation, the secretary of the corporation usually handles all transfers of stock and also the canceling of old certificates and issuing of new. Large corporations, in which there are hundreds and even thousands of transactions, employ transfer agents. The transfer agents transfer stock, cancel old certificates, issue new ones, prepare and keep up-to-date the names of the shareholders of the corporation, distribute dividends, mail out shareholders' notices, and perform many functions to assist the corporation secretary. Stock exchange rules provide that corporations listing stock for sale must maintain a transfer agency and registry, operated and maintained under exchange regulations. The registrar of stock is an agent of the corporation whose duty is to see that no stock certificates are issued in excess of the authorized capitalization of the corporation.

The volume of transactions in stock sold publicly is so large that many techniques have been developed to reduce the cost and confusion of transfers. One such technique is for the title to the stock to be held in the "house" name of a brokerage firm. If the firm has transactions with both buyers and sellers in the same stock, a transfer can be effected by a bookkeeping entry, and new certificates need not be issued. The firm will, however, solicit proxies and vote the stock in accordance with the instructions of the actual owner. As another means of reducing transfers, many companies are discouraging small shareholders from investing. For example, a company may try to purchase back the stock of every holder of ten shares or less. Such a policy will greatly reduce corporate administrative expenses.

Many people are advocating replacing stock certificates with "punch cards" that can be easily transferred by computer. It is anticipated that in the near future, formal stock certificates may disappear from use by large corporations.

Article 8 of the Uniform Commercial Code deals with investment securities. It must be considered along with the blue-sky laws on issues concerning the transfer of stock.

The general approach of Article 8 is that securities are negotiable instruments and that bona fide purchasers thereof have greater rights than they would have "if the things bought were chattels or simple contracts." The particular rules of Article 3 that relate to the establishment of preferred status for commercial paper are applied to securities. Defenses of the issuer are generally not effective against a purchaser for value who has received the securities without being given notice of the particular defense raised.

600

A bona fide purchaser is one who purchases in good faith and without notice of any adverse claim. He is the equivalent of a holder in due course. A bona fide purchaser takes free "adverse claims," which include a claim that a transfer was wrongful or that some other person is the owner of, or has an interest in, the security.

REVIEW QUESTIONS AND PROBLEMS

1. What is the principal matter on which shareholders are entitled to vote?

2. Define the following terms: *cumulative voting, preemptive right, derivative suit, stock dividend, watered stock*, and *treasury stock*.

3. Give two examples of exceptions to the preemptive right.

4. Give three examples of situations in which directors of corporations will have personal liability.

5. P was a stockholder in X corporation. He desired to obtain a list of stockholders before the annual stockholders' meeting so that he could contact and try to persuade them to vote for a corporate merger that the board of directors of X corporation opposed. Is P entitled to inspect the books' and records of the company and prepare a list of stockholders? Why?

6. A was a vice-president of XYZ company. In his contract of employment was a provision saying that if he remained an employee for forty-eight months he would have an option to purchase stock. After thirty-nine months A resigned to take the position of director. Will A be entitled to the option if he remains a director for nine months? Why?

7. The ABC company authorized a director, Z, to negotiate the purchase of some land. Instead Z secretly bought the land himself and sold it to the corporation at a profit. After learning of the deceit, the corporation failed to act. Does B, a minority shareholder, have any cause of action? Explain.

8. On March 1, Y company declared a cash divided of 5 percent, payable on June 1 to all stockholders of record on May 1. On April 10, A sold ten shares of Y stock to B, but the transfer was not recorded on the corporation's books until May 15. To whom will the company pay the dividend? Who is entitled to the dividend? Explain.

9. X company adopted the policy of allowing employees to purchase treasury stock in the company at its par value, which was 50 percent of its actual value. P, a 10 percent shareholder, files suit to enjoin the sale on the alternative that he be allowed to purchase, at the same price, 10 percent of all stock sold. What result? Why?

10. Three of the five directors of the ABC corporation decided among themselves to call a special meeting for the purpose of hiring a new president. The other two directors were not given any notice of the meeting, but one of them attended anyway. At the meeting, the four who attended unanimously elected a new president. Was their action legal? Why?

11. A, the president of XYZ corporation, negligently misplaced some documents belonging to a customer. The customer sued XYZ for damages. The resulting judgment so seriously weakened XYZ's financial status that XYZ was unable to pay C, a creditor of XYZ. May C hold A personally liable for any loss to C? Why?

CORPORATE

41 DISSOLUTIONS, MERGERS, AND CONSOLIDATIONS

Introduction   Corporate existence terminates upon the expiration of the period set forth in the charter, if any, and upon the voluntary or involuntary dissolution of the corporation. In a *consolidation* corporate existence technically ceases for both corporations when the new corporation is formed. In a *merger* it does so for the corporation that is merged into the continuing one. This chapter will discuss these various methods for terminating the corporate existence.

Most corporate charters provide for perpetual existence. However, where the charter stipulates that the corporation shall exist for a definite period, it automatically terminates at the expiration of the period, unless application to continue the corporation is made and approved by the authority granting the charter.

Voluntary   A corporation that has obtained its charter but has not
Dissolutions   commenced business may be dissolved by its incorporators. The incorporators file articles of dissolution with the state, and a certificate of dissolution is issued if all fees are paid and the articles are in order.

A corporation that has commenced business may be voluntarily dissolved either by the written consent of *all* its shareholders or by corporate action instituted by its board of directors and approved by two-thirds of the shareholders. The board action is usually in the form of a recommendation, and it directs that the issue be submitted to the shareholders. A meeting of shareholders is called to consider the dissolution issue, and if the vote is at least two-thirds in favor of it, the officers follow the statutory procedures for dissolution.

These procedures require that the corporate officers file a statement of intent to dissolve with the state of incorporation. This statement of intent includes the consent of all shareholders if that method is used, or the resolutions if the dissolution was instituted by board action. Upon filing the statement of intent to dissolve, the corporation must cease to carry on its business, except for winding up its affairs. However, corporate existence continues until a certificate of dissolution is issued by the state.

In winding up its affairs, the corporation must give notice to all creditors of the corporation. Directors become personally liable for any debt about which notice is not given.

Case: D had been a director of the Parker Laundry Company, a corporation. Personal property taxes levied against the corporation were not paid for the last two years of the corporation's existence. The corporation filed a notice of intent to dissolve with the state but failed to mail a notice of such action to the county taxing authorities. The county brought this action against D personally after the corporation was dissolved.

Issue: Is the director personally liable?

Decision: Yes.

Reason: A director is personally liable for debts of the corporation when the required procedures (notice to creditors in this case) on dissolution are not followed.

People v. Parker, 197 N.E.2d 30 (Ill.) 1964.

In dissolution proceedings, corporate assets are first used to pay debts. After all debts are paid, the remainder is distributed proportionately among the shareholders. If there are insufficient assets to pay all debts, a receiver will be appointed by a court and the proceedings will be similar to those of involuntary dissolutions, discussed later.

When all funds are distributed, the corporation will prepare duplicate "articles of dissolution" and forward them to the state for approval. When signed by the appropriate state official, usually the secretary of state, one copy is filed with state records, and one copy is returned to the corporation to be kept with the corporate records.

INVOLUNTARY DISSOLUTIONS

Proceedings Commenced by the State   The state, having created the corporation, has the right to institute proceedings to cancel the charter. Suits by a state to cancel or forfeit a charter are known as *quo warranto* proceedings. They are filed by the attorney general, usually at the request of the secretary of state.

Quo warranto proceedings may be brought by the attorney general if a corporation (1) fails to file its annual report; (2) fails to pay its franchise tax and license fees; (3) procured its charter by fraud; (4) abuses and misuses its authority; (5) fails to appoint and maintain a registered agent for the service of notices and process, or fails to inform the state of the name and address of its registered agent; or (6) ceases to perform its corporate functions for a long period of time. The attorney general may also, without charter forfeiture, by proper proceedings enjoin a corporation from engaging in a business not authorized by its charter.

Proceedings Commenced by Shareholders Involuntary dissolution may be ordered by a court of equity at the request of a shareholder when it is established that the directors are deadlocked in the management of the corporate affairs or that the shareholders are deadlocked and unable to elect a board of directors. Deadlocks require proof that irreparable injury is likely and that the deadlock cannot be broken.

Courts will also liquidate a corporation at the request of a shareholder when it is proved that those in control of the corporation are acting illegally, oppressively, or fraudulently. It is difficult to define oppressive conduct, and each case must be decided on its own facts. In the early law, courts followed what has been described as the "robber baron" theory. This theory allowed the majority to do anything, including a "squeeze out" of minority stockholders, so long as no specific laws were violated and no actual fraud was committed. The robber baron theory was based on the concept that the majority owed no fiduciary duty to minority shareholders.

Modern decisions tend to reject the robber baron theory. Actions intended to "squeeze out" or "freeze out" minority shareholders may provide grounds for dissolution or other equitable relief. For example, relief has been granted minority shareholders where the majority have refused to declare dividends but have paid out all profits to themselves in the form of salaries and bonuses. Relief was also granted in a recent case where the majority shareholders of a corporation that was *not* in need of funds sold additional stock in order to dilute the percentage of control of the minority, who the majority knew were unable financially to exercise their preemptive right.

Today conduct that is not illegal or fraudulent may be held to be oppressive. Oppressive conduct may be summarized as conduct that is burdensome, harsh, and wrongful. It is a substantial deviation from fair dealing and a violation of fair play. It is a violation of the fiduciary duty of good faith in those states that recognize such a duty.

All states allow minority shareholders to obtain dissolution when it is established that corporate assets are being wasted or looted or that the corporation is unable to carry out its purposes. In addition, a few states by statute have broadened the grounds for court-ordered dissolution. These states allow courts to order dissolution when it is reasonably necessary for the protection of the rights or interests of minority shareholders.

Case: A father and his two sons formed a corporation to conduct a general contracting business. The business had previously been conducted as a partnership, and each shareholder had an equal number of shares in the corporation. Three years later, P, one of the sons, ceased to be employed by the corporation. There had been a dispute, and P had been removed as an officer and director of the corporation. The corporation pays no dividends but invests its profits in real estate. There was no evidence of abuse of authority or persistent unfairness toward P.

P filed suit to dissolve the corporation. California law allows courts to order dissolution where "liquidation is reasonably necessary" for the protection of the rights or interests of any substantial number of shareholders.

Issue: Will the corporation be dissolved?

Decision: Yes.

Reasons: 1. Under the statute, dissolution is not limited to cases of deadlock, persistent mismanagement, or proof of unfairness.

2. Dissolution may be ordered when required to assure fairness to minority shareholders. The law does not authorize dissolution at will. The minority shareholders must convince the court that fairness requires the drastic relief of dissolution.

3. Here, the hostility between the family members was extreme. P received no salary, dividends, or other return on his investment. In all fairness, his investment should be returned.

Stumpf v. C.S. Stumpf & Sons, Inc., 120 Cal. Rptr. 671 (1975).

Even in states with laws similar to the one in the foregoing case, a corporation will not be dissolved by a court for errors of judgment or because the court confronted with a question of policy would decide it differently than would the directors. Dissolutions by decree at the request of a shareholder are rare, but as previously noted the trend is to give greater protection to the minority shareholders.

Proceedings Commenced by Creditors   A corporation is in the same position as a natural person insofar as its creditors are concerned. A suit may be brought against it, and upon judgment being obtained, an execution may be levied against its property, which may then be sold. Also corporate existing prior to dissolution. Suits against the dissolved corporation may be prosecuted and defended in the corporate name. The statutory

605

assets may be attached, and if the corporation has no property subject to execution, its assets may be traced by a bill in a court of equity.

The creditors have no right, because they are creditors, to interfere with the management of the business. A creditor who has an unsatisfied judgment against a corporation may bring a bill in equity to set aside conveyances and transfers of corporate property that have been fraudulently transferred for the purpose of delaying and hindering creditors. Creditors may also, under the above circumstances, ask for a receiver to take over the assets of the corporation and to apply them to the payment of debts.

When there is an unsatisfied execution and it is established that the corporation is insolvent, a court may order a dissolution. The same is true if the corporation admits its insolvency. Dissolution in such cases proceeds in the same manner as if instituted by the state or by voluntary proceedings when insolvent. These procedures are discussed in the next section.

Procedure on Involuntary Dissolution   In liquidating a corporation, courts have the full range of judicial powers at their disposal. They may issue injunctions, appoint receivers, and take whatever steps are necessary to preserve the corporate assets for the protection of creditors and shareholders. The receiver will usually collect the assets, including any amount owed to the corporation for shares. The receiver will then sell the assets, pay the debts and expenses of liquidation, and, if any funds are left, divide them proportionately among the shareholders. Courts usually require creditors to prove their claims in court in a manner similar to that in bankruptcy proceedings. When all funds in the hands of a receiver are paid out, the court issues a decree of dissolution that is filed with the secretary of state. Funds due persons who cannot be located are deposited with the state treasurer and held for a stated number of years. If not claimed within the stated period by the creditor or shareholder, the funds belong to the state.

Liability of Shareholders on Dissolution   As a general rule, shareholders are not liable for the debts of the firm. However, a shareholder who has not paid for his stock in full is liable to the receiver or to a creditor for the unpaid balance.

Statutes in most states allow creditors to reach the assets of the corporation in the hands of the shareholders when the assets have been transferred in fraud of creditors.

These statutory provisions usually provide for survival for a stated period after dissolution of remedies against a corporation, for claims

period is not a statute of limitation but is simply the period during which claims survive. A judgment on such a claim may be collected from property distributed to shareholders on dissolution, or the creditor may proceed directly against the shareholder receiving the property.

Case: D, Simmer Oil Corporation, had been sued by the state of Ohio, and the state had obtained a judgment against the corporation. The corporation then transferred certain parcels of property to its stockholders.

Issue: Is the property available for execution and payment of the judgment?

Decision: Yes.

Reason: In general, corporate creditors are entitled in equity to the payment of their debts before any distribution of corporate property is made to the stockholders. Here there is a legal fraud, and the transaction must be set aside.

State ex rel. Safeguard Ins. Co. v. Vorys, 167 N.E.2d 910 (Ohio) 1960.

CONSOLIDATIONS AND MERGERS

Definitions *Consolidation* is the uniting of two or more corporations, whereby a new corporation is created and the old entities are dissolved. The new corporation takes title to all the property, rights, powers, and privileges of the old corporations, subject to the liabilities and obligations of the old corporations.

In a *merger*, however, one of the corporations continues its existence but absorbs the other corporation, which ceases to have an independent existence. The continuing corporation may expressly or impliedly assume and agree to pay the debts and liabilities of the absorbed corporation. If so, such creditors become third-party creditor beneficiaries. By statute in most states, the surviving corporation is deemed to have assumed all the liabilities and obligations of the absorbed corporation.

Acquisitions comprise a major segment of the antitrust laws. This aspect will be discussed more fully in the next chapter.

Procedures The procedures for consolidations and mergers are statutory. The usual procedure is for the board of directors of each corporation to approve the plan by resolution. The resolution will set forth in detail all the facts of the planned merger or consolidation. The plan is then submitted to the shareholders of each corporation for approval. Notice is given of the meeting, and the resolution passed by the directors is usually a part of the notice. The shareholders are entitled to be informed of all facts that may affect their vote. Shareholders must be given the full picture prior to a vote. The shareholders must approve the plan by a two-thirds vote of all shares and two-thirds of each class if more than one class of stock is voting. If the consolidation or merger is approved by the shareholders of both corporations, articles of consolidation or articles of merger will be prepared and filed with the state. If the papers are in order and all fees are paid, a certificate of consolidation or a certificate of merger will be issued.

A shareholder who dissents to a consolidation or merger, and who makes his dissent a matter of record by serving a written demand that the corporation purchase his stock, is entitled to be paid the fair value of his stock on the day preceding the vote on the corporate action. Procedures are established for ascertaining the fair value and for a judicial decision of that issue if necessary. It is noted that a shareholder who dissents from a sale or exchange of all or substantially all the assets or property of the corporation, other than in the usual course of business, has the same right to be paid for his stock. When the statutory procedures are followed, the dissenting shareholder ceases to be a shareholder when notice is given, and he becomes a creditor at that point in time.

Case: D was a closely held corporation. The owners of a majority of the stock voted to merge the corporation with another corporation. P, a minority stockholder, dissented. The statute provides that a dissenting shareholder who objects to a merger is entitled to be paid the "fair value" of his shares on the date preceding the vote. P contended that the stock was worth $322 per share, but the corporation took the position that it was worth only $100 per share. The lower court found that the fair value was $230 per share.

Issue: Was the lower court's determination of the fair value of the stock correct?

Decision: No. (The "fair value" of the stock was $138.65 per share.)

Reasons: 1. There are three methods used by the court in determining the fair value of shares of dissenting shareholders: (a) the market value method, (b) the asset value method, and (c) the investment or earnings value method.

2. While there is no established market for the stock, the average sale price over four years was $69 per share.

3. Using the fair market value of all assets and subtracting all liabilities, the asset value is $242.81 per share.

4. Using the earnings value or investment value method, the value is zero because the corporation had lost money for several years.

5. The court then assigned weights to each system and computed the value as follows:

	Value	X	Weight	=	Result
Asset	$242.81		50%		$121.40
Market	69.00		25		17.25
Earnings	0		25		0
					$138.65

Brown v. Hedahl's QB&R, Inc., 185 N.W.2d 249 (N.Dak.) 1971.

REVIEW QUESTIONS AND PROBLEMS

1. What steps are required for a voluntary dissolution?

2. List four grounds on which the state may obtain involuntary dissolution.

3. Compare the characteristics of a merger with those of a consolidation.

4. What are the rights of a dissenting shareholder to a merger or consolidation?

5. D owed X corporation $10,000. X corporation's directors and shareholders voted to dissolve. Thereafter X corporation sued D, and D contended that he had no liability because of the dissolution. What result? Why?

6. X corporation entered into a contract to purchase linseed oil from Y. Subsequently X corporation merged with Z corporation, and the latter refused to purchase linseed oil from Y. Does Y have a cause of action against Z corporation? Why?

7. A corporation had not made a profit for twenty years and no dividends had been paid for that period. The preferred stockholders brought suit to obtain a decree of dissolution. What result? Why?

8. A, the owner of all the capital stock of the XYZ corporation, a newspaper business, sold all his shares to B and promised to serve as adviser to the newspaper for a period of five years, in return for $11,000. After three years B petitioned for dissolution, which was obtained. Only $4,000 had been paid to A. Does A have a remedy against the corporation? Explain.

9. A, B, and C were owners of some orange groves in Florida. X wished to enter the orange-growing business and approached A, B, and C with an offer to form a corporation. The corporation was formed and the land owned by A, B, and C was transferred to the corporation. X was to manage the corporation, and A, B, and C were to retire, leaving the operation of the groves to X. X failed to manage the groves; in fact, he did nothing. May A, B, and C dissolve the corporation? Why?

10. A and B, father and son, entered into an agreement whereby each was a 50 percent stockholder of a close corporation, operating a luncheonette. The agreement provided that in the event of the death of either party, this would constitute an automatic option to the survivor to purchase, at book value, the

shares of stock of the deceased. Upon A's death, C, B's brother and administrator of A's estate, refuses to sell for the value shown on the books and creates a deadlock in management. C then petitions for dissolution. Should it be granted? Why?

11. C had sold the XYZ corporation some supplies and had not yet received payment. The corporation was later dissolved, but C was never notified of the dissolution proceeding. What remedy is available to C? Explain.

GOVERNMENT
42 REGULATION OF
BUSINESS
ORGANIZATIONS

Introduction The business environment is the product of political, social, economic, and legal forces. While each of these forces has its own substantial impact on our society, it is the law that possesses the cohesive quality to unite them and make our private property system and competitive economic system workable. The law not only creates and protects property rights, it also regulates business activity in an infinite variety of ways. It ensures that the system is viable and strives to be of maximum benefit to the society it serves.

In earlier periods of history, the law was primarily concerned with enforcing contracts, protecting property, and maintaining order. Today the role of law is much broader, with a primary emphasis on the various aspects of regulation of business. Government regulation affects every aspect of business. Solutions to many of the significant problems confronting society today will be sought by the use of law to regulate all aspects of business.

Regulation of business is the result of statutes enacted by the legislative branch and the execution of the policies set forth in such statutes by the executive branch of government. In other words, the policies of statutes enacted by the legislative branch are carried out by administrative agencies exercising their rule-making, enforcing, and quasi-judicial powers. The determination of the constitutionality and legality of all regulatory activities, as well as the application of the rules issued, ultimately rests with the courts. Therefore, as a practical matter, all branches of government are actively engaged in placing limitations on business activity.

In this chapter we focus on (1) the legal bases for the role government plays in the regulation of business and (2) the field of antitrust law.

611

The Federal Power to Regulate Business The power of the federal government to regulate business activity is found in the commerce clause of the Constitution: "Congress shall have the power to regulate commerce with foreign nations, among the several States and with the Indian tribes." The key language is the phrase "among the several States." This language has been construed to give Congress power to enact laws covering any business activity in interstate commerce, and any intrastate business activity that has a substantial effect on interstate commerce. The effect on interstate commerce may be positive or negative. The effect of any individual business on interstate commerce need not be substantial, if the cumulative effect of all similar businesses is substantial. In recent years this power has been used in a variety of ways. One of the more important pieces of legislation was the public accommodation provisions of the Civil Rights Act of 1964.

In addition, activities such as gambling, discrimination in the sale or rental of housing, and loansharking have been regulated under the commerce clause.

Case: D was convicted of violating the Federal Consumer Credit Protection Act by engaging in "loansharking." D claimed that the federal law passed as a regulation of interstate commerce was unconstitutional because his activities were purely local.

Issue: Does the power of the federal government extend to regulation of intrastate activities?

Decision: Yes.

Reasons: 1. A long line of Supreme Court cases holds that intrastate activities may be regulated where they have an impact on interstate business.

2. The activity of loansharking is within the class of activities regulated and Congress, in enacting this legislation properly, considered the "total incidence" of the practice on commerce. "Extortionate credit transactions, though purely intrastate, do have a substantial affect on interstate commerce."

Perez v. United States, 91 S.Ct. 1357 (1971).

While the power of Congress to regulate an infinite variety of business activities by use of the commerce clause is quite broad, it is subject to some limitations. These limitations are found in other provisions of the Constitution, such as the Sixth Amendment's guarantee of a right to a trial by jury and the Fifth Amendment's due process clause. In addition, a recent decision has made it clear that the power to regulate commerce cannot be used to destroy state and local governments.

Case: The 1974 amendments to the Fair Labor Standards Act extended the minimum wage law to almost all employees of state and local governments. Several cities and states challenged the constitutionality of the law, which was passed under the commerce clause.

Issue: Are these amendments a valid exercise of the commerce clause?

Decision: No.

Reasons: 1. These amendments were beyond the power of Congress under the commerce clause. They operated to displace the states' ability to structure employer-employee relationships in areas of traditional governmental functions such as police and fire protection.

2. Congress sought to wield its power in a fashion that would impair the ability of the various states to function effectively within the federal system.

3. Congress may not exercise its power to regulate commerce so as to force directly upon the states its choices as to how essential decisions regarding the conduct of integral government functions are to be made.

National League of Cities v. Usery, 96 S.Ct. 2465 (1976).

State Regulation of Business

State and local governments use their "police power" to enact laws to promote the public health, safety, morals, and general welfare. Of necessity such laws frequently result in the regulation of business activity. The commerce clause does not expressly prohibit the use of a state's police power merely because it has the effect of regulating business activity. However, the commerce clause and the supremacy clause do impose several restrictions on the use of police power by the states as it affects business.

The first restriction is that state and local governments cannot enact laws on subjects that are considered to be exclusively federal. For example, a state could not pass a law establishing the width of a railroad track or a law concerning air traffic because such subjects require national uniformity. For this reason, any state law concerning a subject that is exclusively under the federal government's jurisdiction is unconstitutional under the commerce and supremacy clauses. This is true even if there is no federal law on the subject.

The second limitation concerns subject matters over which the federal government has taken exclusive jurisdiction by enacting legislation. Federal laws that assert exclusive jurisdiction over a subject are said to preempt the field. Preemption may result from express language or by comprehensive regulation showing an intent by Congress to exercise exclusive dominion over the subject matter. When a federal statute has preempted the field, *any* state or local law pertaining to the same subject matter is unconstitutional and the state regulation is void.

Case: P is the owner and operator of an airport which serves interstate air carriers. D, the city of Burbank, enacted an ordinance prohibiting jet aircraft from taking off between the hours of 11:00 P.M. and 7:00 A.M. P sought an injunction against the enforcement of the ordinance. A federal law provides that the United States of America possesses complete and exclusive national sovereignty of air space in the United States, including the authority to regulate the use of such air space.

Issue: Is the city ordinance constitutional?

Decision: No.

Reasons: 1. The pervasive nature of the scheme of federal regulation of aircraft noise leads us to conclude that there is preemption.

2. Federal control is intensive and exclusive. Planes do not wander about in the sky like vagrant clouds. They move only by federal permission, subject to federal inspection, in the hands of federally certified personnel, and under an intricate system of federal commands. The moment an airplane taxis onto a runway it is caught up in an elaborate and detailed system of controls.

3. The interdependence of the factors of safety and efficiency requires a uniform and exclusive system of federal regulation if the congressional objectives underlying the federal law are to be fulfilled.

City of Burbank v. Lockheed Air Terminal, Inc., 93 S.Ct. 1854 (1973).

Not every federal regulatory statute preempts the field. When a federal law does not preempt the field and the subject matter is not exclusively federal, state regulation under the police power is permitted. However, when a state law is inconsistent or irreconcilably in conflict with a federal statute, it is unconstitutional and void because of the supremacy clause that makes federal laws supreme over state laws. Moreover, state laws are unconstitutional under the commerce clause if they discriminate against interstate commerce or impose an undue burden on it.

In addition to the commerce clause limitations previously discussed, a state's exercise of police power may be challenged under the constitutional provisions relating to "due process," "equal protection of the laws," or under any provisions of the Bill of Rights. Challenges to the constitutionality of a law based on "due process" and "equal protection" are most frequently used to challenge a tax imposed on interstate commerce but may also be used to challenge a regulation or licensing statute. The Bill of Rights provisions are employed to challenge such laws as "Sunday Closing" statutes or ordinances aimed at obscenity.

It should be observed that every tax is to some extent regulatory. The commerce clause also imposes limitations on the taxing power of state and local governments. Although the issues involved are varied and complex, it may be said as a general rule that a state may impose a tax such as an income tax or a property tax on a business engaged in interstate commerce provided that the tax is *apportioned* by some reasonable formula to local activities within the state and does not discriminate against interstate commerce in favor of intrastate commerce. There must be a connection between the tax and the local enterprise being taxed (*nexus*), or the tax will violate the commerce clause. The concepts of nexus and apportionment are used to ensure that interstate commerce pays its fair share for benefits received from the state.

THE ANTITRUST LAWS

Sherman Act   In 1890, under its power to regulate interstate commerce, Congress passed the Sherman Antitrust Act. The Sherman Act was directed essentially at two areas: (1) contracts, combinations, or conspiracies in restraint of trade; and (2) monopoly and attempts to monopolize. The law sought to preserve competition. This was to be achieved by utilization of three basic sanctions. First of all, violation was made a federal crime punishable by fine or imprisonment or both. Second, the Sherman Act authorizes injunctions to prevent and restrain violations or continued violations of its provisions. Failure to obey may be punished by contempt proceedings. Third, a remedy is given to those persons who have been injured by violation of the act. Such persons are given the right, in a civil action, to collect treble damages plus court costs and reasonable attorney's fees.[1] Normally the objective of money damages is to place the injured party in the position he would have enjoyed, as nearly as this can be done with money, had his rights not been invaded. The treble-damage provision serves not only as a means of punishing the defendant for his wrongful act but also as a means of compensating the plaintiff for his actual injury.

The most common type of Sherman Act violation is price-fixing. Price-fixing is as a matter of law in restraint of trade. It is no defense that the prices fixed are fair or reasonable. It also is no defense that price-fixing is engaged in by small competitors to allow them to compete with larger competitors. It is just as illegal to fix a low price as it is to fix a high price. Today it is as illegal to fix the price of services as it is to fix the price of goods. Price-fixing in the service sector has been engaged in by professional persons as well as by service

[1] A 1976 amendment allowed the attorneys general of the various states to seek these treble damages on behalf of the consumers of their state.

occupations such as automobile and TV repair workers, barbers, and refuse collectors. For many years it was contended that persons performing services were not engaged in trade or commerce.

Case: D, a county bar association, developed a schedule of minimum fees to be charged by all lawyers in the county. P contacted several lawyers when he was about to buy a home. All of the lawyers quoted P the same fee for the legal services to be performed. P sued the bar association, alleging that the use of the minimum-fee schedule was a violation of the Sherman Act. D contended that legal services were not "trade or commerce."

Issue: Is it a violation of the Sherman Act for professional persons to agree on minimum fees to be charged for services?

Decision: Yes.

Reasons: 1. The examination of a land title is a service; the exchange of such a service for money is "commerce" in the most common usage of that word. It is not disparagement of the practice of law as a profession to acknowledge that it has this business aspect.

2. Section 1 of the Sherman Act on its face shows a carefully studied attempt to bring within the act every person engaged in business whose activities might restrain or monopolize commercial intercourse among the states. In the modern world it cannot be denied that the activity of lawyers plays an important part in commercial intercourse, and that anticompetitive activities by lawyers may exert a restraint on commerce.

3. Given the substantial volume of commerce involved, and the inseparability of this particular legal service from the interstate aspects of real estate transactions, we conclude that interstate commerce has been sufficiently affected.

Goldfarb et ux. v. Virginia State Bar et al., 95 S.Ct. 2004 (1975).

There are many other examples of Sherman Act violations. Many of these involve concerted activities among competitors. For example, an exchange of price information has been held to be a Sherman Act violation.

Case: The United States brought a civil antitrust action against Ds, who were manufacturers of containers. Ds had entered into an agreement that they would exchange price information with regard to specific sales of their product. The evidence showed that by exchanging this information the prices were kept within a fairly narrow range and tended to stabilize the prices.

616

Issue: Was this arrangement to exchange price information a violation of the Sherman Act?

Decision: Yes.

Reasons: 1. The result of this reciprocal exchange of prices was to stabilize prices though at a downward level. Knowledge of a competitor's price usually meant matching that price.

2. Stabilizing prices as well as raising them is within the ban of §1 of the Sherman Act. In terms of market operations, stabilization is but one form of manipulation. The inferences are irresistible that the exchange of price information has had an anticompetitive effect in the industry, chilling the vigor of price competition.

United States v. Container Corporation of America, 89 S.Ct. 510 (1969).

From its adoption the Sherman Act proved unable to accomplish all its goals. This resulted from its very broad language and from the favorable treatment given "big business" by the courts early in this century. Various amendments designed to make the act more specific have been enacted through the years. These amendments and some other statutes are discussed more fully in the sections that follow.

Clayton Act   In 1914 Congress enacted the Clayton Act, which was designed to make the Sherman Act more specific. The act declared illegal certain practices that might have an adverse effect on competition, but that were something less than violations of the Sherman Act. The practices it enumerated were outlawed if their effect *might* be to substantially lessen competition, or tend to create a monopoly. This effect is sometimes referred to as the prohibited effect of the Clayton Act.

The Clayton Act contained four major provisions. Section 2 made it unlawful for a seller to discriminate in price between purchasers of commodities when the prohibited effect or tendency might result. Price discrimination is lawful if due to differences in the grade, quality, or quantity of the product sold, or to differences in cost of transportation.

Section 3 made it unlawful for a person engaged in commerce to lease or sell commodities or fix a price charged, on the condition that the lessee or purchaser shall not use or deal in the commodities of a competitor of the lessor or seller when the prohibited effect or tendency might result. This section concerning tying and exclusive contracts prevents a seller of a product that is in high demand from forcing a purchaser to purchase a less-desirable product in order to obtain the former. In theory, every product should stand on its merits. For example, a seller or lessor of a computer could not require that the

617

buyer or lessee purchase all punch cards from it. Such a requirement is an unreasonable restraint that might substantially lessen competition by foreclosing competitors from a substantial market.

Section 7 prohibited the acquisition of all or part of the stock of other corporations, where the effect *might* be to lessen competition substantially or to *tend* to create a monopoly. This section has been substantially amended and its provisions will be discussed later in this chapter.

Section 8 of the Clayton Act was aimed at interlocking directorates. It prohibits a person from being a member of the board of directors of two or more corporations at the same time, when one of them has capital, surplus, and undivided profits totaling more than $1 million where elimination of competition by agreement between such corporations would amount to a violation of any of the antitrust laws.

Federal Trade Commission Act Congress enacted a second antitrust law in 1914. This law created the Federal Trade Commission as one of the expert independent regulatory agencies. The Federal Trade Commission was given jurisdiction over cases arising under Section 2, 3, 7, and 8 of the Clayton Act. In addition, the commission was directed to prevent unfair methods of competition in commerce. This directive was amended later to make "unfair methods of competition in commerce and unfair or deceptive acts or practices in commerce" unlawful. The commission has to determine what methods, acts, or practices are "unfair" or "deceptive" and thus illegal. Historically, the major role of the FTC has been in the area of unfair and deceptive business practices. Great deference is given to the decisions of the commission. That is to say that the commission has a wide variety of corrective actions it may require in correcting violations of the law. For example, the FTC sometimes requires that a party guilty of deceptive advertising run a corrective ad admitting the deception. The FTC also has a policy of ad substantiation. Advertisers must be able to prove the truthfulness of their ads. The government is not required to prove that an ad is false for the FTC act to be violated. An activity may be an unfair method of competition without being a violation of the Sherman or Clayton acts.

Case: The company in question manufactures and sells paint. The company made representations in advertisements that stated in various ways that for every can of paint purchased the buyer would get a "free" can of equal quality and quantity. The price paid for the original can of paint was higher than the usual price, and thus the second can was not in fact "free."

Issue: Is this a violation of Section 5 of the FTC Act?

Decision: Yes.

Reasons: 1. A businessman may advertise an article as "free," even though purchase of another article is required, so long as the terms of the offer are clearly stated, the price of the article required to be purchased is not increased, and its quality and quantity are not diminished.

2. In two-for-the-price-of-one offers, the sales price for the two must be the advertiser's usual and customary retail price for the single article in the recent, regular course of his business, or the ad is deceptive.

3. The seller was marketing twins, and in allocating what is in fact the price of two cans to one can, yet calling one "free," it misrepresented the facts.

FTC v. Mary Carter Paint Co., 382 U.S. 46 (1965).

Robinson-Patman Act   In 1936 Congress enacted the Robinson-Patman amendment of Section 2 of the original Clayton Act, dealing with price discrimination. This amendment, sometimes referred to as "the chain-store act," was designed to ensure equality of treatment to all buyers of a seller, in those cases when the result of unequal treatment might substantially lessen competition or tend to create a monopoly in any line of commerce. Section 2 of the Clayton Act had not accomplished this end, partly due to the legality of quantity discounts under it, and partly because some buyers were able to obtain indirect benefits such as promotional or brokerage allowances. Such allowances were actually discounts that gave competitive advantage of one buyer over the other buyers dealing with the same seller.

The Robinson-Patman Act made it a crime for a seller to sell at lower prices in one geographical area than in another in the United States in order to eliminate competition or a competitor, or to sell at unreasonably low prices to drive out a competitor. In addition, the Federal Trade Commission was given jurisdiction and authority to eliminate quantity discounts and to forbid brokerage allowances, except to independent brokers. The statute also prohibited promotional allowances, except on an equal basis. As a result of Robinson-Patman, the small businessman is able to purchase his merchandise at essentially the same price as the large business. He is entitled to the same price for identical goods and to proportionately equal promotional allowances. A large competitor cannot legally reduce his price to drive out the small competitor.

Celler-Kefauver Act   This act, passed in 1950, amends Section 7 of the Clayton Act so that it prohibits the acquisition of the stock or *assets* of other corporations when the effect may be or tend to create a thirty days' notice before the proposed merger is consummated. This enables the government to take action to stop any merger in advance. Mergers meeting these tests are likely to have anticompetitive effects.

619

monopoly *in any line of commerce* in any section of the country. Section 7 as originally written covered horizontal mergers—those between competitors. It did not cover vertical (those between a buyer and a seller) or conglomerate mergers and acquisitions (those between companies that are economically unrelated). Moreover, a major gap existed in the original language preventing the purchase of stock of another company because the term *stock* did not include assets. Acquisitions could occur without violating the Clayton Act simply by the purchase of a plant or other assets of the company to be acquired instead of a purchase of its corporate stock. The Celler-Kefauver amendment plugged this loophole by adding "assets to stock." It also was broadened to cover vertical and conglomerate mergers with the deletion of the language "of a competitor" and the insertion of the language "any line of commerce." Thus today Section 7 of the Clayton Act is applicable to all mergers and acquisitions that may have the prohibited effect.

Section 7 requires only a finding and conclusion that a given acquisition or merger have a reasonable probability of lessening competition or tending toward monopoly. It does not deal with certainties, only with probabilities. The goal of the law is to arrest anticompetitive effects and trends toward undue concentration of economic power at their incipiency. In determining whether or not a given merger or acquisition is illegal, courts examine both the product market and the geographic market affected.

A significant concept in the merger field today is the "potential entrant" doctrine. This doctrine finds that the prohibited effect may exist where an acquisition or a merger involves a potential entrant into a market. An acquisition of a competitor by a potential competitor is thus illegal where the effect may be substantially to lessen competition. The potential entrant doctrine has been used to prevent a soap company from acquiring a major bleach company. Since the soap company was a potential entrant into the bleach business, the acquisition was viewed as anticompetitive. The same doctrine may also be used to stop geographic expansion by mergers and acquisitions. The potential entrant doctrine is applied not only because if entry does occur there is an additional competitor but also because the mere presence of a potential competitor at the edge of the market has positive effects on those companies actually competing.

By a 1976 amendment, a company with annual net sales amounting to $10 million or more that is being acquired by a firm with total annual sales of $100 million or more must give the Justice Department notice of the intended acquisition.

REVIEW QUESTIONS AND PROBLEMS

1. What are the limitations on the federal power to regulate business?

2. Discuss the limitations on the power of state government to regulate business.

3. What was the purpose of the Clayton Act?

4. What was the primary purpose of the Robinson-Patman amendment to the Clayton Act?

5. Why was it necessary to amend (1) the Sherman Act; (2) Section 2 of the Clayton Act; and (3) Section 7 of the Clayton Act?

6. What are the primary objectives and duties of the FTC?

7. The state of Arizona by statute under its police powers imposed maximum lengths of fourteen cars on passenger trains and seventy cars on freight trains, for the purpose of encouraging railroad safety. No other state imposes such regulations. Is the legislation constitutional? Why?

8. South Carolina, concerned with the condition of its highways, passed legislation banning from the highways all trucks over ninety inches in width and over 20,000 lbs. gross weight. Evidence shows 85 percent of all semitrailer trucks exceed that limit. Is the statute constitutional? Why?

9. The Department of Agriculture has set up minimum standards of ripeness based on size and weight for the marking of avocados. A California statute was enacted that provided standards of ripeness based on minimum oil content for the distribution and sale of avocados in California. Is the California statute preempted by the federal legislation? Why?

10. A, a fortune teller, moved to X city and applied for a city occupational license. There was a city ordinance that required applicants of fortune-telling licenses to prove residency in X city for three years prior to the application. City officials refused to grant the license on the basis of the ordinance. Is the ordinance constitutional? Why?

11. The XYZ company manufactured and sold photocopy machines. In order to purchase one of its machines, a buyer had to agree to purchase copy paper only from XYZ. Is this agreement legal? Explain.

621

GLOSSARY

Abandonment: The term applies to many situations. Abandonment of property is the giving up of the dominion and control over it with the intention to relinquish all claim to the same. Losing property is an involuntary act; abandonment is voluntary.

When used with duty, the word *abandonment* is synonymous with *repudiation.*

Abatement of a nuisance: An action to end any act detrimental to the public, such as a suit to enjoin a plant from permitting the escape of noxious vapors.

Acceptance:* Under Article 3—Commercial Paper, this is the drawee's signed engagement to honor a draft as presented. It must be written on the draft and may consist of his signature alone. It becomes operative when completed by delivery or notification.

Accord and satisfaction: An agreement between two persons, one of whom has a right of action against the other, that the latter should do or give, and the former accept, something in satisfaction of the right of action different from, and usually less than, what might legally be enforced.

Account:* Any right to payment for goods sold or leased or for services rendered which is not evidenced by an instrument or chattel paper.

Account:* Under Article 4—Bank Deposits and Collections, this means any account with a bank and includes a checking, time, interest, or savings account.

Account debtor: The person who is obligated on an account, chattel paper, contract right, or general intangible.

Accretion: The gradual and imperceptible accumulation of land by natural causes, usually next to a stream or river.

Action ex contractu: An action at law to recover damages for the breach of a duty arising out of contract. There are two types of causes of action: those arising out of contract, ex contractu, and those arising out of tort, ex delicto.

Action ex delicto: An action at law to recover damages for the breach of a duty existing by reason of a general law. An action to recover damages for an injury caused by the negligent use of an automobile is an ex delicto

---

*The terms followed by an asterisk are defined in the Uniform Commercial Code, and therefore these terms have significance in connection with Code materials. They are often given a particular meaning as related to the Code, and the definitions are therefore not necessarily in conformity with meanings outside the framework of the Code.

action. Tort or wrong is the basis of the action. See *Action ex contractu.*

Adjudicate: The exercise of judicial power by hearing, trying, and determining the claims of litigants before the court.

Administrator: A person to whom letters of administration have been issued by a probate court, giving such person authority to administer, manage, and close the estate of a deceased person.

Adverse possession: To acquire, by adverse possession, the legal title to another's land, the claimant must be in continuous possession during the period prescribed in the statute. This possession must be actual, visible, known to the world, with an intention by the possessor to claim the title as owner as against the rights of the true owner. The claimant usually must pay the taxes and liens lawfully charged against the property. Cutting timber or grass from time to time on the land of another is not such adverse possession as to confer title.

Advising Bank:* A bank that gives notification of the issuance of a credit by another bank.

Affidavit: A voluntary statement of facts formally reduced to writing, sworn to, or affirmed before, some officer authorized to administer oaths. Such officer is usually a notary public.

A fortiori: Latin words meaning "by a stronger reason." The phrase is often used in judicial opinions to say that, since specific proven facts lead to a certain conclusion, there are for this reason other facts that logically follow which make stronger the argument for the conclusion.

Agency coupled with an interest: When an agent has possession or control over the property of his principal and has a right of action against interference by third parties, an agency with an interest has been created. A, an agent, advances freight for goods sent him by his principal. He thus has an interest in the goods.

Agent: An agent is a person authorized to act for another (principal). The term may apply to a person in the service of another, but in the strict sense an agent is one who stands in place of his principal. A works for B as a gardener and is thus a servant; but he may be an agent. If A sells goods for B he becomes more than a servant. He acts in the place of B.

Agreement:* This means the bargain of the parties in fact as found in their language or by implication from other circumstances, including course of dealing or usage of trade or course of performance as provided in the Uniform Commercial Code.

Annuity: A sum of money paid yearly to a person during his lifetime, which sum arises out of a contract by which the recipient or another had previously deposited sums in whole or in part with the grantor—the grantor to return a designated portion of the principal and interest in periodic payments upon the arrival of the beneficiary at a designated age.

Appellant: The party who takes an appeal from one court or jurisdiction to another.

Appellee: The party in a cause against whom an appeal is taken.

A priori: A generalization resting on presuppositions and not upon proven facts.

Arbitration: The submission for determination of disputed matter to private unofficial persons selected in a manner provided by law or agreement.

Architect's certificate: A formal statement signed by an architect that a contractor has performed under his contract and is entitled to be paid. The construction contract provides when and how such certificates shall be issued.

Artisan's lien: One who has expended labor upon or added to another's property is entitled to the possession of such property as security until reimbursed for the value of labor or material. A repairs B's watch. A may keep the watch in his possession until paid by B for such repairs.

Assignee: An assign or assignee is one to whom an assignment has been made.

Assignment: An assignment is the transfer by one person to another of a right that usually arises out of a contract. Such rights are called choses in action. A sells and assigns his contract right to purchase B's house to C. A is an assignor. C is an assignee. The transfer is an assignment.

Assignment:* A transfer of the "contract" or of "all my rights under the contract" or an assignment in similar general terms is an assignment of rights, and unless the language or the circumstances (as in an assignment for security) indicate the contrary, it is a delegation of performance of the duties of the assignor, and its acceptance by the assignee constitutes a promise by him to perform those duties. This promise is enforceable by either the assignor or the other party to the original contract.

Assignment for the benefit of creditors: A, a debtor, has many creditors. An assignment of his property to X, a third party, with directions to make distribution of his property to his creditors is called an assignment for the benefit of creditors. See *Composition of creditors.*

Assignor: An assignor is one who makes an assignment.

Attachment: A legal proceeding accompanying an action in court by which a plaintiff may acquire a lien on a defendant's property as a security for the payment of any judgment that the plaintiff may recover. It is provisional and independent of the court action and is usually provided for by statute. A sues B. Before judgment, A attaches B's automobile in order to make sure of the payment of any judgment that A may secure.

Attorney at law: A person who has been granted a license by the state giving him the privilege of practicing law.

Attorney in fact: A person acting for another under a grant of special power created by an instrument in writing. B, in writing, grants special power to A to execute and deliver for B a conveyance of B's land to X.

Bad faith: The term means "actual intent" to mislead or deceive another. It does not mean misleading by an honest, inadvertent, or careless misstatement.

Bail (verb): To set at liberty an arrested or imprisoned person upon security's being given to the state by himself or at least two other persons that will appear at the proper time and place for trial.

Bailee: A person into whose possession personal property is delivered.

Bailee:* The person who by a warehouse receipt, bill of lading, or other document of title acknowledges possession of goods and contracts to deliver them.

Bailment: A bailment is the delivery of personal property to another for a special purpose. Such delivery is made under a contract, either expressed or implied, that upon the completion of the special purpose, the property shall be redelivered to the bailor or placed at his disposal. A loans B his truck. A places his watch with B for repair. A places his furniture in B's warehouse. A places his securities in B bank's safety deposit vault. In each case, A is a bailor and B is a bailee.

Bailor: One who delivers personal property into the possession of another.

Banking day:* Under Article 4—Bank Deposits and Collections, this means that part of any day on which a bank is open to the public for carrying on substantially all of its banking functions.

Bearer:* The person in possession of an instrument, document of title, or security payable to bearer or indorsed in blank.

Bearer form:* A security is in bearer form when it runs to bearer according to its terms and not by reason of any indorsement.

Beneficiary: A person (not a promisee) for whose benefit a trust, an insurance policy, a will, or a contract promise is made.

Beneficiary:* A person who is entitled under a letter of credit to draw or demand payment.

Bequest: A term used in a will to designate a gift of personal property.

Bid: An offering of money in exchange for property placed for sale. At an ordinary auction sale, a bid is an offer to purchase. It may be withdrawn before acceptance is indicated by the fall of the hammer.

Bilateral contract: One containing mutual promises, with each party being both a promisor and a promisee.

Bill of lading:* A document evidencing the receipt of goods for shipment issued by a person engaged in the business of transporting or forwarding goods, and includes an airbill. "Airbill" means a document serving for air transportation as a bill of lading does for marine or rail transportation, and includes an air consignment note or air way-bill.

Bill of sale: A written evidence that the title to personal property has been transferred from one person to another. It must contain words of transfer and be more than a receipt.

Blue-sky laws: Popular name for acts providing for the regulation and supervision of investment securities.

Bona fide purchaser:* A purchaser of a security for value in good faith and without notice of any adverse claim who takes delivery of a security in bearer form or of one in registered form issued to him or indorsed to him or in blank.

Bond: A promise under seal to pay money. The term is generally used to designate the promise made by a corporation, either public or private, to pay money to bearer. U.S. government bonds; Illinois Central Railroad bonds.

The term also describes an obligation by which one person promises to answer for the debt or default of another—a surety bond.

Broker: A person employed to make contracts with third persons on behalf of his principal. Such contracts involve trade, commerce, buying and selling for a fee (called brokerage or commission).

Broker:* A person engaged for all or part of his time in the business of buying and selling securities, who in the transaction concerned acts for, or buys a security from, or sells a security to a customer. Nothing in this Article determines the capacity in which a person acts for purposes of any other statute or rule to which such person is subject.

Bulk Transfer:* Any transfer in bulk and not in the ordinary course of the transferor's business of a major part of the materials, supplies, merchandise or other inventory of an enterprise subject to this Article.

Buyer:* A person who buys or contracts to buy goods.

Buyer in ordinary course of business:* A person who in good faith and without knowledge that the sale to him is in violation of the ownership rights or security interest of a third party in the goods buys in ordinary course from a person in the business of selling goods of that kind but does not include a pawnbroker. "Buying" may be for cash or by exchange of other property or on secured or unsecured credit and includes receiving goods or documents of title under a preexisting contract for sale but does not include a transfer in bulk or as security for or in total or partial satisfaction of a money debt.

Bylaws: The rules adopted by the members or the board of directors of a corporation or other organization for its government. These rules must not be contrary to the law of the land, and they affect only the rights and duties of the members of the corporation or organization. They are not applicable to third persons.

Call: An assessment upon a subscriber for partial or full payment on shares of unpaid stock of a corporation. The term may also mean the power of a corporation to make an assessment, notice of an assessment, or the time when the assessment is to be paid.

Cancellation:* When either party puts an end to the contract for breach by the other. Its effect is the same as that of "termination" except that the canceling party also retains any remedy for breach of the whole contract or any unperformed balance.

Capital: The net assets of an individual enterprise, partnership, joint stock company, corporation, or business institution, including not only the original investment but also all gains and profits realized from the continued conduct of the business.

Carrier: A natural person or a corporation who receives goods under a contract to transport for a consideration from one place to another. A railroad, a truckline, a busline, an airline.

Cashier's check: A bill of exchange drawn by the cashier of a bank, for the bank, upon the bank. After the check is delivered or issued to the payee or holder, the drawer bank cannot put a "stop order" against itself. By delivery of the check, the drawer bank has accepted, and thus becomes the primary obligor.

Cause of action: When one's legal rights have been invaded either by a breach of a contract or by a breach of a legal duty toward one's person or property, a cause of action has been created.

Caveat: Literally this means "let him beware." It is used generally to mean a warning.

Caveat emptor: These words express an old idea at common law—"let the buyer beware"—and mean that when goods are sold without an express warranty by the vendor as to their quality and capacity for a particular use and purpose, the buyer must take the risk of loss as to all defects in the goods.

Caveat venditor: These words mean "let the seller beware" (In contradistinction to caveat emptor—"let the buyer beware"). Caveat venditor means that unless the seller by express language disclaims any responsibility, he shall be liable to the buyer if the goods delivered are different in kind, quality, use, and purpose from those described in the contract of sale.

Certiorari: An order issuing out of an appellate court to a lower court, at the request of an appellant directing that the record of a case pending in the lower court be transmitted to the upper court for review.

Cestui que trust: A person who is the real or beneficial owner of property held in trust. The trustee holds the legal title to the property for the benefit of the cestui que trust.

Charter: As to a private corporation, the word *charter* includes the contract between the created corporation and the state, the act creating the corporation, and the articles of association granted to the corporation by authority of the legislative act.

As to municipal corporations, charter does not mean a contract between the legislature and the city created. A city charter is a delegation of powers by a state legislature to the governing body of the city. The term includes the creative act, the powers enumerated, and the organization authorized.

Chattel: The word *chattel* is derived from the word *cattle*. It is a very broad term and includes every kind of property that is not real property. Movable properties, such as horses, automobiles, choses in action, stock certificates, bills of lading, and all "good wares, and merchandise," are chattels personal. Chattels real concern real property such as a lease for years—in which case the lessee owns a chattel real.

Chattel paper:* A writing or writings that evidence both a monetary obligation and a security interest in or a lease of specific goods. When a transaction is evidenced both by such a security agreement or a lease and by an instrument or a series of instruments, the group of writings taken together constitutes chattel paper.

Chose in action: Words used to define the "right" one person has to recover money or property from another by a judicial proceeding. Such right arises out of contract, claims for money, debts, and rights against property. Notes, drafts, stock certificates, bills of lading, warehouse receipts, and insurance policies are illustrations of choses in action. They are called tangible choses. Book accounts, simple debts, and obligations not evidenced by formal writing are called intangible choses. Choses in action are transferred by assignment.

Circumstantial evidence: If from certain facts and circumstances, according to the experience of mankind, an ordinary, intelligent person may infer that other connected facts and circumstances must necessarily exist, the latter facts and circumstances are considered proven by circumstantial evidence. Proof of fact *A* from which fact *B* may be inferred is proof of fact *B* by circumstantial evidence.

Civil action: A proceeding in a law court or a suit in equity by one person against another for the enforcement or protection of a private right or the prevention of a wrong. It includes actions on contract, ex delicto, and all suits in equity. Civil action is in contradistinction to criminal action in which the state prosecutes a person for breach of a duty.

Clearinghouse:* Under Article 4—Bank Deposits and Collections, this means any association of banks or other payors regularly clearing items.

Cloud on title: Words used to express the idea that there is some evidence of record that shows a third person has some prima facie interest in another's property.

Code: A collection or compilation of the statutes passed by the legislative body of a state. Such codes are often annotated with citations of cases decided by the state supreme courts. These decisions construe the statutes. Example—Oregon Compiled Laws Annotated, United States Code Annotated.

Codicil: An addition to or a change in an executed last will and testament. It is a part of the original will and must be executed with the same formality as the original will.

Coinsurer: A term in a fire insurance policy that requires the insured to bear a certain portion of the loss when he fails to carry complete coverage. For example, unless the insured carries insurance that totals 80 percent of the value of the property, the insurer shall be liable for only that portion of the loss that the total insurance carried bears to 80 percent of the value of the property.

Collateral: With reference to debts or other obligations, the term *collateral* means security placed with a creditor to assure the performance of the obligator. If the obligator performs, the collateral is returned by the creditor. A owes B $1,000. To secure the payment, A places with B a $500 certificate of stock in X company. The $500 certificate is called collateral security.

Collateral:* The property subject to a security interest, and includes accounts, contract rights, and chattel paper which have been sold.

Collecting bank:* Under Article 4—Bank Deposits and Collections, is any bank handling the item for collection except the payor bank.

Commercial unit:* Such a unit of goods as by commercial usage is a single whole for purposes of sale and division of which materially impairs its character or value on the market or in use. A commercial unit may be a single article (as a machine) or a set of articles (as a suite of furniture or an assortment of sizes) or a quantity (as a bale, gross, or carload) or any other unit treated in use or in the relevant market as a single whole.

Commission: The sum of money, interest, brokerage, compensation, or allowance given to a factor or broker for carrying on the business of his principal.

Commission merchant: An agent or factor employed to sell "goods, wares, and merchandise" consigned or delivered to him by his principal.

Common carrier: One who is engaged in the business of transporting personal property from one place to another for a compensation. Such person is bound to carry for all who tender their goods and the price for transportation. A common carrier operates as a public utility and is subject to state and federal regulations.

Community property: All property acquired after marriage by husband and wife other than separate property acquired by devise, bequest, or from the proceeds of noncommunity property. Community property is a concept of property ownership by husband and wife inherited from the civil law. The husband and wife are somewhat like partners in their ownership of property acquired during marriage.

Complaint: The first paper a plaintiff files in a court in a lawsuit. It is called a pleading. It is a statement of the facts upon which the plaintiff rests his cause of action.

Composition of creditors: An agreement between creditors and their debtors by which they agree that the creditors will take a lesser amount in complete satisfaction of the total debt due. A owes B and C $500 each. A agrees to pay B and C $250 each in complete satisfaction of the $500 due each. B and C agree to take $250 in satisfaction. Such agreement is called a composition of creditors.

Compromise: An agreement between two or more persons, usually opposing parties in a lawsuit, to settle the matters of the controversy without further resort to hostile litigation. An adjustment of issues in dispute by mutual concessions before resorting to a lawsuit.

Condemnation proceedings: An action or proceeding in court authorized by legislation (federal or state) for the purpose of taking private property for public use. It is the exercise by the judiciary of the sovereign power of eminent domain.

Condition: A clause in a contract, either expressed or implied, that has the effect of investing or divesting the legal rights and duties of the parties to the contract. In a

628

deed, a condition is a qualification or restriction providing for the happening or non-happening of events that on occurrence will destroy, commence, or enlarge an estate. "A grants Blackacre to B so long as said land shall be used for church purposes." If it ceases to be used for church purposes, the title to Blackacre will revert to the grantor

Condition precedent: A clause in a contract providing that immediate rights and duties shall vest only upon the happening of some event. Securing an architect's certificate by a contractor before he (the contractor) is entitled to payment is a condition precedent.

A condition is not a promise; hence, its breach will not give rise to a cause of action for damages. A breach of a condition is the basis for a defense. In the above illustration, if the contractor sues the owner without securing the architect's certificate, the owner has a defense.

Conditions concurrent: Conditions concurrent are conditions that are mutually dependent and must be performed at the same time by the parties to the contract. Payment of money and delivery of goods in a cash sale are conditions concurrent. Failure to perform by one party permits a cause of action upon tender by the other party. If S refuses to deliver goods in a cash sale, B, upon tender but not delivery of the money, places S in default and thus may sue S. B does not part with his money without getting the goods. If S sued B, B would have a defense.

Condition subsequent: A clause in a contract providing for the happening of an event that divests legal rights and duties. A clause in a fire insurance policy providing that the policy shall be null and void if combustible material is stored within ten feet of the building is a condition subsequent. If a fire occurs and combustible material was within ten feet of the building, the insurance company is excused from its duty to pay for the loss.

Confirming bank: A bank that engages either that it will itself honor a credit already issued by another bank or that such a credit will be honored by the issuer or a third bank.

Conforming:* Goods or conduct including any part of a performance are "conforming" or conform to the contract when they are in accordance with the obligations under contract.

Consideration: An essential element in the creation of contract obligation. A detriment to the promisee and a benefit to the promisor. One promise is consideration for another promise. The creates a bilateral contract. An act is consideration for a promise. This creates a unilateral contract. Performance of the act asked for by the promisee is a legal detriment to the promisee and a benefit to the promisor.

Consignee: A person to whom a shipper usually directs a carrier to deliver goods. Such person is generally the buyer of goods and is called a consignee on a bill of lading.

Consignee:* The person named in a bill to whom or to whose order the bill promises delivery.

Consignment: The delivery, sending, or transferring of property, "goods, wares, and merchandise" into the possession of another, usually for the purpose of sale. Consignment may be a bailment or an agency for sale.

Consignor: The person who delivers freight to a carrier for shipment and who directs the bill of lading to be executed by the carrier is called a consignor or shipper. Such person may be the consignor-consignee if the bill of lading is made to his own order.

Consignor:* The person named in a bill as the person from whom the goods have been received for shipment.

Conspicuous:* A term or clause is conspicuous when it is so written that a reasonable person against whom it is to operate ought to have noticed it. A printed heading in capitals (as: NONNEGOTIABLE BILL OF LADING) is conspicuous. Language in the body of a form is "conspicuous" if it is in larger or other contrasting type or color. But in a telegram any stated term is "conspicuous." Whether a term or clause is "conspicuous" or not is for decision by the court.

Constitution: The Constitution of the United States constitutes the rules of organization of the United States and enumerates the powers and duties of the federal government thereby created. The constitutions of the several states prescribe the organization of each of the states and in general enumerate those powers not delegated to the federal government.

Constructive delivery: Although physical delivery of personal property has not occurred, yet by the conduct of the parties it may be inferred that as between them possession and title has passed. A sells large and bulky goods to B. Title and possession may pass by the act and conduct of the parties.

Consumer goods:* Goods that are used or bought for use primarily for personal, family, or household purposes.

Contract:* The total obligation that results from the parties' agreement as affected by the Code and any other applicable rules of law.

Contract right:* Any right to payment under a contract not yet earned by performance and not evidenced by an instrument or chattel paper.

Conversion:* Under Article 3—Commercial Paper, an instrument is converted when a drawee to whom it is delivered for acceptance refuses to return it on demand; or any person to whom it is delivered for payment refuses on demand either to pay or to return it; or it is paid on a forged indorsement.

Conveyance: A formal written instrument usually called a deed by which the title or other interests in land (real property) is transferred from one person to another. The word expresses also the fact that the title to real property has been transferred from one person to another.

Corporation: A collection of individuals created by statute as a legal person, vested with powers and capacity to contract, own, control, convey property, and transact business within the limits of the powers granted.

Corporation de facto: If persons have attempted in good faith to organize a corporation under a valid law (statute) and have failed in some minor particular, but have thereafter exercised corporate powers, such is a corporation de facto. Failure to have incorporators' signatures on applications for charter notarized is an illustration of noncompliance with statutory requirements.

Corporation de jure: A corporation that has been formed by complying with the mandatory requirements of the law authorizing such a corporation.

Corporeal: Physical things that are susceptible to the senses are corporeal. Automobiles, grain, fruit, and horses are corporeal and tangible and are called "chattels." The word corporeal is used in contradistinction to incorporeal or intangible. A chose in action (such as a check) is corporeal and tangible, or a chose in action may be a simple debt, incorporeal and intangible.

Costs: Costs, in litigation, are an allowance authorized by statute to a party for the expenses incurred in prosecuting or defending a lawsuit. The word *costs*, unless specifically designated by statute or contract, does not include attorney's fees.

Counterclaims: A claim by the defendant by way of cross-action that the defendant is entitled to recover from the plaintiff. It must arise out of the same transaction set forth in the plaintiff's complaint, and be connected with the same subject matter. S sues B for the purchase price. B counterclaims that the goods were defective, and that he thereby suffered damages.

Course of dealing: This is a sequence of previous conduct between the parties to a particular transaction which is fairly to be regarded as establishing a common basis of understanding for interpreting their expressions and other conduct.

Covenant: A promise in writing under seal. It is often used as a substitute for the word contract. There are convenants (promises) in deeds, leases, mortgages, and other instruments under seal. The word is used sometimes to name promises in unsealed instruments such as insurance policies.

Cover:* After a breach by a seller, the buyer may "cover" by making in good faith and without unreasonable delay any reasonable purchase of or contract to purchase goods in substitution for those due from the seller.

Credit:* ("Letter of credit") This means an engagement by a bank or other person made at the request of a customer and of a kind within the scope of Article 5—Letters of Credit that the issuer will honor drafts or other demands for payment upon compliance with the conditions specified in the credit. A credit may be either revocable or irrevocable. The engagement may be either an agreement to honor or a statement that the bank or other person is authorized to honor.

Creditor:* This includes a general creditor, a secured creditor, a lien creditor, and any representative of creditors, including an assignee for the benefit of creditors, a trustee in bankruptcy, a receiver in equity, and an executor or administrator of an insolvent debtor's or assignor's estate.

Creditor beneficiary: If a promisee is under a duty to a third party and, for a consideration, secures a promise from a promisor which promise, if performed, discharges the promisee's duty to the third party, such third party is a creditor beneficiary. A owes C $100. B, for a consideration, promises A to pay A's debt to C. C is a creditor beneficiary.

Cumulative voting: A stockholder in voting for a director may cast as many votes for one candidate for given office as there are offices to be filled multiplied by the number of shares of his stock, or he may distribute this same number of votes among the other candidates as he sees fit.

Custodian bank:* Any bank or trust company that is supervised and examined by state or federal authority having supervision over banks and which is acting as custodian for a clearing corporation.

Custody (personal property): The words *custody* and *possession* are not synonymous. Custody means in charge of, to keep and care for under the direction of the true owner, without any interest therein adverse to the true owner. A servant is in custody of his master's goods. See *Possession.*

Customer:* Under Article 4—Bank Deposits and Collections, this means any person having an account with a bank or for whom a bank has agreed to collect items and includes a bank carrying an account with another bank.

Customer:* As used in Letters of Credit, a customer is a buyer or other person who causes an issuer to issue a credit. The term also includes a bank that procures issuance or confirmation on behalf of that bank's customer.

Damages: A sum of money the court imposes upon a defendant as compensation for the plaintiff because the defendant has injured the plaintiff by breach of a legal duty.

d.b.a.: An abbreviation of "doing business as." A person who conducts his business under an assumed name is designated "John Doe d.b.a. Excelsior Co."

Debenture: A term used to name corporate obligations that are sold as investments. It is similar to a corporate bond. However, it is not secured by a trust deed. It is not like corporate stock.

Debtor:* The person who owes payment or other performance of the obligation secured, whether or not he owns or has rights in the collateral, and includes the seller of accounts, contract rights, or chattel paper. Where the debtor and the owner of the collateral are not the same person, the term *debtor* means the owner of the collateral in any provision of the Article dealing with the obligation, and may include both where the context so requires.

Deceit: A term to define that conduct in a business transaction by which one man, through fraudulent representations, misleads another who has a right to rely on such representations as the truth, or, who by reason of an unequal station in life, has no means of detecting such fraud.

Declaratory judgment: A determination by a court on a question of law which simply declares the rights of the parties without ordering anything to be done.

Decree: The judgment of the chancellor (judge) in a suit in equity. Like a judgment at law, it is the determination of the rights between the parties and is in the form of an order that requires the decree to be carried out. An order that a contract be specifically enforced is an example of a decree.

Deed: A written instrument in a special form signed, sealed, and delivered, that is used to pass the legal title of real property from one person to another. See *Conveyance.*

In order that the public may know about the title to real property, deeds are recorded in the Deed Record office of the county where the land is situated.

Deed of trust: An instrument by which title to real property is conveyed to a trustee to hold as security for the holder of notes or bonds. It is like a mortgage except the security title is held by a person other than the mortgagee-creditor. Most corporate bonds are secured by a deed of trust.

De facto: Arising out of, or founded upon, fact, although merely apparent or colorable. A de facto officer is one who assumes to be an officer under some color of right, acts as an officer, but in point of law is not a real officer. See *Corporation de facto.*

Defendant: A person who has been sued in a court of law; the person who answers the plaintiff's complaint. The word is applied to the defending party in civil actions. In criminal actions, the defending party is referred to as the accused.

Deficiency judgment: If, upon the foreclosure of a mortgage, the mortgaged property does not sell for a sufficient amount to pay the mortgage indebtedness, such difference is called a "deficiency" and is chargeable to the mortgagor or to any person who has purchased the property and assumed and agreed to pay the mortgage. Illus.: M borrows $10,000 from B and as security gives a mortgage on Blackacre. At maturity M does not pay the debt. B forecloses, and at public sale Blackacre sells for $8,000. There is a deficiency of $2,000, chargeable against M. If M had sold Blackacre to C and C had assumed and agreed to pay the mortgage, he would also be liable for the deficiency.

Defraud: To deprive one of some right by deceitful means. To cheat or withhold wrongfully that which belongs to another. Conveying one's property for the purpose of avoiding payment of debts is a transfer to "hinder, delay, or defraud creditors."

Del credere agency: When an agent, factor, or broker undertakes to guarantee to his principal the payment of a debt due from a buyer of goods, such agent, factor, or broker is operating under a del credere commission or agency.

Delivery: A voluntary transfer of the possession of property, actual or constructive, from one person to another with the intention that title vests in the transferee. In the law of sales, delivery contemplates the absolute giving up of control and dominion over the property by the vendor, and the assumption of the same by the vendee.

Delivery:* With respect to instruments, documents of title, chattel paper, or securities, this means voluntary transfer of possession.

Delivery order:* A written order to deliver goods directed to a warehouseman, carrier, or other person who in the ordinary course of business issues warehouse receipts or bills of lading.

Demand: A request by a party entitled, under a claim of right, that a particular act be performed. In order to bind an indorser on a negotiable instrument, a demand must first be made by the holder on the primary party and such person must dishonor the instrument. Demand notes mean "due when demanded." The word *demand* is also used to mean a claim or legal obligation.

Demurrage: Demurrage is a sum, provided for in a contract of shipment, to be paid for the delay or detention of vessels or railroad cars beyond the time agreed upon for loading or unloading.

Demurrer: A common-law procedural method by which the defendant admits all the facts alleged in the plaintiff's complaint but denies that such facts state a cause of action. It raises a question of law on the facts, which must be decided by the court.

Dependent covenants (promises): In contracts, covenants are either concurrent or mutual, dependent or independent. Dependent covenants mean the performance of one promise must occur before the performance of the other promise. In a cash sale, the buyer must pay the money before the seller is under a duty to deliver the goods.

Depositary bank:* Under Article 4—Bank Deposits and Collections, this means the first bank to which an item is transferred for collection even though it is also the payor bank.

Descent: The transfer of the title of property to the heirs upon the death of the ancestor, heredity; succession. If a person dies without making a will, his property will "descend" according to the Statute of Descent of the state wherein the property is located.

Detriment: Legal detriment that is sufficient consideration constitutes change of position or acts of forbearance by a promisee at the request of a promisor. See *Consideration.*

Devise: A gift, usually of real property, by a last will and testament.

Devisee: The person who receives title to real property by will.

Dictum: An expression of an idea, argument, or rule in the written opinion of a judge that is not essential for the determination of the issues. It lacks the force of a decision in a judgment.

Directed verdict: If it is apparent to reasonable men and the court that the plaintiff by his evidence has not made out his case, the court may instruct the jury to bring in a verdict for the defendant. If, however, different inferences may be drawn from the evidence by reasonable men, then the court cannot direct a verdict.

Discharge: The word has many meanings. A servant or laborer upon being released from his employment is discharged. A guardian or trustee, upon termination of his trust, is discharged by the court. A debtor released from his debts is discharged in bankruptcy. A person who is released from any legal obligation is discharged.

Discovery practice: The disclosure by one party of facts, titles, documents, and other things which are in his knowledge or possession and which are necessary to the party seeking the discovery as a part of a cause of action pending.

Dishonor: A negotiable instrument is dishonored when it is presented for acceptance or payment, and acceptance or payment is refused or cannot be obtained.

Distress for rent: The taking of personal property of a tenant in payment of rent on real estate.

Dividend: A dividend is a stockholder's pro rata share in the profits of a corporation. Dividends are declared by the board of directors of a corporation. Dividends are cash, script, property, and stock.

Documentary draft:* Under Article 4—Bank Deposits and Collections, this means any negotiable or nonnegotiable draft with accompanying documents, securities, or other papers to be delivered against honor of the draft.

Documentary draft:* ("Documentary demand for payment.") A draft the honor of which is conditioned upon the presentation of a document or documents. "Document" means any paper including document of title, security, invoice, certificate, notice of default, and the like.

Document of title:* This term includes bill of lading, dock warrant, dock receipt, warehouse receipt, or order for the delivery of goods, and also any other document that in the regular course of business or financing is treated as adequately evidencing that the person in possession of it is entitled to receive, hold, and dispose of the document and the goods it covers. To be a document of title, a document must purport to be issued by or addressed to a bailee and purport to cover goods in the bailee's possession which are either identified or are fungible portions of an identified mass.

Domicile: That place that a person intends as his fixed and permanent home and establishment and to which, if he is absent, he intends to return. A person can have but one domicile. The old one continues until the acquisition of a new one. One can have more than one residence at a time, but only one domicile. The word is not synonymous with *residence.*

Dominion: As applied to the delivery of property by one person to another, the word means the separation by the transferor or donor from all control over the possession and ownership of the property and the endowing of the transferee or donee with such control of possession and ownership. See *Gift.*

Donee: A recipient of a gift.

633

Donee beneficiary: If a promisee is under no duty to a third party, but for a consideration secures a promise from a promisor for the purpose of making a gift to a third party, such third party is a donee beneficiary. A, promisee for a premium paid, secures a promise from the insurance company, the promisor, to pay A's wife $10,000 upon A's death. A's wife is a donee beneficiary.

Donor: One that gives, donates, or presents.

Dormant partner: A partner who is not known to third persons but is entitled to share in the profits and is subject to the losses. Since credit is not extended upon the strength of such partner's name, he may withdraw without notice and is not subject to debts contracted after his withdrawal.

Duress (of person): Duress means a threat of bodily injury, criminal prosecution, or imprisonment of a contracting party or his near relative to such extent that the threatened party is unable to exercise freely his will at the time of entering into or discharging a legal obligation.

Duress (of property): The seizure by force or the withholding of goods by one not entitled, and the demanding by such person of something as a condition for the release of the goods.

Duty (in law): A legal obligation imposed by general law or voluntarily imposed by the creation of a binding promise. For every legal duty there is a corresponding legal right. By general law, A is under a legal duty not to injure B's person or property. B has a right that A not injure his person or property. X may voluntarily create a duty in himself to Y by a promise to sell Y a horse for $100. If Y accepts, X is under a legal duty to perform his promise. See *Right.*

Earnest money: A term used to describe money that one contracting party gives to another at the time of entering into the contract in order to "bind the bargain" and which will be forfeited by the donor if he fails to carry out the contract. Generally, in real estate contracts such money is used as part payment of the purchase price.

Easement: An easement is an interest in land —a right that one person has to some profit, benefit, or use in or over the land of another. Such right is created by a deed, or it may be acquired by prescription (the continued use of another's land for a statutory period).

Ejectment: An action to recover the possession of real property. It is now generally defined by statute and is a statutory action. See *Forcible entry and detainer.*

Ejusdem generis: Of the same class. General words taking their meaning from specific words which precede the general words. General words have the same meaning as specific words mentioned.

Embezzlement: The fraudulent appropriation by one person, acting in a fiduciary capacity, of the money or property of another. See *Conversion.*

Eminent domain: The right that resides in the United States, state, county, city, school, or other public body, to take private property for public use, upon payment of just compensation.

Entirety (Tenancy by): Property acquired by husband and wife whereby upon the death of one, the survivor takes the whole property. The tenancy exists in only a few states. The husband and wife are both vested with the whole estate so that the survivor takes no new title upon death of the other but remains in possession of the whole as originally granted. For the legal effect of such estate, the state statute should be consulted. See *Joint tenants.*

Entity: The word means "in being" or "existing." The artificial person created when a corporation is organized is "in being" or "existing" for legal purposes; thus, an entity. It is separate from the stockholders. The estate of a deceased person while in administration is an entity. A partnership for many legal purposes is an entity.

Equipment:* Goods that are used or bought for use primarily in business (including farming or a profession) or by a debtor who is a non-profit organization or a governmental subdivision or agency, or if the goods are not included in the definitions of inventory, farm products or consumer goods.

Equitable action: In Anglo-American law there have developed two types of courts and procedures for the administration of justice: law courts and equity courts. Law courts give as a remedy money damages only, whereas equity courts give the plaintiff what he bargains for. A suit for specific performance of a contract is an equitable action. In many states these two courts are now merged.

Equitable conversion: An equitable principle that, for certain purposes, permits real property to be converted into personalty. Thus real property owned by a partnership is, for the purpose of the partnership, personal property because to ascertain a partner's interest, the real property must be reduced to cash. This is an application of the equitable maxim, "Equity considers that done which ought to be done."

Equitable mortgage: A written agreement to make certain property security for a debt, and upon the faith of which the parties have acted in making advances, loans, and thus creating a debt. Example: an improperly executed mortgage, one without seal where a seal is required. An absolute deed made to the mortgagee and intended for security only is an equitable mortgage.

Equity: Because the law courts in early English law did not always give an adequate remedy, an aggrieved party sought redress from the king. Since this appeal was to the king's conscience, he referred the case to his spiritual adviser, the chancellor. The chancellor decided the case according to rules of fairness, honesty, right, and natural justice. From this there developed the rules in equity. The laws of trusts, divorce, rescission of contracts for fraud, injunction, and specific performance are enforced in courts of equity.

Equity of redemption: The right a mortgagor has to redeem or get back his property after it has been forfeited for nonpayment of the debt it secured. By statute, within a certain time before final foreclosure decree, a mortgagor has the privilege, by paying the amount of the debt, interest, and costs, of redeeming his property.

Escrow: An agreement under which a grantor, promisor, or obligor places the instrument upon which he is bound with a third person called escrow holder, until the performance of a condition or the happening of an event stated in the agreement permits the escrow holder to make delivery or performance to the grantee, promisee, or obligee. A (grantor) places a deed to C (grantee) accompanied by the contract of conveyance with B bank, conditioned upon B bank delivering the deed to C (grantee) when C pays all moneys due under contract. The contract and deed have been placed in "escrow."

Estate: A word used to name all the property of a living, deceased, bankrupt, or insane person. It is also applied to the property of a ward. In the law of taxation, wills, and inheritance, the word has a broad meaning. Historically, the word was limited to an interest in land: i.e., estate in fee simple, estate for years, estate for life, and so forth.

Estoppel: When one ought to speak the truth, but does not, and by one's acts, representations, or silence intentionally or through negligence induces another to believe certain facts exist, and such person acts to his detriment on the belief that such facts are true, the first person is estopped to deny the truth of the facts. B, knowingly having kept and used defective goods delivered by S under a contract of sale, is estopped to deny the goods are defective. X holds out Y as his agent. X is estopped to deny Y is not his agent. Persons are estopped to deny the legal effect of written instruments such as deeds, contracts, bills and notes, court records, and judgments. A man's own acts speak louder than his words.

Et al.: Literally translated means "and other persons." Words used in pleadings and cases to indicate that persons other than those specifically named are parties to a lawsuit.

Eviction: An action to expel a tenant from the estate of the landlord. Interfering with the tenant's right of possession or enjoyment amounts to an eviction. Eviction may be actual or constructive. Premises made uninhabitable because the landlord maintains a nuisance is constructive eviction.

Evidence: In law the word has two meanings. First, that testimony of witnesses and facts presented to the court and jury by way of writings and exhibits, which impress the minds of the court and jury, to the extent that an allegation has been proven. *Testimony* and *evidence* are not synonymous Testimony is a broader word and includes all the witness says. *Proof* is distinguished from *evidence* in that proof is the legal consequence of evidence. Second, the rules of law, called the law of evidence, that deter what evidence shall be introduced at a trial and what shall not; also what importance shall be placed upon the evidence.

Ex contractu: See *Action ex contractu.*

Ex delicto: See *Action ex delicto.*

Executed: As applied to contracts or other written instruments, means signed, sealed, and delivered. Effective legal obligations have thus been created. The term is also used to mean that the performances of a contract have been completed. The contract is then at an end. All is done that is to be done.

Execution: Execution of a judgment is the process by which the court through the sheriff enforces the payment of the judgment received by the successful party. The sheriff by a "writ" levies upon the unsuccessful party's property and sells it to pay the judgment creditor.

Executor (of an estate): The person, named or appointed in a will by a testator (the one who makes the will), who by authority of the will has the power to administer the estate upon the death of the testator and to dispose of it according to the intention of the testator. The terms *executor* and *administrator* are not synonymous. An executor is appointed by the deceased to administer an estate. An administrator is appointed by the court to administer the estate of a person who dies without having made a will. See *Intestate.*

Executory (contract): Until the performance required in a contract is completed, it is said to be executory as to that part not executed. See *Executed.*

Exemplary damages: A sum assessed by the jury in a tort action (over and above the compensatory damages) as punishment in order to make an example of the wrongdoer and to deter like conduct by others. Injuries caused by willful, malicious, wanton, and reckless conduct will subject the wrongdoers to exemplary damages.

Exemption: The condition of a person who is free or excused from a duty imposed by some rule of law, statutory or otherwise.

Express warranty: When a seller makes some positive representation concerning the nature, quality, character, use, and purpose of goods, which induces the buyer to buy, and the seller intends the buyer to rely thereon, the seller has made an express warranty.

Factor: A factor is an agent for the sale of merchandise. He may hold possession of the goods in his own name or in the name of his principal. He is authorized to sell and to receive payment for the goods. See *Agent.*

Factor's lien: A lien or right that a factor has to keep the possession of goods consigned to him for the purpose of reimbursing himself for all advances previously made to the consignor.

Farm products:* Goods that are crops or livestock or supplies used or produced in farming operations or if they are products of crops or livestock in their unmanufactured states (such as ginned cotton, wool-clip, maple syrup, milk and eggs), and if they are in the possession of a debtor engaged in raising, fattening, grazing, or other farming operations. If goods are farm products, they are neither equipment nor inventory.

Featherbedding: A term used in labor relations to describe the situation in which demand is made for the payment of wages for a particular service not actually rendered.

Fee simple estate: A term describing the total interest a person may have in land. Such an estate is not qualified by any other interest and passes upon the death of the owners to the heirs free from any conditions.

Felony: A term including all those criminal offenses that are punishable by death or imprisonment in a penitentiary.

Fiduciary: In general, a person is a fiduciary when he occupies a position of trust or confidence in relation to another person or his property. Trustees, guardians, and executors are illustrations of persons occupying fiduciary positions.

Financing agency:* A bank, finance company, or other person who in the ordinary course of business makes advances against goods or documents of title or who by arrangement with either the seller or the buyer intervenes in ordinary course to make or collect payment due or claimed under the contract for sale, as by purchasing or paying the seller's draft or making advances against it or by merely taking it for collection whether or not documents of title accompany the draft. "Financing agency" includes also a bank or other person who similarly intervenes between persons who are in the position of seller and buyer in respect to the goods.

Fine: A sum of money collected by a court from a person guilty of some criminal offense. The amount may be fixed by statute or left to the discretion of the court.

Firm offers:* An offer by a merchant to buy or sell goods in a signed writing which by its terms gives assurance that it will be held open.

Forbearance: Giving up the right to enforce what one honestly believes to be a valid claim in return for a promise is called forbearance and is sufficient "consideration" to make binding a promise.

Forcible entry and detainer: A remedy given to a landowner to evict persons unlawfully in possession of his land. A landlord may use such remedy to evict a tenant in default.

Forfeiture: Loss of money or property by way of compensation and punishment for injury or damage to the person or property of another or to the state. One may forfeit interest earnings for charging a usurious rate.

Forgery: Forgery is the false writing or alteration of an instrument with the fraudulent intent of deceiving and injuring another. Writing, without his consent, another's name upon a check for the purpose of securing money, is a forgery.

Franchise: A right conferred or granted by a legislative body. It is a contract right and cannot be revoked without cause. A franchise is more than a license. A license is only a privilege and may be revoked. A corporation exists by virtue of a "franchise." A corporation secures a franchise from the city council to operate a waterworks within the city. See *License.*

Franchise tax: A tax on the right of a corporation to do business under its corporate name.

Fraud: An intentional misrepresentation of the truth for the purpose of deceiving another person. The elements of fraud are (1) false representation of fact, not opinion, intentionally made; (2) intent that the deceived person act thereon; (3) knowledge that such statements would naturally deceive; and (4) that the deceived person acted to his injury.

Fraudulent conveyance: A conveyance of property by a debtor for the intent and purpose of defrauding his creditors. Such conveyance is of no effect, and such property may be reached by the creditors through appropriate legal proceedings.

Freehold: An estate in fee or one for life is a "freehold." A freeholder is usually a person who has a property right in the title to real estate amounting to an estate of inheritance (in fee), or one who has title for life, or for an indeterminate period.

Fungible:* With respect to goods or securities this means goods and securities of which any unit is, by nature or usage of trade, the equivalent of any other like unit. Goods which are not fungible shall be deemed fungible for the purposes of this Act to the extent that under a particular agreement or document unlike units are treated as equivalents.

Fungible goods: Fungible goods are those "of which any unit is from its nature of mercantile usage treated as the equivalent of any other unit." Grain, wine, and similar items are examples.

Future goods:* Goods that are not both existing and identified.

Futures: Contracts for the sale and delivery of commodities in the future, made with the intention that no commodity be delivered or received immediately.

Garnishee: A person upon whom a garnishment is served. He is a debtor of a defendant and has money or property that the plaintiff is trying to reach in order to satisfy a debt due from the defendant.

Garnishment: A proceeding by which a plaintiff seeks to reach the credits of the defendant that are in the hands of a third party, the garnishee. A garnishment is distinguished from an attachment in that by an attachment an officer of the court takes actual possession of property by virtue of his writ. In a garnishment, the property or money is left with the garnishee until final adjudication.

General agent: An agent authorized to do all the acts connected with carrying on a particular trade, business, or profession.

General intangibles:* Any personal property (including things in action) other than goods, accounts, contract rights, chattel paper, documents, and instruments.

Gift: A gift is made when a donor delivers the subject matter of the gift into the donee's hands, or places in the donee the means of obtaining possession of the subject matter, accompanied by such acts as show clearly that the donor intends to divest himself of all dominion and control over the property.

Gift causa mortis: A gift made in anticipation of death. The donor must have been in sickness and have died as expected; otherwise no effective gift has been made. If the donor survives, the gift is revocable.

Gift inter vivos: A gift inter vivos is an effective gift made during the life of the donor. By a gift inter vivos, property vests immediately in the donee at the time of delivery; whereas a gift causa mortis is made in contemplation of death and is effective only upon the donor's death.

Good faith:* In the case of a merchant this means honesty in fact and the observance of reasonable commercial standards of fair dealing in the trade.

Good faith:* Honesty in fact in the conduct or transaction concerned.

Goods:* All things (including specially manufactured goods) that are movable at the time of identification to the contract for sale other than the money in which the price is to be paid, investment securities, and things in action. "Goods" also includes the unborn young animals and growing crops and other identified things attached to realty as described in the section on goods to be severed from realty.

Grant: A term used in deeds for the transfer of the title to real property. The words *convey*, *transfer*, and *grant* as operative words in a deed to pass title are equivalent. The words *grant*, *bargain*, and *sell* in a deed, in absence of statute, mean the grantor promises he has good title to transfer free from incumbrances and warrants it to be such.

Grantee: A grantee is a person to whom a grant is made; one named in a deed to receive title.

Grantor: A grantor is a person who makes a grant. The grantor executes the deed by which he divests himself of title.

Gross negligence: The lack of even slight or ordinary care.

Guarantor: One who by contract undertakes "to answer for the debt, default, and miscarriage of another." In general, a guarantor undertakes to pay if the principal debtor does not; a surety, on the other hand, joins in the contract of the principal and becomes an original party with the principal.

Guardian: A person appointed by the court to look after the property rights and person of minors, the insane, and other incompetents or legally incapacitated persons.

Guardian ad litem: A special guardian appointed for the sole purpose of carrying on litigation and preserving the interests of a ward. He exercises no control or power over property.

Habeas corpus: A writ issued to a sheriff, warden, or official having custody of a person, directing the official to return the person, alleged to be unlawfully held, before a court in order to determine the legality of the imprisonment.

Hearsay evidence: Evidence that is learned from someone else. It does not derive its value from the credit of the witness testifying but rests upon the veracity of another person. It is not good evidence because there is no opportunity to cross-examine the person who is the source of the testimony.

Hedging contract: A contract of purchase or sale of an equal amount of commodities in the future by which brokers, dealers, or manufacturers protect themselves against the fluctuations of the market. It is a type of insurance against changing prices. A grain dealer, to protect himself, may contract to sell for future delivery the same amount of grain he has purchased in the present market.

Heirs: Those persons upon whom the statute of descent casts the title to real property upon the death of the ancestor. See statutes of descent for the particular state. See *Descent.*

Holder:* A person who is in possession of a document of title or an instrument or an investment security drawn, issued, or indorsed to him or to his order or to bearer or in blank.

Holding company: A corporation organized for the purpose of owning and holding the stock of other corporations. Shareholders of underlying corporations receive in exchange for their stock, upon an agreed value, the shares in the holding corporation.

Homestead: A parcel of land upon which a family dwells or resides, and which to them is home. The statute of the state or federal governments should be consulted to determine the meaning of the term as applied to debtor's exemptions, federal land grants, and so forth.

Honor:* This means to pay or to accept and pay, or where a creditor so engages to purchase or discount a draft complying with the terms of the instrument.

Illegal: Conduct that is contrary to public policy and the fundamental principles of law is illegal. Such conduct includes not only violations of criminal statutes but also the creation of agreements that are prohibited by statute and the common law.

Illusory: That which has a false appearance. If that which appears to be a promise is not a promise, it is said to be illusory. For example: "A promises to buy B's horse, if A wants to," is no promise. Such equivocal statement would not justify reliance; thus, it is not a promise.

Immunity: Freedom from the legal duties and penalties imposed upon others. The "privileges and immunities" clause of the United States Constitution means no state can deny to the citizens of another state the same rights granted to its own citizens. This does not apply to office holding. See *Exemption.*

Implied: The finding of a legal right or duty by inference from facts or circumstances. See *Warranty.*

Imputed negligence: Negligence that is not directly attributable to the person himself, but which is the negligence of a person who is in privity with him and with whose fault he is chargeable.

Incidental beneficiary: If the performance of a promise would indirectly benefit a person not a party to a contract, such person is an incidental beneficiary. A promises B, for a consideration, to plant a valuable nut orchard on B's land. Such improvement would increase the value of the adjacent land. C, the owner of the adjacent land, is an incidental beneficiary. He has no remedy if A breaches his promise with B.

Incumbrance: A burden on either the title to land or thing, or upon the land or thing itself. A mortgage or other lien is an incumbrance upon the title. A right of way over the land is an incumbrance upon the land and affects its physical condition.

Indemnify: Literally it means "to save harmless." Thus one person agrees to protect another against loss.

Indenture: A deed executed by both parties, as distinguished from a deed poll that is executed only by the grantor.

Independent contractor: The following elements are essential to establish the relation of independent contractor in contradistinction to principal and agent. An independent contractor must (1) exercise his independent judgment as to the means used to accomplish the result; (2) be free from control or orders from any other person; (3) be responsible only under his contract for the result obtained.

Indictment: An indictment is a finding by a grand jury that it has reason to believe the accused is guilty as charged. It informs the accused of the offense with which he is charged in order that he may prepare its defense. It is a pleading in a criminal action.

Indorsement: Writing one's name upon paper for the purpose of transferring the title. When a payee of a negotiable instrument writes his name on the back of the instrument, such writing is an indorsement.

Infringement: Infringement of a patent on a machine is the manufacturing of a machine that produces the same result by the same means and operation as the patented machine. Infringement of a trademark consists in the reproduction of a registered trademark and its use upon goods in order to mislead the public to believe that the goods are the genuine, original product.

Inherit: The word is used in contradistinction to acquiring property by will. See *Descent*.

Inheritance: An inheritance denotes an estate that descends to heirs. See *Descent*.

Injunction: A writ of judicial process issued by a court of equity by which a party is required to do a particular thing or to refrain from doing a particular thing.

In personam: A legal proceeding, the judgment of which binds the defeated party to a personal liability.

In rem: A legal proceeding, the judgment of which binds, affects, or determines the status of property.

Insolvent:* Refers to a person who either has ceased to pay his debts in the ordinary course of business or cannot pay his debts as they become due or is insolvent within the meaning of the federal bankruptcy law.

Installment contract:* One which requires or authorizes the delivery of goods in separate lots to be separately accepted, even though the contract contains a clause "each delivery is a separate contract" or its equivalent.

Instrument:* This means a negotiable instrument or a security or any other writing that evidences a right to the payment of money and is not itself a security agreement or lease and is of a type that is in ordinary course of business transferred by delivery with any necessary indorsement or assignment.

Insurable interest: A person has an insurable interest in a person or property if he will be directly and financially affected by the death of the person or the loss of the property.

Insurance: By an insurance contract, one party, for an agreed premium, binds himself to another, called the insured, to pay the insured a sum of money conditioned upon the loss of life or property of the insured.

Intent: A state of mind that exists prior to or contemporaneous with an act. A purpose or design to do or forbear to do an act. It cannot be directly proven but is inferred from known facts.

Interlocutory decree: A decree of a court of equity that does not settle the complete issue but settles only some intervening part, awaiting a final decree.

Intermediary bank:* Under Article 4—Bank Deposits and Collections, is a bank to which an item is transferred in course of collection except the depositary or payor bank.

Interpleader: A procedure whereby a person who has an obligation, e.g., to pay money, and does not know which of two or more claimants are entitled to performance, can bring a suit that requires the contesting parties to litigate between themselves.

Intestate: The intestate laws are the laws of descent or distribution of the estate of a deceased person. A person dies intestate who has not made a will.

Inventory:* Goods that are held by a person who holds them for sale or lease or to be furnished under contracts of service or if he has so furnished them, or if they are raw materials, work in process or materials used or consumed in a business. Inventory of a person is not to be classified as his equipment.

Irreparable damage or injury: Irreparable does not mean such injury as is beyond the possibility of repair, but it does mean that it is so constant and frequent in occurrence that no fair or reasonable redress can be had in a court of law. Thus the plaintiff must seek a remedy in equity by way of an injunction.

Issue:* Under Article 3—Commercial Paper, "issue" means the first delivery of an instrument to a holder or a remitter.

Issuer:* A bailee who issues a document except that in relation to an unaccepted delivery order it means the person who orders the possessor of goods to deliver. Issuer includes any person for whom an agent or employee purports to act in issuing a document if the agent or employee has real or apparent authority to issue documents, notwithstanding that the issuer received no goods or that the goods were misdescribed or that in any other respect the agent or employee violated his instructions.

Item:* Under Article 4—Bank Deposits and Collections, this means any instrument for the payment of money even though it is not negotiable but does not include money.

Jeopardy: A person is in jeopardy when he is regularly charged with a crime before a court properly organized and competent to try him. If acquitted, he cannot be tried again for the same offense.

Joint and several: Two or more persons have an obligation which binds them individually as well as jointly. The obligation can be enforced either by joint action against all of them or by separate actions against one or more.

Joint ownership: The interest that two or more parties have in property. See *Joint tenants.*

Joint tenants: Two or more persons to whom is deeded land in such manner that they have "one and the same interest, accruing by one and the same conveyance, commencing at one and the same time, and held by one and the same undivided possession." Upon the death of one joint tenant, his property passes to the survivor or survivors.

Joint tortfeasors: When two persons commit an injury with a common intent, they are joint tortfeasors.

Judgment (in law): A judgment is the decision, pronouncement, or sentence rendered by a court upon an issue in which it has jurisdiction.

Judgment in personam: A judgment against a person directing the defendant to do or not to do something, is a judgment in personam. See *In personam.*

Judgment in rem: A judgment against a thing, as distinguished from a judgment against a person. See *In rem.*

Judicial sale: A judicial sale is a sale authorized by a court that has jurisdiction to grant such authority. Such sales are conducted by an officer of the court.

Jurisdiction: The authority conferred upon a court by the Constitution to try cases and determine causes.

Jury: A group of persons, usually twelve, sworn to declare the facts of a case as they are proved from the evidence presented to them and, upon instructions from the court, to find a verdict in the cause before them.

Laches: Laches is a term used in equity to name that conduct that is neglect to assert one's rights or to do what by the law a person should have done and did not do. Such failure on the part of one to assert a right will give an equitable defense to another party.

Latent defect: A defect in materials not discernible by examination. Used in contradistinction to patent defect, which is discernible.

Lease: A contract by which one person divests himself of possession of lands or chattels and grants such possession to another for a period of time. The relationship were land is involved is called landlord and tenant.

Leasehold: The land held by a tenant under a lease.

Legacy: Personal property disposed of by a will. Sometimes the term is synonymous with *bequest.* The word *devise* is used in connection with real property distributed by will. See *Bequest, Devise.*

Legatee: A person to whom a legacy is given by will.

Liability: In its broadest legal sense, the word means any obligation one may be under by reason of some rule of law. It includes debt, duty, and responsibility.

Libel: The malicious publication of a defamation of a person by printing, writing, signs, or pictures, for the purpose of injuring the reputation and good name of such person. "The exposing of a person to public hatred, contempt, or ridicule."

License (governmental regulation): A license is a privilege granted by a state or city upon the payment of a fee, which confers authority upon the licensee to do some act or series of acts, which otherwise would be illegal. A license is not a contract and may be revoked for cause. It is a method of governmental regulation exercised under the police power.

License (privilege): A license is a mere personal privilege given by the owner to another to do designated acts upon the land of the owner. It is revocable at will, creates no estate in the land, and such licensee is not in possession. "It is a mere excuse for what otherwise would be a trespass."

Lien: A right one person, usually a creditor, has, to keep possession of or control the property of another for the purpose of satisfying a debt. There are many kinds of liens: judgment liens, attorney's liens, innkeeper's liens, logger's liens, vendor's liens. Consult statute of state for type of liens. See *Judgment.*

Lien creditor:* A creditor who has acquired a lien on the property involved by attachment, levy, or the like and includes an assignee for benefit of creditors from the time of assignment, and a trustee in bankruptcy from the date of the filing of the petition or a receiver in equity from the time of appointment. Unless all the creditors represented had knowledge of the security interest, such a representative of creditors is a lien creditor without knowledge even though he personally has knowledge of the security interest.

Limitation of actions: Statutes of limitations exist for the purpose of bringing to an end old claims. Because witnesses die, memory fails, papers are lost, and the evidence becomes inadequate, stale claims are barred. Such statutes are called statutes of repose. Within a certain period of time, action on claims must be brought; otherwise, they are barred. The period varies from six months to twenty years.

Liquidated: A claim is liquidated when it has been made fixed and certain by the parties concerned.

Liquidated damages: A fixed sum agreed upon between the parties to a contract, to be paid as ascertained damages by that party who breaches the contract. If the sum is excessive, the courts will declare it to be a penalty and unenforceable.

Liquidation: The process of winding up the affairs of a corporation or firm for the purpose of paying its debts and disposing of its assets. May be done voluntarily or under the orders of a court.

Lis pendens: The words mean "pending the suit nothing should be changed." The court, having control of the property involved in the suit, issues notice "lis pendens," that persons dealing with the defendant regarding the subject matter of the suit, do so subject to final determination of the action.

Lot:* A parcel or a single article that is the subject matter of a separate sale or delivery, whether or not it is sufficient to perform the contract.

Magistrate: A public officer, usually a judge, "who has power to issue a warrant for the arrest of a person charged with a public offense." The word has wide application and includes justices of the peace, notaries public, recorders, and other public officers who have power to issue executive orders.

Malice: Malice is a term to define a wrongful act done intentionally without excuse. It does not necessarily mean ill will, but it indicates a state of mind that is reckless concerning the law and the rights of others. Malice is distinguished from negligence in that in *malice* there is always a purpose to injure, whereas such is not true of the word *negligence.*

Malicious prosecution: The prosecution of another at law with malice and without probable cause to believe that such legal action will be successful.

Mandamus: A writ issued by a court of law, in the name of the state, directed to some inferior court, officer, corporation, or person commanding them to do a particular thing that appertains to their office or duty.

Mandatory injunction: An injunctive order issued by a court of equity that compels affirmative action by the defendant.

Marketable title: A title of such character that no apprehension as to its validity would occur to the mind of a reasonable and intelligent person. The title to goods in litigation, subject to incumbrances, in doubt as to a third party's right, or subject to lien, is not marketable.

Marshaling assets: A principle in equity for a fair distribution of a debtor's assets among his creditors. For example, when a creditor of A, by reason of prior right, has two funds X and Y belonging to A out of which he may satisfy his debt, but B, also a creditor of A, has a right to X fund, the first creditor will be compelled to exhaust Y fund before he will be permitted to participate in X fund.

Master in chancery: An officer appointed by the court to assist the court of equity in taking testimony, computing interest, auditing accounts, estimating damages, ascertaining liens, and doing such other tasks incidental to a suit, as the court may require. The power of a master is merely advisory and his tasks largely fact finding.

Maxim: A proposition of law that because of its universal approval needs no proof or argument, and the mere statement of which gives it authority. Example: "A principal is bound by the acts of his agent, when the agent is acting within the scope of his authority."

Mechanic's lien: A mechanic's lien is created by statute to assist suppliers and laborers in collecting their accounts and wages. Such lien has for its purpose to subject the land of an owner to a lien for material and labor expended in the construction of buildings and other improvements.

Merchant: A person who deals in goods of the kind or otherwise by his occupation holds himself out as having knowledge or skill peculiar to the practices or goods involved in the transaction or to whom such knowledge or skill may be attributed by his employment of an agent or broker or other intermediary who by his occupation holds himself out as having such knowledge or skill.

Merger: Two corporations are merged when one corporation continues in existence and the other loses its identity by its absorption into the first. *Merger* must be distinguished from *consolidation*, in which case both corporations are dissolved and a new one is created, which takes over the assets of the dissolved corporations.

Metes and bounds: The description of the boundaries of real property.

Midnight deadline:* Under Article 4—Bank Deposits and Collections, with respect to a bank this is midnight on its next banking day following the banking day on which it receives the relevant item or notice or from which the time for taking action commences to run, whichever is later.

Ministerial duty: The performance of a prescribed duty that requires the exercise of little judgment or discretion. A sheriff performs ministerial duties.

Minutes: The record of a court or the written transactions of the members or board of directors of a corporation. Under the certificate of the clerk of a court or the secretary of a corporation, the minutes are the official evidence of court or corporate action.

Misdemeanor: A criminal offense, less than a felony, that is not punishable by death or imprisonment. Consult the local statute.

Misrepresentation: The affirmative statement or affirmation of a fact that is not true; the term does not include concealment of true facts or nondisclosure or the mere expression of opinion.

Mistake of fact: The unconscious ignorance or forgetfulness of the existence or nonexistence of a fact, past or present, which is material and important to the creation of a legal obligation.

Mistake or law: An erroneous conclusion of the legal effect of known facts.

Mitigation of damages: A plaintiff is entitled to recover damages caused by the defendant's breach, but the plaintiff is also under a duty to avoid increasing or enhancing such damages. Such is called a duty to mitigate damages. If a seller fails to deliver the proper goods on time, the buyer, where possible, must buy other goods, thus mitigating damages.

Monopoly: The exclusive control of the supply and price of a commodity that may be acquired by a franchise or patent from the government; or, the ownership of the source of a commodity or the control of its distribution.

Mortgage: A conveyance or transfer of an interest in property for the purpose of creating a security for a debt. The mortgage becomes void upon payment of the debt, although the recording of a release is necessary to clear the title of the mortgaged property.

Mutual assent: In every contract each party must agree to the same thing. Each must know what the other intends; they must mutually assent or be in agreement.

Mutuality: A word used to describe the situation in every contract that it must be binding on both parties. Each party to the contract must be bound to the other party to do something by virtue of the legal duty created.

Negligence: The failure to do that which an ordinary, reasonable, prudent man would do, or the doing of some act that an ordinary, prudent man would not do. Reference must always be made to the situation, the circumstances, and the knowledge of the parties.

Negotiation:* Under Article 3—Commercial Paper, this is the transfer of an instrument in such form that the transferee becomes a holder. If the instrument is payable to order it is negotiated by delivery with any necessary indorsement; if payable to bearer it is negotiated by delivery.

Net assets: The property or effects of a firm, corporation, institution, or estate, remaining after all its obligations have been paid.

Nexus: Connection, tie, or link used in the law of taxation to establish a connection between a tax and the activity or person being taxed.

Nolo contendere: A plea by an accused in a criminal action. It does not admit guilt of the offense charged, but does equal a plea of guilty for purpose of sentencing.

Nominal damages: A small sum assessed as sufficient to award the case and cover the costs. In such case, no actual damages have been proven.

Nonsuit: A judgment given against the plaintiff when he is unable to prove his case or fails to proceed with the trial after the case is at issue.

Noscitur a sociis: The meaning of a word is or may be known from the accompanying words.

Notary: A public officer authorized to administer oaths by way of affidavits and depositions; also to attest deeds and other formal papers in order that such papers may be used as evidence and be qualified for recording.

Notice:* A person has "notice" of a fact when (a) he has actual knowledge of it; or (b) he has received a notice or notification of it; or (c) from all the facts and circumstances known to him at the time in question he has reason to know that it exists.

A person "knows" or has "knowledge" of a fact when he has actual knowledge of it. "Discover" or "learn" or a word or phrase of similar import refers to knowledge rather than to reason to know.

Novation: The substitution of one obligation for another. When debtor A is substituted for debtor B, and by agreement with the creditor C, debtor B is discharged, a novation has occurred.

Nudum pactum: A naked promise—one for which no consideration has been given.

Nuisance: The word *nuisance* is generally applied to any continuous or continued conduct that causes annoyance, inconvenience, and damage to person or property. It usually applies to the unreasonable and wrongful use of property that produces material discomfort, hurt, and damage to the person or property of another. Example: Fumes from a factory.

Obligee: A creditor or promisee.

Obligor: A debtor or promisor.

Option: A right secured by a contract to accept or reject an offer to purchase property at a fixed price within a fixed time. It is an irrevocable offer sometimes called a "paid-for offer."

Order:* Under Article 3—Commercial Paper, this means a direction to pay and must be more than an authorization or request. It must identify the person to pay with reasonable certainty. It may be addressed to one or more such persons jointly or in the alternative but not in succession.

Ordinance: An ordinance is, generally speaking, the legislative act of a municipality. A city council is a legislative body and passes ordinances that are the laws of the city.

Ordinary care: That care that a prudent man would take under the circumstances of the particular case.

Par value: The words mean "face value." The par value of stocks and bonds on the date of issuance is the principal. At a later date, the par value is the principal plus interest.

Pari delicto: The fault or blame is shared equally.

Pari materia: Latin words that mean "related to the same matter or subject." Statutes and covenants concerning the same subject matter are in pari materia, and as a general rule, for the purpose of ascertaining their meaning, are construed together.

Partition: Court proceedings brought at the request of a party in interest, that real property be taken by the court and divided among the respective owners as their interests appear. If the property is incapable of division in kind, then the property is to be sold and the money divided as each interest appears.

Party:* A person who has engaged in a transaction or made an agreement within the Uniform Commercial Code.

Patent ambiguity: An uncertainty in a written instrument that is obvious upon reading.

Payor bank:* Under Article 4—Bank Deposits and Collections, a bank by which an item is payable as drawn or accepted.

Penal bond: A bond given by an accused, or by another person in his behalf, for the payment of money if the accused fails to appear in court on a certain day.

Pendente lite: A Latin phrase that means "pending during the progress of a suit at law."

Per curiam: A decision by the full court without indicating the author of the decision.

Peremptory challenge: An objection, by a party to a lawsuit, to a person serving as a juror, for which no reason need be given.

Perjury: False swearing upon an oath properly administered in some judicial proceedings.

Per se: Literally it means "by itself." Thus a contract clause may be inherently unconscionable—unconscionable per se.

Personal property: The rights, powers, and privileges a person has in movable things such as chattels, and choses in action. Personal property is used in contradistinction to real property.

Personal representative: The administrator or executor of a deceased person or the guardian of a child or the conservator of an incompetent.

Personal service: The term means that the sheriff actually delivered to the defendant in person a service of process.

Plaintiff: In an action at law, the complaining party or the one who commences the action is called the plaintiff. He is the person who seeks a remedy in court.

Plea: An allegation or answer in a court proceeding.

Pleading: The process by which the parties in a lawsuit arrive at an issue.

Pledge: The deposit or placing of personal property as security for a debt or other obligation with a person called a pledgee. The pledgee has the implied power to sell the property if the debt is not paid. If the debt is paid, the right to possession returns to the pledgor.

Polling jury: To poll the jury is to call the name of each juror and inquire what his verdict is before such is made a matter of record.

Possession: The method, recognized by law, of holding, detaining, or controlling by one's self or by another, property, either personal or real, which will exclude others from holding, detaining, or controlling such property.

Power of attorney: An instrument authorizing another to act as one's agent or attorney in fact.

Precedent: A previously decided case that can serve as an authority to help decide a present controversy. The use of such case is called the doctrine of *stare decisis*, which means to adhere to decided cases and settled principles. Literally, "to stand as decided."

Preference: The term is used most generally in bankruptcy law. Where a bankrupt makes payment of money to certain creditors enabling them to obtain a greater percentage of their debts than other creditors in the same class, and the payment is made within four months prior to the filing of a bankruptcy petition, such payment constitutes illegal and voidable preference. An intention to prefer such creditors must be shown. An insolvent person may lawfully prefer one creditor to another, if done in good faith and without intent to defraud others.

Preferred stock: Stock that entitles the holder to dividends from earnings before the owners of common stock can receive a dividend.

Preponderance: Preponderance of the evidence means that evidence that in the judgment of the jurors is entitled to the greatest weight, which appears to be more credible, has greater force, and overcomes not only the opposing presumptions but also the opposing evidence.

Presenting bank:* Under Article 4—Bank Deposits and Collections, this is any bank presenting an item except a payor bank.

Presentment:* Under Article 3—Commercial Paper, "Presentment" is a demand for acceptance or payment made upon the maker, acceptor, drawee, or other payor by or on behalf of the holder.

Presumption:* "Presumed" means that the trier of fact must find the existence of the fact presumed unless and until evidence is introduced which would support a finding of its nonexistence.

Prima facie: The words literally mean "at first view." Thus, that which first appears seems to be true. A prima facie case is one that stands until contrary evidence is produced.

Privilege: A legal idea or concept of lesser significance than a right. An invitee has only a privilege to walk on another's land because such privilege may be revoked at will; whereas a person who has an easement to go on another's land has a right, created by a grant, which is an interest in land and cannot be revoked at will. To be exempt from jury service is a privilege.

Privity: Mutual and successive relationship to the same interest. Offeror and offeree, assignor and assignee, grantor and grantee are in privity. Privity of estate means that one takes title from another. In contract law, privity denotes parties in mutual legal relationship to each other by virtue of being promisees and promisors. At early common law, third-party beneficiaries and assignees were said to be not in "privity."

Probate: A court that handles the settlement of estates.

Proceeds:* Whatever is received when collateral or proceeds are sold, exchanged, collected or otherwise disposed of. The term also includes the account arising when the right to payment is earned under a contract right. Money, checks, and the like are "cash proceeds." All other proceeds are "non-cash proceeds."

Process: In a court proceeding, a process is an instrument issued by the court in the name of the state before or during the progress of the trial, under the seal of the court, directing an officer of the court to do, act, or cause some act to be done incidental to the trial.

Promise:* Under Article 3—Commercial Paper, it is an undertaking to pay, and must be more than an acknowledgment of an obligation.

Property: All those rights, powers, privileges, and immunities that one has concerning tangibles and intangibles. The term includes everything of value subject to ownership.

Proximate cause: The cause that sets other causes in operation. The responsible cause of an injury.

Proxy: Authority to act for another, used by absent stockholders or members of legislative bodies to have their votes cast by others.

Punitive damages: Damages by way of punishment allowed for an injury caused by a wrong that is willful and malicious.

Purchase:* This includes taking by sale, discount, negotiation, mortgage, pledge, lien, issue or re-issue, gift or any other voluntary transaction creating an interest in property.

Purchase-money security interest:* A security interest that is taken or retained by the seller of the collateral to secure all or part of its price; or taken by a person who by making advances or incurring an obligation gives value to enable the debtor to acquire rights in or the use of collateral if such value is in fact so used.

Quasi contract: The term *quasi contract* is used to define a situation where a legal duty arises that does not rest upon a promise but does involve the payment of money. In order to do justice by a legal fiction, the court enforces the duty as if a promise in fact exists. Thus, if A gives B money by mistake, A can compel B to return the money by an action in quasi contract.

Quiet title: A suit brought by the owner of real property for the purpose of bringing into court any person who claims an adverse interest in the property and requiring him to either establish his claim or be barred from asserting it thereafter. It may be said that the purpose is to remove "clouds" from the title.

Quitclaim: A deed that releases a right or interest in land but does not include any covenants of warranty. The grantor transfers only that which he has.

Quo warranto: A proceeding in court by which a governmental body tests or inquires into the authority or legality of the claim of any person to a public office, franchise, or privilege.

Ratification: The confirmation of one's own previous act or act of another: e.g., a principal may ratify the previous unauthorized act of his agent. B's agent, without authority, buys goods. B, by keeping the goods and receiving the benefits of the agent's act, ratifies the agency.

Real property: The term means land with all its buildings, appurtenances, equitable and legal interests therein. The word is used in contradistinction to personal property, which refers to movables or chattels.

Reasonable care: The care that prudent persons would exercise under the same circumstances.

Receiver: An officer of the court appointed on behalf of all parties to the litigation to take possession of, hold, and control the property involved in the suit, for the benefit of the party who will be determined to be entitled thereto.

Recoupment: A right to deduct from the plaintiff's claim any payment or loss that the defendant has suffered by reason of the plaintiff's wrongful act. The word means "a cutting back."

Redemption: To buy back, a debtor buys back or redeems his mortgaged property when he pays the debt.

Referee: A person to whom a cause pending in a court is referred by the court, to take testimony, hear the parties, and report thereon to the court.

Registered form:* A security is in registered form when it specifies a person entitled to the security or to the rights it evidences and when its transfer may be registered upon books maintained for that purpose by or on behalf of an issuer as security so states.

Reinsurance: In a contract of reinsurance, one insurance company agrees to indemnify another insurance company in whole or in part against risks that the first company has assumed. The original contract of insurance and the reinsurance contract are distinct contracts. There is no privity between the original insured and the reinsurer.

Release: The voluntary relinquishing of a right, lien, or any other obligation. A release need not be under seal, nor does it necessarily require consideration. The words *release, remise, and discharge* are often used together to mean the same thing.

Remand: To send back a cause for the appellate court to the lower court in order that the lower court may comply with the instructions of the appellate court. Also to return a prisoner to jail.

Remedy: The word is used to signify the judicial means or court procedures by which legal and equitable rights are enforced.

Remitting bank:* Under Article 4—Bank Deposits and Collections, is any payor or intermediary bank remitting for an item.

Replevin: A remedy given by statute for the recovery of the possession of a chattel. Only the right to possession can be tried in such action.

Res: A Latin word that means "thing."

Res adjudicata: The doctrine of *res adjudicata*

means that a controversy once having been decided or adjudged upon its merits is forever settled so far as the particular parties involved are concerned. Such a doctrine avoids vexatious lawsuits.

Rescission: (From *rescissio*) Rescission is where an act, valid in appearance, nevertheless conceals a defect, which may make it null and void, if demanded by any of the parties.

Respondent: One who answers another's bill or pleading, particularly in an equity case. Quite similar, in many instances, to defendant in law cases.

Respondeat superior: Latin words that mean the master is liable for the acts of his agent.

Responsible bidder: The word *responsible*, as used by most statutes concerning public works in the phrase "lowest responsible bidder," means that such bidder has the requisite skill, judgment, and integrity necessary to perform the contract involved and has the financial resources and ability to carry the task to completion.

Restraining order: An order issued by a court of equity in aid of a suit to hold matters in abeyance until parties may be heard. A temporary injunction is a restraining order.

Restraint of trade: Monopolies, combinations, and contracts that impede free competition are in restraint of trade.

Right: The phrase "legal right" is a correlative of the phrase "legal duty." One has a legal right if, upon the breach of the correlative legal duty, he can secure a remedy in a court of law.

Right of action: The words are synonymous with *cause of action*: a right to enforce a claim in a court.

Riparian: A person is a riparian owner if his land is situated beside a stream of water, either flowing over or along the border of the land.

Satisfaction: The term *satisfaction* in legal phraseology means the release and discharge of a legal obligation. Such satisfaction may be partial or full performance of the obligation. The word is used with *accord*. Accord means a promise to give a substituted performance for a contract obligation; satisfaction means the acceptance by the obligee of such performance.

Scienter: Knowledge by a defrauding party of the falsity of a representation. In a tort action of deceit, knowledge that a representation is false must be proved.

Seal: A seal is to show that an instrument was executed in a formal manner. At early common law, sealing legal documents was of great legal significance. A promise under seal was binding by virtue of the seal. Today under most statutes any stamp, wafer, mark, scroll, or impression made, adopted, and affixed, is adequate. The printed word "seal" or the letters "L.S." is sufficient.

Seasonably:* An action is taken "seasonably" when it is taken at or within the time agreed or if no time is agreed at or within a reasonable time.

Secondary party:* Under Article 3—Commercial Paper, this means a drawer or indorser.

Secured party:* A lender, seller, or other person in whose favor there is a security interest, including a person to whom accounts, contract rights, or chattel paper have been sold. When the holders of obligations issued under an indenture of trust, equipment trust agreement, or the like are represented by a trustee or other person, the representative is the secured party.

Security: Security may be bonds, stocks, and other property placed by a debtor with a creditor, with power to sell if the debt is not paid. The plural of the term, *securities*, is used broadly to mean tangible choses in action, such as promissory notes, bonds, stocks, and other vendible obligations.

Security:* An instrument that is issued in bearer form or registered form; and is of a type commonly dealt in upon securities exchanges or markets or commonly recognized in any area in which it is issued or dealt in as a medium for investment; and is either one of a class or series or by its terms is divisible into a class or series of instruments; and evidences a share, a participation or other interest in property or in an enterprise or evidences an obligation of the issuer.

648

Security agreement:* An agreement that creates or provides for a security interest.

Security interest:* This means an interest in personal property or fixtures that secures payment or performance of an obligation.

Sell: The words *to sell* mean to negotiate or make arrangement for a sale. A sale is an executed contract *Sell* is the name of the process in executing the contract.

Servant: A person employed by another and subject to the direction and control of the employer in performance of his duties.

Setoff: A matter of defense, called a cross-complaint, used by the defendant for the purpose of making a demand on the plaintiff and which arises out of contract but is independent and unconnected with the cause of action set out in the complaint. See *Counterclaims* and *Recoupment.*

Settle:* Under Article 4—Bank Deposits and Collections, this means to pay in cash, by clearinghouse settlement, in a charge or credit or by remittance, or otherwise as instructed. A settlement may be either provisional or final.

Severable contract: A contract in which the performance is divisible. Two or more parts may be set over against each other. Items and prices may be apportioned to each other without relation to the full performance of all of its parts.

Share of stock: A proportional part of the rights in the management and assets of a corporation. It is a chose in action. The certificate is the evidence of the share.

Situs: Situs means "place, situation." The place where a thing is located. The "situs" of personal property is the domicile of the owner. The "situs" of land is the state or county where it is located.

Slander: Slander is an oral utterance that tends to injure the reputation of another. See *Libel.*

Special appearance: The appearance in court of a person through his attorney for a limited purpose only. A court does not get jurisdiction over a person by special appearance.

Special verdict: A special verdict is one in which the jury finds the facts only, leaving it to the court to apply the law and draw the conclusion as to the proper disposition of the case.

Specific performance: A remedy in personam in equity that compels such substantial performance of a contract as will do justice among the parties. A person who fails to obey a writ for specific performance may be put in jail by the equity judge for contempt of court. Such remedy applies to contracts involving real property. In absence of unique goods or peculiar circumstances, damages generally are an adequate remedy for the breach of contracts involving personal property.

Stare decisis: Translated, the term means "stand by the decision." The law should adhere to decided cases. See *Precedent.*

Statute: A law passed by the legislative body of a state is a statute.

Stock dividend: The issue by a corporation of new shares of its own stock to its shareholders as dividends in order to transfer retained earnings to capital stock.

Stockholders: Those persons whose names appear on the books of a corporation as the owners of the shares of stock and who are entitled to participate in the management and control of the corporation.

Stock split: A readjustment of the financial plan of a corporation whereby each existing share of stock is split into new shares, usually with a lowering of par value.

Stock warrant: A certificate that gives to the holder thereof the right to subscribe for and purchase a given number of shares of stock in a corporation at a stated price.

Stoppage in transitu: The right of a seller of goods, which have not been paid for, upon learning of the insolvency of the buyer, to stop the goods in transit and hold the same as security for the purchase price. It is an extension of the unpaid seller's lien.

Subordinate: In the case of a mortgage or other security interest, the mortgagee may agree to make his mortgage inferior to another mortgage or interest.

Subpoena: A process issued out of a court requiring the attendance of a witness at a trial.

649

Subrogation: The substitution of one person in another's place, whether as a creditor or as the possessor of any lawful right, so that the substituted person may succeed to the rights, remedies, or proceeds of the claim. It rests in equity on the theory that, where a party is compelled to pay a debt for which another is liable, such payment should vest the paying party with all the rights the creditor has against the debtor. For example: X insurance company pays Y for an injury to Y's car by reason of X's negligent act. X insurance company will be subrogated to Y's cause of action against Z.

Subsequent purchaser:* A person who takes a security other than by original issue.

Substantial performance: The complete performance of all the essential elements of a contract. The only permissible omissions or derivations are those that are trivial, inadvertent, and inconsequential. Such performance will not justify repudiation. Compensation for defects may be substituted for actual performance.

Substantive law: A word applied to that law that regulates and controls the rights and duties of all persons in society. It is used in contradistinction to the term *adjective law*, which means the rules of court procedure or remedial law which prescribe the methods by which substantive law is enforced.

Succession: The word means the transfer by operation of law of all the rights and obligations of a deceased person to those who are entitled to take.

Summons: A writ issued by a court to the sheriff directing him to notify the defendant that the plaintiff claims to have a cause of action against the defendant and that he is required to answer. If the defendant does not answer, judgment will be taken by default.

Suspends payments:* Under Article 4—Bank Deposits and Collections, with respect to a bank this means that it has been closed by order of the supervisory authorities, that a public officer has been appointed to take it over, or that it ceases or refuses to make payments in the ordinary course of business.

Tangible: Tangible is a word used to describe property that is physical in character and capable of being moved. A debt is intangible, but a promissory note evidencing such debt is tangible. See *Chose in action, Chattel.*

Tenancy: The interest in property that a tenant acquired from a landlord by a lease is called a tenancy. It may be at will or for a term. It is an interest in land.

Tenant: The person to whom a lease is made. A lessee.

Tender: To offer money in satisfaction of a debt or obligation by producing the same and expressing to the creditor a willingness to pay.

Tender of delivery:* This means that the seller must put and hold conforming goods at the buyer's disposition and give the buyer any notification reasonably necessary to enable him to take delivery.

Testamentary capacity: A person is said to have testamentary capacity when he understands the nature of his business, the value of his property, knows those persons who are natural objects of his bounty, and comprehends the manner in which he has provided for the distribution of his property.

Testator: A male person who has died leaving a will. A female person is called a testatrix.

Testimony: Those statements made by a witness under oath or affirmation in a legal proceeding.

Title: This word has different meanings. It may be limited or broad in its meaning. When a person has the exclusive rights, powers, privileges, and immunities to property, real and personal, tangible and intangible, against all other persons, he may be said to have the complete title thereto. The aggregate of legal relations concerning property is the title. The term is used to describe the means by which a person exercises control and dominion over property. A trustee has a limited title. See *Possession.*

Tort: A wrongful act committed by one person against another person or his property. It is the breach of a legal duty imposed by law other than by contract. The word *tort* means "twisted" or "wrong." A assaults B, thus committing a tort. See *Right, Duty.*

Tortfeasor: One who commits a tort.

Trade fixtures: Personal property placed upon or annexed to leased land by a tenant for the purpose of carrying on a trade or business during the term of the lease. Such property is generally to be removed at the end of the term, providing it can be so removed without destruction or injury to the premises. Trade fixtures include showcases, shelving, racks, machinery, and the like.

Trademark: No complete definition can be given for a trademark. Generally it is any sign, symbol, mark, word, or arrangement of words in the form of a label adopted and used by a manufacturer or distributor to designate his particular goods, and which no other person has the legal right to use. Originally, the design or trademark indicated origin, but today it is used more as an advertising mechanism.

Transfer: In its broadest sense, the word means the act by which an owner sets over or delivers his right, title, and interest in property to another person. A "bill of sale" to personal property is evidence of a transfer.

Treason: The offense of attempting by overt acts to overthrow the government of the state to which the offender owes allegiance; or of betraying the state into the hands of a foreign power.

Treasury stock: Stock or a corporation that has been issued by the corporation for value but is later returned to the corporation by way of gift or purchase or otherwise. It may be returned to the trustees of a corporation for the purpose of sale.

Trespass: An injury to the person, property, or rights of another person committed by actual force and violence, or under such circumstances that the law will imply that the injury was caused by force or violence.

Trust: A relationship between persons by which one holds property for the use and benefit of another. The relationship is called fiduciary. Such rights are enforced in a court of equity. The person trusted is called a trustee. The person for whose benefit the property is held is called a beneficiary or "cestui que trust."

Trustee in bankruptcy: An agent of the court authorized to liquidate the assets of the bankrupt, protect them, and bring them to the court for final distribution for the benefit of the bankrupt and all the creditors.

Trustee (generally): A person who is entrusted with the management and control of another's property and estate. A person occupying a fiduciary position. An executor, an administrator, a guardian.

Ultra vires: Literally the words mean "beyond power." The acts of a corporation are ultra vires when they are beyond the power or capacity of the corporation as granted by the state in its charter.

Unauthorized:* Refers to a signature or indorsement made without actual, implied, or apparent authority and includes a forgery.

Unfair competition: The imitation by design of the goods of another for the purpose of palming them off on the public, thus misleading the public by inducing it to buy goods made by the imitator. It includes misrepresentation and deceit; thus, such conduct is fraudulent not only as to competitors but as to the public.

Unilateral contract: A promise for an act or an act for a promise, a single enforceable promise. A promises B $10 if B will mow A's lawn. B mows the lawn. A's promise now binding is a unilateral contract. See *Bilateral contract*.

Usage of trade:* Any practice or method of dealing having such regularity of observance in a place, vocation, or trade as to justify an expectation that it will be observed with respect to the transaction in question. The existence and scope of such a usage are to be proved as facts. If it is established that such a usage is embodied in a written trade code or similar writing, the interpretation of the writing is for the court.

Usurious: A contract is usurious if made for a loan of money at a rate of interest in excess of that permitted by statute.

Utter: The word means to "put out" or "pass off." To utter a check is to offer it to another in payment of a debt. The words *utter a forged writing* mean to put such writing in circulation, knowing of the falsity of the instrument with the intent to injure another.

Value:* Except as otherwise provided with respect to negotiable instruments and bank collections, a person gives "value" for rights if he acquires them (a) in return for a binding commitment to extend credit or for the extension of immediately available credit whether or not drawn upon and whether or not a chargeback is provided for in the event of difficulties in collection; or (b) as security for or in total or partial satisfaction of a preexisting claim; or (c) by accepting delivery pursuant to a preexisting contract for purchase; or (d) generally, in return for any consideration sufficient to support a simple contract.

Vendee: A purchaser of property. The term is generally applied to the purchaser of real property. The word *buyer* is usually applied to the purchaser of chattels.

Vendor: The seller of property. The term is usually applied to the seller of real property. The word *seller* is applied to the seller of personal property.

Vendor's lien: An unpaid seller's right to hold possession of property until he has recovered the purchase price.

Venire: To come into court, a writ used to summon potential jurors.

Venue: The geographical area over which a court presides. Venue designates the county in which the action is tried. Change of venue means a move to another county.

Verdict: The decision of a jury, reported to the court, on matters properly submitted to it for its consideration.

Void: That which has no legal effect. A contract that is void is a nullity and confers no rights or duties.

Voidable: That which is valid until one party, who has the power of avoidance, exercises such power. An infant has the power of avoidance of his contract. A defrauded party has the power to avoid his contract. Such contract is voidable.

Voir dire: This phrase denotes the preliminary examination of a prospective juror.

Voting trust: A device whereby two or more persons, owning stock, with voting powers, divorce voting rights thereof from ownership, retaining to all intents and purposes the latter in themselves and transferring the former to trustees in whom voting rights of all depositors in the trust are pooled.

Wager: A relationship between persons by which they agree that a certain sum of money or thing owned by one of them will be paid or delivered to the other upon the happening of an uncertain event, which event is not within the control of the parties and rests upon chance.

Waive (verb): To "waive" at law is to relinquish or give up intentionally a known right or to do an act that is inconsistent with the claiming of a known right.

Waiver (noun): The intentional relinquishment or giving up of a known right. It may be done by express words or conduct that involves any acts inconsistent with an intention to claim the right. Such conduct creates an estoppel on the part of the claimant. See *Estoppel.*

Warehouseman:* A person engaged in the business of storing goods for hire.

Warehouse receipt:* A receipt issued by a person engaged in the business of storing goods for hire.

Warehouse receipt: An instrument showing that the signer has in his possession certain described goods for storage, and which obligates the signer, the warehouseman, to deliver the goods to a specified person or to his order or bearer upon the return of the instrument. Consult Uniform Warehouse Receipts Act.

Warrant (noun): An order in writing in the name of the state and signed by a magistrate directed to an officer commanding him to arrest a person.

Warrant (verb): To guarantee, to answer for, to assure that a state of facts exists.

Warranty: An undertaking, either expressed or implied, that a certain fact regarding the subject matter of a contract is presently true or will be true. The word has particular application in the law of sales of chattels. The word relates to title and quality. The word should be distinguished from *guaranty,* which means a contract or promise by one

652

person to answer for the performance of another.

Waste: Damage to the real property so that its value as security is impaired.

Watered stock: Corporate stock issued by a corporation for property at an overvaluation, or stock issued for which the corporation receives nothing in payment therefor.

Will (testament): The formal instrument by which a person makes disposition of his property to take effect upon his death.

Working capital: The amount of cash necessary for the convenient and safe transaction of present business.

Writ: An instrument in writing under seal in the name of the state, issued out of a court of justice the commencement of, or during a legal proceeding, directed to an officer of the court commanding him to do some act, or requiring some person to do or refrain from doing some act pertinent or relative to the cause being tried.

Zoning ordinance: An ordinance passed by a city council by virtue of the police power which regulates and prescribes the kind of buildings, residences, or businesses that shall be built and used in different parts of a city.

UNIFORM COMMERCIAL CODE

UNIFORM COMMERCIAL CODE

AN ACT

To be known as the Uniform Commercial Code, Relating to Certain Commercial Transactions in or regarding Personal Property and Contracts and other Documents concerning them, including Sales, Commercial Paper, Bank Deposits and Collections, Letters of Credit, Bulk Transfers, Warehouse Receipts, Bills of Lading, other Documents of Title, Investment Securities, and Secured Transactions, including certain Sales of Accounts, Chattel Paper, and Contract Rights, Providing for Public Notice to Third Parties in Certain Circumstances; Regulating Procedure, Evidence and Damages in Certain Court Actions Involving such Transactions, Contracts or Documents; to Make Uniform the Law with Respect Thereto; and Repealing Inconsistent Legislation.

ARTICLE 1

GENERAL PROVISIONS

PART 1

SHORT TITLE, CONSTRUCTION, APPLICATION AND SUBJECT MATTER OF THE ACT

Section 1-101. Short Title. This act shall be known and may be cited as Uniform Commercial Code.

Section 1-102. Purposes; Rules of Construction; Variation by Agreement.

(1) This Act shall be liberally construed and applied to promote its underlying purposes and policies.

(2) Underlying purposes and policies of this Act are

(a) to simplify, clarify and modernize the law governing commercial transactions;

(b) to permit the continued expansion

of commercial practices through custom, usage and agreement of the parties;

(c) To make uniform the law among the various jurisdictions.

(3) The effect of provisions of this Act may be varied by agreement, except as otherwise provided in this Act and except that the obligations of good faith, diligence, reasonableness and care prescribed by this Act may not be disclaimed by agreement but the parties may by agreement determine the standards by which the performance of such obligations is to be measured if such standards are not manifestly unreasonable.

(4) The presence in certain provisions of this Act of the words "unless otherwise agreed" or words of similar import does not imply that the effect of other provisions may not be varied by agreement under subsection (3).

(5) In this Act unless the context otherwise requires

(a) words in the singular number include the plural, and in the plural include the singular;

(b) words of the masculine gender include the feminine and the neuter, and when the sense so indicates the words of the neuter gender may refer to any gender.

Section 1-103. Supplementary General Principles of Law Applicable. Unless displaced by the particular provisions of this Act, the principles of law and equity, including the law merchant and the law relative to capacity to contract, principal and agent, estoppel, fraud, misrepresentation, duress, coercion, mistake, bankruptcy, or other validating or invalidating cause shall supplement its provisions.

Section 1-104. Construction Against Implicit Repeal. This Act being a general act intended as a unified coverage of its subject matter, no part of it shall be deemed to be impliedly repealed by subsequent legislation if such construction can reasonable be avoided.

Section 1-105. Territorial Application of the Act; Parties' Power to Choose Applicable Law.

(1) Except as provided hereafter in this section, when a transaction bears a reasonable relation to this state and also to another state or nation the parties may agree that the law either of this state or of such other state or nation shall govern their rights and duties. Failing such agreement this Act applies to transactions bearing an appropriate relation to this state.

(2) Where one of the following provisions of this Act specifies the applicable law, that provision governs and a contrary agreement is effective only to the extent permitted by the law (including the conflict of laws rules) so specified:

Rights of creditors against sold goods. Section 2-402.

Applicability of the Article on Bank Deposits and Collections. Section 4-102.

Bulk transfers subject to the Article on Bulk Transers. Section 6-102.

Applicability of the Article on Investment Securities. Section 8-106.

Policy and scope of the Article on Secured Transactions. Sections 9-102 and 9-103.

Section 1-106. Remedies to be Liberally Administered.

(1) The remedies provided by this Act shall be liberally administered to the end that the aggrieved party may be put in as good a position as if the other party had fully performed but neither consequential or special nor penal damages may be had except as specifically provided in this Act or by other rule of law.

(2) Any right or obligation declared by this Act is enforceable by action unless the provision declaring it specifies a different and limited effect.

Section 1-107. Waiver or Renunciation of Claim or Right After Breach. Any claim or right arising out of an alleged breach can be discharged in whole or in part without consideration by a written waiver or renunciation signed and delivered by the aggrieved party.

Section 1-108. Severability. If any provision or clause of this Act or application thereof to any person or circumstances is held invalid, such invalidity shall not affect other provisions or applications of the Act which can be given effect without the invalid provisions or application, and to this end the provisions of this Act are declared to be severable.

PART 2

GENERAL DEFINITIONS AND PRINCIPLES OF INTERPRETATION

Section 1-201. General Definition. Subject to additional definitions contained in the subsequent Articles of this Act which are applicable to specific Articles or Parts thereof, and unless the context otherwise requires, in this Act:

(1) "Action" in the sense of a judicial proceeding includes recoupment, counterclaim, set-off, suit in equity and any other proceedings in which rights are determined.

(2) "Aggrieved party" means a party entitled to resort to a remedy.

(3) "Agreement" means the bargain of the parties in fact as found in their language or by implication from other circumstances including course of dealing or usage of trade or course of performance as provided in this Act (Sections 1-205 and 2-208). Whether an agreement has legal consequences is determined by the provisions of this Act, if applicable; otherwise by the law of contracts (Section 1-103). (Compare "Contract.")

(4) "Bank" means any person engaged in the business of banking.

(5) "Bearer" means the person in possession of an instrument, document of title, or security payable to bearer or indorsed in blank.

(6) "Bill of lading" means a document evidencing the receipt of goods for shipment issued by a person engaged in the business of transporting or forwarding goods, and includes an airbill. "Airbill" means a document serving for air transportation as a bill of lading does for marine or rail transportation, and includes an air consignment note or air waybill.

(7) "Branch" includes a separately incorporated foreign branch of a bank.

(8) "Burden of establishing" a fact means the burden of persuading the triers of fact that the existence of the fact is more probable than its non-existence.

(9) "Buyer in ordinary course of business" means a person who in good faith and without knowledge that the sale to him is in violation of the ownership rights or security interest of a third party in the goods buys in ordinary course from a person in the business of selling goods of that kind but does not include a pawnbroker. "Buying" may be for cash or by exchange of other property or on secured or unsecured credit and includes receiving goods or documents of title under a pre-existing contract for sale but does not include a transfer in bulk or as security for or in total or partial satisfaction of a money debt.

(10) "Conspicuous": a term or clause is conspicuous when it is so written that a reasonable person against whom it is to operate ought to have noticed it. A printed heading in capitals (as: NON-NEGOTIABLE BILL OF LADING) is conspicuous. Language in the body of a form is "conspicuous" if it is in larger or other contrasting type or color. But in a telegram any stated term is "conspicuous." Whether a term or clause is "conspicuous" or not is for decision by the court.

(11) "Contract" means the total legal obligation which results from the parties' agreement as affected by this Act and any other applicable rules of law. (Compare "Agreement.")

(12) "Creditor" includes a general creditor, a secured creditor, a lien creditor and any representative of creditors, including an assignee for the benefit of creditors, a trustee in bankruptcy, a receiver in equity and an executor or administrator of an insolvent debtor's or assignor's estate.

(13) "Defendant" includes a person in the position of defendant in a cross-action or counterclaim.

(14) "Delivery" with respect to instruments, documents of title, chattel paper or securities means voluntary transfer of possession.

(15) "Document of title" includes bill of lading, dock warrant, dock receipt, warehouse receipt or order for the delivery of goods, and also any other document which

in the regular course of business or financing is treated as adequately evidencing that the person in possession of it is entitled to receive, hold and dispose of the document and the goods it covers. To be a document of title a document must purport to be issued by or addressed to a bailee and purport to cover goods in the bailee's possession which are either identified or are fungible portions of an identified mass.

(16) "Fault" means wrongful act, omission or breach.

(17) "Fungible" with respect to goods or securities means goods or securities of which any unit is, by nature or usage of trade, the equivalent of any other like unit. Goods which are not fungible shall be deemed fungible for the purposes of this Act to the extent that under a particular agreement or document unlike units are treated as equivalents.

(18) "Genuine" means free of forgery or counterfeiting.

(19) "Good faith" means honesty in fact in the conduct or transaction concerned.

(20) "Holder" means a person who is in possession of a document of title or an instrument or an investment security drawn, issued or indorsed to him or to his order or to bearer or in blank.

(21) To "honor" is to pay or to accept and pay, or where a credit so engages to purchase or discount a draft complying with the terms of the credit.

(22) "Insolvency proceedings" includes any assignment for the benefit of creditors or other proceedings intended to liquidate or rehabilitate the estate of the person involved.

(23) A person is "insolvent" who either has ceased to pay his debts in the ordinary course of business or cannot pay his debts as they become due or is insolvent within the meaning of the federal bankruptcy law.

(24) "Money" means a medium of exchange authorized or adopted by a domestic or foreign government as a part of its currency.

(25) A person has "notice" of a fact when
(a) he has actual knowledge of it; or
(b) he has received a notice or notification of it; or
(c) from all the facts and circumstances known to him at the time in question he has reason to know that it exists.

A person "knows" or had "knowledge" of a fact when he has actual knowledge of it. "Discover" or "learn" or a word or phrase of similar import refers to knowledge rather than to reason to know. The time and circumstances under which a notice or notification may cease to be effective are not determined by this Act.

(26) A person "notifies" or "gives" a notice or notification to another by taking such steps as may be reasonably required to inform the other person in ordinary course whether or not such other actually comes to know of it. A person "receives" a notice or notification when
(a) it comes to his attention; or
(b) it is duly delivered at the place of business through which the contract was made or at any other place held out by him as the place for receipt of such communications.

(27) Notice, knowledge or a notice or notification received by an organization is effective for a particular transaction from the time when it is brought to the attention of the individual conducting that transaction, and in any event from the time when it would have been brought to his attention if the organization had exercised due diligence. An organization exercises due diligence if it maintains reasonable routines for communicating significant information to the person conducting the transaction and there is reasonable compliance with the routines. Due diligence does not require an individual acting for the organization to communicate information unless such communication is part of his regular duties or unless he has reason to know of the transaction and that the transaction would be materially affected by the information.

(28) "Organization" includes a corporation, government or governmental subdivision or agency, business trust, estate, trust, partnership or association, two or more persons having a joint or common interest, or any other legal or commercial entity.

(29) "Party," as distinct from "third party," means a person who has engaged in a transaction or made an agreement within this Act.

(30) "Person" includes an individual or an organization (See Section 1-102).

(31) "Presumption" or "presumed" means that the trier of fact must find the existence of the fact presumed unless and until evi-

dence is introduced which would support a finding of its non-existence.

(32) "Purchase" includes taking by sale, discount, negotiation, mortgage, pledge, lien, issue or re-issue, gift or any other voluntary transaction creating an interest in property.

(33) "Purchaser" means a person who takes by purchase.

(34) "Remedy" means any remedial right to which an aggrieved party is entitled with or without resort to a tribunal.

(35) "Representative" includes an agent, an officer of a corporation or association, and a trustee, executor or administrator of an estate, or any other person empowered to act for another.

(36) "Rights" includes remedies.

(37) "Security interest" means an interest in personal property or fixtures which secures payment or performance of an obligation. The retention or reservation of title by a seller or goods notwithstanding shipment or delivery to the buyer (Section 2-401) is limited in effect to a reservation of a "security interest." The term also includes any interest of a buyer of accounts, chattel paper, or contract rights which is subject to Article 9. The special property interest of a buyer of goods on identification or such goods to a contract for sale under Section 2-401 is not a "security interest," but a buyer may also acquire a "security interest" by complying with Article 9. Unless a lease or consignment is intended as security, reservation of title thereunder is not a "security interest" but a consignment is in any event subject to the provisions on consignment sales (Section 2-326). Whether a lease is intended as security is to be determined by the facts of each case; however (a) the inclusion of an option to purchase does not of itself make the lease one intended for security, and (b) an agreement that upon compliance with the terms of the lease the lessee shall become or has the option to become the owner of the property for no additional consideration or for a nominal consideration does make the lease one intended for security.

(38) "Send" in connection with any writing or notice means to deposit in the mail or deliver for transmission by any other usual means of communication with postage or cost of transmission provided for and properly addressed and in the case of an instrument to an address specified thereon or otherwise agreed, or if there be none to any address reasonable under the circumstances. The receipt of any writing or notice within the time at which it would have arrived if properly sent has the effect of a proper sending.

(39) "Signed" includes any symbol executed or adopted by a party with present intention to authenticate a writing.

(40) "Surety" includes guarantor.

(41) "Telegram" includes a message transmitted by radio, teletype, cable, any mechanical method of transmission, or the like.

(42) "Term" means that portion of an agreement which relates to a particular matter.

(43) "Unauthorized" signature or indorsement means one made without actual, implied or apparent authority and includes a forgery.

(44) "Value." Except as otherwise provided with respect to negotiable instruments and bank collections (Sections 3-303, 4-208 and 4-209) a person gives "value" for rights if he acquires them

(a) in return for a binding commitment to extend credit or for the extension of immediately available credit whether or not drawn upon and whether or not a charge-back is provided for in the event of difficulties in collection; or

(b) as security for or in total or partial satisfaction of a pre-existing claim; or

(c) by accepting delivery pursuant to a pre-existing contract for purchase; or

(d) generally, in return for any consideration sufficient to support a simple contract.

(45) "Warehouse receipt" means a receipt issued by a person engaged in the business of storing goods for hire.

(46) "Written" or "writing" includes printing, typewriting or any other intentional reduction to tangible form.

Section 1-202. Prima Facie Evidence by Third Party Documents. A document in due form purporting to be a bill of lading, policy or certificate of insurance, official weigher's or inspector's certificate, consular invoice, or any other document authorized or required by the contract to be issued by a third party shall be prima facie evidence of its own authenticity and genuineness and of the facts stated in the document by the third party.

Section 1-203. Obligation of Good Faith. Every contract or duty within this Act imposes an obligation of good faith in its performance or enforcement.

Section 1-204. Time; Reasonable Time; "Seasonably."

(1) Whenever this Act requires any action to be taken within a reasonable time, any time which is not manifestly unreasonable may be fixed by agreement.

(2) What is a reasonable time for taking any action depends on the nature, purpose and circumstances of such action.

(3) An action is taken "seasonably" when it is taken at or within the time agreed or if no time is agreed at or within a reasonable time.

Section 1-205. Course of Dealing and Usage of Trade.

(1) A course of dealing in a sequence of previous conduct between the parties to a particular transaction which is fairly to be regarded as establishing a common basis of understanding for interpreting their expressions and other conduct.

(2) A usage of trade is any practice or method of dealing having such regularity of observance in a place, vocation or trade as to justify an expectation that it will be observed with respect to the transaction in question. The existence and scope of such a usage are to be proved as facts. If it is established that such a usage is embodied in a written trade code or similar writing the interpretation of the writing is for the court.

(3) A course of dealing between parties and any usage of trade in the vocation or trade in which they are engaged or of which they are or should be aware give particular meaning to and supplement or qualify terms of an agreement.

(4) The express terms of an agreement and an applicable course of dealing or usage of trade shall be construed wherever reasonable as consistent with each other; but wher such construction is unreasonable express terms control both course of dealirg and

usage of trade and course of dealing controls usage of trade.

(5) An applicable usage of trade in the place where any part of performance is to occur shall be used in interpreting the agreement as to that part of the performance.

(6) Evidence of a relevant usage of trade offered by one party is not admissible unless and until he has given the other party such notice as the court finds sufficient to prevent unfair surprise to the latter.

Section 1-206. Statute of Frauds for Kinds of Personal Property Not Otherwise Covered.

(1) Except in the cases described in subsection (2) of this section a contract for the sale of personal property is not enforceable by way of action or defense beyond five thousand dollars in amount or value of remedy unless there is some writing which indicates that a contract for sale has been made between the parties at a defined or stated price, reasonably identifies the subject matter, and is signed by the party against whom enforcement is sought or by his authorized agent.

(2) Subsection (1) of this section does not apply to contracts for the sale of goods (Section 2-201) nor of securities (Section 8-319) nor to security agreements (Section 9-203).

Section 1-207. Performance or Acceptance under Reservation of Rights. A party who with explicit reservation of rights performs or promises performance or assents to performance in a manner demanded or offered by the other party does not thereby prejudice the rights reserved. Such words as "without prejudice," "under protect" or the like are sufficient.

Section 1-208. Option to Accelerate at Will. A term providing that one party or his successor in interest may accelerate payment of performance or require collateral or additional collateral "at will" or "when he deems himself insecure" or in words of similar import shall be construed to mean that he shall have power to do so only if he in good faith believes that the prospect of payment or performance is impaired. The burden of establishing lack of good faith is on the party against whom the power has been exercised.

ARTICLE 2

SALES

PART 1

SHORT TITLE, GENERAL CONSTRUCTION AND SUBJECT MATTER

Section 2-101. Short Title. This Article shall be known and may be cited as Uniform Commercial Code—Sales.

Section 2-102. Scope; Certain Security and Other Transactions Excluded from this Article. Unless the context otherwise requires, this Article applies to transactions in goods; it does not apply to any transaction which although in the form of an unconditional contract to sell or present sale is intended to operate only as a security transaction nor does this Article impair or repeal any statute regulating sales to consumers, farmers or other specified classes of buyers.

Section 2-103. Definitions and Index of Definitions.

(1) In this Article unless the context otherwise requires

(a) "Buyer" means a person who buys or contracts to buy goods.

(b) "Good faith" in the case of a merchant means honesty in fact and the observance of reasonable commercial standards of fair dealing in the trade.

(c) "Receipt" of goods means taking physical possession of them.

(d) "Seller" means a person who sells or contracts to sell goods.

(2) Other definitions applying to this Article or to specified parts thereof, and the sections in which they appear are:

"Acceptance." Section 2-606.
"Banker's credit." Section 2-325.
"Between merchants." Section 2-104.
"Cancellation." Section 2-106(4)
"Commercial unit." Section 2-105.
"Confirmed credit." Section 2-325.
"Conforming to contract." Section 2-106.
"Contract for sale." Section 2-106.
"Cover." Section 2-712.

"Entrusting." Section 2-403.
"Financing agency." Section 2-104.
"Future goods." Section 2-105.
"Goods." Section 2-105.
"Identification." Section 2-501.
"Installment contract." Section 2-612.
"Letter of Credit." Section 2-325.
"Lot." Section 2-105.
"Merchant." Section 2-104.
"Overseas." Section 2-323.
"Person on position of seller." Section 2-707.
"Present sale." Section 2-106.
"Sale." Section 2-106.
"Sale on approval." Section 2-326.
"Sale or return." Section 2-326.
"Termination." Section 2-106.

(3) The following definitions in other Articles apply to this Article:

"Check." Section 3-204.
"Consignee." Section 7-102.
"Consignor." Section 7-102.
"Consumer goods." Section 9-109.
"Dishonor." Section 3-507.
"Draft." Section 3-104.

(4) In addition Article 1 contains general definitions and principles of construction and interpretation applicable throughout this Article.

Section 2-104. Definitions: "Merchant"; "Between Merchants"; Financing Agency."

(1) "Merchant" means a person who deals in goods of the kind or otherwise by his occupation holds himself out as having knowledge or skill peculiar to the practices or goods involved in the transaction or to whom such knowledge or skill may be attributed by his employment of an agent or broker or other intermediary who by his occupation holds himself out as having such knowledge or skill.

(2) "Financing agency" means a bank, finance company or other person who in the ordinary course of business makes advances against goods or documents of title or who by arrangement with either the seller or the buyer intervenes in ordinary course to make or collect payment due or claimed under the contract for sale, as by purchasing or paying the seller's draft or making advances against it or by merely taking it for collection whether or not documents of title accompany the draft. "Financing agency" includes also a bank or other person who similarly intervenes between persons who are in the position of seller and buyer in respect to the goods (Section 2-707).

(3) "Between merchants" means in any transaction with respect to which both parties are chargeable with the knowledge or skill of merchants.

Section 2-105. Definitions: Transferability; "Goods"; "Future" Goods; "Lot"; "Commercial Unit."

(1) "Goods" means all things (including specially ·manufactured goods) which are movable at the time of identification to the contract for sale other than the money in which the price is to be paid, investment securities (Article 8) and things in action. "Goods" also includes the unborn young of animals and growing crops and other identified things attached to realty as described in the section on goods to be severed from realty (Section 2-107).

(2) Goods must be both existing and identified before any interest in them can pass. Goods which are not both existing and identified are "future" goods. A purported present sale of future goods or of any interest therein operates as a contract to sell.

(3) There may be a sale or a part interest in existing identified goods.

(4) An undivided share in an identified bulk of fungible goods is sufficiently identified to be sold although the quantity of the bulk is not determined. Any agreed proportion of such a bulk or any quantity thereof agreed upon by number, weight or other measure may to the extent of the seller's interest in the bulk be sold to the buyer who then becomes an owner in common.

(5) "Lot" means a parcel or a single article which is the subject matter of a separate sale or delivery, whether or not it is usfficient to perform the contract.

(6) "Commercial unit" means such a unit of goods as by commercial usage is a single whole for purposes of sale and division of which materially impairs its character or value on the market or in use. A commercial unit may be a single article (as a machine) or a set of articles (as a suite of furniture or an assortment of sizes) or a quantity (as a bale, gross, or carload) or any other unit treated in use or in the relevant market as a single whole.

Section 2-106. Definitions: "Contract"; "Agreement"; "Contract for Sale"; "Sale"; "Present Sale"; "Conforming" to Contract; "Termination"; "Cancellation."

(1) In this Article unless the context otherwise requires "contract" and "agreement" are limited to those relating to the present or future sale of goods. "Contract for sale" includes both a present sale of goods and a contract to sell goods at a future time. A "sale" consists in the passing of title from the seller to the buyer for a price (Section 2–401). A "present sale" means a sale which is accomplished by the making of the contract.

(2) Goods or conduct including any part of a performance are "conforming" or conform to the contract when they are in accordance with the obligations under the contract.

(3) "Termination" occurs when either party pursuant to a power created by agreement or law puts an end to the contract otherwise than for its breach. On "termination" all obligations which are still executory on both sides are discharged but any right based on prior breach or performance survives.

(4) "Cancellation" occurs when either party puts an end to the contract for breach by the other and its effect is the same as that of "termination" except that the cancelling party also retains any remedy for breach of the whole contract or any unperformed balance.

Section 2-107. Goods to be Severed from Realty: Recording.

(1) A contract for the sale of timber, minerals or the like or a structure or its materials to be removed from realty is a contract for the sale of goods within this Article if they are to be severed by the seller, but until severance a purported present sale thereof which is not effective as

a transfer of an interest in land is effective only as a contract to sell.

(2) A contract for the sale apart from the land of growing crops or other things attached to realty and capable of severance without material harm thereto but not described in subsection (1) is a contract for the sale of goods within this Article whether the subject matter is to be severed by the buyer or by the seller even though it forms part of the realty at the time of contracting, and the parties can by identification effect a present sale before severance.

(3) The provisions of this section are subject to any third party rights provided by the law relating to realty records, and the contract for sale may be executed and recorded as a document transferring an interest in land and shall then constitute notice to third parties of the buyer's rights under the contract for sale.

PART 2

FORM, FORMATION AND READJUSTMENT OF CONTRACT

Section 2-201. Formal Requirements; Statute of Frauds.

(1) Except as otherwise provided in this section a contract for the sale of goods for the price of $500 or more is not enforceable by way of action or defense unless there is some writing sufficient to indicate that a contract for sale has been made between the parties and signed by the party against whom enforcement is sought or by his authorized agent or broker. A writing is not insufficient because it omits or incorrectly states a term agreed upon but the contract is not enforceable under this paragraph beyond the quantity of goods shown in such writing.

(2) Between merchants if within a reasonable time a written confirmation of the contract and sufficient against the sender is received and the party receiving it has reason to know its contents, it satisfies the requirements of subsection (1) against such party unless written notice of objection to its contents is given within ten days after it is received.

(3) A contract which does not satisfy the requirements of subsection (1) but which is valid in other respects is enforceable

(a) if the goods are to be specially manufactured for the buyer and are not suitable for sale to others in the ordinary course of the seller's business and the seller, before notice of repudiation is received and under circumstances which reasonably indicate that the goods are for the buyer, has made either a substantial beginning of their manufacture or commitments for their procurement; or

(b) if the party against whom enforcement is sought admits in his pleading, testimony or otherwise in court that a contract for sale was made, but the contract is not enforceable under this provision beyond the quantity of goods admitted; or

(c) with respect to goods for which payment has been made and accepted or which have been received and accepted (Sec. 2-606).

Section 2-202. Final Written Expression: Parol or Extrinsic Evidence.

Terms with respect to which the confirmatory memoranda of the parties agree or which are otherwise set forth in a writing intended by the parties as a final expression of their agreement with respect to such terms as are included therein may not be contradicted by evidence of any prior agreement or of a contemporaneous oral agreement but may be explained or supplemented.

(a) by course of dealing or usage of trade (Section 1-205) or by course of performance (Section 2-208); and

(b) by evidence of consistent additional terms unless the court finds the writing to have been intended also as a complete and exclusive statement of the terms of the agreement.

Section 2-203. Seals Inoperative.

The affixing of a seal to a writing evidencing a contract for sale or an offer to buy or sell goods does not constitute the writing a sealed instrument and the law with respect to sealed instruments does not apply to such a contract or offer.

Section 2-204. Formation in General.

(1) A contract for sale of goods may be made in any manner sufficient to show agreement, including conduct by both

663

parties which recognizes the existence of such a contract.

(2) An agreement sufficient to constitute a contract for sale may be found even though the moment of its making is undetermined.

(3) Even though one or more terms are left open a contract for sale does not fail for indefiniteness if the parties have intended to make a contract and there is a reasonably certain basis for giving an appropriate remedy.

Section 2-205. Firm Offers. An offer by a merchant to buy or sell goods in a signed writing which by its terms gives assurance that it will be held open is not revocable, for lack of consideration, during the time stated or if no time is stated for a reasonable time, but in no event may such period of irrevocability exceed three months; but any such term of assurance on a form supplied by the offeree must be separately signed by the offeror.

Section 2-206. Offer and Acceptance in Formation of Contract.

(1) Unless otherwise unambiguously indicated by the language or circumstances

(a) an offer to make a contract shall be construed as inviting acceptance in any manner and by any medium reasonable in the circumstances;

(b) an order or other offer to buy goods for prompt or current shipment shall be construed as inviting acceptance either by a prompt promise to ship or by the prompt or current shipment of conforming or non-conforming goods, but such a shipment of non-conforming goods does not constitute an acceptance if the seller reasonably notifies the buyer that the shipment is offered only as an accommodation to the buyer.

(2) Where the beginning of a requested performance is a reasonable mode of acceptance an offeror who is not notified of acceptance within a reasonable time may treat the offer as having lapsed before acceptance.

Section 2-207. Additional Terms in Acceptance or Confirmation.

(1) A definite and seasonable expression of acceptance or a written confirmation which is sent within a reasonable time operates as an acceptance even though it states terms additional to or different from those offered or agreed upon, unless acceptance is expressly made conditional on assent to the additional or different terms.

(2) The additional terms are to be construed as proposals for addition to the contract. Between merchants such terms become part of the contract unless:

(a) the offer expressly limits acceptance to the terms of the offer;

(b) they materially alter it; or

(c) notification of objection to them has already been given or is given within a reasonable time after notice of them is received.

(3) Conduct by both parties which recognizes the existence of a contract is sufficient to establish a contract for sale although the writings of the parties do not otherwise establish a contract. In such case the terms of the particular contract consist of those terms on which the writings of the parties agree, together with any supplementary terms incorporated under any other provisions of this Act.

Section 2-208. Course of Performance or Practical Construction.

(1) Where the contract for sale involves repeated occasions for performance by either party with knowledge of the nature of the performance and opportunity for objection to it by the other, any course of performance accepted or acquiesced in without objection shall be relevant to determine the meaning of the agreement.

(2) The express terms of the agreement and any such course of performance, as well as any course of dealing and usage of trade, shall be construed whenever reasonable as consistent with each other; but when such construction is unreasonable, express terms shall control course of performance and course of performance shall control both course of dealing and usage of trade (Section 1-205).

(3) Subject to the provisions of the next section on modification and waiver, such course of performance shall be relevant to show a waiver or modification of any term inconsistent with such course of performance.

Section 2-209. Modification, Rescission and Waiver.

(1) An agreement modifying a contract within this Article needs no consideration to be binding.

(2) A signed agreement which excludes modification or rescission except by a signed writing cannot be otherwise modified or rescinded, but except as between merchants such a requirement on a form supplied by the merchant must be separately signed by the other party.

(3) The requirements of the statute of frauds section of this Article (Section 2-201) must be satisfied if the contract as modified is within its provisions.

(4) Although an attempt at modification or rescission does not satisfy the requirements of subsection (2) or (3) it can operate as a waiver.

(5) A party who has made a waiver affecting an executory portion of the contract may retract the waiver by reasonable notification received by the other party that strict performance will be required of any term waived, unless the retraction would be unjust in view of a material change of position in reliance on the waiver.

Section 2-210. Delegation of Performance; Assignment of Rights.

(1) A party may perform his duty through a delegate unless otherwise agreed or unless the other party has a substantial interest in having his original promisor perform or control the acts required by the contract. No delegation of performance relieves the party delegating of any duty to perform or any liability for breach.

(2) Unless otherwise agreed all rights of either seller or buyer can be assigned except where the assignment would materially change the duty of the other party, or increase materially the burden or risk imposed on him by his contract, or impair materially his chance of obtaining return performance. A right to damages for breach of the whole contract or a right arising out of the assignor's due performance of his entire obligation can be assigned despite agreement otherwise.

(3) Unless the circumstances indicate the contrary a prohibition of assignment of "the contract" is to be construed as barring only the delegation to the assignee of the assignor's performance.

(4) An assignment of "the contract" or of "all my rights under the contract" or an assignment in similar general terms is an assignment of rights and unless the language or the circumstances (as in an assignment for security) indicate the contrary, it is a delegation of performance of the duties of the assignor and its acceptance by the assignee constitutes a promise by him to perform those duties. This promise is enforceable by either the assignor or the other party to the original contract.

(5) The other party may treat any assignment which delegates performance as creating reasonable grounds for insecurity and may without prejudice to his rights against the assignor demand assurances from the assignee (Section 2-609).

PART 3

GENERAL OBLIGATION AND CONSTRUCTION OF CONTRACT

Section 2-301. General Obligations of Parties. The obligation of the seller is to transfer and deliver and that of the buyer is to accept and pay in accordance with the contract.

Section 2-302. Unconscionable Contract or Clause.

(1) If the court as a matter of law finds the contract or any clause of the contract to have been unconscionable at the time it was made the court may refuse to enforce the contract, or it may enforce the remainder of the contract without the unconscionable clause, or it may so limit the application of any unconscionable clause as to avoid any unconscionable result.

(2) When it is claimed or appears to the court that the contract or any clause thereof may be unconscionable the parties shall be afforded a reasonable opportunity to present evidence as to its commercial setting, purpose and effect to aid the court in making the determination.

Section 2-303. Allocation or Division of Risks. Where this Article allocates a risk or a burden as between the parties "unless otherwise agreed," the agreement may not only shift the allocation but may also divide the risk or burden.

Section 2-304. Price Payable in Money, Goods, Realty, or Otherwise.

(1) The price can be made payable in

money or otherwise. If it is payable in whole or in part in goods each party is a seller of the goods which he is to transfer.

(2) Even though all or part of the price is payable in an interest in realty the transfer of the goods and the seller's obligations with reference to them are subject to this Article, but not the transfer of the interest in realty or the transferor's obligations in connection therewith.

Section 2-305. Open Price Term.

(1) The parties if they so intend can conclude a contract for sale even though the price is not settled. In such a case the price is a reasonable price at the time for delivery if

(a) nothing is said as to price; or

(b) the price is left to be agreed by the parties and they fail to agree; or

(c) the price is to be fixed in terms of some agreed market or other standard as set or recorded by a third person or agency and it is not so set or recorded.

(2) A price to be fixed by the seller or by the buyer means a price for him to fix in good faith.

(3) When a price left to be fixed otherwise than by agreement of the parties fails to be fixed through fault of one party the other may at his option treat the contract as cancelled or himself fix a reasonable price.

(4) Where, however, the parties intend not to be bound unless the price be fixed or agreed and it is not fixed or agreed there is no contract. In such a case the buyer must return any goods already received or if unable to do so must pay their reasonable value at the time of delivery and the seller must return any portion of the price paid on account.

Section 2-306. Output, Requirements and Exclusive Dealings.

(1) A term which measures the quantity by the output of the seller or the requirements of the buyer means such actual output or requirements as may occur in good faith, except that no quantity unreasonably disproportionate to any stated estimate or in the absence of a stated estimate to any normal or otherwise comparable prior output or requirements may be tendered or demanded.

(2) A lawful agreement by either the seller or the buyer for exclusive dealing in the kind of goods concerned imposes unless otherwise agreed an obligation by the seller to use best efforts to supply the goods and by the buyer to use best efforts to promote their sale.

Section 2-307. Delivery in Single Lot or Several Lots.

Unless otherwise agreed all goods called for by a contract for sale must be tendered in a single delivery and payment is due only on such tender but where the circumstances give either party the right to make or demand delivery in lots the price if it can be apportioned may be demanded for each lot.

Section 2-308. Absence of Specified Place for Delivery.

Unless otherwise agreed.

(a) the place for delivery of goods is the seller's place of business or if he has none his residence; but

(b) in a contract for sale of identified goods which to the knowledge of the parties at the time of contracting are in some other place, that place is the place for their delivery; and

(c) documents of title may be delivered through customary banking channels.

Section 2-309. Absence of Specific Time Provisions; Notice of Termination.

(1) The time for shipment or delivery or any other action under a contract if not provided in this Article or agreed upon shall be a reasonable time.

(2) Where the contract provides for successive performances but is indefinite in duration it is valid for a reasonable time but unless otherwise agreed may be terminated at any time by either party.

(3) Termination of a contract by one party except on the happening of an agreed event requires that reasonable notification is invalid if its operation would be unconscionable.

Section 2-310. Open Time for Payment or Running of Credit; Authority to Ship under Reservation.

Unless otherwise agreed

(a) payment is due at the time and place at which the buyer is to receive the goods even though the place of shipment is the place of delivery; and

(b) if the seller is authorized to send the goods he may ship them under reservation, and may tender the documents of title, but the buyer may inspect the goods after their arrival before payment is due unless such inspection is inconsistent with the terms of the contract (Section 2-513); and

(c) if delivery is authorized and made by way of documents of title otherwise than by subsection (b) then payment is due at the time and place at which the buyer is to receive the documents regardless of where the goods are to be received; and

(d) where the seller is required or authorized to ship the goods on credit the credit period runs from the time of shipment but post-dating the invoice or delaying its dispatch will correspondingly delay the starting of the credit period.

Section 2-311. Options and Cooperation Respecting Performance.

(1) An agreement for sale which is otherwise sufficiently definite (subsection (3) of Section 2-204) to be a contract is not made invalid by the fact that it leaves particulars of performance to be specified by one of the parties. Any such specification must be made in good faith and within limits set by commercial reasonableness.

(2) Unless otherwise agreed specifications relating to assortment of the goods are at the buyer's option and except as otherwise provided in subsections (1) (c) and (3) of Section 2-319 specifications or arrangements relating to shipment are at the seller's option.

(3) Where such specification would materially affect the other party's performance but is not seasonably made or where one party's cooperation is necessary to the agreed performance of the other but is not seasonably forthcoming, the other party in addition to all other remedies

(a) is excused for any resulting delay in his own performance; and

(b) may also either proceed to perform in any reasonable manner or after the time for a material part of his own performance treat the failure to specify or to cooperate as a breach by failure to deliver or accept the goods.

Section 2-312. Warranty of Title and Against Infringement; Buyer's Obligation Against Infringement.

(1) Subject to subsection (2) there is in a contract for a sale a warranty by the seller that

(a) the title conveyed shall be good, and its transfer rightful; and

(b) the goods shall be delivered free from any security interest or other lien or encumbrance of which the buyer at the time of contracting has no knowledge.

(2) A warranty under subsection (1) will be excluded or modified only by specific language or by circumstances which give the buyer reason to know that the person selling does not claim title in himself or that he is purporting to sell only such right or title as he or a third person may have.

(3) Unless otherwise agreed a seller who is a merchant regularly dealing in goods of the kind warrants that the goods shall be delivered free of the rightful claim of any third person by way of infringement or the like but a buyer who furnishes specifications to the seller must hold the seller harmless against any such claim which arises out of compliance with the specifications.

Section 2-313. Express Warranties by Affirmation, Promise, Description, Sample.

(1) Express warranties by the seller are created as follows:

(a) Any affirmation of fact or promise made by the seller to the buyer which relates to the goods and becomes part of the basis of the bargain creates an express warranty that the goods shall conform to the affirmation or promise.

(b) Any description of the goods which is made part of the basis of the bargain creates an express warranty that the goods shall conform to the description.

(c) Any sample or model which is made part of the basis of the bargain creates an express warranty that the whole of the goods shall conform to the sample or model.

(2) It is not necessary to the creation of an express warranty that the seller use formal words such as "warrant" or "guarantee" or that he have a specific intention to make a warranty, but an affirmation merely of the value of the goods or a statement purporting to be merely the seller's opinion or commendation of the goods does not create a warranty.

Section 2-314. Implied Warranty: Merchantability; Usage of Trade.

(1) Unless excluded or modified (Section

2-316) a warranty that the goods shall be merchantable is implied in a contract for their sale if the seller is a merchant with respect to goods of that kind. Under this section the serving for value of food or drink to be consumed either on the premises or elsewhere is a sale.

(2) Goods to be merchantable must be at least such as

(a) pass without objection in the trade under the contract description; and

(b) in the case of fungible goods, are of fair average quality within the description; and

(c) are fit for the ordinary purposes for which such goods are used; and

(d) run, within the variations permitted by the agreement, of even kind, quality and quantity within each unit and among all units involved; and

(e) are adequately contained, packaged, and labeled as the agreement may require; and

(f) conform to the promises or affirmations of fact made on the container or label if any.

(3) Unless excluded or modified (Section 2-316) other implied warranties may arise from course of dealing or usage of trade.

Section 2-315. Implied Warranty: Fitness for Particular Purpose. Where the seller at the time of contracting has reason to know any particular purpose for which the goods are required and that the buyer is relying on the seller's skill or judgment to select or furnish suitable goods, there is unless excluded or modified under the next section an implied warranty that the goods shall be fit for such purpose.

Section 2-316. Exclusion or Modification of Warranties.

(1) Words or conduct relevant to the creation of an express warranty and words or conduct tending to negate or limit warranty shall be construed wherever reasonable as consistent with each other; but subject to the provisions of this Article on parol or extrinsic evidence (Section 2-202) negation or limitation is inoperative to the extent that such construction is unreasonable.

(2) Subject to subsection (3), to exclude or modify the implied warranty of merchantability or any part of it the language must mention merchantability and in case of a writing must be conspicuous, and to exclude

or modify any implied warranty of fitness the exclusion must be by a writing and conspicuous. Language to exclude all implied warranties of fitness is sufficient if it states, for example, that "There are no warranties which extend beyond the description on the face hereof."

(3) Notwithstanding subsection (2)

(a) unless the circumstances indicate otherwise, all implied warranties are excluded by expressions like "as is," "with all faults" or other language which in common understanding calls the buyer's attention to the exclusion of warranties and makes plain that there is no implied warranty; and

(b) when the buyer before entering into the contract has examined the goods or the sample or model as fully as he desired or has refused to examine the goods there is no implied warranty with regard to defects which an examination ought in the circumstances to have revealed to him; and

(c) an implied warranty can also be excluded or modified by course of dealing or course of performance or usage of trade.

(4) Remedies for breach of warranty can be limited in accordance with the provisions of this Article on liquidation or limitation of damages and on contractual modification of remedy (Sections 2-718 and 2-719).

Section 2-317. Cumulation and Conflict of Warranties Express or Implied. Warranties whether express or implied shall be construed as consistent with each other and as cumulative, but if such construction is unreasonable the intention of the parties shall determine which warranty is dominant. In ascertaining that intention the following rules apply:

(a) Exact or technical specifications displace an inconsistent sample or model or general language of description.

(b) A sample from an existing bulk displaces inconsistent general language of description.

(c) Express warranties displace inconsistent implied warranties other than an implied warranty of fitness for a particular purpose.

Section 2-318. Third Party Beneficiaries or Warranties Express or Implied. A seller's warranty whether express or implied extends to any natural person who is in the family or household of his buyer or who is a guest in his home if it is reasonable to expect that such person may use, consume or be affected by the goods and who is injured in person by breach of the warranty. A seller may not exclude or limit the operation of this section.

Section 2-319. F.O.B. and F.A.S. Terms.

(1) Unless otherwise agreed the term F.O.B. (which means "free on board") at a named place, even though used only in connection with the stated price, is a delivery term under which

(a) when the term is F.O.B. the place of shipment, the seller must at that place ship the goods in the manner provided in this article (Section 2-504) and bear the expense and risk of putting them into the possession of the carrier; or

(b) when the term is F.O.B. the place of destination, the seller must at his own expense and risk transport the goods to that place and there tender delivery of them in the manner provided in this Article (Section 2-503);

(c) when under either (a) or (b) the term is also F.O.B. vessel, car or other vehicle, the seller must in addition at his own expense and risk load the goods on board. If the term is F.O.B. vessel the buyer must name the vessel and in an appropriate case the seller must comply with the provisions of this Article on the form of bill of lading (Section 2-323).

(2) Unless otherwise agreed the term F.A.S. vessel (which means "free alongside") at a named port, even though used only in connection with the stated price, is a delivery term under which the seller must

(a) at his own expense and risk deliver the goods alongside the vessel in the manner usual in that port or on a dock designated and provided by the buyer; and

(b) obtain and tender a receipt for the goods in exchange for which the carrier is under a duty to issue a bill of lading.

(3) Unless otherwise agreed in any case falling within subsection (1)(a) or (c) or subsection (2) the buyer must seasonably give any needed instructions for making delivery, including when the term is F.A.S. or F.O.B. the loading berth of the vessel and in an appropriate case its name and sailing date.

The seller may treat the failure of needed instructions as a failure of cooperation under this Article (Section 2-311). He may also at his option move the goods in any reasonable manner preparatory to delivery or shipment.

(4) Under the term F.O.B. vessel or F.A.S. unless otherwise agreed the buyer must make payment against tender of the required documents and the seller may not tender nor the buyer demand delivery of the goods in substitution for the documents.

Section 2-320. C.I.F. and C. & F. Terms.

(1) The term C.I.F. means that the price includes in a lump sum the cost of the goods and the insurance and freight to the named destination. The term C. & F. or C.F. means that the price so includes cost and freight to the named destination.

(2) Unless otherwise agreed and even though used only in connection with the stated price and destination, the term C.I.F. destination or its equivalent requires the seller at his own expense and risk to

(a) put the goods into the possession of a carrier at the port for shipment and obtain a negotiable bill or bills of lading covering the entire transportation to the named destination; and

(b) load the goods and obtain a receipt from the carrier (which may be contained in the bill of lading) showing that the freight has been paid or provided for; and

(c) obtain a policy or certificate of insurance, including any war risk insurance, of a kind and on terms then current at the port of shipment in the usual amount, in the currency of the contract, shown to cover the same goods covered by the bill of lading and providing for payment of loss to the order of the buyer or for the account of whom it may concern; but the seller may add to the price the amount of the premium for any such war risk insurance; and

(d) prepare an invoice of the goods and procure any other documents required to effect shipment or to comply with the contract; and

(e) forward and tender with commercial promptness all the documents in due form and with any indorsement necessary to perfect the buyer's rights.

(3) Unless otherwise agreed the term C. & F. or its equivalent has the same effect and imposes upon the seller the same obligations and risks as a C.I.F. term except the obligation as to insurance.

(4) Under the term C.I.F. or C. & F. unless otherwise agreed the buyer must make payment against tender of the required documents and the seller may not tender nor the buyer demand delivery of the goods in substitution for the documents.

Section 2-321. C.I.F. or C. & F.: "Net Landed Weights"; "Payment on Arrival"; Warranty of Condition on Arrival. Under a contract containing a term C.I.F. or C. & F.

(1) Where the price is based on or is to be adjusted according to "net landed weights," "delivered weights," "out turn" quantity or quality or the like, unless otherwise agreed the seller must reasonably estimate the price. The payment due on tender of the documents called for by the contract is the amount so estimated, but after final adjustment of the price a settlement must be made with commercial promptness.

(2) An agreement described in subsection (1) or any warranty of quality or condition of the goods on arrival places upon the seller the risk of ordinary deterioration, shrinkage and the like in transportation but has no effect on the place or time of identification to the contract for sale or delivery or on the passing of the risk of loss.

(3) Unless otherwise agreed where the contract provides for payment on or after arrival of the goods the seller must before payment allow such preliminary inspection as is feasible; but if the goods are lost delivery of the documents and payment are due when the goods should have arrived.

Section 2-322. Delivery "Ex-Ship."

(1) Unless otherwise agreed a term for delivery of goods "ex-ship" (which means from the carrying vessel) or in equivalent language is not restricted to a particular ship and requires delivery from a ship which has reached a place at the named port of destination where goods of the kind are usually discharged.

(2) Under such a term unless otherwise agreed

    (a) the seller must discharge all liens arising out of the carriage and furnish

the buyer with a direction which puts the carrier under a duty to deliver the goods; and

    (b) the risk of loss does not pass to the buyer until the goods leave the ship's tackle or are otherwise properly unloaded.

Section 2-323. Form of Bill of Lading Required in Overseas Shipment; "Overseas."

(1) Where the contract contemplates overseas shipment and contains a term C.I.F. or C. & F. or F. O. B. vessel, the seller unless otherwise agreed must obtain a negotiable bill of lading stating that the goods have been loaded on board or, in the case of a term C.I.F. or C. & F., received for shipment.

(2) Where in a case within subsection (1) a bill of lading has been issued in a set of parts, unless otherwise agreed if the documents are not to be sent from abroad the buyer may demand tender of the full set; otherwise only one part of the bill of lading need be tendered. Even if the agreement expressly requires a full set

    (a) due tender of a single part is acceptable within the provisions of this Article on cure of improper delivery (subsection (1) of Section 2-508); and

    (b) even though the full set is demanded, if the documents are sent from abroad the person tendering an incomplete set may nevertheless require payment upon furnishing an indemnity which the buyer in good faith deems adequate.

(3) A shipment by water or by air or a contract contemplating such shipment is "overseas" insofar as by usage of trade or agreement it is subject to the commercial, financing or shipping practices characteristic of international deep water commerce.

Section 2-324. "No Arrival, No Sale" Term. Under a term "no arrival, no sale" or terms of like meaning, unless otherwise agreed.

    (a) the seller must properly ship conforming goods and if they arrive by any means he must tender them on arrival but he assumes no obligation that the goods will arrive unless he has caused the non-arrival; and

    (b) where without fault of the seller the goods are in part lost or have so deteriorated as no longer to conform to the contract or arrive after the contract time, the buyer may proceed as if there had been casualty to identified goods (Section 2-613).

Section 2-325. "Letter of Credit" Term; "Confirmed Credit."

(1) Failure of the buyer seasonably to furnish an agreed letter of credit is a breach of the contract for sale.

(2) The delivery to seller of a proper letter of credit suspends the buyer's obligation to pay. If the letter of credit is dishonored, the seller may on seasonable notification to the buyer require payment directly from him.

(3) Unless otherwise agreed the term "letter of credit" or "banker's credit" in a contract for sale means an irrevocable credit issued by a financing agency of good repute and, where the shipment is overseas, of good international repute. The term "confirmed credit" means that the credit must also carry the direct obligation of such an agency which does business in the seller's financial market.

Section 2-326. Sale on Approval and Sale or Return; Consignment Sales and Rights of Creditors.

(1) Unless otherwise agreed, if delivered goods may be returned to the buyer even though they conform to the contract, the transaction is.

(a) a "sale on approval" if the goods are delivered primarily for use; and

(b) a "sale or return" if the goods are delivered primarily for resale.

(2) Except as provided in subsection (3), goods held on approval are not subject to the claims of the buyer's creditors until acceptance; goods held on sale or return are subject to such claims while in the buyer's possession.

(3) Where goods are delivered to a person for sale and such person maintains a place of business at which he deals in goods of the kind involved, under a name other than the name of the person making delivery, then with respect to claims of creditors of the person conducting the business the goods are deemed to be on sale or return. The provisions of this subsection are applicable even though an agreement purports to reserve title to the person making delivery until payment or resale or uses such words as "on consignment" or "on memoran-

dum." However, this subsection is not applicable if the person making delivery

(a) complies with an applicable law providing for a consignor's interest or the like to be evidenced by a sign, or

(b) establishes that the person conducting the business is generally known by his creditors to be substantially engaged in selling the goods of others, or

(c) complies with the filing provisions of the Article on Secured Transactions (Article 9).

(4) Any "or return" term of a contract for sale is to be treated as a separate contract for sale within the statute of frauds section of this Article (Section 2-201) and as contradicting the sale aspect of the contract within the provisions of this Article on parol or extrinsic evidence (Section 2-202).

Section 2-327. Special Incidents of Sale on Approval and Sale or Return.

(1) Under a sale on approval unless otherwise agreed

(a) although the goods are identified to the contract the risk of loss and the title do not pass to the buyer until acceptance; and

(b) use of the goods consistent with the purpose of trial is not acceptance but failure seasonably to notify the seller of election to return the goods is acceptance, and if the goods conform to the contract acceptance of any part is acceptance of the whole; and

(c) after due notification of election to return, the return is at the seller's risk and expense but a merchant buyer must follow any reasonable instructions.

(2) Under a sale or return unless otherwise agreed

(a) the option to return extends to the whole or any commercial unit of the goods while in substantially their original condition, but must be exercised seasonably; and

(b) the return is at the buyer's risk and expense.

Section 2-328. Sale by Auction.

(1) In a sale by auction if goods are put up in lots each lot is the subject of a separate sale.

(2) A sale by auction is complete when the auctioneer so announces by the fall of the hammer or in other customary manner.

671

Where a bid is made while the hammer is falling in acceptance of a prior bid the auctioneer may in his discretion reopen the bidding or declare the goods sold under the bid on which the hammer was falling.

(3) Such a sale is with reserve unless the goods are in explicit terms put up without reserve. In an auction with reserve the auctioneer may withdraw the goods at any time until he announces completion of the sale. In an auction without reserve, after the auctioneer calls for bids on an article or lot, that article or lot cannot be withdrawn unless no bid is made within a reasonable time.

In either case a bidder may retract his bid until the auctioneer's announcement of completion of the sale, but a bidder's retraction does not revive any previous bid.

(4) If the auctioneer knowingly receives a bid on the seller's behalf or the seller makes or procures such a bid, and notice has not been given that liberty for such bidding is reserved, the buyer may at his option avoid the sale or take the goods at the price of the last good faith bid prior to the completion of the sale. This subsection shall not apply to any bid at a forced sale.

PART 4

TITLE, CREDITORS AND GOOD FAITH PURCHASERS

Section 2-401. Passing of Title; Reservation for Security; Limited Application of this Section. Each provision of this Article with regard to the rights, obligations and remedies of the seller, the buyer, purchasers or other third parties applies irrespective of title to the goods except where the provision refers to such title. Insofar as situations are not covered by the other provisions of this Article and matters concerning title become material the following rules apply:

(1) Title to goods cannot pass under a contract for sale prior to their identification to the contract (Section 2-501), and unless otherwise explicitly agreed the buyer acquires by their identification a special property as limited by this Act. Any retention or reservation by the seller of the title (property) in goods shipped or delivered to the buyer is limited in effect to a reservation of a security interest. Subject to these provisions and to the provisions of the Article on Secured Transactions (Article 9), title to goods passes from the seller to the buyer in any manner and on any conditions explicitly agreed on by the parties.

(2) Unless otherwise explicitly agreed title passes to the buyer at the time and place at which the seller completes his performance with reference to the physical delivery of the goods, despite any reservation of a security interest and even though a document of title is to be delivered at a different time or place; and in particular and despite any reservation of a security interest by the bill of lading

(a) if the contract requires or authorizes the seller to send the goods to the buyer but does not require him to deliver them at destination, title passes to the buyer at the time and place of shipment;

(b) if the contract requires delivery at destination, title passes on tender there.

(3) Unless otherwise explicitly agreed where delivery is to be made without moving the goods,

(a) if the seller is to deliver a document of title, title passes at the time when and the place where he delivers such documents; or

(b) if the goods are at the time of contracting already identified and no documents are to be delivered, title passes at the time and place of contracting.

(4) A rejection or other refusal by the buyer to receive or retain the goods, whether or not justified, or a justified revocation of acceptance revests title to the goods in the seller. Such revesting occurs by operation of law and is not a "sale."

Section 2-402. Rights of Seller's Creditors Against Sold Goods.

(1) Except as provided in subsections (2) and (3), rights of unsecured creditors of the seller with respect to goods which have been identified to a contract for sale are subject to the buyer's rights to recover the goods under this Article (Sections 2-502 and 2-716).

(2) A creditor of the seller may treat a sale or an identification of goods to a contract

for sale as void if as against him a retention of possession by the seller is fraudulent under any rule of law of the state where the goods are situated, except that retention of possession in good faith and current course of trade by a merchant-seller for a commercially reasonable time after a sale or identification is not fraudulent.

(3) Nothing in this Article shall be deemed to impair the rights of creditors of the seller

(a) under the provisions of the Article on Secured Transactions (Article 9); or

(b) where identification to the contract or delivery is made not in current course of trade but in satisfaction of or as security for a pre-existing claim for money, security or the like and is made under circumstances which under any rule of law of the state where the goods are situated would apart from this Article constitute the transaction a fraudulent transfer or voidable preference.

Section 2-403. Power to Transfer; Good Faith Purchase of Goods; "Entrusting."

(1) A purchaser of goods acquires all title which his transferor had or had power to transfer except that a purchaser of a limited interest acquires rights only to the extent of the interest purchased. A person with voidable title had power to transfer a good title to a good faith purchaser for value. When goods have been delivered under a transaction of purchase the purchaser has such power even though

(a) the transferor was deceived as to the identity of the purchaser, or

(b) the delivery was in exchange for a check which is later dishonored, or

(c) it was agreed that the transaction was to be a "cash sale," or

(d) the delivery was procured through fraud punishable as larcenous under the criminal law.

(2) Any entrusting of possession of goods to a merchant who deals in goods of that kind gives him power to transfer all rights of the entruster to a buyer in ordinary course of business.

(3) "Entrusting" includes any delivery and any acquiescence in retention of possession regardless of any condition expressed between the parties to the delivery or acquiescence and regardless of whether the procurement of the entrusting or the possessor's disposition of the goods have been such as to be larcenous under the criminal law.

(4) The rights of other purchasers of goods and of lien creditors are governed by the Articles on Secured Transactions (Article 9), Bulk Transfers (Article 6) and Documents of Title (Article 7).

PART 5

PERFORMANCE

Section 2-501. Insurable Interest in Goods; Manner of Identification of Goods.

(1) The buyer obtains a special property and an insurable interest in goods by identification of existing goods as goods to which the contract refers even though the goods so identified are non-conforming and he has an opinion to return or reject them. Such identification can be made at any time and in any manner explicitly agreed to by the parties. In the absence of explicit agreement identification occurs

(a) when the contract is made if it is for the sale of goods already existing and identified;

(b) if the contract is for the sale of future goods other than those described in paragraph (c), when goods are shipped, marked or otherwise designated by the seller as goods to which the contract refers;

(c) when the crops are planted or otherwise become growing crops or the young are conceived if the contract is for the sale of unborn young to be born within twelve months after contracting or for the sale of crops to be harvested within twelve months or the next normal harvest season after contracting whichever is longer.

(2) The seller retains an insurable interest in goods so long as title to or any security interest in the goods remains in him and where the identification is by the seller alone he may until default or insolvency or notification to the buyer that the identifica-

tion is final substitute other goods for those identified.

(3) Nothing in this section impairs any insurable interest recognized under any other statute or rule of law.

Section 2-502. Buyer's Right to Goods on Seller's Insolvency.

(1) Subject to subsection (2) and even though the goods have not been shipped a buyer who has paid a part or all of the price of the goods in which he has a special property under the provisions of the immediately preceding section may on making and keeping good a tender of any unpaid portion of their price recover them from the seller if the seller becomes insolvent within ten days after receipt of the first installment on their price.

(2) If the identification creating his special property has been made by the buyer he acquires the right to recover the goods only if they conform to the contract for sale.

Section 2-503. Manner of Seller's Tender of Delivery.

(1) Tender of delivery requires that the seller put and hold conforming goods at the buyer's disposition and give the buyer any notification reasonably necessary to enable him to take delivery. The manner, time and place for tender are determined by the agreement and this Article, and in particular

(a) tender must be at a reasonable hour, and if it is of goods they must be kept available for the period reasonably necessary to enable the buyer to take possession; but

(b) unless otherwise agreed the buyer must furnish facilities reasonably suited to the receipt of the goods.

(2) Where the case is within the next section respecting shipment tender requires that the seller comply with its provisions.

(3) Where the seller is required to deliver at a particular destination tender requires that he comply with subsection (1) and also in any appropriate case tender documents as described in subsections (4) and (5) of this section.

(4) Where goods are in the possession of a bailee and are to be delivered without being moved

(a) tender requires that the seller either

tender a negotiable document of title covering such goods or procure acknowledgment by the bailee of the buyer's right to possession of the goods; but

(b) tender to the buyer of a non-negotiable document of title or of a written direction to the bailee to deliver is sufficient tender unless the buyer seasonably objects, and receipt by the bailee of notification of the buyer's rights fixes those rights as against the bailee and all third persons; but risk of loss of the goods and of any failure by the bailee to honor the non-negotiable document of title or to obey the direction remains on the seller until the buyer has had a reasonable time to present the document or direction, and a refusal by the bailee to honor the document or to obey the direction defeats the tender.

(5) Where the contract requires the seller to deliver documents

(a) he must tender all such documents in correct form, except as provided in this Article with respect to bills of lading in a set (subsection (2) of Section 2-323); and

(b) tender through customary banking channels is sufficient and dishonor of a draft accompanying the documents constitutes non-acceptance or rejection.

Section 2-504. Shipment by Seller.
Where the seller is required or authorized to send the goods to the buyer and the contract does not require him to deliver them at a particular destination, then unless otherwise agreed he must

(a) put the goods in the possession of such a carrier and make such a contract for their transportation as may be reasonable having regard to the nature of the goods and other circumstances of the case; and

(b) obtain and promptly deliver or tender in due form any document necessary to enable the buyer to obtain possession of the goods or otherwise required by the agreement or by usage of trade; and

Failure to notify the buyer under paragraph (c) or to make a proper contract under paragraph (a) is a ground for rejection only if material delay or loss ensued.

Section 2-505. Seller's Shipment Under Reservation.

(1) Where the seller has identified goods to the contract by or before shipment:

(a) his procurement of a negotiable bill of lading to his own order or otherwise reserves in him a security interest in the goods. His procurement of the bill to the order of a financing agency or of the buyer indicates in addition only the seller's expectation of transferring that interest to the person named.

(b) a non-negotiable bill of lading to himself or his nominee reserves possession of the goods as security but except in a case of conditional delivery (subsection (2) of Section 2-507) a non-negotiable bill of lading naming the buyer as consignee reserves no security interest even though the seller retains possession of the bill of lading.

(2) When shipment by the seller with reservation of a security interest is in violation of the contract for sale it constitutes an improper contract for transportation within the preceding section but impairs neither the rights given to the buyer by shipment and identification of the goods to the contract nor the seller's powers as a holder of a negotiable document.

Section 2-506. Rights of Financing Agency.

(1) A financing agency by paying or purchasing for value a draft which relates to a shipment of goods acquires to the extent of the payment or purchase and in addition to its own rights under the draft and any document of title securing it any rights of the shipper in the goods including the right to stop delivery and the shipper's right to have the draft honored by the buyer.

(2) The right to reimbursement of a financing agency which has in good faith honored or purchased the draft under commitment to or authority from the buyer is not impaired by subsequent discovery of defects with reference to any relevant document which was apparently regular on its face.

Section 2-507. Effect of Seller's Tender; Delivery on Condition.

(1) Tender of delivery is a condition to the buyer's duty to accept the goods and, unless otherwise agreed, to his duty to pay for them. Tender entitles the seller to acceptance of the goods and to payment according to the contract.

(2) Where payment is due and demanded on the delivery to the buyer of goods or documents of title, his right as against the seller to retain or dispose of them is conditional upon his making the payment due.

Section 2-508. Cure by Seller of Improper Tender or Delivery; Replacement.

(1) Where any tender or delivery by the seller is rejected because non-conforming and the time for performance has not yet expired, the seller may seasonably notify the buyer of his intention to cure and may then within the contract time make a conforming delivery.

(2) Where the buyer rejects a non-conforming tender which the seller had reasonable grounds to believe would be acceptable with or without money allowance the seller may if he seasonably notifies the buyer have a further reasonable time to substitute a conforming tender.

Section 2-509. Risk of Loss in the Absence of Breach.

(1) Where the contract requires or authorizes the seller to ship the goods by carrier

(a) if it does not require him to deliver them at a particular destination, the risk of loss passes to the buyer when the goods are duly delivered to the carrier even though the shipment is under reservation (Section 2-505); but

(b) if it does require him to deliver them at a particular destination and the goods are there duly tendered while in the possession of the carrier, the risk of loss passes to the buyer when the goods are there duly so tendered as to enable the buyer to take delivery.

(2) Where the goods are held by a bailee to be delivered without being moved, the risk of loss passes to the buyer

(a) on his receipt of a negotiable document of title covering the goods; or

(b) on acknowledgement by the bailee of the buyer's right to possession of the goods; or

(c) after his receipt of a non-negotiable document of title or other written direction to deliver, as provided in subsection (4) (b) of Section 2-503.

(3) In any case not within subsection (1) or (2), the risk of loss passes to the buyer on his receipt of the goods if the seller is a merchant; otherwise the risk passes to the buyer on tender of delivery.

(4) The provisions of this section are subject to contrary agreement of the parties and to the provisions of this Article on sale on approval (Section 2-327) and on effect of breach on risk of loss (Section 2-510).

Section 2-510. Effect of Breach on Risk of Loss.

(1) Where a tender or delivery of goods so fails to conform to the contract as to give a right of rejection the risk of their loss remains on the seller until cure or acceptance.

(2) Where the buyer rightfully revokes acceptance he may to the extent of any deficiency in his effective insurance coverage treat the risk of loss as having rested on the seller from the beginning.

(3) Where the buyer as to conforming goods already identified to the contract for sale repudiates or is otherwise in breach before risk of their loss has passed to him the seller may to the extent of any deficiency in his effective insurance coverage treat the risk of loss as resting on the buyer for a commercially reasonable time.

Section 2-511. Tender of Payment by Buyer; Payment by Check.

(1) Unless otherwise agreed tender of payment is a condition to the seller's duty to tender and complete any delivery.

(2) Tender of payment is sufficient when made by any means or in any manner current in the ordinary course of business unless the seller demands payment in legal tender and gives any extension of time reasonably necessary to procure it.

(3) Subject to the provisions of this Act on the effect of an instrument on an obligation (Section 3-802), payment by check is conditional and is defeated as between the parties by dishonor of the check on due presentment.

Section 2-512. Payment by Buyer Before Inspection.

(1) Where the contract requires payment before inspection non-conformity of the goods does not excuse the buyer from so making payment unless

(a) the non-conformity appears without inspection; or

(b) despite tender of the required documents the circumstances would justify injunction against honor under the provisions of this Act (Section 5-114).

(2) Payment pursuant to subsection (1) does not constitute an acceptance of goods or impair the buyer's right to inspect or any of his remedies.

Section 2-513. Buyer's Right to Inspection of Goods.

(1) Unless otherwise agreed and subject to subsection (3), where goods are tendered or delivered or identified to the contract for sale, the buyer has a right before payment or acceptance to inspect them at any reasonable place and time and in any reasonable manner. When the seller is required or authorized to send the goods to the buyer, the inspection may be after their arrival.

(2) Expenses of inspection must be borne by the buyer but may be recovered from the seller if the goods do not conform and are rejected.

(3) Unless otherwise agreed and subject to the provisions of this Article on C.I.F. contracts (subsection (3) of Section 2-321), the buyer is not entitled to inspect the goods before payment of the price when the contract provides

(a) for delivery "C.O.D." or on other like terms; or

(b) for payment against documents of title, except where such payment is due only after the goods are to become available for inspection.

(4) A place or method of inspection fixed by the parties is presumed to be exclusive but unless otherwise expressly agreed it does not postpone identification or shift the place for delivery or for passing the risk of loss. If compliance becomes impossible, inspection shall be as provided in this section unless the place or method fixed was clearly intended as an indispensable condition failure of which avoids the contract.

Section 3-514. When Documents Deliverable on Acceptance; When on Payment.
Unless otherwise agreed documents against which a draft is drawn are to be delivered to the drawee on acceptance of the draft if it is payable more than three days after presentment; otherwise, only on payment.

Section 2-515. Preserving Evidence of Goods in Dispute. In furtherance of the adjustment of any claim or dispute

(a) either party on reasonable notification to the other and for the purpose of ascertaining the facts and preserving evidence has the right to inspect, test and sample the goods including such of them as may be in the possession or control of the other; and

(b) the parties may agree to a third party inspection or survey to determine the conformity or condition of the goods and may agree that the findings shall be binding upon them in any subsequent litigation or adjustment.

PART 6

BREACH, REPUDIATION AND EXCUSE

Section 2-601. Buyer's Rights on Improper Delivery. Subject to the provisions of this Article on breach in installment contracts (Section 2-612) and unless otherwise agreed under the sections on contractual limitations of remedy (Sections 2-718 and 2-719), if the goods or the tender of delivery fail in any respect to conform to the contract, the buyer may may

(a) reject the whole; or

(b) accept the whole; or

(c) accept any commercial unit or units and reject the rest.

Section 2-602. Manner and Effect of Rightful Rejection.

(1) Rejection of goods must be within a reasonable time after their delivery or tender. It is ineffective unless the buyer seasonably notifies the seller.

(2) Subject to the provisions of the two following sections on rejected goods (Sections 2-603 and 2-604),

(a) after rejection any exercise of ownership by the buyer with respect to any commercial unit is wrongful as against the seller; and

(b) if the buyer has before rejection taken physical possession of goods in which he does not have a security interest under the provisions of this Article (subsection (3) of Section 2-711), he is under a duty after rejection to hold them with reasonable care at the seller's disposition for a time sufficient to permit the seller to remove them; but

(c) the buyer has no further obligations with regard to goods rightfully rejected.

(3) The seller's rights with respect to goods wrongfully rejected are governed by the provisions of this Article on Seller's remedies in general (Section 2-703).

Section 2-603. Merchant Buyer's Duties as to Rightfully Rejected Goods.

(1) Subject to any security interest in the buyer (subsection (3) of Section 2-711), when the seller has no agent or place of business at the market of rejection a merchant buyer is under a duty after rejection of goods in his possession or control to follow any reasonable instructions received from the seller with respect to the goods and in the absence of such instructions to make reasonable efforts to sell them for the seller's account if they are perishable or threaten to decline in value speedily. Instructions are not reasonable if on demand indemnity for expenses is not forthcoming.

(2) When the buyer sells goods under subsection (1), he is entitled to reimbursement from the seller or out of the proceeds for reasonable expenses of caring for and selling them, and if the expenses include no selling commission then to such commission as is usual in the trade or if there is none to a reasonable sum not exceeding ten per cent on the gross proceeds.

(3) In complying with this section the buyer is held only to good faith and good faith conduct hereunder is neither acceptance nor conversion nor the basis of an action for damages.

Section 2-604. Buyer's Options as to Salvage of Rightfully Rejected Goods. Subject to the provisions of the immediately preceding section on perishables if the seller gives no instructions within a reasonable time after notifcation of rejection the buyer may store the rejected goods for the seller's account or reship them to him or resell them for the seller's account with reimbursement as provided in the preceding section. Such action is not acceptance or conversion.

Section 2-605. Waiver of Buyer's Objections by Failure to Particularize.

(1) The buyer's failure to state in connection with rejection a particular defect which is ascertainable by reasonable inspection precludes him from relying on the unstated defect to justify rejection or to establish breach

(a) where the seller could have cured it if stated seasonably; or

(b) between merchants when the seller has after rejection made a request in writing for a full and final written statement of all defects on which the buyer proposes to rely.

(2) Payment against documents made without reservation of rights precludes recovery of the payment for defects apparent on the fact of the documents.

Section 2-606. What Constitutes Acceptance of Goods.

(1) Acceptance of goods occurs when the buyer

(a) after a reasonable opportunity to inspect the goods signifies to the seller that the goods are conforming or that he will take or retain them in spite of their non-conformity; or

(b) fails to make an effective rejection (subsection (1) of Section 2-602), but such acceptance does not occur until the buyer has had a reasonable opportunity to inspect them; or

(c) does any act inconsistent with the seller's ownership but if such act is wrongful as against the seller it is an acceptance only if ratified by him.

(2) Acceptance of a part of any commercial unit is acceptance of that entire unit.

Section 2-607. Effect of Acceptance; Notice of Breach; Burden of Establishing Breach After Acceptance; Notice of Claim or Litigation to Person Answerable Over.

(1) The buyer must pay at the contract rate for any goods accepted.

(2) Acceptance of goods by the buyer precludes rejection of the goods accepted and if made with knowledge of a non-conformity cannot be revoked because of it unless the acceptance was on the reasonable assumption that the non-conformity would be seasonably cured but acceptance does not of itself impair any other remedy provided by this Article for non-conformity.

(3) Where a tender has been accepted

(a) the buyer must within a reasonable time after he discovers or should have discovered any breach notify the seller of breach or be barred from any remedy; and

(b) if the claim is one for infringement or the like (subsection (3) of Section 2-312) and the buyer is sued as a result of such a breach he must so notify the seller within a reasonable time after he receives notice of the litigation or be barred from any remedy over for liability established by the litigation.

(4) The burden is on the buyer to establish any breach with respect to the goods accepted.

(5) Where the buyer is used for breach of a warranty or other obligation for which his seller is answerable over

(a) he may give his seller written notice of the litigation. If the notice states that the seller may come in and defend and that if the seller does not do so he will be bound in any action against him by his buyer by any determination of fact common to the two litigations, then unless the seller after seasonable receipt of the notice does come in and defend he is so bound.

(b) if the claim is one for infringement or the like (subsection (3) of Section 2-312) the original seller may demand in writing that his buyer turn over to him control of the litigation including settlement or else be barred from any remedy over and if he also agrees to bear all expense and to satisfy any adverse judgment, then unless the buyer after seasonable receipt of the demand does turn over control the buyer is so barred.

(6) The provisions of subsections (3), (4) and (5) apply to any obligation of a buyer to hold the seller harmless against infringement or the like (subsection (3) of Section 2-312).

Section 2-608. Revocation of Acceptance in Whole or in Part.

(1) The buyer may revoke his acceptance of a lot or commercial unit whose non-conformity substantially impairs its value to him if he has accepted it

(a) on the reasonable assumption that

its non-conformity would be cured and it has not been seasonably cured; or

(b) without discovery of such non-conformity if his acceptance was reasonably induced either by the difficulty of discovery before acceptance or by the seller's assurances.

(2) Revocation of acceptance must occur within a reasonable time after the buyer discovers or should have discovered the ground for it and before any substantial change in condition of the goods which is not caused by their own defects. It is not effective until the buyer notifies the seller of it.

(3) A buyer who so revokes has the same rights and duties with regard to the goods involved as if he had rejected them.

Section 2-609. Right to Adequate Assurance of Performance.

(1) A contract for sale imposes an obligation on each party that the other's expectation of receiving due performance will not be impaired. When reasonable grounds for insecurity arise with respect to the performance of either party the other may in writing demand adequate assurance of due performance and until he receives such assurance may if commercially reasonable suspend any performance for which he has not already received the agreed return.

(2) Between merchants the reasonableness of grounds for insecurity and the adequacy of any assurance offered shall be determined according to commercial standards.

(3) Acceptance of any improper delivery or payment does not prejudice the aggrieved party's right to demand adequate assurance of future performance.

(4) After receipt of a justified demand failure to provide within a reasonable time not exceeding thirty days such assurance of due performance as is adequate under the circumstances of the particular case is a repudiation of the contract.

Section 2-610. Anticipatory Repudiation.
When either party repudiates the contract with respect to a performance not yet due the loss of which will substantially impair the value of the contract to the other, the aggrieved party may

(a) for a commercially reasonable time await performance by the repudiating party; or

(b) resort to any remedy for breach (Section 2-703 or Section 2-711), even though he has notified the repudiating party that he would await the latter's performance and has urged retraction; and

(c) in either case suspend his own performance or proceed in accordance with the provisions of this Article on the seller's right to identify goods to the contract notwithstanding breach or to salvage unfinished goods (Section 2-704).

Section 2-611. Retraction of Anticipatory Repudiation.

(1) Until the repudiating party's next performance is due he can retract his repudiation unless the aggrieved party has since the repudiation cancelled or materially changed his position or otherwise indicated that he considers the repudiation final.

(2) Retraction may be by any method which clearly indicates to the aggrieved party that the repudiating party intends to perform, but must include any assurance justifiably demanded under the provisions of this Article (Section 2-609).

(3) Retraction reinstates the repudiating party's rights under the contract with due excuse and allowance to the aggrieved party for any delay occasioned by the repudiation.

Section 2-612. "Installment Contract"; Breach.

(1) An "installment contract" is one which requires or authorizes the delivery of goods in separate lots to be separately accepted, even though the contract contains a clause "each delivery is a separate contract" or its equivalent.

(2) The buyer may reject any installment which is non-conforming if the non-conformity substantially impairs the value of that installment and cannot be cured or if the non-conformity is a defect in the required documents; but if the non-conformity does not fall within subsection (3) and the seller gives adequate assurance of its cure the buyer must accept that installment.

(3) Whenever non-conformity or default with respect to one or more installments substantially impairs the value of the whole contract there is a breach of the whole. But

the aggrieved party reinstates the contract if he accepts a non-conforming installment without seasonably notifying of cancellation or if he brings an action with respect only to past installments or demands performance as to future installments.

Section 2-613. Casualty to Identified Goods. Where the contract requires for its performance goods identified when the contract is made, and the goods suffer casualty without fault of either party before the risk of loss passes to the buyer, or in a proper case under a "no arrival, no sale" term (Section 2-324) then

(a) if the loss is total the contract is avoided; and

(b) if the loss is partial or the goods have so deteriorated as no longer to conform to the contract the buyer may nevertheless demand inspection and at his option either treat the contract as avoided or accept the goods with allowance from the contract price for the deterioration or the deficiency in quantity but without further right against the seller.

Section 2-614. Substituted Performance.

(1) Where without fault of either party the agreed berthing, loading, or unloading facilities fail or an agreed type of carrier becomes unavailable or the agreed manner of delivery otherwise becomes commercially impracticable but a commercially reasonable substitute is available, such substitute performance must be tendered and accepted.

(2) If the agreed means or manner of payment fails because of domestic or foreign governmental regulation, the seller may withhold or stop delivery unless the buyer provides a means or manner of payment which is commercially a substantial equivalent. If delivery has already been taken, payment by the means or in the manner provided by the regulation discharges the buyer's obligation unless the regulation is discriminatory, oppressive or predatory.

Section 2-615. Excuse by Failure of Presupposed Conditions. Except so far as a seller may have assumed a greater obligation and subject to the preceding section on substituted performance:

(a) Delay in delivery or non-delivery in whole or in part by a seller who complies with paragraphs (b) and (c) is not a breach of his duty under a contract for sale if performance as agreed has been made impracticable by the occurrence of a contingency and the non-occurrence of which was a basic assumption on which the contract was made or by compliance in good faith with any applicable foreign or domestic governmental regulation or order whether or not it later proves to be invalid.

(b) Where the causes mentioned in paragraph (a) affect only a part of the seller's capacity to perform, he must allocate production and deliveries among his customers but may at his option include regular customers not then under contract as well as his own requirements for further manufacture. He may so allocate in any manner which is fair and reasonable.

(c) The seller must notify the buyer seasonably that there will be delay or non-delivery and, when allocation is required under paragraph (b), of the estimated quota thus made available for the buyer.

Section 2-616. Procedure on Notice Claiming Excuse.

(1) Where the buyer receives notification of a material or indefinite delay or an allocation justified under the preceding section he may by written notification to the seller as to any delivery concerned, and where the prospective deficiency substantially impairs the value of the whole contract under the provisions of this Article relating to breach of installment contracts (Sections 2-612), then also as to the whole,

(a) terminate and thereby discharge any unexecuted portion of the contract; or

(b) modify the contract by agreeing to take his available quota in substitution.

(2) If after receipt of such notification from the seller the buyer fails so to modify the contract within a reasonable time not exceeding thirty days the contract lapses with respect to any deliveries affected.

(3) The provisions of this section may not be negated by agreement except in so far as the seller has assumed a greater obligation under the preceding section.

PART 7

REMEDIES

Section 2-701. Remedies for Breach of Collateral Contracts Not Impaired. Remedies for breach of any obligation or promise collateral or ancillary to a contract for sale are not impaired by the provisions of this Article.

Section 2-702. Seller's Remedies on Discovery of Buyer's Insolvency.

(1) Where the seller discovers the buyer to be insolvent he may refuse delivery except for cash including payment for all goods theretofore delivered under the contract, and stop delivery under this Article (Section 2-705).

(2) Where the seller discovers that the buyer has received goods on credit while insolvent he may reclaim the goods upon demand made within ten days after receipt, but if misrepresentation of solvency has been made to the particular seller in writing within three months before delivery the ten day limitation does not apply. Except as provided in this subsection the seller may not base a right to reclaim goods on the buyer's fraudulent or innocent misrepresentation of solvency or of intent to pay.

(3) The seller's right to reclaim under subsection (2) is subject to the rights of a buyer in ordinary course or other good faith purchaser or lien creditor under this Article (Section 2-403). Successful reclamation of goods excludes all other remedies with respect to them.

Section 2-703. Seller's Remedies in General. Where the buyer wrongfully rejects or revokes acceptance of goods or fails to make a payment due on or before delivery or repudiates with respect to a part or the whole, then with respect to any goods directly affected and, if the breach is of the whole contract (Section 2-612), then also with respect to the whole undelivered balance, the aggrieved seller may

(a) withhold delivery of such goods;

(b) stop delivery by any bailee as hereafter provided (Section 2-705);

(c) proceed under the next section respecting goods still unidentified to the contract;

(d) resell and recover damages as hereafter provided (Section 2-706);

(e) recover damages for non-acceptance (Section 2-708) or in a proper case the price (Section 2-709);

(f) cancel.

Section 2-704. Seller's Right to Identify Goods to the Contract Notwithstanding Breach or to Salvage Unfinished Goods.

(1) An aggrieved seller under the preceding section may

(a) identify to the contract conforming goods not already identified if at the time he learned of the breach they are in his possession or control;

(b) treat as the subject of resale goods which have demonstrably been intended for the particular contract even though those goods are unfinished.

(2) Where the goods are unfinished an aggrieved seller may in the exercise of reasonable commercial judgment for the purposes of avoiding loss and of effective realization either complete the manufacture and wholly identify the goods to the contract or cease manufacture and resell for scrap or salvage value or proceed in any other reasonable manner.

Section 2-705. Seller's Stoppage of Delivery in Transit or Otherwise.

(1) The seller may stop delivery of goods in the possession of a carrier or other bailee when he discovers the buyer to be insolvent (Section 2-702) and may stop delivery of carload, truckload, planeload or larger shipments of express or freight when the buyer repudiates or fails to make a payment due before delivery or if for any other reason the seller has a right to withhold or reclaim the goods.

(2) As against such buyer the seller may stop delivery until

(a) receipt of the goods by the buyer; or

(b) acknowledgement to the buyer by any bailee of the goods except a carrier

681

that the bailee holds the goods for the buyer; or

(c) such acknowledgement to the buyer by a carrier by reshipment or as warehouseman; or

(d) negotiation to the buyer of any negotiable document of title covering the goods.

(3) (a) To stop delivery the seller must so notify as to enable the bailee by reasonable diligence to prevent delivery of the goods.

(b) After such notification the bailee must hold and deliver the goods according to the directions of the seller but the seller is liable to the bailee for any ensuing charges or damages.

(c) If a negotiable document of title has been issued for goods the bailee is not obliged to obey a notification to stop until surrender of the document.

(d) A carrier who has issued a non-negotiable bill of lading is not obliged to obey a notification to stop received from a person other than the consignor.

Section 2-706. Seller's Resale Including Contract for Resale.

(1) Under the conditions stated in Section 2-703 on seller's remedies, the seller may resell the goods concerned or the undelivered balance thereof. Where the resale is made in good faith and in a commercially reasonable manner the seller may recover the difference between the resale price and the contract price together with any incidental damages allowed under the provisions of this Article (Section 2-710), but less expenses saved in consequence of the buyer's breach.

(2) Except as otherwise provided in subsection (3) or unless otherwise agreed resale may be at public or private sale including sale by way of one or more contracts to sell or of identification to any existing contract of the seller. Sale may be as a unit or in parcels and at any time and place and on any terms but every aspect of the sale including the method, manner, time, place and terms must be commercially reasonable. The resale must be reasonably identified as referring to the broken contract, but it is not necessary that the goods be in existence or that any or all of them have been identified to the contract before the breach.

(3) Where the resale is at private sale the seller must give the buyer reasonable notification of his intention to resell.

(4) Where the resale is at public sale

(a) only identified goods can be sold except where there is a recognized market for a public sale of futures in goods of the kind; and

(b) it must be made at a usual place or market for public sale if one is reasonably available and except in the case of goods which are perishable or threaten to decline in value speedily the seller must give the buyer reasonable notice of the time and place of the resale; and

(c) if the goods are not to be within the view of those attending the sale the notification of sale must state the place where the goods are located and provide for their reasonable inspection by prospective bidders; and

(d) the seller may buy.

(5) A purchaser who buys in good faith at a resale takes the goods free of any rights of the original buyer even though the seller fails to comply with one or more of the requirements of this section.

(6) The seller is not accountable to the buyer for any profit made on any resale. A person in the position of a seller (Section 2-707) or a buyer who has rightfully rejected or justifiably revoked acceptance must account for any excess over the amount of his security interest, as hereinafter defined (subsection (3) of Section 2-711).

Section 2-707. "Person in the Position of a Seller."

(1) A "person in the position of a seller" includes as against a principal an agent who has paid or become responsible for the price of goods on behalf of his principal or anyone who otherwise holds a security interest or other right in goods similar to that of the seller.

(2) A person in the position of a seller may as provided in this Article withhold or stop delivery (Section 2-705) and resell (Section 2-706) and recover incidental damages (Section 2-710).

Section 2-708. Seller's Damages for Non-Acceptance or Repudiation.

(1) Subject to subsection (2) and to the provisions of this Article with respect to

proof of market price (Section 2-723), the measure of damages for non-acceptance or repudiation by the buyer is the difference between the market price at the time and place for tender and the unpaid contract price together with any incidental damages provided in this Article (Section 2-710), but less expenses saved in consequence of the buyer's breach.

(2) If the measure of damages provided in subsection (1) is inadequate to put the seller in as good a position as performance would have done then the measure of damages is the profit (including reasonable overhead) which the seller would have made from full performance by the buyer, together with any incidental damages provided in this Article (Section 2-710), due allowance for costs reasonably incurred and due credit for payments or proceeds of resale.

Section 2-709. Action for the Price.

(1) When the buyer fails to pay the price as it becomes due the seller may recover, together with any incidental damages under the next section, the price

(a) of goods accepted or of conforming goods lost or damaged within a commercially reasonable time after risk of their loss has passed to the buyer; and

(b) of goods identified to the contract if the seller is unable after reasonable effort to resell them at a reasonable price or the circumstances reasonably indicate that such effort will be unavailing.

(2) Where the seller sued for the price he must hold for the buyer any goods which have been identified to the contract and are still in his control except that if resale becomes possible he may resell them at any time prior to the collection of the judgment. The net proceeds of any such resale must be credited to the buyer and payment of the judgment entitles him to any goods not resold.

(3) After the buyer has wrongfully rejected or revoked acceptance of the goods or has failed to make a payment due or has repudiated (Section 2-610), a seller who is held not entitled to the price under this section shall nevertheless be awarded damages for non-acceptance under the preceding section.

Section 2-710. Seller's Incidental Damages.
Incidental damages to an aggrieved seller include any commercially reasonable charges, expenses or commissions incurred in stopping delivery, in the transportation, care and custody of goods after the buyer's breach, in connection with return or resale of the goods or otherwise resulting from the breach.

Section 2-711. Buyer's Remedies in General; Buyer's Security Interest in Rejected Goods.

(1) Where the seller fails to make delivery then with respect to any goods involved, and with respect to the whole if the breach goes to the whole contract (Section 2-612), the buyer may cancel and whether or not he has done so may in addition to recovering so much of the price as has been paid

(a) "cover" and have damages under the next section as to all the goods affected whether or not they have been identified to the contract; or

(b) recover damages for non-delivery as provided in this Article (Section 2-713).

(2) Where the seller fails to deliver or repudiates the buyer may also

(a) if the goods have been identified recover them as provided in this Article (Section 2-502); or

(b) in a proper case obtain specific performance or replevy the goods as provided in this Article (Section 2-716).

(3) On rightful rejection or justifiable revocation of acceptance a buyer has a security interest in goods in his possession or control for any payments made on their price and any expenses reasonably incurred in their inspection, receipt, transporation, care and custody and may hold such goods and resell them in like manner as an aggrieved seller (Section 2-706)).

Section 2-712. "Cover"; Buyer's Procurement of Substitute Goods.

(1) After a breach within the preceding section the buyer may "cover" by making in good faith and without unreasonable delay any reasonable purchase of or contract to purchase goods in substitution for those due from the seller.

(2) The buyer may recover from the seller as damages the difference between the cost of cover and the contract price together with any incidental or consequential damages as hereinafter defined (Section 2-715), but less expenses saved in consequence of the seller's breach.

(3) Failure of the buyer to effect cover

683

within this section does not bar him from any other remedy.

Section 2-713. Buyer's Damages for Non-Delivery or Repudiation.

(1) Subject to the provisions of this Article with respect to proof of market price (Section 2-723), the measure of damages for non-delivery or repudiation by the seller is the difference between the market price at the time when the buyer learned of the breach and the contract price together with any incidental and consequential damages provided in this Article (Section 2-715), but less expenses saved in consequence of the seller's breach.

(2) Market price is to be determined as of the place for tender or, in cases of rejection after arrival or revocation of acceptance, as of the place of arrival.

Section 2-714. Buyer's Damages for Breach in Regard to Accepted Goods.

(1) Where the buyer has accepted goods and given notification (subsection (3) of Section 2-607) he may recover as damages for any non-conformity of tender the loss resulting in the ordinary course of events from the seller's breach as determined in any manner which is reasonable.

(2) The measure of damages for breach of warranty is the difference at the time and place of acceptance between the value of the goods accepted and the value they would have had if they had been as warranted, unless special circumstances show proximate damages of a different amount.

(3) In a proper case any incidental and consequential damages under the next section may also be recovered.

Section 2-715. Buyer's Incidental and Consequential Damages.

(1) Incidental damages resulting from the seller's breach include expenses reasonably incurred in inspection, receipt, transportation and care and custody of goods rightfully rejected, any commercially reasonable charges, expenses or commissions in connection with effecting cover and any other reasonable expense incident to the delay or other breach.

(2) Consequential damages resulting from the seller's breach include

(a) any loss resulting from general or particular requirements and needs of which the seller at the time of contract-ing had reason to know and which could not reasonably be prevented by cover or otherwise; and

(b) injury to person or property proximately resulting from any breach of warranty.

Section 2-716. Buyer's Right to Specific Performance or Replevin.

(1) Specific performance may be decreed where the goods are unique or in other proper circumstances.

(2) The decree for specific performance may include such terms and conditions as to payment of the price, damages, or other relief as the court may deem just.

(3) The buyer has a right of replevin for goods identified to the contract if after reasonable effort he is unable to effect cover for such goods or the circumstances reasonably indicate that such effort will be unavailing or if the goods have been shipped under reservation and satisfaction of the security interest in them has been made or tendered.

Section 2-717. Deduction of Damages from the Price. The buyer on notifying the seller of his intention to do so may deduct all or any part of the damages resulting from any breach of the contract from any part of the price still due under the same contract.

Section 2-718. Liquidation or Limitation of Damages; Deposits.

(1) Damages for breach by either party may be liquidated in the agreement but only at an amount which is reasonable in the light of the anticipated or actual harm caused by the breach, the difficulties of proof of loss, and the inconvenience or non-feasibility of otherwise obtaining an adequate remedy. A term fixing unreasonably large liquidated damages is void as a penalty.

(2) Where the seller justifiably withholds delivery of goods because of the buyer's breach, the buyer is entitled to restitution of any amount by which the sum of his payments exceeds

(a) the amount to which the seller is entitled by virtue of terms liquidating the seller's damages in accordance with subsection (1), or

(b) in the absence of such terms, twenty per cent of the value of the total performance for which the buyer is obligated under the contract or $500, whichever is smaller.

(3) The buyer's right to restitution under subsection (2) is subject to offset to the extent that the seller establishes

    (a) a right to recover damages under the provisions of this Article other than subsection (1), and

    (b) the amount or value of any benefits received by the buyer directly or indirectly by reason of the contract.

(4) Where a seller has received payment in goods their reasonable value or the proceeds of their resale shall be treated as payments for the purposes of subsection (2); but if the seller has notice of the buyer's breach before reselling goods received in part performance, his resale is subject to the conditions laid down in this Article on resale by an aggrieved seller (Section 2-706).

Section 2-719. Contractual Modification or Limitation of Remedy.

(1) Subject to the provisions of subsections (2) and (3) of this section and of the preceding section on liquidation and limitation of damages,

    (a) the agreement may provide for remedies in addition to or in substitution for those provided in this Article and may limit or alter the measure of damages recoverable under this Article, as by limiting the buyer's remedies to return of the goods and repayment of the price or to repair and replacement of nonconforming goods or parts; and

    (b) resort to a remedy as provided is optional unless the remedy is expressly agreed to be exclusive, in which case it is the sole remedy.

(2) Where circumstances cause an exclusive or limited remedy to fail of its essential purpose, remedy may be had as provided in this Act.

(3) Consequential damages may be limited or excluded unless the limitation or exclusion is unconscionable. Limitation of consequential damages for injury to the person in the case of consumer goods is prima facie unconscionable but limitation of damages where the loss is commercial is not.

Section 2-720. Effect of "Cancellation" or "Rescission" on Claims for Antecedent Breach.

Unless the contrary intention clearly appears, expressions of "cancellation" or "rescission" of the contract or the like shall not be construed as a renunciation or discharge of any claim in damages for an antecedent breach.

Section 2-712. Remedies for Fraud.

Remedies for material misrepresentation or fraud include all remedies available under this Article for non-fraudulent breach. Neither rescission or a claim for rescission of the contract for sale nor rejection or return of the goods shall bar or be deemed inconsistent with a claim for damages or other remedy.

Section 2-722. Who can sue Third Parties for Injury to Goods.

Where a third party so deals with goods which have been identified to a contract for sale as to cause actionable injury to a party to that contract

    (a) a right of action against the third party is in either party to the contract for sale who has title to or a security interest or a special property or an insurable interest in the goods; and if the goods have been destroyed or converted a right of action is also in the party who either bore the risk of loss under the contract for sale or has since the injury assumed that risk as against the other;

    (b) if at the time of the injury the party plaintiff did not bear the risk of loss as against the other party to the contract for sale and there is no arrangement between them for disposition of the recovery, his suit or settlement is, subject to his own interest, as a fiduciary for the other party to the contract;

    (c) either party may with the consent of the other sue for the benefit of whom it may concern.

Section 2-723. Proof or Market Price: Time and Place.

(1) If an action based on anticipatory repudiation comes to trial before the time for performance with respect to some or all of the goods, any damages based on market price (Section 2-708 or Section 2-713) shall be determined according to the price of such goods prevailing at the time when the aggrieved party learned of the repudiation.

(2) If evidence of a price prevailing at the times or places described in this Article is not readily available the price prevailing within any reasonable time before or after the time described or at any other place which in commercial judgment or under

usage of trade would serve as a reasonable substitute for the one described may be used, making any proper allowance for the cost of transporting the goods to or from such other place.

(3) Evidence of a relevant price prevailing at a time or place other than the one described in this Article offered by one party is not admissible unless and until he has given the other party such notice as the court finds sufficient to prevent unfair surprise.

Section 2-724. Admissibility of Market Quotations. Whenever the prevailing price or value of any goods regularly bought and sold in any established commodity market is in issue, reports in official publications or trade journals or in newspapers or periodicals of general circulation published as the reports of such market shall be admissible in evidence. The circumstances of the preparation of such a report may be shown to affect its weight but not its admissibility.

Section 2-725. Statute of Limitations in Contracts for Sale.

(1) An action for breach of any contract for sale must be commenced within four years after the cause of action has accrued.

By the original agreement the parties may reduce the period of limitation to not less than one year but may not extend it.

(2) A cause of action accrues when the breach occurs, regardless of the aggrieved party's lack of knowledge of the breach. A breach of warranty occurs when tender of delivery is made, except that where a warranty explicitly extends to future performance of the goods and discovery of the breach must await the time of such performance the cause of action accrues when the breach is or should have been discovered.

(3) Where an action commenced within the time limited by subsection (1) is so terminated as to leave available a remedy by another action from the same breach such other action may be commenced after the expiration of the time limited and within six months after the termination of the first action unless the termination resulted from voluntary discontinuance or from dismissal for failure or neglect to prosecute.

(4) This section does not alter the law on tolling of the statute of limitations nor does it apply to causes of action which have accrued before this Act becomes effective.

ARTICLE 3

COMMERCIAL PAPER

PART 1

SHORT TITLE, FORM AND INTERPRETATION

Section 3-101. Short Title. This article shall be known and may be cited as Uniform Commercial Code—Commercial Paper.

Section 3-102. Definitions and Index of Definitions.

(1) In this Article unless the context otherwise requires

(a) "Issue" means the first delivery of an instrument to a holder or a remitter.

(b) An "order" is a direction to pay and must be more than an authorization or request. It must identify the person to pay with reasonable certainty. It may be addressed to one or more such persons jointly or in the alternative but not in succession.

(c) A "promise" is an undertaking to pay and must be more than an acknowledgment of an obligation.

(d) "Secondary party" means a drawer or endorser.

(e) "Instrument" means a negotiable instrument.

(2) Other definitions applying to this Article and the sections in which they appear are:

"Acceptance." Section 3-410.
"Accommodation party." Section 3-415.
"Alteration." Section 3-407.
"Certificate of deposit." Section 3-104.
"Certification." Section 3-411.
"Check." Section 3-104.
"Definite time." Section 3-109.
"Dishonor." Section 3-507.
"Draft." Section 3-104.
"Holder in due course." Section 3-302.
"Negotiation." Section 3-202.
"Note." Section 3-104.

"Notice of dishonor." Section 3-508.

"On demand." Section 3-108.

"Presentment." Section 3-504.

"Protest." Section 3-509.

"Restrictive Indorsement." Section 3-205.

"Signature." Section 3-401.

(3) The following definitions in other Articles apply to this Article:

"Account." Section 4-104.

"Banking Day." Section 4-104.

"Clearing house." Section 4-104.

"Collecting bank." Section 4-105.

"Customer." Section 4-104.

"Depositary Bank." Section 4-105.

"Documentary Draft." Section 4-104.

"Intermediary Bank." Section 4-105.

"Item." Section 4-104.

"Midnight deadline." Section 4-104.

"Payor bank." Section 4-105.

(4) In addition Article 1 contains general definitions and principles of construction and interpretation applicable throughout this Article.

Section 3-103. Limitations on Scope of Article.

(1) This Article does not apply to money, documents of title or investment securities.

(2) The provisions of this Article are subject to the provisions of the Article on Bank Deposits and Collections (Article 4) and Secured Transactions (Article 9).

Section 3-104. Form of Negotiable Instruments: "Draft"; "Check"; "Certificate of Deposit"; "Note."

(1) Any writing to be a negotiable instrument within this Article must

(a) be signed by the maker or drawer; and

(b) contain an unconditional promise or order to pay a sum certain in money and no other promise, order, obligation or power given by the maker or drawer except as authorized by this Article; and

(c) be payable on demand or at a definite time; and

(d) be payable to order or to bearer.

(2) A writing which complies with the requirements of this section is

(a) a "draft" ("bill of exchange") if it is an order;

(b) a "check" if it is a draft drawn on a bank and payable on demand;

(c) a "certificate of deposit" if it is an acknowledgment by a bank of receipt of money with an engagement to repay it;

(d) a "note" if it is a promise other than a certificate of deposit.

(3) As used in other Articles of this Act, and as the context may require, the terms "draft," "check," "certificate of deposit" and "note" may refer to instruments which are not negotiable within this Article as well as to instruments which are so negotiable.

Section 3-105. When Promise or Order Unconditional.

(1) A promise or order otherwise unconditional is not made conditional by the fact that the instrument

(a) is subject to implied or constructive conditions; or

(b) states its consideration, whether performed or promised, or the transaction which gave rise to the instrument, or that the promise or order is made or the instrument matures in accordance with or "as per" such transaction; or

(c) refers to or states that it arises out of a separate agreement or refers to a separate agreement for rights as to prepayment or acceleration; or

(d) states that it is drawn under a letter of credit; or

(e) states that it is secured, whether by mortgage, reservation of title or otherwise; or

(f) indicates a particular account to be debited or any other fund or source from which reimbursement is expected; or

(g) is limited to payment out of a particular fund or the proceeds of a particular source, if the instrument is issued by a government or governmental agency or unit; or

(h) is limited to payment out of the entire assets of a partnership, unincorporated association, trust or estate by or on behalf of which the instrument is issued.

(2) A promise or order is not unconditional if the instrument

(a) states that it is subject to or governed by any other agreement; or

(b) states that it is to be paid only out of a particular fund or source except as provided in this section.

Section 3-106. Sum Certain.

(1) The sum payable is a sum certain even though it is to be paid

(a) with stated interest or by stated installments; or

(b) with stated different rates of interest before and after default or a specified date; or

(c) with a stated discount or addition if paid before or after the date fixed for payment; or

(d) with exchange or less exchange, whether at a fixed rate or at the current rate; or

(e) with costs of collection or an attorney's fee or both upon default.

(2) Nothing in this section shall validate any term which is otherwise illegal.

Section 3-107. Money.

(1) An instrument is payable in money if the medium of exchange in which it is payable is money at the time the instrument is made. An instrument payable in "currency" or "current funds" is payable in money.

(2) A promise or order to pay a sum stated in a foreign currency is for a sum certain in money and, unless a different medium of payment is specified in the instrument, may be satisfied by payment of that number of dollars which the stated foreign currency will purchase at the buying sight rate for that currency on the day on which the instrument is payable or, if payable on demand, on the day of demand. If such an instrument specifies a foreign currency as the medium of payment the instrument is payable in that currency.

Section 3-108. Payable on Demand.

Instruments payable on demand include those payable at sight or on presentation and those in which no time for payment is stated.

Section 3-109. Definite Time.

(1) An instrument is payable at a definite time if by its terms it is payable

(a) on or before a stated date or at a fixed period after a stated date; or

(b) at a fixed period after sight; or

(c) at a definite time subject to any acceleration; or

(d) at a definite time subject to extension at the option of the holder, or to extension to a further definite time at the option of the maker or acceptor or automatically upon or after a specified act or event.

(2) An instrument which by its terms is otherwise payable only upon an act or event

uncertain as to time of occurrence is not payable at a definite time even though the act or event has occurred.

Section 3-110. Payable to Order.

(1) An instrument is payable to order when by its terms it is payable to the order or assigns of any person therein specified with reasonable certainty, or to him or his order, or when it is conspicuously designated on its face as "exchange" or the like and names a payee. It may be payable to the order of

(a) the maker or drawer; or

(b) the drawee; or

(c) a payee who is not maker, drawer or drawee; or

(d) two or more payees together or in the alternative; or

(e) an estate, trust or fund, in which case it is payable to the order of the representative of each estate, trust or fund or his successors; or

(f) an office, or an officer by his title as such in which case it is payable to the principal but the incumbent of the office or his successors may act as if he or they were the holder; or

(g) a partnership or unincorporated association, in which case it is payable to the partnership or association and may be indorsed or transferred by any person thereto authorized.

(2) An instrument not payable to order is not made so payable by such words as "payable upon return of this instrument properly indorsed."

(3) an instrument made payable both to order and to bearer is payable to order unless the bearer words are handwritten or typewritten.

Section 3-111. Payable to Bearer.

An instrument is payable to bearer when by its terms it is payable to

(a) bearer or the order of bearer; or

(b) a specified person or bearer; or

(c) "cash" or the order of "cash," or any other indication which does not purport to designate a specific payee.

Section 3-112. Terms and Omissions Not Affecting Negotiability.

(1) The negotiability of an instrument is not affected by

(a) the omission of a statement of any

consideration or of the place where the instrument is drawn or payable; or

(b) a statement that collateral has been given to secure obligations either on the instrument or otherwise of an obligor on the instrument or that in case of default on those obligations the holder may realize on or dispose of the collateral; or

(c) a promise or power to maintain or protect collateral or to give additional collateral; or

(d) a term authorizing a confession of judgment on the instrument if it is not paid when due; or

(e) a term purporting to waive the benefit of any law intended for the advantage or protection of any obligor; or

(f) a term in a draft providing that the payee by indorsing or cashing it acknowledges full satisfaction of an obligation of the drawer; or

(g) a statement in a draft drawn in a set of parts (Section 3-801) to the effect that the order is effective only if no other part has been honored.

(2) Nothing in this section shall validate any term which is otherwise illegal.

Section 3-113. Seal.
An instrument otherwise negotiable is within this Article even though it is under a seal.

Section 3-114. Date, Antedating, Postdating.
(1) The negotiability of an instrument is not affected by the fact that it is undated, antedated or postdated.

(2) Where an instrument is antedated or postdated the time when it is payable is determined by the stated date if the instrument is payable on demand or at a fixed period after date.

(3) Where the instrument or any signature thereon is dated, the date is presumed to be correct.

Section 3-115. Incomplete Instruments.
(1) When a paper whose contents at the time of signing show that it is intended to become an instrument is signed while still incomplete in any necessary respect it cannot be enforced until completed.

(2) If the completion is unauthorized the rules as to material alteration apply (Section 3-407), even though the paper was not delivered by the maker or drawer; but the burden of establishing that any completion is unauthorized is on the party so asserting.

Section 3-116. Instruments Payable to Two or More Persons.
An instrument payable to the order of two or more persons

(a) if in the alternative is payable to any one of them and may be negotiated, discharged or enforced by any of them who has possession of it;

(b) if not in the alternative is payable to all of them and may be negotiated, discharged or enforced only by all of them.

Section 3-117. Instruments Payable with Words of Description.
An instrument made payable to a named person with the addition of words describing him

(a) as agent or officer of a specified person is payable to his principal but the agent or officer may act as if he were the holder;

(b) as any other fiduciary for a specified person or purpose is payable to the payee and may be negotiated, discharged or enforced by him;

(c) in any other manner is payable to the payee unconditionally and the additional words are without effect on subsequent parties.

Section 3-118. Ambiguous Terms and Rules of Construction.
The following rules apply to every instrument:

(a) Where there is doubt whether the instrument is a draft or a note the holder may treat it as either. A draft drawn on the drawer is effective as a note.

(b) Handwritten terms control typewritten and printed terms, and typewritten control printed.

(c) Words control figures except that if the words are ambiguous figures control.

(d) Unless otherwise specified a provision for interest means interest at the judgment rate at the place of payment from the date of the instrument, or if it is undated from the date of issue.

(e) Unless the instrument otherwise specifies two or more persons who sign as maker, acceptor or drawer or indorser and as a part of the same transaction are jointly and severally liable even though the instrument contains such words as "I promise to pay."

(f) Unless otherwise specified consent to extension authorizes a single extension for not longer than the original period. A consent to extension, expressed in the instrument, is binding on secondary parties and accommodation makers. A holder may not exercise his option to extend an instrument over the objection of a maker or acceptor or other party who in accordance with Section 3-604 tenders full payment when the instrument is due.

Section 3-119. Other Writings Affecting Instrument.

(1) As between the obligor and his immediate obligee or any transferee the terms of an instrument may be modified or affected by any other written agreement executed as a part of the same transaction, except that a holder in due course is not affected by any limitation of his rights arising out of the separate written agreement if he had no notice of the limitation when he took the instrument.

(2) A separate agreement does not affect the negotiability of an instrument.

Section 3-120. Instruments "Payable Through" Bank.

An instrument which states that it is "payable through" a bank or the like designates that bank as a collecting bank to make presentment but does not of itself authorize the bank to pay the instrument.

Section 3-121. Instruments Payable at Bank.

NOTE: *If this Act is introduced in the Congress of the United States this section should be omitted.*

(States to select either alternative)

Alternative A—
A note or acceptance which states that it is payable at a bank is the equivalent of a draft drawn on the bank payable when it falls due out of any funds of the maker or acceptor in current account or otherwise available for such payment.

Alternative B—
A note or acceptance which states that it is payable at a bank is not of itself an order or authorization to the bank to pay it.

Section 3-122. Accrual of Cause of Action.

(1) A cause of action against a maker or an acceptor accrues
    (a) in the case of a time instrument on the day after maturity;
    (b) in the case of a demand instrument upon its date or, if no date is stated, on the date of issue.

(2) A cause of action against the obligor of a demand or time certificate of deposit accrues upon demand, but demand on a time certificate may not be made until on or after the date of maturity.

(3) A cause of action against a drawer of a draft or an indorser of any instrument accrues upon demand following dishonor of the instrument. Notice of dishonor is a demand.

(4) Unless an instrument provides otherwise, interest runs at the rate provided by law for a judgment
    (a) in the case of a maker, acceptor or other primary obligor of a demand instrument, from the date of demand;
    (b) in all other cases from the date of accrual of the cause of action.

PART 2

TRANSFER AND NEGOTIATION

Section 3-201. Transfer: Right to Indorsement.

(1) Transfer of an instrument vests in the transferee such rights as the transferor has therein, except that a transferee who has himself been a party to any fraud or illegality affecting the instrument or who as a prior holder had notice of a defense or claim against it cannot improve his position by taking from a later holder a due course.

(2) A transfer of a security interest in an instrument vests the foregoing rights in the transferee to the extent of the interest transferred.

(3) Unless otherwise agreed any transfer for value of an instrument not then payable to bearer gives the transferee the specifically enforceable right to have the unqualified indorsement of the transferor. Negotiation takes effect only when the indorsement is made and until that time there is no presumption that the transferee is the owner.

Section 3-202. Negotiation.

(1) Negotiation is the transfer of an instrument in such form that the transferee becomes a holder. If the instrument is payable to order it is negotiated by delivery

with any necessary indorsement; if payable to bearer it is negotiated by delivery.

(2) An indorsement must be writted by or on behalf of the holder and on the instrument or on a paper so firmly affixed thereto as to become a part thereof.

(3) An indorsement is effective for negotiation only when it conveys the entire instrument or any unpaid residue. If it purports to be of less it operates only as a partial assignment.

(4) Words of assignment, condition, waiver, guaranty, limitation or disclaimer of liability and the like accompanying an indorsement do not affect its character as an indorsement.

Section 3-203. Wrong or Misspelled Name. Where an instrument is made payable to a person under a misspelled name or one other than his own he may indorse in that name or his own or both; but signature in both names may be required by a person paying or giving value for the instrument.

Section 3-204. Special Indorsement; Blank Indorsement.

(1) A special indorsement specifies the person to whom or to whose order it makes the instrument payable. Any instrument specially indorsed becomes payable to the order of the special indorsee and may be further negotiated only by his indorsement.

(2) An indorsement in blank specifies no particular indorsee and may consist of a mere signature. An instrument payable to order and indorsed in blank becomes payable to bearer and may be negotiated by delivery alone until specially indorsed.

(3) The holder may convert a blank indorsement into a special indorsement by writing over the signature of the indorser in blank any contract consistent with the character of the indorsement.

Section 3-205. Restrictive Indorsements. An indorsement is restrictive which either

(a) is conditional; or

(b) purports to prohibit further transfer of the instrument; or

(c) includes the words "for collection," "for deposit," "pay any bank" or like terms signifying a purpose of deposit or collection; or

(d) otherwise states that it is for the benefit or use of the indorser or of another person.

Section 3-206. Effect of Restrictive Indorsement.

(1) No restrictive indorsement presents further transfer or negotiation of the instrument.

(2) An intermediary bank, or a payor bank which is not the depositary bank, is neither given notice nor otherwise affected by a restrictive indorsement of any person except the bank's immediate transferor or the person presenting for payment.

(3) Except for an intermediary bank, any transferee under an indorsement which is conditional or includes the words "for collection," "for deposit," "pay any bank," or like terms (subparagraphs (a) and (c) of Section 3-205) must pay or apply any value given by him for or on the security of the instrument consistently with the indorsement and to the extent that he does so he becomes a holder for value. In addition such transferee is a holder in due course if he otherwise complies with the requirements of Section 3-302 on what constitutes a holder in due course.

(4) The first taker under an indorsement for the benefit of the indorser of another person (subparagraph (d) of Section 3-205) must pay or apply any value given by him for or on the security of the instrument consistently with the indorsement and to the extent that he does so he becomes a holder for value. In addition such taker is a holder in due course if he otherwise complies with the requirements of Section 3-302 on what constitutes a holder in due course. A later holder for value is neither given notice nor otherwise affected by such restrictive indorsement unless he has knowledge that a fiduciary or other person has negotiated the instrument in any transaction for his own benefit or otherwise in breach of duty (subsection (2) of Section 3-304).

Section 3-207. Negotiation Effective Although it may be Rescinded.

(1) Negotiation is effective to transfer the instrument although the negotiation is

(a) made by an infant, a corporation exceeding its power, or any other person without capacity; or

(b) obtained by fraud, duress or mistake of any kind; or

(c) part of an illegal transaction; or

(d) made in breach of duty.

(2) Except as against a subsequent holder

in due course such negotiation is in an appropriate case subject to rescission, the declaration of a constructive trust or any other remedy permitted by law.

Section 3-208. Reacquisition. Where an instrument is returned to or reacquired by a prior party he may cancel any indorsement which is not necessary to his title and reissue or further negotiate the instrument, but any intervening party is discharged as against the reacquiring party and subsequent holders not in due course and if his indorsement has been cancelled is discharged as against subsequent holders in due course as well.

PART 3

RIGHTS OF A HOLDER

Section 3-301. Rights of a Holder.
The holder of an instrument whether or not he is the owner may transfer or negotiate it and, except as otherwise provided in Section 3-603 on payment or satisfaction, discharge it or enforce payment in his own name.

Section 3-302. Holder in Due Course.
(1)   A holder in due course is a holder who takes the instrument
   (a)   for value; and
   (b)   in good faith; and
   (c)   without notice that it is overdue or has been dishonored or of any defense against or claim to it on the part of any person.
(2)   A payee may be a holder in due course.
(3)   A holder does not become a holder in due course of an instrument:
   (a)   by purchase of it at judicial sale or by taking it under legal process; or
   (b)   by acquiring it in taking over an estate; or
   (c)   by purchasing it as part of a bulk transaction not in regular course of business of the transferor.
(4)   A purchaser of a limited interest can be a holder in due course only to the extent of the interest purchased.

Section 3-303. Taking for Value. A holder takes the instrument for value
   (a)   to the extent that the agreed consideration has been performed or that he acquires a security interest in or a lien on the instrument otherwise than by legal process; or
   (b)   when he takes the instrument in payment of or as security for an antecedent claim against any person whether or not the claim is due; or
   (c)   when he gives a negotiable instrument for it or makes an irrevocable commitment to a third person.

Section 3-304. Notice to Purchaser.
(1)   The purchaser has notice of a claim or defense if
   (a)   the instrument is so incomplete, bears such visible evidence of forgery or alteration, or is otherwise so irregular as to call into question its validity, terms or ownership or to create an ambiguity as the party to pay; or
   (b)   the purchaser has notice that the obligation of any party is voidable in whole or in part, or that all parties have been discharged.
(2)   The purchaser has notice of a claim against the instrument when he has knowledge that a fiduciary has negotiated the instrument in payment of or as security for his own debt or in any transaction for his own benefit or otherwise in breach of duty.
(3)   The purchaser has notice that an instrument is overdue if he has reason to know
   (a)   that any part of the principal amount is overdue or that there is an uncured default in payment of another instrument of the same series; or
   (b)   that acceleration of the instrument has been made; or
   (c)   that he is taking a demand instrument after demand has been made or more than a reasonable length of time after its issue. A reasonable time for a check drawn and payable within the states and territories of the United States and the District of Columbia is presumed to be thirty days.
(4)   Knowledge of the following facts does

not of itself give the purchaser notice of a defense of claim

(a) that the instrument is antedated or postdated;

(b) that it was issued or negotiated in return for an executory promise or accompanied by a separate agreement, unless the purchaser has notice that a defense or claim has arisen from the terms thereof;

(c) that any party has signed for accommodation;

(d) that an incomplete instrument has been completed, unless the purchaser has notice of any improper completion;

(e) that any person negotiating the instrument is or was a fiduciary;

(f) that there has been default in payment of interest on the instrument or in payment of any other instrument, except one of the same series.

(5) The filing or recording of a document does not of itself constitute notice within the provisions of this Article to a person who would otherwise be a holder in due course.

(6) To be effective notice must be received at such time and in such manner as to give a reasonable opportunity to act on it.

Section 3-305. Rights of a Holder in Due Course. To the extent that a holder is a holder in due course he takes the instrument free from

(1) all claims to it on the part of any person; and

(2) all defenses of any party to the instrument with whom the holder has not dealt except

(a) infancy, to the extent that it is a defense to a simple contract; and

(b) such other incapacity, or duress, or illegality of the transaction, as renders the obligation of the party a nullity; and

(c) such misrepresentation as has induced the party to sign the instrument with neither knowledge nor reasonable opportunity to obtain knowledge of its character or its essential terms; and

(d) discharge in insolvency proceedings; and

(e) any other discharge of which the holder has notice when he takes the instrument.

Section 3-306. Rights of One Not Holder in Due Course. Unless he has the rights of a holder in due course any person takes the instrument subject to

(a) all valid claims to it on the part of any person; and

(b) all defenses of any party which would be available in an action on a simple contract; and

(c) the defenses of want or failure of consideration, non-performance of any condition precedent, non-delivery, or delivery for a special purpose (Section 3-408); and

(d) the defense that he or a person through whom he holds the instrument acquired it by theft, or that payment or satisfaction to such holder would be inconsistent with the terms of a restrictive indorsement. The claim of any third person to the instrument is not otherwise available as a defense to any party liable thereon unless the third person himself defends the action for such party.

Section 3-307. Burden of Establishing Signatures, Defenses and Due Course.

(1) Unless specifically denied in the pleadings each signature on an instrument is admitted. When the effectiveness of a signature is put in issue

(a) the burden of establishing it is on the party claiming under the signature; but

(b) the signature is presumed to be genuine or authorized except where the action is to enforce the obligation of a purported signer who has died or become incompetent before proof is required.

(2) When signatures are admitted or established, production of the instrument entitles a holder to recover on it unless the defendant establishes a defense.

(3) After it is shown that a defense exists a person claiming the rights of a holder in due course has the burden of establishing that he or some person under whom he claims is in all respects a holder in due course.

Section 3-401. Signature.

(1) No person is liable on an instrument unless his signature appears thereon.

(2) A signature is made by use of any name, including any trade or assumed name, upon an instrument, or by any word or mark used in lieu of a written signature.

Section 3-402. Signature in Ambiguous Capacity.
Unless the instrument clearly indicates that a signature is made in some other capacity it is an indorsement.

Section 3-403. Signature of Authorized Representative.

(1) A signature may be made by an agent or other representative, and his authority to make it may be established as in other cases of representation. No particular form of appointment is necessary to establish such authority.

(2) An authorized representative who signs his own name to an instrument

(a) is personally obligated if the instrument neither names the person represented nor shows that the representative signed in a representative capacity;

(b) except as otherwise established between the immediate parties, is personally obligated if the instrument names the person represented but does not show that the representative signed in a representative capacity, or if the instrument does not name the person represented but does show that the representative signed in a representative capacity.

(3) Except as otherwise established the name of an organization preceded or followed by the name and office of an authorized individual is a signature made in a representative capacity.

Section 3-404. Unauthorized Signatures.

(1) Any unauthorized signature is wholly inoperative as that of the person whose name is signed unless he ratifies it or is precluded from denying it; but it operates as the signature of the unauthorized signer in favor of any person who in good faith pays the instrument or takes it for value.

(2) Any unauthorized signature may be ratified for all purposes of this Article. Such ratification does not of itself affect any rights of the person ratifying against the actual signer.

Section 3-405. Impostors; Signature in Name of Payee.

(1) An indorsement by any person in the name of a named payee is effective if

(a) an impostor by use of the mails or otherwise has induced the maker or drawer to issue the instrument to him or his confederate in the name of the payee; or

(b) a person signing as or on behalf of a maker or drawer intends the payee to have no interest in the instrument; or

(c) an agent or employee of the maker or drawer has supplied him with the name of the payee intending the latter to have no such interest.

(2) Nothing in this section shall affect the criminal or civil liability of the person so indorsing.

Section 3-406. Negligence Contributing to Alteration or Unauthorized Signature.
Any person who by his negligence substantially contributes to a material alteration of the instrument or to the making of an unauthorized signature is precluded from asserting the alteration or lack of authority against a holder in due course or against a drawee or other payor who pays the instrument in good faith and in accordance with the reasonable commercial standards of the drawee's or payor's business.

Section 3-407. Alteration.

(1) Any alteration of an instrument is material which changes the contract of any party thereto in any respect, including any such change in

(a) the number or relations of the parties; or

(b) an incomplete instrument, by completing it otherwise than as authorized; or

(c) the writing as signed, by adding to it or by removing any part of it.

(2) As against any person other than a subsequent holder in due course

(a) alteration by the holder which is both fraudulent and material discharges any party whose contract is thereby

694

changed unless that party assents or is precluded from asserting the defense;

(b) no other alteration discharges any party and the instrument may be enforced according to its original tenor, or as to incomplete instruments according to the authority given.

(3) A subsequent holder in due course may in all cases enforce the instrument according to its original tenor, and when an incomplete instrument has been completed, he may enforce it as completed.

Section 3-408. Consideration.

Want or failure of consideration is a defense as against any person not having the rights of a holder in due course (Section 3-305), except that no consideration is necessary for an instrument or obligation thereon given in payment of or as security for an antecedent obligation of any kind. Nothing in this section shall be taken to displace any statute outside this Act under which a promise is enforceable notwithstanding lack or failure of consideration. Partial failure of consideration is a defense pro tanto whether or not the failure is in an ascertained or liquidated amount.

Section 3-409. Draft Not an Assignment.

(1) A check or other draft does not of itself operate as an assignment of any funds in the hands of the drawee available for its payment, and the drawee is not liable on the instrument until he accepts it.

(2) Nothing in this section shall affect any liability in contract, tort or otherwise arising from any letter of credit or other obligation or representation which is not an acceptance.

Section 3-410. Definition and Operation of Acceptance.

(1) Acceptance is the drawee's signed engagement to honor the draft as presented. It must be written on the draft, and may consist of his signature alone. It becomes operative when completed by delivery or notification.

(2) A draft may be accepted although it has not been signed by the drawer or is otherwise incomplete or is overdue or has been dishonored.

(3) Where the draft is payable at a fixed period after sight and the acceptor fails to date his acceptance the holder may complete it by supplying a date in good faith.

Section 3-411. Certificate of a Check.

(1) Certification of a check is acceptance.

Where a holder procures certification the drawer and all prior indorsers are discharged.

(2) Unless otherwise agreed a bank has no obligation to certify a check.

(3) A bank may certify a check before returning it for lack of proper indorsement. If it does so the drawer is discharged.

Section 3-412. Acceptance Varying Draft.

(1) Where the drawee's proffered acceptance in any manner varies the draft as presented the holder may refuse the acceptance and treat the draft as dishonored in which case the drawee is entitled to have his acceptance cancelled.

(2) The terms of the draft are not varied by an acceptance to pay at any particular bank or place in the United States, unless the acceptance states that the draft is to be paid only at such bank or place.

(3) Where the holder assents to an acceptance varying the terms of the draft each drawer and indorser who does not affirmatively assent is discharged.

Section 3-413. Contract of Maker, Drawer and Acceptor.

(1) The maker or acceptor engages that he will pay the instrument according to its tenor at the time of his engagement or as completed pursuant to Section 3-115 on incomplete instruments.

(2) The drawer engages that upon dishonor of the draft and any necessary notice of dishonor or protest he will pay the amount of the draft to the holder or to any indorser who takes it up. The drawer may disclaim this liability by drawing without recourse.

(3) By making, drawing or accepting the party admits as against all subsequent parties including the drawee the existence of the payee and his then capacity to indorse.

Section 3-414. Contract of Indorser; Order of Liability.

(1) Unless the indorsement otherwise specifies (as by such words as "without recourse") every indorser engages that upon dishonor and any necessary notice of dishonor and protest he will pay the instrument according to its tenor at the time of his indorsement to the holder or to any subsequent indorser who takes it up, even though the indorser who takes it up was not obligated to do so.

(2) Unless they otherwise agree indorsers

are liable to one another in the order in which they indorse, which is presumed to be the order in which their signatures appear on the instrument.

Section 3-415. Contract of Accommodation Party.

(1) An accommodation party is one who signs the instrument in any capacity for the purpose of lending his name to another party to it.

(2) When the instrument has been taken for value before it is due the accommodation party is liable in the capacity in which he has signed even though the taker knows of the accommodation.

(3) As against a holder in due course and without notice of the accommodation oral proof of the accommodation is not admissible to give the accommodation party the benefit of discharges dependent on his character as such. In other cases the accommodation character may be shown by oral proof.

(4) An indorsement which shows that it is not in the chain of title is notice of its accommodation character.

(5) An accommodation party is not liable to the party accommodated, and if he pays the instrument has a right of recourse on the instrument against such party.

Section 3-416. Contract of Guarantor.

(1) "Payment guaranteed" or equivalent words added to a signature means that the signer engages that if the instrument is not paid when due he will pay it according to its tenor without resort by the holder to any other party.

(2) "Collection guaranteed" or equivalent words added to a signature mean that the signer engages that if the instrument is not paid when due he will pay it according to its tenor, but only after the holder has reduced his claim against the maker or acceptor to judgment and execution has been returned unsatisfied, or after the maker or acceptor has become insolvent or it is otherwise apparent that it is useless to proceed against him.

(3) Words of guaranty which do not otherwise specify guarantee payment.

(4) No words of guaranty added to the signature of a sole maker or acceptor affect his liability on the instrument. Such words added to the signature of one of two or more makers or acceptors create a presumption that the signature is for the accommodation of the others.

(5) When words of guaranty are used presentment, notice of dishonor and protest are not necessary to charge the user.

(6) Any guaranty written on the instrument is enforcible notwithstanding any statute of frauds.

Section 3-417. Warranties on Presentment and Transfer.

(1) Any person who obtains payment or acceptance and any prior transferor warrants to a person who in good faith pays or accepts that

(a) he has a good title to the instrument or is authorized to obtain payment or acceptance on behalf of one who has a good title; and

(b) he has no knowledge that the signature of the maker or drawer is unauthorized, except that this warranty is not given by a holder in due course acting in good faith

(i) to a maker with respect to the maker's own signature; or

(ii) to a drawer with respect to the drawer's own signature, whether or not the drawer is also the drawee; or

(iii) to an acceptor of a draft if the holder in due course took the draft after the acceptance or obtained the acceptance without knowledge that the drawer's signature was unauthorized; and

(c) the instrument has not been materially altered, except that this warranty is not given by a holder in due course acting in good faith

(i) to the maker of a note; or

(ii) to the drawer of a draft whether or not the drawer is also the drawee; or

(iii) to the acceptor of a draft with respect to alteration made prior to the acceptance, even though the acceptance provided "payable as originally drawn" or equivalent terms; or

(iv) to the acceptor of a draft with respect to an alteration made after the acceptance.

(2) Any person who transfers an instrument and receives consideration warrants to

his transferee and if the transfer is by indorsement to any subsequent holder who takes the instrument in good faith that

    (a) he has a good title to the instrument or is authorized to obtain payment or acceptance on behalf of one who has a good title and the transfer is otherwise rightful; and

    (b) all signatures are genuine or authorized; and

    (c) the instrument has not been materially altered; and

    (d) no defense of any party is good against him; and

    (e) he has no knowledge of any insolvency proceeding instituted with respect to the maker or acceptor or the drawer of an unaccepted instrument.

(3) By transferring "without recourse" the transferor limits the obligation stated in subsection (2) (d) to a warranty that he has no knowledge of such a defense.

(4) A selling agent or broker who does not disclose the fact that he is acting only as such gives the warranties provided in this section, but if he makes such disclosure warrants only his good faith and authority.

Section 3-418. Finality of Payment or Acceptance. Except for recovery of bank payments as provided in the Article on Bank Deposits and Collections (Article 4) and except for liability for breach of warranty on presentment under the preceding section, payment or acceptance of any instrument is final in favor of a holder in due course, or a person who has in good faith changed his position in reliance on the payment.

Section 3-419. Conversion of Instrument; Innocent Representative.

(1) An instrument is converted when

    (a) a drawee to whom it is delivered for acceptance refuses to return it on demand; or

    (b) any person to whom it is delivered for payment refuses on demand either to pay or to return it; or

    (c) it is paid on a forged indorsement.

(2) In an action against a drawee under subsection (1) the measure of the drawee's liability is the face amount of the instrument. In any other action under subsection (1) the measure of liability is presumed to be the face amount of the instrument.

(3) Subject to the provisions of this Act concerning restrictive indorsements a representative, including a depositary or collecting bank, who has in good faith and in accordance with the reasonable commercial standards applicable to the business of such representative dealt with an instrument or its proceeds on behalf of one who was not the true owner is not liable in conversion or otherwise to the true owner beyond the amount of any proceeds remaining in his hands.

(4) An intermediary bank or payor bank which is not a depositary bank is not liable in conversion solely by reason of the fact that proceeds of an item indorsed restrictively (Sections 3-205 and 3-206) are not paid or applied consistently with the restrictive indorsement of an indorser other than its immediate transferor.

PART 5

PRESENTMENT, NOTICE OF DISHONOR AND PROTEST

Section 3-501. When Presentment, Notice of Dishonor, and Protest Necessary or Permissible.

(1) Unless excused (Section 3-511) presentment is necessary to charge secondary parties as follows:

    (a) presentment for acceptance is necessary to charge the drawer and indorsers of a draft where the draft so provides, or is payable elsewhere than at the residence or place of business of the drawee, or its date of payment depends upon such presentment. The holder may at his option present for acceptance any other draft payable at a stated date;

    (b) presentment for payment is necessary to charge any indorser;

    (c) in the case of any drawer, the acceptor of a draft payable at a bank or the maker of a note payable at a bank, presentment for payment is necessary, but failure to make presentment discharges such drawer, acceptor or maker only as stated in Section 3-502(1) (b).

(2) Unless excused (Section 3-511)

(a) notice of any dishonor is necessary to charge any indorser;

(b) in the case of any drawer, the acceptor of a draft payable at a bank or the maker of a note payable at a bank, notice of any dishonor is necessary, but failure to give such notice discharges such drawer, acceptor or maker only as stated in Section 3-502(1) (b).

(3) Unless excused (Section 3-511) protest of any dishonor is necessary to charge the drawer and indorsers of any draft which on its face appears to be drawn or payable outside of the states and territories of the United States and the District of Columbia. The holder may at his option make protest of any dishonor of any other instrument and in the case of a foreign draft may on insolvency of the acceptor before maturity make protest for a better security.

(4) Notwithstanding any provision of this section, neither presentment nor notice of dishonor nor protest is necessary to charge an indorser who has indorsed an instrument after maturity.

Section 3-502. Unexcused Delay; Discharge.

(1) Where without excuse any necessary presentment or notice of dishonor is delayed beyond the time when it is due

(a) any indorser is discharged; and

(b) any drawer or the acceptor of a draft payable at a bank or the maker of a note payable at a bank who because the drawee or payor bank becomes insolvent during the delay is deprived of funds maintained with the drawee or payor bank to cover the instrument may discharge his liability by written assignment to the holder of his rights against the drawee or payor bank in respect of such funds, but such drawer, acceptor or maker is not otherwise discharged.

(2) Where without excuse a necessary protest is delayed beyond the time when it is due any drawer or indorser is discharged.

Section 3-503. Time of Presentment.

(1) Unless a different time is expressed in the instrument the time for any presentment is determined as follows:

(a) where an instrument is payable at or a fixed period after a stated date any presentment for acceptance must be made on or before the date it is payable;

(b) where an instrument is payable after sight it must either be presented for acceptance or negotiated within a reasonable time after date or issue whichever is later;

(c) where an instrument shows the date on which it is payable presentment for payment is due on that date;

(d) where an instrument is accelerated presentment for payment is due within a reasonable time after the acceleration;

(e) with respect to the liability of any secondary party presentment for acceptance or payment of any other instrument is due within a reasonable time after such party becomes liable thereon.

(2) A reasonable time for presentment is determined by the nature of the instrument, any usage of banking or trade and the facts of the particular case. In the case of an uncertified check which is drawn and payable within the United States and which is not a draft drawn by a bank the following are presumed to be reasonable periods within which to present for payment or to initiate bank collection:

(a) with respect to the liability of the drawer, thirty days after date or issue which ever is later and

(b) with respect to the liability of an indorser, seven days after his indorsement.

(3) Where any presentment is due on a day which is not a full business day for either the person making presentment or the party to pay or accept, presentment is due on the next following day which is a full business day for both parties.

(4) Presentment to be sufficient must be made at a reasonable hour, and if at a bank during its banking day.

Section 3-504. How Presentment Made.

(1) Presentment is a demand for acceptance or payment made upon the maker, acceptor, drawee or other payor by or on behalf of the holder.

(2) Presentment may be made

(a) by mail, in which even the time of presentment is determined by the time or receipt of the mail; or

(b) through a clearing house; or

(c) at the place of acceptance or payment specified in the instrument or if there be none at the place of business or residence of the party to accept or pay. If neither the party to accept or pay nor anyone authorized to act for him is present or accessible at such place presentment is excused.

(3) It may be made

(a) to any one of two or more makers, acceptors, drawees or other payors; or

(b) to any person who has authority to make or refuse the acceptance or payment.

(4) A draft accepted or a note made payable at a bank in the United States must be presented at such bank.

(5) In the cases described in Section 4-210 presentment may be made in the manner and with the result stated in that section.

Section 3-505. Rights of Party to Whom Presentment is Made.

(1) The party to whom presentment is made may without dishonor require

(a) exhibition of the instrument; and

(b) reasonable identification of the person making presentment and evidence of his authority to make it if made for another; and

. (c) that the instrument be produced for acceptance or payment at a place specified in it, or if there be none at any place reasonable in the circumstances; and

(d) a signed receipt on the instrument for any partial or full payment and its surrender upon full payment.

(2) Failure to comply with any such requirement invalidates the presentment but the person presenting has a reasonable time in which to comply and the time for acceptance or payment runs from the time of compliance.

Section 3-506. Time Allowed for Acceptance or Payment.

(1) Acceptance may be deferred without dishonor until the close of the next business day following presentment. The holder may also in good faith effort to obtain acceptance and without either dishonor of the instrument or discharge of secondary parties allow postponement of acceptance for an additional business day.

(2) Except as a longer time is allowed in the case of documentary drafts drawn under a letter of credit, and unless an earlier time

is agreed to by the party to pay, payment of an instrument may be deferred without dishonor pending reasonable examination to determine whether it is properly payable, but payment must be made in any event before the close of business on the day of presentment.

Section 3-507. Dishonor; Holder's Right of Recourse; Term Allowing Representment.

(1) An instrument is dishonored when

(a) a necessary or optional presentment is duly made and due acceptance or payment is refused or cannot be obtained within the prescribed time or in case of bank collections the instrument is seasonably returned by the midnight deadline (Section 4-301); or

(b) presentment is excused and the instrument is not duly accepted or paid.

(2) Subject to any necessary notice of dishonor and protest, the holder has upon dishonor an immediate right of recourse against the drawers and indorsers.

(3) Return of an instrument for lack of proper indorsement is not dishonor.

(4) A term in a draft or an indorsement thereof allowing a stated time for representment in the event of any dishonor of the draft by nonacceptance if a time draft or by nonpayment if a sight draft gives the holder as against any secondary party bound by the term an option to waive the dishonor without affecting the liability of the secondary party and he may present again up to the end of the stated time.

Section 3-508. Notice of Dishonor.

(1) Notice of dishonor may be given to any person who may be liable on the instrument by or on behalf of the holder or any party who has himself received notice, or any other party who can be compelled to pay the instrument. In addition an agent or bank in whose hands the instrument is dishonored may give notice to his principal or customer or to another agent or bank from which the instrument was received.

(2) Any necessary notice must be given by a bank before its midnight deadline and by any other person before midnight of the third business day after dishonor or receipt of notice of dishonor.

(3) Notice may be given in any reasonable manner. It may be oral or written and in

any terms which identify the instrument and state that it has been dishonored. A misdescription which does not mislead the party notified does not vitiate the notice. Sending the instrument bearing a stamp, ticket or writing stating that acceptance or payment has been refused or sending a notice of debit with respect to the instrument is sufficient.

(4) Written notice is given when sent although it is not received.

(5) Notice to one partner is notice to each although the firm has been dissolved.

(6) When any party is in insolvency proceedings instituted after the issue of the instrument notice may be given either to the party or to the representative of his estate.

(7) When any party is dead or incompetent notice may be sent to his last known address or given to his personal representative.

(8) Notice operates for the benefit of all parties who have rights on the instrument against the party notified.

Section 3-509. **Protest; Noting for Protest.**

(1) A protest is a certificate of dishonor made under the hand and seal of a United States consul or vice consul or a notary public or other person authorized to certify dishonor by the law of the place where dishonor occurs. It may be made upon information satisfactory to such person.

(2) The protest must identify the instrument and certify either that due presentment has been made or the reason why it is excused and that the instrument has been dishonored by a nonacceptance or nonpayment.

(3) The protest may also certify that notice of dishonor has been given to all parties or to specified parties.

(4) Subject to subsection (5) any necessary protest is due by the time that notice of dishonor is due.

(5) If, before protest is due, an instrument has been noted for protest by the officer to make protest, the protest may be made at any time thereafter as of the date of the noting.

Section 3-510. **Evidence of Dishonor and Notice of Dishonor.** The following are admissible as evidence and create a presumption of dishonor and of any notice or dishonor therein shown:

(a) a document regular in form as provided in the preceding section which purports to be a protest;

(b) the purported stamp or writing of the drawee, payor bank or presenting bank on the instrument or accompanying it stating that acceptance or payment has been refused for reasons consistent with dishonor;

(c) any book or record of the drawee, payor bank, or any collecting bank kept in the usual course of business which shows dishonor, even though there is no evidence of who made the entry.

Section 3-511. **Waived or Excused Presentment, Protest or Notice of Dishonor or Delay Therein.**

(1) Delay in presentment, protest or notice of dishonor is excused when the party is without notice that it is due or when the delay is caused by circumstances beyond his control and he exercises reasonable diligence after the cause of the delay ceases to operate.

(2) Presentment or notice or protest as the case may be is entirely excused when

(a) the party to be charged has waived it expressly or by implication either before or after it is due; or

(b) such party has himself dishonored the instrument or has countermanded payment or otherwise has no reason to expect or right to require that the instrument be accepted or paid; or

(c) by reasonable diligence the presentment or protest cannot be made or the notice given.

(3) Presentment is also entirely excused when

(a) the maker, acceptor or drawee of any instrument except a documentary draft is dead or in insolvency proceedings instituted after the issue of the instrument; or

(b) acceptance or payment is refused but not for want of proper presentment.

(4) Where a draft has been dishonored by nonacceptance a later presentment for payment and any notice of dishonor and protest for nonpayment are excused unless in the meantime the instrument has been accepted.

(5) A waiver of protest is also a waiver of presentment and of notice of dishonor even though protest is not required.

(6) Where a waiver of presentment or

notice or protest is embodied in the instrument itself it is binding upon all parties; but where it is written above the signature of an indorser it binds him only.

PART 6

DISCHARGE

Section 3-601. Discharge of Parties.
(1) The extent of the discharge of any party from liability on an instrument is governed by the section on

(a) payment or satisfaction (Section 3-603; or

(b) tender of payment (Section 3-604); or

(c) cancellation or renunciation (Section 3-605); or

(d) impairment of right of recourse or of collateral (Section 3-606); or

(e) reacquisition of the instrument by a prior party (Section 3-208); or

(f) fraudulent and material alteration (Section 3-407); or

(g) certification of a check (Section 3-411); or

(h) acceptance varying a draft (Section 3-412); or

(i) unexcused delay in presentment or notice of dishonor or protest (Section 3-502).

(2) Any party is also discharged from his liability on an instrument to another party by any other act or agreement with such party which would discharge his simple contract for the payment of money.

(3) The liability of all parties is discharged when any party who has himself no right of action or recourse on the instrument

(a) reacquires the instrument in his own right; or

(b) is discharged under any provision of this Article, except as otherwise provided with respect to discharge for impairment of recourse or of collateral (Section 3-606).

Section 3-602. Effect of Discharge Against Holder in Due Course.
No discharge of any party provided by this Article is effective against a subsequent holder in due course unless he has notice thereof when he takes the instrument.

Section 3-603. Payment or Satisfaction.
(1) The liability of any party is discharged to the extent of his payment or satisfaction to the holder even though it is made with knowledge of a claim of another person to the instrument unless prior to such payment or satisfaction the person making the claim either supplies indemnity deemed adequate by the party seeking the discharge or enjoins payment or satisfaction by order of a court of competent jurisdiction in an action in which the adverse claimant and the holder are parties. This subsection does not, however, result in the discharge of the liability

(a) of a party who in bad faith pays or satisfies a holder who acquired the instrument, by theft or who (unless having the rights of a holder in due course) holds through one who so acquired it; or

(b) of a party (other than an intermediary bank or a payor bank which is not a depositary bank) who pays or satisfies the holder of an instrument which has been restrictively indorsed in a manner not consistent with the terms of such restrictive indorsement.

(2) Payment or satisfaction may be made with the consent of the holder by any person including a stranger to the instrument. Surrender of the instrument to such a person gives him the rights of a transferee (Section 3-201).

Section 3-604. Tender of Payment.
(1) Any party making tender of full payment to a holder when or after it is due is discharged to the extent of all subsequent liability for interest, costs and attorney's fees.

(2) The holder's refusal of such tender wholly discharges any party who has a right or recourse against the party making the tender.

(3) Where the maker or acceptor of an instrument payable otherwise than on demand is able and ready to pay at every place of payment specified in the instrument when it is due, it is equivalent to tender.

Section 3-605. Cancellation and Renunciation.
(1) The holder of an instrument may even without consideration discharge any party

701

(a) in any manner apparent on the face of the instrument or the indorsement, as by intentionally cancelling the instrument or the party's signature by destruction or mutilation, or by striking out the party's signature; or

(b) by renouncing his rights by a writing signed and delivered or by surrender of the instrument to the party to be discharged.

(2) Neither cancellation nor renunciation without surrender of the instrument affects the title thereto.

Section 3-606. Impairment of Recourse or of Collateral.

(1) The holder discharges any party to the instrument to the extent that without such party's consent the holder

(a) without express reservation of rights releases or agrees not to sue any person against whom the party has to the knowledge of the holder a right of recourse or agrees to suspend the right to enforce against such person the instrument or collateral or otherwise discharges such person, except that failure or delay in effecting any required presentment, protest or notice of dishonor with respect to any such person does not discharge any party as to whom presentment, protest or notice of dishonor is effective or unnecessary; or

(b) unjustifiably impairs any collateral for the instrument given by or on behalf of the party or any person against whom he has a right of recourse.

(2) By express reservation of rights against a party with a right of recourse the holder preserves

(a) all his rights against such party as of the time when the instrument was originally due; and

(b) the right of the party to pay the instrument as of that time; and

(c) all rights of such party to recourse against others.

PART 7

ADVICE OF INTERNATIONAL SIGHT DRAFT

Section 3-701. Letter of Advice of International Sight Draft.

(1) A "letter of advice" is a drawer's communication to the drawee that a described draft has been drawn.

(2) Unless otherwise agreed when a bank receives from another bank a letter of advice of an international sight draft the drawee bank may immediately debit the drawer's account and stop the running of interest pro tanto. Such a debit and any resulting credit to any account covering outstanding drafts leaves in the drawer full power to stop payment or otherwise dispose of the amount and creates no trust or interest in favor of the holder.

(3) Unless otherwise agreed and except where a draft is drawn under a credit issued by the drawee, the drawee of an international sight draft owes the drawer no duty to pay an unadvised draft but if it does so and the draft is genuine, may appropriately debit the drawer's account.

PART 8

MISCELLANEOUS

Section 3-801. Drafts in a Set.

(1) Where a draft is drawn in a set of parts, each of which is numbered and expressed to be an order only if no other part has been honored, the whole of the parts constitutes one draft but a taker of any part may become a holder in due course of the draft.

(2) Any person who negotiates, indorses or accepts a single part of a draft drawn in a set thereby becomes liable to any holder in due course of that part as if it were the whole set, but as between different holders in due course to whom different parts have been negotiated the holder whose title first accrues has all rights to the draft and its proceeds.

(3) As against the drawee the first presented part of a draft drawn in a set is the part entitled to payment, or if a time draft to acceptance and payment. Acceptance of any subsequently presented part renders the drawee liable thereon under subsection (2). With respect both to a holder and to the drawer payment of a subsequently presented part of a draft payable at sight has the same effect as payment of a check notwithstanding an effective stop order (Section 4-407).

(4) Except as otherwise provided in this section, where any part of a draft in a set is discharged by payment or otherwise the whole draft is discharged.

Section 3-802. Effect of Instrument on Obligation for Which it is Given.

(1) Unless otherwise agreed where an instrument is taken for an underlying obligation

(a) the obligation is pro tanto discharged if a bank is drawer, maker or acceptor of the instrument and there is no recourse on the instrument against the underlying obligor; and

(b) in any other case the obligation is suspended pro tanto until the instrument is due or if it is payable on demand until its presentment. If the instrument is dishonored action may be maintained on either the instrument or the obligation; discharge of the underlying obligor on the instrument also discharges him on the obligation.

(2) The taking in good faith of a check which is not postdated does not of itself so extend the time on the original obligation as to discharge a surety.

Section 3-803. Notice to Third Party.

Where a defendant is sued for breach of an obligation for which a third person is answerable over under this Article he may give the third person written notice of the litigation, and the person notified may then give similar notice to any other person who is answerable over to him under this Article. If the notice states that the person notified may come in and defend and that if the person notified does not do so he will in any action against him by the person giving the notice be bound by any determination of fact common to the two litigations, then unless after seasonable receipt of the notice the person notified does come in and defend he is so bound.

Section 3-804. Lost, Destroyed or Stolen Instruments. The owner of an instrument which is lost, whether by destruction, theft or otherwise, may maintain an action in his own name and recover from any party liable thereon upon due proof of his ownership, the facts which prevent his production of the instrument and its terms. The court may require security indemnifying the defendant against loss by reason of further claims on the instrument.

Section 3-805. Instruments Not Payable to Order or to Bearer. This Article applies to any instrument whose terms do not preclude transfer and which is otherwise negotiable within this Article but which is not payable to order to bearer, except that there can be no holder in due course of such an instrument.

ARTICLE 4

BANK DEPOSITS AND COLLECTIONS

PART 1

GENERAL PROVISIONS AND DEFINITIONS

Section 4-101. Short Title. This Article shall be known and may be cited as Uniform Commercial Code—Bank Deposits and Collections.

Section 4-102. Applicability.

(1) To the extent that items within this Article are also within the scope of Articles 3 and 8, they are subject to the provisions of those Articles. In the event of conflict the provisions of this Article govern those of Article 3 but the provisions of Article 8 govern those of this Article.

(2) The liability of a bank for action or non-action with respect to any item handled by it for purposes of presentment, payment or collection is governed by the law of the place where the bank is located. In the case of action or non-action by or at a branch or separate office of a bank, its liability is gov-

erned by the law of the place where the branch or separate office is located.

Section 4-103. Variation by Agreement; Measure of Damages; Certain Action Constituting Ordinary Care.

(1) The effect of the provisions of this Article may be varied by agreement except that no agreement can disclaim a bank's responsibility for its own lack of good faith or failure to exercise ordinary care or can limit the measure of damages for such lack or failure; but the parties may by agreement determine the standards by which such responsibility is to be measured if such standards are not manifestly unreasonable.

(2) Federal Reserve regulations and operating letters, clearing house rules, and the like, have the effect of agreements under subsection (1), whether or not specifically assented to by all parties interested in items handled.

(3) Action or non-action approved by this Article or pursuant to Federal Reserve regulations or operating letters constitutes the exercise of ordinary care and, in the absence of special instructions, action or non-action consistent with clearing house rules and the like or with a general banking usage not disapproved by this Article, prima facie constitutes the exercise of ordinary care.

(4) The specification or approval of certain procedures by this Article does not constitute disapproval of other procedures which may be reasonable under the circumstances.

(5) The measure of damages for failure to exercise ordinary care in handling an item is the amount of the item reduced by an amount which could not have been realized by the use of ordinary care, and where there is bad faith it includes other damages, if any, suffered by the party as a proximate consequence.

Section 4-104. Definitions and Index of Definitions.

(1) In this Article unless the context otherwise requires

(a) "Account" means any account with a bank and includes a checking, time, interest or savings account;

(b) "Afternoon" means the period of a day between noon and midnight;

(c) "Banking day" means that part of any day on which a bank is open to the public for carrying on substantially all of its banking functions;

(d) "Clearing house" means any association of banks or other payors regularly clearing items;

(e) "Customer" means any person having an account with a bank or for whom a bank has agreed to collect items and includes a bank carrying an account with another bank;

(f) "Documentary draft" means any negotiable or non-negotiable draft with accompanying documents, securities or other papers to be delivered against honor of the draft;

(g) "Item" means any instrument for the payment of money even though it is not negotiable but does not include money;

(h) "Midnight deadline" with respect to a bank is midnight on its next banking day following the banking day on which it receives the relevant item or notice or from which the time for taking action commences to run, whichever is later;

(i) "Properly payable" includes the availability of funds for payment at the time of decision to pay or dishonor;

(j) "Settle" means to pay in cash, by clearing house settlement, in a charge or credit or by remittance, or otherwise as instructed. A settlement may be either provisional or final;

(k) "Suspends payments" with respect to a bank means that it has been closed by order of the supervisory authorities, that a public officer has been appointed to take it over or that it ceases or refuses to make payments in the ordinary course of business.

(2) Other definitions applying to this Article and the sections in which they appear are:

"Collecting bank." Section 4-105.
"Depositary bank." Section 4-105.
"Intermediary bank." Section 4-105.
"Payor bank." Section 4-105.
"Presenting bank." Section 4-105.
"Remitting bank." Section 4-105.

(3) The following definitions in other Articles apply to this Article:

"Acceptance." Section 3-410.
"Certificate of deposit." Section 3-104.
"Certification." Section 3-411.
"Check." Section 3-104.
"Draft." Section 3-104.
"Holder in due course." Section 3-302.

"Notice of dishonor." Section 3-508.
"Presentment." Section 3-504.
"Protest." Section 3-509.
"Secondary party." Section 3-102.

(4) In addition Article 1 contains general definitions and principles of construction and interpretation applicable throughout this Article.

Section 4-105. "Depositary Bank"; "Intermediary Bank"; "Collecting Bank"; "Payor Bank"; "Presenting Bank"; "Remitting Bank." In this Article unless the context otherwise requires:

> (a) "Depositary bank" means the first bank to which an item is transferred for collection even though it is also the payor bank;
> (b) "Payor bank" means a bank by which an item is payable as drawn or accepted;
> (c) "Intermediary bank" means any bank to which an item is transferred in course of collection except the depositary or payor bank;
> (d) "Collecting bank" means any bank handling the item for collection except the payor bank;
> (e) "Presenting bank" means any bank presenting an item except a payor bank;
> (f) "Remitting bank" means any payor or intermediary bank remitting for an item.

Section 4-106. Separate Office of a Bank. A branch or separate office of a bank [maintaining its own deposit ledgers] is a separate bank for the purpose of computing the time within which and determining the place at or to which action may be taken or notices or orders shall be given under this Article and under Article 3.
NOTE: *The words in Brackets are optional.*

Section 4-107. Time of Receipt of Items.

(1) For the purpose of allowing time to process items, prove balances and make the necessary entries on its books to determine its position for the day, a bank may fix an afternoon hour of two P.M. or later as a cut-off hour for the handling of money and items and the making of entries on its books.

(2) Any item or deposit of money received on any day after a cut-off hour so fixed or after the close of the banking day may be treated as being received at the opening of the next banking day.

Section 4-108. Delays.

(1) Unless otherwise instructed, a collecting bank in a good faith effort to secure payment may, in the case of specific items and with or without the approval of any person involved, waive, modify or extend time limits imposed or permitted by this Act for a period not in excess of an additional banking day without discharge of secondary parties and without liability to its transferor or any prior party.

(2) Delay by a collecting bank or payor bank beyond time limits prescribed or permitted by this Act or by instructions is excused if caused by interruption of communication facilities, suspension of payments by another bank, war, emergency conditions or other circumstances beyond the control of the bank provided it exercises such diligence as the circumstances require.

Section 4-109. Process of Posting. The "process of posting" means the usual procedure followed by a payor bank in determining to pay an item and in recording the payment including one or more of the following or other steps as determined by the bank:

> (a) verification of any signature;
> (b) ascertaining that sufficient funds are are available;
> (c) affixing a "paid" or other stamp;
> (d) entering a charge or entry to a customer's account;
> (e) correcting or reversing an entry or erroneous action with respect to the item.

PART 2

COLLECTION OF ITEMS: DEPOSITARY
AND COLLECTING BANKS

Section 4-201. Presumption and Duration of Agency Status of Collecting Banks and Provisional Status of Credits; Applicability of Article; Item Indorsed "Pay any Bank."

(1) Unless a contrary intent clearly appears and prior to the time that a settlement given by a collecting bank for an item is or becomes final (subsection (3) of Section 4-211 and Sections 4-212 and 4-213) the bank is an agent or sub-agent of the owner of the item and any settlement given for the item is provisional. This provision applies regardless of the form of indorsement or lack of indorsement and even though credit given for the item is subject to immediate withdrawal as of right or is in fact withdrawn; but the continuance of ownership of an item by its owner and any rights of the owner to proceeds of the item are subject to rights of .a collecting bank such as those resulting from outstanding advances on the item and valid rights of setoff. When an item is handled by banks for purposes of presentment, payment and collection, the relevant provisions of this Article apply even though action of parties clearly establishes that a particular bank has purchased the item and is the owner of it.

(2) After an item has been indorsed with the words "pay any bank" or the like, only a bank may acquire the rights of a holder

    (a) until the item has been returned to the customer initiating collection; or

    (b) until the item has been specially indorsed by a bank to a person who is not a bank.

Section 4-202. Responsibility for Collection; when Action Seasonable.

(1) A collecting bank must use ordinary care in

    (a) presenting an item or sending it for presentment; and

    (b) sending notice of dishonor or non-payment or returning an item other than a documentary draft to the bank's transferor [or directly to the depositary bank under subsection (2) of Section 4-212] (*see note to Section 4-212*) after learning that the item has not been paid or

accepted, as the case may be; and

    (c) settling for an item when the bank receives final settlement; and

    (d) making or providing for any necessary protest; and

    (e) notifying its transferor of any loss or delay in transit within a reasonable time after discovery thereof.

(2) A collecting bank taking proper action before its midnight deadline following receipt of an item, notice or payment acts seasonably; taking proper action within a reasonably longer time may be seasonable but the bank has the burden of so establishing.

(3) Subject to subsection (1) (a), a bank is not liable for the insolvency, neglect, misconduct, mistake or default of another bank or person or for loss or destruction of an item in transit or in the possession of others.

Section 4-203. Effect of Instructions. Subject to the provisions of Article 3 concerning conversion of instruments (Section 3-429) and the provisions of both Article 3 and this Article concerning restrictive indorsements only a collecting bank's transferor can give instructions which affect the bank or constitute notice to it and a collecting bank is not liable to prior parties for any action taken pursuant to such instructions or in accordance with any agreement with its transferor.

Section 4-204. Methods of Sending and Presenting; Sending Direct to Payor Bank.

(1) A collecting bank must send items by reasonably prompt method taking into consideration any relevant instructions, the nature of the item, the number of such items on hand, and the cost of collection involved and the method generally used by it or others to present such items.

(2) A collecting bank may send

    (a) any item direct to the payor bank;

    (b) any item to any non-bank payor if authorized by its transferor; and

    (c) any item other than documentary drafts to any non-bank payor, if authorized by Federal Reserve regulation or operating letter. clearing house rule or the like.

(3) Presenting may be made by a present-

ing bank at a place where the payor bank has requested that presentment be made.

Section 4-205. Supplying Missing Indorsement; No Notice from Prior Indorsement.

(1) A depositary bank which has taken an item for collection may supply any indorsement of the customer which is necessary to title unless the item contains the words "payee's indorsement required" or the like. In the absence of such a requirement a statement placed on the item by the depositary bank to the effect that the item was deposited by a customer or credited to his account is effective as the customer's indorsement.

(2) An intermediary bank, or payor bank which is not a depositary bank, is neither given notice nor otherwise affected by a restrictive indorsement of any person except the bank's immediate transferor.

Section 4-206. Transfer Between Banks. Any agreed method which identifies the transferor bank is sufficient for the item's further transfer to another bank.

Section 4-207. Warranties or Customer and Collecting Bank on Transfer or Presentment of Items; Time for Claims.

(1) Each customer or collecting bank who obtains payment or acceptance of an item and each prior customer and collecting bank warrants to the payor bank or other payor who in good faith pays or accepts the item that

(a) he has a good title to the item or is authorized to obtain payment of acceptance on behalf of one who has a good title and the transfer is otherwise rightful; and

(b) he has no knowledge that the signature of the maker or drawer is unauthorized, except that this warranty is not given by any customer or collecting bank that is a holder in due course and acts in good faith

(i) to a maker with respect to the maker's own signature; or

(ii) to a drawer with respect to the drawer's own signature, whether or not the drawer is also the drawee; or

(iii) to an acceptor of an item if the holder in due course took the item after the acceptance or obtained the acceptance without knowledge that the drawer's signature was unauthorized; and

(c) the time has not been materially altered, except that this warranty is not given by any customer or collecting bank that is a holder in due course and acts in good faith

(i) to the maker of a note; or

(ii) to the drawer of a draft whether or not the drawer is also the drawee; or

(iii) to the acceptor of an item with respect to an alteration made prior to the acceptance if the holder in due course took the item after the acceptance provided "payable as originally drawn" or equivalent terms; or

(iv) to the acceptor of an item with respect to an alteration made after the acceptance.

(2) Each customer and collecting bank who transfers an item and receives a settlement or other consideration for it warrants to his transferee and to any subsequent collecting bank who takes the item in good faith that

authorized to obtain payment or acceptance on behalf of one who has a good title and the transfer is otherwise rightful; and

(b) all signatures are genuine or authorized; and

(c) the item has not been materially altered; and

(d) no defense of any party is good against him; and

(e) he has no knowledge of any insolvency proceeding instituted with respect to the maker or acceptor or the drawer of an unaccepted item.

In addition each customer and collecting bank so transferring an item and receiving a settlement or other consideration engages that upon dishonor and any necessary notice of dishonor and protest he will take up the item.

(3) The warranties and the engagement to honor set forth in the two preceding subsections arise notwithstanding the absence of indorsement or words of guaranty or warranty in the transfer or presentment and a collecting bank remains liable for their breach despite remittance to its transferor. Damages for breach of such warranties or engagement to honor shall not exceed the consideration received by the customer or collecting bank responsible plus finance

charges and expenses related to the item, if any.

(4) Unless a claim for breach of warranty under this section is made within a reasonable time after the person claiming learns of the breach, the person liable is discharged to the extent of any loss caused by the delay in making claim.

Section 4-208. Security Interest of Collecting Bank in Items, Accompanying Documents and Proceeds.

(1) A bank has a security interest in an item and any accompanying documents or the proceeds of either

(a) in case of an item deposited in an account to the extent to which credit given for the item has been withdrawn or applied;

(b) in case of an item for which it has given credit available for withdrawal as of right, to the extent of the credit given whether or not the credit is drawn upon and whether or not there is a right of charge-back; or

(c) if it makes an advance on or against the item.

(2) When credit which has been given for several items received at one time or pursuant to a single agreement is withdrawn or applied in part the security interest remains upon all the items, any accompanying documents or the proceeds of either. For the purpose of this section, credits first given are first withdrawn.

(3) Receipt by a collecting bank of a final settlement for an item is a realization on its security interest in the item, accompanying documents and proceeds. To the extent and so long as the bank does not receive final settlement for the item or give up possession of the item or accompanying documents for purposes other than collection, the security interest continues and is subject to the provisions of Article 9 except that

(a) no security agreement is necessary to make the security interest enforceable (subsection (1) (b) of Section 9-203); and

(b) no filing is required to perfect the security interest; and

(c) the security interest has priority over conflicting perfected security interests in the item, accompanying documents or proceeds.

Section 4-209. When Bank Gives Value for Purposes of Holder in Due Course. For purposes of determining its status as a holder in due course, the bank has given value to the extent that it has a security interest in an item provided that the bank otherwise complies with the requirements of Section 3-302 on what constitutes a holder in due course.

Section 4-210. Presentment by Notice of Item Not Payable by, through or at a Bank; Liability of Secondary Parties.

(1) Unless otherwise instructed, a collecting bank may present an item not payable by, through or at a bank by sending to the party to accept or pay a written notice that the bank holds the item for acceptance or payment. The notice must be sent in time to be received on or before the day when presentment is due and the bank must meet any requirement of the party to accept or pay under Section 3-505 by the close of the bank's next banking day after it knows of the requirement.

(2) Where presentment is made by notice and neither honor nor request for compliance with a requirement under Section 3-505 is received by the close of business on the day after maturity or in the case of demand items by the close of business on the third banking day after notice was sent, the presenting bank may treat the item as dishonored and charge any secondary party by sending him notice of the facts.

Section 4-211. Media or Remittance; Provisional and Final Settlement in Remittance Cases.

(1) A collecting bank may take in settlement of an item

(a) a check of the remitting bank or of another bank on any bank except the remitting bank; or

(b) a cashier's check or similar primary obligation of a remitting bank which is a member of or clears through a member of the same clearing house or group as the collecting bank; or

(c) appropriate authority to charge an account of the remitting bank or of another bank with the collecting bank; or

(d) if the item is drawn upon or payable by a person other than a bank, a cashier's check, certified check or other bank check or obligation.

(2) If before its midnight deadline the collecting bank properly dishonors a remittance check or authorization to charge on itself or presents or forwards for collection a remittance instrument of or on another bank which is of a kind approved by subsection (1) or has not been authorized by it, the collecting bank is not liable to prior parties in the event of the dishonor of such check, instrument or authorization.

(3) A settlement for an item by means of a remittance instrument or authorization to charge is or becomes a final settlement as to both the person making and the person receiving the settlement

(a) if the remittance instrument or authorization to charge is of a kind approved by subsection (1) or has not been authorized by the person receiving the settlement and in either case the person receiving the settlement acts seasonably before its midnight deadline in presenting, forwarding for collection or paying the instrument or authorization is finally paid by the payor by which it is payable;

(b) if the person receiving the settlement has authorized remittance by a non-bank check or obligation or by a cashier's check or similar primary obligation of or a check upon the payor or other remitting bank which is not of a kind approved by subsection (1)(b),—at the time of the receipt of such remittance check or obligation; or

(c) if in case not covered by sub-paragraphs (a) or (b) the person receiving the settlement fails to seasonably present, forward for collection, pay or return a remittance instrument of authorization to it to charge before its midnight deadline,—at such midnight deadline.

Section 4-212. Right of Charge-Back or Refund.

(1) If a collecting bank has made provisional settlement with its customer for an item and itself fails by reason of dishonor, suspension of payments by a bank or otherwise to receive a settlement for the item which is or becomes final, the bank may revoke the settlement given by it, charge back the amount of any credit given for the item to its customer whether or not it is able to return the items if by its midnight deadline or within a longer reasonable time after it learns the facts it returns the item or sends notification of the facts. These rights to revoke, charge-back and obtain refund terminate if and when a settlement for the item received by the bank is or becomes final (subsection (3) of Section 4-211 and subsections (2) and (3) of Section 4-213).

[(2) Within the time and manner prescribed by this section and Section 4-301, an intermediary or payor bank, as the case may be, may return an unpaid item directly to the depositary bank and may send for collection a draft on the depositary bank and obtain reimbursement. In such case, if the depositary bank has received provisional settlement for the item, it must reimburse the bank drawing the draft and any provisional credits for the item between banks shall become and remain final.]

NOTE: *Direct returns is recognized as an innovation that is not yet established bank practice, and therefore, Paragraph 2 has been bracketed. Some lawyers have doubted whether it should be included in legislation or left to development by agreement.*

(3) A depositary bank which is also the payor may charge-back the amount of an item to its customer's account or obtain refund in accordance with the section governing return of an item received by a payor bank for credit on its books (Section 4-301).

(4) The right to charge-back is not affected by

(a) prior use of the credit given for the item; or

(b) failure by any bank to exercise ordinary care with respect to the item but any bank so failing remains liable.

(5) A failure to charge-back or claim refund does not affect other rights of the bank against the customer or any other party.

(6) If credit is given in dollars as the equivalent of the value of an item payable in a foreign currency the dollar amount of any charge-back or refund shall be calculated on the basis of the buying site rate for the foreign currency prevailing on the day when the person entitled to the charge-back or refund learns that it will not receive payment in ordinary course.

Section 4-213. Final Payment of Item by Payor Bank; When Provisional Debits and Credits become Final; When Certain Credits become Available for Withdrawal.

(1) An item is finally paid by a payor bank when the bank has done any of the following whichever happens first:

(a) paid the item in cash; or

(b) settled for the item without reserving a right to revoke the settlement and without having such right under statute, clearing house rule or agreement; or

(c) completed the process of posting the item to the indicated account of the drawer, maker or other person to be charged therewith; or

(d) made a provisional settlement for the item and failed to revoke the settlement in the time and manner permitted by statute, clearing house rule or agreement.

Upon a final payment under subparagraphs (b), (c) or (d) the payor bank shall be accountable for the amount of the item.

(2) If provisional settlement for an item between the presenting and payor banks is made through a clearing house or by debits or credits in an account between them, then to the extent that provisional debits or credits for the item are entered in accounts between the presenting and payor banks or between the presenting and successive prior collecting banks seratim, they become final upon final payment of the item by the payor bank.

(3) If a collecting bank receives a settlement for an item which is or becomes final (subsection (3) of Section 4-211, subsection (2) of Section 4-213) the bank is accountable to its customer for the amount of the item and any provisional credit given for the item in an account with its customer becomes final.

(4) Subject to any right of the bank to apply the credit to an obligation of the customer, credit given by a bank for an item in an account with its customer becomes available for withdrawal as of right

(a) in any case where the bank has received a provisional settlement for the item,—when such settlement becomes final and the bank has had a reasonable time to learn that the settlement is final;

(b) in any case where the bank is both a depositary bank and a payor bank and the item is finally paid,—at the opening of the bank's second banking day following receipt of the item.

(5) A deposit of money in a bank is final when made but, subject to any right of the bank to apply the deposit to an obligation of the customer, the deposit becomes available for withdrawal as of right at the opening of the bank's next banking day following receipt of the deposit.

Section 4-214. Insolvency and Preference.

(1) Any item in or coming into the possession of a payor or collecting bank which suspends payment and which item is not finally paid shall be returned by the receiver, trustee or agent in charge of the closed bank to the presenting bank or the closed bank's customer.

(2) If a payor bank finally pays an item and suspends payments without making a settlement for the item with its customer or the presenting bank which settlement is or becomes final, the owner of the item has a preferred claim against the payor bank.

(3) If a payor bank gives or a collecting bank gives or receives a provisional settlement for an item and thereafter suspends payments, the suspension does not prevent or interfere with the settlement becoming final if such finality occurs automatically upon the lapse of certain time or the happening of certain events (subsection (3) of Section 4-211, subsections (1)(d), (2) and (3) of Section 4-213).

(4) If a collecting bank receives from subsequent parties settlement for an item which settlement is or becomes final and suspends payments without making a settlement for the item with its customer which is or becomes final, the owner of the item has a preferred claim against such collecting bank.

PART 3

COLLECTION OF ITEMS: PAYOR BANKS

Section 4-301. Deferred Posting; Recovery of Payment by Return of Items; Time of Dishonor.

(1) Where an authorized settlement for a demand item (other than a documentary draft) received by a payor bank otherwise than for immediate payment over the counter has been made before midnight of the banking day of receipt the payor bank may revoke the settlement and recover any payment if before it has made final payment (subsection (1) of Section 4-213) and before its midnight deadline it

(a) returns the item; or

(b) sends written notice of dishonor or nonpayment if the item is held for protest or is otherwise unavailable for return.

(2) If a demand item is received by a payor bank for credit on its books it may return such item or send notice of dishonor and may revoke any credit given or recover the amount thereof withdrawn by its customer, if it acts within the time limit and in the manner specified in the preceding subsection.

(3) Unless previous notice of dishonor has been sent an item is dishonored at the time when for purposes of dishonor it is returned or notice sent in accordance with this section.

(4) An item is returned:

(a) as to an item received through a clearing house, when it is delivered to the presenting or last collecting bank or to the clearing house or is sent or delivered in accordance with its rules; or

(b) in all other cases, when it is sent or delivered to the bank's customer or transferor or pursuant to his instructions.

Section 4-302. Payor Bank's Responsibility for Late Return of Item. In the absence of a valid defense such as breach of a presentment warranty (subsection (1) of Section 4-207), settlement effected or the like, of an item is presented on and received by a payor bank the bank is accountable for the amount of

(a) a demand item other than a documentary draft whether properly payable or not if the bank, in any case where it is not also the depositary bank, retains the item beyond midnight of the banking day of receipt without settling for it or, regardless of whether it is also the depositary bank, does not pay or return the item or send notice of dishonor until after its midnight deadline; or

(b) any other properly payable item unless within the time allowed for acceptance or payment of that item the bank either accepts or pays the item or returns it and accompanying documents.

Section 4-303. When Items Subject to Notice, Stop-Order, Legal Process or Setoff; Order in which Items may be Charged or Certified.

(1) Any knowledge, notice or stop-order received by, legal process served upon or setoff exercised by a payor bank, whether or not effective under other rules of law to terminate, suspend or modify the bank's right or duty to pay an item or to charge its customer's account for the item, comes too late to so terminate, suspend or modify such right or duty if the knowledge, notice, stop-order or legal process is received or served and a reasonable time for the bank to act thereon expires or the setoff is exercised after the bank has done any of the following:

(a) accepted or certified the item;

(b) paid the item in cash;

(c) settled for the item without reserving the right to revoke the settlement and without having such right under statute, clearing house rule or agreement;

(d) completed the process of posting the item to the indicated account of the drawer, maker or other person to be charged therewith or otherwise has evidenced by examination of such indicated account and by action its decision to pay the item; or

(e) become accountable for the amount of the item under subsection (1) (d) of Section 4-213 and Section 4-302 dealing with the payor bank's responsibility for late return of items.

(2) Subject to the provisions of subsection (1) items may be accepted, paid, certified or charged to the indicated account of its customer in any order convenient to the bank.

PART 4

RELATIONSHIP BETWEEN PAYOR BANK AND ITS CUSTOMER

Section 4-401. When Bank May Charge Customer's Account.

(1) As against its customer, a bank may charge against his account any item which is otherwise properly payable from that account even though the charge creates an overdraft.

(2) A bank which in good faith makes payment to a holder may charge the indicated account of its customer according to

(a) the original tenor of his altered item; or

(b) the tenor of his completed item, even though the bank knows the item has been completed unless the bank has notice that the completion was improper.

Section 4-402. Bank's Liability to Customer for Wrongful Dishonor. A payor bank is liable to its customer for damages proximately caused by the wrongful dishonor of an item. When the dishonor occurs through mistake liability is limited to actual damages proved. If so proximately caused and proved damages may include damages for an arrest or prosecution of the customer or other consequential damages. Whether any consequential damages are proximately caused by the wrongful dishonor is a question of fact to be determined in each case.

Section 4-403. Customer's Right to Stop Payment; Burden of Proof of Loss.

(1) A customer may by order to his bank stop payment of any item payable for his account but the order must be received at such time and in such manner as to afford the bank a reasonable opportunity to act on it prior to any action by the bank with respect to the item described in Section 4-303.

(2) An oral order is binding upon the bank only for fourteen calendar days unless confirmed in writing within that period. A written order is effective for only six months unless renewed in writing.

(3) The burden of establishing the fact and amount of loss resulting from the payment of an item contrary to a binding stop payment order is on the customer.

Section 4-404. Bank not Obligated to Pay Check more than Six Months old. A bank is under no obligation to a customer having a checking account to pay a check, other than a certified check, which is presented more than six months after its date, but it may charge its customer's account for a payment made thereafter in good faith.

Section 4-405. Death or Incompetence of Customer.

(1) A payor or collecting bank's authority to accept, pay or collect an item or to account for proceeds of its collection if otherwise effective is not rendered ineffective by incompetence of a customer of either bank existing at the time the item is issued or its collection is undertaken if the bank does not know of an adjudication of incompetence. Neither death nor incompetence of a customer revokes such authority to accept, pay, collect or account until the bank knows of the fact of death or of an adjudication of incompetence and has reasonable opportunity to act on it.

(2) Even with knowledge a bank may for ten days after the date of death pay or certify checks drawn on or prior to that date unless ordered to stop payment by a person claiming an interest in the account.

Section 4-406. Customer's Duty to Discover and Report Unauthorized Signature or Alteration.

(1) When a bank sends to its customer a statement of account accompanied by items paid in good faith in support of the debit entries or holds the statement and items

pursuant to a request or instructions of its customer or otherwise in a reasonable manner makes the statement and items available to the customer, the customer must exercise reasonable care and promptness to examine the statement and items to discover his unauthorized signature or any alteration on an item and must notify the bank promptly after discovery thereof.

(2) If the bank establishes that the customer failed with respect to an item to comply with the duties imposed on the customer by subsection (1) the customer is precluded from asserting against the bank

(a) his unauthorized signature or any alteration on the item of the bank also establishes that it suffered a loss by reason of such failure; and

(b) an unauthorized signature or alteration by the same wrongdoer on any other item paid in good faith by the bank after the first item and statement was available to the customer for a reasonable period not exceeding fourteen calendar days and before the bank receives notification from the customer of any such unauthorized signature or alteration.

(3) The preclusion under subsection (2) does not apply if the customer establishes lack of ordinary care on the part of the bank in paying the item(s).

(4) Without regard to care or lack of care of either the customer or the bank a customer who does not within one year from the time the statement and items are made available to the customer (subsection (1)) discover and report his unauthorized signature or any alteration on the fact or back of the item or does not within three years from that time discover and report any unauthorized indorsement is precluded from asserting against the bank such unauthorized signature or indorsement or such alteration.

(5) If under this section a payor bank has a valid defense against a claim of a customer upon or resulting from payment of an item and waives or fails upon request to assert the defense the bank may not assert against any collecting bank or other prior party presenting or transferring the item a claim based upon the unauthorized signature or alteration giving rise to the customer's claim.

Section 4-407. Payor Bank's Right to Subrogation on Improper Payment. If a payor bank has paid an item over the stop payment order of the drawer or maker, or otherwise under circumstances giving a basis for objection by the drawer or maker, to present unjust enrichment and only to the extent necessary to prevent loss to the bank by reason of its payment of the item, the payor bank shall be subrogated to the rights

(a) of any holder in due course on the item against the drawer or maker; and

(b) of the payee or any other holder of the item against the drawer or maker either on the item or under the transaction out of which the item arose; and

(c) of the drawer or maker against the payee or any other holder of the item with respect to the transaction out of which the item arose.

PART 5

COLLECTION OF DOCUMENTARY DRAFTS

Section 4-501. Handling of Documentary Drafts; Duty to Send for Presentment and to Notify Customer of Dishonor. A bank which takes a documentary draft for collection must present or send the draft and accompanying documents for presentment and upon learning that the draft has not been paid or accepted in due course must seasonably notify its customer of such fact even though it may have discounted or bought the draft or extended credit available for withdrawal as if right.

Section 4-502. Presentment of "On Arrival" Drafts. When a draft or the relevant instructions require presentment "on arrival," "when goods arrive" or the like, the collecting bank need not present until in its judgment a reasonable time for arrival of the goods has expired. Refusal to pay or accept because the goods have not arrived is not dishonor; the bank must notify its transferor of such refusal but need not present the draft again until it is instructed to do so or learns of the arrival of the goods.

Section 4-503. Responsibility of Presenting Bank for Documents and Goods; Report or Reasons for Dishonor; Referee in Case of Need. Unless otherwise instructed and except as provided in Article 5 a bank presenting a documentary draft

(a) must deliver the documents to the drawee on acceptance of the draft if it is payable more than three days after presentment; otherwise, only on payment; and

(b) upon dishonor, either in the case of presentment for acceptance or presentment for payment, may seek and follow instructions from any referee in case of need designated in the draft or if the presenting bank does not choose to utilize his services it must use diligence and good faith to ascertain the reason for dishonor, must notify its transferor of the dishonor and of the results of its effort to ascertain the reasons therefor and must request instructions.

But the presenting bank is under no obligation with respect to goods represented by the documents except to follow any reasonable instructions seasonably received; it has a right to reimbursement for any expense incurred in following instructions and to prepayment of or indemnity for such expenses.

Section 4-504. Privilege of Presenting Bank to Deal with Goods, Security Interest for Expenses.

(1) A presenting bank which, following the dishonor of a documentary draft, has seasonably requested instructions but does not receive them within a reasonable time may store, sell, or otherwise deal with the goods in any reasonable manner.

(2) For its reasonable expenses incurred by action under subsection (1) the presenting bank has a lien upon the goods or their proceeds, which may be foreclosed in the same manner as an unpaid seller's lien.

ARTICLE 5

LETTERS OF CREDIT

Section 5-101. Short Title. This Article shall be known and may be cited as Uniform Commercial Code—Letters of Credit.

Section 5-102. Scope.

(1) This Article applies

(a) to a credit issued by a bank if the credit requires a documentary draft or a documentary demand for payment; and

(b) to a credit issued by a person other than a bank if the credit requires that the draft or demand for payment be accompanied by a document of title; and

(c) to a credit issued by a bank or other person if the credit is not within subparagraphs (a) or (b) but conspicuously states that it is a letter of credit or is conspicuously so entitled.

(2) Unless the engagement meets the requirements of subsection (1), this Article does not apply to engagements to make advances or to honor drafts or demands for payment, to authorities to pay or purchase, to guarantees or to general agreements.

(3) This Article deals with some but not all of the rules and concepts of letters of credit

as such rules or concepts have developed prior to this act or may hereafter develop. The fact that this Article states a rule does not by itself require, imply or negate application of the same or a converse rule to a situation not provided for or to a person not specified by this Article.

Section 5-103. Definitions.

(1) In this Article unless the context otherwise requires

(a) "credit" or "letter of credit" means an engagement by a bank or other person made at the request of a customer and of a kind within the scope of this Article (Section 5-201) that the issuer will honor drafts or other demands for payment upon compliance with the conditions specified in the credit. A credit may be either revocable or irrevocable. The engagement may be either an agreement to honor or a statement that the bank or other person is authorized to honor.

(b) a "documentary draft" or a "documentary demand for payment" is one honor of which is conditioned upon the

714

presentation of a document or documents. "Document" means any paper including document of title, security, invoice, certificate, notice of default and the like.

(c) an "issuer" is a bank or other person issuing a credit.

(d) a "beneficiary" of a credit is a person who is entitled under its terms to draw or demand payment.

(e) an "advising bank" is a bank which gives notification of the issuance of a credit by another bank.

(f) a "confirming bank" is a bank which engages either that it will itself honor a credit already issued by another bank or that such a credit will be honored by the issuer or a third bank.

(g) a "customer" is a buyer or other person who causes an issuer to issue a credit. The term also includes a bank which procures issuance or confirmation on behalf of that bank's customer.

(2) Other definitions applying to this Article and the sections in which they appear are:

"Notation of Credit." Section 5-108.
"Presenter." Section 5-112(3).

(3) Definitions in other Articles applying to this Article and the sections in which they appear are:

"Accept" or "Acceptance." Section 3-410.
"Contract for sale." Section 2-106.
"Draft." Section 3-104.
"Holder in due course." Section 3-302.
"Midnight deadline." Section 4-104.
"Security." Section 8-102.

(4) In addition, Article 1 contains general definitions and principles of construction and interpretation applicable throughout this Article.

Section 5-104. Formal Requirements; Signing.

(1) Except as otherwise required in subsection (1) (c) of Section 5-102 on scope, no particular form of phrasing is required for a credit. A credit must be in writing and signed by the issuer and a confirmation must be in writing and signed by the confirming bank. A modification of the terms of a credit or confirmation must be signed by the issuer or confirming bank.

(2) A telegram may be a sufficient signed writing if it identifies its sender by an authorized authentication. The authentication may be in code and the authorized naming of the issuer in an advice of credit is a sufficient signing.

Section 5-106. Time and Effect of Establishment of Credit.

(1) Unless otherwise agreed a credit is established

(a) as regards the customer as soon as a letter of credit is sent to him or the letter of credit or an authorized written advice of its issuance is sent to the beneficiary; and

(b) as regards the beneficiary when he receives a letter of credit or an authorized written advice of its issuance.

(2) Unless otherwise agreed once an irrevocable credit is established as regards the customer it can be modified or revoked only with the consent of the customer and once it is established as regards the beneficiary it can be modified or revoked only with his consent.

(3) Unless otherwise agreed after a revocable credit is established it may be modified or revoked by the issuer without notice to or consent from the customer or beneficiary.

(4) Notwithstanding any modification or revocation of a revocable credit any person authorized to honor or negotiate under the terms of the original credit is entitled to reimbursement for or honor of any draft or demand for payment duly honored or negotiated before receipt of notice of the modification or revocation and the issuer in turn is entitled to reimbursement from its customer.

Section 5-107. Advice of Credit; Confirmation: Error in Statement of Terms.

(1) Unless otherwise specified an advising bank by advising a credit issued by another bank does not assume any obligation to honor drafts drawn or demands for payment made under the credit but it does assume obligation for the accuracy of its own statement.

(2) A confirming bank by confirming a credit becomes directly obligated on the credit to the extent of its confirmation as though it were its issuer and acquires the rights of an issuer.

(3) Even though an advising bank incor-

rectly advises the terms of a credit it has been authorized to advise the credit is established as against the issuer to the extent of its original terms.

(4) Unless otherwise specified the customer bears as against the issuer all risks of transmission and reasonable translation or interpretation of any message relating to a credit.

Section 5-108. "Notation Credit"; Exhaustion of Credit.

(1) A credit which specifies that any person purchasing or paying drafts drawn or demands for payment made under it must note the amount of the draft or demand on the letter or advice of credit is a "notation credit."

(2) Under a notation credit

(a) a person paying the beneficiary or purchasing a draft or demand for payment from him acquires a right to honor only if the appropriate notation is made and by transferring or forwarding for honor the documents under the credit such a person warrants to the issuer that the notation has been made; and

(b) unless the credit or a signed statement that an appropriate notation has been made accompanies the draft or demand for payment the issuer may delay honor until evidence of notation has been procured which is satisfactory to it but its obligation and that of its customer continue for a reasonable time not exceeding thirty days to obtain such evidence.

(3) If the credit is not a notation credit

(a) the issuer may honor complying drafts or demands for payment presented to it in the order in which they are presented and is discharged pro tanto by honor of any such draft or demand;

(b) as between competing good faith purchasers of complying drafts or demands the person first purchasing has priority over a subsequent purchaser even though the later purchased draft or demand has been first honored.

Section 5-109. Issuer's Obligation to its Customer.

(1) An issuer's obligation to its customer includes good faith and observance of any general banking usage but unless otherwise agreed does not include liability or responsibility

(a) for performance of the underlying contract for sale or other transaction between the customer and the beneficiary; or

(b) for any act or omission of any person other than itself or its own branch or for loss or destruction of a draft, demand or document in transit or in the possession of others; or

(c) based on knowledge or lack of knowledge or any usage of any particular trade.

(2) An issuer must examine documents with care so as to ascertain that on their face they appear to comply with the terms of the credit but unless otherwise agreed assumes no liability or responsibility for the genuineness, falsification or effect of any document which appears on such examination to be regular on its face.

(3) A non-bank issuer is not bound by any banking usage of which it has no knowledge.

Section 5-110. Availability of Credit in Portions; Presenter's Reservation of Lien or Claim.

(1) Unless otherwise specified a credit may be used in portions in the discretion of the beneficiary.

(2) Unless otherwise specified a person by presenting a documentary draft or demand for payment under a credit relinquishes upon its honor all claims to the documents and a person by transferring such draft or demand or causing such presentment authorizes such relinquishment. An explicit reservation of claim makes the draft or demand non-complying.

Section 5-111. Warranties on Transfer and Presentment.

(1) Unless otherwise agreed the beneficiary by transferring or presenting a documentary draft or demand for payment warrants to all interested parties that the necessary conditions of the credit have been complied with. This is in addition to any warranties arising under Articles 3, 4, 7 and 8.

(2) Unless otherwise agreed a negotiating, advising, confirming, collecting or issuing bank presenting or transferring a draft or demand for payment under a credit warrants only the matters warranted by a collecting bank under Article 4 and any such bank transferring a document warrants only the matters warranted by an intermediary under Articles 7 and 8.

Section 5-112. Time Allowed for Honor or Rejection; Withholding Honor or Rejection by Consent; Presenter.

(1) A bank to which a documentary draft or demand for payment is presented under a credit may without dishonor of the draft, demand or credit

    (a) defer honor until the close of the third banking day following receipt of the documents; and

    (b) further defer honor if the presenter has expressly or impliedly consented thereto.

Failure to honor within the time here specified constitutes dishonor of the draft or demand and of the credit [except as otherwise provided in subsection (4) of Section 5-114 on conditional payment].

> NOTE: *The bracketed language in the last sentence of subsection (1) should be included only if the optional provisions of Section 5-114(4) and (5) are included.*

(2) Upon dishonor the bank may unless otherwise instructed fulfill its duty to return the draft or demand and the documents by holding them at the disposal of the presenter and sending him an advice to that effect.

(3) "Presenter" means any person presenting a draft or demand for payment for honor under a credit even though that person is a confirming bank or other correspondent which is acting under an issuer's authorization.

Section 5-113. Indemnities.

(1) A bank seeking to obtain (whether for itself or another) honor, negotiation or reimbursement under a credit may give an indemnity to induce such honor, negotiation or reimbursement.

(2) An indemnity agreement inducing honor, negotiation or reimbursement

    (a) unless otherwise explicitly agreed applies to defects in the documents but not in the goods; and

    (b) unless a longer time is explicitly agreed expires at the end of ten business days following receipt of the documents by the ultimate customer unless notice of objection is sent before such expiration date. The ultimate customer may send notice of objection to the person from whom he received the documents and any bank receiving such notice is

under a duty to send notice to its transferor before its midnight deadline.

Section 5-114. Issuer's Duty and Privilege to Honor; Right to Reimbursement.

(1) An issuer must honor a draft or demand for payment which complies with the terms of the relevant credit regardless of whether the goods or documents conform to the underlying contract for sale or other contract between the customer and the beneficiary. The issuer is not excused from honor of such a draft or demand by reason of an additional general term that all documents must be satisfactory to the issuer, but an issuer may require that specified documents must be satisfactory to it.

(2) Unless otherwise agreed when documents appear on their face to comply with the terms of a credit but a required document does not in fact conform to the warranties made on negotiation or transfer of a document of title (Section 7-507) or of a security (Section 8-306) or is forged or fraudulent or there is fraud in the transaction

    (a) the issuer must honor the draft or demand for payment if honor is demanded by a negotiating bank or other holder of the draft or demand which has taken the draft or demand under the credit and under circumstances which would make it a holder in due course (Section 3-302) and in an appropriate case would make it a person to whom a document of title has been duly negotiated (Section 7-502) or a bona fide purchaser of a security (Section 8-302); and

    (b) in all other cases as against its customer, an issuer acting in good faith may honor the draft or demand for payment despite notification from the customer of fraud, forgery or other defect not apparent on the face of the documents but a court of appropriate jurisdiction may enjoin such honor.

(3) Unless otherwise agreed an issuer which has duly honored a draft or demand for payment is entitled to immediate reimbursement of any payment made under the credit and to be put in effectively available funds not later than the day before maturity of any acceptance made under the credit.

[(4) When a credit provides for payment by the issuer on receipt of notice that the required documents are in the possession of a correspondent or other agent of the issuer

    (a) any payment made on receipt of such notice is conditional; and

    (b) the issuer may reject documents which do not comply with the credit if it does so within three banking days following its receipt of the documents; and

    (c) in the event of such rejection, the issuer is entitled by charge back or otherwise to return of the payment made.]

[(5) In the case covered by subsection (4) failure to reject documents within the time specified in sub-paragraph (b) constitutes acceptance of the documents and makes the payment final in favor of the beneficiary.]

    NOTE: *Subsections (4) and (5) are bracketed as optional. If they are included the bracketed language in the last sentence of Section 5-112(1) should also be included.*

Section 5-115. Remedy for Improper Dishonor or Anticipatory Repudiation.

(1) When an issuer wrongfully dishonors a draft or demand for payment under a credit the person entitled to honor has with respect to any documents the rights of a person in the position of a seller (Section 2-707) and may recover from the issuer the face amount of the draft or demand together with incidental damages under Section 2-710 on seller's incidental damages and interest but less any amount realized by resale or other use or disposition of the subject matter of the transaction. In the event no resale or other utilization is made the documents, goods or other subject matter involved in the transaction must be turned over to the issuer on payment of judgment.

(2) When an issuer wrongfully cancels or otherwise repudiates a credit before presentment of a draft or demand for payment drawn under it the beneficiary has the rights of a seller after anticipatory repudiation by the buyer under Section 2-610 if he learns of the repudiation in time reasonably to avoid procurement of the required documents. Otherwise the beneficiary has an immediate right of action for wrongful dishonor.

Section 5-116. Transfer and Assignment.

(1) The right to draw under a credit can be transferred or assigned only when the credit is expressly designated as transferable or assignable.

(2) Even though the credit specifically states that it is nontransferable or nonassignable the beneficiary may before performance of the conditions of the credit assign his right to proceeds. Such an assignment is an assignment of a contract right under Article 9 on Secured Transactions and is governed by that Article except that

    (a) the assignment is ineffective until the letter of credit or advice of credit is delivered to the assignee which delivery constitutes perfection of the security interest under Article 9; and

    (b) the issuer may honor drafts or demands for payment drawn under the credit until it receives a notification of the assignment signed by the beneficiary which reasonably identifies the credit involved in the assignment and contains a request to pay the assignee; and

    (c) after what reasonably appears to be such a notification has been received the issuer may without dishonor refuse to accept or pay even to a person otherwise entitled to honor until the letter of credit or advice of credit is exhibited to the issuer.

(3) Except where the beneficiary has effectively assigned his right to draw or his right to proceeds, nothing in this section limits his right to transfer or negotiate drafts or demands drawn under the credit.

Section 5-117. Insolvency of Bank Holding Funds for Documentary Credit.

(1) Where an issuer or an advising or confirming bank or a bank which has for a customer procured issuance of a credit by another bank becomes insolvent before final payment under the credit and the credit is one to which this Article is made applicable by paragraphs (a) or (b) of Section 5-102(1) on scope, the receipt or allocation of funds or collateral to secure or meet obligations under the credit shall have the following results:

    (a) to the extent of any funds or collateral turned over after or before the insolvency as indemnity against or specifically for the purpose of payment of drafts or demand for payment drawn under the designated credit, the drafts or demands are entitled to payment in preference over depositors or other general creditors of the issuer or bank; and

(b) on expiration of the credit or surrender of the beneficiary's rights under it unused any person who has given such funds or collateral is similarly entitled to return thereof; and

(c) a change to a general or current account with a bank if specifically consented to for the purpose of indemnity against or payment of drafts or demands for payment drawn under the designated credit falls under the same rules as if the funds had been drawn out in cash and then turned over with specific instructions.

(2) After honor or reimbursement under this section the customer or other person for whose account the insolvent bank has acted is entitled to receive the documents involved.

ARTICLE 6

BULK TRANSFERS

Section 6-101. Short Title. This Article shall be known and may be cited as Uniform Commercial Code—Bulk Transfers.

Section 6-102. "Bulk Transfers"; Transfers of Equipment; Enterprises Subject to this Article; Bulk Transfers Subject to this Article.

(1) A "bulk transfer" is any transfer in bulk and not in the ordinary course of the transferor's business of a major part of the materials, supplies, merchandise or other inventory (Section 9-109) of an enterprise subject to this Article.

(2) A transfer of a substantial part of the equipment (Section 9-109) of such an enterprise is a bulk transfer if it is made in connection with a bulk transfer of inventory, but not otherwise.

(3) The enterprises subject to this Article are all those whose principal business is the sale of merchandise from stock, including those who manufacture what they sell.

(4) Except as limited by the following section all bulk transfers of goods located within this state are subject to this Article.

Section 6-103. Transfers Excepted from this Article. The following transfers are not subject to this Article:

(1) Those made to give security for the performance of an obligation;

(2) General assignments for the benefit of all the creditors of the transferor, and subsequent transfers by the assignee thereunder;

(3) Transfers in settlement or realization of a lien or other security interest;

(4) Sales by executors, administrators, receivers, trustees in bankruptcy, or any public officer under judicial process;

(5) Sales made in the course of judicial or administrative proceedings for the dissolution or reorganization of a corporation and of which notice is sent to the creditors of the corporation to order of the court or administrative agency;

(6) Transfers to a person maintaining a known place of business in this State who becomes bound to pay the debts of the transferor in full and gives public notice of that fact, and who is solvent after becoming so bound;

(7) A transfer to a new business enterprise organized to take over and continue the business, if public notice of the transaction is given and the new enterprise assumes the debts of the transferor and he receives nothing from the transaction except an interest in the new enterprise junior to the claims of creditors;

(8) Transfers of property which is exempt from execution.

Public notice under subsection (6) or subsection (7) may be given by publishing once a week for two consecutive weeks in a newspaper of general circulation where the transferor had its principal place of business in this state an advertisement including the names and addresses of the transferor and transferee and the effective date of the transfer.

Section 6-104. Schedule of Property, List of Creditors.

(1) Except as provided with respect to auction sales (Section 6-108), a bulk transfer subject to this Article is ineffective against any creditor of the transferor unless:

(a) The transferee requires the transferor to furnish a list of his existing creditors prepared as stated in this section; and

(b) The parties prepare a schedule of the property transferred sufficient to identify it; and

(c) The transferee preserves the list and schedule for six months next following the transfer and permits inspection of either or both and copying therefrom at all reasonable hours by any creditor of the transferor, or files the list and schedule in (a public office to be here identified).

(2) The list of creditors must be signed and sworn to or affirmed by the transferot or his agent. It must contain the names and business addresses of all creditors of the transferor, with the amounts when known, and also the names of all persons who are known to the transferor to assert claims against him even though such claims are disputed. If the transferor is the obligor of an outstanding issue of bonds, debentures or the like as to which there is an indenture trustee, the list of creditors need include only the name and address of the indenture trustee and the aggregate outstanding principal amount of the issue.

(3) Responsibility for the completeness and accuracy of the list of creditors rests on the transferor, and the transfer is not rendered ineffective by errors or omissions therein unless the transferee is shown to have had knowledge.

Section 6-105. Notice to Creditors. In addition to the requirements of the preceding section, any bulk transfer subject to this Article except one made by auction sale (Section 6-108) is ineffective against any creditor of the transferor unless at least ten days before he takes possession of the goods or pays for them, whichever happens first, the transferee gives notice of the transfer in the manner and to the persons hereafter provided (Section 6-107).

Section 6-106. Application of the Proceeds. In addition to the requirements of the two preceding sections:

(1) Upon every bulk transfer subject to this Article for which new consideration becomes payable except those made by sale at auction it is the duty of the transferee to assure that such consideration is applied so far as necessary to pay those debts of the transferor which are either shown on the list

furnished by the transferor (Section 6-104) or filed in writing in the place stated in the notice (Section 6-107) within thirty days after the mailing of such notice. This duty of the transferee runs to all the holders of such debts, and may be enforced by any of them for the benefit of all.

(2) If any of said debts are in dispute the necessary sum may be withheld from distribution until the dispute is settled or adjudicated.

(3) If the consideration payable is not enough to pay all of the said debts in full distribution shall be made pro rata]

NOTE: *This section is bracketed to indicate division of opinion as to whether or not it is a wise provision, and to suggest that this is a point on which state enactments may differ without serious damage to the principle of uniformity.*

In any State where this section is omitted, the following parts of sections also bracketed in the text, should also be omitted, namely:
Section 6-107(2)(e).
6-108(3)(c).
6-109(2).

In any State where this section is enacted, these other provisions should be also.

Optional Subsection (4) [(4) The transferee may within ten days after he takes possession of the goods pay the consideration into the (specify court) in the county where the transferor had its principal place of business in this state and thereafter may discharge his duty under this section by giving notice by registered or certified mail to all the persons to whom the duty runs that the consideration has been paid into that court and that they should file their claims there. On motion of any interested party, the court may order the distribution of the consideration to the persons entitled to it.]

NOTE: *Optional subsection (4) is recommended for those states which do not have a general statute providing for payment of money into court.*

Section 6-107. The Notice.

(1) The notice to creditors (Section 6-105) shall state:

(a) that a bulk transfer is about to be made; and

(b) the names and business addresses of the transferor and transferee, and all other business names and addresses used by the transferor within three years last past so far as known to the transferee; and

(c) whether or not all the debts of the transferor are to be paid in full as they fall due as a result of the transaction, and if so, the address to which creditors should send their bills.

(2) If the debts of the transferor are not to be paid in full as they fall due or if the transferee is in doubt on that point then the notice shall state further:

(a) the location and general description of the property to be transferred and the estimated total of the transferor's debts;

(b) the address where the schedule of property and list of creditors (Section 6-104) may be inspected;

(c) whether the transfer is to pay existing debts and if so the amount of such debts and to whom owing;

(d) whether the transfer is for new consideration and if so the amount of such consideration and the time and place of payment; [and]

[(e) if for new consideration the time and place where creditors of the transferor are to file their claims.]

(3) The notice in any case shall be delivered personally or sent by registered mail to all the persons shown on the list of creditors furnished by the transferor (Section 6-104) and to all other persons who are known to the transferee to hold or assert claims against the transferor.

NOTE: *The words in brackets are optional.*

Section 6-108. Auction Sales; "Auctioneer."

(1) A bulk transfer is subject to this Article even though it is by sale at auction, but only in the manner and with the results stated in this section.

(2) The transferor shall furnish a list of his creditors and assist in the preparation of a schedule of the property to be sold, both prepared as before stated (Section 6-104).

(3) The person or persons other than the transferor who direct, control or are responsible for the auction are collectively called the "auctioneer." The auctioneer shall:

(a) receive and retain the list of creditors and prepare and retain the schedule

of property for the period stated in this Article (Section 6-104);

(b) give notice of the auction personally or by registered or certified mail at least ten days before it occurs to all persons shown on the list of creditors and to all other persons who are known to him to hold or assert claims against the transferor; [and]

[(c) assure that the net proceeds of the auction are applied as provided in this Article (Section 6-106).]

(4) Failure of the auctioneer to perform any of these duties does not affect the validity of the sale or the title of the purchasers, but if the auctioneer knows that the auction constitutes a bulk transfer such failure renders the auctioneer liable to the creditors of the transferor as a class for the sums owing to them from the transferor up to but not exceeding the net proceeds of the auction. If the auctioneer consists of several persons their liability is joint and several.

NOTE: *The words in brackets are optional.*

Section 6-109. What Creditors Protected; Credit for Payment to Particular Creditors.

(1) The creditors of the transferor mentioned in this Article are those holding claims based on transactions or events occurring before the bulk transfer, but creditors who become such after notice to creditors is given (Sections 6-105 and 6-107) are not entitled to notice.

[(2) Against the aggregate obligation imposed by the provisions of this Article concerning the application of the proceeds (Section 6-106 and subsection (3) (c) of 6-108) the transferee or auctioneer is entitled to credit for sums paid to particular creditors of the transferor, not exceeding the sums believed in good faith at the time of the payment to be properly payable to such creditors.]

Section 6-110. Subsequent Transfers. When the title of a transferee to property is subject to a defect by reason of his noncompliance with the requirements of this Article, then:

(1) a purchaser of any of such property from such transferee who pays no value or who takes with notice of such non-compliance takes subject to such defect, but

(2) a purchaser for value in good faith and

without such notice takes free of such defect.

Section 6-111. Limitation of Actions and Levies. No action under this Article shall be brought nor levy made more than six months after the date on which the transferee took possession of the goods unless the transfer has been concealed. If the transfer has been concealed, actions may be brought or levies made within six months after its discovery.

NOTE TO ARTICLE 6: *Section 6-106 is bracketed to indicate division of opinion as to whether or not it is a wise provision, and to suggest that this is a point on which State enactments may differ without serious damage to the principle of uniformity.*

In any State where Section 6-106 is not enacted, the following parts of sections, also bracketed in the text, should also be omitted, namely:

Sec. 6-107(2)(e)
6-109(3)(c)
6-109(2).

In any State where Section 6-106 is enacted, these other provisions should be also.

ARTICLE 7

WAREHOUSE RECEIPTS, BILLS OF LADING AND OTHER DOCUMENTS OF TITLE

PART 1

GENERAL

Section 7-101. Short Title. This Article shall be known and may be cited as Uniform Commercial Code—Documents of Title.

Section 7-102. Definitions and Index of Definitions.

(1) In this Article, unless the context otherwise requires:

(a) "Bailee" means the person who by a warehouse receipt, bill of lading or other document of title acknowledges possession of goods and contracts to deliver them.

(b) "Consignee" means the person named in a bill to whom or to whose order the bill promises delivery.

(c) "Consignor" means the person named in a bill as the person from whom the goods have been received for shipment.

(d) "Delivery order" means a written order to deliver goods directed to a warehouseman, carrier or other person who in the ordinary course of business issues warehouse receipts of bills of lading.

(e) "Document" means document of title as defined in the general definitions in Article 1 (Section 1-201).

(f) "Goods" means all things which are treated as movable for the purposes of a contract of storage or transportation.

(g) "Issuer" means a bailee who issues a document except that in relation to an unaccepted delivery order it means the person who orders the possessor of goods to deliver. Issuer includes any person for whom an agent or employee purports to act in issuing a document if the agent or employee has real or apparent authority to issue documents, notwithstanding that the issuer received no goods or that the goods were misdescribed or that in any other respect the agent or employee violated his instructions.

(h) "Warehouseman" is a person engaged in the business of storing goods for hire.

(2) Other definitions applying to this Article or to specified Parts thereof, and the sections in which they appear are:

"Duly negotiate." Section 7-501.

"Person entitled under the document." Section 7-403(4).

(3) Definitions in other Articles applying to this Article and the sections in which they appear are:

"Contract for sale." Section 2-106.

"Overseas." Section 2-323.

"Receipt" of goods. Section 2-103.

(4) In addition Article 2 contains general

definitions and principles of construction and interpretation applicable throughout this Article.

Section 7-103. Relation of Article to Treaty, Statute, Tariff, Classification or Regulation. To the extent that any treaty or statute of the United States, regulatory statute of this State or tariff, classification or regulation filed or issued pursuant thereto is applicable, the provisions of this Article are subject thereto.

Section 7-104. Negotiable and Non-Negotiable Warehouse Receipt, Bill of Lading or Other Document of Title.

    (1) A warehouse receipt, bill of lading or other document of title is negotiable

        (a) if by its terms the goods are to be delivered to bearer or to the order of a named person; or

        (b) where recognized in overseas trade, if it runs to a named person or assigns.

    (2) Any other document is non-negotiable. A bill of lading in which it is stated that the goods are consigned to a named person is not made negotiable by a provision that the goods are to be delivered only against a written order signed by the same or another named person.

Section 7-105. Construction Against Negative Implication. The omission from either Part 2 or Part 3 of this Article of a provision corresponding to a provision made in the other Part does not imply that a corresponding rule of law is not applicable.

PART 2

WAREHOUSE RECEIPTS: SPECIAL PROVISIONS

Section 7-201. Who may issue a Warehouse Receipt; Storage under Government Bond.

    (1) A warehouse receipt may be issued by any warehouseman.

    (2) Where goods including distilled spirits and agricultural commodities are stored under a statute requiring a bond against a withdrawal or a license for the issuance of receipts in the nature of warehouse receipts, a receipt for the goods has like effect as a warehouse receipt even though issued by a person who is the owner of the goods and is not a warehouseman.

Section 7-202. Form of Warehouse Receipt; Essential Terms; Optional Terms.

    (1) A warehouse receipt need not be in any particular form.

    (2) Unless a warehouse receipt embodies within its written or printed terms each of the following, the warehouseman is liable for damages caused by the omission to a person injured thereby:

        (a) the location of the warehouse where the goods are stored;

        (b) the date of issue of the receipt;

        (c) the consecutive number of the receipt;

        (d) a statement whether the goods received will be delivered to the bearer, to a specified person, or to a specified person or his order;

        (e) the rate of storage and handling charges, except that where goods are stored under a field warehousing arrangement a statement of that fact is sufficient on a non-negotiable receipt;

        (f) a description of the goods or of the packages containing them;

        (g) the signature of the warehouseman, which may be made by his authorized agent;

        (h) if the receipt is issued for goods of which the warehouseman is owner, either solely or jointly or in common with others, the fact of such ownership; and

        (i) a statement of the amount of advances made and of liabilities incurred for which the warehouseman claims a lien or security interest (Section 7-209). If the precise amount of such advances made or of such liabilities incurred is, at the time of the issue of the receipt, unknown to the warehouseman or to his agent who issues it, a statement of the fact that advances have been made or liabilities incurred and the purpose thereof is sufficient.

    (3) A warehouseman may insert in his receipt any other terms which are not contrary to the provisions of this Act and do not impair his obligation of delivery (Sec-

tion 7-403) or his duty to care (Section 7-204). Any contrary provisions shall be ineffective.

Section 7-203. Liability for Non-Receipt or Misdescription. A party to or purchaser for value in good faith of a document of title other than a bill of lading relying in either case upon the description therein of the goods may recover from the issuer damages caused by the non-receipt or misdescription of the goods, except to the extent that the document conspicuously indicates that the issuer does not know whether any part or all of the goods in fact were received or conform to the description, as where the description is in terms of marks or labels or kind, quantity or condition, or the receipt or description is qualified by "contents, condition and quality unknown," "said to contain" or the like, if such indication be true, or the party or purchaser otherwise has notice.

Section 7-204. Duty of Care: Contractual Limitation of Warehouseman's Liability.

(1) A warehouseman is liable for damages for loss of or injury to the goods caused by his failure to exercise such care in regard to them as a reasonably careful man would exercise under like circumstances but unless otherwise agreed he is not liable for damages which could not have been avoided by the exercise of such care.

(2) Damages may be limited by a term in the warehouse receipt or storage agreement limiting the amount of liability in case of loss or damage, and setting forth a specific liability per article or item, or value per unit of weight, beyond which the warehouseman shall not be liable; provided, however, that such liability may on written request of the bailor at the time of signing such storage agreement or within a reasonable time after receipt of the warehouse receipt be increased on part or all of the goods thereunder, in which event increased rates may be charged based on such increased valuation, but that no such increase shall be permitted contrary to a lawful limitation of liability contained in the warehouseman's tariff, if any. No such limitation is effective with respect to the warehouseman's liability for conversion to his own use.

(3) Reasonable provisions as to the time

and manner of presenting claims and instituting actions based on the bailment may be included in the warehouse receipt or tariff.

(4) This section does not impair or repeal . .

> NOTE: *Insert in subsection (4) a reference to any statute which imposes a higher responsibility upon the warehouseman or invalidates contractual limitations which would be permissible under this Article.*

Section 7-205. Title Under Warehouse Receipt Defeated in Certain Cases. A buyer in the ordinary course of business of fungible goods sold and delivered by a warehouseman who is also in the business of buying and selling such goods takes free of any claim under a warehouse receipt even though it has been duly negotiated.

Section 7-206. Termination of Storage at Warehouseman's Option.

(1) A warehouseman may on notifying the person on whose account the goods are held and any other person known to claim an interest in the goods require payment of any charges and removal of the goods from the warehouse at the termination of the period of storage fixed by the document, or, if no period is fixed, within a stated period not less than thirty days after the notification. If the goods are not removed before the date specified in the notification, the warehouseman may sell them in accordance with the provisions of the section on enforcement of a warehouseman's lien (Section 7-210).

(2) If a warehouseman in good faith believes that the goods are about to deteriorate or decline in value to less than the amount of his lien within the time prescribed in subsection (1) for notification, advertisement and sale, the warehouseman may specify in the notification any reasonable shorter time for removal of the goods and in case the goods are not removed, may sell them at public sale held not less than one week after a single advertisement or posting.

(3) If as a result of a quality or condition of the goods of which the warehouseman had no choice at the time of deposit the goods are a hazard to other property or to the warehouse or to persons, the warehouseman may sell the goods at public or private

sale without advertisement on reasonable notification to all persons known to claim an interest in the goods. If the warehouse man after a reasonable effort is unable to sell the goods he may dispose of them in any lawful manner and shall incur no liability by reason of such disposition.

(4) The warehouseman must deliver the goods to any person entitled to them under this Article upon due demand made at any time prior to the sale or other disposition under this section.

(5) The warehouseman may satisfy his lien from the proceeds of any sale or disposition under this section but must hold the balance for delivery on the demand of any person to whom he would have been bound to deliver the goods.

Section 7-207. Goods Must be Kept Separate; Fungible Goods.

(1) Unless the warehouse receipt otherwise provides, a warehouseman must keep separate the goods covered by each receipt so as to permit at all times identification and delivery of those goods except that different lots of tungible goods may be commingled.

(2) Fungible goods so commingled are owned in common by the persons entitled thereto and the warehouseman is severally liable to each owner for that owner's share. Where because of overissue a mass of fungible goods is insufficient to meet all the receipts which the warehouseman has issued against it, the persons entitled include all holders to whom overissued receipts have been duly negotiated.

Section 7-208. Altered Warehouse Receipts.
Where a blank in a negotiable warehouse receipt has been filled in without authority, a purchaser for value and without notice of the want of authority may treat the insertion as authorized. Any other unauthorized alteration leaves any receipt enforceable against the issuer according to its original tenor.

Section 7-209. Lien of Warehouseman.

(1) A warehouseman has a lien against the bailor on the goods covered by a warehouse receipt or on the proceeds thereof in his possession for charges for storage or transportation (including demurrage and terminal charges), insurance, labor, or charges present or future in relation to the goods, and for expenses necessary for preservation of the goods or reasonably incurred in their sale pursuant to law. If the person on whose account the goods are held is liable for like charges or expenses in relation to other goods whenever deposited and it is stated in the receipt that a lien is claimed for charges and expenses in relation to other goods, the warehouseman also has a lien against him for such charges and expenses whether or not the other goods have been delivered by the warehouseman. But against a person to whom a negotiable warehouse receipt is duly negotiated a warehouseman's lien is limited to charges in an amount or at a rate specified on the receipt or if no charges are so specified then to a reasonable charge for storage of the goods covered by the receipt subsequent to the date of the receipt.

(2) The warehouseman may also reserve a security interest against the bailor for a maximum amount specified on the receipt for charges other than those specified in subsection (1), such as for money advanced and interest. Such a security interest is governed by the Article on Secured Transactions (Article 9).

(3) A warehouseman's lien for charges and expenses under subsection (1) or a security interest under subsection (2) is also effective against any person who so entrusted the bailor with possession of the goods that a pledge of them by him to a good faith purchaser for value would have been valid but is not effective against a person as to whom the document confers no right in the goods covered by it under Section 7-503.

(4) A warehouseman loses his lien on any goods which he voluntarily delivers or which he unjustifiably refuses to deliver.

Section 7-210. Enforcement of Warehouseman's Lien.

(1) Except as provided in subsection (2), a warehouseman's lien may be enforced by public or private sale of the goods in block or in parcels, at any time or place and on any terms which are commercially reasonable, after notifying all persons known to claim an interest in the goods. Such notification must include a statement of the amount due, the nature of the proposed sale and the

time and place of any public sale. The fact that a better price could have been obtained by a sale at a different time or in a different method from that selected by the warehouseman is not of itself sufficient to establish that the sale was not made in a commercially reasonable manner. If the warehouseman either sells the goods in the usual manner in any recognized market therefore, or if he sells at the price current in such market at the time of his sale, or if he has otherwise sold in conformity with commercially reasonable practices among dealers in the type of goods sold, he has sold in a commercially reasonable manner. A sale of more goods than apparently necessary to be offered to insure satisfaction of the obligation is not commercially reasonable except in cases covered by the preceding sentence.

(2) A warehouseman's lien on goods other than goods stored by a merchant in the course of his business may be enforced only as follows:

(a) All persons known to claim an interest in the goods must be notified.

(b) The notification must be delivered in person or sent by registered or certified letter to the last known address of any person to be notified.

(c) The notification must include an itemized statement of the claim, a description of the goods subject to the lien, a demand for payment within a specified time not less than ten days after receipt of the notification, and a conspicuous statement that unless the claim is paid within that time the goods will be advertised for sale and sold by auction at a specified time and place.

(d) The sale must conform to the terms of the notification.

(e) The sale must be held at the nearest suitable place to that where the goods are held or stored.

(f) After the expiration of the time given in the notification, an advertisement of the sale must be published once a week for two weeks consecutively in a newspaper of general circulation where the sale is to be held. The advertisement must include a description of the goods, the name of the person on whose account they are being held, and the time and place of the sale. The sale must take place at least fifteen days after the first publication. If there is no newspaper of general circulation where the sale is to be held, the advertisement must be posted at least ten days before the sale in not less than six conspicuous places in the neighborhood of the proposed sale.

(3) Before any sale pursuant to this section any person claiming a right in the goods may pay the amount necessary to satisfy the lien and the reasonable expenses incurred under this section. In that event the goods must not be sold, but must be retained by the warehouseman subject to the terms of the receipt and this Article.

(4) The warehouseman may buy at any public sale pursuant to this section.

(5) A purchaser in good faith of goods sold to enforce a warehouseman's lien takes the goods free of any rights of persons against whom the lien was valid, despite noncompliance by the warehouseman with the requirements of this section.

(6) The warehouseman may satisfy his lien from the proceeds of any sale pursuant to this section but must hold the balance, if any, for delivery on demand to any person to whom he would have been bound to deliver the goods.

(7) The rights provided by this section shall be in addition to all other rights allowed by law to a creditor against his debtor.

(8) Where a lien is on goods stored by a merchant in the course of his business the lien may be enforced in accordance with either subsection (1) or (2).

(9) The warehouseman is liable for damages caused by failure to comply with the requirements for sale under this section and in case of willful violation is liable for conversion.

PART 3

BILLS OF LADING: SPECIAL PROVISIONS

Section 7-301. Liability for Non-receipt or Mis-description; "Said to Contain"; "Shipper's Load and Count"; Improper Handling.

(1) A consignee of a non-negotiable bill who has given value in good faith or a holder to whom a negotiable bill has been duly negotiated relying in either case upon the description therein of the goods, or upon the date therein shown, may recover from the issuer damages caused by the misdating of the bill or the nonreceipt or misdescription of the goods, except to the extent that the document indicates that the issuer does not know whether any part or all of the goods in fact were received or conform to the description, as where the description is in terms of marks or labels or kind, quantity, or condition of the receipt or description is qualified by "contents or condition of contents of packages unknown," "said to contain," "shipper's weight, load and count" or the like, if such indication be true.

(2) , When goods are loaded by an issuer who is a common carrier, the issuer must count the packages of goods if package freight and ascertain the kind and quantity if bulk freight. In such cases "shipper's weight, load and count" or other words indicating that the description was made by the shipper are ineffective except as to freight concealed by packages.

(3) When bulk freight is loaded by a shipper who makes available to the issuer adequate facilities for weighing such freight, an issuer who is a common carrier must ascertain the kind and quantity within a reasonable time after receiving the written request of the shipper to do so. In such cases "shipper's weight" or other words of like purport are ineffective.

(4) The issuer may by inserting in the bill the words "shipper's weight, load and count" or other words of like purport indicate that the goods were loaded by the shipper; and if such statement be true the issuer shall not be liable for damages caused by the improper loading. But their omission does not imply liability for such damages.

(5) The shipper shall be deemed to have guaranteed to the issuer the accuracy at the time of shipment of the description, marks, labels, number, kind, quantity, condition and weight, as furnished by him; and the shipper shall indemnify the issuer against damage caused by inaccuracies in such particulars. The right of the issuer to such indemnity shall in no way limit his responsibility and liability under the contract of carriage to any person other than the shipper.

Section 7-302. Through Bills of Lading and Similar Documents.

(1) The issuer of a through bill of lading or other document embodying an undertaking to be performed in part by persons acting as its agents or by connecting carriers is liable to anyone entitled to recover on the document for any breach by such other persons or by a connecting carrier of its obligation under the document but to the extent that the bill covers an undertaking to be performed overseas or in territory not contiguous to the continental United States or an undertaking including matters other than transportation this liability may be varied by agreement of the parties.

(2) Where goods covered by a through bill of lading or other document embodying an undertaking to be performed in part by persons other than the issuer are received by any such person, he is subject with respect to his own performance while the goods are in his possession to the obligation of the issuer. His obligation is discharged by delivery of the goods to another such person pursuant to the document, and does not

include liability for breach by any other such persons or by the issuer.

(3) The issuer of such through bill of lading or other document shall be entitled to recover from the connecting carrier or such other person in possession of the goods when the breach of the obligation under the document occurred, the amount it may be required to pay to anyone entitled to recover on the document therefor, as may be evidenced by any receipt, judgment, or transcript thereof, and the amount of any expense reasonably incurred by it in defending any action brought by anyone entitled to recover on the document therefor.

Section 7-303. Diversion; Reconsignment; Change of Instructions.

(1) Unless the bill of lading otherwise provides, the carrier may deliver the goods to a person or destination other than that stated in the bill or may otherwise dispose of the goods on instructions from

    (a) the holder of a negotiable bill; or

    (b) the consignor on a non-negotiable bill notwithstanding contrary instructions from the consignee; or

    (c) the consignee on a non-negotiable bill in the absence of contrary instructions from the consignor, if the goods have arrived at the billed destination or if the consignee is in possession of the bill; or

    (d) the consignee on a non-negotiable bill if he is entitled as against the consignor to dispose of them.

(2) Unless such instructions are noted on a negotiable bill of lading, a person to whom the bill is duly negotiated can hold the bailee according to the original terms.

Section 7-304. Bills of Lading in a Set.

(1) Except where customary in overseas transportation, a bill of lading must not be issued in a set of parts. The issuer is liable for damages caused by violation of this subsection.

(2) Where a bill of lading is lawfully drawn in a set of parts, each of which is numbered and expressed to be valid only if the goods have not been delivered against any other part, the whole of the parts constitute one bill.

(3) Where a bill of lading is lawfully issued in a set of parts and different parts are negotiated to different persons, the title of the holder to whom the first due negotiation is made prevails as to both the document and the goods even though any later holder may have received the goods from the carrier in good faith and discharged the carrier's obligation by surrender of his part.

(4) Any person who negotiates or transfers a single part of a bill of lading drawn in a set is liable to holders of that part as if it were the whole set.

(5) The bailee is obliged to deliver in accordance with Part 4 of this Article against the first presented part of a bill of lading lawfully drawn in a set. Such delivery discharges the bailee's obligation on the whole bill.

Section 7-305. Destination Bills.

(1) Instead of issuing a bill of lading to the consignor at the place of shipment a carrier may at the request of the consignor procure the bill to be issued at destination or at any other place designated in the request.

(2) Upon request of anyone entitled as against the carrier to control the goods while in transit and on surrender of any outstanding bill of lading or other receipt covering such goods, the issuer may procure a substitute bill to be issued at any place designated in the request.

Section 7-306. Altered Bills of Lading. An unauthorized alteration or filling of a blank in a bill of lading leaves the bill enforceable according to its original tenor.

Section 7-307. Lien of Carrier.

(1) A carrier has a lien on the goods covered by a bill of lading for charges subsequent to the date of its receipt of the goods for storage or transportation (including demurrage and terminal charges) and for expenses incurred in their sale pursuant to law. But against a purchaser for value of a negotiable bill of lading a carrier's lien is limited to charges stated in the bill or the applicable tariffs, or if no charges are stated then to a reasonable charge.

(2) A lien for charges and expenses under subsection (1) on goods which the carrier was required by law to receive for transportation is effective against the consignor or any person entitled to the goods unless the carrier had notice that the consignor lacked authority to subject the goods to

such charges and expenses. Any other lien under subsection (1) is effective against the consignor and any person who permitted the bailor to have control or possession of the goods unless the carrier had notice that the bailor lacked such authority.

(3) A carrier loses his lien on any goods which he voluntarily delivers or which he unjustifiably refuses to deliver.

Section 7-308. Enforcement of Carrier's Lien.

(1) A carrier's lien may be enforced by public or private sale of the goods, in bloc or in parcels, at any time or place and on any terms which are commercially reasonable, after notifying all persons known to claim an interest in the goods. Such notification must include a statement of the amount due, the nature of the proposed sale and the time and place of any public sale. The fact that a better price could have been obtained by a sale at a different time or in a different method from that selected by the carrier is not of itself sufficient to establish that the sale was not made in a commercially reasonable manner. If the carrier either sells the goods in the usual manner in any recognized market therefor or if he sells at the price current in such market at the time of his sale or if he has otherwise sold in conformity with commercially reasonable practices among dealers in the type of goods sold he has sold in a commercially reasonable manner. A sale of more goods than apparently necessary to be offered to ensure satisfaction of the obligation is not commercially reasonable except in cases covered by the preceding sentence.

(2) Before any sale pursuant to this section any person claiming a right in the goods may pay the amount necessary to satisfy the lien and the reasonable expenses incurred under this section. In that event the goods must not be sold, but must be retained by the carrier subject to the terms of the bill and this Article.

(3) The carrier may buy at any public sale pursuant to this section.

(4) A purchaser in good faith of goods sold to enforce a carrier's lien takes the goods free of any rights of persons against whom the lien was valid, despite non-compliance by the carrier with the requirements of this section.

(5) The carrier may satisfy his lien from the proceeds of any sale pursuant to this section but must hold the balance, if any, for delivery on demand to any person to whom he would have been bound to deliver the goods.

(6) The rights provided by this section shall be in addition to all other rights allowed by law to a creditor against his debtor.

(7) A carrier's lien may be enforced in accordance with either subsection (1) or the procedure set forth in subsection (2) of Section 7-210.

(8) The carrier is liable for damages caused by failure to comply with the requirements for sale under this section and in case of willful violation is liable for conversion.

Section 7-309. Duty of Care; Contractual Limitation of Carrier's Liability.

(1) A carrier who issues a bill of lading whether negotiable or non-negotiable must exercise the degree of care in relation to the goods which a reasonably careful man would exercise under like circumstances. This subsection does not repeal or change any law or rule of law which imposes liability upon a common carrier for damages not caused by its negligence.

(2) Damages may be limited by a provision that the carrier's liability shall not exceed a value stated in the document if the carrier's rates are dependent upon value and the consignor by the carrier's tariff is afforded an opportunity to declare a higher value or a value as lawfully provided in the tariff, or where no tariff is filed he is otherwise advised of such opportunity; but no such limitation is effective with respect to the carrier's liability for conversion to its own use.

(3) Reasonable provisions as to the time and manner of presenting claims and instituting actions based on the shipment may be included in a bill of lading or tariff.

Section 7-401. Irregularities in Issue of Receipt or Bill or Conduct of Issue. The obligations imposed by this Article on an issuer apply to a document of title regardless of the fact that

(a) the document may not comply with the requirements of this Article or of any other law or regulation regarding its issue, form or content; or

(b) the issuer may have violated laws regulating the conduct of his business; or

(c) The goods covered by the document were owned by the bailee at the time the document was issued; or

(d) the person issuing the document does not come within the definition of warehouseman if it purports to be a warehouse receipt.

Section 7-402. Duplicate Receipt or Bill; Overissue. Neither a duplicate nor any other document of title-purporting to cover goods already represented by an outstanding document of the same issuer confers any right in the goods, except as provided in the case of bills in a set, overissue of documents for fungible goods and substitutes for lost, stolen or destroyed documents. But the issuer is liable for damages caused by his overissue or failure to identify a duplicate document as such by conspicuous notation on its face.

Section 403. Obligation of Warehouseman or Carrier to Deliver; Excuse.

(1) The bailee must deliver the goods to a person entitled under the document who complies w h subsection (2) and (3), unless and to the extent that the bailee establishes any of the following:

(a) delivery of the goods to a person whose receipt was rightful as against the claimant;

(b) damage to or delay, loss or destruction of the goods for which the bailee is not liable [,but the burden of establishing negligence in such cases is on the person entitled under the document];

NOTE: *The brakets in (1) (b) indicate that State enactments may differ on this point without serious damage to the principle of uniformity.*

(c) previous sale or other disposition of the goods in lawful enforcement of a lien or on warehouseman's lawful termination of storage;

(d) the exercise by a seller of his right to stop delivery pursuant to the provisions of the Article on Sales (Section 2-705);

(e) a diversion, reconsignment or other disposition pursuant to the provisions of this Article (Section 7-303) or tariff regulating such right;

(f) release, satisfaction or any other fact affording a personal defense against the claimant;

(g) any other lawful excuse.

(2) A person claiming goods covered by a document of title must satisfy the bailee's lien where the bailee so requests or where the bailee is prohibited by law from delivering the goods until the charges are paid.

(3) Unless the person claiming is one against whom the document confers no right under Sec. 7-503 (1), he must surrender for cancellation or notation of partial deliveries any outstanding negotiable document covering the goods, and the bailee must cancel the document or conspicuously note the partial delivery thereon or be liable to any person to whom the document is duly negotiated.

(4) "Person entitled under the document" means holder in the case of a negotiable document, or the person to whom delivery is to be made by the terms of or pursuant to written instructions under a non-negotiable document.

Section 7-404. No Liability for Good Faith Delivery Pursuant to Receipt or Bill. A bailee who in good faith including observance of reasonable commercial standards has received goods and delivered or otherwise disposed of them according to the terms of the document of title or pursuant to this Article is not liable therefor. This rule applies even though the person from whom he received the goods had no authority to procure the document or to dispose of the goods and even though the person to whom he delivered the goods had no authority to receive them.

PART 5

WAREHOUSE RECEIPTS AND BILLS OF LADING: NEGOTIATION AND TRANSFER

Section 7-501. Form of Negotiation and Requirements of "Due Negotiation."

(1) A negotiable document of title running to the order of a named person is negotiated by his indorsement and delivery. After his indorsement in blank or to bearer any person can negotiate it by delivery alone.

(2)(a) A negotiable document of title is also negotiated by delivery alone when by its original terms it runs to bearer.

(b) When a document running to the order of a named person is delivered to him the effect is the same as if the document had been negotiated.

(3) Negotiation of a negotiable document of title after it has been indorsed to a specified person requires indorsement by the special indorsee as well as delivery.

(4) A negotiable document of title is "duly negotiated" when it is negotiated in the manner stated in this section to a holder who purchases it in good faith without notice of any defense against or claim to it on the part of any person and for value, unless it is established that the negotiation is not in the regular course of business or financing or involves receiving the document in settlement or payment of a money obligation.

(5) Indorsement of a non-negotiable document neither makes it negotiable nor adds to the transferee's rights.

(6) The naming in a negotiable bill of a person to be notified of the arrival of the goods does not limit the negotiability of the bill nor constitute notice to a purchaser thereof of any interest of such person in the goods.

Section 7-502. Rights Acquired by Due Negotiation.

(1) Subject to the following section and to the provisions of Section 7-205 on fungible goods, a holder to whom a negotiable document of title has been duly negotiated acquires thereby:

(a) title to the document;

(b) title to the goods;

(c) all rights accruing under the law of agency or estoppel, including rights to goods delivered to the bailee after the document was issued; and

(d) the direct obligation of the issuer to hold or deliver the goods according to the terms of the document free of any defense or claim by him except those arising under the terms of the document or under this Article. In the case of a delivery order the bailee's obligation accrued only upon acceptance and the obligation acquired by the holder is that the issuer and any indorser will procure the acceptance of the bailee.

(2) Subject to the following section, title and rights so acquired are not defeated by any stoppage of the goods represented by the document or by surrender of such goods by the bailee, and are not impaired even though the negotiation or any prior negotiation constituted a breach of duty or even though any person has been deprived of possession of the document by misrepresentation, fraud, accident, mistake, duress, loss, theft or conversion, or even though a previous sale or other transfer of the goods has been made to a third person.

Section 7-503. Documents of Title to Goods Defeated in Certain Cases.

(1) A document of title confers no right in goods against a person who before issuance of the document had a legal interest or a perfected security interest in them and who neither

(a) delivered or entrusted them or any document of title covering them to the bailor or his nominee with actual or apparent authority to ship, store or sell or with power to obtain delivery under this Article (Section 7-403) or with power of disposition under this Act (Sections 2-403 and 9-307) or other statute or rule of law; nor

(b) acquiesced in the procurement by the bailor or his nominee of any document of title.

(2) Title to goods based upon an unaccepted delivery order is subject to the rights of anyone to whom a negotiable warehouse receipt or bill of lading covering the goods has been duly negotiated. Such a title may be defeated under the next section to the same extent as the rights of the issuer or a transferee from the issuer.

(3) Title to goods based upon a bill of lading issued to a freight forwarder is subject to the rights of anyone to whom a bill issued by the freight forwarder is duly negotiated; but delivery by the carrier in accordance with Part 4 of this Article pursuant to its own bill of lading discharges the carrier's obligation to deliver.

Section 7-504. Rights Acquired in the Absence of Due Negotiation; Effect of Diversion; Seller's Stoppage of Delivery.

(1) A transferee of a document, whether negotiable or non-negotiable, to whom the document has been delivered but not duly negotiated, acquires the title and rights which his transferor had or had actual authority to convey.

(2) In the case of a non-negotiable document, until but not after the bailee receives notification of the transfer, the rights of the transferee may be defeated

(a) by those creditors of the transferor who could treat the sale as void under Section 2-402; or

(b) by a buyer from the transferor in ordinary course of business if the bailee has delivered the goods to the buyer or received notification of his rights; or

(c) as against the bailee by good faith dealings of the bailee with the transferor.

(3) A diversion or other change of shipping instructions by the consignor in a non-negotiable bill of lading which causes the bailee not to deliver to the consignee defeats the consignee's title to the goods if they have been delivered to a buyer in ordinary course of business and in any event defeats the consignee's rights against the bailee.

(4) Delivery pursuant to a non-negotiable document may be stopped by a seller under Section 2-705, and subject to the requirement of due notification there provided. A bailee honoring the seller's instructions is entitled to be indemnified by the seller against any resulting loss or expense.

Section 7-505. Indorser Not a Guarantor for Other Parties. The indorsement of a document of title issued by a bailee does not make the indorser liable for any default by the bailee or by previous indorsers.

Section 7-506. Delivery Without Indorsement: Right to Compel Indorsement. The transferee of a negotiable document of title has a specifically enforceable right to have his transferor supply any necessary indorsement but the transfer becomes a negotiation only as of the time the indorsement is supplied.

Section 7-507. Warranties on Negotiation or Transfer of Receipt or Bill. Where a person negotiates or transfers a document of title for value otherwise than as a mere intermediary under the next following section, then unless otherwise agreed he warrants to his immediate purchaser only in addition to any warranty made in selling the goods

(a) that the document is genuine; and

(b) that he has no knowledge of any fact which would impair its validity or worth; and

(c) that his negotiation or transfer is rightful and fully effective with respect to the title to the document and the goods it represents.

Section 7-508. Warranties of Collecting Bank as to Documents. A collecting bank or other intermediary known to be entrusted with documents on behalf of another or with collection of a draft or other claim against delivery of documents warrants by such delivery of the documents only its own good faith and authority. This rule applies even though the intermediary has purchased or made advances against the claim or draft to be collected.

Section 7-509. Receipt or Bill: When Adequate Compliance with Commercial Contract. The question whether a document is adequate to fulfill the obligations of a contract for sale or the conditions of a credit is governed by the Articles on Sales (Article 2) and on Letters of Credit (Article 5).

PART 6

WHAREHOUSE RECEIPTS AND BILLS OF LADING: MISCELLANEOUS PROVISIONS

Section 7-601. Lost and Missing Documents.

(1) If a document has been lost, stolen or destroyed, a court may order delivery of the goods or issuance of a substitute document and the bailee may without liability to any person comply with such order. If the document was negotiable the claimant must post security approved by the court to indemnify any person who may suffer loss as a result of non-surrender of the document. If the

document was not negotiable, such security may be required at the discretion of the court. The court may also in its discretion order payment of the bailee's reasonable costs and counsel fees.

(2) A bailee who without court order delivers goods to a person claiming under a missing negotiable document is liable to any person injured thereby, and if the delivery is not in good faith becomes liable for conversion. Delivery in good faith is not conversion if made in accordance with a filed classification or tariff or, where no classification or tariff is filed, if the claimant posts security with the bailee in an amount at least double the value of the goods at the time of posting to indemnify any person injured by the delivery who files a notice of claim within one year after the delivery.

Section 7-602. Attachment of Goods Covered by a Negotiable Document. Except where the document was originally issued upon delivery of the goods by a person who had no power to dispose of them, no lien attaches by virtue of any judicial process to goods in the possession of a bailee for which a negotiable document of title is outstanding unless the document be first surrendered to the bailee or its negotiation enjoined, and the bailee shall not be compelled to deliver the goods pursuant to process until the document is surrendered to him or impounded by the court. One who purchases the document for value without notice of the process or injunction takes free of the lien imposed by judicial process.

Section 7-603. Conflicting Claims; Interpleader. If more than one person claims title or possession of the goods, the bailee is excused from delivery until he has had a reasonable time to ascertain the validity of the adverse claims or to bring an action to compel all claimants to interplead and may compel such interpleader, either in defending an action for non-delivery of the goods, or by original action, whichever is appropriate.

ARTICLE 8

INVESTMENT SECURITIES

PART 1

SHORT TITLE AND GENERAL MATTERS

Section 8-101. Short Title. This Article shall be known and may be cited as Uniform Commercial Code—Investment Securities.

Section 8-102. Definitions and Index of Definitions.

(1) In this Article unless the context otherwise requires

  (a) A "security" is an instrument which

    (i) is issued in bearer or registered form; and

    (ii) is of a type commonly dealt in upon securities exchanges or markets or commonly recognized in any area in which it is issued or dealt in as a medium for investment; and

    (iii) is either one of a class or series or by its terms is divisible into a class or series of instruments; and

    (iv) evidences a share, participation or other interest in property or in an enterprise or evidences an obligation of the issuer.

  (b) A writing which is a security is governed by this Article and not by Uniform Commercial Code-Commercial Paper even though it also meets the requirements of that Article. This Article does not apply to money.

  (c) A security is in "registered form" when it specifies a person entitled to the security or to the rights it evidences and when its transfer may be registered upon books maintained for that purpose by or on behalf of an issuer or the security so states.

  (d) A security is in "bearer form" when it runs to bearer according to its terms and not by reason of any indorsement.

(2) A "subsequent purchaser" is a person who takes other than by original issue.

(3) A "clearing corporation" is a corporation all of the capital stock of which is held by or for a national security exchange or association registered under a statute of the United States such as the Securities Exchange Act of 1934.

(4) A "custodian bank" is any bank or trust company which is supervised and examined by state or federal authority having supervision over banks and which is acting as custodian for a clearing corporation.

(5) Other definitions applying to this Article or to specified Parts thereof and the sections in which they appear are:

"Adverse claim." Section 8-301.

"Bona fide purchaser." Section 8-302.

"Broker." Section 8-303.

"Guarantee of
   the signature." Section 8-402.

"Intermediary bank." Section 4-105.

"Issuer." Section 8-201.

"Overissue." Section 8-104.

(6) In addition Article 1 contains general definitions and principles of construction and interpretation applicable throughout this Article.

Section 8-103. Issuer's Lien. A lien upon a security in favor of an issuer thereof is valid against a purchaser only if the right of the issuer to such lien is noted conspicuously on the security.

Section 8-104. Effect of Overissue; "Overissue."

(1) The provisions of this Article which validate a security or compel its issue or reissue do not apply to the extent that validation, issue or reissue would result in overissue; but

   (a) if an identical secuirty which does not constitute an overissue is reasonably available for purchase, the person entitled to issue or validation may compel the issuer to purchase and deliver such a security to him against surrender of the security, if any, which he holds; or

   (b) if a security is not so available for purchase, the person entitled to issue or validation may recover from the issuer the price he or the last purchaser for value paid for it with interest from the date of his demand.

(2) "Overissue" means the issue of securities in excess of the amount which the issuer has corporate power to issue.

Section 8-105. Securities Negotiable; Presumptions.

(1) Securities governed by this Article are negotiable instruments.

(2) In any action on a security

   (a) unless specifically denied in the pleadings, each signature on the security or in a necessary indorsement is admitted;

   (b) when the effectiveness of a signature is put in issue the burden of establishing it is on the party claiming under the signature but the signature is presumed to be genuine or authorized;

   (c) when signatures are admitted or established production of the instrument entitles a holder to recover on it unless the defendant establishes a defense or a defect going to the validity of the security; and

   (d) after it is shown that a defense or defect exists the plaintiff has the burden of establishing that he or some person under whom he claims is a person against whom the defense or defect is ineffective (Section 8-202).

Section 8-106. Applicability. The validity of a security and the rights and duties of the issuer with respect to registration of transfer are governed by the law (including the conflict of laws rules) or the jurisdiction of organization or the issuer.

Section 8-107. Securities Deliverable; Action for Price.

(1) Unless otherwise agreed and subject to any applicable law or regulation respecting short sales, a person obligated to deliver securities may deliver any security of the specified issue in bearer form or registered in the name of the transferee or indorsed to him or in blank.

(2) When the buyer fails to pay the price as it comes due under a contract of sale the seller may recover the price

   (a) of securities accepted by the buyer; and

   (b) of other securities if efforts at their resale would be unduly burdensome or if there is no readily available market for their resale.

Section 8-201. "Issuer."

(1) With respect to obligations on or defenses to a security "issuer" includes a person who

(a) places or authorizes the placing of his name on a security (otherwise than as authenticating trustee, registrar, transfer agent or the like) to evidence that it represents a share, participation or other interest in his property or in an enterprise or to evidence his duty to perform an obligation evidenced by the security; or

(b) directly or indirectly creates fractional interests in his rights or property which fractional interests are evidenced by securities; or

(c) becomes responsible for or in place of any other person described as an issuer in this section.

(2) With respect to obligations on or defenses to a security a guarantor is an issuer to the extent of his guaranty whether or not his obligation is noted on the security.

(3) With respect to registration of transfer (Part 4 of this Article) "issuer" means a person on whose behalf transfer books are maintained.

Section 8-202. Issuer's Responsibility and Defenses; Notice of Defect or Defense.

(1) Even against a purchaser for value and without notice, the terms of a security include those stated on the security and those made part of the security by reference to another instrument, indenture or document or to a constitution, statute, ordinance, rule, regulation, order or the like to the extent that the terms so referred to do not conflict with the stated terms. Such a reference does not of itself charge a purchaser for value with notice of a defect going to the validity of the security even though the security expressly states that a person accepting it admits such notice.

(2) (a)   A security other than one issued by a government or governmental agency or unit even though issued with a defect going to its validity is valid in the hands of a purchaser for value and without notice of the particular defect unless the defect involves a violation of constitutional provisions in which case the security is valid in the hands of a subsequent purchaser for value and without notice of the defect.

(b) The rule of subparagraph (a) applies to an issuer which is a government or governmental agency or unit only if either there has been substantial compliance with the legal requirements governing the issue or the issuer has received a substantial consideration for the issue as a whole or for the particular security and a stated purpose of the issue is one for which the issuer has power to borrow money or issue the security.

(3) Except as otherwise provided in the case of certain unauthorized signatures on issue (Section 8-205), lack of genuineness of a security is a complete defense even against a purchaser for value and without notice.

(4) All other defenses of the issuer including nondelivery and conditional delivery of the security are ineffective against a purchaser for value who has taken without notice of the particular defense.

(5) Nothing in this section shall be construed to affect the right of a party to a "when, as and if issued" or a "when distributed" contract to cancel the contract in the event of a material change in the character of the security which is the subject of the contract or in the plan or arrangement pursuant to which such security is to be issued or distributed.

Section 8-203. Staleness as Notice of Defects or Defenses.

(1) After an act or event which creates a right to immediate performance of the principal obligation evidenced by the security or which sets a date on or after which the security is to be presented or sur-

rendered for redemption or exchange, a purchaser is charged with notice of any defect in its issue or defense of the issuer

(a) if the act or event is one requiring the payment of money or the delivery of securities or both on presentation or surrender of the security and such funds or securities are available on the date set for payment or exchange and he takes the security more than one year after that date; and

(b) if the act or event is not covered by paragraph (a) and he takes the security more than two years after the date set for surrender or presentation or the date on which such performance became due.

(2) A call which has been revoked is not within subsection (1).

Section 8-204. Effect of Issuer's Restrictions on Transfer. Unless noted conspicuously on the security a restriction on transfer imposed by the issuer even though otherwise lawful is ineffective except against a person with actual knowledge of it.

Section 8-205. Effect of Unauthorized Signature on Issue. An unauthorized signature placed on a security prior to or in the course of issue is ineffective except that the signature is effective in favor of a purchaser for value and without notice of the lack of authority if the signing has been done by

(a) an authenticating trustee, registrar, transfer agent or other person entrusted by the issuer with the signing of the security or of similar securities or their immediate preparation for signing; or

(b) an employee of the issuer or of any of the foregoing entrusted with responsible handling of the security.

Section 8-206. Completion or Alteration of Instrument.

(1) Where a security contains the signatures necessary to its issue or transfer but is incomplete in any other respect

(a) any person may complete it by filling in the blanks as authorized; and

(b) even though the blanks are incorrectly filled in, the security as completed is enforceable by a purchaser who took it for value and without notice of such incorrectness.

(2) A complete security which has been improperly altered even though fraudulently remains enforceable but only according to its original terms.

Section 8-207. Rights of Issuer with Respect to Registered Owners.

(1) Prior to due presentment for registration of transfer of a security in registered form the issuer or indenture trustee may treat the registered owner as the person exclusively entitled to vote, to receive notifications and otherwise to exercise all the rights and powers of an owner.

(2) Nothing in this Article shall be construed to affect the liability of the registered owner of a security for calls, assessments or the like.

Section 8-208. Effect of Signature of Authenticating Trustee, Registrar or Transfer Agent.

(1) A person placing his signature upon a security as authenticating trustee, registrar, transfer agent or the like warrants to a purchaser for value without notice of the particular defect that

(a) the security is genuine; and

(b) his own participation in the issue of the security is within his capacity and within the scope of the authorization received by him from the issuer; and

(c) he has reasonable grounds to believe that the security is in the form and within the amount the issuer is authorized to issue.

(2) Unless otherwise agreed, a person by so placing his signature does not assume responsibility for the validity of the security in other respects.

PART 3

PURCHASE

Section 8-301. Rights Acquired by Purchaser; "Adverse Claim"; Title Acquired by Bona Fide Purchaser.

(1) Upon delivery of a security the purchaser acquires the rights in the security which his transferor had or had actual authority to convey except that a purchaser who has himself been a party to any fraud or illegality affecting the security or who as a prior holder had notice of an adverse claim cannot improve his position by taking from a later bona fide purchaser. "Adverse claim"

includes a claim that a transfer was or would be wrongful or that a particular adverse person is the owner of or has an interest in the security.

(2) A bona fide purchaser in addition to acquiring the rights of a purchaser also acquires the security free of any adverse claim.

(3) A purchaser of a limited interest acquires rights only to the extent of the interest purchased.

Section 8-302. "Bona Fide Purchaser." A "bona fide purchaser" is a purchaser for value in good faith and without notice of any adverse claim who takes delivery of a security in bearer form or of one in registered form issued to him or indorsed to him or in blank.

Section 8-303. "Broker." "Broker" means a person engaged for all or part of his time in the business of buying and selling securities, who in the transaction concerned acts for, or buys a security from or sells a security to a customer. Nothing in this Article determines the capacity in which a person acts for purposes of any other statute or rule to which such person is subject.

Section 8-304. Notice to Purchaser of Adverse Claims.

(1) A purchaser (including a broker for the seller or buyer but excluding an intermediary bank) of a security is charged with notice of adverse claims if

(a) the security whether in bearer or registered form has been indorsed "for collection" or "for surrender" or for some other purpose not involving transfer; or

(b) the security is in bearer form and has on it an unambiguous statement that it is the property of a person other than the transferor. The mere writing of a name on a security is not such a statement.

(2) The fact that the purchaser (including a broker for the seller or buyer) has notice that the security is held for a third person or is registered in the name of or indorsed by a fiduciary does not create a duty of inquiry into the rightfulness of the transfer or constitute notice of adverse claims. If, however, the purchaser (excluding an intermediary bank) has knowledge that the proceeds are being used or that the transaction is for the individual benefit of the fiduciary or otherwise in breach of duty, the purchaser is charged with notice of adverse claims.

Section 8-305. Staleness as Notice of Adverse Claims. An act or event which creates a right to immediate performance of the principal obligation evidenced by the security or which sets a date on or after which the security is to be presented or surrendered for redemption or exchange does not of itself constitute any notice of adverse claims except in the case of a purchase

(a) after one year from any date set for such presentment or surrender for redemption or exchange; or

(b) after six months from any date set for payment of money against presentation or surrender of the security if funds are available for payment on that date.

Section 8-306. Warranties on Presentment and Transfer.

(1) A person who presents a security for registration on transfer or for payment or exchange warrants to the issuer that he is entitled to the registration, payment or exchange. But a purchaser for value without notice of adverse claims who receives a new, reissued or registered security on registration of transfer warrants only that he has no knowledge of any unauthorized signature (Section 8-311) in a necessary indorsement.

(2) A person by transferring a security to a purchaser for value warrants only that

(a) his transfer is effective and rightful; and

(b) the security is genuine and has not been materially altered; and

(c) he knows no fact which might impair the validity of the security.

(3) Where a security is delivered by an intermediary known to be entrusted with delivery of the security on behalf of another or with collection of a draft or other claim against such delivery, the intermediary by such delivery warrants only his own good faith and authority even though he has purchased or made advances against the claim to be collected against the delivery.

(4) A pledgee or other holder for security who redelivers the security received, or after payment and on order of the debtor delivers that security to a third person makes only the warranties of an intermediary under subsection (3).

(5) A broker gives to his customer and to

the issuer and a purchaser the warranties provided in this section and has the rights and privileges of a purchaser under this section. The warranties of and in favor of the broker acting as an agent are in addition to applicable warranties given by and in favor of his customer.

Section 8-307. Effect of Delivery Without Indorsement; Right to Compel Indorsement. Where a security in registered form has been delivered to a purchaser without a necessary indorsement he may become a bona fide purchaser only as of the time the indorsement is supplied, but against the transferor the transfer is complete upon delivery and the purchaser has a specifically enforceable right to have any necessary indorsement supplied.

Section 8-308. Indorsement, How Made; Special Indorsement; Indorser Not a Guarantor; Partial Assignment.

(1) An indorsement of a security in registered form is made when an appropriate person signs on it or on a separate document an assignment or transfer of the security or a power to·assign or transfer it or when the signature of such person is written without more upon the back of the security.

(2) An indorsement may be in blank or special. An indorsement in blank includes an indorsement to bearer. A special indorsement specifies the person to whom the security is to be transferred, or who has power to transfer it. A holder may convert a blank indorsement into a special indorsement.

(3) "An appropriate person" in subsection (1) means

(a) the person specified by the security or by special indorsement to be entitled to the security; or

(b) where the person so specified is described as a fiduciary but is no longer serving in the described capacity,—either that person or his successor; or

(c) where the security or indorsement so specifies more than one person as fiduciaries and one or more are no longer serving in the described capacity,—the remaining fiduciary or fiducaries, whether or not a successor has been appointed or qualified; or

(d) where the person so specified is an individual and is without capacity to act by virtue of death, incompetence, in-

fancy or otherwise,—his executor, administrator, guardian or like fiduciary; or

(e) where the security or indorsement so specifies more than one person as tenants by the entirety or with right of survivorship and by reason of death all cannot sign,—the survivor or survivors; or

(f) a person having power to sign under applicable law or controlling instrument; or

(g) to the extent that any of the foregoing persons may act through an agent,—his authorized agent.

(4) Unless otherwise agreed the indorser by his indorsement assumes no obligation that the security will be honored by the issuer.

(5) An indorsement purporting to be only a part of a security representing units intended by the issuer to be separately transferable is effective to the extent of the indorsement.

(6) Whether the person signing is appropriate is determined as of the date of signing and an indorsement by such a person does not become unauthorized for the purposes of this Article by virtue of any subsequent change of circumstances.

(7) Failure of a fiduciary to comply with a controlling instrument or with the law of the state having jurisdiction of the fiduciary relationship, including any law requiring the fiduciary to obtain court approval of the transfer, does not render his indorsement unauthorized for the purposes of this Article.

Section 8-309. Effect of Indorsement Without Delivery. An indorsement of a security whether special or in blank does not constitute a transfer until delivery of the security on which it appears or if the indorsement is on a separate document until delivery of both the document and the security.

Section 8-310. Indorsement of Security in Bearer Form. An indorsement of a security in bearer form may give notice of adverse claims (Section 8-304) but does not otherwise affect any right to registration the holder may possess.

Section 8-311. Effect of Unauthorized Indorsement. Unless the owner has ratified an unauthorizeindorsement or is otherwise precluded from asserting its ineffectiveness

(a) he may assert its ineffectiveness against the issuer or any purchaser other than a purchaser for value and without notice of adverse claims who has in good faith received a new, reissued or re-registered security on registration of transfer; and

(b) an issuer who registers the transfer of a security upon the unauthorized indorsement is subject to liability for improper registration (Section 8-404).

Section 8-312. Effect of Guaranteeing Signature or Indorsement.

(1) Any person guaranteeing a signature of an indorser of a security warrants that at the time of signing

(a) the signature was genuine; and

(b) the signer was an appropriate person to indorse (Section 8-308); and

(c) the signer had legal capacity to sign. But the guarantor does not otherwise warrant the rightfulness of the particular transfer.

(2) Any person may guarantee an indorsement of a security and by so doing warrants not only the signature (subsection 1) but also the rightfulness of the particular transfer in all respects, but no issuer may require a guarantee of indorsement as a condition to registration of transfer.

(3) The foregoing warranties are made to any person taking or dealing with the security in reliance on the guarantee and the guarantor is liable to such person for any loss resulting from breach of the warranties.

Section 8-313. When Delivery to the Purchaser Occurs; Purchaser's Broker as Holder.

(1) Delivery to a purchaser occurs when

(a) he or a person designated by him acquires possession of a security; or

(b) his broker acquires possession of a security specially indorsed to or issued in the name of the purchaser; or

(c) his broker sends him confirmation of the purchase and also by book entry or otherwise identifies a specific security in the broker's possession as belonging to the purchaser; or

(d) with respect to an identified security to be delivered while still in the possession of a third person when that person acknowledges that he holds for the purchaser; or

(e) appropriate entries on the books of a clearing corporation are made under Section 8-320.

(2) The purchaser is the owner of a security held for him by his broker, but is not the holder except as specified in subparagraphs (b), (c) and (e) of subsection (1). Where a security is part of a fungible bulk the purchaser is the owner of a proportionate property interest in the fungible bulk.

(3) Notice of an adverse claim received by the broker or by the purchaser after the broker takes delivery as a holder for value is not effective either as to the broker or as to the purchaser. However, as between the broker and the purchaser the pruchaser may demand delivery of an equivalent security as to which no notice of an adverse claim has been received.

Section 8-314. Duty to Deliver, When Completed.

(1) Unless otherwise agreed where a sale of a security is made on an exchange or otherwise through brokers

(a) the selling customer fulfills his duty to deliver when he places such a security in the possession of the selling broker or of a person designated by the broker or if requested causes an acknowledgement to be made to the selling broker that it is held for him; and

(b) the selling broker including a correspondent broker acting for a selling customer fulfills his duty to deliver by placing the security or a like security in the possession of the buying broker or a person designated by him or by effecting clearance of the sale in accordance with the rules of the exchange on which the transaction took place.

(2) Except as otherwise provided in this section and unless otherwise agreed, a transferor's duty to deliver a security under a contract of purchase is not fulfilled until he places the security in form to be negotiated by the purchaser in the possession of the purchaser or of a person designated by him or at the purchaser's request causes an acknowledgment to be made to the purchaser that it is held for him. Unless made on an exchange a sale to a broker purchasing for his own account is within this subsection and not within subsection (1).

Section 8-315. Action Against Purchaser Based Upon Wrongful Transfer.

(1) Any person against whom the transfer of a security is wrongful for any reason,

including his incapacity, may against anyone except a bona fide purchaser reclaim possession of the security or obtain possession of any new security evidencing all or part of the same rights or have damages.

(2) If the transfer is wrongful because of an unauthorized indorsement, the owner may also reclaim or obtain possession of the security or new security even from a bona fide purchaser if the ineffectiveness of the purported indorsement can be asserted against him under the provisions of this Article on unauthorized indorsements (Section 8-311).

(3) The right to obtain or reclaim possession of a security may be specifically enforced and its transfer enjoined and the security impounded pending the litigation.

Section 8-316. Purchaser's Right to Requisites for Registration of Transfer on Books. Unless otherwise agreed the transferor must on due demand supply his purchaser with any proof of his authority to transfer or with any other requisite which may be necessary to obtain registration of the transfer of the security but if the transfer is not for value a transferor need not do so unless the purchaser furnishes the necessary expenses. Failure to comply with a demand made within a reasonable time gives the purchaser the right to reject or rescind the transfer.

Section 8-317. Attachment or Levy Upon Security.

(1) No attachment or levy upon a security or any share or other interest evidenced thereby which is outstanding shall be valid until the security is actually seized by the officer making the attachment or levy but a security which has been surrendered to the issuer may be attached or levied upon at the source.

(2) A creditor whose debtor is the owner of a security shall be entitled to such aid from courts of appropriate jurisdiction, by injunction or otherwise, in reaching such security or in satisfying the claim by means thereof as is allowed at law or in equity in regard to property which cannot readily be attached or levied upon by ordinary legal process.

Section 8-318. No Conversion by Good Faith Delivery. An agent or bailee who in good faith (including observance of reasonable commercial standards if he is in the business of buying, selling or otherwise dealing with securities) has received securities and sold, pledged or delivered them according to the instructions of his principal is not liable for conversion or for participation in breach of fiduciary duty although the principal had no right to dispose of them.

Section 8-319. Statute of Frauds. A contract for the sale of securities is not enforceable by way of action or defense unless

(a) there is some writing signed by the party against whom enforcement is sought or by his authorized agent or broker sufficient to indicate that a contract has been made for sale of a stated quantity of described securities at a defined or stated price; or

(b) delivery of the security has been accepted or payment has been made but the contract is enforceable under this provision only to the extent of such delivery or payment; or

(c) within a reasonable time a writing in confirmation of the sale or purchase and sufficient against the sender under paragraph (a) has been received by the party against whom enforcement is sought and he has failed to send written objection to its contents within ten days after its receipt; or

(d) the party against whom enforcement is sought admits in his pleading, testimony or otherwise in court that a contract was made for the sale of a stated quantity of described securities at a defined or stated price.

Section 8-320. Transfer or Pledge Within a Central Depository System.

(1) If a security

(a) is in the custody of a clearing corporation or of a custodian bank or a nominee of either subject to the instructions of the clearing corporation; and

(b) is in bearer form or indorsed in blank by an appropriate person or registered in the name of the clearing corporation or custodian bank or a nominee of either; and

(c) is shown on the account of a transferor or pledgor on the books of the clearing corporation;

then, in addition to other methods, a transfer or pledge of the security or any interest therein may be effected by the making of appropriate entries on the books of the clearing corporation reducing the account of the transferor or pledgor and increasing the account of the transferee or pledgee by the amount of the obligation or the number of shares or rights transferred or pledged.

(2) Under this section entries may be with respect to like securities or interests therein as a part of a fungible bulk and may refer merely to a quantity of a particular security without reference to the name of the registered owner, certificate or bond number or the like, and, in appropriate cases, may be on a net basis taking into account other transfers or pledges of the same security.

(3) A transfer or pledge under this section has the effect of a delivery of a security in bearer form or duly indorsed in blank (Section 8-301) representing the amount of the obligation or the number of shares or rights transferred or pledged. If a pledge or the creation of a security interest is intended, the making of entries has the effect of a taking of delivery by the pledgee or a secured party (Sections 9-304 and 9-305). A transferee or pledgee under this section is a holder.

(4) A transfer or pledge under this section does not constitute a registration of transfer under Part 4 of this Article.

(5) That entries made on the books of the clearing corporation as provided in subsection (1) are not appropriate does not affect the validity or effect of the entries nor the liabilities or obligations of the clearing corporation to any person adversely affected thereby.

PART 4

REGISTRATION

Section 8-401. Duty of Issuer to Register Transfer.

(1) Where a security in registered form is presented to the issuer with a request to register transfer, the issuer is under a duty to register the transfer as requested if

    (a) the security is indorsed by the appropriate person or persons (Section 8-308); and

    (b) reasonable assurance is given that those indorsements are genuine and effective (Section 8-402); and

    (c) the issuer has no duty to inquire into adverse claims or has discharged any such duty (Section 8-403); and

    (d) any applicable law relating to the collection of taxes has been complied with; and

    (e) the transfer is in fact rightful or is to a bona fide purchaser.

(2) Where an issuer is under a duty to register a transfer of a security the issuer is also liable to the person presenting it for registration or his principal for loss resulting from any unreasonable delay in registration or from failure or refusal to register the transfer.

Section 8-402. Assurance that Indorsements are Effective.

(1) The issuer may require the following assurance that each necessary indorsement (Section 8-308) is genuine and effective

    (a) in all cases, a guarantee of the signature (subsection (1) of Section 8-312) of the person indorsing; and

    (b) where the indorsement is by an agent, appropriate assurance of authority to sign;

    (c) where the indorsement is by a fiduciary, appropriate evidence of appointment or incumbency;

    (d) where there is more than one fiduciary, reasonable assurance that all who are required to sign have done so;

    (e) where the indorsement is by a person not covered by any of the foregoing, assurance appropriate to the case corresponding as nearly as may be to the foregoing.

(2) A "guarantee of the signature" in subsection (1) means a guarantee signed by or on behalf of a person reasonably believed by the issuer to be responsible. The issuer may adopt standards with respect to responsibility provided such standards are not manifestly unreasonable.

(3) "Appropriate evidence of appointment or incumbency" in subsection (1) means

    (a) in the case of a fiduciary appointed or qualified by a court, a certificate issued by or under the direction or supervision of that court or an officer thereof and dated within sixty days before the date of presentation for transfer; or

(b) in any other case, a copy of a document showing the appointment or a certificate issued by or on behalf of a person reasonably believed by the issuer to be responsible or, in the absence of such a document or certificate, other evidence reasonably deemed by the issuer to be appropriate. The issuer may adopt standards with respect to such evidence provided such standards are not manifestly unreasonable. The issuer is not charged with notice of the contents of any document obtained pursuant to this paragraph (b) except to the extent that the contents relate directly to the appointment or incumbency.

(4) The issuer may elect to require a reasonable assurance beyond that specified in this section but if it does so and for a purpose other than that specified in subsection (3) (b) both requires and obtains a copy of a will, trust, indenture, articles of co-partnership, by-laws or other controlling instrument it is charged with notice of all matters contained therein affecting the transfer.

Section 8-403. Limited Duty of Inquiry.

(1) An issuer to whom a security is presented for registration is under a duty to inquire into adverse claims if

(a) a written notification of an adverse claim is received at a time and in a manner which affords the issuer a reasonable opportunity to act on it prior to the issuance of a new, reissued or re-registered security and the notification identifies the claimant, the registered owner and the issue of which the security is a part and provides an address for communications directed to the claimant; or

(b) the issuer is charged with notice of an adverse claim from a controlling instrument which it has elected to require under subsection (4) of Section 8-402.

(2) The issuer may discharge any duty of inquiry by any reasonable means, including notifying an adverse claimant by registered or certified mail at the address furnished by him or if there be no such address at his residence or regular place of business that

the security has been presented for registration of transfer by a named person, and that the transfer will be registered unless within thirty days from the date of mailing the notification, either

(a) an appropriate restraining order, injunction or other process issues from a court of competent jurisdiction; or

(b) an indemnity bond sufficient in the issuer's judgment to protect the issuer and any transfer agent, registrar or other agent of the issuer involved, from any loss which it or they may suffer by complying with the adverse claim is filed with the issuer.

(3) Unless an issuer is charged with notice of an adverse claim from a controlling instrument which it has elected to require under subsection (4) of Section 8-402 or receives notification of an adverse claim under subsection (1) of this section, where a security presented for registration is indorsed by the appropriate person or persons the issuer is under no duty to inquire into adverse claims. In particular

(a) an issuer registering a security in the name of a person who is a fiduciary or who is described as a fiduciary is not bound to inquire into the existence, extent, or correct description of the fiduciary relationship and thereafter the issuer may assume without inquiry that the newly registered owner continues to be the fiduciary until the issuer receives written notice that the fiduciary is no longer acting as such with respect to the particular security;

(b) an issuer registering transfer on an indorsement by a fiduciary is not bound to inquire whether the transfer is made in compliance with a controlling instrument or with the law of the state having jurisdiction of the fiduciary relationship, including any law requiring the fiduciary to obtain court approval of the transfer; and

(c) the issuer is not charged with notice of the contents of any court record or file or other recorded or unrecorded documents even though the document is in its possession and even though the transfer is made on the indorsement of a fiduciary to the fiduciary himself or to his nominee.

Section 8-404. Liability and Non-Liability for Registration.

(1) Except as otherwise provided in any law relating to the collection of taxes, the issuer is not liable to the owner or any other person suffering loss as a result of the registration of a transfer of a security if

(a) there were on or with the security the necessary indorsements (Section 8-308); and

(b) the issuer had no duty to inquire into adverse claims or has discharged any such duty (Section 8-403).

(2) Where an issuer has registered a transfer of a security to a person not entitled to it the issuer on demand must deliver a like security to the true owner unless

(a) the registration was pursuant to subsection (1); or

(b) the owner is precluded from asserting any claim for registering the transfer under subsection (1) of the following section; or

(c) such delivery would result in overissue, in which case the issuer's liability is governed by Section 8-104.

Section 8-405. Lost, Destroyed and Stolen Securities.

(1) Where a security has been lost, apparently destroyed or wrongfully taken and the owner fails to notify the issuer of that fact within a reasonable time after he has notice of it and the issuer registerers a transfer of the security before receiving such a notification, the owner is precluded from asserting against the issuer any claim for registering the transfer under the preceding section or any claim to a new security under this section.

(2) Where the owner of a security claims that the security has been lost, destroyed or wrongfully taken, the issuer must issue a new security in place of the original security if the owner

(a) so requests before the issuer has notice that the security has been acquired by a bona fide purchaser; and

(b) files with the issuer a sufficient indemnity bond; and

(c) satisfies any other reasonable requirements imposed by the issuer.

(3) If, after the issue of the new security, a bona fide purchaser of the original security presents it for registration of transfer, the issuer must register the transfer unless registration would result in overissue, in which event the issuer's liability is governed by Section 8-104. In addition to any rights on the indemnity bond, the issuer may recover the new security from the person to whom it was issued or any person taking under him except a bona fide purchaser.

Section 8-406. Duty of Authenticating Trustee, Transfer Agent or Registrar.

(1) Where a person acts as authenticating trustee, transfer agent, registrar, or other agent for an issuer in the registration of transfers of its securities or in the issue of new securities or in the cancellation of surrendered securities

(a) he is under a duty to the issuer to exercise good faith and due diligence in performing his functions; and

(b) he has with regard to the particular functions he performs the same obligation to the holder or owner of the security and has the same rights and privileges as the issuer has in regard to those functions.

(2) Notice to an authenticating trustee, transfer agent, registrar or other such agent is notice to the issuer with respect to the functions performed by the agent.

ARTICLE 9

SECURED TRANSACTIONS; SALES OF ACCOUNTS, CONTRACT RIGHTS AND CHATTEL PAPER

PART 1

SHORT TITLE, APPLICABILITY AND DEFINITIONS

Section 9-101. Short Title. This Article shall be known and may be cited as Uniform Commercial Code–Secured Transactions.

Section 9-102. Policy and Scope of Article.

(1) Except as otherwise provided in Section 9-103 on multiple state transactions

743

and in Section 9-104 on excluded transactions, this Article applies so far as concerns any personal property and fixtures within the jurisdiction of this state

    (a) to any transaction (regardless of its form) which is intended to create a security interest in personal property or fixtures including goods, documents, instruments, general intangibles, chattel paper, accounts or contract rights; and also

    (b) to any sale of accounts, contract rights or chattel paper.

(2) This Article applies to security interests created by contract including pledge, assignment, chattel mortgage, chattel trust, trust deed, factor's lien, equipment trust, conditional sale, trust receipt, other lien or title retention contract and lease or consignment intended as security. This Article does not apply to statutory liens except as provided in Section 9-310.

(3) The application of this Article to a security interest in a secured obligation is not affected by the fact that the obligation is itself secured by a transaction or interest to which this Article does not apply.

    NOTE: *The adoption of this Article should be accompanied by the repeal of existing statutes dealing with conditional sales, trust receipts, factor's liens where the factor is given a non-possessory lien, chattel mortgages, crop mortgages, mortgages on railroad equipment, assignment of accounts and generally statutes regulating security interests in personal property.*

    Where the state has a retail installment selling act or small loan act, that legislation should be carefully examined to determine what changes in those acts are needed to conform them to this Article. This Article primarily sets out rules defining rights of a secured party against persons dealing with the debtor; it does not prescribe regulations and controls which may be necessary to curb abuses arising in the small loan business or in the financing of consumer purchases on credit. Accordingly there is no intention to repeal existing regulatory acts in those fields. See Section 9-203(2) and the Note thereto.

Section 9-103. Accounts, Contract Rights, General Intangibles and Equipment Relating to Another Jurisdiction; and Incoming Goods Already Subject to a Security Interest.

(1) If the office where the assignor accounts or contract rights keeps his records concerning them is in this state, the validity and perfection of a security interest therein and the possibility and effect of proper filing is governed by this Article; otherwise by the law (including the conflict of laws rules) of the jurisdiction where such office is located.

(2) If the chief place of business of a debtor is in this state, this Article governs the validity and perfection of a security interest and the possibility and effect of proper filing with regard to general intangibles or with regard to goods of a type which are normally used in more than one jurisdiction (such as automotive equipment, rolling stock, airplanes, road building equipment, commercial harvesting equipment, construction machinery and the like) if such goods are classified as equipment or classified as inventory by reason of their being leased by the debtor to others. Otherwise, the law (including the conflict of laws rules) of the jurisdiction where such chief place of business is located shall govern. If the chief place of business is located in a jurisdiction which does not provide for perfection of the security interest by filing or recording in that jurisdiction, then the security interest may be perfected by filing in this state. [For the purpose of determining the validity and perfection of a security interest in an airplane, the chief place of business of a debtor who is a foreign air carrier under the Federal Aviation Act of 1958, as amended, is the designated office of the agent upon whom service of process may be made on behalf of the debtor.]

(3) If personal property other than that governed by subsections (1) and (2) is already subject to a security interest when it is brought into this state, the validity of the security interest in this state is to be determined by the law (including the conflict of laws rules) of the jurisdiction where the property was when the security interest attached. However, if the parties to the transaction understood at the time that the

security interest attached that the property would be kept in this state and it was brought into this state within 30 days after the security interest attached for purposes other than transportation through this state, then the validity of the security interest in this state is to be determined by the law of this state. If the security interest was already perfected under the law of the jurisdiction where the property was when the security interest attached and before being brought into this state, the security interest continues perfected in this state for four months and also thereafter if within the four month period it is perfected in this state. The security interest may also be perfected in this state after the expiration of the four month period; in such case perfection dates from the time of perfection in this state. If the security interest was not perfected under the law of the jurisdiction where the property was when the security interest attached and before being brought into this state, it may be perfected in this state; in such case perfection dates from the time of perfection in this state.

(4) Notwithstanding subsections (2) and (3), if personal property is covered by a certificate of title issued under a statute of this state or any other jurisdiction which requires indication on a certificate of title of any security interest in the property as a condition of perfection, then the perfection is governed by the law of the jurisdiction which issued the certificate.

[(5) Notwithstanding subsection (1) and Section 9-302, if the office where the assignor of accounts or contract rights keeps his records concerning them is not located in a jurisdiction which is a part of the United States, its territories or possessions, and the accounts or contract rights are within the jurisdiction of this state or the transaction which creates the security interest otherwise bears an appropriate relation to this state, this Article governs the validity and perfection of the security interest and the security interest may only be perfected by notification to the account debtor.]

NOTE: *The last sentence of subsection (2) and subsection (5) are bracketed to indicate optional enactment. In states engaging in financing of airplanes of foreign carriers and of international open accounts receivable, bracketed language will be of value. In other states not engaging in financing of this type, the bracketed language may not be considered necessary.*

Section 9-104. Transactions Excluded from Article. This Article does not apply

(a) to a security interest subject to any statute of the United States such as the Ship Mortgage Act, 1920, to the extent that such statute governs the rights of parties to and third parties affected by transactions in particular types of property; or

(b) to a landlord's lien; or

(c) to a lien given by statute or other rule of law for services or materials except as provided in Section 9-310 on priority of such liens; or

(d) to a transfer of a claim for wages, salary or other compensation of an employee; or

(e) to an equipment trust covering railway rolling stock; or

(f) to a sale of accounts, contract rights or chattel paper as part of a sale of the business out of which they arose, or an assignment of accounts, contract rights or chattel paper which is for the purpose of collection only, or a transfer of a contract right to an assignee who is also to do the performance under the contract; or

(g) to a transfer of an interest or claim in or under any policy of insurance; or

(h) to a right represented by a judgment; or

(i) to any right of set-off; or

(j) except to the extent that provision is made for fixtures in Section 9-313, to the creation or transfer of an interest in or lien on real estate, including a lease or rents thereunder; or

(k) to a transfer in whole or in part of any of the following: any claim arising out of tort; any deposit, savings, passbook or like account maintained with a bank, savings and loan association, credit union or like organization.

Section 9-105. Definitions and Index of Definitions.

(1) In this Article unless the context otherwise requires:

(a) "Account debtor" means the person who is obligated on an account, chattel paper, contract right or general intangible;

(b) "Chattel paper" means a writing or writings which evidence both a monetary obligation and a security interest in or a lease of specific goods. When a transaction is evidenced both by such a security agreement or a lease and by an instrument or a series of instruments, the group of writings taken together constitutes chattel paper;

(c) "Collateral" means the property subject to a security interest, and includes accounts, contract rights and chattel paper which have been sold;

(d) "Debtor" means the person who owes payment or other performance of the obligation secured, whether or not he owns or has rights in the collateral, and includes the seller of accounts, contract rights or chattel paper. Where the debtor and the owner of the collateral are not the same person, the term "debtor" means the owner of the collateral in any provision of the Article dealing with the collateral, the obligor in any provision dealing with the obligation, and may include both where the context so requires;

(e) "Document" means document of title as defined in the general definitions of Article 1 (Section 1-201);

(f) "Goods" includes all things which are movable at the time the security interest attaches or which are fixtures (Section 9-313), but does not include money, documents, instruments, accounts, chattel paper, general intangibles, contract rights and other things in action. "Goods" also include the unborn young of animals and growing crops;

(g) "Instrument" means a negotiable instrument (defined in Section 3-104), or a security (defined in Section 8-102) or any other writing which evidences a right to the payment of money and is not itself a security agreement or lease and is of a type which is in ordinary course of business transferred by delivery with any necessary indorsement or assignment;

(h) "Security agreement" means an agreement which creates or provides for a security interest;

(i) "Secured party" means a lender, seller or other person in whose favor there is a security interest, including a person to whom accounts, contract rights or chattel paper have been sold. When the holders of obligations issued under an indenture of trust, equipment trust agreement or the like are represented by a trustee or other person, the representative is the secured party.

(2) Other definitions applying to this Article and the sections in which they appear are:

"Account." Section 9-106.
"Consumer goods." Section 9-109(1).
"Contract right." Section 9-106.
"Equipment." Section 9-109(2).
"Farm products." Section 9-109(3).
"General intangibles." Section 9-106.
"Inventory." Section 9-109(4).
"Lien creditor." Section 9-301(3).
"Proceeds." Section 9-306(1).
"Purchase money
   security interest." Section 9-107.

(3) The following definitions in other Articles apply to this Article:
"Check." Section 3-104.
"Contract for sale." Section 2-106.
"Holder in due course." Section 3-302.
"Note." Section 3-104.
"Sale." Section 2-106.

(4) In addition Article 1 contains general definitions and principles of construction and interpretation applicable throughout this Article.

Section 9-106. Definitions: "Account"; "Contract Right"; "General Intangibles."

"Account" means any right to payment for goods sold or leased or for services rendered which is not evidenced by an instrument or chattel paper. "Contract right" means any right to payment under a contract not yet earned by performance and not evidenced by an instrument or chattel paper. "General intangibles" means any personal property (including things in action) other than goods, accounts, contract rights, chattel paper, documents and instruments.

Section 9-107. Definitions: "Purchase Money Security Interest." A security interest is a "purchase money security interest" to the extent that it is

(a) taken or retained by the seller of the collateral to secure all or part of its price; or

(b) taken by a person who by making advances or incurring an obligation gives value to enable the debtor to acquire rights in or the use of collateral if such value is in fact so used.

Section 9-108. When After-Acquired Collateral Not Security for Antecedent Debt. Where a secured party makes an advance, incurs an obligation, releases a perfected security interest, or otherwise gives new value which is to be secured in whole or in part by after-acquired property his security interest in the after-acquired collateral shall be deemed to be taken for new value and not as security for an antecedent debt if the debtor acquires his rights in such collateral either in the ordinary course of his business or under a contract of purchase made pursuant to the security agreement within a reasonable time after new value is given.

Section 9-109. Classification of Goods; "Consumer Goods"; "Equipment"; "Farm Products"; "Inventory." Goods are

(1) "consumer goods" if they are used or bought for use primarily for personal, family or household purposes;

(2) "equipment" if they are used or bought for use primarily in business (including farming or a profession) or by a debtor who is a non-profit organization or a governmental subdivision or agency or if the goods are not included in the definitions of inventory, farm products or consumer goods;

(3) "farm products" if they are crops or livestock or supplies used or produced in farming operations or if they are products of crops or livestock in their unmanufactured states (such as ginned cotton, wool-clip, maple syrup, milk and eggs), and if they are in the possession of a debtor engaged in raising, fattening, grazing or other farming operations. If goods are farm products they are neither equipment nor inventory;

(4) "inventory" if they are held by a person who holds them for sale or lease or to be furnished under contracts of service or if he has so furnished them, or if they are raw materials, work in process or materials used or consumed in a business. Inventory of a person is not to be classified as his equipment.

Section 9-110. Sufficiency of Description. For the purposes of this Article any description of personal property or real estate is sufficient whether or not it is specific if it reasonably identifies what is described.

Section 9-111. Applicability of Bulk Transfer Laws. The creation of a security interest is not a bulk transfer under Article 6 (see Section 6-103).

Section 9-112. Where Collateral is Not Owned by Debtor. Unless otherwise agreed, when a secured party knows that collateral is owned by a person who is not the debtor, the owner of the collateral is entitled to receive from the secured party any surplus under Section 9-502(2) or under Section 9-504(1), and is not liable for the debt or for any deficiency after resale, and he has the same right as the debtor

(a) to receive statements under Section 9-208;

(b) to receive notice of and to object to a secured party's proposal to retain the collateral in satisfaction of the indebtedness under Section 9-505;

(c) to redeem the collateral under Section 9-506;

(d) to obtain injunctive or other relief under Section 9-507(1); and

(e) to recover losses caused to him under Section 9-208(2).

Section 9-113. Security Interests Arising under Article on Sales. A security interest arising solely under the Article on Sales (Article 2) is subject to the provisions of this Article except that to the extent that and so long as the debtor does not have or does not lawfully obtain possession of the goods

(a) no security agreement is necessary to make the security interest enforceable; and

(b) no filing is required to perfect the security interest; and

(c) the rights of the secured party on default by the debtor are governed by the Article on Sales (Article 2).

VALIDITY OF SECURITY AGREEMENT AND RIGHTS OF PARTIES THERETO

Section 9-201. General Validity of Security Agreement. Except as otherwise provided by this Act a security agreement is effective according to its terms between the parties, against purchasers of the collateral and against creditors. Nothing in this Article validates any charge or practice illegal under any statute or regulation thereunder governing usury, small loans, retail installment sales, or the like, or extends the application of any such statute or regulation to any transaction not otherwise subject thereto.

Section 9-202. Title to Collateral Immaterial. Each provision of this Article with regard to rights, obligations and remedies applies whether title to collateral is in the secured party or in the debtor.

Section 9-203. Enforceability of Security Interest; Proceeds, Formal Requisites.

(1) Subject to the provisions of Section 4-208 on the security interest of a collecting bank and Section 9-113 on a security interest arising under the Article on Sales, a security interest is not enforceable against the debtor or third parties unless

    (a) the collateral is in the possession of the secured party; or

    (b) the debtor has signed a security agreement which contains a description of the collateral and in addition, when the security interest covers crops or oil, gas or minerals to be extracted or timber to be cut, a description of the land concerned. In describing collateral, the word "proceeds" is sufficient without further description to cover proceeds of any character.

(2) A transaction, although subject to this Article, is also subject to . . . .*, and in the case of conflict between the provisions of this Article and any such statute, the provisions of such statute control. Failure to comply with any applicable statute has only the effect which is specified therein.

    NOTE: *At* * *in subsection (2) insert reference to any local statute regulating small loans, retail installments sales and the like.*

    The foregoing subsection (2) is designed to make it clear that certain transactions, *although subject to this Article, must also comply with other applicable legislation.*

    This Article is designed to regulate all the "security" aspects of transactions within its scope. There is, however, nuch regulatory legislation, particularly in the consumer field, which supplements this Article and should not be repealed by its enactment. Examples are small loan acts, retail installment selling acts and the like. Such acts may provide for licensing and rate regulation and may prescribe particular forms of contract. Such provisions should remain in force despite the enactment of this Article. On the other hand if a Retail Installment Selling Act contains provisions on filing, rights on default, etc., such provisions should be repealed as inconsistent with this Article.

Section 9-204. When Security Interest Attaches; After-Acquired Property; Future Advances.

(1) A security interest cannot attach until there is agreement (subsection (3) of Section 1-201) that it attach and value is given and the debtor has rights in the collateral. It attaches as soon as all of the events in the preceding sentence have taken place unless explicit agreement postpones the time of attaching.

(2) For the purposes of this section the debtor has no rights

    (a) in crops until they are planted or otherwise become growing crops, in the young of livestock until they are conceived;

    (b) in fish until caught, in oil, gas or minerals until they are extracted, in timber until it is cut;

    (c) in a contract right until the contract has been made;

    (d) in an account until it comes into existence.

(3) Except as provided in subsection (4) a security agreement may provide that collateral, whenever acquired, shall secure all obligations covered by the security agreement.

(4) No security interest attaches under an after-acquired property clause

    (a) to crops which become such more than one year after the security agreement is executed except that a security interest in crops which is given in conjunction with a lease or a land purchase or improvement transaction evidenced by a contract, mortgage or deed of trust may if so agreed attach to crops to be grown on the land concerned during the period of such real estate transaction;

    (b) to consumer goods other than accessions (Section 9-314) when given as additional security unless the debtor acquires rights in them within ten days after the secured party gives value.

(5) Obligations covered by a security agreement may include future advances or other value whether or not the advances or value are given pursuant to commitment.

Section 9-205. Use or Disposition of Collateral Without Accounting Permissible. A security interest is not invalid or fraudulent against creditors by reason of liberty in the debtor to use, commingle or dispose of proceeds, or by reason of the failure of the secured party to require the debtor to account for proceeds or replace collateral. This section does not relax the requirements of possession where perfection of a security interest depends upon possession of the collateral by the secured party or by a bailee.

Section 9-206. Agreement Not to Assert Defenses Against Assignee; Modification of Sales Warranties Where Security Agreement Exists.

(1) Subject to any statute or decision which establishes a different rule for buyers or lessees of consumer goods, an agreement by a buyer or lessee that he will not assert against an assignee any claim or defense which he may have against the seller or lessor is enforceable by an assignee who takes his assignment for value, in good faith and without notice of a claim or defense, except as to defenses of a type which may be asserted against a holder in due course of a negotiable instrument under the Article on Commercial Paper (Article 3). A buyer who as part of one transaction signs both a negotiable instrument and a security agreement makes such an agreement.

(2) When a seller retains a purchase money

security interest in goods the Article on Sales (Article 2) governs the sale and any disclaimer, limitation or modification of the seller's warranties.

Section 9-207. Rights and Duties when Collateral is in Secured Party's Possession.

(1) A secured party must use reasonable care in the custody and preservation of collateral in his possession. In the case of an instrument or chattel paper reasonable case includes taking necessary steps to preserve rights against prior parties unless otherwise agreed.

(2) Unless otherwise agreed, when collateral is in the secured party's possession

    (a) reasonable expenses (including the cost of any insurance and payment of taxes or other charges) incurred in the custody, preservation, use or operation of the collateral are chargeable to the debtor and are secured by the collateral;

    (b) the risk of accidental loss or damage is on the debtor to the extent of any deficiency in any effective insurance coverage;

    (c) the secured party may hold as additional security any increase or profits (except money) received from the collateral, but money so received, unless remitted to the debtor, shall be applied in reduction of the secured obligation;

    (d) the secured party must keep the collateral identifiable but fungible collateral may be commingled;

    (e) the secured party may repledge the collateral upon terms which do not impair the debtor's right to redeem it.

(3) A secured party is liable for any loss caused by his failure to meet any obligation imposed by the preceding subsections but does not lose his security interest.

(4) A secured party may use or operate the collateral for the purpose of preserving the collateral or its value or pursuant to the order of a court of appropriate jurisdiction or, except in the case of consumer goods, in the manner and to the extent provided in the security agreement.

Section 9-208. Request for Statement of Accounts or List of Collateral

(1) A debtor may sign a statement indicating what he believes to be the aggregate amount of unpaid indebtedness as of a specified date and may send it to the se-

cured party with a request that the statement be approved or corrected and returned to the debtor. When the security agreement or any other record kept by the secured party identifies the collateral a debtor may similarly request the secured party to approve or correct a list of the collateral.

(2) The secured party must comply with such a request within two weeks after receipt by sending a written correction or approval. If the secured party claims a security interest in all of a particular type of collateral owned by the debtor he may indicate that fact in his reply and need not approve or correct an itemized list of such collateral. If the secured party without reasonable excuse fails to comply he is liable for any loss caused to the debtor thereby; and if the debtor has properly included in

his request a good faith statement of the obligation or a list of the collateral or both the secured party may claim a security interest only as shown in the statement against persons misled by his failure to comply. If he no longer has an interest in the obligation or collateral at the time the request is received he must disclose the name and address of any successor in interest known to him and he is liable for any loss caused to the debtor as a result of failure to disclose. A successor in interest is not subject to this section until a request is received by him.

(3) A debtor is entitled to such a statement once every six months without charge. The secured party may require payment of a charge not exceeding $10 for each additional statement furnished.

PART 3

RIGHTS OF THIRD PARTIES; PERFECTED AND UNPERFECTED SECURITY INTERESTS; RULES OF PRIORITY

Section 9-301. Persons Who Take Priority Over Unperfected Security Interests: "Lien Creditor."

(1) Except as otherwise provided in subsection (2), an unperfected security interest is subordinate to the rights of

    (a) persons entitled to priority under Section 9-312;

    (b) a person who becomes a lien creditor without knowledge of the security interest and before it is perfected;

    (c) in the case of goods, instruments, documents, and chattel paper, a person who is not a secured party and who is a transferee in bulk or other buyer not in ordinary course of business to the extent that he gives value and receives delivery of the collateral without knowledge of the security interest and before it is perfected;

    (d) in the case of accounts, contract rights, and general intangibles, a person who is not a secured party and who is a transferee to the extent that he gives value without knowledge of the security interest and before it is perfected.

(2) If the secured party files with respect to a purchase money security interest before or within ten days after the collateral comes

into possession of the debtor, he takes priority over the rights of a transferee in bulk or of a lien creditor which arise between the time the security interest attaches and the time of filing.

(3) A "lien creditor" means a creditor who has acquired a lien on the property involved by attachment, levy or the like and includes an assignee for benefit of creditors from the time of assignment, and a trustee in bankruptcy from the date of the filing of the petition or a receiver in equity from the time of appointment. Unless all the creditors represented had knowledge of the security interest such a representative of creditors is a lien creditor without knowledge even though he personally has knowledge of the security interest.

Section 9-302. When Filing is Required to Perfect Security Interest; Security Interests to which Filing Provisions of this Article do not Apply.

(1) A financing statement must be filed to perfect all security interests except the following:

    (a) a security interest in collateral in possession of the secured party under Section 9-305;

    (b) a security interest temporarily perfected in instruments or documents without delivery under Section 9-304 or in proceeds for a 10 day period under Section 9-306;

(c) a purchase money security interest in farm equipment having a purchase price not in excess of $2500; but filing is required for a fixture under Section 9-313 or for a motor vehicle required to be licensed;

(d) a purchase money security interest in consumer goods; but filing is required for a fixture under Section 9-313 or for a motor vehicle required to be licensed;

(e) an assignment of accounts or contract rights which does not alone or in conjunction with other assignments to the same assignee transfer a significant part of the outstanding accounts or contract rights of the assignor;

(f) a security interest of a collecting bank (Section 4-208) or arising under the Article on Sales (see Section 9-113) or covered in subsection (3) of this section.

(2) If a secured party assigns a perfected security interest, no filing under this Article is required in order to continue the perfected status of the security interest against creditors of and transferees from the original debtor.

(3) The filing provisions of this Article do not apply to a security interest in property subject to a statute

(a) of the United States which provides for a national registration or filing of all security interests in such property; or

NOTE: *States to select either Alternative A or Alternative B.*

ALTERNATIVE A—

(b) of this state which provides for central filing of, or which requires indication on a certificate of title of, such security interests in such property.

ALTERNATIVE B—

(b) of this state which provides for central filing of security interests in such property, or in a motor vehicle which is not inventory held for sale for which a certificate of title is required under the statutes of this state if a notation of such a security interest can be indicated by a public official on a certificate or a duplicate thereof.

(4) A security interest in property covered by a statute described in subsection (3) can be perfected only by registration or filing under that statute or by indication of the security interest on a certificate of title or a duplicate thereof by a public official.

Section 9-303. When Security Interest is Perfected; Continuity of Perfection.

(1) A security interest is perfected when it has attached and when all of the applicable steps required for perfection have been taken. Such steps are specified in Sections 9-302, 9-304, 9-305 and 9-306. If such steps are taken before the security interest attaches, it is perfected at the time when it attaches.

(2) If a security interest is originally perfected in any way permitted under this Article and is subsequently perfected in some other way under this Article, without an intermediate period when it was unperfected, the security interest shall be deemed to be perfected continuously for the purposes of this Article.

Section 9-304. Perfection of Security Interests in Instruments, Documents, and Goods Covered by Documents; Perfection by Permissive Filing; Temporary Perfection without Filing or Transfer of Possession.

(1) A security interest in chattel paper or negotiable documents may be perfected by filing. A security interest in instruments (other than instruments which constitute part of chattel paper) can be perfected only by the secured party's taking possession, except as provided in subsections (4) and (5).

(2) During the period that goods are in the possession of the issuer of a negotiable document therefor, a security interest in the goods is perfected by perfecting a security interest in the document, and any security interest in the goods otherwise perfected during such period is subject thereto.

(3) A security interest in goods in the possession of a bailee other than one who has issued a negotiable document therefor is perfected by issuance of a document in the name of the secured party or by the bailee's receipt of notification of the secured party's interest or by filing as to the goods.

(4) A security interest in instruments or negotiable documents is perfected without filing or the taking of possession for a

period of 21 days from the time it attaches to the extent that it arises for new value given under a written security agreement.

(5) A security interest remains perfected for a period of 21 days without filing where a secured party having a perfected security interest in an instrument, a negotiable document or goods in possession of a bailee other than one who has issued a negotiable document therefor

(a) makes available to the debtor the goods or documents representing the goods for the purpose of ultimate sale or exchange or for the purpose of loading, unloading, storing, shipping, transshipping, manufacturing, processing or otherwise dealing with them in a manner preliminary to their sale or exchange; or

(b) delivers the instrument to the debtor for the purpose of ultimate sale or exchange or of presentation, collection, renewal or registration of transfer.

(6) After the 21 day period in subsections (4) and (5) perfection depends upon compliance with applicable provisions of this Article.

Section 9-305. When Possession by Secured Party Perfects Security Interest without Filing. A security interest in letters of credit and advices of credit (subsection (2)(a) of Section 5-116) goods, instruments, negotiable documents or chattel paper may be perfected by the secured party's taking possession of the collateral. If such collateral other than goods covered by a negotiable document is held by a bailee, the secured party is deemed to have possession from the time the bailee receives notification of the secured party's interest. A security interest is perfected by possession from the time possession is taken without relation back and continues only so long as possession is retained, unless otherwise specified in this Article. The security interest may be otherwise perfected as provided in this Article before or after the period of possession by the secured party.

Section 9-306. "Proceeds"; Secured Party's Rights on Disposition of Collateral.

(1) "Proceeds" includes whatever is received when collateral or proceeds is sold, exchanged, collected or otherwise disposed of. The term also includes the account arising when the right to payment is earned under a contract right. Money, checks and the like are "cash proceeds." All other proceeds are "non-cash proceeds."

(2) Except where this Article otherwise provides, a security interest continues in collateral notwithstanding sale, exchange or other disposition thereof by the debtor unless his action was authorized by the secured party in the security agreement or otherwise, and also continues in any identifiable proceeds including collections received by the debtor.

(3) The security interest in proceeds is a continuously perfected security interest if the interest in the original collateral was perfected but it ceases to be a perfected security interest and becomes unperfected ten days after receipt of the proceeds by the debtor unless

(a) a filed financing statement covering the original collateral also covers proceeds; or

(b) the security interest in the proceeds is perfected before the expiration of the ten day period.

(4) In the event of insolvency proceedings instituted by or against a debtor, a secured party with a perfected security interest in proceeds has a perfected security interest

(a) in identifiable non-cash proceeds;

(b) in identifiable cash proceeds in the form of money which is not commingled with other money or deposited in a bank account prior to the insolvency proceedings;

(c) in identifiable cash proceeds in the form of checks and the like which are not deposited in a bank account prior to the insolvency proceedings; and

(d) in all cash and bank accounts of the debtor, if other cash proceeds have been commingled or deposited in a bank account, but the perfected security interest under this paragraph (d) is

(i) subject to any right of set-off; and

(ii) limited to an amount not greater than the amount of any cash proceeds received by the debtor within ten days before the institution of the insolvency proceedings and commingled or deposited in a bank account prior to the insolvency proceedings less the amount of cash proceeds received by the debtor and paid over to the secured party during the ten day period.

(5) If a sale of goods results in an account

or chattel paper which is transferred by the seller to a secured party, and if the goods are returned to or are repossessed by the seller or the secured party, the following rules determine priorities:

(a) If the goods were collateral at the time of sale for an indebtedness of the seller which is still unpaid, the original security interest attaches again to the goods and continues as a perfected security interest if it was perfected at the time when the goods were sold. If the security interest was originally perfected by a filing which is still effective, nothing further is required to continue the perfected status; in any other case, the secured party must take possession of the returned or repossessed goods or must file.

(b) An unpaid transferee of the chattel paper has a security interest in the goods against the transferor. Such security interest is prior to a security interest asserted under paragraph (a) to the extent that the transferee of the chattel paper was entitled to priority under Section 9-308.

(c) An unpaid transferee of the account has a security interest in the goods against the transferor. Such security interest is subordinate to a security interest asserted under paragraph (a).

(d) A security interest of an unpaid transferee asserted under paragraph (b) or (c) must be perfected for protection against creditors of the transferor and purchasers of the returned or repossessed goods.

Section 9-307. Protection of Buyers of Goods.

(1) A buyer in ordinary course of business (subsection (9) of Section 1-201) other than a person buying farm products from a person engaged in farming operations takes free of a security interest created by his seller even though the security interest is perfected and even though the buyer knows of its existence.

(2) In the case of consumer goods and in the case of farm equipment having an original purchase price not in excess of $2500 (other than fixtures, see Section 9-313), a buyer takes free of a security interest even though perfected if he buys without knowledge of the security interest, for the value and for his own personal, family or household purposes or his own farming operations unless prior to the purchase the secured party has filed a financing statement covering such goods.

Section 9-308. Purchase of Chattel Paper and Non-Negotiable Instruments. A purchaser of chattel paper or a non-negotiable instrument who gives new value and takes possession of it in the ordinary course of his business and without knowledge that the specific paper or instrument is subject to a security interest has priority over a security interest which is perfected under Section 9-304 (permissive filing and temporary perfection). A purchaser of chattel paper who gives new value and takes possession of it in the ordinary course of his business has priority over a security interest in chattel paper which is claimed merely as proceeds of inventory subject to a security interest (Section 9-306), even though he knows that the specific paper is subject to the security interest.

Section 9-309. Protection of Purchasers of Instruments and Documents. Nothing in this Article limits the rights of a holder in due course of a negotiable instrument (Section 3-302) or a holder to whom a negotiable document of title has been duly negotiated (Section 7-501) or a bona fide purchaser of a security (Section 8-301) and such holders or purchasers take priority over an earlier security interest even though perfected. Filing under this Article does not constitute notice of the security interest to such holders or purchasers.

Section 9-310. Priority of Certain Liens Arising by Operation of Law.

When a person in the ordinary course of his business furnishes services or materials with respect to goods subject to a security interest, a lien upon goods in the possession of such person given by statute or rule of law for such materials or services takes priority over a perfected security interest unless the lien is statutory and the statute expressly provides otherwise.

Section 9-311. Alienability of Debtor's Rights: Judicial Process.

The debtor's rights in collateral may be voluntarily or involuntarily transferred (by way of sale, creation of a security interest, attachment, levy, garnishment or other judicial process) notwithstanding a provision in the security agreement prohibiting any transfer or making the transfer constitute a default.

Section 9-312. Priorities Among Conflicting Security Interests in the Same Collateral.

(1) The rules of priority stated in the following sections shall govern where applicable: Section 4-208 with respect to the security interest of collecting banks in items being collected, accompanying documents and proceeds; Section 9-301 on certain priorities; Section 9-304 on goods covered by documents; Section 9-306 on proceeds and repossessions; Section 9-307 on buyers of goods; Section 9-308 on possessory against non-possessory interests in chattel paper or non-negotiable instruments; Section 9-309 on security interests in negotiable instrument, documents or securities; Section 9-310 on priorities between perfected security interests and liens by operation of law; Section 9-313 on security interests in fixtures as against interests in real estate; Section 9-314 on security interests in accessions as against interest in goods; Section 9-315 on conflicting security interests where goods lose their identity or become part of a product; and Section 9-316 on contractual subordination.

(2) A perfected security interest in crops for new value given to enable the debtor to produce the crops during the production season and given not more than three months before the crops become growing crops by planting or otherwise takes priority over an earlier perfected security interest to the extent that such earlier interest secures obligations due more than six months before the crops become growing crops by planting or otherwise, even though the person giving new value had knowledge of the earlier security interest.

(3) A purchase money security interest in inventory collateral has priority over a conflicting security interest in the same collateral if

(a) the purchase money security interest is perfected at the time the debtor receives possession of the collateral; and

(b) any secured party whose security interest is known to the holder of the purchase money security interest or who, prior to the date of the filing made by the holder of the purchase money security interest, had filed a financing statement covering the same items or type of inventory, has received notification of the purchase money security interest before the debtor receives possession of the collateral covered by the purchase money security interest; and

(c) such notification states that the person giving the notice has or expects to acquire a purchase money security interest in inventory of the debtor, describing such inventory by item or type.

(4) A purchase money security interest in collateral other than inventory has priority over a conflicting security interest in the same collateral if the purchase money security interest is perfected at the time the debtor receives possession of the collateral or within ten days thereafter.

(5) In all cases not governed by other rules stated in this section (including cases of purchase money security interests which do not qualify for the special priorities set forth in subsections (3) and (4) of this section), priority between conflicting security interests in the same collateral shall be determined as follows:

(a) in the order of filing if both are perfected by filing, regardless of which security interest attached first under Section 9-204(1) and whether it attached before or after filing;

(b) in the order of perfection unless both are perfected by filing, regardless of which security interest attached first under Section 9-204(1) and, in the case of a filed security interest, whether it attached before or after filing; and

(c) in the order of attachment under Section 9-204(1) so long as neither is perfected.

(6) For the purpose of the priority rules of the immediately preceding subsection, a continuously perfected security interest shall be treated at all times as if perfected by filing if it was originally so perfected and it shall be treated at all times as if perfected otherwise than by filing if it was originally perfected otherwise than by filing.

Section 9-313. Priority of Security Interests in Fixtures.

(1) The rules of this section do not apply to goods incorporated into a structure in the manner of lumber, bricks, tile, cement, glass, metal work and the like and no security interest in them exists under this Article unless the structure remains personal property under applicable law. The law of this state other than this Act determines wheth-

er and when other goods become fixtures. This Act does not present creation of an encumbrance upon fixtures or real estate pursuant to the law applicable to real estate.

(2) A security interest which attaches to goods before they become fixtures takes priority as to the goods over the claims of all persons who have an interest in the real estate except as stated in subsection (4).

(3) A security interest which attaches to goods after they become fixtures is valid against all persons subsequently acquiring interests in the real estate except as stated in subsection (4) but is invalid against any person with an interest in the real estate at the time the security interest attaches to the goods who has not in writing consented to the security or disclaimed an interest in the goods as fixtures.

(4) The security interests described in subsections (2) and (3) do not take priority over

(a) a subsequent purchaser for value of any interest in the real estate; or

(b) a creditor with a lien on the real estate subsequently obtained by judicial proceedings; or

(c) a creditor with a prior encumbrance of record on the real estate to the extent that he makes subsequent advances

if the subsequent purchase is made, the lien by judicial proceedings is obtained, or the subsequent advance under the prior encumbrance is made or contracted for without knowledge of the security interest and before it is perfected. A purchaser of the real estate at a foreclosure sale other than an encumbrancer, purchasing at his own foreclosure sale is a subsequent purchaser within this section. (5) When under subsections (2) or (3) and (4) a secured party has priority over the claims of all persons who have interests in the real estate, he may, on default, subject to the provisions of Part 5, remove his collateral from the real estate but he must reimburse any encumbrancer or owner of the real estate who is not the debtor and who has not otherwise agreed for the cost of repair of any physical injury, but not for any diminution in value of the real estate caused by the absence of the goods removed or by any necessity for replacing them. A person entitled to reimbursement may refuse permission to remove until the secured party gives adequate security for the performance of this obligation.

Section 9-314. Accessions.

(1) A security interest in goods which attaches before they are installed in or affixed to other goods takes priority as to the goods installed or affixed (called in this section "accessions") over the claims of all persons to the whole except as stated in subsection (3) and subject to Section 9-315(1).

(2) A security interest which attaches to goods after they become part of a whole is valid against all persons subsequently acquiring interests in the whole except as stated in subsection (3) but is invalid against any person with an interest in the whole at the time the security interest attaches to the goods who has not in writing consented to the security interest or disclaimed an interest in the goods as part of the whole.

(3) The security interests described in subsections (1) and (2) do not take priority over

(a) a subsequent purchaser for value of any interest in the whole; or

(b) a creditor with a lien on the whole subsequently obtained by judicial proceedings; or

(c) a creditor with a prior perfected security interest in the whole to the extent that he makes subsequent advances

if the subsequent purchase is made, the lien by judicial proceedings obtained or the subsequent advance under the prior perfected security interest is made or contracted for without knowledge of the security interest and before it is perfected. A purchaser of the whole at a foreclosure sale other than the holder of a perfected security interest purchasing at his own foreclosure sale is a subsequent purchaser within this section.

(4) When under subsections (1) or (2) and (3) a secured party has an interest in accessions which has priority over the claims of all persons who have interests in the whole, he may on default subject to the provisions of Part 5 remove his collateral from the whole but he must reimburse any encumbrancer or owner of the whole who is not the debtor and who has not otherwise agreed for the cost of repair of any physical injury but not for any diminution in value

of the whole caused by the absence of the goods removed or by any necessity for replacing them. A person entitled to reimbursement may refuse permission to remove until the secured party gives adequate security for the performance of this obligation.

Section 9-315. Priority When Goods are Commingled or Processed.

(1) If a security interest in goods was perfected and subsequently the goods or a part thereof have become part of a product or mass, the security interest continues in the product or mass if

(a) the goods are so manufactured, processed, assembled or commingled that their identity is lost in the product or mass; or

(b) a financing statement covering the original goods also covers the product into which the goods have been manufactured, processed or assembled.

In a case to which paragraph (b) applies, no separate security interest in that part of the original goods which has been manufactured, processed or assembled into the product may be claimed under Section 9-314.

(2) When under subsection (1) more than one security interest attaches to the product or mass, they rank equally according to the ratio that the cost of the goods to which each interest originally attached bears to the cost of the total product or mass.

Section 9-316. Priority Subject to Subordination. Nothing in this Article prevents subordination by agreement by any person entitled to priority.

Section 9-317. Secured Party Not Obligated on Contract of Debtor.

The mere existence of a security interest or authority given to the debtor to dispose of or use collateral does not impose contract or tort liability upon the secured party for the debtor's acts or omissions.

Section 9-318. Defenses Against Assignee: Modification of Contract after Notification of Assignment; Term Prohibiting Assignment Ineffective; Identification and Proof of Assignment.

(1) Unless an account debtor has made an enforceable agreement not to assert defenses or claims arising out of a sale as provided in Section 9-206 the rights of an assignee are subject to

(a) all the terms of the contract between the account debtor and assignor and any defense or claim arising therefrom; and

(b) any other defense or claim of the account debtor against the assignor which accrues before the account debtor receives notification of the assignment.

(2) So far as the right to payment under an assigned contract right has not already become an account, and notwithstanding notification of the assignment, any modification of or substitution for the contract made in good faith and in accordance with reasonable commercial standards is effective against an assignee unless the account debtor has otherwise agreed but the assignee acquires corresponding rights under the modified or substituted contract. The assignment may provide that such modification or substitution is a breach by the assignor.

(3) The account debtor is authorized to pay the assignor until the account debtor receives notification that the account has been assigned and that payment is to be made to the assignee. A notification which does not reasonably identify the rights assigned is ineffective. If requested by the account debtor, the assignee must seasonably furnish reasonable proof that the assignment has been made and unless he does so the account debtor may pay the assignor.

(4) A term in any contract between an account debtor and an assignor which prohibits assignment of an account or contract right to which they are parties is ineffective.

Section 9-401. Place of Filing; Erroneous Filing; Removal of Collateral.

First Alternative Subsection (1)

(1) The proper place to file in order to perfect a security interest is as follows:
(a) when the collateral is goods which at the time the security interest attaches are or are to become fixtures, then in the office where a mortgage on the real estate concerned would be filed or recorded;
(b) in all other cases, in the office of the [Secretary of State].

Second Alternative Subsection (1)

(1) The proper place to file in order to perfect a security interest is as follows:
(a) when the collateral is equipment used in farming operations, or farm products, or accounts, contract rights or general intangibles arising from or relating to the sale of farm products by a farmer, or consumer goods, then in the office of the . . . . in the county of the debtor's residence or if the debtor is not a resident of this state then in the office of the . . . . in the county where the goods are kept, and in addition when the collateral is crops in the office of the . . . . in the county where the land on which the crops are growing or to be grown is located;
(b) when the collateral is goods which at the time the security interest attaches are or are to become fixtures, then in the office where a mortgage on the real estate concerned would be filed or recorded;
(c) in all other cases, in the office of the [Secretary of State].

Third Alternative Subsection (1)

(1) The proper place to file in order to perfect a security interest is as follows:
(a) when the collateral is equipment used in farming operations, or farm products, or accounts, contract rights or general intangibles arising from or relating to the sale of farm products by a farmer, or consumer goods, then in the office of the . . . . in the county of the debtor's residence or if the debtor is not a resident of this state then in the office of the . . . . in the county where the goods are kept, and in addition when the collateral is crops in the office of the . . . . in the county where the land on which the crops are growing is located;
(b) when the collateral is goods which at the time the security interest attaches are or are to become fixtures, then in the office where a mortgage on the real estate concerned would be filed or recorded;
(c) in all other cases, in the office of the [Secretary of State] and in addition, if the debtor has a place of business in only one county of this state, also in the office of . . . . of such county, or, if the debtor has no place of business in this state, but resides in the state, also in the office of . . . . of the county in which he resides.

NOTE: *One of the three alternatives should be selected as subsection (1).*

(2) A filing which is made in good faith in an improper place or not in all of the places required by this section is nevertheless effective with regard to any collateral as to which the filing complied with the requirements of this Article and is also effective with regard to collateral covered by the financing state-

ment against any person who has knowledge of the contents of such financing statement. (3) A filing which is made in the proper place in this state continues effective even though the debtor's residence or place of business or the location of the collateral or its use, whichever controlled the original filing, is thereafter changed.

Alternative Subsection (3)

[(3) A filing which is made in the proper county continues effective for four months after a change to another county of the debtor's residence or place of business or the location of the collateral, whichever controlled the original filing. It becomes ineffective thereafter unless a copy of the financing statement signed by the secured party is filed in the new county within said period. The security interest may also be perfected in the new county after the expiration of the four-month period; in such case perfection dates from the time of perfection in the new county. A change in the use of the collateral does not impair the effectiveness of the original filing.]

(4) If collateral is brought into this state from another jurisdiction, the rules stated in Section 9-103 determine whether filing is necessary in this state.

Section 9-402. Formal Requisites of Financing Statement; Amendments.

(1) A financing statement is sufficient if it is signed by the debtor and the secured party, gives an address of the secured party from which information concerning the security interest may be obtained, gives a mailing address of the debtor and contains a statement indicating the types, or describing the items, of collateral. A financing statement may be filed before a security agreement is made or a security interest otherwise attaches. When the financing statement covers crops growing or to be grown or goods which are or are to become fixtures, the statement must also contain a description of the real estate concerned. A copy of the security agreement is sufficient as a financing statement if it contains the above information and is signed by both parties.

(2) A financing statement which otherwise complies with subsection (1) is sufficient although it is signed only by the secured

party when it is filed to perfect a security interest in

(a) collateral already subject to a security interest in another jurisdiction when it is brought into this state. Such a financing statement must state that the collateral was brought into this state under such circumstances.

(b) proceeds under Section 9-306 if the security interest in the original collateral was perfected. Such a financing statement must describe the original collateral.

(3) A form substantially as follows is sufficient to comply with subsection (1):

Name of debtor (or assignor) . . . .
Address . . . .
Name of secured party (or assignee) . . . .
Address . . . .

1. This financing statement covers the following types (or items) of property:
   (Describe) . . . .
2. (If collateral is crops) The above described crops are growing or are to be grown on:
   (Describe Real Estate) . . . .
3. (If collateral is goods which are or are to become fixtures) The above described goods are affixed or to be affixed to:
   (Describe Real Estate) . . . .
4. (If proceeds or products of collateral are claimed) Proceeds—Products of the collateral are also covered.
   Signature of Debtor (or Assignor)
   Signature of Secured Party (or Assignee)

(4) The term "financing statement" as used in this Article means the original financing statement and any amendments but if any amendment adds collateral, it is effective as to the added collateral only from the filing date of the amendment.

(5) A financing statement substantially complying with the requirements of this section is effective even though it contains minor errors which are not seriously misleading.

Section 9-403. What Constitutes Filing; Duration of Filing; Effect of Lapsed Filing; Duties of Filing Officer.

(1) Presentation for filing of a financing statement and tender of the filing fee or

acceptance of the statement by the filing officer constitutes filing under this Article.

(2) A filed financing statement which states a maturity date of the obligation secured of five years or less is effective until such maturity date and thereafter for a period of sixty days. Any other filed financing statement is effective for a period of five years from the date of filing. The effectiveness of a filed financing statement lapses on the expiration of such sixty day period after a stated maturity date or on the expiration of such five year period, as the case may be, unless a continuation statement is filed prior to the lapse. Upon such lapse the security interest becomes unperfected. A filed financing statement which states that the obligation secured is payable on demand is effective for five years from the date of filing.

(3) A continuation statement may be filed by the secured party (i) within six months before and sixty days after a stated maturity date of five years or less, and (ii) otherwise within six months prior to the expiration of the five year period specified in subsection (2). Any such continuation statement must be signed by the secured party, identify the original statement by file number and state that the original statement is still effective. Upon timely filing of the continuation statement, the effectiveness of the original statement is continued for five years after the last date to which the filing was effective whereupon it lapses in the same manner as provided in subsection (2) unless another continuation statement is filed in the same manner to continue the effectiveness of the original statement. Unless a statute on disposition of public records provides otherwise, the filing officer may remove a lapsed statement from the files and destroy it.

(4) A filing officer shall mark each statement with a consecutive file number and with the date and hour of filing and shall hold the statement for public inspection. In addition the filing officer shall index the statements according to the name of the debtor and shall note in the index the file number and the address of the debtor given in the statement.

(5) The uniform fee for filing, indexing and furnishing filing data for an original or a continuation statement shall be $. . . . .

Section 9-404. Termination Statement.

(1) Whenever there is no outstanding secured obligation and no commitment to make advances, incur obligations or otherwise give value, the secured party must on written demand by the debtor send the debtor a statement that he no longer claims a security interest under the financing statement, which shall be identified by file number. A termination statement signed by a person other than the secured party of record must include or be accompanied by the assignment or a statement by the secured party of record that he has assigned the security interest to the signer of the termination statement. The uniform fee for filing and indexing such an assignment or statement thereof shall be $ . . . . If the affected secured party fails to send such a termination statement within ten days after proper demand therefor he shall be liable to the debtor for one hundred dollars, and in addition for any loss caused to the debtor by such failure.

(2) On presentation to the filing officer of such a termination statement he must note it on the index. The filing officer shall remove from the files, mark "terminated" and send or deliver to the secured party the financing statement and any continuation statement, statement of assignment or statement of release pertaining thereto.

(3) The uniform fee for filing and indexing a termination statement including sending or delivering the financing statement shall be $ . . . .

Section 9-405. Assignment of Security Interest; Duties of Filing Officer; Fees.

(1) A financing statement may disclose an assignment of a security interest in the collateral described in the statement by indication in the statement of the name and address of the assignee or by an assignment itself or a copy thereof on the face or back of the statement. Either the original secured party or the assignee may sign this statement as the secured party. On presentation to the filing officer of such a financing statement the filing officer shall mark the same as provided in Section 9-403(4). The uniform fee for filing, indexing and furnishing filing data for a financing statement so indicating an assignment shall be $ . . . .

(2) A secured party may assign of record all or a part of his rights under a financing

statement by the filing of a separate written statement of assignment signed by the secured party of record and setting forth the name of the secured party of record and the debtor, the file number and the date of filing of the financing statement and the name and address of the assignee and containing a description of the collateral assigned. A copy of the assignment is sufficient as a separate statement if it complies with the preceding sentence. On presentation to the filing officer of such a separate statement, the filing officer shall mark such separate statement with the date and hour of the filing. He shall note the assignment on the index of the financing statement. The uniform fee for filing, indexing and furnishing filing data about such a separate statement of assignment shall be $ . . . .

(3) After the disclosure or filing of an assignment under this section, the assignee is the secured party of record.

Section 9-406. Release of Collateral; Duties of Filing Officer; Fees. A secured party of record may by his signed statement release all or a part of any collateral described in a filed financing statement. The statement of release is sufficient if it contains a description of the collateral being released, the name and address of the debtor, the name and address of the secured party, and the file number of the financing statement. pon presentation of such a statement to the filing officer he shall mark the statement with the hour and date of filing and shall note the same upon the margin of the

index of the filing of the financing statement. The uniform fee for filing and noting such a statement of release shall be $ . . . .

Section 9-407. Information from Filing Officer.

(1) If the person filing any financing statement, termination statement, statement of assignment, or statement of release, furnishes the filing officer a copy thereof, the filing officer shall upon request note upon the copy the file number and date and hour of the filing of the original and deliver or send the copy to such person.

(2) Upon request of any person, the filing officer shall issue his certificate showing whether there is on file on the date and hour stated therein, any presently effective financing statement naming a particular debtor and any statement of assignment thereof and if there is, giving the date and hour of filing of each such statement and the names and addresses of each secured party therein. The uniform fee for such a certificate shall be $ . . . . plus $ . . . . for each financing statement and for each statement of assignment reported therein. Upon request the filing officer shall furnish a copy of any filed financing statement or statement of assignment for a uniform fee of $ . . . . per page.

NOTE: *This new section is proposed as an optional provision to require filing officers to furnish certificates. Local law and practices should be consulted with regard to the advisability of adoption.*

PART 5

DEFAULT

Section 9-501. Default; Procedure when Security Agreement Covers both Real and Personal Property.

(1) When a debtor is in default under a security agreement, a secured party has the rights and remedies provided in this Part and except as limited by subsection (3) those provided in the security agreement. He may reduce his claim to judgment, foreclose or otherwise enforce the security interest by any available judicial procedure. If the collateral is documents the secured party may proceed either as to the documents or as to

the goods covered thereby. A secured party in possession has the rights, remedies and duties provided in Section 9-207. The rights and remedies referred to in this section are cumulative.

(2) After default, the debtor has the rights and remedies provided in this Part, those provided in the security agreement and those provided in Section 9-207.

(3) To the extent that they give rights to the debtor and impose duties on the secured party, the rules stated in the subsections referred to below may not be waived or

varied except as provided with respect to compulsory disposition of collateral (subsection (1) of Section 9-505) and with respect to redemption of collateral (Section 9-506) but the parties may by agreement determine the standards by which the fulfillment of these rights and duties is to be measured if such standards are not manifestly unreasonable:

(a) subsection (2) of Section 9-502 and subsection (2) of Section 9-504 insofar as they require accounting for surplus proceeds of collateral;

(b) subsection (3) of Section 9-504 and subsection (1) of Section 9-505 which deal with disposition of collateral;

(c) subsection (2) of Section 9-505 which deals with acceptance of collateral as discharge of obligation;

(d) Section 9-506 which deals with redemption of collateral; and

(e) subsection (1) of Section 9-507 which deals with the secured party's liability for failure to comply with this Part.

(4) If the security agreement covers both real and personal property, the secured party may proceed under this Part as to the personal property or he may proceed as to both the real and the personal property in accordance with his rights and remedies in respect of the real property in which case the provisions of this Part do not apply.

(5) When a secured party has reduced his claim to judgment the lien of any levy which may be made upon his collateral by virtue of any execution based upon the judgment shall relate back to the date of the perfection of the security interest in such collateral. A judicial sale, pursuant to such execution, is a foreclosure of the security interest by judicial procedure within the meaning of this section, and the secured party may purchase at the sale and thereafter hold the collateral free of any other requirements of this Article.

Section 9-502. Collection Rights of Secured Party.

(1) When so agreed and in any event on default the secured party is entitled to notify an account debtor or the obligor on an instrument to make payment to him whether or not the assignor was theretofore making collections on the collateral, and

also to take control of any proceeds to which he is entitled under Section 9-306.

(2) A secured party who by agreement is entitled to charge back uncollected collateral or otherwise to full or limited recourse against the debtor and who undertakes to collect from the account debtors or obligors must proceed in a commercially reasonable manner and may deduct his reasonable expenses of realization from the collections. If the security agreement secures an indebtedness, the secured party must account to the debtor for any surplus, and unless otherwise agreed, the debtor is liable for any deficiency. But, if the underlying transaction was a sale of accounts, contract rights, or chattel paper, the debtor is entitled to any surplus or is liable for any deficiency only if the security agreement so provides.

Section 9-503. Secured Party's Right to take Possession after Default.

Unless otherwise agreed a secured party has on default the right to take possession of the collateral. In taking possession a secured party may proceed without judicial process if this can be done without breach of the peace or many proceed by action. If the security agreement so provides the secured party may require the debtor to assemble the collateral and make it available to the secured party at a place to be designated by the secured party which is reasonably convenient to both parties. Without removal a secured party may render equipment unusable, and may dispose of collateral on the debtor's premises under Section 9-504.

Section 9-504. Secured Party's Right to Dispose of Collateral after Default; Effect of Disposition.

(1) A secured party after default may sell, lease or otherwise dispose of any or all of the collateral in its then condition or following any commercially reasonable preparation or processing. Any sale of goods is subject to the Article on Sales (Article 2). The proceeds of disposition shall be applied in the order following to

(a) the reasonable expenses of retaking, holding, preparing for sale, selling and the like and, to the extent provided for in the agreement and not prohibited by law, the reasonable attorney's fees and legal expenses incurred by the secured party;

(b) the satisfaction · of indebtedness

secured by the security interest under which the disposition is made;

(c) the satisfaction of indebtedness secured by any subordinate security interest in the collateral if written notification of demand therefor is received before distribution of the proceeds is completed. If requested by the secured party, the holder of a subordinate security interest must seasonably furnish reasonable proof of his interest, and unless he does so, the secured party need not comply with his demand.

(2) If the security interest secures an indebtedness, the secured party must account to the debtor for any surplus, and, unless otherwise agreed, the debtor is liable for any deficiency. But if the underlying transaction was a sale of accounts, contract rights, or chattel paper, the debtor is entitled to any surplus or is liable for any deficiency only if the security agreement so provides.

(3) Disposition of the collateral may be by public or private proceedings and may be made by way of one or more contracts. Sale or other disposition may be as a unit or in parcels and at any time and place, and on any terms but every aspect of the disposition including the method, manner, time, place and terms must be commercially reasonable. Unless collateral is perishable or threatens to decline speedily in value or is of a type customarily sold on a recognized market, reasonable notification of the time and place of any public sale or reasonable notification of the time after which any private sale or other intended disposition is to be made shall be sent by the secured party to the debtor, and except in the case of consumer goods to any other person who has a security interest in the collateral and who has duly filed a financing statement indexed in the name of the debtor in this state or who is known by the secured party to have a security interest in the collateral is of a type customarily sold in a recognized market or is of a type which is the subject of widely distributed standard price quotations he may buy at private sale.

(4) When collateral is disposed of by a secured party after default, the disposition transfers to a purchaser for value all of the debtor's rights therein, discharges the security interest under which it is made and any

security interest or lien subordinate thereto. The purchaser takes free of all such rights and interests even though the secured party fails to comply with the requirements of this Part or of any judicial proceedings

(a) in the case of a public sale, if the purchaser has no knowledge of any defects in the sale and if he does not buy in collusion with the secured party, other bidders or the person conducting the sale; or

(b) in any other case, if the purchaser acts in good faith.

(5) A person who is liable to a secured party under a guaranty, indorsement, repurchase agreement or the like and who receives a transfer of collateral from the secured party or is subrogated to his rights has thereafter the rights and duties of the secured party. Such a transfer of collateral is not a sale or disposition of the collateral under this Article.

Section 9-505. Compulsory Disposition of Collateral; Acceptance of the Collateral as Discharge of Obligation.

(1) If the debtor has paid sixty per cent of the cash price in the case of a purchase money security interest in consumer goods or sixty per cent of the loan in the case of another security interest in consumer goods, and has not signed after default a statement renouncing or modifying his rights under this Part a secured party who has taken possession of collateral must dispose of it under Section 9-504 and if he fails to do so within ninety days after he takes possession the debtor at his option may recover in conversion or under Section 9-507(1) on secured party's liability.

(2) In any other case involving consumer goods or any other collateral a secured party in possession may, after default, propose to retain the collateral in satisfaction of the obligation. Written notice of such proposal shall be sent to the debtor and except in the case of consumer goods to any other secured party who has a security interest in the collateral and who has duly filed a financing statement indexed in the name of the debtor in this state or is known by the secured in possession to have a security interest in it. If the debtor or other person entitled to receive notification objects in writing within thirty days from the receipt

of the notification or if any other secured party objects in writing within thirty days after the secured party obtains possession the secured party must dispose of the collateral under Section 9-504. In the absence of such written objection the secured party may retain the collateral in satisfaction of the debtor's obligation.

Section 9-506. Debtor's Right to Redeem Collateral. At any time before the secured party has disposed of collateral or entered into a contract for its disposition under Section 9-504 or beforethe obligation has been discharged under Section 9-505(2) the debtor or any other secured party may unless otherwise agreed in writing after default redeem the collateral by tendering fulfillment of all obligations secured by the collateral as well as the expenses reasonably incurred by the secured party in retaking, holding and preparing the collateral for disposition, in arranging for the sale, and to the extent provided in the agreement and not prohibited by law, his reasonable attorney's fees and legal expenses.

Section 9-507. Secured Party's Liability for Failure to Comply with this Part.

(1) If it is established that the secured party is not proceeding in accordance with the provisions of this Part disposition may be ordered or restrained on appropriate terms and conditions. If the disposition has occurred the debtor or any person entitled to notification or whose security interest has been made known to the secured party prior to the disposition has a right to recover from the secured party any loss caused by a failure to comply with the provisions of this Part. If the collateral is consumer goods, the debtor has a right to recover in any event an amount not less than the credit service charge plus ten per cent of the principal amount of the debt or the time price differential plus ten per cent of the cash price.

(2) The fact that a better price could have been obtained by a sale at a different time or in a different method from that selected by the secured party is not of itself sufficient to establish that the sale was not made in a commercially reasonable manner. If the secured party either sells the collateral in the usual manner in any recognized market therefor or if he sells at the price current in such market at the time of his sale or if he has otherwise sold in conformity with reasonable commercial practices among dealers in the type of property sold he has sold in a commercially reasonable manner. The principles stated in the two preceding sentences with respect to sales also apply as may be appropriate to other types of disposition. A disposition which has been approved in any judicial proceeding or by any bona fide creditors' committee or representative of creditors shall conclusively be deemed to be commercially reasonable, but this sentence does not indicate that any such approval must be obtained in any case nor does it indicate that any disposition not so approved is not commercially reasonable.

ARTICLE 10

EFFECTIVE DATE AND REPEALER

Section 10-101. Effective Date. This Act shall become effective at midnight on December 31st following its enactment. It applies to transactions entered into and events occurring after that date.

Section 10-102. Specific Repealer; Provision for Transition.

(1) The following acts and all other acts and parts of acts inconsistent herewith are hereby repealed:
(Here should follow the acts to be specifically repealed including the following:
Uniform Negotiable Instruments Act
Uniform Warehouse Receipts Act
Uniform Sales Act
Uniform Bills of Lading Act
Uniform Stock Transfer Act
Uniform Trust Receipts Act
Also any acts regulating:
Bank collections
Bulk sales
Chattel mortgages
Conditional sales
Factor's lien acts
Farm storage of grain and similar acts
Assignment of accounts receivable)

(2) Transactions validly entered into before the effective date specified in Section

10-101 and the rights, duties and interests flowing from them remain valid thereafter and may be terminated, completed, consummated or enforced as required or permitted by any statute or other law amended or repealed by this Act as though such repeal or amendment had not occurred.

NOTE: *Subsection (1) should be separately prepared for each state. The foregoing is a list of statutes to be checked.*

Section 10-103. General Repealer.

Except as provided in the following section, all acts and parts of acts inconsistent with this Act are hereby repealed.

Section 10-104. Laws Not Repealed.

(1) The Article on Documents of Title (Article 7) does not repeal or modify any laws prescribing the form or contents of regulating bailees' businesses in respects not specifically dealt with herein; but the fact that such laws are violated does not affect the status of a document of title which otherwise complies with the definition of a document of title (Section 1-201).

[(2) This Act does not repeal . . . . *, cited as the Uniform Act for the Simplification of Fiduciary Security Transfers, and if in any respect there is any inconsistency between that Act and the Article of this Act on investment securities (Article 8) the provisions of the former Act shall control.]

NOTE: *At * in subsection (2) insert the statutory reference to the Uniform Act for the Simplification of Fiduciary Security Transfers if such Act has previously been enacted. If it has not been enacted, omit subsection (2).*

INDEX